POLITICS AND THE NATION

Politics and the Nation

Britain in the Mid-Eighteenth Century

BOB HARRIS

OXFORD
UNIVERSITY PRESS

OXFORD
UNIVERSITY PRESS

Great Clarendon Street, Oxford OX2 6DP

Oxford University Press is a department of the University of Oxford.
It furthers the University's objective of excellence in research, scholarship,
and education by publishing worldwide in

Oxford New York

Athens Auckland Bangkok Bogotá Buenos Aires Cape Town
Chennai Dar es Salaam Delhi Florence Hong Kong Istanbul Karachi
Kolkata Kuala Lumpur Madrid Melbourne Mexico City Mumbai Nairobi
Paris São Paulo Shanghai Singapore Taipei Tokyo Toronto Warsaw

with associated companies in Berlin Ibadan

Oxford is a registered trade mark of Oxford University Press
in the UK and in certain other countries

Published in the United States
By Oxford University Press Inc., New York

British Library Cataloguing in Publication Data
Data available

Library of Congress Cataloging in Publication Data
Harris, Bob, 1964–
Politics and the nation : Britain in the mid-eighteenth century / Bob Harris.
p. cm.
Includes bibliographical references.
1. Great Britain–Politics and government–18th century. I. Title.
DA480 H26 2002   941.07′2   dc21   2001036595

ISBN 0-19-924693-9

1 3 5 7 9 10 8 6 4 2

Typeset in Baskerville
by Florence Production Ltd, Stoodleigh, Devon
Printed in Great Britain
on acid-free paper by
T.J. International Ltd, Padstow, Cornwall

Preface

THIS BOOK IS an attempt to reconstruct the politics and political culture of Britain in the mid-eighteenth century in a way which helps to highlight the main issues, feelings, ideologies, and realities which gave distinctive form and shape to them. What it is not is a detailed narrative of events. This does not reflect any scepticism about the value of such an approach; such narratives provide the essential foundation for works such as this. Yet the mid-eighteenth century in Britain has perhaps too often been studied from this perspective, and this has helped reinforce an impression that politics in this period was consumed with little more than factional and individual rivalries amongst a small number of politicians. What I have tried to do is to provide a fuller, more rounded picture of political life in this period, and in so doing challenge long-standing preconceptions about it.

Recent years have seen much exciting published and unpublished work which has provided fresh perspectives from which to view the mid-eighteenth century in Britain, and I have benefited enormously from this. The attempt to write a history which includes at least three, and occasionally four, of the nations which made up the eighteenth-century British state is also working with the grain of recent scholarship. That said, the development of 'British history' is still at a relatively early stage, and we lack many maps or guides about how to do it. Yet if the result involves quite a few compromises, and many gaps, the challenge is a stimulating one, and one which helps to reveal more clearly than any other several important threads in British politics in this period. This is especially true of the main themes explored in this book.

The book is designed to be read as a whole, but chapters pursue particular topics and can be read separately. There is a limited amount of repetition, but this is only because certain topics bear reconsideration from different stand-points. I have sought not simply to replicate the work of other historians—although in several places the debts to this will be obvious—but to present new material which either confirms and extends the findings of this work, or which places it in a new perspective. I have also sought to include new insights, based on a decade of research on politics and political culture on mid-eighteenth-century Britain but also on the fact that this book covers a comparatively short period, enabling me to pursue details which wider-ranging studies of necessity must pass over quickly if not ignore completely. I have tried to write with three main groups of readers in mind—specialists, students, and those with a general interest in history and the eighteenth century in particular.

Acknowledgements

IN THE COURSE of researching and writing this book, I have received assistance and encouragement from several institutions, and individuals. The final stages of writing were completed whilst on sabbatical leave made possible by an award from the Arts and Humanities Research Board. The terms of this award required the University of Dundee to provide leave for a second term, and I am grateful to the Dean of the Faculty of Arts and Humanities, Professor Huw Jones, for agreeing to this. The Carnegie Endowment for the Scottish Universities provided two awards of money to finance research trips. Material from the Lonsdale Papers is reproduced with the kind permission of the Earl of Lonsdale. Staff of various libraries and archives have provided invaluable assistance, especially those at the British Library, the University of Dundee, the Greater London Record Office, the National Library of Scotland, the National Archives of Scotland, the University of Nottingham, the University of St Andrew's, and the Cumberland Record Office in Carlisle.

Of individuals who have provided support and advice, I would particularly like to thank Jeremy Black, Harry Dickinson, and Joanna Innes. Jeremy Black read early drafts of several chapters, and his comments were, as always, helpful and stimulating. Eoin Magennis also deserves special mention for his great generosity in sharing his expertise and enthusiasm for Irish politics in the mid-eighteenth century with me on a visit to Belfast in the summer of 1999. Much shorter versions of Chapter 3 were read in 1998 to the North West Branch of the British Society for Eighteenth Century Studies and the Imperial History seminar at the Institute of Historical Research, and I am grateful for comments made by several individuals on both occasions. A version of Chapter 7 was read in the spring of 1999 at a joint meeting of the Economic and Social History and History Department seminars at the University of Edinburgh, and again remarks made on that occasion have helped to sharpen my ideas. Various colleagues in the History Department at Dundee have provided moral and practical support, notably Julie Flavell and Charles McKean. Professor Chris Whatley has read and commented on various drafts of chapters over the course of the last two years, and his advice and support have been much appreciated. My forays into Scottish history have owed much to his enthusiasm for eighteenth-century Scottish history and his generosity in sharing his findings and thoughts with me.

I am also very grateful to Ruth Parr at Oxford University Press for her encouragement to complete this book and to Kay Rogers for guiding it through production.

Finally, to Rachel, Andrew, Charlotte, and Harriet thanks are due for putting up with my periodic visits to them in London. They have made their home a wonderful base from which to make forays into archives in London and the south.

This book is for Tess.

Contents

List of Maps

Abbreviations

BL	British Library
Bodl.	Bodleian Library, Oxford
CLRO	Corporation of London Record Office, Guildhall, London
CRO (Carlisle)	Cumberland Record Office, Carlisle
EHR	*English Historical Review*
Gent. Mag.	*Gentleman's Magazine*
GLRO	Greater London Record Office, London
HJ	*Historical Journal*
JBS	*Journal of British Studies*
Lond. Ev. P.	*London Evening Post*
NAS	National Archives of Scotland
NLS	National Library of Scotland
NUL	Nottingham University Library
Parl. Hist.	William Cobbett, *The Parliamentary History of England* (36 vols., 1806–20)
Scots Mag.	*Scots Magazine*
TRHS	*Transactions of the Royal Historical Society*
Walpole, *Correspondence*	*The Yale Edition of Horace Walpole's Correspondence*, ed. W. S. Lewis, *et al.* (34 vols., New Haven, Conn., 1937–70)
Walpole, *Memoirs of King George II*	Horace Walpole, *Memoirs of the Reign of King George II*, ed. John Brooke (3 vols., New Haven, Conn. and London, 1985)

Introduction

POLITICS IN MID-EIGHTEENTH-CENTURY Britain has traditionally not
attracted the greatest amount of attention from historians. Until relatively
recently, this reflected a perception that politics in this period lacked the
drama and wider historical importance of politics in other decades in the
eighteenth century. A story can, and has been, told of how Whig politicians
from the early 1720s—pre-eminently Sir Robert Walpole, leading minister
between 1720 and 1742—succeeded in constructing a stable system of
oligarchical rule, and in eliminating or marginalizing potential sources of
opposition to this rule.[1] Politics had, as a consequence, become an activity
engaged in by a narrow, exclusive elite fighting over the spoils of power and
office, usually undisturbed by popular pressures.

It is a crude sketch, but not an unduly distorted one. It also contains
important elements of truth. National politics in the 1740s and 1750s from one
perspective did become a game, fiercely conducted at times, played by small
coteries of Whig politicians; opposition coalitions were loose and fissile;
national politics also lacked the coherence and depth that party divisions lent
it in earlier periods, particularly between c1701 and 1722, and were to do so
again from the end of the century. As John Owen showed in his masterly, if
narrowly conceived, study of politics in the 1740s, *The Rise of the Pelhams* (1957),
with party allegiances becoming looser and looser, political battles were characterized by a marked degree of individualism. The essential conflict was
between ministries and groups of usually opposition Whig politicians seeking
to force their way into office or between Whig rivals in office. Politics became,
in short, more than was usual in an eighteenth-century context, dominated by
the narrow ambitions of a handful or so of politicians. It is a political world
which has been painstakingly and exhaustively chronicled by J. C. D. Clark in
his *The Dynamics of Change: The Crisis of the 1750s and English Party Systems*
(Cambridge, 1982).

Mid-century politics can seem to lack the intensity and personalities of
surrounding periods. Many political debates have an air of shadow boxing, or
at least of stereotyped exchanges. Walpole's successors in office were not made
from the same giant mould, with the exception perhaps of Lord Carteret (the
Earl of Granville as he became in 1744). Even the reputation of Pitt the Elder,
the most compelling politician of the period, and certainly the one to have

---

[1] See esp. J. H. Plumb, *The Growth of Political Stability in England, 1675–1725* (1967).

stimulated the greatest interest,[2] owes more to the myth-making of a generation of imperial historians who came to maturity at the turn of twentieth
century than to the historical facts.[3]

However, the lack of apparent unity in political life was not only a function
of the personalized nature of political rivalries. This was a period of political
transition, something which has further encouraged the habit of seeing it as
either a coda to the Walpole years or as a prelude to the politics of the new reign
after 1760. Especially in the 1750s, an older political world—one shaped by
party identities, by the Jacobite threat, and by a generation of politicians
formed in the political conflict of Augustan England—was disintegrating.
George II was born in 1683, while many of the leading political figures—the
Duke of Newcastle, the third Duke of Argyll, Lord Hardwicke—were also of a
generation who reached maturity in the world of Queen Anne and who took
its dimensions as the natural shape of the political world. A younger generation was now pressing its claims to office and power, led by Pitt, Henry Fox, the
Duke of Bedford, and, at the end of our period, the Earl of Bute, from 1756
Groom of the Stole to the future George III. Theirs was the political world
which was to emerge much more clearly after 1760, a world in which landed
society was finally united, and long-standing distinctions of Whig and Tory
eradicated or completely disrupted, in which the tempo of politics 'without
doors' became more insistent and clamorous, and in which demands for political reform took on a new force. The acquisition of a much-expanded territorial empire at the Peace of Paris (1763) also created a series of new issues and
challenges regarding the retention and government of different parts of this
empire, which were to consume an increasing amount of time and energy of
leading politicians from the early 1760s.[4] There is often a sense in the mid-eighteenth century of two political worlds colliding against one another, of the older
political world resurfacing and submerging newer issues. Which, for example,
tells us more about the character of politics in this period—the Jacobite demonstrations which occurred in parts of the West Midlands in the later 1740s and
early 1750s, and which Paul Monod has recently sought to portray (unconvinc-
ingly perhaps) as a near insurrection,[5] or the widespread celebrations produced
by the capture of French and Spanish colonies in the great mid-century wars,
the War of the Austrian Succession (1740–8) and the Seven Years War (1756–63)?

---

[2] Brief historiographical studies of writing on Pitt are to be found in R. Middleton, *The Bells of
Victory: the Pitt–Newcastle Ministry and the Conduct of the Seven Years' War, 1757–1762* (Cambridge, 1985);
Marie Peters, 'The Myth of William Pitt, Earl of Chatham, Great Imperialist. Part I: Pitt and Imperial
Expansion 1738–1763', *Journal of Imperial and Commonwealth History*, 21 (1993), 31–4. See also Karl W.
Schweizer (ed.), *William Pitt, Earl of Chatham 1708–1778. A Bibliography* (Westport, Conn., 1993).

[3] See Peters, 'The Myth of William Pitt'; *ead.*, *The Elder Pitt* (Harlow, 1998).

[4] For a recent overview, see P. J. Marshall, 'Britain and the World in the Eighteenth Century. I:
Reshaping the Empire', *TRHS*, 6th ser., 8 (1998), 1–18.

[5] Paul Kleber Monod, *Jacobitism and the English People 1688–1788* (Cambridge, 1989), 208–9. For a
different interpretation, see Nicholas Rogers, *Crowds, Culture and Politics in Georgian Britain* (Oxford,
1998), 50.

Important work in the last two decades has begun to reveal some of the limitations of the traditional view of this period, although without over-turning it completely. The main challenges have come in the form of new histories of Jacobitism, foreign policy and diplomacy, popular politics, and national identities. All have offered fresh perspectives from which to view the period; they have also served to reveal a political world which was far from devoid of creative forces, serious issues, powerful emotions, and deeper histor-ical significance, especially once we move the focus away from the battles for political supremacy amongst national politicians. Broadening our field of vision still further, to include developments in Scotland and Ireland, only further reinforces this conclusion.

Recent work on Jacobitism has failed as yet to produce a consensus about the nature and scope of the threat which support for the Stuarts posed to the Hanoverian regime after the early 1720s.[6] One thing, however, is clear: minis-ters and their supporters never stopped believing that Jacobitism constituted a serious threat, and if anything their fears about this only grew after 1739.[7] Jacobite fortunes were inextricably linked to the contemporary conditions of diplomacy and foreign politics, as both Jacobites and their opponents fully recognized. This was because without foreign support a restoration attempt was very unlikely to succeed. In 1741, Britain was to enter a major European war, the War of the Austrian Succession, for the first time since 1713. Conflict with France was now unavoidable, although war between the two powers was only officially declared in the spring of 1744. The prospect of France, or another foreign power, supporting a restoration attempt was one which continued to exercise ministers (and many Britons) even after the crushing of the Young Pretender's army at the battle of Culloden (16 April 1746). Indeed, the Jacobite Rebellion of 1745–6 simply served as a dramatic reminder of the dangers such an attempt continued to hold, especially in the middle of war when British forces were committed overseas. The disaffected clans in the Highlands remained a potentially potent threat to the regime, hence the energy and the resources which ministers committed to eradicating this threat once and for all after 1746. As ministers were only too aware, disaffected clansmen, stirred up by visits from attainted rebels, continued to entertain hopes of further risings in 1747–8 and again in the early 1750s.[8] Whether such a rising could actually have brought about anything other than further disaster and suffering in the Highlands is only partly the point; there was no compla-cency amongst ministers and the Whig establishment in Edinburgh that the Jacobite menace had been eliminated, and Jacobite activity in Scotland continued to be very closely watched and policed into the 1750s.

---

[6] For a very useful, balanced summary, see Daniel Szechi, *The Jacobites* (1994).
[7] See Paul Fritz, *The English Ministers and Jacobitism between the Rebellions of 1715 and 1745* (Toronto, 1975).
[8] See Ch. 4, below, pp. 165–8.

The political stability, therefore, which some historians have seen in this period was a quality which for most of it eluded contemporaries. For ministers, and for most contemporaries, the Jacobite Rebellion of 1745–6 raised fundamental and troubling questions about the security of the Hanoverian and Protestant Succession, and the political, economic, and religious order it was held to underpin. Was disaffection in the Highlands likely to threaten again the prosperity and security of Hanoverian Britain? Was the British navy capable of protecting Britain's extended coastline against invasion? The uncomfortable memory of the Young Pretender's army marching down the spine of the country to Derby, without significant resistance either from military forces under Sir John Cope or elements of the civilian population, provoked debates about whether a rapidly commercializing society, such as Britain in this period, could maintain the values and commitments—or, as contemporaries termed it, the 'public spirit'—to rebuff international enemies and rivals and to sustain military security and strength. It was the '45 which also raised very clearly a fear that recurs throughout debate and perceptions in the mid-eighteenth century—that God's chosen people and latter-day Israel, Britain, had lost his favour, or faced his imminent judgment on their sins and lax religious observance. Hugh Blair, a moderate minister of the Church of Scotland, was voicing a commonplace when he argued that the Jacobite rebels were instruments of Providence for punishing a people that had responded to his bountiful blessings with sinfulness.[9]

Any convincing account of this period needs, therefore, to reconstruct a world of insecurity and challenge which faced contemporaries, and the complex range of emotions which this elicited. It needs also to integrate foreign and domestic politics, to examine the impact on domestic perceptions and emotions of the period's two major European and global wars—the War of the Austrian Succession (1740–8) and the Seven Years War (1756–63)—together with the rivalry between Britain and France which gave these conflicts their unity as far as the British were concerned. There is, in this context, a strong temptation to write the history of this period from the perspective of our knowledge that, eventually, Britain was to emerge from this rivalry the clear victor. In 1763, the Peace of Paris set the seal on the emergence of Britain as the most powerful, global power the world, ancient or modern, had hitherto witnessed. It also signalled an important shift towards territorial, as opposed to maritime, empire, a shift underlined in 1765 when the East India Company effectively took control of Bengal in India. British military success in the Seven Years War after 1758 was, however, unanticipated and indeed had seemed most unlikely in the early stages of the Seven Years War. It is worth reminding ourselves that the French had threatened, or appeared immediately and directly to threaten, the security of the Protestant

---

[9] Hugh Blair, *The Wrath of Man Praising Man* (Edinburgh, 1746).

Succession in Britain in the winter of 1743–4, 1745–6, and that their armies had conquered the strategically vital territories of the Austrian Netherlands in the later 1740s. The years between the end of the War of the Austrian Succession and the outbreak of the Seven Years War had seen major efforts on the part of the Bourbon powers to reconstruct and increase their naval power, as well as French expansion and aggression in North America, the Caribbean, India, and West Africa. Britain's much vaunted 'empire of the seas'—the bulwark of her security and prosperity—appeared to be under formidable challenge. For the British, the Seven Years War began as a struggle to defend the security of its North American colonies. There was relief that conflict had been renewed, since it was widely believed that further delay would have only strengthened French military power. The military failures and setbacks of the early phases of the war appeared to confirm the worst apprehensions of contemporaries about French power and ambition. They also produced an acute sense of vulnerability in Britain, a feeling compounded by a perception of financial weakness. In 1757, ministers were openly speculating about being compelled to conclude an unfavourable peace with France. In July of that year, Charles Townshend lamented to his mother, 'Indeed, Lady Townshend we are undone.'[10] Two years after that, the British were to face another major Franco-Jacobite invasion threat from France.[11]

For much of the mid-eighteenth century, Britain appeared, in short, to be locked in a conflict for international standing and even survival with a much more populous and therefore, according to contemporary thinking on these matters, powerful state. Contemporaries were haunted by the scope and rest-lessness of French ambition. There was also a strengthening perception that the French state might be a more effective promoter of economic and commercial expansion than the much less centralized British state heralded in so much loyal propaganda in this period; freedom and the rule of law, it appeared, did not uniquely promote commercial vitality. As one of Newcastle's correspondents wrote in early October 1754:

France now seems to be pushing for Universal Commerce, as Lewis the 14th for what we call Universal Monarchy. I own my self to be more afraid at this hour of French credit and French commerce than of French Fleets and French Armys.[12]

French cultural influence was also pervasive amongst the upper ranks, and was easily seen in terms of a betrayal of the nation and national interest.[13] The French challenge was, therefore, much more than a military one, although it was, whatever Newcastle's correspondent said, most immediately threatening

[10] Quoted in Jeremy Black, *America or Europe? British Foreign Policy, 1739–63* (1998), 151.
[11] See Claude Nordmann, 'Choiseul and the Last Jacobite Attempt of 1759', in Eveline Cruickshanks (ed.), *Ideology and Conspiracy: Aspects of Jacobitism, 1689–1759* (Edinburgh, 1982), 201–17.
[12] BL, Add. MS 32737 (Newcastle Papers), fo. 99: Page to Newcastle, 10 Oct. 1754.
[13] See Gerald Newman, *The Rise of English Nationalism: A Cultural History, 1740–1830* (New York, 1987), esp. ch. 4.

in its military and diplomatic guise. The construction of the massive Fort George at Ardersier Point; the renewal of a road building programme in the Highlands; the military, judicial, and legislative assault on the disaffected clans; the construction of the military road between Newcastle and Carlisle; persistent concerns about the defensibility of Ireland, with its majority Catholic population; each and all speak eloquently of the apprehensions of contemporaries about the continuing survival of an independent, free, Protestant, and prosperous Britain. So too in a different way do fears, referred to above, and very widely expressed, that God had an argument with his chosen nation. The sense of alarm and nervousness was compounded by a very widely shared outlook or mentality which bordered on the paranoid. A strong ingredient in this was the loose but deeply ingrained ideology of anti-popery, which constructed the forces of international Catholicism, represented by the Pretender but also by an axis of Rome, Paris, and Madrid, as infinitely devious and protean in nature, as well as dedicated to the suppression of Protestant heresy.[14] Jacobites, like Catholic agents, worked through disguise; the fact that none identified himself publicly as Jacobite did not mean that they were not present. There was, in short, much to fear, and, where there was not, contemporaries were eminently capable of conjuring up imaginary fears. As George Lyttleton wrote in a slightly different context at the end of the Seven Years War, 'Britannia is like a nervous lady seldom well long together, but not dangerously ill'.[15] Not everyone was so sanguine.

If the British nation faced grave challenges from within and without in this period, historians of popular politics have also in recent years revealed a political world beyond Westminster and St James's which was only superficially calm and tranquil. Following the fall of Sir Robert Walpole, in February 1742, the popular opposition to Whig oligarchy which had built up from the later 1720s, and which helped crucially to sustain an often divided parliamentary opposition in the period 1740–2, did fracture and lose coherence.[16] Successive political betrayals by opposition politicians entering office, starting with, and most importantly by, William Pulteney and his allies in 1742, also produced intense public disillusionment with national politics and politicians. Edward Turner wrote in May 1746, after witnessing Pitt, hero of the opposition of 1742–4, supporting the employment of Hanoverian troops: 'My patience is worn out, in seeing Patriots swallow down Ministerial Puddings piping hot without so much blistering their tongues.'[17] Some sections of the opposition

---

[14] For this ideology, see Colin Haydon, *Anti-Catholicism in Eighteenth-Century England c. 1714–80: A Political and Social Study* (Manchester, 1994).

[15] Quoted in Jeremy Black, 'The Struggle of Politics in Hanoverian England from the Perspective of the Huntingdon Library', *Archives* (1999), 26.

[16] See esp. Nicholas Rogers, *Whigs and Cities: Popular Politics in the Age of Walpole and Pitt* (Oxford, 1989), ch. 3.

[17] Quoted in Richard Trevanion Connors, 'Pelham, Parliament and Public Policy, 1746–1754', Ph.D. thesis (Cambridge University, 1993), 42.

became much more pessimistic about the possibilities of effecting major political change, and of eradicating the corruption which supposedly characterized Whig oligarchy. From the later 1740s until the mid-1750s, national politics also retreated as a topic of press and public discussion. In May 1752, Horace Walpole wrote, looking back to the England of his father's administration, 'England is no longer England . . . news, madness, parties, whims, and twenty other causes, that used to produce perpetual events are at an end.'[18]

The institutional bases for widespread discussion of politics and popular interest in political life in England and Wales did not, however, disappear in the early 1740s. This was most obviously the case in respect of the press, although it was also true of the City of London and Westminster, important centres of anti-oligarchical politics throughout the early-Hanoverian period. War and factional fighting amongst Whig politicians served to reanimate the press between 1742–1746 and again in the mid- to later 1750s.[19] Even in the later 1740s and early 1750s, during the supremacy of the Pelhams, there were papers, most notably the influential tri-weekly evening paper, the *London Evening Post*, which kept up a strong flow of hostile commentary on the personnel and politics of the Hanoverian regime. In the mid-1750s, calls were made in Parliament for tighter regulation of the press, such was the scurrilous and abusive discourse on politics offered by writers in the *London Evening Post*. Those who wrote for the paper included several Jacobites, and while ministers resisted the temptation to impose tighter restrictions on the press, in the following year (1755), the paper's publisher, Richard Nutt, was prosecuted before the Court of King's Bench for seditious libel.

The press also represented an important vehicle for the construction and dissemination of patriotic and national identities. The contents of the majority of newspapers were dominated by foreign news and reports of the course of war and diplomacy. Through the press, a wide cross-section of society was encouraged to view British fortunes overseas as a proper sphere for the exercise of their imaginations and opinions. A background of continual war and heightened international rivalry only made this politically more important and sensitive; these were conditions too in which patriotic feelings and emotions assumed a new importance. As Linda Colley has observed: 'The two decades which followed the Battle of Culloden were an intensely creative period in terms of patriotic initiatives and discussion of national identities'.[20] The idea that Britain's destiny was as a maritime power with global interests and influence came into much sharper focus, especially from the later stages of the War of the Austrian Succession. It was in part Pitt

---

[18] Walpole, *Correspondence*, xx. 315.

[19] Bob Harris, *Politics and the Rise of the Press: Britain and France 1620–1800* (1996), 16. See also Marie Peters, *Pitt and Popularity: The Patriot Minister and London Opinion during the Seven Years War* (Oxford, 1980).

[20] Linda Colley, *Britons: Forging the Nation, 1707–1837* (New Haven, Conn. and London, 1992), 85.

the Elder who, as Marie Peters has argued, personified this shift in the later 1750s and helped further to expedite it:

Pitt came to personify and articulate, with unique panache, the national mood of growing self-confidence. At this major milestone in Britain's emergence as a great power, he epitomized that competition with France which now added a new dimension of clear imperial supremacy to Britain's status.[21]

Kathleen Wilson has talked about the noisy popular enthusiasm for colonial aggrandisement and military victory after 1758 as the 'fulfilment and ultimate expression of mercantilist imperial aspirations'.[22] She has also portrayed these aspirations as one political expression of the growing prosperity and influence of the urban middling ranks in English society. Through imperialist feelings and aims, these groups staked their claim ever more insistently from the later 1730s to greater political recognition and status.[23] Contemporary reactions to the changing conditions of international conflict and rivalry, were, however, more volatile and changeable than Wilson has implied. They were also more ambivalent and, on certain crucial aspects, contradictory. Britons might agree that Britain was a trading nation, that her identity was increasingly that of a commercial society. They might also, in this vein, appreciate the commercial potential of existing and new colonial markets. Equally, however, they might argue that peace represented the optimum conditions in which to promote further growth in overseas trade. A commercial society was not simply one, moreover, of growing refinement and prosperity; it was one in which money and new social habits threatened the integrity, moral health, and stability of the social order. The mid-eighteenth century was also seen as an 'age of pleasure'. The pursuit of pleasure through what contemporaries termed 'public diversions'—pleasure gardens, gaming, masquerades—and the grip of fashion amongst a broad cross-section of especially metropolitan society were undermining well-understood social roles and identities; they were other forces threatening to undermine the commercial and military strength of the nation.

These dilemmas were not easily, if ever, resolved, either intellectually or practically. Important attempts were made, nevertheless, to square the circle. One such means was philanthropy, a vital and expanding force in this period. A key figure here was the traveller, merchant, and indefatigable philanthropist, Jonas Hanway. In his life and writings, Hanway embodies the ambiguities, contradictions, and conflicting emotions prevailing in this period. As one historian has recently written: 'Hanway's thought and prose is full of

---

[21] Peters, *The Elder Pitt*, 114.

[22] Kathleen Wilson, 'Empire of Virtue: The Imperial Project and Hanoverian Culture c.1720–1785', in Lawrence Stone (ed.), *An Imperial State at War: Britain from 1689–1815* (1994), 148.

[23] Kathleen Wilson, 'Empire, Trade and Popular Politics in Mid-Hanoverian Britain: The Case of Admiral Vernon', *Past and Present*, 212 (1988), 74–109; ead., *The Sense of the People: Politics, Culture and Imperialism in England, 1715–1785* (Cambridge, 1995).

ambiguities, alternately very prolix and very muddled, optimistic and wildly fearful, resigned and constantly urging to action.'[24] Through philanthropy, Hanway sought personal respectability and status; he also sought to reconcile, on the one hand, commerce and the pursuit of profit with, on the other, concern for national interest and the public good. He sought to prove, in short, that commerce could be 'virtuous'. Others, as Harriet Guest has recently argued, sought to displace their anxieties by contrasting commerce with the excesses of a fashionable society   what Arthur Murphy was to call in 1753 the 'happy disposition for luxury, gaming, and every vice, folly, whim, foible, Humour and Extravagance'—which was, in reality, commerce's own creation.[25]

This book is not a conventional narrative history; nor does it pretend to be exhaustive. Some episodes—for example, the Jacobite Rebellion or the course of war and international rivalry—are referred to in passing rather than described in detail. Readers requiring such descriptions should look in several recent, admirable studies of them.[26] How Britain was able to mobilize unprecedented resources to fight France and, eventually, to emerge pre-eminent is also a question left to other historians better qualified to answer it.[27] There are other gaps which await detailed research. One is local government, which began to show signs of renewed energy and ambition in this period. Local acts establishing some form of incorporation of the poor showed a new upsurge in the 1750s, while in 1753 an act incorporating the Suffolk hundreds of Colneis and Carlford was the first such act relating to a rural district.[28] Mid-eighteenth-century Scottish politics and society have been far from exhaustively studied. We know relatively little, for example, about the state in eighteenth-century Scotland or about politics at the level of the burghs, including Edinburgh. There is no modern study of the Scottish press. There is room too for a detailed new investigation of the final phases of Scottish

---

[24] Donna T. Andrew, *Philanthropy and Police: London Charity in the Eighteenth Century* (Princeton, NJ, 1989), 92.

[25] *Gray's Inn Journal*, 29 Dec. 1753; Harriet Guest, ' "Those Neuter Somethings": Gender Difference and Commercial Culture in Mid Eighteenth Century England', in Kevin Sharpe and Steven N. Zwicker (eds.), *Refiguring Revolution: Aesthetics and Politics from the English Revolution to the Romantic Revolution* (Berkeley, Calif. and London, 1998), 174.

[26] For the '45, see esp. W. A. Speck, *The Butcher: The Duke of Cumberland and the Suppression of the '45*, new edn. (Gwynedd, 1995): Jeremy Black, Culloden and the '45 (Stroud, 1990); Frank McLynn, *The Jacobite Army in England* (Edinburgh, 1981). For the course of war and diplomacy, see Jeremy Black, *A System of Ambition: British Foreign Policy 1660–1793* (Harlow, 1991), esp. ch 10; id., *America or Europe?*; Paul Langford, *The Eighteenth Century* (1976).

[27] See *inter alia* Middleton, *The Bells of Victory*; John Brewer, *The Sinews of Power: War, Money, and the English State, 1688–1783* (1989); Lawrence Stone (ed.), *An Imperial State at War: Britain from 1689 to 1815* (1994). See also many of the works cited in Jeremy Black, 'Britain as a Military Power, 1688–1815', *Journal of Military History*, 64 (2000), 159–78.

[28] See Joanna Innes, 'The "Mixed Economy" of Welfare in Early Modern England: Assessments of the Options from Hale to Malthus (c.1683–1803)', in Martin Daunton (ed.), *Charity, Self-Interest and Welfare in the English Past* (1996), 161.

Jacobitism. Wales receives no separate discussion, although in this period, as throughout the eighteenth century, one can argue that there was no 'Welsh' politics apart from the English politics of which it was a part.[29]

The main purpose of the book is to uncover (or rather recover) a series of unifying patterns and themes from what is often portrayed as, and what can easily seem, a very fragmented and confusing period in British political history. The Irish poet and writer Ciaron Carson has written in an entirely different context:

> Of necessity, the story they had entered comprised many stories, yet their diverse personal narratives and many-layered time-scales evinced glimpses of an underlying structure, like a traffic flow chart with its arteries, veins and capillaries.[30]

It is the arteries, veins, and capillaries of mid-eighteenth-century British politics and political culture which are this book's main subject.

The chapters are thematic, and each can be read separately. The book is organized, nevertheless, around several main themes. The most important is 'national revival', but closely related to this is the strengthening contemporary recognition that commerce and the consequences of commercial progress were changing British society irreversibly—for better and for worse—and, allied to this, the belief that trade represented Britain's foremost national interest.

The presence of the concept of 'national revival' in British politics was nothing new, and can easily be found in other periods in the eighteenth century. What was singular, nevertheless, was the specific ways in which, under the impact of the changing conditions and course of domestic and international politics, and of economic development, different strands of it combined and recombined. The impact of continuous war and international rivalry from 1739 also gave it special salience. The argument which runs through this book is simply stated: it is that it is in the way in which the various elements of 'national revival' were constituted and reconstituted, the links between them, the attempted reconciliations or pairings, that a great deal of what was characteristic of the period is to be discerned.

The revival or 'restoration' of the primitive constitution, and of the liberty and virtue which supported it, was the ultimate goal of the constitutional opposition to Whig oligarchical rule. This opposition—usually labelled the 'Patriots' or the 'Country Interest'—comprised a broad, unstable alliance of Whigs, Tories, Jacobites, and independents. Whig oligarchy was portrayed by it as corrupt, and as a betrayal of the principles of freedom which defined England's unique constitutional heritage. What exactly a revived politics would look like differed according to political allegiance and, perhaps even,

---

[29] See Peter D. G. Thomas, *Politics in Eighteenth-Century Wales* (Cardiff, 1998). See also Philip Jenkins, *The Making of a Ruling Class: The Glamorgan Gentry 1640–1790* (Cambridge, 1983).

[30] Cairan Carson, *The Star Factory* (1997), 62.

social position. For Tories, it meant a restoration of the natural rulership of the landed classes; for Jacobites, who included some Tories amongst their number, it also meant a restoration of the Stuart Pretender to the thrones of Britain and Ireland; for the mercantile and middling classes greater recognition of their interests and value to society and the state. Other hopes for transformation were readily subsumed within these overlapping visions, hopes for religious and moral revival, for a flowering of national culture, for legal and others reforms, for further commercial progress, and for Britain to realize its supposed national destiny as a trans-oceanic empire devoted to trade and peace. The discourse of restoration came, therefore, to carry hopes for improvement, not simply renovation, without any sense of possible contradiction.

Walpole's fall (in 1742) promised, briefly, to be the new dawn which the Patriot opposition had dreamt of for several decades, only for hopes to be dashed by the narrow ambition of Pulteney and his allies. As the prospect of fundamental political change in national politics receded after 1742, so the sense that political and national renewal was imperative only deepened amongst different strands of opposition opinion, albeit it lacked a strong parliamentary focus. Some argued the need for a hero figure to bring about the reform which normal political processes had failed to produce. In the later 1740s and before his death in 1751, the most likely candidate for this role was Frederick, Prince of Wales. From 1747, and looking forward to a new reign, Frederick began to reconstruct his political identity as a healer of political divisions and ills, and as a focus for national renewal, an identity which his son was to revive on his accession (in 1760). In the later 1750s, Pitt the Elder was the beneficiary of many of the emotions and aspirations which Frederick had begun to harness. But it was the accession of George III in 1760 which led to their fullest expression. As Henry Baker wrote of the new King: 'The surprise begins now to be turned to Joy after the succession of a Prince, sober, sensible, and virtuous, under whom there is a fair Prospect of becoming a happy People.'[31]

National revival was also a major theme in Irish politics. This reflected a definite quickening of economic activity from the later 1740s and a related strengthening of confidence about national economic improvement. The deep pessimism which had characterized Irish thinking on economic development in the 1720s and early 1730s was disappearing, to be replaced by the early 1750s with a more confident outlook. It also directly reflected the influence of an Irish variant of Patriot politics, together with the crisis which overtook Irish politics and relations between London and Dublin in the mid-1750s, the money bill crisis. The language and ideological roots of the Patriot

---

[31] Quoted in D. G. C. Allan, 'The Society For the Encouragement of Arts, Manufactures and Commerce: Organization, Membership and Objectives in the First Three Decades 1755–84', Ph.D. thesis (London University, 1979), 112.

political platform in Ireland were similar to the Patriot platform in England and Wales. A markedly different political and religious context, however, lent it a distinctive set of meanings. National revival in Ireland meant a reduction of English influence in the Irish parliament and Irish politics; it also meant, paradoxically perhaps, the recreation in Ireland of English liberties as the political expression of the equal status of the Protestant nation in Ireland. The crisis of the mid-1750s did not last, and a political accommodation between the different factions and politicians involved was reached in 1756. In this way too, Irish politics mirrored English, in that Patriot hopes of major reform were undermined by the all-too-obvious frailties and mercenary motivations of parliamentary politicians. Yet the episode was not without very important consequences. In the mid-1750s, we see much more clearly than hitherto—even than during the political campaigns of Charles Lucas in the 1740s which galvanized Dublin politics and which Jacqueline Hill has recently documented with great authority[32]—the germination of a new political world in Ireland. It was a development in which the press, as well as Patriotism, had a large role to play. Under the impact of Lucas's interventions in politics and the money bill crisis, a new sort of press emerged in Ireland, one which was much more direct and critical in its commentary on politics. In November 1754, the Irish Lord Chancellor wrote to the Duke of Newcastle:

The spirit of Dissension was for some months, amongst other methods, fomented by licentious & scandalous libels; some of the Publishers of which were apprehended, but the Prosecution stopt with the Grand Jury; & tho' this Evil is of late much abated & several well wrote Papers in defence of his Majesty's Rights have been of undoubted sense in disabusing Persons of Candor, yet the notion of a National Interest, distinct from that of the English Government in this Kingdom, has been so industriously propagated, that the infection has spread itself in every part of this country.[33]

As the Jacobite threat was extinguished in this period, and as Ireland experienced the startling transformation of British fortunes in the Seven Years War, so the question of Ireland's standing within the British state was going to be subject henceforth to unexampled scrutiny, within the Irish parliament and without.

In Ireland, then, as at Westminster, we can discern new political forces and structures emerging. The disappearance of Jacobitism as a major threat was always going to have major repercussions in Ireland with its majority Catholic population. Propertied Catholics and the Catholic Church showed themselves to be solidly loyal during the '45 and during the Seven Years War. More important, however, in the short to medium term was the fact that Protestants—Anglicans and Dissenters—also found repeated opportunities

---

[32] Jacqueline Hill, *From Patriots to Unionists: Dublin Civic Politics and Irish Protestant Patriotism, 1660–1840* (Oxford, 1997).
[33] BL, Add. MS 32377, fos. 245–8.

to demonstrate their staunch loyalty to the Hanoverian and Protestant Succession. Against this background, sections of the Protestant communities gained greater confidence about asserting their goals and hopes. Under the impact of the money bill crisis, and dissent and division amongst Ireland's Protestant political establishment, ministers in London also began to reassess their attitudes towards the political management of Ireland. As evidence of restiveness in Irish politics mounted, there was also a strengthening sense in London that political control needed to be reasserted over Ireland. Only continuing war with France prevented London adopting a more determined strategy with respect to Dublin and Irish politics. We also see the airing of a notion at the very end of the Seven Years War that was to have huge repercussions in coming decades—the idea that the Catholic population represented a potential source of manpower for the armies of an expanding British empire. What Thomas Bartlett has recently called the 'Catholic question'—the question of the status of the Catholic population within Ireland and Britain's empire—was to loom over Irish politics in the second half of the eighteenth century.[34] It was also to introduce a new element of tension into the 'uneasy harmony' which characterized eighteenth-century Irish political life before the French Revolution of 1789 ignited passions and hopes in Irish society which shattered many of the brittle accommodations on which it rested.

The politics of patriotism in Scotland showed several important similarities with that in England and Wales and, even more so perhaps, in Ireland. Yet, in retrospect, it is the differences which stand out. From the later 1730s, Scotland witnessed the development of a strengthening anti-Walpolian opposition politics. It is a politics we currently know rather little about, but it embraced the 2nd Duke of Argyll, who went into open opposition to the ministry in 1739, the Squadrone, the traditional Whig opponents of the Argathelian faction, and Jacobites.[35] After the fall of Walpole, however, it appears to have quickly unravelled. This reflected the extent to which Scottish politics and society were unusually susceptible to elite control and influence; after the '45 it also reflected a mood of accommodation and unity amongst Whigs, and the reuniting of the Argathelian interest behind the third Duke of Argyll.[36]

Insofar as patriotism was a crucial force in Scotland in this period it was, therefore, patriotism of a different sort, a patriotism which expressed not opposition to the politics and personnel of the Hanoverian regime, but rather the reverse. It was a patriotism which sought to sunder the nation's relationship to its past, real and as imagined, to recreate Scotland as an exemplar of

[34] Thomas Bartlett, *The Fall and Rise of the Irish Nation: The Catholic Question 1690–1830* (Dublin, 1992).

[35] See J. S. Shaw, *The Political History of Eighteenth-Century Scotland* (1999). See also Richard Scott, 'The Politics and Administration of Scotland, 1725–1748', Ph.D. thesis (Edinburgh University, 1981). See also the very useful comments in Colin Kidd, 'North Britishness and the Nature of Eighteenth-Century British Patriotisms', *HJ* 39 (1996), 370–3.

[36] See Shaw, *Political History of Eighteenth-Century Scotland*, ch. 4.

modernity, or presumed modernity. The essential contexts for its mid-century manifestation were, as in Ireland, a definite acceleration of economic activity and, unlike in Ireland, a major transformation in Scotland's place within the British state. The defeat of the Jacobite Rebellion was a crucial turning point here. In the first place, the emotions, energies, and intent which went into finally and fully integrating the Highlands into the union with England after the '45 were formidable ones. They also had their origins in Scotland as well as in England. The English in the eighteenth century liked to forget about the Scots; the Jacobite Rebellion jolted some of them at least out of their complacency. It also inaugarated the greatest episode of state-sponsored social engineering in the history of the eighteenth-century British state, as ministers and their supporters throughout Britain sought to transform the Highlands from an outpost of barbarity into an important part of Britain's commercial society. This campaign was, in some respects, misjudged and limited in its effects, but its importance to the history of the period should not be underestimated. Amongst other things, it produced a relatively rapid transformation in perceptions of the threat posed by Scottish Jacobitism.

Secondly, the scare induced by the Jacobite Rebellion caused some Scots, as John Robertson has emphasized elsewhere, to revive a debate which had flourished at the turn of the century   about Scottish national identity, the bonds of society, and the impact of commercial progress.[37] The years after 1745 saw the efflorescence of what Colin Kidd has recently portrayed as 'emulative patriotism' amongst Scots.[38] Examples of this included plans for improvements to Edinburgh, in which the development of the New Town was a central feature; diverse and multiplying schemes of commercial improvement; and the unfolding agitation for the revival of the Scottish militia after 1759. This activity was designed to 'wipe away the stain of the '45' and assert Scotland's place and importance within the strengthening British state and empire. Underpinning it were complex emotions, and while it looked to English society and insititutions as models of progress, especially in economic affairs, it was also fuelled by a competitive dynamic, a sense of possibility about Scotland's future, and confidence about what Scotland had to offer to the Union.

The goal of national revival can also be discerned behind much contemporary parliamentary and voluntarist activity throughout Britain and Ireland. In this context, it can be clearly seen that it was a goal which cut across normal political divisions, or perhaps more helpfully one which took on a variety of overlapping, but distinct, forms. In some cases, these were aligned with either opposition or ministerial politics; in others, they transcended, without eliminating, such divisions. This activity included wide-ranging parliamentary and extra-parliamentary efforts to promote national economic and commercial

---

[37] John Robertson, *The Scottish Enlightenment and the Militia Question* (Edinburgh, 1985).
[38] Kidd, 'North Britishness and the Nature of Eighteenth-Century British Patriotisms'.

development, culture, and the arts; to ensure the continued development of the British colonies in North America as pillars of British prosperity and power; to reduce the British national debt after 1748; and more broadly to put the British state and society in a condition to combat the threat from an expansionist France.

To a significant degree, the state and voluntary initiatives worked in tandem with one another. The Free British Fishery Society, for example, which was founded in 1749 primarily to boost British naval power and commerce, relied on bounty payments funded by the customs to provide financial incentives to encourage merchants and others to engage in deep-sea fishing for herring. Parliament from 1756 provided public funding to the Foundling Hospital, a philanthropic foundation established in 1740 to protect infants who might otherwise be abandoned to die. The Society for the Promotion of Arts, Manufactures and Commerce provided premiums to encourage the develop-ment of better design and skills in British manufacturing, an improving trade balance, and greater employment amongst the poor. Another aim of the Society was supporting the colonial production of raw materials needed by British manufacturers, such as silk in North America. The state, meanwhile, through fiscal policy, provided bounties and drawbacks to facilitate similar ends. Behind many of these efforts was the sense of heightened economic and military rivalry with France. The British state was, as referred to earlier, compared unfavourably in this period with the French as a promoter of over-seas trade and colonial development. Voluntary initiatives were seen as one response to this, one which was more in keeping with English liberties. Debates about poor relief and 'police', in the eighteenth-century meaning of the term, were similarly shaped by fears about French competition. In the latter context, several far-reaching proposals were made which, if implemented, would have had the effect of turning Britain into a much more intensely 'policed' society. The aim was, usually, to ensure that the labouring classes fulfilled their presumed function in society—to work hard and cheaply—and thus ensure continued British prosperity, but also to prevent unwanted social and moral consequences of further economic development. To this extent, the authors were trying to square the same circle which Hanway and the philanthropists were confronted with.

As far as the timing of many of the parliamentary and voluntary initia-tives to revive Britain's economy and society is concerned, a crucial period was between the end of the War of the Austrian Succession and the renewal of conflict between Britain and France in 1754. The end of war meant that there was time for ministers and politicians to devote to domestic and reform issues. Under the Earl of Halifax, for example, the Board of Trade was re-vitalized after 1748 as a force in colonial government and politics, sponsoring far-reaching proposals for a tightening up, and rationalization, of colonial administration and security in North America. When Britain was at war, such proposals tended rapidly to become submerged under the pressure of mobilizing resources for conflict and of the conduct of war and diplomacy. That military forces were rapidly demobilized at the end of each war in the eighteenth century, for reasons of economy and important political constraints on expenditure, only reinforced this pattern. In terms of the chronology of reform, there are strong parallels with developments on the continent, and indeed with events after subsequent wars, the Seven Years War, and, even more markedly, the War of American Independence. British perceptions and actions in this period form, in short, part of a general European pattern; they represent the British dimension of the renewed phase of European state building which followed the end of the War of the Austrian Succession.[39]

Finally, moral and social reform can also helpfully be seen in terms of the theme of national revival. A major argument of this book is that the mid-eighteenth century in England, and to a lesser extent in Scotland, saw a reformation of manners movement, or perhaps more accurately, a strong impetus to one, which has important similarities with the much better known movements of the 1690s and 1780s. This development has eluded most historians, partly simply because they have failed to look for it, or at least look for it in the right places, and partly because, rather than resulting in any major institutional innovations similar to the Societies of the Reformation of Manners in 1690s or the Proclamation Society of the 1780s it came to a relatively short-lived peak of intensity in 1757 before retreating fairly rapidly under the impact of the astonishing British victories in the Seven Years War from 1758. In both the 1690s and 1780s the sense of disruption, challenge, and crisis in the life of the nation was both more profound and longer lasting. Had Britain's military fortunes not been transformed after 1758, there might well, however, have been similar developments to the reforming societies of the other periods. The epicentre of mid-century moral reforming was London and its environs, and the impulses behind it were as various as its forms. Crucial to its emergence and nature were a major crime wave which followed the Peace of Aix-la-Chapelle, perceptions of rivalry with and the threat from France, the revival of a sense of an active providence, and deeper-lying awareness that British society was undergoing crucial structural changes, that trade and commerce were reshaping social relations. Whatever the terms in which it was conceived, the challenge remained fundamentally the same: could Britain restore to her society moral health, order and discipline, economic competitiveness, and, last but by no means least, regain the favour of God.

The approach adopted in this book is, as referred to above, broadly thematic. Chapter 1 explores the nature and changing conditions of national politics in mid-eighteenth-century England and Wales. This provides a basic framework

[39] For an overview, see H. M. Scott, *Enlightened Absolutism: Reform and Reformers in Later Eighteenth-Century Europe* (1990).

for what follows, beginning also to disclose why national revival became such a significant theme in political life in this period. Emphasis is placed too on the main forces shaping political life, especially party identities, and the degree of political stability which existed. The second chapter examines the nature and content of Patriot argument and ideology in England and Wales. A major theme is how far the focus and content of Patriot argument in England and Wales, always a more diverse and complex tradition of argument than is often recognized, changed during this period. Put simply, under the impact of political disillusionment from the later 1740s, Patriot writers focused their attention much more closely than during the years of Walpolian rule on society rather than politics as the source and well-spring of corruption. They also focused renewed attention on irreligion and declining morals as debilitating political ills. Such themes were in themselves hardly new; what was striking, none the less, was the insistence on how deeply and widely luxurious habits had penetrated throughout society, together with the general mood of pessimism which infused their commentaries on society and politics.

The third chapter reconstructs debates about foreign affairs and British participation in war in this period. Two aims are uppermost: first, mapping the ways in which Britain's shifting military and international fortunes were registered in public debate in this period; and secondly, related to this, identifying the ways in which different elements of the political nation responded to these wars. Major themes are the relative rapidity with which North America emerged as the centre of attention in much discussion of war and foreign affairs, how it came to be viewed as the primary locus of British maritime, commercial, and financial power, and the extent to which this changed conceptions of British national identity. A secondary theme is how far issues arising from war and international rivalry engrossed the attention of many different groups throughout society well beyond the confines of the parliamentary classes. In this sphere, as in several others, it was the influence of the press which was crucial. It also, however, reflected the issues and interests which contemporaries thought were at stake. War and rivalry with France became an unfolding drama on to which Britons projected their hopes and anxieties not just about the standing and identity of their nation, but also deeper-lying concerns about the state of society, the political system, overseas trade, popular morals, and religion. The Seven Years War was not just about whether Britain would remain, or fulfil her destiny as, a great power; it was also a war in which fears about the morals and courage of the landed elites pressed hard on contemporary perceptions of the conduct of Britain's military forces; it was a war too in which Scotland particularly, but also Ireland, sought to demonstrate their value and contribution to the cause of Britain and British power overseas.

Chapter 4 concentrates on developments in Scotland after the '45. The starting point is the impact of the rebellion in Scotland and the ways in which different sections of Scottish society responded to the Jacobite threat. Scotland's loyalists, long overlooked by historians, are identified and placed alongside the Jacobites and the apathetic or frightened who comprised the Scottish political nation in 1745–6. The chapter then goes on to examine the consequences of the rebellion and in particular the sustained and broad-based campaign to subdue and transform the Jacobite clans of the Highlands. This campaign served to focus debates about the nature of Scottish society in general as well the position of the Highlands within Scotland and Britain. Commerce and commercial progress were identified even more strongly with loyalty to the Hanoverian Succession. At the same time, writers sought to reaffirm the commercial nature of Scottish society. Scots were, in this period, seeking a sense of national identity which was forward-looking and compatible with their commitment to the Union and growing sense of British identity.

Chapter 5 explores developments in Irish politics in this period. The main focus is on how the money bill crisis worked to politicize Protestant public opinion in Ireland, and in so doing begin to change the underlying nature of Irish political life. Much attention is focused, therefore, on the ways in which Patriots in Ireland in the mid-1750s sought to fashion a sense of crisis in politics, and on the creation of so-called Patriot Clubs, particularly in Ulster and Leinster, to sustain the patriot cause. These clubs, which have never been systematically investigated, became the organizational basis and focus for the development of a more independent, restive public opinion in Irish politics in this period, a force which was to demonstrate its importance (and its limitations) in the general election of 1761, called because of the death of George II. The relationship between developments in, on the one hand, Irish politics and political culture and, on the other, British politics and political culture is also explored.

Chapters 6 and 7 examine a whole series of projects and proposals to revive British commerce, military strength, and security, and to revitalize society which arose in this period. Chapter 6 focuses on schemes to promote British commercial power and in particular to match efforts being made in France and elsewhere on the continent to strengthen their trading and economic base. As economic nationalism waxed strong in Europe, the British legislature was pressed to respond. There were also efforts outside Parliament to promote British manufactures and commerce. The relationship of these extra-parliamentary efforts to party and normal political divisions was complex. Several bodies—for example, the Free British Fishery Society—were broadly aligned with the opposition. The Society for the Promotion of Arts, Manufactures and Commerce was, however, non-partisan. In this, it reflects how far by the mid-1750s partisan politics at the national level were becoming more fluid and confused, but also the degree to which the cause of supporting British commerce, in the face of French competition and the French threat to British security, had become a genuinely national goal.

The final chapter seeks to reconstruct the mid-century campaign for the reformation of manners. The principal focus is on England, but similar developments in Scotland are also examined briefly. The drive to reform morals and manners was closely shaped by perceptions of the commercial and military threat from France. It was also, as already noted, diverse in inspiration and form. A crucial strand was the disciplining of the lower orders. Like so much else in the politics of 'national revival', it was backward looking. It sought to restore the respect for hierarchy, the social disciplines, and 'industry' amongst the lower orders, which gave society its health and stability and which also underpinned economic and commercial prosperity. Not all, however, saw the reformation of manners in this way. For others, it was primarily a religious problem and the solution lay in religion or restoring the influence of the Anglican church and the Kirk in Scotland. Clergymen and bishops also argued that national security and the nation's future depended on restoring a proper relationship to God and God's laws. Britain's destiny was conceptualized in the mid-century in religious as well as secular terms.

The period of the mid-century is interpreted with some flexibility in this book, although the main focus is on the years between the fall of Walpole (1742) and the accession of George III (1760). This reflects the conviction of the author that this period has a particular coherence and unity to it. The accession of George III, as many studies have made clear, overturned many of the assumptions and conventions on which Whig oligarchy had operated from 1714. It also created intense hopes and expectations about political, social, and cultural change. The story of the disappointment of these hopes, and the frustrations this aroused, is one that is separate from the story which unfolds in this book. It has also been largely told elsewhere. I have, however, where it seemed sensible and themes demanded it, extended the chronological span at both ends.

This book is also an attempt to write an inclusive British history. This poses considerable challenges. Those writing British history constantly face the difficulty of how or where to centre the narrative or discussion.[40] The histories of England, Scotland, Ireland, and indeed Wales were overlapping, but separate. Time and time again, developments resist a common interpretative framework. Ireland poses a particular difficulty in this regard. Its relationship to Britain and Britishness was riven with ambiguity; familar concepts, for example, 'the Protestant interest' or 'Patriotism', take on different meanings in Ireland, reflecting its distinctive constitutional and religious identity (or rather identities). Even the term 'Briton' is peculiarly problematic when applied to Irish society. Anglicans would almost certainly have been more happy to be described as part of the 'English interest'; it was Presbyterians of

[40] See the comments of Raphael Samuel, 'Four Nations History', in id., *Island Stories: Unravelling Britain. Theatres of Memory*, ii (1988), 21–40.

Scottish origin who were 'British'.[41] Scotland retained a distinctive institutional, religious, and legal identity at the Union of 1707; indeed, it was this which helped to smooth the further integration of Scotland within the British state as the eighteenth-century proceeded. The chronologies of economic growth and urbanization also differed between the nations which made up the British state. Critics of British history rightly warn of the danger that it might simply become a vehicle for an expanded empire of English history because many accounts choose to place England and London at the centre of their narratives, or serve to elide the important differences between, say, English and Scottish forms of government and political culture. There is no easy solution to the problem, and my approach has been a pragmatic one. Some themes are tackled through the prism of politics at Westminster and St James's and as reflected in the London press, and through it, the provincial, Scottish, and indeed Irish presses; there are also separate chapters on Irish and Scottish developments. In writing in this way, I do so in the conviction that, first, there is great merit in comparing and contrasting the interlinking, but different, histories of England, Wales, Scotland, and Ireland. Secondly, it is a natural perspective to adopt, and one which would have sense to many contemporaries in all four nations. Thirdly, this was a period in which important convergent forces were at work throughout Britain and Ireland. As Alexander Murdoch has recently argued, British history is not an alternative to English, Scottish, Irish, or indeed Welsh history; they are complementary to each other.[42] Others interpret British history differently, as a history with a distinct subject, the always problematic and always incomplete creation of Britain and a sense of Britishness.[43] Much of what I say has relevance to this history, but the main focus of this book is rather different—to offer an interpretation of the forces, ideologies, emotions, events, and some of the personalities out of which was formed the distinctive character of politics and political culture in this period and to bring out the broader significance of this period for an understanding of eighteenth-century British political history.

Lastly, this book is also primarily about the attitudes, interests, hopes, and projects of the upper and diverse middling ranks of society, those groups stretching from the nobility at one end to the tenant farmers, lesser free-

---

[41] David Hayton, 'Anglo-Irish Attitudes: Changing Perceptions of National Identity Among the Protestant Ascendancy in Ireland, ca 1690–1750', *Eighteenth Century Culture*, 17 (1987), 151.

[42] Alexander Murdoch, *British History 1660–1832: National Identity and Local Culture* (1998).

[43] See J. G. A. Pocock, 'British History: A Plea for a New Subject', *Journal of Modern History*, 47 (1975), 601–28; id., 'The Limits and Divisions of British History', *American Historical Review*, 87 (1982), 311–36; 'AHR Forum: The New British History in Atlantic Perspective', *American Historical Review*, 104 (1999), 426–500; S. G. Ellis and Sarah Barber (eds.), *Conquest and Union: Fashioning a British State 1485–1725* (1995); Alexander Grant and Keith J. Stringer (eds.), *Uniting the Kingdom? The Making of British History* (1995); Lawrence Brockliss and David Eastwood (eds.), *A Union of Multiple Identities: The British Isles c1750–1850* (Manchester, 1997); S. J. Connolly (ed.), *Kingdoms United? Great Britain and Ireland Since 1500: Integration and Diversity* (Dublin, 1998); Tony Claydon and Ian McBride (eds.), *Protestantism and National Identity: Britain and Ireland c.1650–1850* (Cambridge, 1998).

holders, shopkeepers, tradesmen, and skilled artisans at the other. These represented about the top third of the population in England, and rather less in Scotland and Ireland. Other sections of the population make less of an appearance, or do so as the subjects of policy and proposals. It is a book, in short, about those who formed the contemporary 'political nation', a population which extended far into and across society but which almost certainly excluded the bulk of the labouring classes and the poor. The experiences of these latter groups, for whom politics and war often meant the unwelcome intrusion of the state in the form of recruitment or impressment, are not ignored because they are unimportant, but because they are not central to the themes of this book.

CHAPTER ONE

The Political World

All Great Men are alike. The only difference is that some are less scrupulous to avow themselves than others. (Bodleian Library, MS Don c 105, fo. 200: John Tucker, MP for Weymouth, to his brother, Richard, 16 December 1742.)

12. Good Friday.—Lord Egmont came [to Bridgewater] with trumpets, noise &c.
13. Saturday. He, and we walk'd the town: we found nothing unexpected, as far as we went.
14. Sunday
15. Monday.
Spent in the infamous and disagreeable compliance with the low habits of venal wretches.
16. Tuesday.
17. Wednesday. Came on the election, which I lost, by the injustice of the Returning Officer . . .
18. Thursday. Left Bridgewater for ever . . .' (Entries for April 1754 in *The Political Journal of George Bubb Dodington*, ed. John Carswell and Lewis A. Dralle (Oxford, 1965), 264.)

John Tucker was reacting to the ministerial changes which had followed the fall of Sir Robert Walpole in February 1742. The resignation of Walpole, who had been in office since 1720 and who in his person and political dominance had come to symbolize all that was supposedly wrong with early-Hanoverian politics, led to expectations of major reform. What occurred amounted to no more than a reshuffle of offices amongst ambitious politicians. As the Revd Francis Ayscough, then clerk of the closet to Frederick, Prince of Wales, recorded in his political journal in May 1742: 'It was all a scramble for Employments.'[1]

George Bubb Dodington was John Tucker's political patron and ally; he was also one of the 'great men' for whom politics was primarily about the pursuit of office and influence. When his political journal was first published, in 1784, it was to support the case for reform of politics and to indict the narrow concerns and cynical manœuvring of the political elite. Dodington's

[1] 'A Leicester House Political Diary 1742–3', ed. R. Harris, *Camden Miscellany*, xxxi, 4th Ser., 44 (1992), 392.

disapproval of the 'low habits' of Bridgewater's voters no doubt reflected the fact that he lost the election. That he lost it to a keen personal rival, the Earl of Egmont, can only have made it worse.

Negative views of mid-eighteenth-century British politics are easy to find. For many historians, the period was characterized above all by political stability. A picture can be created of political battles continuing, but conducted by a narrow elite, and little understood or influenced by those outside this exclusive circle. It was a world in which issues and principles were subordinate to manœuvre and tactics.[2] Threats to political stability were limited. Jacobitism was bloodily and decisively defeated at the battle of Culloden (16 April 1746). Partly because of this, and partly because the religious heats and divisions of the early eighteenth century had passed, Whig and Tory party loyalties, which might have given politics more depth, were unravelling. Against this background, and without major issues to divide the political nation, local elites decided to accommodate or suspend their differences at elections, one result of which was that after the general election of 1741 the number of contests diminished significantly. The occasional irruption of electoral activity and violence, such as occurred in Bristol or Oxfordshire in 1754, only served to remind the rest of the country what it was missing. As John Cannon has recently put it, the electoral system was running on 'vicarious excitement'.[3]

This chapter (and indeed the rest of the book) presents a different picture of mid-eighteenth-century political life and of the mood of politics. Whatever the degree of political stability achieved in Britain in this period, it was not accompanied by lengthy periods of political tranquillity or an absence of widespread and often intense fears about the nation's present and future, except perhaps for a few years in the early 1750s and at the very end of our period. To this extent, the sharp reduction in the number of election contests after 1741 is a poor, or at least limited, index of wider political conditions.

At times during the mid-eighteenth century, the political authority of Whig oligarchy appeared notably fragile, and its course was far from smooth. The years 1742–6 and 1754–7 saw acute governmental instability. Both coincided with major wars—the War of the Austrian Succession (1740–8) and the Seven Years War (1756–63)—which acted to excite and destabilize politics. These wars also produced major challenges to Hanoverian rule in Britain, and to the integrity, security, and prosperity of the British state. The Jacobite rebellion of 1745–6 represented perhaps the most serious threat which the Hanoverian

[2] Such a portrayal of politics is to be found in J. C. D. Clark's *The Dynamics of Change: The Crisis of the 1750s and English Party Systems* (Cambridge, 1982). Clark does not deny the existence of a lively extra-parliamentary politics, but argues that it lacked sophistication and, more importantly, any influence. The central aim of politics, in his view, was power; ideology was secondary. The differences between this and the view of politics being offered here will become quickly obvious in the course of this chapter, and the rest of the book.

[3] John Cannon, *Samuel Johnson and the Politics of Hanoverian England* (Oxford, 1994), 267.

regime had to face during the whole of the eighteenth century; its failure, moreover, did not—as was indicated in the introduction—eradicate the threat of Jacobitism, at least in the minds of many (perhaps most) contemporaries. The landed elite, together with a considerable part of the rest of society, also remained fundamentally divided politically, albeit the fault lines were sometimes not so readily perceived as in earlier decades. Against a background of continuing international uncertainty and tension, of sullen displays of Tory disaffection and alienation in several parts of England, and of the survival of hopes for a further rising amongst disaffected clans in the Highlands, the ideological stereotypes and suspicions which underpinned Whig and Tory party divisions lived on into the 1750s. It was because such divisions continued to fracture the political world, that the political and patriotic unity achieved at the end of the 1750s appeared so striking to contemporaries.

The political world of the mid-eighteenth century was a world too in which vital issues continued to exercise the fears, hopes, and energies of the political elites and wider political nation. Several of these issues reflected long-standing political and religious divisions. Others, however, had their origins in contemporary international conditions and threats. A key question in this latter context was whether the British state and British society had the capacity to repel the challenge posed by French power and international ambition after 1740, the year in which the War of the Austrian Succession broke out. At several times, many (perhaps most) contemporaries would probably have been forced to give a negative answer to this question. In 1758, the Patriot city politician, Richard Glover—admittedly a much disappointed man by this time—wrote of the 'nation's fall, which my ill-boding judgement foresees to be inevitable'.[4] As we will see in Chapter 3, what people came to fear, at least before the later 1750s and the spectacular military victories of British arms in the later stages of the Seven Years War, was that France would finally achieve her supposedly long-standing international ambition—'universal monarchy' or European and global hegemony.

The chapter has three sections. The first examines political life from the point of view of the politicians who dominated ministerial office—the old corps Whigs, together with Whig politicians and factions who sought office, the 'flying squadons' as Lord Hardwicke was to call them on one occasion.[5] The second focuses on the opposition to Whig oligarchical government, which included the Jacobites, Tories, who comprised a majority of opposition MPs throughout this period, opposition Whig and independent MPs, and the press. The press of the later 1740s to later 1750s has been little studied, yet it

---

[4] Richard Glover, *Memoirs of a Celebrated Literary and Political Character from the Resignation of Sir Robert Walpole, in 1742, to the Establishment of Lord Chatham's Second Administration, in 1757, containing Strictures on some of the most Distinguished men of that Time* (1873), 40.

[5] P. C. Yorke, *The Life and Correspondence of Philip Yorke, Earl of Hardwicke, High Lord Chancellor of Britain* 2nd edn., (3 vols., New York, 1977), i. 380–4.

continued to be an important and episodically influential base for dissent from Whig rule. The third section looks briefly at the changes which took place in national politics and political life in the mid-1750s, together with the political unity and consensus which fell on political life in the final years of the mid-century. An important theme throughout is the various constraints which existed on political stability. The focus of the chapter is on England and Wales; Scottish and Irish developments are explored in detail in Chapters 4 and 5 respectively.

MINISTRIES AND THE WHIG INTEREST

From the perspective of competition for high office and political supremacy, the political history of Britain in the mid-eighteenth century is essentially one of rivalries for power amongst the leaders of the old corps Whigs and various Whig factions and politicians. The recent rediscovery of the early-Hanoverian Tory party has not fundamentally altered this fact.[6] The Court was one important site of factional and personal rivalries; the Duke of Cumberland's emergence as an important political actor between 1746 and his military and political disgrace in 1757 only reinforced this fact. George II was far from the cypher of the Pelhams depicted in much opposition propaganda, especially that which emerged from Leicester House, and his favour was crucial to political advancement. As John Owen has emphasized, the events in 1744, when Lord Carteret was forced from office, despite the King's favour, and again in early 1746, when, through the Earl of Bath, he attempted briefly and unsuccessfully to free himself from the Pelhams, were the outcome of special factors favouring the Pelhams; they also easily detract from the King's underlying political influence.[7] Whigs who found themselves out of office, or frustrated about their lack of advancement, used often outspoken attacks on the ministry or particular ministers in Parliament and less often in the press as means to attempt to force their way into office or into new positions. These attacks might involve them in alliances with Tories and independent Whigs, but such alliances were inherently unstable; they were also readily disgarded once the Whigs were admitted to the ministry. This fact created, as John Tucker's comments quoted above begin to reveal, considerable alienation from national politics. Evident from 1742, the pattern became even more marked in the 1750s, although it was complicated to some extent by awareness that a new monarch would reign before long, which gave new political salience to the

[6] Linda Colley, *In Defiance of Oligarchy: The Tory Party 1714–60* (Cambridge, 1982).

[7] J. B. Owen, 'George II Reconsidered', in A. Whiteman, J. S. Bromley, and P. G. M. Dickson (eds.), *Statesmen, Scholars and Merchants* (Oxford, 1983), 113–34. See also Aubrey Newman's reappraisal of George II's political importance in id., *The World Turned Inside Out: New Views on George II* (Leicester, 1988).

junior courts of, first, Prince Frederick before his death in 1751 and, subsequently from 1756, his son, the future George III.

The struggles for office in this period, which had a marked personal dimension, have contributed to the considerable cynicism which exists about political motivations in the eighteenth century. There were those amongst the Whigs who had come to see politics almost entirely in terms of personal ambition and advantage. George Bubb Dodington was probably one of these. So easily and repeatedly did Dodington switch political sides from the later 1730s that Horace Walpole was to dub him on one occasion the 'reprostituted prostitute'.[8] One of Pitt the Elder's foremost characteristics was the ability increasingly to convince himself that his own interest and the national interest were one and the same. Notwithstanding this, his route to office in the 1740s and early 1750s displayed a keen sense of political opportunism, as Namier and others have not been slow to observe.[9] Several steps below such individuals on the political ladder were men like John Olmius. Olmius' main aim in politics was a peerage, and he did not seem to mind who would secure it for him. In the general election of 1741, he acted as Walpole's agent in hard-fought, dirty, and disputed elections in Weymouth and Colchester.[10] In 1751, seeing no prospect of favour from the Pelhams, Olmius was gravitating towards the Court of Prince Frederick and the reversionary interest. In 1757, he sent the Duke of Newcastle a querulous little petition soliciting a peerage as acknowledgement of his 'family, fortune and principles'. This was 'to be laid before the king when there was any design to create knights of the Bath'.[11] It would be easy to multiply these examples. In a political system and society in which patronage was a crucial currency, matters of personal interest did often loom large in politics. The strength of Whig oligarchy also rested, to a significant degree in many parts of the country, on access to patronage.[12] In May 1754, Hans Stanley pleaded with the Duke of Newcastle, in the course of a letter about the disposal of places in his constituency: 'I need not repeat to your Grace, that with the strong Tory bias at Southampton, no Whig can ever be chose without helps of this sort.'[13] Three years later, in December 1757, John White wrote regarding the appointment of a new vicar to the parish of St Alkmond in Shrewsbury. The previous incumbent, who had just died, had been 'since the time of Sachaverall and since a zealous Whig' who

---

[8]   Quoted in Clark, *The Dynamics of Change*, 223.

[9]   See also the judgement reached in E. J. S. Fraser, 'The Pitt–Newcastle Ministry and the Conduct of the Seven Years War, 1757–1760', D.Phil. thesis (Oxford University, 1976).

[10]   The contest in Colchester is fully described in Shani D'Cruze, 'The Middling Sort in Provincial England: Politics and Social Relations in Colchester 1700–1800', Ph.D. thesis (Essex University, 1990), ch. 6.

[11]   BL, Add. MS 32, 874 (Newcastle Papers), fo. 209.

[12]   See esp. J. H. Plumb, *The Growth of Political Stability in England, 1675–1725* (1967); Peter D. G. Thomas, *Politics in Eighteenth-Century Wales* (Cardiff, 1988), chs. 4 and 5; Philip Jenkins, *The Making of a Ruling Class: The Glamorgan Gentry 1640–1790* (Cambridge, 1983).

[13]   BL, Add. MS 32, 734 (Newcastle Papers), fo. 310.

had used his power of nominating churchwardens to give the Whigs locally a majority in setting and levying church and poor rates. In Shrewsbury, the right of election lay in the burgesses paying scot and lot (church and poor rates).[14]

Such facts need to be placed in perspective, however. Most of those who held ministerial office in this period had a strong sense of political duty, as well as a clear conception of the 'national interest'. Newcastle's remarkable longevity in office (1724–56, 1757–61) owed not a little to the fact that he was a dutiful and competent servant of his country and the Hanoverian regime.[15] A recent detailed study of church patronage in the gift of the crown has concluded that while its disposal in this period reflected a concern to reinforce the 'Whig interest', it was not therefore used irresponsibly or without genuine regard for the interests of the Church.[16] The 'Whig interest', which Newcastle and the old corps saw themselves as particular guardians of, also continued to mean more than narrow party or personal interest. It stood, above all, for the security of the Hanoverian and Protestant Succession and the system of balanced government brought into being by the Glorious Revolution of 1688. For ministers and their supporters, the constitution, stable government, and the Hanoverian succession needed to be defended against a licentious press and popular clamour; they also needed protecting from the Jacobite threat and from the Tories.[17] Factious allegations of Jacobitism, such as those made against the former Tories and now important allies of Newcastle, Andrew Stone, William Murray and against certain individuals responsible for the eduction of Prince George, the future George III, in the early 1750s—or indeed those made by the Duke of Bedford against government in Scotland in 1752—had political salience precisely because the integrity of the Hanoverian and Protestant succession continued to be such a touchstone of Whiggism. As Archbishop Herring observed in 1752, with reference to the allegations about 'Jacobite' principles being taught to the young prince:

as to the sentiments of the old whigs, of great account in the kingdom, I know it goes to the Heart of them, That the Education of the Princes should be at all trusted to men, who were brought up in the school of Bolingbroke . . . & I have some reason to say, that, one of the bad man's Principles, is already stirring in the P[rince's] family, viz. That a king of Eng[land] is a King of his People, not of Whigs & Tories—This

[14] BL, Add. MS 32, 881 (Newcastle Papers), fos. 479–80.

[15] See the conclusions on this reached in R. Middleton, *The Bells of Victory: The Pitt–Newcastle Ministry and the Conduct of the Seven Years' War, 1757–1762* (Cambridge, 1985). See also W. A. Speck, *The Butcher: The Duke of Cumberland and the Suppression of the '45*, 2nd edn. (Gwynned, 1995).

[16] Stephen Taylor, ' "The Fac Totum in Ecclesiastical Affairs"? The Duke of Newcastle and the Crown's Ecclesiastical Patronage', *Albion*, 24 (1992), 409–33.

[17] For the views of one old corps' supporter, William Hay, see *Tory and Whig: The Parliamentary Papers of Edward Harley, Third Earl of Oxford and William Hay, MP for Seaford, 1716–1753*, ed. Stephen Taylor and Clyve Jones (Bury St Edmunds, 1998). See also Reed Browning, *Political and Constitutional Ideas of the Court Whigs* (Baton Rouge, La., 1982); Simon Targett, 'Government and Ideology During the Age of Whig Supremacy: The Political Argument of Sir Robert Walpole's Newspaper Propagandists', *HJ* 37 (1994), 289–317.

is a noble Principle, it must be own'd & I would to God, it took Effect truly, but what must be the consequence, when it is only made the Vehicle of Jacobitism and tends to overturn a Government w[hi]ch began and can only be supported upon Whig Principles?[18]

One the first acts of the Rockingham Club, which was founded in 1754 to focus the 'Whig interest' in Yorkshire on the young Marquis of that name, was to offer a reward for the discovery of those responsible for removing the heads of executed Jacobite rebels from the Micklegate Bar in York.[19] Another of these acts was to commission portraits of William III, hero of the Revolution settlement, and George II.

The years of Pelhamite supremacy (1746–54) saw Whig oligarchical government at its most untroubled, at least by parliamentary and popular opposition, as is demonstrated further below. It is this fact which has helped to entrench the notion that political stability had been achieved by the mid-eighteenth century. The basic political strategy pursued by the ministry was one which reflected how well Henry Pelham, First Lord of the Treasury and Chancellor, had absorbed the lessons of Walpolian politics; Pelham pursued a path of cautious, moderate reform and political conciliation.[20] Alongside this path, and occasionally in conflict with it, ministers and MPs also grappled with the problems of restoring British fortunes following the end of the War of the Austrian Succession in 1748, and of dealing with disruptive and disturbing social dislocations caused by the consequent military demobilization.[21] The war left Britain encumbered with a much increased national debt and taxation. It also left Britain's position with respect to France and her traditional allies on the continent, Austria and the United Provinces, dangerously weak. Britain's 'barrier' in the Low Countries, comprising fortresses manned by Dutch and Austrian troops, had been overrun by the French from 1745. The Dutch state, which had seen a revolution in 1747, was in a chaotic and weakened state; Austria's attentions were firmly focused on major administrative and military reform and retrieving Silesia from the Prussians, seized in 1741. The war had also revealed the ability of the disaffected clans in the Highlands, in alliance with France, to threaten the very existence of the Hanoverian

[18] BL, Add. MS 35599 (Hardwicke Papers), fos. 64–5: Herring to Hardwicke, 14 Sept. 1752.

[19] The club offered a reward of 50 guineas for the discovery of those responsible. The Lord Mayor of York offered a reward of £10. The culprit was a Roman Catholic tailor, William Arundel. He was caught when his journeyman, John Moffat, confessed. The 50 guineas paid off Moffat's debt in gaol and he was released. Arundel was fined £5 and imprisoned for 2 years. He was also bound by sureties of £200 for good behaviour for 2 years following his release. See *Scots Mag.* (1754), 46; *ibid.* (1755), 258; BL, Add. MS 32734 (Newcastle Papers), fos. 146–7, 160–3; Paul Monod, *Jacobitism and the English People, 1688–1788* (Cambridge, 1989), 120.

[20] There is no satisfactory up-to-date biography of Pelham, but see John Wilkes, *A Whig in Power, The Political Career of Henry Pelham* (Evanston, Ill, 1964).

[21] For the most recent discussion of Pelhamite politics and policies, see R. T. Connors, 'Pelham, Parliament and Public Policy, 1746–1754', Ph.D. thesis (Cambridge University, 1993).

regime. What can be easily forgotten in discussions of the '45 is that what created most alarm amongst ministers in late 1745 was not the spectacle of the Young Pretender's largely Highland army marching south as far as Derby, but the probability and reality that France was mobilizing a major invasion force to support the rebellion.[22] On 15 December 1745, Cumberland was actually ordered to return to London and desist from chasing the Young Pretender's army, because of reports that the French had landed on the south coast. The order was only countermanded when the reports were discovered to have been false.[23]

From 1748, Pelham focused on a politics of financial reconstruction—consolidating and reducing the interest on the national debt, which he successfully and skilfully did between 1749 and 1751—and of economy, so far as this could be achieved. This also made sound political sense—it allowed Pelham to reduce the land tax from 4 shillings to 2 shillings in the pound in 1753, always a crucial issue with the country gentry; it was also a programme consistent with promoting commercial expansion through easing taxation on trade—a major goal of fiscal policy throughout this period.[24] There was discussion about improving the efficiency of tax collection. Corbyn Morris was dispatched to Edinburgh as secretary of the customs and salt duty in Scotland, where he worked to introduce greater efficiency into revenue collection north of the border and to combat fraud in imports of tobacco and French wines.[25] At the Board of Trade, the Earl of Halifax strove to introduce greater order and economy into the government of British colonies in North America. He also promoted a forward policy in defence of the British empire in North America, a policy which included settlement of Nova Scotia from 1749, land speculation in the Ohio river valley, and ambitious plans for inter-colonial cooperation in their defence against the French.[26] Behind the stance

[22] Recent studies of the '45 include Speck, *The Butcher*; Jeremy Black, *Culloden and the '45* (Stroud, 1990).

[23] Speck, *The Butcher*, 97–8.

[24] For a detailed discussion of Pelham's conversion plan, see Lucy Sutherland, 'Sampson Gideon and the Reduction of Interest, 1749–50', in Aubrey Newman (ed.), *Politics and Finance in the Eighteenth Century: Lucy Sutherland* (London, 1984), 399–413. See also P. G. M. Dickson, *The Financial Revolution in England: A Study in the Development of Public Credit, 1688–1756* (1967), 228–43.

[25] For Morris' role, see BL, Add. MS 32860 (Newcastle Papers), fo. 46; Add. MS 32871, fo. 452; Add. MS 32872, fos. 198–9; Add. MS 33049, fos. 289–90; NUL, NeC (Newcastle (Clumber) Papers), fos. 2042–4, 2047/1, 2048, 2134. Morris reported to Pelham on issues other than those relating to management of the revenue. Various reports on maladministration and common frauds in the Scottish revenue departments are to be found in the Newcastle (Clumber) Papers and in the Treasury Board Papers (T1 series) in the Public Record Office. Morris remained in Edinburgh until 1763 when he was appointed commissioner of customs in London.

[26] J. P. Greene, *Peripheries and Centre: Constitutional Development in the Extended Polities of the British Empire and United States 1607–1788* (New York, 1986), 54–76: id., ' "A Posture of Hostility"; A Reconsideration of Some Aspects of the American Revolution', *Proceedings of the American Antiquarian Society*, 87 (1977), 27–68; id., 'The Seven Years War and the American Revolution: The Causal Relationship Reconsidered', *Journal of Imperial and Commonwealth History*, 8 (1979–80), 85–105; D. M. Clark, *The Rise of the British Treasury: Colonial Administration in the Eighteenth Century* (Newton Abbot, 1960), 76–98.

of Halifax and the Board lay the strengthening perception that Britain's American empire, in which North America occupied a growing importance, was crucial to the country's present and future prosperity and influence; it was also a perception very strongly supported by other ministers, including Pelham and Newcastle.[27] The Admiralty Board, under Anson and, before 1751, the Earl of Sandwich, focused its attention on manning and discipline in the navy; there were also continuing efforts to improve administration and control of the Navy Board and the dockyards.[28] Reform of army discipline was controlled by Cumberland and George II.[29] In Scotland, ministers, persuaded that Jacobitism continued to pose a major threat to the regime, pursued an ambitious programme of eradicating disaffection and the tyranny of clanship, and the poverty on which it allegedly thrived, from the Highlands and ensuring that English (or British) rule was effective north of the border.[30]

The achievements of reform were more limited than many of the ambitions which lay behind them. The reasons for this include the intrinsic difficulties of some of what was attempted, but also the political constraints which shaped what was possible or desirable. Pelham, for example, was not going to experiment with bold fiscal reform, the results of which would be unknown, and which might endanger his efforts to reduce and simplify the national debt. The only significant revenue reform was the Tobacco Act, passed in 1751. This was designed to limit frauds in customs administration in that trade, but was much less far-reaching in its measures (and likely effects) than some English merchants hoped for.[31] Inexpensive reforms were also always most likely to succeed. Plans to create a naval reserve in 1749, for example, came to nothing because of Treasury parsimony.[32] Underlying all these strands in ministerial policy was, nevertheless, an awareness that the outbreak of another major war amongst Europe's great powers was only a matter of time. In the late 1740s and early 1750s, it was feared that Baltic politics and rivalries would precipitate renewed conflict. French post-war reconstruction, politics, and commercial activities were anxiously and suspi-

---

[27] For ministerial attitudes towards North America, see T. R. Clayton, 'The Duke of Newcastle, the Earl of Halifax, and the American Origins of the Seven Years' War', *HJ* 24 (1981), 571–603. See also the comments in Chapter 3, below, p. 121.

[28] See esp. N. A. M. Rodger, *The Insatiable Earl: A Life of John Montagu, Fourth Earl of Sandwich 1718–1792* (London, 1993), chs. 11 and 15. Reform in the navy and navy administration represented a continuation of efforts instigated by a new admiralty board under the Duke of Bedford appointed in 1744. One of the principal achievements of these years was the development of the Western squadron, which was to form the principal feature of Britain's naval strategy in the Seven Years War and for many years thereafter.

[29] A. Guy, *Oeconomy and Discipline: Officership and the British Army, 1714–63* (Manchester, 1985).

[30] See Ch. 4, below.

[31] This established a rigid system of controls concerning the internal movement of tobacco; unmanufactured tobacco could not change hands or move from place to place without a special permit. See Jacob M. Price, *Tobacco in Atlantic Trade: The Chesapeale, London and Glasgow, 1675–1775* (Aldershot and Brookfield, V., 1995), 186–7.

[32] See Ch. 6, below, pp. 254–5.

ciously watched. In July 1750, Pelham declared to his brother that he was

too sensible of the state of that great kingdom [i.e. France] already; which (if they apply themselves steadily to their manufactures and commerce also, in my poor opinion, ought to make us, by oeconomy and proper encouragement to Trade, endeavour to be before hand with them in these great views. . . .[33]

The politics of peace was the politics of war by other means, a pattern familiar throughout Europe in the eighteenth century. Even Newcastle's much-maligned Imperial Election scheme (1749–54), which created continual frictions between him and the economisers, led by his brother, should be seen in terms of national reconstruction and revival. Newcastle was convinced that the opportunities of peace had to be grasped to create a strong anti-French alliance system in Europe. He was equally convinced that the fate of America would, ultimately, rest on events and the conditions of diplomacy in Europe.[34] The diagnosis was astute, albeit the solution—subsidies to German electors to encourage them to vote for an Austrian candidate as King of the Romans, successor to the German imperial throne—was flawed.[35] To a degree that is often underestimated, Britain's eventual successes in the Seven Years War owed a great deal to Prussia's unforeseen invasion of Saxony in 1756, and the astonishing military campaigns conducted by Frederick the Great.

The course of politics following Pelham's death (in 1754) tells us much about the nature of Whig oligarchy and about constraints on the stability with which it has become associated. Factional conflict, which broke out after 1754, was endemic in Whig politics throughout the period. Between 1742 and 1746, within the ministry the most important rivalry was that between the Pelhams and Lord Carteret, or the Earl of Granville as he became on his mother's death in 1744. Before late 1744, the opposition included, and was to a significant degree led by, Whig politicians excluded from the political settlement which followed Walpole's fall. In late 1744, most of these politicians were brought into the ministry, although Pitt was still excluded. In the winter of 1745–6, he, therefore, renewed his parliamentary opposition in order to remind ministers of the need to find him office. In early 1746, he entered the ministry, albeit in a relatively junior capacity, as part of the events by which the Pelhams finally achieved the elimination of Granville as an important influence at Court. In 1750–1, the ministry was destabilized by tension and rivalry between Newcastle and the Duke of Bedford, Newcastle's fellow secretary of state from 1748. Bedford was supported at Court by the Duke of Cumberland and Princess Amelia. In early 1751, a major political realignment

[33] BL, Add. MS 32721 (Newcastle Papers), fo. 358: Pelham to Newcastle, 13 July 1750.

[34] See esp. BL, Add. MS 32719 (Newcastle Papers), fos. 69–74: Newcastle to Hardwicke, 25 Aug. 1749. See also BL, Add. MS 32721, fos. 79–84: Newcastle to Pelham, 9 June 1750.

[35] For Newcastle's diplomacy in this period, see Reed Browning, 'The Duke of Newcastle and the Imperial Election Plan, 1749–1754', *JBS* 1 (1967), 28–47.

briefly threatened, with Newcastle, through Pitt, making overtures to the junior court. It was only the death of the Prince of Wales in March 1751 which allowed the Pelhams to force Bedford from office. What made the rivalries of 1754–7 so damaging to governmental, if not political, stability was unfolding conflict between Britain and France in North America and the outbreak in 1756 of general war in Europe. As in the period 1742–6, rivalries between Whig factions and politicians became closely intertwined in issues raised by British participation in war. Renewed conflict also served to excite political debate and life inside and outside Parliament. In the mid-1750s, popular opinion again became a significant force in politics.

Following his brother's death, Newcastle sought to continue the broad thrust of policy pursued since 1748—economy, firm defence of British interests in North America, and ensuring the writ of British government was fully effective in Scotland.[36] As he declared in June 1754:

I am as strong as any Body for preserving Peace, but I will endeavour to prevent our either being insulted at Home, or our Trade & possessions invaded abroad, & particularly in America by any power whatsoever. Scotland shall be treated as part of our government—but the laws shall be put in Execution there, if I can bring it about, & the King's real Friends supported & promoted.[37]

What prevented him from achieving these goals, or two of them at least, was the accelerating slide into renewed conflict with France.

Newcastle wanted limited military action in response to French expansionism in North America, hoping to keep the conflict confined to that continent. Pressure for a more bellicose strategy came from Fox, then secretary at war, Halifax at the Board of Trade, and the Duke of Cumberland, an influential voice in military matters at this stage. In September 1754, a decision was taken to send two regiments from the Irish establishment to North America under Major General Braddock. Newcastle did succeed, however, in ensuring that the navy had orders in 1755 not to intercept French vessels in European waters, for fear that this might be used as *casus belli* by the French. What ultimately frustrated Newcastle's plan was Braddock's famous defeat in July 1755 *en route* to Fort Duquesne. In the previous month, Vice Admiral Boscawen, cruising with a small squadron off the mouth of the St Lawrence river, failed to intercept a French fleet sailing to Canada to reinforce the fortress of Louisbourg on the island of Cape Breton. With the prospect of full-scale war against France now likely, Newcastle and his colleagues had to confront squarely the possibility that France would attack Hanover, the Low Countries, or mainland Britain, and that it would support Prussian action against Hanover. They were forced to embark, therefore, on a desperate search for defensive treaties with European

[36] For Scotland, see Alexander Murdoch, *'The People Above': Politics and Administration in Mid-Eighteenth-Century Scotland* (Edinburgh, 1980).
[37] BL, Add. MS 32736, fos. 681–2.

powers. While responses from the United Provinces and Austria were unhelpful, treaties were signed in 1755 with Hesse-Cassel and Russia; in January of the following year, a similar treaty would be signed with Prussia. The purpose was to protect Hanover, not to bring Britain into a 'general war' in Europe. These developments created promising issues and conditions for opposition, and for impatient politicians within the ministry. Even before the parliamentary session of 1755–6, when the treaties would need to be supported, Newcastle had decided that his Commons' position needed further strengthening. What he feared was not the size of the opposition, but the lack of strong speakers to support ministerial policy in debates. Between July and the opening of the parliamentary session, a desperate effort was made to shore up the ministry's forces in the Commons, including 'feeling the pulse of the Great Pitt'.[38] Overtures were made to the Duke of Argyll, which ended in Newcastle conceding entirely Argyll's demands relative to Scottish administration; the assault on Scottish autonomy was ended. Finally, on the eve of the session, agreement was reached with Fox, who was to be leader of the ministry in the house with full authority—a position he had been denied in 1754—and, once the session was begun, secretary of state in place of Sir Thomas Robinson.[39]

Unlike his immediate predecessors, Walpole and Pelham, Newcastle was attempting to lead the ministry from the Lords. In recent years, there has been some debate about whether this was, as is often assumed, doomed to failure or was, in fact, practical.[40] Following an unusually heavy effort to whip in ministerial supporters for the opening of the session, Newcastle's majority in the Commons held firm in the winter of 1755–6, despite a violent and often intemperate assault against the subsidy treaties led by Pitt, for which he was dismissed from office, along with Henry Bilson Legge and George Grenville. There was little evidence yet that popular opinion was becoming alienated from the ministry and its conduct of the war, beyond a small faction within the City. Even Braddock's defeat and Boscawen's failure did not cause mercantile and popular opinion to turn against the ministry. In the early months of 1756, fears of invasion from France dampened the impact of an often outspoken parliamentary and press opposition to the stationing of Hanoverian and Hessian troops in England.[41]

However, the event which decisively transformed the balance of political forces facing Newcastle, and exposed the underlying weaknesses of his political position, was the loss of Minorca in June 1756. The military setback provoked an upsurge of popular outrage and clamour, which was to last at least until the end of the year. Popular anger and alarm was to be further

[38] BL, Add. MS 32858 (Newcastle Papers), fo. 40.
[39] For Fox's role in this period, see esp P. A. Luff, 'Henry Fox and the "Lead" in the House of Commons, 1754–1755', *Parliamentary History*, 6 (1987), 33–46.
[40] See esp. Clark, *The Dynamics of Change*.
[41] See esp. Marie Peters, *Pitt and Popularity: The Patriot Minister and London Opinion during the Seven Years War* (Oxford, 1980), 40–6.

stirred during the summer and autumn by continued military and diplomatic failures. These included the dramatic conclusion of a treaty between France and Britain's old ally, Austria; Prussia's invasion of Saxony at the end of August; and the fall of Fort Oswego on Lake Ontario in North America to the French in October. It was a dismal scene, which appeared full of menace to British interests and security. The failure successfully to defend Minorca, and the gale of popular anger demanding political retribution for the loss, raised uncomfortable issues of political responsibility. Both Newcastle and Fox feared they would be forced, personally, to shoulder the blame for the setback. Unable to hold on to the services of Fox, who chose to resign rather than face the ire of the Commons, or to entice Pitt back into office—Pitt had been developing strong links with the junior Court at Leicester House from the summer—Newcastle himself resigned in early November. What seems to have weighed most heavily with him was his and his ministry's now exposed position in the Commons. He had lost another major debating talent to the Lords in the summer, Lord Mansfield (formerly William Murray), and MPs could be expected to reflect the concern and agitation of popular opinion. As Newcastle declared to Hardwicke at the beginning of September:

I could have wished in this Time of Difficulty, Danger, and almost Universal Uneasiness and Discontent, thro' out the whole Kingdom; (of which I receive fresh Accounts from all Quarters, and from undoubted Hands) That your Lordship could have suggested some adequate Expedient, for stemming the Torrent, and Effect, of this ill-Humour, in the House of Commons.[42]

Pitt, now allied with Leicester House, also appeared much more likely to be able to impose a degree of unity on what had hitherto been a divided, weak opposition.

A return to ministerial stability had to wait well over a year. The Newcastle ministry was followed in office by a relatively short-lived coalition led by the Whig peer, the Duke of Devonshire—who had most recently been Lord Lieutenant of Ireland—and Pitt. Lacking the essential ingredients for longevity in office—parliamentary strength and the firm support of George II—it was dismissed in April 1757. The challenge which now faced the Whig elite, and which had in a sense faced them since Newcastle's dismissal at the end of the previous year, was essentially one of how to reconcile the power and influence of Newcastle, with his large parliamentary support and continuing favour of George II, with the ambition of Pitt and Fox. This was complicated by a lack of trust amongst these politicians, uncertainties about their goals and nature of their ambitions, but also by dynastic tensions between the court of Prince George, under the management of the Princess Dowager and Lord Bute, and Fox's royal patron, the Duke of Cumberland. The eventual outcome was the Pitt–Newcastle ministry, formed in June. This brought not only a new

---

[42] BL, Add. MS 32867 (Newcastle Papers), fos. 175–85: Newcastle to Hardwicke, 2 Sept. 1756.

measure of political stability—it was to endure until 1761—it was also to oversee a remarkable turnaround in Britain's international and military fortunes. It is crucial to recognize, however, that neither could have been predicted in 1757. As George Bubb Dodington was to write three years later, 'This country has undergone such a surprizing variety of changes of late, that the imagination can hardly keep pace with it . . .'.[43] In the early summer of 1757, the spectacle of Whig politicians squabbling over power and the spoils of office, when Britain was facing defeat and ruin in a major war for the nation's survival as a major international and commercial power, left the reputation of the personnel and politics of the Hanoverian regime at perhaps its lowest ebb since the early 1720s and the collapse of the South Sea Bubble. Whig oligarchy appeared to be not just irresponsible and corrupt, but inept as well. It is no accident, as we will see below, that 1756–7 saw a revival of demands for the kind of major political reform last called for at the time of Walpole's fall.

OPPOSITION TO WHIG OLIGARCHY

The history of opposition to Whig oligarchy in this period is, from one persective, a history of increasing impotence. One source of opposition which has attracted a great deal of attention amongst historians in recent years, but little consensus about its nature, was support for a restoration of the Stuarts. The evidence, which is fragmentary and controversial, is not such as is likely ever to admit of a definitive conclusion. Several points can, nevertheless, be made with confidence. First, ministers took the challenge of Jacobitism very seriously indeed. As was emphasized at the beginning of this chapter, Britain's entry into war with Spain in 1739 and the outbreak of the War of the Austrian Succession in 1740, into which Britain was quickly drawn in 1741, very significantly increased the chances that Jacobitism would find major foreign support, most probably from France, Britain's principal international rival. Britain faced major invasion scares in 1740, 1743–4, and 1745 during the War of the Austrian Succession and in 1755–6 and again in 1759 during the Seven Years War. Nor was it by any means certain that the British navy would be able to intercept a French invasion force.[44] Secondly, Scotland, and a number of the Highland clans, remained the main source of potential and actual military support for a restoration attempt, as the events of the Jacobite Rebellion of 1745–6 demonstrated.[45] Whatever the levels of Lowland support in 1745–6 for the Young Pretender, it was clansmen who bore the brunt of the fighting

---

[43] *Dodington Political Journal*, 389.

[44] See J. Black, 'British Naval Power and International Commitments: Political and Strategic Problems, 1688–1770', in M. Duffy (ed.), *Parameters of British Naval Power 1650–1850* (Exeter, 1992), 39–59.

[45] A point emphasized recently by Allan Macinnes (id., 'Scottish Jacobitism: In Search of a Movement', in T. M. Devine and J. R. Young (eds.), *Eighteenth-Century Scotland: New Perspectives* (East Linton, 1998), 70–89.

and on whose determination and fighting prowess Jacobite fortunes turned.[46] Jacobite hopes, as is made clear in Chapter 4 below, were also far from extinguished by the defeat at Culloden and its bloody aftermath as the British army swept through disaffected areas. There were displays and signs of continued disaffection in Episcopalian north-east Scotland, for example in Montrose.[47] In Leith, the Scottish capital's port, the Young Pretender's birthday appears to have been celebrated in 1746; a major attempt to hold similar celebrations in Edinburgh itself was only foiled by determined action by magistrates and soldiery.[48] Jacobite pamphlets and ballads also appear to have circulated on a considerable scale.[49] Catholic priests were said to be disseminating 'Popish books, rebellious songs, pamphlets, Declarations and Manifestoes' in the Highlands. They also carried 'pieces' printed in 1715 and 1745 with them.[50] Ministers and the administration in Edinburgh maintained close surveillance of disaffected areas and of any sign of conspiracy amongst the clans, just as they sought information about Jacobite activities abroad. From this, and their diplomats and informants in Europe, they were fully aware that Jacobites were continuing to fish in troubled international waters after the Peace of Aix-la-Chapelle (1748). In the early 1750s, Prussia appeared to the Jacobites to offer the most likely source of foreign support for a further restoration attempt.

Ministers were far from complacent, therefore, about the Jacobite threat after 1746, continuing to believe that Jacobitism posed a potentially very grave threat to the regime. It was for this reason that Pelham and his colleagues decided in 1753 to execute Dr Archibald Cameron, brother of Donald Cameron of Lochiel. Taken up in the Highlands by troops from the Inversnaid garrison, Cameron was condemned under act of attainder for his role in the '45.[51] In June, he had the distinction of being the last Jacobite to be executed on British soil. To his death, which he faced with exemplary bravery, Cameron maintained his innocence.[52] In reality, he was up to his neck (if this is an appropriate word given his end) in what was a confused episode of plotting known as the Elibank plot. Unfortunately for Cameron, the plot had been fully known to ministers through information provided by the well-placed spy.[53]

[46]   For a recent attempt to underline lowland support for the Young Pretender in 1745–6, see Murray G. H. Pittock, *The Myth of the Jacobite Clans* (Edinburgh, 1995).

[47]   'Extracts from the Diary of the Rev John Bisset, Minister at Aberdeen, 1745–6', *The Miscellany of the Spalding Club*, i (Aberdeen, 1891), 397; NLS, MS 304 (Letter Book of General Bland, 1747–54), fos. 41–4, 50.

[48]   NLS, MS 17527 (Saltoun Papers), fo. 114; PRO, SP 54/34/55A-C.

[49]   NAS, GD 248/565 (Seafield Papers), fo. 49; NAS, RH 2/4/370, fos. 207, 223; *General Evening Post*, 1 Jan 1748; NLS, MS 309 (Erskine-Murray Papers), fos. 32–3; RACP, Cumberland Papers, 43/287.

[50]   BL, Add. MS 32731, fo. 406.

[51]   The act excepted named individuals from an act of general pardon passed in 1747.

[52]   Sir James Lowther noted that, 'Dr Cameron behav'd very undaunted & dyed with great resolution' (CRO (Carlisle), D/Lons/W2/115, Lowther to John Spedding, 7 June 1753). See also *Scots Mag.* (1753), 279–81; Walpole, *Correspondence*, xx. 384.

[53]   For Archibald Cameron, see Bruce Lenman, 'Physicians and Politics in the Jacobite Era', in Eveline Cruickshanks and Jeremy Black (eds.), *The Jacobite Challenge* (Edinburgh, 1989), 86–7. The spy, whose codename was 'Pickle', was Alastair Ruadh MacDonnell of Glengarry.

Ministers also remained very concerned about Jacobitism south of the border. This was despite the fact that English support for the '45 had been insubstantial. Ironically, in the years after the suppression of the rebellion, ostensible signs of support for the Stuarts in different parts of England became much more visible. Ministers and their supporters were alarmed in 1748 by drunken Jacobite demonstrations amongst undergraduates at Oxford University, which led to plans being discussed in 1748 for a visitation of the University in order to bring it under closer political discipline.[54] In 1754, further stories were circulated about Jacobite activities and affiliations at the University. That the sources of these stories were Whig politicians, William Pitt and the staunch Oxford Whig, Richard Blacow, and that they surfaced against the background of a vicious and hugely expensive election contest for Oxfordshire in the 1754 general election fought on Whig and Tory party lines, is the best guide to their nature and the partisan motivation which lay behind them.[55] Staffordshire and the West Midlands also saw a series of Jacobite, or apparently Jacobite disturbances, culminating in an episode of substantial unrest in and around Walsall in 1750.[56] There were also other, more minor episodes of disaffection. In 1750, for example, the Pretender was proclaimed by a group of keelmen in a field outside of Newcastle.[57]

Ministers and their supporters took such incidents seriously. As Pelham wrote to Newcastle on 28 June 1750: 'I don't like these overt acts of disaffection for tho' low people only appear in 'em, they must be promoted and countenanced by some of the better sort. I wish to God we may find them out; and I hope they will then be severely trounced.'[58] Ministers were determined to see those involved punished. Responsibility for punishing the drunken Oxford undergraduates was removed from the University, and their cases prosecuted in the Court of King's Bench by the Attorney General. The Vice Chancellor of the University was also faced with the prospect of prosecution for his failure to take the incidents sufficiently seriously.[59] In 1754, ministers were impatient with Oxford magistrates when they failed to discover those who ministers believed were the true authors of the 'Rag Plot'—so called because it concerned a series of seditious verses

---

[54] W. R. Ward, *Georgian Oxford: University Politics in the Eighteenth Century* (Oxford, 1958), 170–91.

[55] Ibid., 192–206.

[56] See esp. Nicholas Rogers, *Crowds, Culture and Politics in Georgian Britain* (Oxford, 1998), 48–50; Paul Kleber Monod, *Jacobitism and the English People 1688–1788* (Cambridge, 1989), 198–209. For further incidents of 'disaffection in Staffordshire in this period, see BL, Add. MS 35599 (Hardwicke Papers), fos. 23–4, for drinking Young Pretender's health in the autumn of 1750; and BL, Add. MS 32766, fo. 195, for attacks on Dissenters and the pulling down of a dissenting meeting house in 1752.

[57] *Gent. Mag.*, 20 (1750), 232.

[58] BL, Add. MS 32721, fos. 194–5: Pelham to Newcastle, 28 June 1750.

[59] Ward, *Georgian Oxford*, 171.

found in a pile of rags in Oxford market place.[60] Magistrates in Newcastle were offered the assistance of troops in response to the 'disaffection' of the keelmen.[61] In the West Midlands in July 1750, three troops of horse were sent to Birmingham, two to Walsall and one to Wednesbury. The cases of several rioters were also conveyed from the local assizes to the King's Bench, to increase the chances of securing a conviction.[62] Apparently minor incidents such as the removal from the top of the Micklegate Bar in York of the heads of Jacobite rebels executed after the '45, referred to earlier in this chapter, were not allowed to pass unnoticed or unpunished.

How historians should interpret such incidents is an interesting issue. Several of the episodes of Jacobite rioting in the West Midlands reflected Tory alienation and disgruntlement in the later 1740s. They also reflected Tory anger at the defection of one of their leaders to the ministry in 1745, the Staffordshire peer, Lord Gower.[63] The keelmen included a substantial Scots Presbyterian element; they had also demonstrated their loyalty during the '45. It is also significant that the incident took place during a labour protest.[64] Tokens of disaffection were not uncommon in popular protests. In 1753, Newcastle, for example, received reports of anti-turnpike riots in Wiltshire in which talk surfaced of the imminence of French support for the protestors. In 1756, food rioters in Warwickshire refused to disperse until the 'Pretender came to stop them'.[65] One recent re-examination of the disturbances in Walsall and around the West Midlands in 1750 has concluded that they are better seen in the context of local politics and rivalries than in terms of organized support for a Stuart restoration.[66] In Shrewsbury, where there was a Jacobite demonstration in 1750, Pelham acknowledged the role of provocation from soldiers stationed there; they had, he noted, been a 'little indiscreet'.[67]

There did remain a determined Jacobite presence in the press. It was a world, in London at least, of marginal, dependent figures, often mired in debt, and which often remains largely hidden from our view.[68] Several were part of

---

[60] See BL, Egerton MS 3440, fos. 77, 82, 126–7.

[61] BL, Add. MS 35870 (Hardwicke papers), fos. 138–9. A proclamation was also published in the *London Gazette* offering a pardon to anyone who could bring evidence to capture and prosecute those involved, except the individual who had actually proclaimed the Pretender.

[62] Monod, *Jacobitism and the English People*, 206–7. Again, this was partly done because ministers were convinced that the defendants were supported by people of higher social standing than themselves.

[63] See esp. ibid., 199.

[64] *Gent. Mag.*, 20 (1750), 232; *Newcastle Gazette*, 6 Nov. 1745; Joyce Ellis, 'A Dynamic Society: Social Relations in Newcastle-upon-Tyne 1660–1760', in Peter Clark (ed.), *The Transformation of English Provincial Towns* (1984), 209–14.

[65] BL Add. MS 32732, fo. 343; Monod, *Jacobitism and the English People*, 197.

[66] Rogers, *Crowds, Culture and Politics*, 50.

[67] BL, Add. MS 32721, fos. 194–6: Pelham to Newcastle, 28 June 1750.

[68] Outside of London, the only Jacobite paper which remained in this period was Elizabeth Adams' *Chester Courant*. Various articles which first appeared in the *Courant* were reprinted in pamphlet form. See *Manchester Vindicated: Being a Compleat Collection of Papers Lately Published in Defence of that Town, in the Chester Courant* (Chester, 1749); *The Chester Miscellany. Being a Collection of Several Pieces, both in Prose and Verse,*

a world of popular publishing, often working on the fringes of legality. These included Dr Gaylord, who had been an apprentice of Nathaniel Mist—an influential Jacobite newspaper printer in the 1710s and early 1720s—Abraham Illive and William Rayner.[69] In 1747, the ministry sought the printer and publisher of two pamphlets of dying speeches of Jacobites executed after the '45. These included comments designed to highlight the barbarity of 'Whig justice' and the Hanoverian regime. The main suspect was the Catholic bookseller, Thomas Meighan.[70] Jacobite prints of the Young Pretender also appear to have been quite widely available after the '45, and several seditious maps were printed and distributed.[71] There were also several narratives or 'chronicles' of the exploits of the Young Pretender in 1745–6.[72]

One figure in the Jacobite press for whom we have more information than most was a man called George Gordon. Gordon was involved in two overtly Jacobite papers, the *National Journal; or, the Country Gazette* (1746) and the *True Briton* (1751–3) and a paper, the *London Evening Post* which had Jacobite connections and which provided several hints of, in one contemporary's rather neat phrase, 'a higher allegiance'.[73] The Reverend Samuel Eccles, another Jacobite, worked on both the *True Briton* and the *London Evening Post*. Eccles became a deputy reader in 1753 at the Chapel of the Bridewell hospital, a Tory-dominated establishment; he also published a sermon in that year against the Jewish Naturalization Act, the proceeds of which were to be given

which were in the Chester Courant from January 1745, to May 1750 (Chester and London, 1750); A Brief Account of the Martyrdom of K. Charles I of Blessed Memory [extracted from the Chester Courant] (Chester, 1752).

[69] PRO, SP 83, fos. 471–5, 478, 480; SP 36/77, fo. 51; SP 36/84, fo. 138. For a general discussion of these individuals and the world in which they operated, see Michael Harris, London Newspapers in the Age of Walpole: A Study in the Origins of the Modern English Press (London and Ontario, 1987), ch. 5. Rayner was behind the printing and publication of Archibald Cameron's dying speech in 1753 (BL, Add. MS 32733, fo. 207).

[70] The pamphlets were: A True Copy of the Papers, Wrote by Arthur Lord Balmerino, Thomas Syddal, David Morgan, George Fletcher, John Berwick, Thomas Deacon, Thomas Chadwick, James Dawson, and Andrew Blyde, and delivered to the Sheriffs by them at the Places of their Execution; A True Copy of the Paper read by Mr James Bradshaw and delivered by him to the Sheriff of Surry just before his Execution at Kennington Common on Friday, November the 28th 1746 (1746). PRO, SP 36/93, fos. 4–9 159–61, 163–5, 167–8, 169–72; SP 44/84, fo. 127.

[71] In 1747, a warrant was issued for the seizure of persons and papers of individuals involved in importing prints of the Young Pretender into Britain (PRO, SP 44/84, fos. 164–5). In 1749, print seller and publisher, George Bickham, of Mays Buildings, St Martin in the Fields, was implicated in the sale of prints of the Young Pretender and several seditious maps (Monod, Jacobitism and the English People, 83). Early in 1750, the press also reported that an unnamed engraver and print seller had been taken up for selling a new print of the Young Pretender imported from France (Bristol Journal, 24 Feb. 1750).

[72] Monod, Jacobitism and the English People, 37.

[73] For the London Evening Post, see my, 'The "London Evening Post" and Mid Eighteenth Century British Politics', EHR 110 (1995), 1132–56. In 1743, Gordon's name had been put forward to organize a Jacobite paper to exploit the intense anti-Hanoverian sentiment of the time (Michael Harris, London Newspapers in the Age of Walpole, 131). He was also responsible for seeing through the printing and publishing stages of Jacobite Thomas Carte's important defence of Tory participation in the Broad-Bottom ministry, The Case Fairly Stated in a Letter from a Member of Parliament in the Country Interest to One of his Constituents (1745) (Robert (Bob) Harris, A Patriot Press: National Politics and the London Press in the 1740s (Oxford, 1993), 73). The phrase 'Higher' allegiance was James Ralph's (id., A Critical History of the Late Administration of Sir Robert Walpole (1743), 516).

to Archibald Cameron's widow.[74] The *National Journal* was short-lived, being brought to an early end by Gordon's imprisonment for treasonable libel.[75] The *True Briton* was the second of two Jacobite periodical publications conducted by George Osborne, the first being the *Mitre and Crown* (1748–50). The *True Briton* was never very successful, although it did fire the enthusiasm of one Jacobite in exile, Andrew Lumisden.[76] Its content of serious political and religious commentary never caught the enthusiasm of London newspaper readers, as Osborne acknowledged in a verse he wrote in the spring of 1753:

> But for True Brit two pence to spare,
> The fat Cit thinks would be waste,
> What's the good of Mind a Year,
> Compar'd with one Venison Feast?[77]

Osborne wrote and sought to manage the paper from the Fleet prison, where he had removed himself because of a suit against him for debt. Although he did receive some encouragement from John Caryll, Edward Gibbon (father of the historian), and James Edward Oglethorpe, this was limited and insufficient to maintain the paper. Osborne also became embroiled in arguments with Eccles about money and the conduct of the paper.[78] The fact that the paper does not appear to have attracted the attention of ministers, or ministerial supporters, is perhaps the strongest indication of its lack of influence.

Osborne, Eccles, and Gordon were part of a shadowy world of metropolitan Jacobitism. It was a world which included several aldermen and common council men of the City of London, and appears to have been focused on a series of clubs and taverns.[79] Before his death in 1755, William Benn, Lord Mayor in 1747, was a leading Jacobite figure in City politics. At the meeting in the City to nominate candidates for election in 1747, Benn not only failed to gain any support, but was 'great hissed on account of his being suspected to be a Jacobite'.[80] Another City politician whose path to Jacobitism was more

[74] The sermon, entitled *The Candid Determination of the Jews in Preferring a Thief and a Robber before our Saviour*, was advertised in the *London Evening Post* on 19 June 1753. 'Pickle', or Young Glengarry, reported in 1751: 'That a clergyman of the Church of England, who belongs to one of the Hospitals, but whose name he cant at present recollect, 'tho' he will endeavour to recover it, is one of the principal persons employed in collecting the money that is rais'd here for the Pretender's service.' It is almost certain that he is referring to Eccles (NUL, Newcastle (Clumber) Papers, Nec 2088/1). See also NUL, Nec 2091, for a further allusion by Glengarry to Eccles.

[75] See Jeremy Black, 'A Short-Lived Jacobite Newspaper: The *National Journal* of 1746', in Karl Schweizer and Jeremy Black (eds.), *Politics and the Press in Hanoverian Britain* (Lewiston, NY, 1989), 77–87.

[76] NLS, Acc. 11328: Lumisden to Capt Edgar, 26 Sept. 1752; Lusmisden to Robert Strange, 20 Mar. 1753.

[77] BL, Add. MS 28236, fo. 38.

[78] See ibid., *passim*. See also Monod, *Jacobitism and the English People*, 33–4.

[79] Nicholas Rogers has argued that the notion that London was a disaffected capital is to strain the evidence too far. Jacobitism was an element in City opposition politics, but not the dominant one (id., *Whigs and Cities: Popular Politics in the Age of Walpole and Pitt* (Oxford, 1989), esp. p. 81). See also Monod, *Jacobitism and the English People*, 181–2.

[80] NLS, MS 16647 (Saltoun Papers), fos. 134–5.

tortuous was George Heathcote. Heathcote emerged in the later 1730s as an outspoken opposition Whig, influential in the later stages of the anti-Walpolian opposition; his involvement in the politics of disloyalty appears to have been motivated primarily by disillusionment with the successive betrayals of parliamentary opposition leaders after 1742. The inns and meeting places of metropolitan Jacobitism are imperfectly glimpsed in the reports of spies, such as Newcastle's semi-literate informant, John Gordon.[81] In 1753, the King's Messenger, Nathan Carrington, was sent to Wapping to report on the Thistle and Crown, an alleged haunt of the disaffected.[82] Three years earlier, John Blachford, another alderman, was reported to have attended a Jacobite club in Fenchurch Street.[83] Another present at this club was his colleague, Matthew Blakiston.[84] It was from the metropolitan Jacobites, and their landed allies, that the Young Pretender saw, surprisingly, the best hopes of a new restoration attempt after the failure of the '45.[85] In 1750, he even visited London. Jacobite politics in this guise was a politics with a distinctly Whiggish colouration. The metropolitan Jacobite taxed Whig oligarchy with its betrayal of the promise of 1688 and of English liberties. The issue was how to effect Britain's deliverance from corrupt and tyrannical government. Henry Fielding's Jacobite-Republican alderman was not merely a polemical fiction designed to aid the cause of the Whigs in the 1747 general election; it was also testimony to the complexity and ambiguity of opposition politics in this period.[86] As Paul Monod has noted, Jacobite prints in this period depicted the Young Pretender as a true Whig hero, the guardian and saviour of English liberties.[87] Jacobites blended into a broader opposition in the 1740s and 1750s, one that transcended narrow partisan divisions without undermining them. That Jacobitism took this form only makes it more elusive to the historian.

Turning now to constitutional opposition to Whig oligarchy, a clear contrast needs to be drawn between the years of Pelhamite supremacy and the early 1740s. In the early 1740s, a vigorous opposition, comprising opposition Whigs, Tories, and Jacobites, faced a divided and uncertain ministry. They had other powerful political resources. These included a politically maturing

[81] Gordon's reports, written in a spiky, awkward hand, 'litter' Newcastle's papers for this period. Gordon had first been employed by Walpole. Sir Lewis Namier caustically remarks that 'his reports show what nonsense will be paid for in the 'secret services' (id., *The Structure of Politics at the Accession of George III*, 2nd edn. (1957), 428 n. 1). Gordon was receiving an annual payment of £120.

[82] BL, Add. MS 32731, fos. 415–16.

[83] NUL, Nec 2091 (Newcastle Clumber Papers).

[84] NUL, Nec 2091. The club comprised a majority of, according to Glengarry, 'low ordinary people'. See also BL, Add. MS, 32735, fo. 453, where John Gordon informs Newcastle that Blakiston and around 60 others had been at a Jacobite gathering in 1754 at the Morning Buck, without Aldersgate.

[85] The standard account of the final years of Jacobite conspiracy remains Sir Charles Petrie, *The Jacobite Movement: The Last Phase, 1717–1807* (1950).

[86] Henry Fielding, *A Dialogue between a Gentleman of London and an Honest Alderman of the Country Party* (1747).

[87] Monod, *Jacobitism and the English People*, 84–5.

metropolitan and provincial press which had developed rapidly in the last three decades, and which tended to be aligned politically, if at all, with the opposition.[88] It was also a press over which government control was limited, despite the availability of what in theory was a powerful panoply of policing powers.[89] Another major factor helping them was the existence of an influential metropolitan opposition embracing Whigs, Tories, independents, and Jacobites. This had played a prominent and important role in the final years of opposition to Walpole. Thomas Hay, a Walpole supporter, was to assert in the aftermath of Walpole's defeat, 'I believe there is no one Cause, to which the fall of the Minister [i.e. Walpole] is to be more ascribed, than to the hatred of the City of London.'[90] Prominent opposition politicians in 1742–5 also developed strong links with another focus for metropolitan opposition which had come into existence in the final months of Walpolian rule, the Westminster Society of Independent Electors, a body whose composition was to reflect closely the fluctuating elements of opposition politics in these years.[91] The Walpolian opposition had also left a legacy of political strategy and tactics—intervention in the press, petitioning, addresses, and campaigns of constituency instructions to MPs—which a new opposition could readily exploit.

The opposition between 1742 and 1744 also had an issue of great political potential and sensitivity with which to harass ministers—Hanoverian influence on British foreign policy. This issue had initially came into prominence as a result of the Hanoverian Neutrality, negotiated in November 1741 by George II as elector to protect Hanover from invasion by France and her allies, and the first clear demonstration that the French might use Hanover as lever against Britain.[92] It re-emerged in the summer of 1742 when 16,000 Hanoverian troops were taken into British pay. Their purpose was to support Britain's main allies in Europe—Austria and the United Provinces—in the War of the Austrian Succession. In 1743, the battle of Dettingen, the last battle in British history in which a reigning monarch was present on the battlefield, raised further controversy. Initially viewed, even by the opposition, as a great military victory over the French, as further details emerged so opinion quickly altered. Arguments raged about the circumstances of the battle (the allied army had been in danger of being outmanœuvred before the engagement); the role of the Hanoverians and their commanders (the Hanoverians had been stationed in the rear); George II's decision to sport the yellow sash of

[88] See esp. Harris, *London Newspapers in the Age of Walpole*; G. A. Cranfield, *The Development of the Provincial Newspaper, 1700–1760* (Oxford, 1962); H. T. Dickinson, *The Politics of the People in Eighteenth Century Britain* (1994), ch. 6; Harris, *A Patriot Press*.

[89] See the comments in my *Politics and the Rise of the Press: Britain and France, 1620–1800* (1996), 34–7.

[90] Taylor and Jones *Whig and Tory*, 181. For an invaluable modern study of London politics, see Nicholas Rogers, *Whigs and Cities*.

[91] See Rogers, *Whigs and Cities*, 193–5. See also the comments in Harris, *A Patriot Press*, 41–3.

[92] See Harris, *A Patriot Press*, 103–9.

Hanover during the battle; and the failure to exploit any military advantages seemingly offered by the victory.[93] The noise of popular indignation and protest, stirred by uninhibited, bitter, and frequently populist anti-Hanoverian printed propaganda, much of it traceable to opposition Whigs, reached a climax of intensity in the winter of 1743–4. To make opposition to Hanoverian influence the touchstone of politics was to ministerial supporters a development pregnant with menace. As Charles Hanbury Williams declared in October 1743: 'Had Machiavel been a Jacobite now tis a Distinction he would have been proud to have the Father of.'[94] Jacobite agents reported back to Rome and Paris in excited and optimistic mood.[95] On 10 November 1743, the Marquis of Hartington wrote to his father, the Duke of Devonshire, currently the Lord Lieutenant of Ireland, about the *Old England, or the Broad-Bottom Journal*, the leading opposition essay paper of the early 1740s:

I suppose you have seen the Broadbottom journals. They are direct treason, and almost within the letter of the law, but as yet no notice has been taken of him [*sic*]. If they do not, there must an end of government, for they do not attack the administration, but are directly pointed at the king.[96]

In Parliament, Pitt praised the essays in the *Old England Journal* as 'wrote with a truly British constitutional spirit and what he would adopt and support'.[97] In January 1744, the Duke of Marlborough was to claim to his fellow Lords that, 'Hanover is now become a name which cannot be mentioned without provoking rage and malignity . . .'.[98]

The parliamentary session of 1743–4 saw several big set-piece debates on the Hanoverian troops at the end of which the division lobbies were as full as at any time in the early Hanoverian period.[99] The ministerial majority remained firm, although it was reduced. The experience of the session left its mark, however, on the rivalry between the Pelhams and Lord Carteret. John Owen has written that it was a division of the Commons on 18 January, when on a vote on the Hanoverian troops, the ministerial majority fell to 45 in a house of 500, which first made Carteret's fall 'inevitable'.[100]

Carteret's removal from office, which came ten months later, led to the formation of the Broad-Bottom ministry, so called because it included Tories, former opposition Whigs, as well as the old corps. Presented to George II as a national coalition which would support and strengthen the conduct of the

[93] For details of the battle, see Rohan Butler, *Choiseul: Father and Son, 1719–1754* (Oxford, 1980), 409–18. See also Harris, *A Patriot Press*, 153–62.

[94] BL, Add. MS 51390 (Holland House Papers), fo. 127: Charles Hanbury Williams to Henry Fox, 9 Oct. 1743.

[95] Rogers, *Whigs and Cities*, 69.

[96] PRONI, T 3158 (Transcripts of the Chatsworth Papers)/251.

[97] Ibid. 259.

[98] *Parl. Hist.*, xiii. 564–5, quoted in Black, *America or Europe?*, 40.

[99] Owen, *Rise of the Pelhams*, 207, 212.

[100] Ibid., 211.

war, the experiment in political inclusiveness proved short-lived, lasting for little more than six months. With hindsight, its significance was twofold: it furthered, as referred to earlier, the process of bringing Whigs who had been in opposition to Walpole back into the ministry; secondly, it revealed how difficult it was to contrive a political accommodation which would satisfy Tory and Whig sensitivities, at both the national and local levels.[101]

It also revealed how ill-suited for office the Tories were. Whether they actually sought this as a party in this period is a moot point.[102] The evidence is ambiguous. Given their suspect and in some cases actual disloyalty, and their deep-rooted antipathy to the Hanoverian connection, the possibility of George II admitting them to office as anything other than individuals was remote.[103] The Tories were also a far from unified force. Indeed, their politics was characterized by a high level of individualism, as well as a deep suspicion of power. From the early 1740s, they also lacked unified and consistent leadership.

Toryism is, in fact, a slippery quarry. This is not because it is impossible to identify who the Tories were; contemporary division lists frequently do this. There also remained, throughout this period, a network of distinctively Tory institutions and clubs—for example, the Cocoa Tree coffee house, the Bean Club in Birmingham, the Steadfast Society in Bristol, various metropolitan philanthropic bodies (St Bartholomew's Hospital, Christ Church, and Bethlem Hospitals). What is difficult is to determine exactly what the Tories stood for as a national force. A significant minority of Tories had Jacobite connections, as alluded to above, and in several cases these continued even after the crushing defeat of their cause at Culloden.[104] Yet in parliamentary terms, Toryism meant little more than 'country' politics by this period. Indeed, some Tories, for example, Edward Harley, 3rd Earl of Oxford or Sir Roger Newdigate, did not refer to themselves as Tories at all, preferring other labels, such as the 'country interest' or the 'old interest'.[105] When Charles Gray, Tory MP for Colchester, wrote to the Earl of Egmont in 1749 about the possibilities of a Tory alliance with Egmont's political master, the Prince of Wales, he talked of the cause of 'disinterested country

---

[101] Tory demands focused primarily on the creation of Tory JPs in the counties. Pelham and Hardwicke moved slowly and cautiously on this demand. Even then, their moves were greeted with strong opposition from Whigs in the counties affected. The most detailed analysis of this is contained in Norma Landau, *The Justices of the Peace 1679–1760* (Berkeley, Calif. and London, 1984), 108–36.

[102] For the view that they did, see Colley, *In Defiance of Oligarchy*.

[103] See G. C. Gibbs, 'English Attitudes towards Hanover and the Hanoverian Succession in the First Half of the Eighteenth Century', in A. M. Birke and Kurt Kluxen (eds.), *England and Hanover* (Munich, 1986), 33–50.

[104] See Thomas, *Politics in Eighteenth Century Wales*, 148. The questions of what proportion of Tories were Jacobites or what their Jacobitism meant are particularly vexed ones. For one attempt to shed light on them, see Ian Christie, 'The Tory Party, Jacobitism and the '45: A Note', *HJ* 30 (1987), 921–31.

[105] For Harley, see Taylor and Jones, *Whig and Tory*, pp. xlii–lv. Newdigate stood (unsuccessfully) on the 'old interest' at Middlesex in the 1747 general election (Warwickshire Record Office, Newdigate Papers, CR 136/B 2517).

gentlemen'.[106] When Peniston Powney, MP for Berkshire, urged his fellow Tories to respond positively to overtures from the Prince of Wales two years previously one argument he stressed was that under Frederick as monarch, power and the principles of the 'landed interest' would be reconciled.[107] What Tories sought was to protect landed independence and interest in Parliament and in local government—which meant their admission to the ranks of county Justices of the Peace—and to eliminate corruption from politics. It was a platform which could easily be supported by other independent opposition politicians, and throughout this period it was. It was also a platform which required opposition Whig support if it was to pose a serious threat to Whig oligarchy.

The elusiveness of a Tory party runs still deeper. As we move into the 1750s, at the national level the Tories are probably best characterized as a loose alliance of backbench MPs bound together by a common wish to see a cleansing and regeneration of national politics. It was project riven with ambiguity; indeed for a party which still included a Jacobite element, however small and ineffectual, its ambiguity was perhaps its major strength. There was about Toryism an ideological fuzziness, or at least Toryism reflected and held in tension contradictory goals and hopes. Tories continued, as they had done earlier in the century, to idealize the rule and higher integrity of the landed gentry, yet elements within the party also had connections with metropolitan radicalism and the politics of trade and imperial expansion. They also remained susceptible to the vision of a strong patriot monarch healing the divisions and scars left by Whig oligarchical rule, and imbuing politics with a higher dignity and morality. This monarch might be the Young Pretender, but could equally well be Prince Frederick (before his death in 1751). Different elements of this politics were fairly easily reconciled by some individuals, for example, William Beckford and Sir John Philipps, both of whom in their lives and connections straddled the world of land and trade.[108] In others, the more traditional loyalty to an identification with the landed interest remained uppermost. It was a politics only possible because of protracted and near complete political exclusion.

Prospects for national political opposition after 1746 were poor. Ministerial majorities in Parliament were large, and increased at the 1747 and 1754 general elections.[109] These elections saw fewer contests than at any other time during the eighteenth century, itself a good index of the enfeebled condition of opposition.[110] Well before 1747, the growing strength of ministerial and oligarchical

[106] 'Leicester House Politics, 1750–60, From the Papers of John, Second Earl of Egmont', ed. Aubrey Newman, *Camden Miscellany*, xxiii, Camden 4th Ser. (1967), 180–2.

[107] BL, Add. MS 35870 (Hardwicke Papers), fos. 129–30.

[108] For a recent essay on Philipps, see Thomas, *Politics in Eighteenth-Century Wales*, ch. 8.

[109] After the 1747 election, government members numbered 351 and the opposition 207. In 1754, Lord Dupplin calculated that government support stood at 368 MPs, the Tories 106, opposition Whigs 42, with 26 described as doubtful.

[110] See Frank O'Gorman, *Voters, Patrons and Parties: The Unreformed Electorate of Hanoverian England, 1734–1832* (Oxford, 1989), 108–10.

control over small, close boroughs had been clearly demonstrated at the 1734 and 1741 general elections. Electoral attacks against Whig oligarchy in the Walpolian period were concentrated in larger, open boroughs and in the counties. This resistance tended to weaken and dissipate in the years after 1742, in part as a consequence of the fracturing and loss of cohesion of the political forces which had overthrown Walpole.[111] The precise set of circumstances shaping electoral activity, or its absence, varied according to local conditions and personalities, as throughout the eighteenth century. In Colchester, the local Tories sought to build an opposition which embraced Whigs as well as Tories to the sitting Whig MP on the basis of a campaign to restore the corporation charter, removed in 1742.[112] In Northumberland, Berwick and Morpeth, electoral peace coincided with Whig supremacy and the elimination of the Tories as serious electoral rivals; only Whig divisions could produce a contest in Northumberland in 1747. In Newcastle, Whigs and Tories divided the representation following the unanimity displayed locally in reaction to the Jacobite Rebellion.[113] Where contests did occur, they could still be violent, bitter affairs involving whole communities; several of them also reveal the continuing limitations of elite political control in this period. They also show how traditional party rancour could still break out, especially where underpinned with sectarian tensions. In Nottingham, a large freeman borough, Dissenters and Tories clashed in 1747 and again in 1754.[114] One of the best documented contests of the period occurred in Bristol in 1754 where the Whig Union club supported Robert Nugent and the Tory Steadfast Society put forward Sir John Philipps and Richard Beckford, a wealthy West Indian planter and younger brother of William, referred to earlier. As Rogers writes, it was an election 'full of party invective and caustic aspersions'; it was also hugely expensive. Two years later, on Beckford's death, deep-seated party loyalties and animosities, underpinned by sectarian divisions, prevented any political accommodation at a by-election.[115] The most notorious contest of the period, and indeed perhaps of the whole of the eighteenth century, took place in Oxfordshire in 1754. This was more than a contest for a county; it engaged the energies, pockets, and interest of Tories and Whigs nationally. Fought along party lines, it also produced a welter of printed propaganda, including ballads and the establishment of a local paper, *Jackson's Oxford*

---

[111] Rogers, *Whigs and Cities*, ch. 7.

[112] See D'Cruze, 'The Middling Sort in Provincial England', ch. 6.

[113] W. A. Speck, 'Northumberland Elections in the Eighteenth Century', *Northern History*, 28 (1992), 164–77.

[114] Namier, *The Structure of Politics*, 91–5. Namier presents the contest in 1754 as simply a product of the decision of John Plumtree, the sitting Whig MP, to contest the election. Newcastle was supporting Lord Howe, and representation was usually split with the Tories, led by Lord Middleton. Contemporary press comment indicates, however, that against this background, sectarian tensions burst out. The Whig corporation was also reluctant to follow Newcastle's directions. See BL, Add. MS 32733, fos. 397–8.

[115] Rogers, *Whigs and Cities*, 293–9.

Journal.[116] It was the last contest to be fought in the county until 1826; in Oxfordshire the peace of the mid century was the peace of exhaustion.

Where there were no contests, national issues could still impinge on electoral politics. In 1753–4, Tory and opposition hostility towards the Jewish Naturalization Act had an impact in several constituencies. Humphrey Sydenham lost his seat at Tory Exeter because of his vote for the bill. This was despite efforts to prove to his constituents his staunch support for Christianity. Norborne Berkeley, MP for Gloucestershire, faced with criticism of his support for the measure at the Gloucester races in 1753, offered to stand down in favour of another candidate if this was necessary, an offer which, fortunately for him, he was not required to see through.[117] In Kent, Edward Deering sought election to one of the county seats as a staunch opponent of the Jew Bill.[118] The Tory-controlled corporation of Reading, meanwhile, sought to extract pledges from the three candidates in 1753 that they would vote for its repeal, a pledge all three candidates gave in one form or another.[119] The decision in favour of repeal was also taken by Pelham and ministers in order to protect Whigs against any potential electoral repercussions of the furore stirred up by the measure's opponents. In 1747, Parliament had been dissolved a year early, partly to undermine the efforts of a new opposition led by the Prince of Wales to organize a concerted challenge at the polls, but also to deny this opposition the opportunity to canvas a popular question in the final session as had occurred in both 1734 and 1740.[120] Joseph Yorke, youngest son of Lord Hardwicke, called the dissolution of 1747 'a master stroke of politics'.[121]

Attendance and organization in Parliament amongst opposition MPs was from the later 1740s limited and fluctuating. In 1749, the Earl of Egmont was talking about creating an opposition comprising around 100 MPs.[122] What is striking is how the opposition struggled to find issues with which to harass the ministry, together with the small size of their vote when matters were pushed to a division. In 1749 and 1750, reforms to the Mutiny Acts, which included extending martial law to half-pay officers, provided the main issue for opposition. Behind this lay fears about the political influence of the Duke of Cumberland. Much of the suspicion about Cumberland reflected dynastic tensions between him and the Prince of Wales; and Leicester House was the source of much bitter anti-Cumberland propaganda.[123] There appears to

[116] See Ward, *Georgian Oxford*, ch. 12; R. J. Robson, *The Oxfordshire Election of 1754* (Oxford, 1949).
[117] BL, Add. MS 35398, fo. 166.
[118] See *Advice to the Freeholders of Kent* (1754); *The Kentish Candidates* (1754); *Advice to the Freeholders of Kent. A New Ballad* (1754).
[119] Berkshire County Record Office, R/AC 1/1/22 (Reading Corporation Diary), fo. 173.
[120] In 1734, the issue was a Septennial Bill; in 1740, a Place Bill.
[121] BL, Add. MS 35360 (Hardwicke Papers), fos. 166–7: Joseph Yorke to Lord Hardwicke, 16 June 1747.
[122] 'Leicester House Politics', 182–8.
[123] The Leicester House essay paper the *Remembrancer* was an important vehicle for anti-Cumberland propaganda. Leicester House was also probably the source of the handbill *Constitutional Queries*,

have been, nevertheless, a genuine fear that Cumberland was striving to create the conditions for military rule in Britain in the later 1740s. Sir James Lowther, the independent Whig MP for Cumberland, provides a good barometer of the growth of this opinion. On 7 March 1749, he reported 'great' debates in the Commons on 'these bold attempts that tend to sett up a military power beyond anything known in the Kingdom'. Two days later, he wrote: 'This contest now in Parl[iamen]t w[hi]ch is like to be one of the greatest that ever was known, & w[hi][ch the Ministry has so rashly brought upon themselves is like to lengthen the session. The Town is in a vast ferment ab[ou]t it & so will the whole Kingdom in all Likelyhood.'[124] Some of the most lively debates in the parliament of 1747–54 took place on non-partisan lines—for example, on the Bedford Turnpike bill in January 1750 or the Lord Chancellor's Marriage Act of 1753.[125] In 1751, ministers faced a temporary difficulty on numbers of seamen voted for the year, but largely because Pitt and a number of other office holders voted with the opposition against the proposed reduction. This also took place against a widespread expectation that ministerial changes were imminent.[126] The most controversial piece of legislation of these years—the Jewish Naturalization Act—was a minor measure which began life in the Lords; nor did opposition to it have any significant effect on ministerial support in the Commons.

Several factors lay behind the debility of opposition. One was the morale of the Tories. The Tories emerged from the confused politics of the early 1740s bruised and uncertain as a national political force. Several of their leading figures were tainted with Jacobitism or vulnerable to allegations of disloyalty. Sir Watkin William Wynn and Sir John Hynde Cotton and Lord Barrymore were named as Jacobite conspirators by the Young Pretender's secretary, John Murray of Broughton, who turned King's evidence in the trial of the Scottish rebel peer, Lord Lovat in 1747. Others, including Sir John Philipps and Sir Roger Newdigate, had opposed subscriptions to raise loyal troops during the Jacobite Rebellion of 1745–6.[127] In the general election of 1747, the number of Tory MPs was reduced from 136 to 117. In the later 1740s, they appear, by turns, apathetic, disgruntled, and suspicious. Their

Earnestly Recommended to the Serious Consideration of Every True Briton, which was voted by the Lords a 'false, malicious, scandalous, infamous and seditious libel' and ordered to be burnt by the common hangman. The Commons also passed a resolution calling on the King to discover and punish those responsible for it (*Commons Journals*, 26 (1750–4), 9). This handbill portrayed the Mutiny Act as part of a wider scheme to impose tyrannical rule on Britain under Cumberland.

[124] CRO (Carlisle), D/Lons/W2/1/110: Lowther to John Spedding, 7 Mar., 9 Mar. 1750.

[125] For a recent examination of the Marriage Act, see David Lemmings, 'Marriage and the Law in the Eighteenth Century: Harwicke's Marriage Act of 1753', *HJ* 39 (1996), 339–60. The vote on the Bedford Turnpike bill attracted an attendance of nearly 400, the largest of the session. Interest in it reflected divisions in the ministry and at Court, in particular the struggle between Bedford and the Pelhams.

[126] See Peters, *The Elder Pitt*, 57–9.

[127] See Colley, *In Defiance of Oligarchy*, ch. 9.

enthusiasm for continued opposition, in alliance with the court of Prince Frederick, was limited; participation in earlier oppositions had only produced betrayal by opposition Whigs and they were wary of committing themselves again.[128] Where they, or some of their number, were more enthusiastic, was in demonstrating their disgust at Gower's betrayal, which they did at the 1747 Staffordshire election and again in a by-election at Westminster in 1749–50, caused by the elevation of Lord Trentham, Gower's son, to office in the Admiralty. Some of their number also, as alluded to above, indulged in very public displays of disaffection and alienation from the Hanoverian regime.[129]

A second obstacle was the state of opposition 'without doors'. Popular opinion was disillusioned about national politics and politicians in this period, as emphasized earlier. This did not mean, however, an absence of considerable popular alienation and discontent. Some of this was created by mounting evidence in the late 1740s and early 1750s of French aggression in colonial spheres, especially the Caribbean, where they were threatening to seize control of the so-called neutral islands, and the apparent inability or unwillingness of the ministry to do anything decisive about this.[130] The passage of the Jewish Naturalization Act, a minor measure of religious liberalization, also provoked a major popular outcry.[131] The motivation behind this was in part factious—it was used by opposition politicians to stir up opposition to the ministry. But it also reflected again how easily religious issues could, if given an opportunity, reignite Tory and popular passions. Prominent amongst the bill's opponents were Tory lesser clergy, a political force which had been largely dormant for decades. Prominent clergy in Tory Oxford preached against the bill. The Bishop of Norwich, who had been absent from the Lords when the bill was voted on, was berated by his lesser clergy in Suffolk for not having been present and opposed it.[132] Ministers, alarmed by the outcry and, most importantly its potential effects on the general election in 1754, as referred to above, repealed it at the beginning of the susbsequent session of

---

[128] See esp. Charles Gray's comments, which show the depth of Tory mistrust of alliances with opposition Whigs after the events of 1742, and 1745–6, in a letter to Lord Egmont in 1749, reprinted in 'Leicester House Politics', 180–2.

[129] For such displays in the north west, see Jan Albers, ' "Papist traitors" and "Presbyterian rogues": Religious Identities in Eighteenth-century Lancashire', in John Walsh, Colin Haydon, and Stephen Taylor (eds), *The Church of England c.1689–c1833: From Toleration to Tractarianism* (Cambridge, 1993), 317–33. On 6 May 1749, *The Whitehall Evening Post* printed an extract from a letter from Manchester, dated 21 April. This told of 'great rejoycings' in Manchester on the birth of a son to the Tory leader, Sir Watkin Williams Wynn. There had apparently been no similar demonstrations on either the birthday of the Duke of Cumberland or the anniversary of Culloden. Soldiers stationed in the town had made their own demonstrations, but these had pointedly not been attended by any of the town's officers.

[130] See e.g. CRO (Carlisle), D/Lons/W2/1/114: Lowther to John Spedding, 1 Apr. 1752.

[131] See esp. T. W. Perry, *Public Opinion, Propaganda and Politics in Eighteenth Century England* (Cambridge, Mass., 1962).

[132] BL, Add. MS 35398, fo. 128: Birch to Yorke, 7 July 1753.

the Parliament. The Earl of Halifax, for one, worried that so obvious a concession to popular clamour set a dangerous precedent for government.[133]

The outcry provoked by the Jewish Naturalization Act also demonstrated that the press had far from disappeared as a significant force in political life in this period. The political liveliness and influence of the press did decline somewhat in the later 1740s and early 1750s, reflecting the wider contemporary disillusionment with national politics, but also the fact that, after 1748 and the end of the War of the Austrian Succession, it did not have a war to provide it with copy and controversial issues. The first main phase of growth in the provincial press also ended around 1746.[134] The parliamentary reporting of the monthly magazines was also, in the case of the *Gentleman's Magazine*, brought to an end, and, in the case of the *London Magazine*, substantially curtailed by a reprimand by the House of Lords in 1747 for their reporting on the Lovat trial.[135] Yet political papers still existed, and continued to offer strong criticism of Whig oligarchical politics. In early 1750, Sir James Lowther recommended two opposition essay papers, the *Remembrancer*, a paper sponsered by Leicester House, and the *Old England Journal* for their 'plain English' views.[136] The *Remembrancer* of 18 November 1749 provoked the ministry to take action against it and its editor, James Ralph.[137] In 1753, the Tories William Beckford, brother of Richard referred to earlier, and Sir John Philipps, together with the Duke of Bedford, financed an essay paper entitled *The Protestor, on Behalf of the People*. Written and edited by Ralph, who had been a prominent opposition journalist since the 1730s, this was a major vehicle for attacks on the Jewish Naturalization Act. Scottish and Irish newspapers also regularly printed letters from London correspondents which included parliamentary news. Several opposition politicians also appear to have supplied the press with copies of what they thought (or hoped) were important parliamentary speeches.[138]

The most influential opposition paper of the period was the *London Evening Post*, a tri-weekly evening paper which had been founded as long ago as 1727.

---

[133] BL, Add. MS 32733 (Newcastle Papers), fos. 236–9: Earl of Halifax to Newcastle, 12 Nov. 1753.

[134] See R. M. Wiles, *Freshest Advices: Early Provincial Newspapers in England* (Columbia, 1965).

[135] See *Lords Journals*, xxvii. 94, 98, 101, 103, 107, 108. See also Cannon, *Samuel Johnson*, 280–1. In the early 1750s, the *Gentleman's Magazine* had resumed printing summaries of parliamentary debates and transactions. In 1751, for example, it included as summary of arguments on the regency bill (*Gent. Mag.*, 21 (1751), 386–90, 435–8).

[136] CRO (Carlisle), D/Lons/W2/1/111, Lowther to John Spedding, 9 Jan. 1750.

[137] *Dodington's Political Journal*, 27; PRO, SP 36/111, fo. 186; PRO, T1/343/81.

[138] See e.g. *Country Advertiser*, 11, 25 May, 8, 23 June, 20 July 1745 (Lord Polwarth's speech on the report of the Hanoverian troops); *Bristol Journal*, 1 Apr. 1749 (Admiral Vernon's speech concerning the navy); *Gent. Mag.*, 21 (1751), 339–43 (Speech of William Beckford on the report of the Regency bill, 20 May 1751); *Gent. Mag.*, 22 (1752), 247–50 (speech of William Thornton on the number of troops to be deployed abroad in 1751), 295–300 (speech of William Beckford on commitment of the bill to prohibit insurances on foreign East India ships), 343–6 (speeches of William Thornton on augmentation of seamen and on lowering of the land tax), 391–3, 439–41 (speeches of William Thornton on bringing in bill to make the militia more useful).

This was read by country gentleman and city politician alike.[139] The tri-week-lies were published on post days, and circulated widely throughout England and Wales. Paragraphs from them were also much reprinted in the contemporary provincial and Scottish press. Its style was decidedly populist and outspoken, which led one ministerial supporter to dismiss its political contents as 'bald and ill digested stuff'. Thomas Birch, meanwhile, described it as a 'sink of ribaldry', and John Gordon informed Newcastle that it was the chosen paper of the Jacobites and extreme faction in City politics.[140] As well as Eccles and Gordon, other contributors to it may have included the High Churchman William Romaine and Paul Whitehead, whose politics were of a very different order. Whitehead's eighteenth-century biographer was to note that the 'company which he kept, laid him [Whitehead] under suspicion of being a Tory; though no man speaks which such zeal and warmth against Kings and Courts, or breathes a more genuine spirit of Independence.'[141] Whitehead had links with Prince Frederick and Leicester House before the Prince's death, and with Sir Francis Dashwood, an independent opposition MP with close Tory connections. He was also a member of the Westminster Society of Independent Electors.[142] Whitehead may have been 'Britannicus', the pseudonymous author of the paper's most important articles in the 1750s; he also appears to have been the author of a pamphlet defence of Alexander Murray in 1751, for which the printer and publisher, William Owen, was arrested and tried at the Middlesex Guildhall in 1752.[143] The paper's power was demonstrated in 1753, when, alongside the *Protestor*, it led the vicious press campaign against the Jewish Naturalization Act. Its outspoken comment was usually in the form of small verses and paragraphs, bogus news items, or short articles, which probably had greater impact and immediacy than lengthy, often abstract essays on political theory or political allegories and visions which tended to prevail in many essay papers.

Both the *Protestor* and the *London Evening Post* provoked great concern amongst ministers and their supporters. This concern went to the highest level—the King. The *Protestor* was brought to a close when Ralph, who had actually been on a government pension in the 1740s, was threatened with prosecution, and failed to receive assurances that he would be supported in the costs defending himself would entail. Interestingly, in the light of ministers'

[139] See Harris, 'The "London Evening Post" '. For its influence amongst country gentry, see BL, Add. MS 32731, fos. 13–14: Earl of Leicester to Newcastle, Holkham, 3 Jan. 1753.

[140] BL, Add. MS 35599, fos. 96–7; Archbishop Herring to Lord Hardwicke, 19 Aug. 1753; BL, Add. MS 35398, fo. 219: Thomas Birch to Philip Yorke, 1 Oct. 1754; BL, Add. MS 32737, fos. 154–5: John Gordon to Newcastle, 14 Oct. 1754.

[141] Captain Edward Thompson, *The Poems and Miscellaneous Compositions of Paul Whitehead with Explanatory Notes on his Writings and Life* (1777), pp. vi–vii.

[142] See 'Leicester House Politics', 101.

[143] See my, 'The "London Evening Post" ', 1138. The pamphlet, *The Case of Alexander Murray* was described by Thomas Birch as 'one of the highest Insults upon Authority which even our own Times & Country have produc'd' (BL, Add. MS 35398, fo. 24). For Owen's trial, see below, p. 54.

sensitivity about the dangers of such actions—they could prove politically counterproductive or even fail—the issue chosen for prosecution was one which was deemed to impugn the legitimacy of the Glorious Revolution. It was chosen with care, and due caution about the pitfalls which could attend efforts to police the press. In the event, no prosecution was necessary, and Ralph was silenced with an annual pension of £300.[144] The *London Evening Post* provoked an even more concerted response. Since Walpole's fall, the ministry had been poorly represented in the press.[145] In 1753, ministerial supporters appear to have been able to place articles in two papers, the *Whitehall Evening Post* and the *General Evening Post*.[146] In 1754, however, a new paper was founded to oppose the *London Evening Post*, entitled the *Evening Advertiser*. A major contributor to this paper was the Oxford Whig, Richard Blacow.[147] In the same year, the ministry decided to take more direct action against the paper. Already in the autumn of 1753, Lord Hardwicke had told the Lords 'that the Lords and Commons might trust themselves with looking into the licence of the press'.[148] In October 1754 the circulation of the paper via the post office was stopped; its publisher, Richard Nutt, was also arrested for an item which appeared in the paper on 10 September which cast doubt on the legitimacy of the Glorious Revolution.[149] The success of Nutt's prosecution in 1755 was hailed by Treasury Solicitor John Sharpe and by ministers as a 'great victory'.[150] It failed, however, to neuter the paper, which continued to be a major vehicle for opposition opinion and comment throughout the later 1750s. Two years later, the Duke of Newcastle was again contemplating a prosecution over one particularly offensive issue.[151]

The pages of the *London Evening Post* provide further evidence, therefore, that political discontent did not disappear in the early 1750s, and could on occasion take an extreme form. Discontent of this sort was not, however,

---

[144] BL, Add. MS 32732, fos. 295–300; 322–3; 628–9; 645–6; 651–3; *Dodington Political Journal*, 27, 218. Other writers in receipt of government pensions in the 1750s were Ralph Courteville, who had been prominent in the pro-Walpole press, and William Guthrie, whose silence had been bought in late 1744.

[145] Harris, *A Patriot Press*, 33–8; Jeremy Black, *The English Press in the Eighteenth Century* (1987), 170.

[146] BL, Add. MS 35398, fo. 147.

[147] See BL, Add. MS 35398, fos. 193–4, 219, 228, 229, 240. The establishment of the paper was under discussion in the summer of 1753 (BL, Add. MS 35599, fos. 96–7). In one advertisement, the paper boasted of an extensive correspondence which gave it access to news which was unavailable to other newspapers. It also declared that part of the paper would be devoted to opposing 'those wicked and destructive Principles, so long and so daringly propagated in the London Evening Post; an infamous Paper that hath set itself up to be a vehicle of Lyes and Scandal upon most of the good and amiable characters of this Kingdom'. (Advertisement on back page of *A Voyage to the Island of Ceylon: on Board a Dutch Indiaman* (1754).)

[148] Walpole, *Memoirs of King George II*, i. 241. See also BL, Add. MS 35364, fos. 1–2 for further comment by Joseph Yorke on the virulence of the press at the beginning of 1754.

[149] PRO, SP 36/79, fos. 82–3; SP 44/84, fo. 234; TS 11/944; T1/377, fos. 61–4.

[150] BL, Add. MS 32857, fos. 110, 187–8. For material on the prosecution, see PRO, T1/357/80; T1/360/61–4. Nutt was sentenced to a £500 fine, to stand in the pillory at Charing Cross for 1 hour, to 2 years' imprisonment, and to find security for good behaviour on his release for 5 years of £2,000.

[151] BL, Add. MS 32867 (Newcastle Papers), fos. 135–6: John Sharpe to Newcastle, 28 Aug. 1756.

readily mobilized in support of a concerted national opposition to Whig oligarchy. The opposition alliance in the City, which had been such a prominent element of the anti-Walpolian opposition, had fragmented and lost cohesion by this period. Symptomatic of this was the disillusioned resignation from the Board of Aldermen of George Heathcote in January 1749.[152] Opposition within the City still retained an important hold, and included, as referred to above, an extreme Tory-Jacobite element. But it lacked leadership and focus. The City's potential importance as an instrument and focus of opposition also did not entirely disappear, as City petitions against a general naturalization in 1751 and the Jewish Naturalization Act of 1753 indicate.[153] In 1752, William Beckford, first elected for the borough of Shaftesbury in 1747, began to build a political base in the City, being elected as an alderman for Billingsgate in that year. Beckford's ceaseless political activity (of which more below), and seemingly boundless wealth and ambition, raised suspicions in City circles that he was a fortune hunter. This was not to prevent his election as a City MP in 1754. Undoubtedly his background, as a West Indian planter, and his commercial expertise and interests were very important in this context. Beckford was a frequent speaker in parliamentary debates, seeing himself as a spokesman for trade and the world of commerce. He also courted Tory opinion in the City through support for the controversial practice of selecting Dissenters for the office of sheriff, which they in conscience could not assume, and then extorting a fine from them for failure to serve.[154] From the end of 1756, it was Beckford who was to provide Pitt with his main line of communication with the City opposition.

The picture in Westminster was essentially similar. The history of the Westminster Society of Independent Electors, a focus of independent opposition in the constituency, can only be glimpsed in fragments in the historical sources for the period. What appears to have happened is that its support drained away, not least because in 1747 it was strongly tainted with suspicions of disloyalty. One of its members, the Welshman, David Morgan, was executed for his involvement in the Jacobite Rebellion. In 1747, the society was investigated for treasonable oaths said to have been drunk at its annual dinner.[155] The allegations of Jacobitism had considerable substance. Its leader

---

[152] Heathcote's letter of resignation disillusionment was first printed in the *London Evening Post* and then widely reprinted. See e.g. *Scots Mag.*, 11 (1749), 51–2; *Gent. Mag.*, 19 (1749), 30–1.

[153] Rogers, *Whigs and Cities*, 87–91.

[154] This practice, which intensified in the mid-1740s, was to be declared illegal by Lord Mansfield in 1768. See NAS, GD 248/182 (Seafield Papers), fo. 53, where William Grant writes in 1754: 'The great Topick in the City is a Dispute between High & [MS torn at this point] church. The office of sheriff you know is expensive. Alderman Beckford & his high Church friends want to elect two Pr[es]b[yte]rians into it.' Grant also reported that the purpose was to get them to pay the fine of £500 to be excused from the office. Interestingly, in 1754, the Quakers were to the fore in opposing Beckford in the general election (BL, Add. MS 32735, fos. 48–9). Beckford was labelled a Jacobite by opponents in the 1754 election. See esp *Old Nick To the Liverymen of London* (1754).

[155] See Rogers, *Whigs and Cities*, ch. 5. The following paragraph owes much to Rogers' account.

in this period was an attorney called Samuel Johns, who had strong Jacobite connections.[156] Other members, such as the alderman Matthew Blakiston, referred to earlier, were also suspected Jacobites. Jacobitism did not bring influence or importance, however, and the cause of independence in Westminster, with which it was inseparably intertwined, was soundly defeated at the 1747 general election. Two years later its revival was owing to a series of accidents, not least the fact that Lord Trentham's need for re-election—he had been appointed to the Admiralty—provided an opportunity for the Tories to display once again their hatred of Lord Gower. Leicester House also brought its influence to bear against Trentham, while the Pelhams may have been slow to support a candidate backed by Bedford House. The election was a noisy, violent affair. Trentham was elected, but only with a majority of 170 out of 9,500 votes cast. Arguments about the conduct of the election reached the floor of the Commons. Alexander Murray, brother to the Jacobite Lord Elibank, charged with one other individual of using threatening language towards the High Baillif, who oversaw the conduct of the poll, defied the censure of the Commons. This defiance of the 'tyranny' of the Commons became an opposition *cause célèbre*, and his incarceration in Newgate for the duration of the parliamentary session won him the status of popular hero. His case also led, as referred to earlier, to the arrest and trial of William Owen, printer and publisher of a pamphlet defence of Murray. In 1752, Owen was acquitted because of the refusal of a city jury to limit their deliberations to the fact of publication alone. It was a decision which alarmed George II and his ministers, not solely because of the challenge it posed them in policing the activities of the press, but also because it was feared that it too portended a revival of metropolitan opposition.[157] Yet the practical effects of the cause of 'Murray and Liberty' were limited, apart from providing a cause which temporarily united the disparate strands of opposition in this period. It did not, moreover, stimulate a revival of the Westminster Independents; in 1753, they were unable to find a candidate to stand in a by-election occasioned by the death of one of the sitting MPs, Sir Peter Warren.[158] In 1754, they also struggled to find candidates, fixing first on Edward Vernon and Sir Francis

[156] See BL, Add. MS 32737, fos. 304–5, where John Gordon described Johns to Newcastle as 'intimate with the principal Jacobites all over the Kingdom'. Johns also supposedly told Gordon that the 'life of Jacobitism was to mingle and influence every opposition to the Court let who would be at the helme'. In 1757, Gordon reported that Johns, on the Grocer's barge, had serenaded Kew House with 'the old remarkable Jacobite tune of the King shall enjoy his own again' when the royal family had been walking on the river bank (BL, Add. MS 32876 (Newcastle Papers), fos. 31–4).

[157] See Jeremy Black, 'George II and the Juries Act: Royal Concern about the Control of the Press', *Historical Research*, 61 (1988), 359–62; BL, Add. MS 32728, fos. 345–6; BL, Add. MS 32729, fo. 44.

[158] There is some evidence that Johns was seeking to revive the Independents in 1753 against the background of popular concern about the Jewish Naturalization Act. See Walpole, *Memoirs of King George II*, i. 210. See also BL, Add. MS 35398, fo 143: Birch to Yorke, 4 Aug. 1753, where Birch writes, 'The Independent Electors of Westminster have in their last Advertisement assum'd a new Pretence for meeting "to exert themselves in the great causes of Xtianity & National Birth-right, against all Jewish schemes that are or may be introduc'd for the Introduction of *Foreigners* into this Nation".'

Delaval and, subsequently, on almost the day of polling, Lord Middlesex and James Edward Oglethorpe. On the second day of polling, lack of support led Middlesex and Oglethorpe to beg to be excused from further efforts in the election.[159]

The final obstacle facing opposition from the later 1740s was the quality and nature of leadership available to it. This meant, between 1747 and 1751, Prince Frederick and the loose coalition of the hopeful and excluded he built up around him at Leicester House, those who Horace Walpole unkindly described as 'the refuse of every party'.[160] The Prince was more effective as a figurehead than a strong political leader; he was always susceptible to manipulation by stronger political intelligences and personalities than his own.[161] His Court also presented a scene of political division and confusion. From 1749, two of his major advisers, the Earl of Egmont and George Bubb Dodington, were bitter rivals. It was a rivalry which stemmed from personal vanity—in both cases substantial—but also from the advocacy of different political strategies. Dodington sought a measured, temperate opposition which looked forward to the next reign; Egmont sought to harry Pelham and the ministers at every opportunity.[162] As Aubrey Newman has emphasized, the Leicester House opposition was more a divided unstable faction than anything else.[163] In 1750–1, the Prince's enthusiasm for Newcastle's continental diplomacy, which had also been evident in the early 1740s, created further confusion and political incoherence amongst his supporters.[164] Against this background, it is hardly surprising that the Tories remained wary about too close an alliance with the Prince.

However, the political importance of the Leicester House opposition derived primarily from the fact that George II was elderly, not from its capacity to embarass the Pelhams in the present. The question of what would happen on his death overshadowed much of the politics of the later 1740s and 1750s. (It was this question which made Cumberland's role in politics so important following Prince Frederick's death, at least before 1757.) Given their divisions, and failure to mount an effective opposition, Leicester House politicians were very fortunate to have a new reign to dream of. Egmont's papers include many memorandums about plans for this reign.[165] It was to be the beginning of a bright new Patriot dawn in which old party divisions would fall

---

[159] The independents appear to have determined, initially, to continue polling to 'plague the court' until the 29 May, that is the anniversary of the Restoration, but were forced to give the election up (NAS, GD 248/183, fos. 28, 40).

[160] Walpole, *Memoirs of King George II*, i. 32.

[161] More positive reassessments of the Prince have tended to focus on his literary, intellectual, and cultural interests and patronage. On this, see esp. Christine Gerrard, *The Patriot Opposition to Walpole: Politics, Poetry and National Myth 1725–1742* (Oxford, 1994), ch. 3.

[162] Dodington's view of this division is amply described in his political journal.

[163] 'Leicester House Politics', 577.

[164] See ibid., 193–4.

[165] See ibid.

away, and politics would enter a simpler, purer future. Egmont and Frederick also strove to project a platform of patriot reform and revival before the latter's death. It was a platform defined in part by its criticism of Pelhamite reconstruction after 1748. A major element was a call for greater financial reform and economy. The latter was necessary if Britain's commercial fortunes and prosperity were to revive. As James Ralph wrote in the *Remembrancer* in December 1749:

There is not a class of man in this whole Community (except such as, in the m[inis-teria]l land of Goschen, live on the Fat of the land) who is not overtaxed: And the same load of Oppressions which has been so hard on Individuals, does the same on our Manufactures, Navigation, and Commerce: and will, in the End, as infallibly ruin the one, as the other . . .

Several months earlier, Ralph was calling for economy to alleviate the present 'calamitous state of the commonwealth'.[166] The Prince also strove to demonstrate very visible support for other contemporary patriotic totems—namely, commerce and the navy. He became governor of the Free British Fishery Society, a major popular patriotic initiative of the early 1750s which sought to boost British prosperity and naval power.[167] In 1750, he undertook a series of progresses through the south west, which served to emphasize his patronage of domestic manufactures and commerce. These had an aspect of pageantry and spectacle which was usually singularly absent at the court of George II.[168] We can also see in them, and the popular reaction to them, the lineaments of and potential for popular Protestant patriotic monarchy which were to be even more strongly revived at the accession of his son, George III. Frederick's death, in March 1751, was seen a major blow to patriotic hopes, at least amongst the opposition. In the outpouring of verse composed to mark his passing, he was portrayed as a heroic and, at the same time, benevolent figure, and as patron and protector of national interests and culture.[169] Britain had lost a future 'father of the people'; the implicit contrast was with George II.

The Prince's death brought about the collapse too of hopes of future advancement amongst many of his former servants, and there was a rush amongst their number to return to the ministerial fold. The Princess Dowager also made her peace with the Court, although tension still remained between her and Cumberland. Those looking for a new leadership of opposition forces were forced to turn after 1751 to the Duke of Bedford and his faction before 1754, and after 1754 and before 1757, Pitt or Fox. In 1756, Prince George reached his majority, and Leicester House also re-emerged as an important

---

[166] *Remembrancer*, 30 Dec. 1749; 4 Feb. 1749.

[167] See Ch. 6, below, pp. 253–64.

[168] They are described in some detail in the *Whitehall Evening Post*, 12–14, 19–21, 21–4, 24–6 July, 14–6, 16–18, 18–21 Aug 1750.

[169] See e.g. *General Evening Post*, 19–21 Mar.; 21–3 Mar.; 4–6 Apr. 1751; *Old England, or the National Gazette*, 6 Apr. 1751.

political force. The opposition of Bedford, Pitt, and Fox was all-too-evidently factious, a further factor limiting its popularity amongst independent and Tory MPs, as well as popular opinion. This did not prevent the Tories William Beckford and Sir John Philipps supporting Bedford's opposition in 1753–4. Beckford's was a strange political odyssey which looked beyond Toryism, and is indicative of the greater fluidity of opposition politics in these years. In November 1754, James Ralph was reporting that Beckford was to join a 'flying squadron' to be headed by the independent city MP, Sir John Barnard.[170] In the same year, Beckford was prepared to support Fox on the Mitchell election petition, unlike most other Tories, perhaps because Fox, in alliance with Bedford and Cumberland, seemed more likely to favour a strong line in opposition to the French advance in North America. In late 1755, he was continuing to show signs of favouring Fox.[171] In the same year, his brother, Richard, helped found a new essay paper entitled the *Monitor*, which sought to defend and promote Patriot views on politics.[172] It was only in late 1756 that Beckford and the *Monitor* showed signs of being convinced that Pitt represented the best prospect for securing Patriot reforms and policies.[173]

Beckford's ceaseless activity, his willingness to ally with those he became convinced would genuinely support Patriot policies, and his frequent interventions in Commons debates, did not represent, however, the behaviour of the typical Tory, if such a thing can be said to have existed. Others sought to trace out different political paths. Some Tories, alongside some independents—for example, the Earl of Oxford and Lord Shaftesbury—considered aligning themselves with Newcastle in 1754 as the lesser of the evils which faced them politically.[174] The plain fact was that by 1754, as a party the Tories found themselves politically impotent; they were irrelevant to the struggles of Whigs over power and office which consumed the next few years. In 1762, one pamphleteer described their plight in cruel but fundamentally accurate words: 'You have been wandering about, gentlemen, for some years past, in search of a minister, under whom you might recover your importance, without giving up the absurdities of your ancestors. The general decay of your party reduced you to this vagrant state.'[175] Tory support for Pitt in office, after late 1756, was a victory for realism and hope in equal measure; there was nowhere else for

---

[170] BL, Add. MS 32737, fos. 272–5: Ralph to Newcastle, 5 Nov. 1754.

[171] Colley, *In Defiance of Oligarchy*, 270; Walpole, *Memoirs of the Reign of George II*, ii. 43, 76. See also BL, Add. MS 32861, fos. 55–6, where John West reports, on 21 Nov. 1755, that Beckford 'talked much against ministers, that he regarded only measures and not men tho' he must own he had a great opinion of the abilities of Mr Fox which if exerted should have his support'. See also BL, Add. MS 32867, where Beckford is described as Fox's 'profess'd Friend'.

[172] Marie Peters, ' "Names and Cant": Party Labels in English Political Propaganda, c.1753–1763', *Parliamentary History*, 7 (1984), 103–27. Peters has described the *Monitor* as a Tory paper. For a slightly different view, see my 'The "London Evening Post" ', 1154.

[173] See esp. Peters, *Pitt and Popularity*, 45–57.

[174] See Taylor and Jones, *Whig and Tory*, p. lv. See also BL, Add. MS 32374, fo. 179.

[175] *An Address to the Cocoa Tree, from a Whig* (1762), 6.

Tories to go. Even then, not all Tories supported Pitt, and what support they did provide was far from unconditional.[176]

PITT AND THE POLITICS OF UNITY

The mid-1750s were a turning point in British politics, as well as in British military fortunes. As emphasized earlier, the combination of Pelham's death in 1754 and the renewal of conflict with France galvanized political life. Factionalism and war also led to a further surge in the growth of the press. Fortunately, we possess figures for stamp duties levied on newspapers for the period 1750–6. These indicate a significant rise in 1756 in the numbers of newspapers produced. In 1755, the total number of newspapers on which duty had been paid stood at 8,639,864; in the following year, this figure climbed to 10,746,146.[177] Even an increase in stamp duty in 1757, which forced most newspapers to raise their prices by a halfpenny, did not interrupt the expansion. In 1760, 9.4 million newspaper stamps were issued, a slight fall on 1756, but the latter was a year of unusual political excitement. The mid-1750s also saw a flurry of new provincial papers, and the upward path of growth in this section of the press, which had fallen back after 1746, was resumed.[178]

Popular and press opinion was, as we saw earlier, initially supportive of ministerial actions to repulse French aggression in North America. As evidence of military misfortune and misadventure grew from 1755, however, ministers were increasingly faced with a vocal, angry, and alienated political nation, led by papers such as the *London Evening Post* and the *Monitor*. In 1755–6, there was strong criticism of the employment and stationing in England of Hessian and Hanoverian troops to protect Britain against French invasion. The virulent anti-Hanoverianism of the early 1740s resurfaced, finding new expression in the rich metaphors and vivid rhetoric of Dr John Shebbeare.[179] In June 1756, again as noted above, the loss of Minorca created a major popular and press outcry. Once it began, the tempest refused to die down. In the late summer and autumn, addresses and instructions began to be issued and find their way on to the pages of metropolitan and provincial newspapers. These were overwhelmingly critical of the ministry. By the end of the year, thirty-six had appeared calling for an enquiry into the loss of Minorca. A substantial minority, led by the City of London, also revived calls for major political reform which had last been heard at the time of Walpole's fall.[180]

[176] The complex turns and shifts in Tory relations with Pitt are traced in detail in Peters, *Pitt and Popularity*, esp. chs. 2–8. Peters shows very clearly how far Tory support for Pitt waned from as early as 1758 as their anxiety about the rising costs of the war outweighed their enthusiasm for colonial aggrandisement and the periodical political sops which Pitt was able to throw them.

[177] *Commons Journals*, xxvii (1754–7), 769

[178] R. M. Wiles, *Freshest Advices*.

[179] See Ch. 2, below, pp. 89–96.

[180] The addresses and instructions are examined in Rogers, *Whigs and Cities*, 99–104.

A popular image in the opposition press was of a diseased and corrupt political system, or constitution, requiring drastic measures to revive it. A print
published in July 1756, entitled 'A Grand Consultation of Physicians: or an
Attempt to assign the Cause of a Sickly & languishing Constitution; prescrib-
ing the most Salutary & probably methods for effecting a Cure', showed a
group of physicians counselling against 'tinkering' cures. The verse appended
to the print included the lines:

> From their close Coverts drag the Sons of Guilt,
> And be their Blood with large Effusion spilt.[181]

The spontaneity and impact of the outcry in 1756 have been questioned by
Jonathan Clark.[182] Several of the instructions and addresses certainly betray
the influence of Tories and other opposition politicians. Some popular
demonstrations of anger towards Byng and Whig oligarchy were also
supported, if not organized, by members of the elite.[183] Yet, as Nicholas
Rogers has emphasized, much more striking is how far ministers and their
supporters sought to prevent or moderate expressions of popular anger
throughout England and Wales, and how far popular and public anger was
not to be deflected, despite their best efforts. In the City, Sir John Barnard—
who had been a very popular politician in London since the later 1730s—earnt
himself only enmity and a sudden loss of political influence when he tried to
moderate a hostile City address on the setback.[184] John West, one of the
undersecretaries of state, sought to organize a counter-address amongst City
merchants, but was forced to desist because of an inability to find merchants
willing to support such a move.[185] The story was essentially similar elsewhere.
Only Bristol produced counter-addresses, while attempts at issuing hostile
addresses were quashed in Surrey and Cambridgeshire.[186] Sir William
Harbord reported from Norwich that his opposition to an address from the
corporation had been ineffective; he had also been forced to sign the address
because of the need to protect his 'popularity'. That the corporation at
Norwich was dominated by the Whigs, natural supporters of the ministry, only
made this action more significant.[187] Edward Willes, Justice of the King's
Bench, was asked by ministers to observe the general disposition of the people
when he was on circuit; his reports offered Newcastle no comfort.[188]

The crisis also exposed the essential weakness of the ministry's position relative to the press when faced with an upsurge of popular hostility. Against a

---

[181] Bodl., Johnson Ballads, fol. 51.
[182] Clark, *The Dynamics of Change*, esp. p. 232.
[183] See Rogers, *Crowds, Culture and Politics in Georgian Britain*, 60–4.
[184] Peters, *Pitt and Popularity*, 55.
[185] BL, Add. MS 32866, fos. 496–8: West to Newcastle, 20 Aug. 1756.
[186] For Cambridgeshire, see BL, Add. MS 35351 (Hardwicke Papers), fos. 343–4, 347–8. For Surrey,
see BL, Add. MS 35416, fos. 1–2, 37.
[187] BL, Add. MS 32867, fo. 482: Sir William Harbord to Newcastle, 30 Sept. 1756.
[188] BL, Add. MS 32867, fos. 1–2.

background of popular fury, there was little point in seeking to still the press through harassment or prosecutions; the chances of a jury reaching a guilty verdict in a trial for seditious libel in 1756 were negligible. Ministers and their supporters worried about their ability (or inability) to mount a defence of themselves in a form which would reach a substantial audience. In June, the poet and writer David Mallet offered his services as a 'writer of plain sense and common honesty' to Newcastle. Two months later, Robert Nugent was volunteering the pen of Josiah Tucker, the Bristol cleric and future Dean of Gloucester.[189] In late August, Hardwicke wrote to Newcastle from his Cambridgeshire home, Wimpole Hall, 'I hope Mr M[allet] is hard at work. Indeed it is necessary to hasten some justification into the world.' Two days later, Newcastle replied calling for the prosecution of libels in the press. This provoked Hardwicke, in turn, to respond:

One Thing I am sure ought to be done, & set about immediately: – I mean printing *Short Papers*, in some of the Daily News Papers, in vindication or by way of true Representations of the Measures of Administration upon some of these popular points. I really believe these short diurnal libels do more harm than the larger Pamphlets, because they are more read, & spread more amongst the common People. This would be following the Opposition in their own way; whereas now the People meet with that scandal every day & no contradiction or answer to it.[190]

Hardwicke's comments reflected an important change which was underway in the way in which the press intervened in and commented on politics. During the later 1740s and 1750s there was a tendency for anonymous or pseudonymous letters on political topics to assume greater prominence and importance; the long-standing dominance of the essay paper and the pamphlet were steadily being eroded. It was an uneven process, and essay papers, such as John Wilkes's famous paper the *North Briton*, continued to achieve great prominence in the early 1760s. The underlying trend was, none the less, clear.

   The outcry provoked by the loss of Minorca did not by itself bring down the Newcastle ministry, although it was an important part of the context in which the ministry fell apart. It also brought into sharp focus the influence of popular opinion on parliamentary and ministerial politics. For the rest of the war, 'popularity', as Marie Peters has emphasized, remained a factor in government, one which was inextricably linked with the rise to political pre-eminence of Pitt in 1756–7.[191] It was a force which was ill understood by ministers and politicians, not least by Pitt himself. It was also inherently volatile. Yet its very lack of precise definition, its intangibility, probably added

   [189] BL, Add. MS 32866, fos. 256, 347–9.
   [190] BL, Add. MS 32867, fos. 72–3: Hardwicke to Newcastle, 20 Aug. 1756; fos. 117–18: Newcastle to Hardwicke, 28 Aug. 1756; fos. 143–9, Hardwicke to Newcastle, 29 Aug. 1756.
   [191] See esp. Peters, *Pitt and Popularity*, *passim*.

to rather than subtracted from its impact. Other ministers were very aware of Pitt's 'popularity'; they also saw it as a political asset they did not wish to be without while the war lasted.

The final years of the 1750s were characterized by unprecedented political and patriotic unity. The ministry faced little opposition in Parliament, not least because most influential Whig politicians were included within it. Political controversies and frictions did not disappear. There were frequent tensions between Pitt and Newcastle and his old corps colleagues. Lacking conventional political support—direct influence over a number of boroughs or MPs—Pitt cultivated a stance of personal independence, which at times bordered on wilful political irresponsibility. He also insisted on maintaining links with and courting Tory and Patriot opinion.[192] The course and conduct of the war also continued to create controversial issues and debates, not least with regard to the degree of British commitment to the European theatre and her main ally, Frederick the Great. There were also further military setbacks in 1757–8. As we will see in a later chapter, the changing conditions of the war, and issues and debates arising from them, fully exercised the attention of the press and political nation. The unity of the later 1750s was also comparatively short-lived, it reached its height in 1759–60, and was only achieved under the impact of unusual conditions: first, the spectacular series of British military successes across the globe; and secondly, buoyant overseas trade. That the successes of the years after 1758 were largely unanticipated at the beginning and during the early phases of the conflict only magnified their political effects. The consensus also began to unravel with remarkable rapidity after 1760, when a new reign, and the emergence of Lord Bute, George III's favourite, created new political conditions, and began to undermine the delicate balances and accommodations which held together the Pitt–Newcastle coalition. The prospect of the end of the Seven Years War, which contemporaries debated from at least 1759, and the issue of what sort of peace Britain should negotiate, also served to fracture the temporary consensus which had fallen on political life after 1758.

This consensus was, in any case, perhaps more apparent than real. Within it, contradictory political hopes and expectations continued to be maintained and nurtured. These were to find expression at the beginning of the new reign, when hopes for political change, and the dismantling of Whig oligarchy began to be passed from Pitt to the new King. In bringing popular and city opinion into closer alignment to government in the later 1750s, Pitt also increased expectations for their influence. In this and indeed in other ways, the turbulence and instability of politics in the 1760s had their origins firmly in the previous decade. The unity of the later 1750s can also disguise the continuing limitations of political authority and consent in Britain in this

---

[192] See ibid.; id., *The Elder Pitt*, chs. 3 and 4.

period. In this context, it is the contrast between 1758–60 and the years immediately preceding which is instructive. In the course of a few years, Britons
passed from being convinced that they faced national ruin to intoxication on
visions of national apotheosis. What made 1756–7 years of such anxiety for
the political elites, and many others, was that failure in war coincided with
widespread domestic unrest and protest. 1756–7 saw outbreaks of food rioting
across many areas of the country unmatched in scale and scope by anything
in recent history; this was followed in 1757 by violent protests against the
implementation of the Militia Act, carried through Parliament with the reluctant support of the old corps but led by two opposition Whigs, George and
Charles Townshend.[193] These protests—which took place across Yorkshire,
the Midlands, East Anglia, and in Middlesex, Gloucestershire, and Kent—
exposed fractures and tensions within society that had been largely hidden
from view in previous decades, although shortages in 1740 had produced
several serious disturbances. They were marked by the scale of intimidation
employed to deter implementation of the act, and a signal lack of deference
towards authority. Recent and continuing problems regarding grain shortages
and prices fuelled a sense of popular grievance, and underlying the protests
was a sense of class hostility rarely evident in the eighteenth century. In several
places, but particularly in the East Riding of Yorkshire, the elites were
alarmed by what they saw as a 'levelling spirit'. Armed mobs demanded drink
and money from constables and local justices; constables and justices who
insisted on going ahead with implementing the act had their houses attacked
and, in some cases, destroyed.[194] Following a 'prodigious riot' at Royston in
Hertfordshire, where a mob of 800 had attacked the house of two deputy lieutenants, extorting from them money, drink, and provisions, Lord Hardwicke
wrote: 'This grows a serious thing; a spirit of Plunder & levying contributions
is gone forth, as well as of opposition to this Act of Parliament.'[195] Sir
Rowland Wynn reported from Yorkshire in September about the destruction
of mills near to Sheffield. Those responsible 'now publickly declare', Wynn
wrote, 'that ye Gentlemen have been long enough in possession of their
Estates but that it shall now be their Turn . . .'.[196] Local JPs and elites struggled, often only partially successfully, to reassert their authority in the face of
remarkably determined popular protest in these years. Efforts to implement
the act were postponed; rioters often escaped punishment owing to timidity
(or prudence) on the part of local authorities.[197] The efforts to implement the
Militia Act also further revealed that, at the local level, the partisan fissures of
landed society remained. To Newcastle and many other old corps Whigs, the

---

[193] See Rogers, *Crowds, Culture and Politics*, ch. 2.
[194] See the correspondence on the riots in the East Riding in BL, Egerton MS 3476.
[195] BL, Add. MS 32873, fos. 510–11.
[196] BL, Add. MS 32874, fos. 222–3.
[197] See e.g. BL, Add. MS 32875, fos. 331–2.

reformed militia was in danger of becoming an instrument to reintroduce Tories into positions of local power and influence. Many English counties did not raise a militia until 1759–60, and this was only after several of the popular grievances about the militia had been redressed; it was also against the background of another major invasion scare.[198]

The mid-eighteenth-century political world in Britain defies simple characterization. In reality, there was not one political world, but a series of overlapping and interlinking ones. Some of these have been referred to in the account provided above, but by no means all. The world of commercial and special interest lobbies, such as the West India lobby or the linen interest in Scotland, has not been mentioned. The responsiveness of oligarchical government to these pressures was an important and often underestimated feature of political life throughout the eighteenth century, as recent work has shown.[199] William Beckford cut his political teeth in the West India lobby. In Scotland, the Convention of the Royal Burghs constituted a national lobbying body for Scottish economic interests of considerable scope and sophistication, a role which awaits detailed study. At the local level, political interests required to be carefully nurtured, and were more often than not readily susceptible to challenge or collapse. Their creation and survival also usually required cooperation and consent from more than a small, exclusive elite.[200] Oligarchical politics may have been dominated by a small, landed elite, but it never stopped with this elite. The appropriate question may also be what this elite did with political power, not its social composition.

Struggles for office and the spoils of office loomed large in mid-century politics. To some, it was a distasteful spectacle. The Jacobite Andrew Lumisden responded to a correspondent in early December 1755: 'I am concerned but not surprised at the account you give me of the generality of the people at home. Paltry immediate interest is the idol to w.ch the world bows.'[201] Perhaps it took a Jacobite overseas to express this view so clearly; were it otherwise Lumisden would not have been in Rome with his King. But principles were not absent from the calculations of Whig politicians, and on one issue they were entirely united—the need to ensure the survival of the Hanoverian and Protestant Succession and the balanced system of government created in 1689. Whig principles may have been dimmed by years of office, but the continued spectre of a Jacobite restoration, and fears and suspicions about Tory allegiances, sustained traditional party loyalties well into the mid-eighteenth century. The Jacobite Rebellion reminded Whigs of

---

[198] J. R. Western, *The English Militia in the Eighteenth Century* (London and Toronto, 1965), esp. pp. 154–61. See also BL, Add. MS 32873 and 32874, for letters expressing Whig fears about Tory exploitation of the revived militia. See also Ch. 3, below, pp.142–4.

[199] See e.g. H. T. Dickinson, *The Politics of the People in Eighteenth-Century Britain* (1994), ch. 2.

[200] For an exemplary local study, see D'Cruze, 'The Middling Sort in Provincial England'.

[201] NLS, Acc. 11328, Lumisden to Capt Edgar, 2 Dec. 1755.

the essence of their political faith, and in the years which immediately followed its suppression, many Whigs sought to demonstrate their loyalty with renewed intent.

Whig oligarchy in the mid-eighteenth century also demonstrated very clearly both its resilience and limitations as a form of government. The crises which faced it at various points were severe ones. The years 1745–6 and 1756–7 produced challenges to and strains on government which were not often matched in earlier or later decades. These crises were, nevertheless, overcome, albeit with a significant measure of good fortune as well as political skill and determination. Ministers and old corps Whigs naturally saw themselves as the only guardians of the national interest, and they generally pursued this role responsibly and with some notable successes, for example, Pelham's reduction of the national debt or Lord Anson's leadership of the navy in the Seven Years War.[202] The personnel and politics of the Hanoverian regime rarely, however, commanded popular consent or support. This was partly owing to George II, whose all too obvious liking for his Hanoverian electorate, and near annual trips to it, antagonized a deeply xenophobic English political nation. The two mid-century wars also served to highlight the Anglo-Hanoverian connection and its influence on British diplomatic and international fortunes. Whig oligarchical rule also alienated major sections of opinion from it. Hanoverian stability was on occasion based on nothing more than the realization that the most obvious alternative—a Stuart restoration—promised less and threatened more, not least the status and security of the Anglican Church and Protestant religion. Only spectacular and unforeseen military victories, and buoyant overseas trade, brought the Hanoverian regime a measure of popularity in the later 1750s, and even then much of this mood was focused on Pitt, whose singular political feat was to manage to maintain a reputation of being a political outsider whilst in office.

The opposition to Whig oligarchy, which embraced disparate political groups and politicians, Whig, Tory, Jacobite, and independent, was frequently disunited after 1742. It also included politicians whose primary motivation was factious, or simply forcing themselves into office. Insofar as it did achieve coherence, it was as a Patriot alliance, an alliance which sought a regeneration and cleasing of national politics. This was to be achieved through the creation of a national ministry, not a narrow Whig one, and through the elimination of corruption from politics. By the 1750s, the Tories stood for nothing else at the national level. William Beckford's rapid rise to prominence in Tory ranks in the 1750s is suggestive of how little traditional party identities meant

---

[202] For the latter, see R. Middleton, *The Bells of Victory: The Pitt–Newcastle Ministry and the Conduct of the Seven Years' War, 1757–1762* (Cambridge, 1985); S. F. Gradish, *The Manning of the British Navy During the Seven Years' War* (1980). See also John Brewer's very positive assessment of Henry Pelham's stewardship of national finances in id., *The Sinews of Power: War, Money and the English State, 1688–1783* (1989), esp. p. 124.

at the national level by that stage; so too is the fact that he could so happily and readily call himself a Whig in the new reign.

The press was also a sporadically powerful instrument for criticism of Whig oligarchy. Its importance in the development of popular politics in the years of Walpolian rule has been emphasized elsewhere. It was a role which continued after 1742. It was also one which, as we have seen, ministers had notably limited control over. The weakness of the ministry in 1756 faced with a hostile press, backed by hostile popular opinion, looks forward to problems Grenville and his colleagues were to face in the early 1760s when confronted with the journalistic talents of John Wilkes. The opposition press, led by the *London Evening Post*, continued to harass ministers even during the political calm which prevailed in the later 1740s and early 1750s. In 1756, it was the *London Evening Post*, aided by the *Monitor* and several other papers, which helped to orchestrate and direct the outcry created by the fall of Minorca against Newcastle and his fellow old corps Whigs. In the following year, Newcastle referred to the newspapers as being full of the 'most dangerous impertinence'.[203] That opposition to the Hanoverian regime lacked clear and effective leadership for much of the 1750s only underlines how important the contribution of the press was to sustaining popular involvement in politics in this period.

What, finally, of the 'stability' of Whig oligarchy at its height? To contemporaries, for anything other than one or two years, this would probably have been lost on them. The political world they inhabited was one which continued to present visions of threat and calamity. French power and international ambition haunted contemporaries, at least before the end of the period. This is not the same as saying that stability did not exist; but it does allow us to be clear about what it was not. It did not mean tranquillity, an absence of crisis, or an absence of at times very disruptive political and sectarian divisions. The landed elites remained fundamentally politically divided until 1760, although this did not prevent cooperation between Whigs and Tories, and there was a strong tendency towards political accommodations between Whigs and Tories in electoral politics. If the pulse of the political nation beat slower in many places in the 1750s, this was a consequence of the weakness of opposition at the national level, and the entrenchment of Whig supremacy at a local one. It was the continuing reality of divisions along party lines which made the cooperation between many Whigs and Tories during the crisis of the Jacobite Rebellion so striking to contemporaries. As Joseph Yorke wrote in early October 1745, in the context of comment about the strength of the loyal reaction to the Young Pretender's invasion, 'what is more extraordinary his Conduct & Behaviour has been such as to unite both Whigs and Torys in him as in aliquo fortio.'[204] Two years later, Charles Yorke, another of Hardwicke's sons, was at Bedford for the county assizes. The

---

[203] BL, Add. MS 32870, fo. 389.
[204] BL, Add. MS 35363 (Hardwicke Papers), fos. 101–2.

picture he sketched for his father was one of a local society still segregated along party lines:

None of the Tory gentlemen appeared upon the occasion, but some of the Ladies could not contain themselves, and found nature too strong for Grace; for tho' they had great scruples of conscience about going (as they expressed it) to a presbyterian Ball, yet they were so eager to share in the gaiety of it, that they came without any seeming Remorse.[205]

The era when the empire of polite manners would reign supreme, and party divisions be a thing of the past, or subordinate to it, was fast approaching, but it had not yet come. The political stability of the period was of a different sort, and partly masked by continuing party divisions. It was a product of widespread acceptance of the religious settlement which had emerged partly by accident in the decades which followed 1689; it was the product of a strong, but flexible and dynamic social order and of widespread (but not unconditional) acquiescence in and respect for the leadership of the landed classes; it was also the product of a strengthening consensus, as later chapters will demonstrate, that Britain's national interest was her trade.

[205] BL, Add. MS 35353 (Hardwicke Papers), fos 29–30: Joseph Yorke to Lord Hardwicke, 9 Aug. 1747.

CHAPTER TWO

Virtue, Liberty, and
the 'Country Interest'

Give me leave likewise to wish you Joy of ye choice ye County of Middlesex has made—I am very glad you are so early in life to mount ye Theatre of Liberty since I am sure you cannot but Act your Part with applause—Exert yourself, my Friend, Dare to shew a good example to a corrupt & degenerate Age—Let ye Publick & Private virtues go Hand in hand together, & mutually support & set off each other.

So wrote George Shakerley to Sir Roger Newdigate, newly elected, in the summer of 1742, as an MP standing on the 'Country' or 'Old' interest.[1] Newdigate was to stand forth in the cause of liberty and virtue, to act, by his virtuous and uncorrupt conduct, as a reproach to a corrupt and corrupted society. Seven years later, on 13 April 1749, Dr William King, the Jacobite Principal of St Mary's Hall, Oxford University, delivered a Latin oration at the formal dedication of the Radcliffe Camera. The occasion was attended by most of the leading Tories of the period, including Newdigate.[2] According to two eyewitnesses, King had led his audience to believe that this would be his last great public oration; it was to be the final, despairing stand of an ageing patriot.[3] There had been a time, King declared, when Britons had retained their ancient frugality and strictness of manners, together with a fierce zeal for liberty. MPs had been chosen with the utmost care and foresight. No candidate had been elected who was susceptible to bribery or the threats of ministers. Yet today everything was different. The people had grown corrupt; they showed no signs of shame, especially when it came to elections. The source of corruption was luxury. Only God could now rescue the nation from calamity and ruin. King finished his oration with a series of five prayers. Here he flirted with controversy by, as one modern historian has put it, 'punctuating

---

[1] Warwickshire County Record Office, CR 136, B 2252: George Shakerley to Sir Roger Newdigate, 28 Aug. 1742.

[2] For a description of the ceremonies associated with the dedication, see *Lond. Ev. P.*, 13–15 Apr. 1749.

[3] See 'The Opening of the Radcliffe Library in 1749', *Bodleian Library Quarterly*, 1 (1915), 165–72. King was wrong. In 1754, he was also to give an address to Convocation, similarly replete with reproachful language about the condition of society and politics. See BL, Egerton MS 3440, fos. 66–70.

his litany of modern wickedness with cries of *REDEAT ILLE MAGNUS GENIUS BRITANNIAE* (restore the great genius of Britain)'.[4] The cry was ambiguous, deliberately so. Many there, and amongst those who subsequently read the line, would have been in no doubt that King was referring to a restoration of the Stuarts to the British throne. His oration could also be interpreted more innocently, however, as a call for the eradication of corruption and the restoration of virtue in the nation.

The twin perceptions of the pervasiveness of corruption and the need for a restoration of virtue united many of those who sought political change in mid-eighteenth-century Britain. The perceptions were not new. Under Walpole, Tory poets—for example, Alexander Pope—had used their verse to comment on what they saw as the degeneration of society and culture. Henry St John, Viscount Bolingbroke also gave them powerful expression in his main political works of the later 1730s, the *Letters on the Spirit of Patriotism* and the *Idea of a Patriot King*.[5] Yet from the early 1740s, they became ever more important. Indeed, the story of opposition politics in this period is, from a certain perspective, as we began to see in the previous chapter, the story of the relationship between increasingly desperate hopes for national renewal and revival, and a deepening disenchantment with the politics of the Hanoverian regime and a growing conviction that parliamentary politics was incapable of delivering reform. As the disillusionment grew, so did a tendency to look for heroic figures to effect reform. A minority, like William King, looked to the Young Pretender. Before his death in March 1751, a larger number looked to Frederick, Prince of Wales. In the later 1750s, under the impact of unprecedented and unanticipated military success, Pitt the Elder became the focus of such hopes. It was also the role of the Patriot King, the true 'father of his people', which George III sought to play, with momentous if unintended consequences, on his accession in 1760.

This chapter explores the ideological construction and content of the politics of virtue in the mid-eighteenth century. This politics was known at the time as the 'Country Interest' or 'Patriotism'. It also sometimes went under different labels, for example, the cause of 'Old England', or even, amongst the Tories, the 'old interest' or the 'honest party'. Many of the major concepts, assumptions, values, and attitudes which lent this interest what structure and coherence it possessed were well established in political debate by the begin-

[4] Paul Kleber Monod, *Jacobitism and the English People, 1688–1788* (Cambridge, 1989), 36. The fullest discussion of King's oration and its subsequent English translations is contained in David Greenwood, *William King, Tory and Jacobite* (Oxford, 1969), 197–203.

[5] These were not published or widely disseminated until 1749. See *Bolingbroke's Political Writings: The Conservative Enlightenment*, ed. Bernard Cottret (1997); Simon Varey, *Henry St John, Viscount Bolingbroke* (Boston, Mass., 1984); Isaac Kramnick, *Bolingbroke and his Circle: The Politics of Nostalgia in the Age of Walpole* (1968); H. T. Dickinson, *Bolingbroke* (1970).

ning of our period. As J. G. A. Pocock has shown, a 'civic humanist' tradition
of political argument, which looked to classical republicanism for its sources
and inspiration, provided a common language and set of concepts for those
who found themselves excluded from the political system from the later seventeenth century.[6] Much of the political argument of the mid-century opposition can, therefore, seem repetitive, even stale, which perhaps raises the issue
of why examine it at all. Yet the 'Country Interest' was never a unified or
stable force in politics. Just as there was no Country Party in early Hanoverian
politics—it was always a coalition of diverse, unstable even contradictory
elements—so there was no unchanging Country interest.[7] Indeed, one of the
major themes of this chapter will be how far the content of Country argument shifted to bring into much sharper focus the threat to English liberties
and national destiny from luxury, immorality, and irreligion.

There was another way of perceiving the same problem. This was in terms
of a crisis of 'public spirit'. Public spirit—a key concept in Country thinking—
was defined as devotion to the common good of the *patria*, the disposition to
disregard self-interest and sectional advantage for the sake of national interest.
The condition and display of public spirit were portrayed by Country writers
as being crucial to the defence of liberty and to the power and influence of
the nation abroad. What lent the goal of reviving public spirit great urgency
in this period was the very direct and immediate threat which France posed
to national survival and prosperity, especially from the later 1740s.[8] On this
view, the major task facing the Country Interest was how to recreate the social
and moral basis for a cohesive, prosperous, and *powerful* Britain. The weak
condition of public spirit threatened, or could be represented as so doing,
the loss of everything that was dear to Britons—their independence, their
freedom, their commerce, and their religion.

[6] J. G. A. Pocock, *The Machiavellian Moment: Florentine Political Thought and the Atlantic Republican Tradition* (Princeton, NJ, 1975); id., 'The Varieties of Whiggism from Exclusion to Reform. A History of Ideology and Discourse', in id., *Virtue, Commerce and History: Essays on Political Thought, Chiefly Eighteenth Century* (Cambridge, 1985), 215–310.

[7] Much of the debate about the 'Country Interest' in early-Hanoverian politics has concerned how far, if at all, it subsumed and undermined Whig and Tory party identities. Several historians have been dismissive of the importance of the 'Country Interest', seeing it as no more than an unstable tactical alliance between the Tories and different groups of opposition Whigs. For more balanced views, which, while acknowledging the persistence of traditional party identities, take the shifting and multiple meanings of Country politics seriously, see esp. H. T. Dickinson, *The Politics of the People in Eighteenth-Century Britain* (1994), 197–203; Nicholas Rogers, *Whigs and Cities: Popular Politics in the Age of Walpole and Pitt* (Oxford, 1989), 394–7; Kathleen Wilson, *The Sense of the People: Politics, Culture and Imperialism in England, 1715–1785* (Cambridge, 1995), chs. 2 and 3; Bob Harris, 'The "London Evening Post" and Mid Eighteenth Century British Politics', *EHR* 110 (1995), 1132–56; Bob Harris and Jeremy Black, 'John Tucker, MP, and Mid-Eighteenth-Century British Politics', *Albion*, 29 (1997), 15–38.

[8] See Ch. 3, below.

COUNTRY IDEOLOGY

At the heart of the political outlook of the Country Interest was concern with freedom and 'English liberties', their condition and prospects.[9] Corruption, in the form of illegitimate influence—bribery, the disposal of places and favours—was seen as the major threat to these liberties. It weakened the spirit or essence of the constitution, while leaving its form intact. It was also assumed that tyranny could only be established by stealth; this was the lesson of the turbulent struggle between liberty and tyranny of the previous century. Under Walpole, government had become a system of corruption. Ministerial MPs, under the influence of corruption, formed a unified and uniformly compliant force in the Commons. The executive also sought to extend its powers through legislation—the Riot and Black Acts, for example—and the maintenance of a standing army. The revolution in public finance in the later seventeenth century had both expanded the opportunities for corruption and laid the basis for the impoverishment of the bulk of the population. The high levels of taxation required to fund this debt, especially in the form of duties on consumer goods and trade, not only expanded the size and influence of the revenue departments, a powerful source of government patronage, it also depressed the prosperity of the population and rendered it more susceptible to corruption. Corrupt rule was denuding the wealth of the nation, as well as undermining its virtue and liberties.

Country ideology was neither rural nor urban; it expressed rather the views and interests of a diverse range of social and political groups and individuals who found (or felt themselves to be) excluded from power in early-Hanoverian Britain. These included gentry; freeholders; farmers; tradesmen; merchants; artisans and shopkeepers; Whigs; Tories; Jacobites; independents.[10] The political vision underlying Country ideology was at bottom, however, a conservative one, and the view of society which most Country propagandists cleaved to was profoundly traditional and backward looking. Whig oligarchy was often portrayed by these writers as a system or union of 'unnatural interests'. At one level, this simply referred to the network of interests and associations that were allegedly parasitic on the state and the country's wealth over which Walpole and his successors presided. What defined these interests was their supposed common opposition to 'national interest'; they represented self-interest in the service of corruption. Yet the term also

---

[9] In addition to n. 7 above, see Hugh Cunningham, *The Language of Patriotism: The Making and Unmaking of British National Identity*, i, *History and Politics*, ed. Raphael Samuel (1989), 57–66; Quentin Skinner, 'The Principles and Practice of Opposition: The Case of Bolingbroke versus Walpole', in Neil McKendrick (ed.), *Historical Perspectives: Studies in English Thought and Society in Honour of J H Plumb* (1974), 113–21; J. A. W. Gunn, *Beyond Liberty and Property: The Process of Self-Recognition in Eighteenth Century Political Thought* (Kingston and Montreal, 1983); Shelley Burtt, *Virtue Transformed: Political Argument in England, 1688–1740* (Cambridge, 1992).

[10] See esp. Pocock, 'The Varieties of Whiggism'.

had deeper meanings. Whig oligarchy threatened to overturn the legitimate interests and influence on government of property, especially landed property, and the values with which this was associated—honour, virtue, and public spirit. It represented the subversion of the normal, proper social basis of politics, and its replacement by the rule of the 'lowborn and upstart'.

In recent years, historians have tended to pass over or ignore this aspect of Country politics, choosing instead to emphasize how far the Country Interest absorbed and expressed the grievances and aspirations of non-landed sections of society from the 1730s.[11] As these historians have demonstrated, the interests of trade became more strongly and insistently represented in Country argument and politics in this period, as is also amply demonstrated elsewhere in this book.[12] Commerce, unlike stockjobbing, constituted another legitimate or natural interest in the body politic. Thus the *Remembrancer*, the essay paper supported by Leicester House after 1747, could draw a clear line in 1748 between the 'm[inisteria]l posse of stock-jobbers, contractors, remitters . . . etc., and the fair and upright exporter'.[13] There remained, however, a significant tension in Country ideology between supporting trade as an important national interest and a vision of society and social values that were essentially pre-commercial. Country writers were, as we will see, often critical of or at least ambivalent about commercialization, seeing in it the rise of the power of money and self-interest in society. As Paul Monod has suggested, the elevation of commerce as a national interest was one way of resolving the contradiction, or appearing to do so.[14]

If the political outlook of the Country interest was conservative—change being conceived of as restoration—it also developed a strong populist, even republican edge. Country propagandists frequently asserted the popular origins of government and liberties, espousing delegatory theories of political sovereignty. As one writer in the Tory-Patriot essay paper, the *Monitor, or British Freeholder*, put it in 1755: 'For our Liberties and privileges were not the gift of our princes; but are original rights, and as much a part of the constitution, as the prerogative, and powers of the Crown'.[15] On 29 October 1754, 'Britannicus', the leading writer in the influential *London Evening Post*, advised his readers: 'That the Supreme Power of this Kingdom is in the People cannot be denied by any one who approves of the Revolution Principles; all other Power is but delegated, is but intrusted to them for their Good . . .'. In some cases, the principle of popular sovereignty was used to defend striking claims.

[11] See esp. Dickinson, *The Politics of the People*, 197–203; Wilson, *The Sense of the People*, ch. 3; Rogers, *Whigs and Cities, passim.*

[12] See Ch. 3, below.

[13] *Remembrancer*, 10 Sept. 1748, quoted in Lucy Sutherland, 'The City of London in Eighteenth-Century Politics', in Aubrey Newman (ed.), *Politics and Finance in the Eighteenth Century: Lucy Sutherland* (1984), 53.

[14] Monod, *Jacobitism and the English People*, 82.

[15] *Monitor*, 9 Aug. 1755.

In 1757, for example, in the context of the ministerial instability which followed the collapse of the Devonshire–Pitt ministry, 'Britannicus' argued that the 'people' had the right to 'interfere' in the appointment of ministers should ministers use powers which had been delegated to them for purposes which were contrary to those for which they had been so delegated.[16] As Kathleen Wilson has emphasized, the Glorious Revolution of 1689 was portrayed by the same writers as an example of the principles of popular sovereignty in action, as well as a warning to future would-be tyrants.[17] Thus, one pamphleteer declared in 1757:

> Then [during the Revolution] it was that *Britons* behaved like *Britons*, and shewed themselves to be worthy successors of their great and noble spirited Progenitors, that would not suffer their Birth-rights to be taken from them.[18]

Contractual notions of political obligation and sovereignty also lay behind an emphasis on the so-called fundamental laws in much Country propaganda— Magna Carta, the Bill of Rights, and the Act of Settlement. These laws were portrayed as permanent contracts between monarchs and the English people. The Act of Settlement served as a very visible reminder of the basis on which the Hanoverians occupied the English throne. The same pamphleteer quoted above asserted that the Act was 'the compact between the House of Hanover and the People of Great Britain' and that it 'ought to be religiously observed and adhered to'.[19] By repealing or ignoring parts of the Act of Settlement the Hanoverian regime was imperilling its own legitimacy.

Patriot writers insisted that the nation had flourished in the past (and would only do so again) when the monarch based his or her rule on the confidence and interests of the 'people'. The source of corruption was usually, although not always, identified as ministers. There was also a deep-seated suspicion and hostility towards royal favourites, who stood between the monarch and the people. The iconic status of Elizabeth I in this period derived precisely from the assumption that the monarch should pursue, even personify, the interests of the people or nation.[20] Elizabeth's reign supposedly represented the period in recent English history when the monarch had most fully embodied in her rule the interests of her free people. It was against this mythic vision of Elizabeth's reign that the present was often judged and always found wanting.

The main reforms sought by supporters of the Country interest continued to be those sought under Walpole—place and pension bills and repeal of the Septennial Act. It was argued that only these reforms would restore the

---

[16] *Lond. Ev. P.*, 28–31 May 1757.

[17] Kathleen Wilson, 'Inventing Revolution: 1688 and Eighteenth-century Popular Politics', *JBS*, 28 (1989), 349–86.

[18] *A Guide to the Knowledge of the Rights and Privileges of Englishmen* (1757), 73.

[19] Ibid., 88.

[20] See Christine Gerrard, *The Patriot Opposition to Walpole: Politics, Poetry and National Myth, 1725–1742* (Oxford, 1994), ch. 6.

independence of the House of Commons and allow it to resume its proper constitutional functions—to represent the 'grievances of the nation' and to defend the liberties of the people. The reforming ambitions of the Country Interest also began, however, to expand to embrace electoral reform, as well as, as we will see later, various other reforms. The focus of disquiet in this context was ministerial control of small, closed borough constituencies, or what the essay paper the *Protestor, on Behalf of the People* called in 1753 the 'Borough System'.[21] Control of such constituencies had enabled Walpole to maintain his parliamentary majority at the general elections of 1734 and 1741, despite losses in county and larger, more open urban constituencies. Borough elections were depicted as characterized by riot, misrule, and flagrant corruption. The ministerial interest in them was alleged to be the product of money, intimidation and 'unnatural' influence. The large body of laws against electoral bribery and corruption were also viewed as hopelessly ineffective.[22]

Against this background, some opposition writers began to call for reform of the electoral system. In the 1750s, 'Britannicus' recommended on a number of occasions a 'fair and equal representation of property'. On 29 January 1754, he argued that

the Boroughs, which have the Privilege of sending members to Parliament, are, very many of them, fallen into great decay, and certainly have now a trifle of property . . . For though the Boroughs constitute above Two-Thirds of the Representative of this Kingdom, they be at present, no manner of Proportion, (hardly one to a hundred) in Point of Property, to the rest of the Nation: And therefore, is it not contrary to all Reason and Equity, that they should elect so great a Part of its Representative?

The thrust of the case was that the system of representation needed to reflect better the distribution of property in the country in order to reduce the susceptibility of the electorate to corruption. This was in line with other reforms of the electoral system recommended in the 1740s and 1750s, such as payment of MPs, the introduction of the secret ballot, and residency requirements for MPs.[23]

Some care is needed when trying to characterize arguments about electoral reform in this period. What lay behind them was a creative tension between a recognition that London and certain other large urban constituencies were by the later 1730s providing an important source of opposition to Whig oligarchy and a continuing respect for landed property. Land continued to be seen as the strongest basis of political virtue and independence, and landed political leadership as the best guarantor of the national interest. 1747, for example, saw the publication of a remarkable pamphlet advocating reform

[21] *Protestor*, 16 Aug. 1753.
[22] *Lond. Ev. P.*, 9–13 Mar. 1754; 18–20 Aug. 1757.
[23] *Lond. Ev. P.*, 12–14 Sept., 5–7 Dec. 1751; 26–9 Jan., 18–20 Apr. 1754; 17–20 Mar., 14–17 Apr. 1759. See also below.

entitled *Liberty and Right: or, An Essay, Historical and Political, on The Constitution and Administration of Great Britain*. The author urged the regulation of property inheritance—to prevent too unequal a distribution of landed wealth in society—as the bedrock on which to build a reformed and newly virtuous polity. MPs were to be salaried, subject to a strictly enforced property qualification, and were not to hold places from government. A third of MPs were to be re-elected every year. The distribution of seats was to be changed to increase the representation of London from four to twelve MPs, while each county was to gain an additional MP. Elsewhere, voters were called upon to support candidates who were independent, resident, and of 'old family'.[24] The author of *The Independent Freeholder's Letter to the People of England* (1757) declared:

> Your parliaments well know that the independent gentry of England, not the servants of the crown, were at all times, particularly at such a time, the proper persons to constitute that branch of the legislature belonging to the people. For this end we may find many antient statutes provide, that members shall be chose of the gentlemen born in the county; again, that they shall be resident in the counties and boroughs.[25]

In June 1751, the essay paper, *Old England* called for the imposition of tighter property qualifications for MPs. MPs would be required to take oaths that they would 'obey' any directions and instructions they received from their constituents. They were also to be disqualified from holding any post or pension from the government. No MP was to represent the same constituency in two successive parliaments. Parliaments, meanwhile, were to be limited to three-year terms and a third of MPs subject to re-election each year. MPs were also to be salaried.[26]

Insofar, therefore, as new forms of property were to be admitted to the electorate, it was because they offered no overt challenge to the political supremacy of land. The crucial factor was independence, and this was most likely to be associated with land ownership. Following the infamous Oxfordshire election contest of 1754, there were calls for legislation to prevent copyholders, a tenurial status that implied dependency, voting in county elections. (Such legislation was passed in 1758.[27]) It was precisely the low social status of the degraded borough electorates, their susceptibility to bribery and influence, that was the burden of the attack on them. As 'Britannicus' remarked, the borough franchise was in the 'hands of poor, sordid, unthinking wretches that are wholly ignorant and careless of their country's interest'.[28] Property was to be brought into the balance against the court. As a writer in the *Westminster Journal* declared in 1747:

---

[24] *Lond. Ev. P.*, 29 Nov.–1 Dec. 1753.
[25] *The Independent Freeholder's Letter*, 12.
[26] *Old England*, 22 June 1751.
[27] *Monitor*, 9 Aug., 23 Aug. 1755; 15 Jan. 1757. For the background to the Freeholders' Qualification Act (1758), see Linda Colley, *In Defiance of Oligarchy: The Tory Party 1714–60* (Cambridge, 1982), 70–1, 284.
[28] *Lond. Ev. P.*, 26–9 Jan. 1754.

Upon the whole, it is the opinion of discerning unbiass'd men throughout the kingdom, that the People of *Great Britain* can never be *justly represented*, without a *more equal Distribution of the Right of Electing*, without conferring it on *greater* Number, and at the same Time restraining it more to *men of large Property*.[29]

No social dilution of the electorate was envisaged; if anything, exactly the opposite.

Country propagandists and writers were keen to defend the political rights of 'the people' in other ways. Popular scrutiny of government was represented as a facet or symptom of 'public spirit'; as such, it was another important 'fence of liberty'. The liberty of the press was also forcefully defended in this context. Several writers argued that freedom of the press was the precondition of all other freedoms.[30] Perhaps unsurprisingly, it was when press freedom appeared to be under attack that such arguments became prominent. In 1748, a hint dropped in a pamphlet by George Lyttleton, which seemed to indicate the likelihood of tighter regulation of the press, acted as the trigger.[31] In 1752, it was the trial of printer and publisher William Owen. During Owen's trial and in subsequent years, opposition pamphlets and letters and essays in newspapers argued in favour of the widest possible definition of jury competence in libel trials as essential to safeguarding press freedom. (Owen had been acquitted because the jury had resisted the judge's instruction that they should confine themselves to deliberating about the fact of publication and not about whether the pamphlet constituted a libel.) Other concerns about actions for libel, notably the use by ministers of ex-officio informations lodged in the Court of King's Bench (these allowed them to forego the usual defence of a bill of indictment before a grand jury prior to trial proper), the use of special juries selected by the City sheriffs for libel trials (these were of a higher social status than normally impanelled juries and, therefore, more likely to favour ministerial interests), the status and legality of general warrants under which authors, printers, and publishers were taken up by servants of the ministry (general warrants, which empowered the seizure of unnamed individuals, had originated under the Star Court, a prerogative court abolished in 1641), and the doctrine of 'innuendoes' (which allowed the judge to determine the meaning of the allusive language and devices of political essays writers)—all were fully aired in this period.[32] It was these issues which John Wilkes and his supporters were to raise

[29] *Westminster Journal*, 25 July 1747.

[30] See e.g. *Lond. Ev. P.*, 5–7 July 1755.

[31] See esp. *The Importance of The Liberty of the Press . . . Being Six Papers, Publish'd in the OLD ENGLAND . . .* (1748).

[32] See esp. *Lond. Ev. P.*, 10–12 Jan. 1751; 28–30 May 1752; 28 June–1 July, 3–5 July, 5–8 July 1755; 2–4 Mar., 14–16 Mar., 4–6 Apr. 1758; *An Address to the Jurymen of London. By a Citizen* (1755); *A Guide to the Knowledge of the Rights and Privileges of Englishmen* (1757); *Old England*, 9 May, 4 July 1752; *True Briton*, 13 May, 11 Oct. 1752. 1752 also saw the reissue of the famous *The Trial of Peter Zenger, of New York, Printer*. Zenger's trial was a cause célèbre in the history of press freedom in the North American colonies. It also raised many of the issues which concerned those thinking about regulation of the press in the mother country.

again in the 1760s, and to much greater effect, following the use in 1763 of a general warrant to arrest Wilkes and several printers and publishers for Number 45 of the *North Briton*.[33] With Jacobitism defunct after 1760 as a political and military threat to the regime, defending ministerial powers over the press was to become a much more difficult challenge.

If Country writers were strongly critical of the powers available to ministers to harass the press, more striking still were their defences of popular involvement in politics in the context of the opposition practice of issuing constituency instructions to MPs. During this period, six separate waves of instructions were issued by the opposition: in 1739–40 in favour of a place bill; in 1742 before and following the fall of Sir Robert Walpole calling for widespread political reform and punishment of Walpole; in 1753 demanding repeal of the Jewish Naturalization Act; and in 1756 calling for punishment of the authors of the disaster and political reform during the outcry which accompanied the loss of Minorca.[34] Constituency instructions were primarily devices used by parliamentary politicians for channelling popular opinion against the ministry. They were blatantly propagandist in intent, being very widely reprinted in the opposition press and even collected together in pamphlet form.[35] Historians have, therefore, debated how far they actually reflected popular opinion. In some cases they were clearly the result of political manipulation and influence from above. This was true, for example, in the narrow and closely managed Scottish burgh constituencies. Linda Colley has also emphasized the role of the Tory party in securing instructions.[36] As their most recent historian has shown, in many, particularly larger urban constituencies, they do appear, however, to have represented the views of important components of the electorate and even opinion outside of this.[37] Their authenticity, status, and legitimacy were contested by ministerial supporters, who argued that the 'voice of the nation' was represented by Parliament. These same individuals also argued that MPs, on the principle of virtual representation later defended by Edmund Burke, represented the 'nation' and not their constituents in an immediate sense. Country or Patriot writers responded by arguing that the right of issuing instructions flowed from the delegatory basis of government and representation.[38] Several also argued that the people had a stake in government through their contribution to taxation and the costs of government. This gave them the right to information about the activities of

---

[33] See esp. R. R. Rea, *The English Press in Politics, 1760–1774* (Lincoln, Nebr., 1963).

[34] Rogers, *Whigs and Cities*, 244.

[35] Robert (Bob) Harris, *A Patriot Press: National Politics and the London Press in the 1740s* (Oxford, 1993), 26–7; *Great Britain's Memorial: A Collection of Instructions etc. to the Members of Parliament, Part I* (1741); *Great Britain's Memorial . . . Part II* (1742); *The Voice of the People: A Collection of Addresses to His Majesty and Instructions to Members of Parliament by their Constituents* (1756).

[36] Colley, 'Eighteenth Century English Radicalism Before Wilkes', *TRHS*, 5th ser., 31 (1981), 1–19.

[37] Rogers, *Whigs and Cities*, 245–6.

[38] *Common Sense*, 3, 10 Jan., 7 Feb. 1741; *Craftsman*, 22 Dec. 1739; 10 Jan., 7 Feb. 1741; [Lord Marchmont] *A Serious Exhortation to the Electors of Great Britain* (1740). See also Kathleen Wilson, 'Inventing Revolution'.

government, but also the right to make their views known on issues of importance to them.[39] The gap between this and the radical slogan of 'No taxation
without representation' raised by Patriots in the North American colonies
from the mid-1760s and echoed by several radicals and reformers in England
in the following decade, was, as Harry Dickinson has recently emphasized, not
a notably wide one.[40] Yet, it is also worth noting that this was an area in which
logical consistency and constitutional clarity were frequently absent. Against
the background of limited popular support for Whig oligarchy, it was easy for
Country writers to portray popularity and corruption as opposing forces; the
role of popular opinion was being defended insofar as it represented another
obstacle to the undermining of freedom. Emphasis also continued to be
placed in Country propaganda on the importance of the independence of
judgement of MPs.[41] This was another crucial 'fence of liberty'. The heat of
political debate also tended to disguise assumptions about politics which were
common to both ministers and opposition. In this instance, the issue was not
really about whether popular opinion had any role to play in political life, but
about its constitutional status and the weight of influence it should have on
parliamentary deliberations on specific issues.[42]

There is an important sense too in which Country propagandists always
looked beyond politics. We will return to this later. Suffice it to say here, the
ultimate goal of Country politics was national reconciliation and reform, even
national apotheosis. Country ideologists or writers looked to the creation of
conditions in which freedom would be secure, corruption would be eliminated
or tamed, and the nation united, prosperous, powerful, and virtuous under
the rule of a Patriot ruler. The image was one of restoration leading to the
reinvigoration of society and its institutions, and thereby to prosperity
and improvement. One of the most famous expressions of this vision was
Bolingbroke's *Idea of a Patriot King*. Although written in 1738–9, the tract
was first published in 1749 and was widely extracted and discussed in the
press.[43] Bolingbroke's political purpose in writing it has often been debated;

[39] *The Livery Man: or Plain Thoughts on Public Affairs* (1740); [John Campbell] *The Case of the Opposition Impartially Stated* (1742), 51–2.

[40] Dickinson, *The Politics of the People*, 203.

[41] On this point, see Marie Peters, 'The "Monitor" on the Constitution, 1755–65: New Light on the Ideological Origins of English Radicalism', *EHR* 82 (1971), 715.

[42] David Hume called the controversy 'frivolous'. As he noted, the way in which it was conducted tended to obscure areas of agreement. The key issue was how much weight constituents' opinions should have on MPs. This was matter of degree and not of rigidly opposed positions (Hume, *Essays: Moral, Political and Literary* (Oxford, 1963), 33–4). See also the comments on the relative merits of instructing and petitioning in *A Letter to a Member of Parliament Concerning the Present State of Affairs at Home and Abroad* (1740) and *A Second Letter to a Member of Parliament Concerning the Present State of Affairs* (1741). Something of the confusion which could characterize this debate is suggested by the recommendation of the essay paper *Old England* on 8 Aug. 1752, 'That the favourite maxim, which declares the Elected Independent of the Electors, be no longer a Maxim than where the general Good evidently require it.'

[43] *Old England*, 6 July, 14 Dec. 1751; *Scots Mag.*, 11 (1749), 378–405, 429–38, 473–80, 532–8, 581–1; *Mitre and Crown*, 1749, 479–89, 509–20, 557–73, 605–19.

similarly the ambiguities and equivocations of its arguments and rhetoric have led to protracted arguments about which possible Patriot prince—Stuart or Hanoverian—Bolingbroke may have had in mind.[44] The *Patriot King* was certainly susceptible to different readings, something which was probably intrinsic to its polemical purpose.[45] It was, however, as a powerful imaginative vision of a people and nation reunified and revitalized by the example and leadership of a reformist and virtuous monarch that its real contemporary importance lay. As Bolingbroke wrote:

A Patriot King is the most powerful of all reformers; for he is himself a sort of standing miracle, so rarely seen and so little understood, that the sure effects of his appearance will be admiration and love in every honest breast, confusion and terror to every guilty conscience, but submission and resignation in all. A new people will seem to arise with a new king. Innumerable metamorphoses, like those which poets feign, will happen in the very deed: and, while men are conscious that they are the same individuals, the difference of their sentiments will almost persuade them that they are changed into different beings.[46]

It was, as we will see below, a political vision which formed a sharp counterpoint to the alienation from and dissatisfaction with national politics and politicians amongst opposition opinion which took hold during the 1740s and which was to prevail for much of the following decade.

PATRIOTISM AND THE COURSE OF POLITICS

So far we have discussed Country ideology in terms of a series of perceptions, attitudes, and values. To reveal its nature more fully, and the ways in which it changed over the course of this period, we need to map its shifting content on to the changing conditions of national politics. We also need to look more closely at some individual voices within the 'Country Interest'.

Casting a long shadow over the fortunes of the Country Interest in the mideighteeth century was the narrow political settlement which followed the fall of Sir Robert Walpole. On this settlement rested the hopes of a popular political opposition that had been building, albeit unevenly, for at least sixteen years and which had identified all political ills and setbacks with Walpole's iron grip on power. From 1738, under the impact of, first, agitation for war against Spain and, then, the lack of success in that war once it began in October of the following year, popular hostility to Walpole had intensified markedly. As Nicholas Rogers amongst others has shown, the issues arising from the

[44] Dickinson, *Bolingbroke*, 262–4; Kramnick, *Bolingbroke and his Circle*, 166–9; Simon Varey, 'Hanover, Stuart and "The Patriot King" ', *British Journal for Eighteenth Century Studies*, 6 (1983), 163–72; Christine Gerrard, *The Patriot Opposition to Walpole*, ch. 7; David Armitage, 'A Patriot for Whom? The Afterlives of Bolingbroke's Patriot King', *JBS*, 36 (1997), 397–418.

[45] See J. C. D. Clark, *English Society, 1688–1832* (Cambridge, 1985), 182.

[46] Quoted ibid.

military setbacks in the war became personalized to a striking degree.[47] Admiral Vernon, who led the combined expedition against the Spanish American empire in 1740–1 and who claimed an early success at Portobello, was portrayed as a Patriot and national hero frustrated by the enmity and opposition of Walpole. When Walpole's fall finally came (in early February 1742) the popular reaction was first one of celebration and then expectation of far-reaching political change.

Hopes for change had already been very strongly expressed in a pamphlet published on the eve of the parliamentary session which saw Walpole finally dislodged from power. Entitled *A Key to the Business of the Present S[essio]n*, this was designed, as its title indicates, as a guide to the crucial political battles which lay ahead. The author represented the new session as one of historic importance; on its outcome depended the future of liberty and national well-being. A 'golden period' was finally within reach of the opposition; all the grievances, economic, social, and political, that had been so long complained about could be redressed. The immediate task was to destroy Walpole and then 'cleanse the Augean stable', in other words demolish the political foundations of Whig oligarchy. Change was not viewed solely in negative terms, however. Walpole's fall also promised the proper stewardship of commerce and manufactures and of Britain's international fortunes, as well as a revival of proper national spirit, morals, and culture. The stain of Walpolian mismanagement and venality was to be wiped away, ushering in a new era of national prosperity, strength, and virtue. Other writers expressed similar hopes and in similarly striking terms. Walpole's punishment was to be an act of patriotic catharsis, a wiping away of national humiliations, a prelude to restoring the political system and the constitution to its original purity and the nation to its proper influence in international affairs and diplomacy.[48]

In the event, hopes for far-reaching change were dashed—rapidly and decisively. The former opposition Whig heroes of the Country Interest, pre-eminently William Pulteney, turned villains as they accepted office and honours—Pulteney was created Earl of Bath in July 1742—without securing the punishment of Walpole or the passage of significant political reforms.[49] (The only reform measure which reached the statute book was a very limited place bill.) The popular disillusionment and outrage were commensurate with the weight of expectation that had followed Walpole's fall, and can be traced in detail in newspapers, pamphlets, and a profusion of ballads published during 1742 and early 1743.[50] The deep sense of disgust created by events also

[47] Rogers, *Whigs and Cities*, 59–68, 235–40; Kathleen Wilson, 'Empire, Trade and Popular Politics in Mid-Hanoverian Britain: The Case of Admiral Vernon', *Past and Present*, 121 (1988), 74–109.

[48] See e.g. *Common Sense*, 20 Feb., 10 Apr., 15 May, 22 May 1742; *Champion*, 6 Feb., 16 Feb., 4 Mar., 9 Mar., 11 Mar. 1742; *Daily Post*, 11 Feb. 1742; *Lond. Ev. P.*, 9–11 Feb., 16–18 Mar. 1742. See also the constituency instructions of 1742 collected together in *Great Britain's Memorial . . . Part II* (1742).

[49] See J. B. Owen, *The Rise of the Pelhams* (1957).

[50] Harris, *A Patriot Press*, 59–61; *The New Ministry. Containing a Collection of all the Satyrical Poems, Songs, &c since the Beginning of 1742* (1742).

emerges very clearly in the contemporary correspondence of several opposition supporters. Sir James Lowther, the independent Whig MP for Cumberland, wrote on 18 May 1742:

People are so sordid & rapacious there is hardly any thing but corruption from the highest to the lowest & it has bin Sr Rob[er]ts master peice [*sic*] to make it so universal that honest men w[oul]d be torn to peices [*sic*] if God Almighty did not preserve them in a wonderful manner.[51]

John Tucker, one of the MPs for Weymouth, and closely aligned at this stage to the Country Interest, wrote at around the same time that 'the loaves and fishes work so strongly on the minds of People that Patriotism seems to be forgot'.[52]

The 'great betrayal' of 1742 set the pattern, or so it appeared in retrospect, for further betrayals of hopes for reform by opposition politicians in the 1740s. Late 1744 saw these hopes and a change of direction in politics revive with the formation of the Broad-Bottom ministry, which included amongst its members several opposition Whigs and Tories. Again, however, such hopes went unrealized.[53] Early 1746 saw the admission of Pitt the Elder into the ministry. Between 1742 and 1744, Pitt had gained notoriety and popularity because of his scathing parliamentary denunciations of Hanoverian influence on British politics and policies. In 1746, following his admission to office, he defended the employment in the War of the Austrian Succession of Hanoverian troops by Britain.[54] Pitt was just the last of a succession of cynical, flawed, and unapologetic opposition politicians prepared to use Patriotism as a lever to force their way into office, or so it seemed.[55]

The ideological and political effects of these betrayals were enduring and fundamental. In the first place, the intense and widespread public interest in national politics that had characterized the final years of Walpole's rule diminished. Especially in the later 1740s, politics retreated as a topic of public and press debate, making way for an efflorescence of magazine-style publications and journals devoted to polite letters, social manners, and entertainment. Secondly, there was much greater cynicism about national politics and, more particularly, Patriotism. The alienation from, even disinterest in, national politics from the early 1740s made popular support for new Country or Patriot oppositions difficult to mobilize. The lack of such support was to be a recurring theme in the *Remembrancer*, the essay paper associated with the Leicester House opposition of 1747–51.[56] It was also a common theme in other major opposition papers of the period: for example, the *Protestor, on Behalf of the People,*

---

[51] CRO (Carlisle), D/Lons/W2/103 (Lonsdale MS): Lowther to John Spedding, 18 May 1742.
[52] Bodl., MS Don c. 105, fo. 109 (Tucker MS): John to Richard Tucker, 13 May 1742.
[53] Harris, *A Patriot Press*, 69–75.
[54] Marie Peters, *The Elder Pitt* (1997), 27–40; Jeremy Black, *Pitt the Elder*, 2nd edn. (1999), ch. 2.
[55] For contemporary press attacks on Pitt, see Harris, *A Patriot Press*, 77–8.
[56] *Remembrancer*, 23 Sept. 1749; 3 Feb., 7 Apr. 1750.

the relatively short-lived essay paper subsidized by the Duke of Bedford and William Beckford in 1753.[57] The case for opposition also now had to be more carefully made. The *London Evening Post*, as we saw in the last chapter, perhaps the most influential Patriot paper of the 1750s, repeatedly commented on the debased currency of Patriotism. In November 1756, for example, referring to the events which followed Walpole's fall, it commented, 'From that infamous Period, how hath all Patriotism and Publick Spirit been ridiculed and laugh'd at'.[58] The paper also repeatedly, and for this reason, claimed to be interested in measures, not in particular politicians.[59] The famous letter writer and youngest son of Sir Robert Walpole, Horace Walpole, was one of those who were surprised when popular opposition to Whig oligarchy re-emerged as a significant force in politics in the mid-1750s because Patriotism had become so discredited as a national political force after the events of the 1740s.[60]

There were other more subtle, less easily documented, ideological effects of the 'great betrayal' of 1742. M. M. Goldsmith had argued that the events of 1742 led to more sceptical attitudes towards government and politics.[61] These were revealed in the work of such literary luminaries as Henry Fielding, who moved away from opposition and towards the ministry during the 1740s, and Samuel Johnson, who withdrew from partisan political writing in the early 1740s, and by the reception of David Hume's *Essays: Moral, Political and Literary*, published in London in 1741. Hume was fortunate, Goldsmith suggests, to launch his sceptical or moderate Whiggism at this moment. He also suggests that greater scepticism about politics and politicians may have promoted a deepening acceptance of party as a permanent and desirable feature of politics. In a world where ambitions were more limited, where political virtue seemed out of reach, and where self-interest and conflict were natural, party had an important constitutional role to play in checking the executive.

Such views probably remained those of a minority, however. More important at the time was a wider shift in the ways in which corruption was perceived. Before Walpole's fall, corruption had commonly been portrayed as a tool of government. After 1742, and particularly from the later 1740s, society rather than the ministry or the court became seen as the major source of corruption, as attention became focused more sharply on 'luxury', or the degeneration of morals and manners, as a major political problem confronting the nation. This in itself was hardly a new perception. As referred to at the start of this chapter, Bolingbroke, for one, had expressed similar views in his unpublished manuscripts on politics in the later 1730s. The problem of 'luxury' as a force undermining public spirit and the public good had also

---

[57] See e.g. *Protestor*, 16 June 1753; 15 Sept. 1753.
[58] *Lond. Ev. P.*, 2–4 Nov. 1756.
[59] Ibid., 3 Apr. 1755; 24–6 June 1756.
[60] See Paul Langford, *A Polite and Commercial People: England 1727–1783* (Oxford, 1989), 230.
[61] M. M. Goldsmith, 'Faction Detected: Ideological Consequences of Robert Walpole's Decline and Fall', *History*, 64 (1979), 1–19.

been raised in several pamphlets in the final years of Walpolian rule.[62] Yet it was the amount of attention devoted to 'luxury', to a perceived crisis of 'public spirit', and the clarity and insistence with which the problem of 'luxury' was debated, which distinguishes the later 1740s and 1750s from the preceding two decades.

Several other factors lay behind the shift in the terms of political debate. Amongst these, important were the impact of the Jewish Naturalization Act (1753) and the Marriage Act (1753). These two measures, but the Jewish Naturalization Act especially, have been correctly seen as bringing to the fore again sentiments and views which had long remained hidden or suppressed at a national level. By raising the issue of religion, and the standing and authority of the Church of England, they provided a context in which traditional Tory attitudes and prejudices could find expression.[63] These attitudes had, for the most part, lain dormant for thirty years, partly because of a lack of issues to act as a focus for them, but also because the Tories were committed to alliance with opposition Whigs as part of a Country opposition. Yet, as Horatio Walpole, Sir Robert's brother, emphasized in 1750, they, and the political constituency which lay behind them—the Tory lower clergy espe-cially—retained considerable disruptive potential.[64] The Jewish Natural-ization Act also acted as a spur to a campaign in the opposition press calling for its repeal of almost unprecedented vituperation, racism, and populism. What is, however, less often emphasized about both acts is that they also brought to the surface of debate anxieties amongst some elements of the Country opposition about the impact of money and materialism on society.

It is a development which can be followed in the pages of the *London Evening Post*, which led the opposition press campaign against the two acts.[65] On 29 June 1754, the paper observed of the Jewish Naturalization Act:

[this] led us to consider the Necessity of standing up for the great and fundamental Articles of our Faith, the Doctrine of the Trinity, and Divinity of our Lord Jesus, and made Christianity more the subject of conversation that it had been for some years past.

The paper published frequent letters from the mid-1750s concerning the role of the Church and the need to recovene Convocation, the legislative and deliberative body of the Church, and the threats posed by free-thinking and irreligion and enthusiasm.[66] As early as September 1753, the paper was

---

[62] See e.g. *A Serious Address to the Electors of Great Britain* (n.d., 1740?).

[63] See esp. T. W. Perry, *Public Opinion, Propaganda and Politics in Eighteenth-Century England: A Study of the Jew Bill of 1753* (Camb., Mass., 1962).

[64] BL, Add. MS 32721 (Newcastle Papers), fos. 60–8: Horatio Walpole to Thomas Sherlock, Bishop of London, 7 June 1750 (copy). See also the comments in Stephen Taylor, 'Whigs, Bishops and America: The Politics of Church Reform in Mid-Eighteenth-Century England', *HJ* 36 (1993), 331–56.

[65] See Harris, 'The "London Evening Post" '. See also Ch. 1, above, pp. 50–2.

[66] Harris, 'The "London Evening Post" ', 1143–5.

arguing that it had 'justly acquired the character of the champion of Christianity against corruption'.[67] Equally striking, however, were the ways in which writers in the paper and elsewhere in the mid-1750s also sought to make strong connections between the religious condition of the country and luxury and corruption. Restoring the vitality of the Anglican church was the means to regenerate society, to re-instil virtue and public spirit. A revived, influential Anglican church was projected as the bedrock of a revived nation and society.[68] The Jewish Naturalization Act and the Marriage Act symbolized for the same writers how far society had become debased by the influence of money and materialism. This criticism of the Marriage Act, which prevented clandestine marriages of heirs and heiresses under the age of 21 without parental consent, was perhaps more important than the criticism more usually associated with it—the closure of elite society to entry from those from classes and groups below.[69] As we will see below, the Marriage Act was also seen as a rake's charter, a licence for adultery and the debasement of the virtue and chastity of English womanhood. The Jew, meanwhile, was represented as an embodiment of the values of a corrupt, debased society. Lacking the moral codes of the Christian, Jews were adepts in the murky, deceitful world of finance; they were also allegedly allies of corrupt government. As one writer asked: 'Would not these spread Dishonesty and Fraud yet farther amongst us, and hold Riches in their Hands for those who have, and ever will be ready to supply the Great with money for their private Interest, and the public Ruin.'[70] Admitting Jews to full citizenship was both symptom and cause of society's departure from the ways of virtue and honour.[71]

The new levels of concern about 'luxury' also reflected the influence of the crime wave which followed the end of the War of the Austrian Succession—the impact of which is explored in Chapter 7—as well as the contemporary international context. Public spirit, or commitment to the public good, were, as referred to at the beginning of this chapter, viewed by the Country opposition as crucial to national strength and military power. Failure in war was seen not just as a consequence of inept and corrupt leadership, and of the misuse of patronage in the military forces by ministers for corrupt ends, but also a consequence of a cowardly and selfish population. From the mid-1740s, anxiety about public spirit, and the potential consequences for the defensibility of the nation and its fortunes in war, became a pressing issue. The events

---

[67] *Lond. Ev. P.*, 25–7 Sept. 1753.

[68] Harris, 'The "London Evening Post" ', 1145.

[69] For a recent discussion of the Marriage Act and its contemporary opponents, see David Lemmings, 'Marriage and the Law in the Eighteenth Century: Hardwicke's Marriage Act of 1753', *HJ* 39 (1996), 339–60. Lemmings tends to discount the opposition to the act on the grounds that its opponents failed to live up to the principles they were enunciating. My view is that the principles had an importance independent of the philandering of men such as William Beckford and Robert Nugent.

[70] John Shebbeare, *The Marriage Act. A Novel containing a Series of Interesting Adventures* (1754), 377.

[71] *Lond. Ev. P.*, 22–4 May, 30 Aug.–1 Sept. 1753.

of the '45, as several historians have noted elsewhere, were crucial in this context.[72] In the panic which greeted the '45, the ability of the Jacobite invading forces to march through Scotland and much of England uninterrupted by the civilian population, Britons had appeared to reveal, in only too alarming fashion, the enfeebled condition of public spirit amongst them. The campaign which unfolded following the '45 to revive the militia in Britain was in significant measure an attempt to remedy the perceived crisis of public spirit. The militia was to be the vehicle for re-calling the population to its duty and commitment to the nation and to public good. (It was also to be the vehicle for restoring social hierarchy by allowing the landed classes to assume their role as leaders of the rest of society.) William Thornton, author of the pro-militia pamphlet, *The Counterpoise* (1752), prefaced his tract with the claim that 'the depravity and selfishness of those in a higher class was never more remarkable than at present'. He also argued that the militia would revive the martial spirit of the nation and prevent it from sinking to the effeminacy of the Chinese.[73] In the mid-1750s, when the militia agitation in England was at its height, the perception of a continuing crisis in public spirit was further sharpened by the French invasion scare of 1755–6, when foreign mercenaries, Hessians and Hanoverians, were deployed in Britain to defend its shores. This was portrayed in opposition propaganda as a national disgrace, as well as an alarming threat to English liberties.[74] The Smuggling and Game Acts were also portrayed as depressing the military and public spirit of the population by undermining familiarity amongst the population with the use of arms.

The state, or Whig oligarchy, continued to be seen, therefore, as a major source of political ills. Indeed promoting luxury was one of the means by which it extended its corrupt rule. Yet the degeneration of contemporary manners and morals was also seen as deep-rooted. John Brown attempted a balanced assessment in 1757:

It hath been much debated, whether the Ministers or the People have contributed more to the Establishment of this System of Self Interest and Faction. On Enquiry it would probably appear, that at different Periods the Pendulum hath swung at large on both sides. It came down, in former Times, from the Minister to the Representative, from the Representative to the managing Alderman, from the Alderman to the Cobler. In later Times, the Impulse seems to have been chiefly in the contrary Direction: From the Cobler to the managing Alderman; from him to the Member; from the Member, to the great Man who ruled the Borrough; and thence to the Minister.[75]

---

[72] Linda Colley, *Britons: Forging the Nation, 1707–1837* (New Haven, Conn. and London 1992), 85–100; Richard B. Sher, *Church and University in the Scottish Enlightenment: The Moderate Literati of Edinburgh* (Edinburgh, 1985), esp. ch. 6; John Robertson, *The Scottish Enlightenment and the Militia Issue* (Edinburgh, 1985).

[73] Quoted in Robertson, *The Scottish Enlightenment and the Militia Issue*, 82.

[74] *Monitor*, 26 Oct., 1 Nov. 1755; 13 Mar., 10 Apr., 24 Apr., 29 May, 5 June, 13 Nov. 1756; *A Guide to the Knowledge of the Rights and Privileges of Englishmen* (1757), 101; *German Cruelty: A Fair Warning to the People of Great Britain* (1757).

[75] John Brown, *An Estimate of the Manners and Principles of the Times* (1757), 112–13.

Another writer declared:

The *real fact* is, that we have let in such an inundation of *corruption* upon us, that all orders of men are so much more ambitious of acquiring wealth than virtue, and of gratifying their luxurious inclination, that of living as the laws of God direct, destruction seems already to gape wide upon us.[76]

Against this background, political reform might be urged as much for its anticipated effects on society and morals as for its own sake. The problem had shifted from political corruption to the corruption of society; political reform was now a precondition of wider social and moral reform.[77]

Another symptom of the same underlying shift in debate and perceptions was a sharpened focus in the 1750s on the role of the elites as a source of social and moral degeneration. Gerald Newman has recently portrayed this development in terms of the emergence of a nascent bourgeois nationalism.[78] The higher orders were increasingly attacked for cultural betrayal from the later 1740s, for their cosmopolitan habits and patronage of foreign goods and craftsmen. This attack contained a marked anti-aristocratic strand. Amongst writers in the Country or Patriot interest, this was most evident in criticisms of the Game Laws and in debates about the issue of access to Richmond Park. What brought the Game Laws, which had been passed in the early 1670s and which sought to restrict hunting for game to a landed elite, back into public debate was the formation in 1752 of the Society of Noblemen and Gentlemen for the Preservation of Game. For several Country writers, the Game Laws appeared to symbolize how far national interests were being sacrificed for the purpose of elite pleasure and enjoyment. Not only did the laws inconvenience farmers and lesser landowners, they also, as alluded to above, supposedly contributed to the population losing their capacity to use firearms. This also disabled them from protecting their freedoms from hostile assault whether from abroad, in the form of an invasion, or from within in the form of a standing army used to enforce tyranny.[79] The issue of access to Richmond Park had rumbled on throughout Walpole's time, and concerned rights of way through the park, as well as common rights.[80] In 1749, the curate of Richmond and several parishioners pulled down part of the wall when attempting to walk the bounds of the parish.[81] The cause was that of 'Old England', and concerned gentry, merchants, tradespeople, and artisans.[82] It was fought through

---

[76] *The Morning's Thoughts on Reading The Test and Contest* (1757), 25.

[77] See e.g. *Lond. Ev. P.*, 25–7 Oct. 1757.

[78] Gerald Newman, *The Rise of English Nationalism: A Cultural History 1740–1830* (New York, 1987), esp. ch. 4.

[79] *Lond. Ev. P.*, 23–5 Aug. 1753; *Monitor*, 13 Mar. 1755, 29 May 1756; *An Alarm to the People of England* (1757).

[80] E. P. Thompson, *Customs in Common* (1990), 111–13.

[81] PRO, T1/343/58.

[82] See *Two Historical Accounts of the Making of the New Forest in Hampshire, by King William the Conqueror; And Richmond New Park in Surry* (1751).

the press and in the courts in a manner which prefigures the political tactics later adopted by John Wilkes. In 1754, a prosecution was brought against a gatekeeper for denying admission to the park. The council for the prosecution included Sir John Philipps and Richard Beckford. The attorney for the prosecution was Arthur Beardmore, future under-sheriff of the City of London and Patriot.[83] One commentator observed of the case, which involved right of highway between Richmond and Croydon and right of footway between Richmond and Wimbledon:

It might be observed that the witnesses were low poor people, and that the Defendants were men of character and Fortune: But, Gentlemen, if you were once to discourage or give way on the Evidence of common People, all our Rights and Properties would be very insecure.[84]

In 1755, another case was instigated, this time regarding access to ancient footways. Tried before the Surrey Assizes in 1758, this was won. Country propagandists argued that the attempts to prevent access inconvenienced farmers and traders, again for the purpose of protecting the enjoyments, in this case deer hunting, of 'gentlemen of figure and fortune'. They also symbolized the oppressiveness of the Hanoverian regime—the ranger of the park was Princess Amelia—and the regime's disregard for the customary rights of the people.[85]

The critique of elite manners amongst Patriot writers of the 1750s needs to be seen primarily in terms of the changes in political debate discussed above. Elite luxury and immorality were attacked because of their contaminating influence, through the effect of emulation, on society as a whole. As Newman recognizes, it was primarily a political critique.[86] Even the attacks on the Game Laws were principally political. As one of their most ferocious critics commented:

Might we not ask, who are Those Associators for the Preservation of Game all over *England?* Are they not in general a Tribe of Placemen, Pensioners, and fawning Sycophants (unauthorised by Parliament) assembled, without the Fear of God before their Eyes, to rob us of those Blessings given by the All-wise creator?[87]

---

[83] See the narrative in *Merlin's Life and Prophecies . . . His Prediction Relating to the Late Contest about the Rights of Richmond Park* (1755).

[84] Ibid., 71.

[85] *Advice to Posterity Concerning a Point of the Last Importance* (1755); *A Tract on the National Interest, and Depravity of the Times* (1757); *Lond. Ev. P.*, 31 July–2 Aug., 11–13 Oct. 1753.

[86] Newman, *Rise of English Nationalism*, 74 where the author writes: 'There was an element of class warfare here in the fifties, a battle mounted by the London man of letters against the London man of fashion . . . But we must keep things in proportion . . . The artist's target was not yet the aristocracy itself but rather aristocracy as a corrupted and corrupting moral system . . .'. See also comments in W. A. Speck, *Literature and Society in Eighteenth-Century England: Ideology, Politics and Culture, 1680–1820* (1998), chs. 6 and 7.

[87] *An Alarm to the People of England: shewing Their Rights, Liberties and Properties to be in the utmost Danger from the present destructive, and unconstitutional Association for the Preservation of Game all over England, which is proved to be illegal* (1757), 12.

As this quotation shows, 'the Great' were defined as much in terms of their relationship to the corrupt political system as in more conventional social terms. The upper ranks, in their addiction to gaming, their adultery, their neglect and disdain for religion, were abdicating their function as leaders of society. In their degenerate and effeminate condition, they were primarily responsible for the feeble state of 'public spirit'. The wellspring of reform had to be found, therefore, amongst the elites; they needed to resume their proper role as founts of honour, virtue, and courage.

It was this conviction which was the principal message of John Brown's famous *Estimate of the Manners and Principles of the Times*, published in 1757. Often viewed simply as a jeremiad, this tract encapsulated the conflicting emotions which prevailed in the mid-1750s, the fears about moral decline and corruption, and the sense that Britain's fortunes were recuperable. The tract also shows how far attacks on elite manners became conflated with a broader critique of the pervasiveness of materialist values in society. Brown produced a lengthy and formidable indictment of elite manners and immorality. Fashionable polite culture was attacked as a source of effeminacy in society. Polite diversions, literary, artistic, and musical taste—the favouring of Italian opera above the 'manly, pathetic, the astonishing Strains of Handel'—the disregard for religion and for honour, and the decay more generally of public spirit amongst the elites were condemned. The clergy were criticized for their submission to materialist values or narrow pursuit of advancement. The '45 had presented the pathetic spectacle of a cowardly and spineless social elite:

How far this dastard Spirit of Effeminacy hath crept upon use, and destroyed the national Spirit of Defence, may appear from the general Panic the Nation was thrown into, at the late Rebellion. When those of every rank above a Constable, instead of arming themselves and encouraging the People, generally fled before the Rebels; while a Mob of ragged Highlanders marched unmolested to the heart of a populous Kingdom.[88]

France, Brown argued—again illustrating the importance of the international context to perceptions of social and moral conditions in this period—escaped the worst effects of luxury because of the spirit of unity and union imparted to society by French absolute monarchy. France also educated its elites in principles of military honour and discipline. It ensured, moreover, that different ranks and groups in society were separated from one another in respect of their activities. Most importantly, the aristocracy were prevented from engaging in trade. Luxury was also a consequence of the progress of commerce. Commerce undermined public spirit by promoting an all-consuming love of money once its ends exceeded 'Self Preservation and moderate Enjoyment'. It also led to luxury by increasing the value of landed estates and unearned incomes amongst the landed elites. As Brown wrote:

[88] Brown, *Estimate*, 91.

THESE Ranks of men being not bred up to Habits of Industry; on the contrary, their increased Rents coming in unfought for, and their Times being often a Load upon them, thro' want of Capacity and Employment, the Habit of Indulgence comes on, and grow of Course. Additional Wealth gives the Power to gratify every Desire that rises, Leisure improves these Desires into Habits; thus Money is at length considered as no more than the Means of Gratification; and hence the genuine Character of a rich Nobility of Gentry, is that of Expence and Luxury.[89]

The attitudes towards commerce and commercial progress expressed by Brown were at best ambivalent. For Brown, as for many other writers in the Country tradition, virtue was most easily associated with rural society, modest wealth, and the influence of religion.

TWO PATRIOT WRITERS: JAMES BURGH AND JOHN SHEBBEARE

Similar themes and anxieties appear in the works of James Burgh and John Shebbeare. Burgh's main contribution to eighteenth-century political argu-ment was to come after this period, with the publication of his famous bible of reformist and radical argument, the *Political Disquisitions, or An Enquiry into Public Errors, Defects and Abuses* (3 vols., 1774–5).[90] He finds a place, nevertheless, in the broad political stream which was the mid-eighteenth-century Country Interest; through him and his writings we can also pursue the importance of this interest as a formative influence on the perceptions and arguments of the radicals of the 1760s and early 1770s.

Burgh was a Presbyterian Scot by birth. In 1746, at which time he was a Dissenting schoolmaster in London, he was to achieve notoriety through the publication of a stern call for the reformation of manners in the aftermath of the '45, entitled *Britain's Remembrancer, or the Danger Not Over*. The first of the many indictments of British 'public spirit' which followed the rebellion, it was firmly providentialist in perspective, arguing that a reformation of manners was necessary if Britain was to avoid national disaster as a consequence of the loss of God's favour. Such arguments became increasingly important in this period, as is demonstrated in Chapter 7. They also provide a further reason why attention focused more heavily on social manners and morals from the later 1740s. Like Brown, Burgh gave expression to anxieties which were widely felt at the time about the impact of commerce and materialist values on society. In the later 1740s and early 1750s, he looked to education to restore public spirit and virtue in society. In 1762, he wrote and submitted to the Court 'Remarks Historical and Political Collected from Books and Observations. Humbly presented to the King's Most Excellent Majesty'.[91] The express

[89] Ibid., 156–7.
[90] See Carla H. Hay, *James Burgh: Spokesman for Reform in Hanoverian England* (Washington, DC, 1979).
[91] BL, King's MS 433.

purpose was to encourage the new king to become a reforming Patriot monarch. Two year later, he published *An Account of the First Settlement, Laws, Form of Government, and Police, of the Cessares, A People of South America* (1764). A Utopian tract, this allowed him the freedom to express fully his vision of what a virtuous polity might look like and how it would be governed. Commerce was to be strictly regulated so as not to introduce luxury into society; land was to be divided equally amongst the inhabitants as a solution to the problem of poverty and also to eliminate luxury or excessive wealth leading to luxury. The social principles underlying the vision were authoritarian and tutelary; public manners were to be closely policed and constantly supervised.

Burgh's purpose in publishing this tract is, as with much writing in this genre, difficult to state with certainty. He claimed that it was timely given the recent acquisition of new colonial territories. Utopian colonies were not novel; Georgia had been founded as one such in the mid-1730s. It seems as likely, however, that the tract was designed as a mirror to contemporary social problems and the degeneration of manners and morals in Britain. It also illustrates how deep-rooted the contradictions and tensions were in Patriot ideology in this period. Contemporaries were fully aware that British society was developing in ways which made the language of Patriotism seem increasingly out of step with social and economic conditions. Britain was becoming a society in which commerce and commercial values and practices assumed ever increasing importance. It was the gap between, on the one hand, Patriot conceptions of virtue and society and, on the other, the direction of economic and social progress in Britain that lent hopes of national or Patriotic renewal their essential fragility. What stands out, however, is how such hopes continued to shape very powerfully contemporary attitudes and emotions.

Differences between John Shebbeare and James Burgh were substantial. Burgh was a Dissenter and Whig, whereas Shebbeare was a high Anglican Tory-Jacobite.[92] While Burgh is today remembered as a leading proponent of parliamentary reform, Shebbeare's fame (or infamy) stems from his six *Letters to the People of England* and especially the violently anti-Hanoverian *Sixth Letter*.[93] It was this last outpouring of disaffection and anti-Hanoverianism which finally provoked the ministry to haul him before the Court of King's Bench, where he was found guilty of seditious libel and severely punished for the latest

---

[92] For Shebbeare, see Margaret Avery, 'Toryism in the Age of the American Revolution: John Lind and John Shebbeare', *Historical Studies*, 18 (1978), 24–36; James R. Foster, 'Smollet's Pamphleteering Foe Shebbeare', *Publications of the Modern Languages Association*, 62 (Baltimore, 1942), 1053–100.

[93] *A Letter to the People of England, on the present Situation and Conduct of National Affairs* (1755); *A Second Letter to the People of England, on Foreign Subsidies, Subsidiary Armies, and their Consequences to this Nation* (1755); *A Third Letter to the People of England. On Liberty, Taxes and the Application of Public Money* (1756); *A Fourth Letter to the People of England. On the Conduct of the M[iniste]rs in Alliances, Fleets and Armies, since the First Differences on the Ohio to the taking of Minorca by the French* (1756); *A Fifth Letter to the People of England. On the Subversion of the Constitution, and the Necessity of its being Restored* (1757); *A Sixth Letter to the People of England, on the Progress of National Ruin* (1757)

literary indiscretion.[94] His output was prodigious, comprising numerous occasional pamphlets, several medical tracts, two novels, a short-lived essay paper, and an abortive history of England.[95] This output was also frequently seditious.[96]

The influence of Shebbeare's writings, especially the six letters, was considerable. All the letters went through several editions, with several of them going into a sixth edition.[97] There were also pirate editions published, perhaps the surest sign of popularity. Several of the letters provoked direct refutations, and some more than one.[98] Contemporary views of Shebbeare's writings were hostile and dismissive, even from among his political allies. A report on Shebbeare in one of the under-secretaries' papers suggested that Shebbeare had turned to abuse because he was unable to earn a living from any other sort of writing. It went on:

He must write as this is his only dependence, and the booksellers will now pay him for nothing but scandal. And in this Article he is found to excel. His Blood appears to be

[94] Shebbeare was sentenced to a £5 fine and three years in prison. He also had to find security for good behaviour for seven years, and stand in the pillory at Charing Cross for one hour on 5 December. For details of his trial, see BL, Add. MS 36202 (Hardwicke Papers), fos. 261–315.

[95] In addition to the six *Letters*, in the 1750s and early 1760s Shebbeare wrote: *The Marriage Act. A Novel containing a Series of Interesting Adventures* (1754); *Lydia, or Filial Piety* (1756); *An Answer to a Pamphlet call'd, The Conduct of the Ministry Impartially Examined* (1756); *Letters on the English Nation* (1755); *An Appeal to the People, Containing the Genuine and Entire Letter of Admiral Byng to the Secr. of the A[dmiralt]y* (1756); *The Occasional Critic* (1757); *An Appendix to the Occasional Critic* (1757); *The Practice of Physic* (1755); *The History of the Excellence and Decline of the Constitution, Religion, Laws, Manners and Genius of the Sumatrans* (1762); *A Letter to the Right Honourable Author of a Letter to a Citizen* (1761); *One More Letter to the People of England* (1762); *Another Answer to the Letter of the Right Honourable William Pitt to Ralph Allen* (1763); *Invincible Reason for the Earl of Bute's Immediate Resignation* (1763). Shebbeare had a very short-lived connection to the *Monitor*. He may also have been behind the short-lived paper, the *Citizen*, in 1758. No copies of this have survived, but extracts were printed in the *London Evening Post*. There is a list of Shebbeare's works in 'An Account of the Life and Writings of Dr. John Shebbeare', *European Magazine*, Aug 1788, 83–7, 167–8; 'Further Particulars Concerning Dr J Shebbeare, from a Correspondent', ibid., 244–5.

[96] Warrants were issued against the first of his novels, *The Marriage Act: A Novel* (1754) and the *Third Letter*. His *Fourth Letter* was considered for prosecution, but such a course of action was rejected because of the judgement that a London jury were unlikely to find him guilty. Eleven days after a general warrant was issued for taking up the author, printer, and publisher of the *Sixth Letter*, all copies of a seventh letter were seized and suppressed. On 24 January 1758, the attorney general also advised Lord Holdernesse, one of the two secretaries of state, that there was 'sufficient ground' to take up and prosecute the author, publisher, and printer of the *Fifth Letter* and the author and printer of the *Seventh Letter* (PRO, SP 44/83, fos. 245, 246, 264–6, 267; BL, Add. MS 32867 (Newcastle Papers)), fos. 135–6, 143–8).

[97] Establishing the number of editions with any certainty is extremely difficult given the existence of variant and pirate editions. The first three letters may have reached sixth editions. The *Fifth Letter* went through at least four editions, while the *Sixth Letter* was published in two editions as well as at least two further variant editions. The publication history of these pamphlets can be traced using the Eighteenth-Century Short-Title Catalogue.

[98] *An Answer to a Pamphlet called A Second Letter to the People* (1755); *The Nature and Use of Subsidiary Forces fully Considered: In an Answer to a Pamphlet intitled A Second Letter to the People of England* (1755); *An Answer to a Pamphlet called A Third Letter to the People of England* (1756); *A Fifth Letter to the People of England, on M[inis]teria]l Influence and Management of National Treasure* (1756) [This was an answer to Shebbeare's *Fourth Letter*]; *A Full and Particular Answer to all the Calumnies, Misrepresentations and Falsehoods contained in a Pamphlet, called A Fourth Letter to the People of England* (1756); *A Refutation of the Sixth Letter to the People of England* (1757); *A Letter of Consolation to Dr Shebbeare* (1758?); *A Seventh Letter to the People of England. Upon Political Writing, True Patriotism, Jacobitism, and Evil and Corrupt Adm[inistratio]ns* (1757).

fully maturated & ready always to burst out of his Face. He has some memory, a lively but incorrect and desultory imagination, furious in his Passions, but vain & arrogant beyond Example.[99]

Critics argued, perhaps predictably, that the extravagance of his language and metaphors mirrored the disorder of his mind. His populism and personalization of politics also led to equally unsurprising accusations that he was a vulgarizer, that he found his readership amongst a credulous and easily misled mob. At the same time, however, critics tended to acknowledge that Shebbeare did possess some qualities as a political writer, a capacity at the very least for producing an arresting metaphor or image.[100] The success of his pamphlets required some explanation apart from the supposed gullibility of his readership.

Shebbeare had a talent for disaffection and for hating, and it was this that principally characterized his writing. He encapsulated, or reflected back at the public, the mood of anger and disillusionment about national politics which prevailed in the mid-1750s. The main sources of popular alienation from the politics and personnel of the Hanoverian regime have already been referred to. Yet events in the mid-1750s only added further to this mood, as Linda Colley has noted and as was emphasized in the previous chapter.[101] Politics appeared to be a game played without regard to national interest by corrupt and self-interested individuals. It was the conjunction of failure in the early phases of the Seven Years War, the sense of vulnerability and unease which this created in Britain, and the fragmentation and instability in national politics which followed the death of Henry Pelham in 1754 which lay behind this image of national politics and the emotions which it gave rise to. Popular anger about the conduct of the war and condition of national politics boiled over in the outcry created by the loss of Minorca to the French in May 1756. It also expressed itself in virulent anti-Hanoverian sentiment, which on occasion took on a republican edge. This was what Lord Waldegrave characterized in 1758, in conversation with George II, as 'a mutinous spirit in the lower class of people'.[102] Shebbeare's violent attacks on the Hanoverian regime and the conduct of the early stages of the Seven Years War gave expression to, and were part of, this spirit.

Underpinning Shebbeare's writings was a deep alienation from or ambivalence about the way in which society was developing. Shebbeare saw the sources of national degeneration not just in the corrupt, oppressive, and inept politics of the Hanoverian regime but in irreligion and the debasement of society through the power of money. These themes resurface again and again

---

[99] BL, Add. MS 36202, fos. 300–1.

[100] *A Refutation of the Sixth Letter to the People of England* (1757), 61–2.

[101] Colley, *In Defiance of Oligarchy*, 274.

[102] *The Memoirs and Speeches of James, 2nd Earl Waldegrave, 1742–63*, ed. J. C. D. Clark (Cambridge, 1986), 206.

in his writing. His attitudes towards religion were, in some respects, an anachronism, especially in respect of his religious intolerance. His hatred of Dissent was unremmitting and was fuelled by visions of seventeeth-century sectarian politics and conflict. He was an opponent of the Toleration Act (1689), which had granted limited religious freedoms to orthodox Protestant Dissenters.[103] What he sought was the restoration of the Anglican church to a dominant position in society. A revived Church was to revive society and social manners and values.

Shebbeare's concern about money and the influence of materialism was expressed very clearly in his novel, *The Marriage Act. A Novel* (1754). Insofar as this possesses a main plot, it concerns two sisters, children of James and Molly Barter. James was a Presbyterian fortune hunter, who had been apprenticed to Thomas Stem, a rich London tobacconist. Stem's ambition was to see his nephew and heir become Mayor of London. Barter corrupts Stem's nephew into seeking to live like a gentleman and uses his master's love of money to alienate him from his newly profligate heir. Stem disinherits his nephew and on his death his wealth passes to his apprentice, Barter, who marries his master's former maid, Molly. Once rich, the Barters set about seeking social position and status. One of their daughters, Mary, corrupted by the influence of her worldy tutor and the social aspiration of her parvenu parents, marries the fashionable and degenerate son of Earl Wormeaten, Lord Sapplin. Sapplin is the archetypal dissolute noble buck:

My Lord, being indulged in all Things, was, a Buck of the First Head; he kept Running Horse, Fighting Cocks, Pack of Hounds, and Women; in truth, for I hate to belie any man, Noble or Commoner, he kept everything but Three, his Church, his Honour, and his Money.[104]

The marriage is unhappy, and Mary runs away to Paris with her valet de chambre, Samuel Wentwell. In Paris, in a polite society in which appearance is everything and nothing is what it seems, the valet acquires a title, and abandons Mary, upon which Mary enters a convent. Her sister, Eliza, has had the good fortune to be brought up in the country by a clergyman and his family, and has, therefore, been untainted by the corruptions of society and city life. She is, in Shebbeare's words, one of those 'poor Country Girls . . . [that] really imagine that Virtue, good nature, good Sense and Beauty, confined to the Possession and Praise of one Man, is true Happiness.'[105] Eliza refuses her parent's entreaties to marry Sir Roger Ramble, who has dissipated his fortune and ruined his health—like several sons of the nobility and gentry, he has contracted venereal disease in the fleshpots of Rome—on a grand tour of the continent. Instead, she marries her father's clerk, William Worthy, who is, in

---

[103] See esp. *Letters on the English Nation*, 76, 79, 85–6.
[104] *The Marriage Act*, i. 95.
[105] Ibid., ii, 42.

fact, son to Sir Simon Worthy, a member of the Cornish gentry. Worthy is true inheritor of the values of 'old England'; he also later inherits a fortune.

The Marriage Act. A Novel is, as one commentator has put it, 'ramshackle' and the plot contrived.[106] Everything—plot and character—is subordinated to polemical purpose. Shebbeare constructs a series of narratives and caricatures to illustrate the dangers to female chastity, virtue, and the clergy posed by the Marriage Act. Yet there are consistent principles, or at least prejudices, under-pinning it. According to Shebbeare, the Act encourages immorality; it also defies the law of nature and religion in the interests of material ambition and greed. It is not just degenerate members of the aristocracy who are satirized, but also merchants and tradesmen who subordinate everything, including the interests of their country and the happiness of their daughters, to accumu-lating wealth and to achieving social position and status. The world in which the Marriage Act operates is one where the values of religion, virtue, and honour have lost their influence, a world where even the language of praise has become detached from any secure and appropriate meaning.[107]

Shebbeare was accused by another of his critics of 'senseless and virulent Jacobitism'.[108] The charge has substance, although he often clothed his Jacobitism in slippery and often deliberately ambiguous meaning. He was also inconsistent. He acknowledged that the Revolution had brought about greater liberty in England, yet he also saw the Revolution as a product of Whig decep-tion and manipulation. James II was the deceived party, who was forced to abdicate his throne and who had, albeit too late, offered to change his poli-cies.[109] He portrayed Whig oligarchy as a system of parliamentary tyranny more absolute and menacing that anything attempted under the Stuarts in the later seventeenth century. He compared present conditions in England unfavourably with those that had pertained in 1688.[110] The implication was that Britons had exchanged one form of tyranny for another, even more destructive and damaging form. A further implication might be that if revolu-tion was justified in 1688, it was justified under present conditions. His hostility to William III was unalloyed and savage. It was William who had yoked Britain's fortunes, with disastrous consequences and unacceptable costs, to the continent.[111] He was also violently anti-Hanoverian, nowhere more so than in the *Sixth Letter*. This was an extended rehearsal of criticisms of policy and politics under the first of the Hanoverian Kings, George I. British foreign policy and interests had, Shebbeare asserted, been subordinated firmly to

---

[106] Foster, 'Smollet's Pamphleteering Foe', 1073.
[107] See the discussion of the meaning of the term 'good' in the City and in the West End (*The Marriage Act*, i 112–13).
[108] *A Fourth Letter to the People of England*, 8.
[109] *Second Letter*, 3–4; *Third Letter*, 25; *Fourth Letter*, 10–11; *Fifth Letter*, 10–11, 15, 25, 52.
[110] *Fourth Letter*, 25; *Sixth Letter*, *passim*.
[111] *Third Letter*, 22.

Hanoverian aggrandisement. British wealth and prosperity were being depleted to secure this end. At one point, Shebbeare asked:

What Evils a Stuart on the Throne of England would have produced, can be but a speculative Consideration at present; however it may be perfectly discerned what are the Blessings which came with a North-East Wind from Germany, and the Effects of them were never more conspicuous than at this unparallel'd Moment.[112]

In the *Third Letter* he asserted, 'It cannot suffer this Kingdom to be wedded for her Wealth subservient to another more favourite Wife, taken for Love alone.'[113] The implication did not need spelling out: what he was saying was that the Anglo-Hanoverian union was incompatible with the well-being and prosperity of Britain. In the early 1740s, other Patriot writers had made similar assertions.[114]

Shebbeare's rhetorical technique was constantly to suggest a gap between his language and meaning, to engage with his readers in a 'conspiracy of meaning'. Readers of his pamphlets might easily have reached the conclusion that political salvation would only arrive with a Stuart restoration. In the first letter, Shebbeare praised Frederick the Great as an exemplary Patriot king.[115] In the *Third* and *Fifth* letters, however, his hopes for reform were invested in Pitt the Elder, who sought, with some success and considerable political sleight of hand, to maintain a Patriot reputation in office in 1756 and again after 1757.[116] He was also able to transfer his hopes very easily after 1760 to the figure of George III. In this, Shebbeare was part of a wider Tory rapprochement with the Hanoverian regime after 1760. In 1763, Sir John Phillips interceded successfully with George Grenville to get him a goverment pension.[117] Contemporaries were not insensitive to the irony of a former Jacobite finding favour at the Hanoverian court only five years after being imprisoned for seditious libel against the Hanoverian regime.

Shebbeare's most substantial and interesting political work in our period was itself a product of the Tory rapprochement with the Court. Entitled *The History of the Excellence and Decline of the Constitution, Religion, Laws, Manners and Genius of the Sumatrans, And the Restoration thereof in the Reign of Amaurath the Third, surnamed The Legislator*, it was published in two volumes in 1762. It was a lightly disguised expression of Shebbeare's hopes that, under the new king, Britain would enter a new age of patriotic government and that her society would be reformed, as well as being a commentary on what had happened following his accession. There were to be three major planks of reform. Religion in the form of the Church of England, which had been 'so long and so fatally

---

[112] *Sixth Letter*, 38.
[113] *Third Letter*, 23.
[114] See Harris, *A Patriot Press*, ch. 5.
[115] *First Letter*, 6–7.
[116] *Third Letter*, 62–4; *Fifth Letter*, 62, 88.
[117] Peter D. G. Thomas, *Politics in Eighteenth-Century Wales* (Cardiff, 1998), 199.

neglected and despised', was to resume its dominant position and influence in society. Toleration was described as an 'ensnaring proposition', and 'swarms of sectaries' as responsible for eroding the majesty and authority of the Church and her officers. It was the lack of influence of religion that had caused the degeneration of morals and manners in the previous forty or so years. As Shebbeare wrote:

Pleasure reigned with full Powers, and the Means of indulging it became the general Pursuit. In consequence of this Propensity Money was deemed the sole Good, in order to obtain what all desired; and all Things were confounded in its meritricious and delusive Glare.[118]

Alongside a revived Anglican Church, prosperity and economic health were to be restored through changes in taxation—the introduction of a graduated income tax—the economic incorporation of Ireland within the fiscal and customs union of Britain, and elimination of the national debt.[119] It was a vision of wealth and economic well-being which rested on the domestic economy as opposed to possession and exploitation of the colonies. As such, it was also opposed to the bellicose, imperialist patriotism associated with Pitt and his city allies and which expressed itself in hostility to the peace policy of Bute and the King and the Peace of Paris which brought the Seven Years War to a close in 1763.

The third element of reform was legal. The law had become, according to Shebbeare, an instrument of oppression; through its complexity and mystifications, it had also become a tool of the rich. It was to restored to its proper role in society through codification, simplification, and the exercise of proportionality in punishment. It was a vision of legal reform which combined humanitarianism and toughness. For example, all theft, of whatever value, was to carry a capital tariff, although guilt had to be proved by the evidence of two positive witnesses. This penal strategy, Shebbeare argued, was the 'most humane and commiserating'.[120]

Shebbeare's vision of a reformed Britain was conservative and hierarchical in inspiration, as well as containing humanitarian and utilitarian elements. Honour and virtue were to reimpose their sway on society from the top downward. A reformed nobility was a crucial component of the newly virtuous society. Noble rank was to reacquire dignity and respect. Aristocratic dissoluteness was to disappear as the nobility re-assumed their role as patrons of learning, the arts, and polite letters, and as promoters of improvement in society and purveyors of hospitality. This was to be the basis for the restoration of respect for noble rank in society: 'The Interest of the Nobles was founded on the Laudableness of their Actions, and the People who had so long

[118] *The History of the Excellence and Decline of the Constitution*, i 63, 241–63.
[119] Ibid., ii. 100–7.
[120] Ibid., ii. 160–5.

detested them as Tyrants at present revered and loved them as their common Parents'.[121] Where desire for wealth and personal enrichment had once governed society, Shebbeare was conjuring into existence a vision of a society where honour, and the principles of virtue and religion associated with this, governed behaviour. From one perspective, he was another seeking to reconcile commercial progress and an older set of social and moral values. His society was governed and arranged to mitigate the potential ill effects of commercialization: for example, the confounding of ranks which it produced. Society was to be divided at the level of localities ('districts, cities, and towns') into classes of nobility, clergy, gentry, merchants, tradesmen, mechanics, artisans, and husbandmen. Each company of local class was to be policed by a local court, which was responsible for maintaining the 'honour' of the company, as well as regulating the quality of the goods it produced. The end was moral as much as economic reform, to re-instil the principles of 'pride and shame' throughout the population.[122] This was commerce without avarice or greed, or even perhaps 'virtuous commerce'. As Shebbeare argued about the policy and intentions of his Patriot King:

In a commercial State to have depressed the Desire of Riches, had been adequate to the Banishment of Commerce; and in some Degree subversive of the End he was proposing to obtain. The Esteem of them was for that Reason to be proportioned to the Means by which they were gotten, and the Uses to which they were applied. To be rich with probity was scandalous, and to be illiberal was to be contemned. By these Means the rapacious Spirit of Avarice became much allayed.[123]

Seen as a whole, Shebbeare's vision was every bit as Utopian as Burgh's. From another perspective, however, it was simply the summation of hopes for reform which had been widely expressed by various Country writers during the final years of George II's reign.

The Country interest was a complex, unstable, but important force in British politics in the mid-eighteenth century. It was not the vehicle principally of any single group in society, but rather encompassed the hopes, anxieties, interests, and goals of all who felt themselves to be excluded or alienated from national politics and structures of power under George II. Underneath its broad umbrella, different ideological traditions, Whig and Tory, Jacobite and Republican, came together, mixed and became intertwined. There was something more than ideological cross-dressing going on here. Under the pressure of events, tactical political considerations, common perceptions, the Country Interest subsumed and blurred, without ever completely eradicating, traditional political boundaries. Henry Fielding captured something of this reality

[121] Ibid., ii. 227.
[122] Ibid., ii. 177–84.
[123] Ibid., ii. 212–13.

in the figure of the Jacobite-Republican alderman in his 1747 election pamphlet, *A Dialogue between a Gentleman of London and an Honest Alderman of the Country Party*. So did the conception of the 'Modern Tory' which was used by the essay paper the *Monitor* to indicate the distance between its political principles and those of traditional Toryism.[124]

Ambiguity, even contradiction, were intrinsic to the Country interest. The terms 'Patriot' or 'the honest party' might mean one thing to a Jacobite-Patriot and another to a Whig-Patriot. Country writers sought to promote trade as in the national interest, even as *the* national interest, yet the same writers could also express ambivalence about the social, moral, and political repercussions of commercial progress and commercialization. In this, they were reflecting wider concerns about the social impact of commercial progress.[125] But this ambivalence also reflected the fact that the social vision of most Country writers was, as has been emphasized in a number of places in this chapter, backward looking and conservative. The national revival Country propagandists looked for was a revival of traditional values and principles in society; these would reinvigorate society, and also facilitate progress in a range of spheres—culture, the law, the economy. To this extent, 'restoration' was seen as the prelude or basis for 'improvement'. There was also a strong paternalistic element in Country ideology, evident in, for example, criticism of the adverse social effects of enclosure—depopulation and loss of rights amongst the poorer sections of rural society—support for the laws against re-grating and fore-stalling in the grain market, or celebration of the role of charity and hospitality as productive of social harmony and subordination.[126]

Patrick Joyce has talked recently about the openness and flexibility of narratives used to describe social and political orders in nineteenth-century England. He writes:

It is paradoxically true that only the most open and unfixed narratives could secure the fixity necessary to achieve coherent identities and a workable sense of political agency. To encompass different and sometimes competing narratives, and the instabilities inherent within narrative itself, stories were needed that did not foreclose options.[127]

The Country interest can be seen in similar terms. The identities it 'fixed' were inclusive and flexible; this is what gave them power and agency in politics and political debate. Country writers valorized 'the people' and their role in the political process. But it was a group which they rarely felt the need to define with precision. There was some, albeit infrequent, mention of the

---

[124] *Monitor*, 23 Aug. 1755. See also Marie Peters, ' "Names and Cant": Party Lables in English Political Propaganda c1753–1763', *Parliamentary History*, 7 (1984), 103–27.

[125] See esp. Ch. 7, below.

[126] *Lond. Ev. P.*, 21–4 Jan., 15–18 Apr., 27–9 Apr., 22–4 June 1758; *Monitor*, 18 Jan., 5 Mar. 1757.

[127] Patrick Joyce, *Democratic Subjects: The Self and the Social in Nineteenth-Century England* (Cambridge, 1994), 155.

'middling state' or even 'middle class', and it was on this group that some Country writers began to place their hopes for the restoration of virtue and reform.[128] On 8 August 1752, the essay paper *Old England* remarked:

It has been observed, that Persons in the Middle Ranks of Life are more to be confided in, have less Timidity, can suffer less influence, than any other. We shall not deny it. But may the next general Election produce an illustrious Example to verify the Observation.

But it was not a middle class in any modern sense; nor was it a specifically or even primarily urban group. Rather it was defined in contradistinction to both 'the Great' and to the lower orders. It encompassed the gentry, freeholders, farmers, professionals, merchants, and tradesmen. It was those who, in William Beckford's phrase in 1761, 'bore the heat of the day', those on whom national prosperity and national strength and well-being rested.[129] (There is something here of a prefigurement of the division between the 'idle' and the 'industrious' classes which was to play such an important role in shaping radical perceptions and argument from the 1790s in Britain.) It was the strengthening perception that 'the Great' were betraying the national interest, through their luxury, immorality, and devotion to pleasure, that caused—or perhaps even enabled—this notably disparate and diverse series of groups to be seen collectively as an important force in society and politics.

The balance and nature of political forces behind the Country Interest shifted in this period. This was a consequence of changes in the condition and nature of national politics described in the previous chapter, especially the creation under Henry Pelham of a broad Whig ministerial coalition, and the growing incoherence and weakness from the later 1740s of the Tories as a collective political force. The recreation of a strong Patriot coalition encompassing Whigs and Tories, as well as Jacobites and Independents after 1742 proved elusive, without which the Tories were rendered politically impotent at the national level. It was against this background that, paradoxically, a stronger Tory and Jacobite-Tory element in the patriot press of the 1750s emerged, one which sometimes combined republican or extreme Whig political argument with calls for the revival of the influence of the Church in society. John Shebbeare was an influential representative of this strand in political debate, but it was also represented in the pages of the *London Evening Post* and the *Monitor*. It also reflected how far public opinion became alienated from the politics of the Hanoverian regime in this period, a process which reached a climax in 1756–7.

The 1740s and 1750s produced strident criticisms from Country writers (and

---

[128] See e.g. *Protestor*, 9 June, 11 Aug. 1753.

[129] BL, Add. MS 38344, fo. 29, quoted in Lucy Sutherland, 'The City of London in Eighteenth-Century Politics', 58. See also the *Protestor* of 9 June 1753, where the 'middle ranks' are defined as the 'Gentry, the Liberal Professions, the whole Mercantile Interest'.

indeed from others) of the degeneration of manners and morals in Hanoverian Britain. Against this background, and the perception that the normal processes of politics were unable to produce reform, more and more people amongst the Country opposition looked to or dreamed of heroic interventions to effect reform and save their country. One of those who looked to play just such a role in the early 1750s was the Young Pretender. As Paul Monod has noted, however, 'the title of Patriot Prince was not monopolized by Charles Edward Stuart'.[130] Prince Frederick was also trying to assume a similar role from 1747 until his death in March 1751. As several historians have pointed out, he sought in his person to reconcile the contradictions and ambiguities of opposition politics in this period.[131] He also sought to revive charismatic monarchy in Britain, partly looking back to aspects of Stuart monarchy as his model. His death was a major blow to the Country Interest and hopes for reform in Britain. His popular political style—his royal progresses in the summer of 1750, his support for initiatives to strengthen British commerce— appeared to represent the future for the Country Interest and for national reconciliation and revival.[132] It was Prince George and Bute who together sought to take on the mantle of this role in the later 1750s and on George's accession in 1760.

The appeal of the figure of the Patriot prince grew, therefore, from the patterns of change in perceptions, emotions, and hopes which have formed the subject of this chapter. As disenchantment with opposition politicians crystalized from the early 1740s, so did alienation from the politics and personnel of the existing regime. Emotions towards politics became more unstable. To some extent, the presence of a Jacobite or Tory-Country strand in political debate in the 1750s was a consequence of the lack of credibility in public eyes of parliamentary oppositions. Yet, as suggested above, the violence of their alienation and disaffection in the mid-1750s also reflected wider feelings and anger about the incompetence, corruption, and mismanagement of government under Whig oligarchy.

It was Pitt the Elder who helped to rescue the popularity of the Hanoverian regime in the later 1750s, or at least Pitt and the unfolding spectacle of British military success in the Seven Years War after 1758. The latter helped to allay (but not undermine completely) many of the anxieties which Britons had been feeling about their society and political system in recent years. Why Pitt came to embody the hopes of Patriots and the Country Interest in the mid 1750s, is, as Lucy Sutherland argued some years ago, not easily explained.[133] As we have seen, he had attracted criticism and hostility for his defence of ministerial

[130] Monod, *Jacobitism and the English People*, 85.
[131] Clark, *English Society*, 182–4; Colley, *In Defiance of Oligarchy*, 257–8.
[132] See Ch. 1, above, pp. 56.
[133] Lucy Sutherland, 'London and the Pitt–Devonshire Administration', in *Politics and Finance in the Eighteenth Century*, esp. p. 82.

policy when he entered the ministry in early 1746. His path in politics in the early 1750s was tortuous and reflected the fluidity of politics at particular moments, especially before the death of the Prince of Wales in 1751. Until Pelham's death, however, his support for the Duke of Newcastle was fairly strong and consistent; nor was he a critic of Newcastle's foreign policy initiatives on the continent in the form of the Imperial Election Scheme. Perhaps the answer lies in part in the fact that there was nowhere else for Patriotism to go in the mid-1750s, apart from disillusionment with or disinterest in national politics. Prince George was too young to construct a reversionary interest around; Jacobites were increasingly disillusioned with the profligate and drunken Bonnie Prince Charlie, while Jacobitism was essentially bankrupt as a practical political force or option. Pitt had the confidence, the theatrical talent, perhaps as Jeremy Black has suggested, the necessary air of being an outsider to play the role of Patriot hero at this point.[134] As perceptions of national decline and degeneration intensified in the mid-1750s, as fears of national dissolution grew, so also perhaps Patriots and public opinion created out of Pitt a hero in the image they desired. In 1757, one writer asked:

And by whom will such abuses, by whom can such abused be corrected, but by men who are superior to the love of money; superior to the false glory of a misemployed authority; superior even to the love of power upon any other than upright principles? If these have the courage to stand forth and employ all their strength and abilities to divert the torrent of venality, and guard the fabric, whose foundations have been undermined, we may yet hope to repair the breaches and save it from falling.[135]

As Sutherland pointed out, the circumstances in which the Pitt–Devonshire ministry was dismissed, when its Patriot credentials, although sullied, had not been completely undermined, also helped Pitt to sustain a reputation for having pursued Patriot policies in office as well as in opposition.[136] Pitt's popularity in 1757 is, in any case, easy to exaggerate; the majority of people were probably waiting on events.[137]

What of hopes for a fundamental reform of politics and national revival? What happened to these after the end of our period? To some extent, the intensity of these hopes, or the anxieties that gave rise to them, declined under the impact of military success and expansion overseas in the later 1750s and early 1760s. The political forces and conditions which had fuelled these also fragmented and were transformed as the old political parties and alignments

---

[134] Black, *Pitt the Elder*, esp. ch. 2.

[135] *The Morning's Thoughts on Reading the Test and Contest*, 13.

[136] Sutherland, 'London and the Pitt–Devonshire Adminstration'.

[137] The issue of the extent of Pitt's popularity in 1756–7 has been debated by historians. Paul Langford offered a sceptical account of this some years ago in an examination of the freedoms of cities and boroughs, beginning with the Corporation of London, conferred on Pitt and his chancellor, Henry Legge, in the summer of 1757 (Langford, 'William Pitt and Public Opinion, 1757', *EHR* 88 (1973), 58–71). Nicholas Rogers offers a balanced assessment in his *Whigs and Cities*, 107, where he notes that 'it remained to be seen whether public opinion would coalesce around London leadership'.

which had shaped large areas of politics from the later seventeenth century finally collapsed after 1760.[138] The Country Interest also fragmented to all points on the political spectrum, to the Rockingham Whigs, the Court, and to metropolitan radicalism. The Association Movement of the later 1770s and early 1780s was also the inheritor of several strands and elements in the early-Hanoverian Country Interest. This dispersal is a further indication of the intrinsic instabilities and diverse tendencies embraced by the early-Hanoverian Country Interest. George III's attempts on his accession to play the Patriot king were ill conceived and poorly executed.[139] His accession was greeted with huge popular enthusiasm from many different sections of opinion as they looked forward to a new age of prosperity and virtue in Britain. Different people and different groups, however, saw national revival in different ways. Squaring the political circle was impossible; George III was a victim, in this context, of the tensions and contradictions that had been held in dynamic balance in the Country Interest in the final years of his grandfather's reign. Some Tories saw in George III the force for a revived politics of Anglicanism and order, and continued to support him on this basis. These principles were also given added relevance by the nature of opposition to his and his ministers' rule as his reign developed, in which urban and Dissenting radicals played a very visible role. Shebbeare's reconciliation with the Court was symptomatic of this wider development. Other elements of the mid-eighteenth-century Country Interest followed very different trajectories. As we have seen, this interest was not without radical elements or tendencies, although these were of a basically conservative stripe. Indeed, as several other historians have emphasized in recent years, the political foundations on which John Wilkes and his supporters built in the 1760s were deep ones.[140] In terms of perception and argument, there was little that was new about the Wilkite political platform; what had changed was the context. Hopes that a Patriotic king would eliminate corruption and revive political virtue acted to some degree as a lightening conductor for radical or reformist tendencies in the Country interest in the final years of George II's reign. After the early 1760s, there was no such figure to look to embody hopes and aspirations for political reform. With most parliamentary politicians also distancing themselves from reform and populism, those who sought, or who came to see the need for, change to the political system were forced to look to their own devices and organization to secure their political goals. The stage was set for parliamentary reform to emerge for the first time in eighteenth-century England as an organized, independent force.

---

[138] For a useful overview, see Ian R. Christie, 'The Changing Nature of Parliamentary Politics, 1742–1789', in Jeremy Black (ed.), *British Politics from Walpole to Pitt 1742–1789* (1990), 101–22, 250–4.

[139] See John Brooke, *King George III* (1972).

[140] See esp. Dickinson, *The Politics of the People*, ch. 6; Rogers, *Whigs and Cities*; Wilson, *The Sense of the People*.

CHAPTER THREE

Britain and France and the 'Empire of the Seas'

every Briton ought to be acquainted with the ambitious views of France, her eternal thirst after universal dominion, and her continual encroach-ments on the properties of her neighbours . . . (Extract from a review of a pamphlet entitled *The Progress of the French, in their Views of Universal Monarchy* (1756) in the *Critical Review*, 14 (1756), 265–6.)

In 1741, Britain entered a major European war for the first time since 1713, the War of the Austrian Succession, and although war with France was officially declared only in 1744, military conflict between the two powers was open and unavoidable. What followed was over two decades in which Britain strug-gled, through the use of military power and diplomacy, to curb French inter-national power and ambition.

The course of the mid-century Anglo-French battle for security—or supremacy (they effectively amounted to the same thing)—lies beyond the scope of this work.[1] Several basic points are worth emphasizing, however. In the first place, it was a fight which was to extend across the globe, and which would force Britons to confront with unexampled clarity the nature of their relationship to the 'old world' (i.e. Europe) and the 'new' one rising across the Atlantic. This was not immediately evident. The War of the Austrian Succession (1740–8) began as a conflict in the mould of the wars against Louis XIV's France, as a war to prevent French hegemony in Europe, and to defend European liberties and the 'balance of power'.[2] The decisive events were also ultimately those which took place in Europe. Between 1745 and 1748, never-theless, a new sort of rivalry between Britain and France did begin to become apparent, a competition for trade and empire. In July 1745, a combined British and British-colonial naval and military force captured the island of Cape Breton in the mouth of the St Lawrence river from the French. British naval power also became a much more influential factor in the war, a fact signalled

---

[1] It is well described in Jeremy Black, *A System of Ambition: British Foreign Policy 1660–1793* (1991). See also Bruce Lenman, *Britain's Colonial Wars 1688–1783* (Harlow, 2001).

[2] Jeremy Black, *America or Europe? British Foreign Policy, 1739–63* (1998), ch. 3. See also Reed Browning, *The War of the Austrian Succession* (New York, 1993); M.S. Anderson, *The War of the Austrian Succession, 1740–1748* (Harlow, 1995).

by major naval victories over the French in 1747 and, as importantly, the destruction inflicted on French overseas trade in the final phases of the war. By contrast, the Seven Years War (1756–63) began, for Britain and France, in North America and as a battle to secure their respective territories on that continent, and the prosperity which was seen to flow from this. From North America, conflict spread back to Europe, and from thence to India, West Africa, and the Caribbean. There was a crucial continental dimension to the war, but, with regard to the fight against French power and ambition, it was for Britain secondary to the war across the seas. It was, paraphrasing William Pitt in 1761, following his resignation from office, a case of fighting for the 'new world' in the 'old'.[3]

Secondly, that Britain would emerge victorious could not have been foreseen by contemporaries and was in serious doubt certainly before 1759. The question, therefore, of whether Britain had the capacity and resources— economic, political, social, and moral—to combat the French was an open one for most of our period. There were moments of impending calamity. In the first of the period's two great wars—the War of the Austrian Succession— the darkest of these came in the second half of 1745. The French defeated Britain and her allies at the battle of Fontenoy (11 May) in the Austrian Netherlands. This was swiftly followed by the capitulation to French forces of Ghent (15 July), Bruges (19 July), and, most alarmingly, Ostend (23 August). (The Low Countries were viewed throughout the eighteenth century as strategically vital to Britain, given their proximity to its coasts, and it was a major goal of British foreign policy to prevent France gaining control of the area.) In the summer of 1745, Britain's main ally, Austria, was also facing defeat at the hands of Prussia. Public opinion was alienated from the conduct of the war, and angry about the role of Britain's allies, especially the Dutch, who were refusing to enter the war in anything other than an auxiliary capacity.[4] Even before the Young Pretender landed off the west coast of Scotland in late July, therefore, British prospects in the War of the Austrian Succession appeared dismal; ministers and their supporters were beginning to talk in alarmist tones of Britain's inability to continue to carry the fight to France.[5] Had France invaded in late 1745, as it was poised to do, civil war might well have broken out throughout Britain and not just in Scotland. In the Seven Years War, British prospects reached a new low point in the summer and autumn of 1757. In May 1757, a French army invaded George II's Hanover.

[3] R. Middleton, *The Bells of Victory: The Pitt–Newcastle Ministry and the Conduct of the Seven Years' War, 1757–1762* (Cambridge, 1985). For Pitt's retrospective rationalization of his conduct of the war since 1757, see Marie Peters, *The Elder Pitt* (Harlow, 1998), 140–1.

[4] Robert (Bob) Harris, *A Patriot Press: National Politics and the London Press in the 1740s* (Oxford, 1993), 178–93.

[5] *Letters to Henry Fox, Lord Holland, with a Few Addressed to his Brother Stephen, Earl of Ilchester*, ed. Earl of Ilchester (1915), 4–5: Henry Pelham to Fox, 22 July 1745; HMC, Fourteenth Report, Appendix 9 (1895), 118–19: Henry Pelham to Robert Trevor, 9 July 1745.

In the following month, the electorate appeared to be at the mercy of French forces following the defeat of a British-financed army of observation—comprising largely Hessian and Hanoverian troops and led by the Duke of Cumberland—at the battle of Hastenbeck. With Prussia, Britain's only significant European ally in the war, facing the threat of being overwhelmed by Austrian, Russian, and Swedish forces, and making overtures for peace with France, Britain once again appeared to face the uncomfortable prospect of being forced to accept a peace dictated on French terms. The fact that its armies had had little success by that time in North America only deepened the gloomy prospect. The period between April and June, moreover, was one of protracted and confused political manœuvring in Britain as George II and the politicians struggled to form a ministry to replace the short-lived Devonshire–Pitt administration. Public opinion was also again angry and deeply disillusioned with the politics and personnel of the Hanoverian regime; many parts of Britain were also wracked with popular disturbances caused by food shortages, and as summer moved into autumn, attempts to implement the new Militia Act. Elizabeth Anson, wife of the First Lord of the Admiralty, was expressing a commonly held view in the autumn of 1757 when she declared: 'God grant us a tolerable peace if possible before we are more undone, for to go on is sure not possible'.[6] Newcastle wrote around the same time of the 'Nation plunged into endless Ruin'.[7]

However, in the following year (1758), the conditions of military conflict and international rivalry changed sharply once again and in a way which was decisively to transform the balance of European power politics in Britain's favour in the final stages of the Seven Years War. In 1758, Cape Breton fell to a British and British-colonial expeditionary force. Between 1758 and 1762, British arms were to carry all before them across the globe. In the process, France was to lose its main colonies in North America and the West Indies to British naval and military power. The list of captured colonies is a long one: Goree, the West African slaving base in 1758; Quebec and the important West Indian island of Guadeloupe in 1759; Montreal in 1760; Pondicherry, the main French base in India, in 1761; and Martinique, another important Caribbean colony in 1762. In 1762, Britain also captured Manilla and Havanna from the Spanish, who finally entered the war in that year. In 1763, when the Seven Years War ended, Britain emerged as the greatest military and imperial power the world had yet seen. At the Peace of Paris, France ceded to Britain, Canada, Senegal in West Africa, and the West Indian islands of Grenada, Tobago, Dominica, and St Vincent; while Spain relinquished West and East Florida. Such was the shift in international power that in terms of international politics Britain's story during the rest of the century can be portrayed

---

[6] BL, Add. MS 35756 (Hardwicke Papers), fos. 143–4: Elizabeth Anson to Lord Royston, 31 Oct. 1757.

[7] BL, Add. MS 32874 (Newcastle Papers), fo 356: Newcastle to Dupplin, 28 Sept. 1757.

as one of how British ministers, diplomats, and armed forces fought to retain British hegemony in Europe and overseas, not that contemporaries saw it in these terms.

The main purpose of the rest of this chapter is to explore the ways in which contemporaries in different parts of the British Isles reacted to the course and changing conditions of diplomacy and war between c.1740 and 1763. Kathleen Wilson has recently argued that this period saw the flowering in England, against the background of war and heightened international rivalry, of a belli-cose popular imperialism.[8] She portrays this as signalling the increasing political visibility and maturity of the English urban middling ranks, who had been growing in number and prosperity since the later seventeenth century. She argues that from this group there emerged an exciteable, noisy enthusiasm for imperial expansion, and for the multiplying opportunities for trade and profit which followed in its wake. The cause of empire also provided them with a powerful vehicle for mounting a fundamental critique of aristocratic leadership in Hanoverian Britain, and for pressing their own claims to greater political recognition.

Such a brief summary does little justice to the power and richness of Wilson's arguments. Her portrayal of popular imperialism captures much about the nature, dynamics, and mood of popular politics in this period. It fully recognizes—as is further emphasized below—that the conduct of war and foreign policy were made to carry a notably heavy political load. It is also consistent with a great deal of recent writing on eighteenth-century British society which has stressed the dynamism and growing influence of the middling ranks and the connections which increasingly bound British society and culture to the nation's expanding overseas trade and empire.[9] Yet several problems do remain. At times, Wilson tends to discuss 'empire' as if it existed as a set of realities, imagined as well as real, which were detached from the world of European power politics, something which leads her to underplay important continuities in views of Britain's role overseas. It is also striking how

[8] Kathleen Wilson, 'Empire, Trade and Popular Politics in Mid-Hanoverian Britain: The Case of Admiral Vernon', *Past and Present*, 121 (1988), 74–109; ead., ' "Empire of Virtue": The Imperial Project and Hanoverian Culture c.1720–1785', in Lawrence Stone (ed.), *An Imperial State at War: Britain from 1689–1815* (1994), 128–64; ead., *The Sense of the People: Politics, Culture and Imperialism in England, 1715–1785* (Cambridge, 1995); ead., 'The Good, the Bad and the Impotent: Imperialism and the Politics of Identity in Georgian England', in Ann Bermingham and John Brewer (eds.), *The Consumption of Culture 1600–1800: Image, Object, Text* (1995), 237–62.

[9] See e.g. James Walvin, *Fruits of Empire: Exotic Produce and British Taste, 1660–1800* (Basingstoke, 1997); Margaret R. Hunt, 'Racism, Imperialism, and the Traveler's Gaze in Eighteenth-Century England', *JBS* 32 (1993), 333–57; Karen O'Brien, 'Protestantism and the Poetry of Empire 1660–1800', in Jeremy Black (ed.), *Culture and Society in Britain 1660–1800* (Manchester, 1997), 146–62; Christine Gerrard, *The Patriot Opposition to Walpole: Politics, Poetry, and National Myth, 1725–1742* (Oxford, 1994); Philip Lawson, *A Taste for Empire and Glory: Studies in British Overseas Expansion, 1660–1800* (Aldershot, 1997). Recent work on the middling sort is summarized in Jonathan Barry and Christopher Brooks (eds.), *The Middling Sort of People: Culture, Society and Politics in England, 1550–1800* (1994).

far many of the attitudes she identifies as focused on empire found equally strong expression in other, non-imperial contexts, pointing to the conclusion that it was war rather than empire per se which provided the principal context and focus for their expression. Attitudes towards war were notably volatile and in several important respects marked by strong ambivalence. Many Britons, for example, applauded the capture of colonies from the Bourbon powers in war, and called for their retention at peace settlements. At the same time, imperial expansion was not usually viewed as a national goal. Merchants were notably unsteady in their support for British military action overseas, supporting it insofar as it was consistent with their economic interests. They also expected the state to protect their interests in wartime; they were much less ready to strengthen the power of the state if this imposed additional costs or burdens on them.

The rivalry with France, which overshadowed perceptions of war and empire in this period, was also, in the last resort, strategic and political as much as economic. What was at stake was the survival of Britain as an independent and Protestant power. This does not mean that economic factors were unimportant in shaping attitudes towards the conflict, but they need to be placed in context.

WAR, THE PRESS, AND PUBLIC OPINION

As the main activities of the eighteenth-century state, war and diplomacy occupied a prominent place in political debate. This debate took place, moreover, on a remarkably wide social and geographical basis. Several factors help to explain this—economic, political, and religious.[10] Yet insofar as a broad geographical cross-section of the upper and middling ranks, and some below these on the social scale in larger towns and cities, participated in discussions about war and diplomacy, it was a consequence principally of the expanding reach of print culture, and in particular one element of this—the newspaper press.

The vitality and growing maturity of the London press were emphasized in Chapter 1, as was the further surge in its growth from the mid-1750s. One historian has recently estimated that by 1750 around a quarter of the capital's residents probably read newspapers.[11] These readers would have included members of the skilled labouring classes, as well as the middling ranks (shop-

[10] See esp. John Brewer, 'Commercialization and Politics', in Neil McKendrick, John Brewer, and J. H. Plumb, *The Birth of a Consumer Society: The Commercialization of Eighteenth-Century England* (Cambridge, 1982), 197–262. Brewer emphasizes the economic motives behind widespread interest in foreign affairs. Political motives may, however, have weighed more heavily with many, given the close connections between domestic and international politics. Jacobites throughout Britain and Ireland, for example, watched the course of diplomacy and war with special interest, in the knowledge that the fortunes of the exiled Stuart dynasty would ultimately depend on this.

[11] Michael Harris, *London Newspapers in the Age of Walpole: A Study in the Origins of the Modern English Press* (1987), 190.

keepers, tradesmen, professionals, and merchants) and the social and political elites. Beyond the capital, an increasingly extensive network of provincial papers was in existence. The first main phase of expansion in the English provincial press, which had begun in the 1720s, came to an end after the Jacobite Rebellion, which created a new surge in demand for provincial papers.[12] There followed a period of retrenchment before growth resumed in the middle of the next decade. By 1760, there were around thirty-five provincial papers. (In the mid-1740s there had been over forty.) Beneath the pattern of overall growth, there was still considerable instability, with many papers being comparatively short lived. In some places—Bristol or Norwich, for example—this reflected saturated markets; in others, such as Cumberland, weakness of demand. Several sizeable towns were also without a paper for long periods. Liverpool had no paper between 1713 and 1756. The trend was clear, however, and was to continue after 1760, reflecting the accumulating strength and dynamism of urban society.

Purchasers of provincial papers (if not readers) came from a relatively select group, comprising typically country gentry, lesser landowners, farmers, professionals and tradesmen.[13] Hannah Barker has recently suggested a figure of around 4 per cent of the population outside London for readers of these papers.[14] Provincial and London papers were available in coffee houses and taverns with newsrooms in cities and larger towns, as well as in circulating libraries and reading rooms. From around 1730, the number of coffee houses in provincial urban society appears to have grown quite rapidly, although data on this is patchy.[15] The circulating libraries and reading rooms, which began to spring up in significant numbers slightly later—from the 1740s and 1750s—were designed for a largely fashionable and commercial clientele;[16] lesser coffee houses and some taverns were probably patronized, however, by skilled artisans and craftsmen. There were also other ways of gaining access to newspapers which further extended the social ambit of their readership outside the

[12] See Bob Harris, 'England's Provincial Papers and the Jacobite Rebellion of 1745–6' *History*, 80 (1995), 5–21.

[13] See C. Y. Ferdinand, *Benjamin Collins and the Provincial Newspaper Trade in the Eighteenth Century* (Oxford, 1997). Shopkeeper Thomas Turne)r, who was resident in the Sussex village of East Hoathly, appears to have bought (or acquired) copies of the *Lewes Journal* (*The Diary of Thomas Turner 1754–65*, ed. David Vaisey (Oxford, 1984), 80–1, 153).

[14] Hannah Barker, *Newspapers, Politics and English Society, 1695–1855* (Harlow, 2000), 47. Such an estimate is necessarily reliant on several heroic assumptions about readers per issue and about average circulation.

[15] For Bristol, see Jonathan Barry, 'The Cultural Life of Bristol 1640–1775', D.Phil. thesis (Oxford University, 1985), 100.

[16] Alan McKillop, 'English Circulating Libraries, 1725–50', *Library*, 4th ser., 14 (1934), 477–85; Paul Kaufman, 'The Community Library: A Chapter in English Social History', *Transactions of the American Philosophical Society*, 57 (1967), 3–67; James Raven, 'From Promotion to Proscription: Arrangements for Reading and Eighteenth-Century Libraries', in James Raven, Helen Small, and Naomi Tadmor (eds.), *The Practice and Representation of Reading in England* (Cambridge, 1996), 175–201.

capital—collective purchase, borrowing, and hiring papers. In 1757, several Bristol papers complained about the practice of hiring papers from hawkers and vendors.[17] In villages and smaller towns, passing newspapers around between readers may have been relatively commonplace. In one rural village in Berkshire, for example, 'ye Politicians of ye Village' met at the blacksmith's to discuss the news. Their number included, in addition to the blacksmith, a wheelwright, an exciseman, and several farmers.[18]

Scotland saw considerable development in the press in the mid-eighteenth century. Scottish newspaper publishing was dominated in this period by Edinburgh and Glasgow; the only other major town to boast a successful paper before the final decade of the eighteenth century was Aberdeen, where from 1748 James Chalmers printed the *Aberdeen Journal*. Between 1752 and 1757, it was also joined by the *Aberdeen Intelligencer*. The main Edinburgh papers had been founded in the 1720s—the *Edinburgh Evening Courant* (1718–) and the *Caledonian Mercury* (1720–). In the 1750s, two new Edinburgh papers were founded: the *Edinburgh Weekly Journal* (1757–) and *The Edinburgh Chronicle: or, Universal Intelligencer* (1759–60). Mid-eighteenth-century Glasgow boasted two successful papers, the *Glasgow Journal* (1741–) and the *Glasgow Courant* (1745–60). Through the post office, Edinburgh papers circulated throughout Scotland, and Glasgow ones up and down the west coast. Outside of the two main cities, they were probably confined to a socially more restricted readership than many papers south of the border.[19] Newcastle papers were also widely available in the south of Scotland, while London papers were available in larger burghs. Many Scottish burghs also had coffee houses where newspapers could be read.[20] In Ireland, Dublin retained a striking dominance in newspaper publishing. As Robert Munter has shown, between 1685 and 1760, there were only seventeen papers started outside of the Irish capital; and of these only three lasted more than a year. In the same period, 160 newspapers were begun in Dublin.[21] Nevertheless, in this period, several papers beyond

[17] Austin Gee, 'English Provincial Newspapers and the Politics of the Seven Years War, 1756–1763', MA thesis (Canterbury University, New Zealand, 1983), 46.

[18] John Mullan and Christopher Reid (eds.), *Eighteenth-Century Popular Culture. A Selection* (Oxford, 2000), 21–2.

[19] There is no satisfactory detailed modern study of the Scottish press in this period. But see M. E. Craig, *The Scottish Periodical Press 1750–1789* (Edinburgh, 1931). See also the comments in Bob Harris, *Politics and the Rise of the Press: Britain and France 1620–1800* (1996), ch. 2. In 1765, thirty towns in Scotland enjoyed a daily postal service; five received mail five times a week; fifty-five three times a week. Other towns which received mail did so once or twice a week (A. R. B. Haldane, *Three Centuries of Scottish Posts: An Historical Survey to 1836* (Edinburgh, 1971)). Scottish society was less urbanized than south of the border, while Scottish rural society lacked a substantial middle stratum.

[20] W. J. Couper, *The Edinburgh Periodical Press* (2 vols., Stirling, 1908), i. 129. Burgh councils throughout Scotland had since the later seventeenth century subscribed for London and Edinburgh newspapers and newsletters. Circulating libraries were, outside of Edinburgh, relatively rare in Scotland before the final third of the century. See Couper, *The Edinburgh Periodical Press*, i. 81. See also R. A. Houston, 'Literacy, Education and the Culture of Print in Enlightenment Edinburgh', *History*, 78 (1993), 384.

[21] Robert Munter, *The History of the Irish Newspaper 1685–1760* (Cambridge, 1967), 16.

the capital did achieve stability and success, notably the *Belfast Newsletter* (1737–) and the *Cork Evening Post* (1737–). London papers, particularly tri-weekly evening papers, but weeklies as well, were, thanks to a developing and increasingly extensive postal service, also available throughout Britain. In 1764, a little over a million London papers were sent via the post office to other parts of Britain.[22] They were also regularly dispatched to Dublin, and at least one London paper in the 1750s, the *London Chronicle*, was republished in the Irish capital as a weekly pamphlet.

The importance which the newspapers of this period accorded news of diplomatic and military events is striking.[23] Considerable efforts were made to provide ever greater quantities of information about the course of the wars and diplomacy, and as quickly as possible. Newspapers printed in ports—London, Belfast, Glasgow, Bristol, Liverpool—had a distinct advantage in this context. Thanks to merchant ships arriving with letters and colonial newspa-pers, they were on occasion able to furnish news of campaigns in North America and the Caribbean in advance of official sources. Several papers printed inland used express services to bring the London papers, on which they relied for news and comment, more quickly than they would arrive through the post.[24] In 1759, *Aris' Birmingham Gazette* brought forward its day of publication by two days to furnish readers with the earliest possible account of the capitulation of Quebec to British forces.[25] In the same year, an account of the fall of Guadeloupe, extracted from the *London Gazette*, filled five pages out of a total of eight in the *Edinburgh Chronicle*.[26] The contents of the *Gazette*, which was produced by an official in the secretary of state's office, and which was the vehicle for official news and proclamations, were eagerly awaited and read in wartime, and then widely extracted in other papers and in pamphlet form. In the summer of 1743, ministers in London were irritated at Lord Carteret's failure to ensure that sufficiently detailed official accounts of the battle of Dettingen were sent back to London, where they would be reprinted in the *Gazette*.[27] Edward Owen, printer of the *Gazette*, reacted with equanimity to the new Stamp Act in 1757, which forced him, like many others, to put up the price of the paper:

---

[22] Kenneth Ellis, *The Post Office in the Eighteenth Century* (Oxford, 1958), 47–69.

[23] For an excellent general discussion, see Jeremy Black, *The English Press in the Eighteenth Century* (1987), 197–243.

[24] See Gee, 'English Provincial Newspapers', 36.

[25] Ibid., 58.

[26] *The Edinburgh Chronicle: or, Universal Intelligencer*, 16–21 June 1759.

[27] On 1 July 1743, Newcastle wrote to the Duke of Richmond, 'My Lord Carteret's saying nothing of the English in His first letter, raised a great outcry against Him, and as there was not one word of the English, particularly in the second Account sent by the Court Messenger, we were forced to make a little addition to the paper printed by authority, or there would have been a clamour against Lord Carteret not to have been withstood' (*The Correspondence of the Dukes of Richmond and Newcastle 1724–1750*, ed. T. J. McCann, Sussex Record Society, 73 (Gloucester, 1984), 104–5). See also BL, Add. MS 35396 (Hardwicke Papers), fos. 115–16, 117–18; BL, Add. MS 35360 (Hardwicke Papers), fo. 114.

[the] high price will doubtless diminish the sale, and greatly reduce it, I am certain, in time of peace; for in war time we always keep up a little; for though there is scarce ever anything in it, yet the continual lies that are thrown out by other papers, keep up the expectations of the people, who are eternally damning the printer for not giving them more news; and some times, when there has been great expectations, they have not only broke the windows, but threatened to pull down the house.[28]

It is worth recalling that before the 1770s, press reporting of parliamentary proceedings, which in the later eighteenth century was to form a very important element of press coverage, was prohibited by parliamentary privilege and prevented by watchful MPs and Peers.[29] This served further to underline the dominance of foreign and military news in newspapers before the final third of the century.

Newspapers also provided readers with a great deal of supplementary material designed to aid understanding of the main events of war. In this task, they were powerfully aided by the growing number of periodicals from the 1740s. The most successful of these, the *Gentleman's Magazine* and the *London Magazine*, had been founded in the early 1730s, and by the 1740s were achieving print runs of between seven and thirteen thousand. Such success inspired many imitators, including the *British Magazine* and the *Universal Magazine*. In Scotland, the *Scots Magazine* commenced publication in 1739, and was joined by the rather less successful *Edinburgh Magazine* (1757–62) and the *Aberdeen Magazine* (1761). Newspapers and periodicals formed parts of an interlinking information industry reliant on rampant extraction, replication, and emulation for its existence and expansion. Each siege, battle, or capture of a colony in wartime produced a stream of paragraphs in newspapers and periodicals describing the important features of the fortress, terrain, or, in the case of colonies, topography, economy, and natural resources.[30] Plans and maps also began to appear at regular intervals from the 1740s. One of the earliest was published in 1746 in the *Westminster Journal*, a successful weekly essay paper. This was of the Brittany coast and port of L'Orient, the scene of an unsuccessful combined British military operation in September of that year.[31] In the Seven Years War maps and plans of the main theatres of war and of important battles became far more common.[32]

The print trade also produced large numbers of pamphlets on military and diplomatic affairs and issues. Between 1760 and 1763, over sixty were published, for example, on the peace terms to be settled with France at the end of the

[28] Owen to Edward Weston, Writer of the *Gazette*, 26 Mar. 1757, Iden Green, Kent, home of John Weston-Underwood, papers of Edward Weston. I owe this reference to Jeremy Black.

[29] See L. Hanson, *Government and the Press 1695–1763* (Oxford, 1936).

[30] See Philip Lawson, ' "The Irishman's Prize": Views of Canada from the British Press, 1760–1774', *HJ* 28 (1985), 575–6.

[31] *Westminster Journal*, 8 Nov. 1746. The earliest plans were of Cape Breton, captured from the French in July 1745. Plans of Culloden were also fairly common.

[32] The *London Magazine* included 31 maps and charts between 1755 and 1759.

Seven Years War. The circulation of these pamphlets was usually quite low; the typical edition size was 500, rising to 1,500 for the more successful or even perhaps above this on occasion.[33] The vast majority were published in London, where most of them were probably sold and read, many by the political and social elite who converged on the capital during parliamentary sessions. Outside of the capital, their circulation beyond the ranks of the political elite—MPs or those with close contacts with national politics—was probably limited, although evidence for this is fragmentary. In 1760, Samuel Mountford, a bookseller in Worcester, claimed to have in stock 'most of the Political Pamphlets published since the Beginning of the Present War'.[34] Some circulating libraries also appear to have carried a selection of the most important pamphlets.[35] In subsequent decades, book clubs, which purchased significant numbers of pamphlets on political issues and foreign affairs, would be formed in many places, although membership of these was often very small and confined to members of the local social elite. Many pamphlets appeared and disappeared equally rapidly, making little or no impression on public debate and perceptions. Others did have considerable influence, however, although none probably matched in this regard Israel Mauduit's *Considerations on the Present German War* (1760). With a total print run of over 5,000, Mauduit's pamphlet helped shape debates in Parliament as well as outside Westminster on the final stages of the Seven Years War.[36] Pamphlets were also widely extracted in newspapers and periodicals throughout Britain and Ireland, thereby ensuring that at least their main points were familiar to more than those with time, money, and the inclination to read what were often lengthy, densely argued pieces of writing. They were also commented on in the contemporary reviews—the *Monthly Review*, founded in 1749, and the *Critical Review*, first published seven years later. Ralph Courteville reported in 1758 on abridgements of pamphlets appearing in coffee houses in London.[37] A considerable number were also published in separate editions in Edinburgh and Dublin.

War also provided subject matter for prints, ballads, and other printed ephemera, although again their production and circulation was in this period heavily concentrated in London.[38] In 1743, the victory over the French at the

---

[33] Marie Peters, *Pitt and Popularity: The Patriot Minister and London Opinion during the Seven Years War* (Oxford, 1980), 17. Low edition sizes reflected the relatively high costs of production. Only when a pamphlet had proved its success in the market place were new editions printed.

[34] John Feather, *The Provincial Book Trade in Eighteenth-Century England* (Cambridge, 1985), 78.

[35] Robert Goadby, a bookseller in Bath, announced in 1744 that he was opening a shop at Hotwells in Bristol where subscribers would have access to books and pamphlets 'as at other places' (*Lond. Ev. P.*, 22 May 1744).

[36] Karl Schweizer, 'Israel Mauduit: Pamphleteering and Foreign Policy in the Age of the Elder Pitt', in Stephen Taylor, Richard Connors, and Clyve Jones (eds.), *Hanoverian Britain and Empire: Essays in Memory of Philip Lawson* (Woodbridge, 1998), 198–209.

[37] BL, Add. MS 32877, fos. 285–6.

[38] The lack of evidence for the production of similar material outside of London may simply reflect its failure to survive. One study of ephemera printed in Exeter concludes that such material can only

battle of Dettingen was widely celebrated in verse and ballads.[39] The loss of Minorca in 1756 appears to have led to an unusual quantity of handbills, posters, ballads, and prints.[40] Some of these items were very clearly aimed at a popular readership or audience, either bridging the literate–oral divide, as in the case of ballads, or conveying a simple political message in a form which was accessible to those with limited reading skills, as in the case of posters and several prints and cheap pamphlets. In 1742, a Jacobite verse on the Hanoverian Neutrality of the previous year published in London was sold at only a penny a copy.[41]

The appetite amongst the public for news and information about war and foreign affairs appears to have been insatiable. Printers and publishers fought to exploit the opportunities for profit this created. Instant histories—summaries of recent international events—were evidently popular. Typical of these was *An Historical Review of the Transactions of Europe for Six Years Past*, which first appeared in June 1746, and which was printed in Reading by David Henry, printer of the *Reading Mercury*. Like other items aimed at a popular market, it was published in weekly instalments costing 2*d*. Each significant event or episode in the mid-eighteenth-century wars produced a profusion of similar sorts of publications—journals and eyewitness accounts, as well as poems, maps, and other illustrations. Heroes of the wars—General Wolfe, Major-General Blakeney, and Frederick the Great—were the subject of biographies, as well as prints and a host of other commemorative items—busts, ceramics, snuff boxes, medals, handkerchiefs, even fans. There was also a separate genre of publications—for example, *The news-reader's pocket book, or military dictionary* (1759)—which was designed to help the reader find their way through the torrents of news about military and foreign affairs which dominated the pages of the newspapers.

A lively, developing print culture reflected and sustained, therefore, a large, at times intense demand for up-to-date information and comment about Britain's fortunes in war and diplomacy. The course and conduct of the wars provoked other, very visible marks of public favour and disfavour, which together only reinforce the impression that war and international

be found there from the 1780s. Ian Maxted, 'Single Sheets from a County Town: Exeter', in Robin Myers and Michael Harris (eds.), *Spreading the Word: The Distribution Networks of Print 1550–1850* (Winchester, 1990), 109–29.

[39]   *BRITAIN'S Triumph, or Monsieur Defeated* (1743); *A New Bloody Ballad on the Bloody Battle of Dettingen* (1743); *A New Song on the Sharp and Bloody Battle of Dettingen* (1743).

[40]   *A Rueful Story, Admiral B——g's Glory, or Who Ran Away First. A New Ballad* (1756); *The Block and Yard Arm: A New Ballad* (1756); *Admiral B—— Seiz'd with Pannick, at Captain A——s Ghost; or Who is Afraid to Come Home* (1756?); *Admiral Byng's Letter to Secretary Cleveland; or Who will Kick at the Coward* (1756); *The Wonder of Surry! Or, Who Perswaded A——l B——g to run away?* (1756) [published in several editions, including one with a woodblock illustration]. See also BL, Add. MS 32866 (Newcastle Papers), fos. 275, 278–9 for Newcastle's alarm about a hostile handbill on the loss of Minorca stuck up on St Margaret's hill.

[41]   *A Poem* (1742). A copy is held in the St Andrews University Special Collections (Typ BG D45XC, 199, 723).

affairs consistently galvanized the interest and hopes of diverse groups and individuals across many parts of the British Isles. In 1740 and 1741, as Wilson has shown, the birthday of Admiral Vernon, popular hero of the war against Spain which had broken out in October 1739, was the occasion for anti-Walpolian demonstrations throughout England, Wales and Scotland. Wilson has noted around fifty such demonstrations in twenty-five different English and Welsh counties and two Scottish counties.[42] The celebrations which accompanied the news that Cape Breton had fallen to British arms in 1758 were equally widespread and numerous. This was, as alluded to at the beginning of this chapter, the first major British victory in the Seven Years War, and followed two years of persistent military setbacks and misadventure, which may help to account for the scale of the response. Fifty congratulatory addresses flowed into the Crown and on to the pages of the *London Gazette*, from towns and bodies across Britain and Ireland, including from the tinners of Cornwall, as well as from several merchant bodies.[43] The *London Evening Post* either listed celebrations in, or letters regarding these from, Winchester, Chatham, Salisbury, Brighthelmstone [Brighton], Canterbury, Liverpool, Hull, Poole, Norwich, Edinburgh, Birmingham, and Walsall.[44] On 31 August 1758, the paper declared that it had received

Accounts of great Rejoicings at Bath, and many other places in Somersetshire, Hampshire, Berkshire, Oxfordshire, Northamptonshire, Leicestershire, Derbyshire, Nottinghamshire, Cheshire, Lancashire, Yorkshire, Cumberland, Westmoreland, and Northumberland; and indeed throughout the land.

From Gloucester came the following report:

The same Accounts we have also from Worcester, Hereford, Upton upon Severn, Tewkesbury, Ross, Mitchell-Deane, Newent, Ledbury, Ludlow, Cirencester, Malvern, Cheltenham, Painswick, Stroud, Colford, Chepstow, Newnham, Lidney, Nieuport, &c&c—Wherever the News came the Bells were set to ringing, tho' at Midnight . . . In short, never was a People more agreeably alarmed, not so much as a single village was wanting on this occasion, nothing but Bell ringing, Bonfires, Huzaaing, illuminations, &c, being seen or heard all the Country over.[45]

---

[42] Wilson, 'Empire, Trade and Popular Politics', 83.

[43] Addresses were issued by: the City of London; Exeter; Newcastle upon Tyne; the Merchant Adventurers of Newcastle upon Tyne; the Master, Pilots, and Seamen of Trinity House, Newcastle upon Tyne; Norwich; the University of Cambridge; Bristol; Great Yarmouth; Kings Lynn; Berwick upon Tweed; York; Lincoln; Chester; New Sarum; Glasgow; Dorchester; Shaston; Bath; Dublin; Tewksbury; Wells; Kingston upon Hull; Liverpool; Plymouth; Carlisle; Poole; Boston; Trinity College, Dublin; Huntingdon (county); Huntingdon (borough); Trinity House of Kingston upon Hull; Northampton; University of Oxford; Portsmouth; Island of Jersey; Southampton; Bridport; Renfrew; Nottingham; Taunton; Totnes; Coventry; County of Durham; Helston; Kendal; Guernsey; the tinners of Cornwall; Leicester.

[44] *Lond. Ev. P.*, 26, 28, 31 Aug. 1758.

[45] Ibid., 28 Aug. 1758.

In Scotland, similar scenes were repeated in many burghs, apart from Edinburgh.[46]

During the Seven Years War, celebrations of military victories, and of several anniversaries relating to the war, came to occupy a prominent position in national and local political life. In 1758, there were several major processions of trophies and spoils of war through the streets of the capital.[47] The Dundee burgh authorities, in the east of Scotland, organized celebrations or had the town's music bells rung for the battle of Rossbach (1757); the capture of Louisbourg (1758), Guadeloupe (1759), Quebec (1759), Montreal (1760), the forts of Crown Point and Niagara in North America (1759); the battle of Minden (1759) and the naval victories off Cape Lagos and Quiberon Bay (1759); the capture of Belleisle and Pondicherry (1761) and of Martinique (1762), Havanna, and Manilla (1762).[48] In 1757–8, Frederick the Great's birthday was celebrated across Britain and in many places in Ireland.[49] Major Irish cities, such as Dublin, Belfast, and Cork, staged celebrations of military victories by British forces and forces on the continent led by Frederick the Great and Prince Ferdinand of Brunswick.[50] As is evident from the reports of reactions to news of the capture of Louisbourg quoted above, celebrations occurred in very different sorts of places—commercial and trading towns, manufacturing centres and dockyard towns, county towns, and even small, rural villages. The Sussex estate of the Duke of Newcastle, Halland, was the scene of several major celebrations during the Seven Years War.[51] In the rural parish of East Hendred in Berkshire, on the arrival of news of the fall of Louisbourg in 1758, the rector spread the news and supplied the bellringers with ale. According to the rector, the 'whole parish was soon got together',

[46] See e.g. University of St Andrews Archives, St Andrews Burgh Records, Supplementary Papers, Box 68: account of 'the charge of the Solemnoly on the Taking of Louisbourg the 23d of August, 1758'; Dundee Archives and Record Centre, Burgh Treasurers' Account Books, 1758. For celebrations in Bo'ness and Jedburgh, see *Edinburgh Evening Courant*, 26 Aug.; 29 Aug. 1758.

[47] The colours captured at Louisbourg were carried in procession on 6 September from Kensington Palace to St Paul's. The cannon from Cherbourg were placed in Hyde Park on 8 September and taken to the Tower in procession on 16 September. Henry Fox, who did not share Pitt's enthusiasm for expeditions against the French coast, described these processions dismissively as 'our most childish canon triumph'. Nevertheless, he also acknowledged their popularity with the London crowd. See BL, Add. MS 51406, fos. 51–2.

[48] Dundee Archives and Records Centre, Dundee Burgh Treasurers' Account Books, 1756–1763.

[49] See e.g. *Evening Advertiser*, 21 Jan.–2 Feb., 2–4 Feb. 1758. For Ireland, see Eda Sagarra, 'Frederick II and his image in eighteenth century Dublin', *Hermathena*, 142 (1987), 50–8.

[50] These can be followed in any of the main Irish newspapers of the period. In 1759, for example, Belfast celebrated the fall of Guadeloupe, the battle of Minden, fall of Quebec, Lagos, Crown Point, Ticonderoga, Niagara, and Hawke's victory over the French fleet at Quiberon Bay. The fall of Louisbourg in 1758 was celebrated in Dublin, Cork, Limerick, Galway, Waterford, Narrow-Water, Busherstown, Mongahan, Ballinasloe (in Galway), Kinsale, Bandon, Donegal Port, Moneymore (in County Londonderry). The pleasure garden attached to the Lying-in-Hospital in Dublin also illuminated its windows and the cupola of the main building. Above the orchestra, a painting was also erected depicting the main events of the seige and capture of the fortress (*Universal Advertiser*, 26 Aug. 1758).

[51] *The Diary of Thomas Turner*, 155–7, 161, 191–2, 194–5, 212.

spending the night rejoicing.[52] Protestant churches throughout Britain and Ireland also held days of fasting and thanksgiving in most years of war; these must have ensured that few people remained completely unaware of the changing military and international fortunes of their country.

ATTITUDES AND IMAGES

Viewed with hindsight, the tone and course of debate, together with public reactions to war and foreign affairs in general, appear to have been governed by hopelessly unrealistic expectations and prejudice. Ministerial supporters frequently characterized popular and opposition views of Britain's role and conduct overseas in such, or very similar, terms. Thus, one ministerial writer referred in 1755 to the 'vulgar inflammatory Rant' which filled the newspapers and pamphlets, and of the 'idle speculations and imaginary triumphs' which filled the heads of the people.[53]

Several main assumptions underpinned popular and opposition attitudes. The most important was that Britain supposedly boasted unequalled international, military, and especially naval power. It was the latter which enabled Britain's rulers to exercise a decisive influence on European power politics, while remaining detached from them, or so Patriot writers and politicians incessantly and insistently urged. Patriots believed that Britain's navy could be used to destroy French and Spanish overseas trade and to capture their colonies, thereby depriving them of the 'sinews of war' and influence in Europe. Such a strategy, when combined with financial subsidies to European allies—the so-called blue-water strategy—constituted the only one consistent with Britain's national interest; it was also cheaper and more effective, and less potentially destructive of domestic political liberties, than committing British land forces to war on the continent.

Such views may have been simplistic—they certainly exaggerated British naval power and capacity—but they were not any the less strongly held for that. To understand why they were so influential, we need to recognize that behind them lay further layers of deeply entrenched attitudes and feelings. Some of these stemmed from hostility towards the political and financial system which had developed in Britain since 1689, and which was ineradicably associated in the minds of many people with continental war and diplomacy. To some extent, antipathy towards the national debt and system of public borrowing had diminished from its high point of the early 1720s during the South Sea crisis.[54] During the Jacobite Rebellion, the Young Pretender was

[52] Mullan and Reid, *Eighteenth-Century Popular Culture. A Selection*, 13.
[53] *The Important Question Concerning Invasions, A Sea War, Raising the Militia and Paying Subsidies for Foreign Troops* (1755), 38, 63.
[54] A point emphasized by Paul Langford in his *Public Life and the Propertied Englishman, 1689–1798* (Oxford, 1991), ch. 5.

careful to suggest that the national debt would not simply be abolished under Stuart rule, and even claimed that public stocks would be safer than under the Hanoverians.[55] Objections to the national debt in this period could also be as much about how government loans were arranged—through open or closed subscriptions—as about the existence of the debt itself. From 1744, however, when, under the impact of the demands of war, public borrowing resumed on a substantial scale, so too did very negative attitudes towards the national debt. Such attitudes were often based on limited understanding and racism— several prominent financiers were Jews, most famously Sampson Gideon. But there was also a strong perception that a relatively small number of individuals and groups were profiting handsomely from investment in and manipulation of public stocks and through contracts to supply the army with goods and specie. As Peter Dickson has emphasized, the notion of a 'sinister plutocracy' was 'based on something more than ignorance and prejudice'.[56] While the ownership of public stocks had broadened significantly in previous decades, in terms of value of stocks held, it was still heavily concentrated amongst a relatively tight-knit group of peers, officeholders, city merchants, and financiers, a few military and naval men, and foreign owners of similar backgrounds. Many of these individuals were beneficiaries of government contracts. The fact that taxes raised to pay interest on the debt fell heavily on trade and the poor only added to the hostility to this group. In 1750, one pamphleteer spoke of the monied interest as the 'very Drones of a Society'.[57]

Patriot views of war also tapped a potent sense of British exceptionalism. The history of this feeling was a complex one with deep roots, being intimately bound up with the history of Protestantism in the British Isles.[58] By the middle of the eighteenth century, it was becoming increasingly freed of its historic religious moorings. Britain's national interests were usually portrayed in the press in secular libertarian, economic, and strategic terms. A free, independent Britain, in its island fastness, was set apart from the messy, narrow quarrels of her European neighbours. As one writer declared very simply: 'This Kingdom is formed to stand alone'.[59] It was this situation which allowed Britain to focus on aggrandisement through trade, to protect and nurture

---

[55] *Considerations Addressed to the Publick* (1745), 9–10; *A Collection of Declarations, Proclamations and other Valuable Papers. Published by Authority at Edinburgh, in the Years 1745 and 1746* (repr. 1748), 15–19, 'Declaration of Charles, Prince of Wales, Holyroodhouse, 10 Oct 1745', where Prince Charles Edward asserts that, on the restoration of his father, the advice of 'a free and legal parliament' would be taken on the national debt.

[56] P. G. M. Dickson, *The Financial Revolution in England: A Study in the Development of Public Credit 1688–1756* (1967), 295.

[57] *A Copy of a Letter wrote to a Member of Parliament* (1750), 8. For similar sentiments, see *The Necessity of Lowering Interest and Continuing Taxes* (1750), 9–10.

[58] See Alexander Murdoch, *British History 1660–1832: National Identity and Local Culture* (1998).

[59] John Butley, *A Sermon Preached in the Church of Greenwich in Kent, on Wednesday the 29th of May, 1754, Before the Laudable Association of AntiGallicans, Established at Greenwich* (1744), 17.

liberty at home, and to maintain Europe free from the domination of any one power.

However, the much less comfortable reality Britons were confronted with was that from 1740 Britain was deeply entangled in European politics and war. It was this reality, together with a formidable strain of xenophobia, which lay behind the acute sensivity of a large element of the political nation to the possibility that Britain's military and international destiny was being subverted by the union with Hanover. It was this fear which dominated debates about the War of the Austrian Succession between late 1742 and the summer of 1745, and about the subsidy treaties with Hesse-Cassel and Russia negotiated in 1755.[60] The Anglo-Hanoverian union—and George II's obvious attachment to his electorate and its interests—threatened, in short, to negate the heaven-sent advantages of Britain's island status. The opposition peer Lord Barrington spoke for many when he remarked in the upper house in 1744, 'if an Angel could come and tell us, I will separate you from Hanover, I will make you an island again.'[61]

The Patriot vision of national destiny was of an 'empire of the seas', an empire built on maritime power and devoted to trade and ever-increasing prosperity. The existing Atlantic colonies formed crucial parts of this network of influence and territories. These colonies were viewed as sources of primary products for domestic manufactures and of maritime power in the form of materials for building ships and experienced seamen. By the mid-eighteenth century, they were also increasingly recognized to be crucial markets for British manufactured exports. Unlike trade with Europe, where the balance of trade was not always in Britain's favour, the colonial trades with the Caribbean and North America were ones in which advantage rested squarely with the mother country. (India was not generally viewed as part of this empire because the balance of trade with it did not rest with Britain. As such, it was a drain on specie. It also attracted unpopularity because it was conducted by a monopoly—the East India Company.[62]) The object of the 'empire of the seas' was not further territorial expansion—a point which needs particular emphasis in the light of Wilson's claims about imperial expansion as a cry of popular opinion—but the accumulation of ever greater wealth, and, through this and the maritime strength which would accompany it, international security. It was an empire devoted to peace and liberty, as well as enrichment. As Karen O'Brien has written, it was 'a cosmopolitan fantasy of the empire as

---

[60] See Harris, *A Patriot Press*, chs. 4–6; Peters, *Pitt and Popularity*, ch. 1. A good, although admittedly rough, indication of just how sensitive the issue was is that between 1740 and 1760 around 160 pamphlets were published on the subject of Hanoverian influence on British foreign policy. This compares with just over 100 on North America.

[61] Walpole, *Memoirs of King George II*, i. 102.

[62] See e.g. *Some Thoughts on the Present State of our Trade to India* (1754); *Remembrancer*, 28 July, 4 Aug., 11 Aug., 18 Aug. 1750.

the bringer of a universal British peace and free trade in an era of navigation acts and continuous warfare.'[63]

Patriot views of Britain's role overseas also need to be seen, finally, in the context of contemporary conceptions of French international power and ambition. These were starkly drawn and remarkably tenacious, being never far from the surface of debate and perceptions. Louis XV and his ministers were depicted as having one overriding ambition—'univeral monarchy' or domination of Europe. French pursuit of this end was unvarying, whether by diplomatic or military means. France was also depicted as an inherently slippery enemy, not worthy of trust. This was the lesson of diplomacy and international politics since 1689; France only entered a peace settlement better to prepare for a renewed effort to achieve its constant international goal.[64] France had always to be watched and suspected; the ambition of its rulers was unceasing. As one writer declared, France had 'no other Principles or Aims than its own Grandeur and the Oppression of others'.[65] France's vaunting ambition was also portrayed as the main source of international uncertainty and instability in Europe. British power and diplomacy were the major obstacles to French realization of its international goals. Indeed, it was Britain's opposition to French ambition which defined its international role—as a bulwark of peace and European liberties; it was this which also accounted for the depth and scope of contemporary Anglo-French rivalry.

It was a set of attitudes, or way of seeing, with a relatively long genealogy, having taken shape in the later seventeenth century in response to Louis XIV's foreign policy and wars.[66] The underlying frame of mind was suspicious, even paranoid. The sense that Britain and France were trapped in a momentous struggle for international pre-eminence was only underlined by certain events and episodes in both wars. In 1741, France and her allies embarked on an ambitious diplomatic and military strategy aimed at reconstructing the political map of Europe. By the end of 1741, these plans looked like succeeding, although the vision of a Europe finally compliant before French power was to recede almost as quickly as it had arisen, during 1742. The Jacobite Rebellion also had a very substantial effect in this context, powerfully concentrating contemporaries' attention on the continuing French threat not just to British power and prosperity, but, as they saw it, to the continuation of Hanoverian

---

[63] O'Brien, 'Protestantism and the Poetry of Empire', 147.

[64] See e.g. *General Advertiser*, 27 Nov. 1747, 'The Political Creed of the French'; *Some Material and Very Important Remarks Concerning the Present Situation of Affairs between Great Britain, France and Spain* (1755), 6, where the author writes: 'The grand characteristic of the French Nation, particularly to this Kingdom, has been, and always will be perfidy and Breach of Faith . . .'. See also *The Present State of North America* (1755), 74–5; *The Progress of the French, in their Views of Universal Monarchy* (1756).

[65] *French Perfidy Illustrated in General, But particularly in the Present Intended Invasion, and the State of Dunkirk* (1744), 52.

[66] See esp. S. C. A. Pincus, 'Popery, Trade and Universal Monarchy: The Ideological Context of the Outbreak of the Second Dutch War', *EHR* 107 (1992), 1–29; John Robertson (ed.), *A Union for Empire: Political Thought and the Union of 1707* (Cambridge, 1995), *passim*.

and Protestant rule in Britain and Ireland, and the liberties on which this rule was founded. The advance of Marshal Saxe's armies through the Low Countries after 1744 had a similar effect—to underline French military power and its potential to threaten vital British interests. In the Seven Years War, the invasion threats of 1756 and 1759 had a similar effect.

From the 1740s, however, new themes did increasingly gain prominence in the portrayal of Anglo-French rivalry. Put simply, Anglo-French rivalry was seen as becoming focused more clearly on control of trade and empire. The origins of the change lie in the 1730s, and perhaps even further back than that. Anxiety about French economic expansion since 1713 was an important, if often neglected, factor in the upsurge in 1738–9 of popular demands for a belligerent response to Spanish attacks on British traders in the Caribbean. There was a sense that the Bourbon powers were winning the peace, and that vital British interests were failing or being neglected.[67] Several writers in the early stages of the War of the Austrian Succession, for example, George Burrington, former colonial governor of North Carolina, also emphasized the importance of the colonial and commercial dimensions to wider Anglo-French rivalry and the balance of power in Europe.[68] It was the capture of Cape Breton in 1745, however, which imparted new momentum to the shift. Calling for the island's retention, opposition writers argued that France was altering her character from a power principally seeking conquest and territorial aggrandisement through military might to one more concerned with cultivating commerce and manufacturing. French commercial, maritime, and imperial activity formed part of a broader plan to remove Britain's independence and ability to prevent France from achieving 'universal monarchy'.

It was a view which was again lent some plausibility by the course of the War of the Austrian Succession, as well as by French efforts to rebuild her international power after 1748. The Peace of Aix-la-Chapelle (1748), at which Cape Breton was returned to the French, was widely seen as signalling no more than a hiatus in the unfolding conflict between the two powers. What particularly alarmed contemporaries was the apparent rapidity with which France appeared after 1748 to be preparing for a renewal of hostilities, and the fact that these efforts were heavily focused on rebuilding its navy. It was a development watched with considerable anxiety in Britain, provoking frequent comment in the press. In 1751, the essay paper the *Old England Journal* observed that only three years previously the French had ten ships of war, a number which had since risen to over one hundred. The prospect was that in fewer than three more years, French naval power would be at least equal if not superior to the British.[69] Another writer warned 'that an equal, or nearly equal Capacity to face us at seas [on the part of the French], will be fully

[67] See also the comments in Ch. 6, below, pp. 240–7.
[68] George Burrington, *Seasonable Considerations on the Expediency of a War with France* (1743).
[69] *Old England Journal*, 26 Oct. 1751.

sufficient to render us Tributaries to those who already command the Continent.'[70] The French were also adopting an aggressive posture in various colonial spheres. In North America from 1749, French colonial forces threatened the new British settlement of Halifax in Nova Scotia; from the same date and into the early 1750s, the French were also seeking to push forward into the Ohio river valley to prevent British expansion westwards. In the Caribbean, meanwhile, in the early 1750s, French subjects were encroaching on Tobago and St Lucia, islands declared 'neutral' under the terms of the Peace of Utrecht. In India, there were repeated clashes between the British and French East India Companies, while even on the coast of West Africa British and French forces came into conflict.[71] In 1749, Admiral Vernon, who saw himself as guardian of the interests of Britain's navy and its seamen, the bulwarks of its 'empire of the seas', was warning that in two years the French would have made themselves masters of Britain's sugar colonies in the Caribbean, and that they would then be in a position to force Britain's North American colonies to sue for French protection.[72] The French appeared to many to have learnt the major lesson of the previous war—that British naval power stood in the way of their achieving their international goals. The contest for 'universal monarchy' was now being fought in the spheres of trade, colonial territories, and maritime power.

Views of French international power and ambition cut across political allegiances. The main line of division was a strategic one. About the principal object of war, and the nature of the national interest—trade—there was no real disagreement. Ministers and their supporters were more ready, nevertheless, to recognize the importance of Britain's markets in mainland Europe, as well as across the Atlantic. They and their supporters also argued that British strategic as well as commercial interest dictated involvement in continental diplomacy and, in certain circumstances, war.[73] As Lord Dupplin wrote, in exasperation, in 1755, when there was much opposition to ministerial efforts to secure allies on the continent to defend Hanover:

I am not a deep Politician, But these Propositions appear clear to me; That if you will in a war with France absolutely disconnect yourselves from all the Powers upon the Continent, France may disband one hundred Thousand men, That she may throw all

---

[70] *Plans and Proposals Submitted on the British Fishery* (1758), 55. The proposals were drawn up in 1749.
[71] Black, *America or Europe?*, ch. 4.
[72] Marshall, 'Britain and the World in the Eighteenth Century', 5.
[73] See *A Letter to a Certain Foreign Minister; in which the Grounds of the Present War are Truly Stated* (1745), 7–8; *The Important Question Concerning Invasions, A Sea War, Raising the Militia, and Paying Subsidies to Foreign Troops; Fairly and Impartially Stated on Both Sides . . . Being a New Edition of the Papers first Published in the Evening Advertiser* (1755); *Some Particular Remarks upon the Affair of the Hanoverian Soldier* (1757), 28–30; *An Appeal to the Sense of the People on the Present Posture of Affairs* (1756), 7; *A Letter Addressed to Two Great Men* (1760); *Occasional Reflections on the Importance of War in America, and the Reasonableness and Justice of Supporting the King of Prussia* (1758); *A Fair and Full Answer to the Author of the Occasional Thoughts on the Present German War, with a Reply to the Consideration on the Same Subject* (1762).

her Men & Money into ye Marine & if she does will soon make it superior to Yours & what Army she has she may use it to subdue you in America or invade you in Britain.[74]

They also recognized that the protection of Hanover was, in the last resort, in Britain's interests.[75]

Changing perceptions of French power and aims from the later 1740s created further convergence between the ministry and opposition about the main aims of British military and foreign policy. The Duke of Newcastle expressed serious concern about French ambitions in Europe *and* America from 1749.[76] In 1750, he and other ministers were seriously concerned about French incursions into British territory in Nova Scotia to the extent that Newcastle could describe them as an affair on which the future peace and security of Britain and Europe depended; ten years earlier, North America had barely featured in ministerial and public debates about foreign policy.[77] Newcastle was, along with other ministerial colleagues (including Pitt), prepared to risk war to defend Nova Scotia and wider British strategic interests in North America. He and other ministers were similarly suspicious of French actions elsewhere in North America, particularly in the Ohio river valley, and in the Caribbean. As Professor Marshall has recently observed: 'The crucial importance to Britain of colonies and long-distance trades had become an article of faith' for ministers; 'They did not need to be taught this by Pitt or any other opposition patriot'.[78]

Patriots called for Britain in the early 1750s to meet threats to her trade and interests, especially French aggression in North America and the West Indies, with decisive naval action.[79] It was a posture of spiky bellicosity which reflected as much profound anxiety about British power and standing as vaunting confidence in the nation's admirals and ships. There was a sense underlying Patriot argument in this period, as the comments on French naval reconstruction quoted earlier reveal, that time was on France's side. The danger was that if Britain failed to act decisively and swiftly, the country would

[74] NAS, GD 248/562/55 (Seafield Papers), fos. 16–19.
[75] This is what ministers argued in defence of the subsidy treaties of 1755. Britain's conflict with France in North America was threatening Hanoverian security and Hanover had, therefore, a right to expect Britain to act to protect the electorate. See Walpole, *Memoirs of King George II*, ii. 96–110. See also *An Impartial View of the Conduct of the M[inistr]y, in Regard to the War in America* (1756); BL, Add. MS 51406 (Holland House Papers), fos. 7–8: John Campbell to Henry Fox, 21 Oct 1755.
[76] T. R. Clayton, 'The Duke of Newcastle, the Earl of Halifax, and the American Origins of the Seven Years' War', *HJ* 24 (1981), 571–603.
[77] See BL, Add. MS 32721 (Newcastle Papers), fos. 79–84: Newcastle to Hardwicke, 9/20 June 1750, Hanover; fos. 129–30: Pitt to Newcastle, 19 June 1750.
[78] Marshall, 'Britain and the World in the Eighteenth Century', 8.
[79] See e.g. *Newcastle Courant*, 18 July 1752; 20 Jan. 1753; *Lond. Ev. P.*, 31 Oct.–2 Nov. 1751; 11–13 June 1752; 1–3 Aug., 12–14 Sept., 17–19 Oct. 1754; *Old England Journal*, 6 Oct., 15 Dec. 1750; *Remembrancer*, 8 July 1749. In Parliament, William Beckford was a prominent spokesman for the 'blue water' strategy (Walpole, *Memoirs of King George II*, ii. 22).

not be in a position to resist French power and ambition in the future.[80] When Newcastle and his fellow ministers dispatched troops to North America in late 1754, and a naval squadron in the spring of 1755 to intercept French reinforcements from Europe, the dominant popular reaction was, therefore, one of relief; Britain was finally showing that it would defend its 'empire of the seas'. It is also the underlying anxieties which help explain why the military setbacks of the early stages of the Seven Years had such a profound impact on public perceptions and opinion.

'PUBLIC SPIRIT' AND MILITARY VALOUR

A strong sense of vulnerability to French ambition and power in the early 1750s was not only, however, a consequence of the course and changing conditions of the rivalry between the two powers; nor was it simply a reflection of anxieties about the 'boundless' scope and relentlessness of French ambition, and the superior resources which the French state had to call on in support of this. It was also symptomatic of how closely reactions to war in this period were shaped by wider concerns about social, moral, religious, and political trends and development. It is this feature of public attitudes and feelings which helps further to explain their often ambivalent and volatile nature.

It was a disposition which derived in part from the tradition of civic humanist political argument which underpinned the Patriot political platform in this period, but which was much more generally diffused throughout society. A key concept was 'public virtue', which embraced a range of individual moral virtues but which achieved its highest expression in commitment to the 'public good'. It was a tradition which lionized patriotic sacrifice. John Hume, the Moderate Edinburgh minister, wrote two successful plays in the 1750s on this theme—'Douglas' (1755) and 'Agis' (1759). In both of these, the hero was an exemplary patriot prepared to die rather than to see his country, and its interests, betrayed. Masculine heroic virtues were also contrasted with feminine virtues of fortitude, and love and loss. In Hume's plays, we can see how the growing influence of values and tropes of sensibility infused patriotic sacrifice and actions with additional meanings, transforming them into compelling domestic as well as national drama. (The same complex of influences can also be discerned in Jacobite imagery in this period.) It was a developing cast of mind which, in turn, judged failure or possible cowardice in war very harshly. Military setbacks in both wars provoked intense demands for enquiries and for severe punishment of supposedly inept military leadership, although this also reflected unrealistic expectations about the likely effectiveness of naval and military action. It was also a posture fed by

---

[80] See esp. *The Present State of North America* (1755), 84.

pervasive suspicion that corruption was undermining the effectiveness of Britain's military forces, that commanders were being chosen for political rather than military reasons. In 1744, an indecisive naval battle between British and French fleets off Toulon in the War of the Austrian Succession led to calls for the senior admirals in the British fleet, Admirals Matthews and Lestock, to be quickly court-martialled and, if found culpable, shot, to redeem the patriotic credentials of the navy and to prove that Britons expected their military leaders to display steadfast courage. Following a parliamentary enquiry into the failure at Toulon in 1745, Lestock was to be acquitted at a court martial in the following year. This only served to confirm suspicions that political motives were undermining the effectiveness of the navy.[81] One writer in the *Westminster Journal* argued: 'In a country where the Reputation of Riches is valued beyond all other, that of military merit will of Necessity be little accounted for; And I have seen no country wherein Riches are more adored than here in England.'[82] In the next war, Byng's failure to relieve Minorca revived anxieties about 'parliamentary admirals'.[83]

The civic humanist tradition portrayed public virtue as constantly imperilled. Through the effects of luxury—in the guise of pleasure and idle diversions—and of political corruption, people became habituated to the gratification of private desires, threatening the integrity of the political system and the liberties it existed to uphold, and ultimately the cohesion and security of the nation. A 'luxurious' nation lacked the capacity to resist political enslavement at home and insignificance abroad. During the 1740s and 1750s, Patriot fears about the effects of luxury and corruption intensified. As we will see in a later chapter (Chapter 7), this reflected domestic political factors, and a deepening sense from the later 1740s that corruption and luxury had spread throughout society. Many of the elements which comprised this perception were not in themselves new; what was distinctive were the ways in which a background of heightened international rivalry and tension, and a crime wave in the capital in the early 1750s, brought them into unexampled focus. The image of the effeminate fop was a recurring one in the press in this period, embodying the growing fear that the British landed classes were betraying their nation's interest and security for pursuit of fine fashions and giddy pleasures. As late as 1759, a writer in the weekly essay paper, the *Monitor*, could remark:

Instead of a manly, robust, and patient bearing of the fatigues and chance of war, which is required to lead forth our armies with honour and success, we scarce find a commander that is not dressed like an ape, stinking with perfumes and ointments, spending more time in settling his toupee, than in the exercise of his men, averse to

[81] See Harris, *A Patriot Press*, 192, 228–9. See also *Westminster Journal*, 8 Nov.; 15 Nov.; 29 Nov. 1746; 14 Feb. 1747; *Old England Journal*, 23 Mar.; 11 May 1745; 8 Nov.; 15 Nov. 1746; 10 Jan.; 24 Jan. 1747.
[82] *Westminster Journal*, 27 Sept. 1746.
[83] See e.g. *Monitor*, 19 June, 10 July, 14, 21 Aug. 1756.

the life a soldier, and ready to risk everything rather than encounter danger or to be deprived of his ease and pleasures.[84]

Concern about 'effeminacy' reflected, in turn, deeper-lying fears that a society dominated by commerce and the pursuit of profit was unable to nurture the values and fortitude necessary to defend the nation's interests in war. In 1756, it was precisely these fears and anxieties which were projected on to Byng. As well as being pilloried as an example of a 'parliamentary admiral'—in other words, one selected for narrow, political reasons—he was portrayed as an effete member of a landed class which, in its pursuit of French fashions and polite sophistication, was betraying natural English character and security.[85]

There was also an important religious dimension to reactions to British fortunes overseas in this period, which lent the conduct and course of war an additional set of meanings. Again, this is explored in greater detail in Chapter 7. Protestant churches throughout Britain and Ireland held fasts and days of thanksgiving in most years of war.[86] On such days, the pulpits resounded with the message that success or failure in war was a consequence of God's disposition and favour towards the nation. The course of war, with its inherently unpredictable character, was portrayed as a major instrument which God used to chastise a people who had fallen away from the proper standards of religious and moral duty. The people of Britain were also portrayed as latter-day Israelites, a chosen people, who had in the past repeatedly benefited from God's protection and who, like the Israel of the Old Testament, were in danger of forfeiting this protection through sin and moral and religious backsliding. Fast sermons also frequently show how readily this religious outlook and elements of civic humanist argument could become intertwined with one another. Public virtue and moral and religious virtues were portrayed as identical; proper religious adherence was the only guarantor of a 'virtuous' society. Religious observance also represented the best guarantee of bravery on the battlefield. Indeed, to the true believer, bravery came easily, as they had learnt to place a proper, lesser value on earthly life and pleasures.[87] John Hume had Lysander, a character in 'Agis', use his religious belief to console himself when expecting to die for his staunch support for his king, the eponymous hero of the play. 'Whilst I live and breathe', declared Lysander, 'by Heaven, I'll act —As if I were immortal'.[88] Dissenters and Anglicans could readily embrace the cause of their nation in war, and exalt patriotic sacrifice in the cause of Britain. The Northampton Dissenter Philip Doddridge wrote a celebratory

---

[84] Repr. in the *Edinburgh Chronicle*, 22–5 Sept. 1759.

[85] Nicholas Rogers, *Crowds, Culture and Politics in Georgian Britain* (Oxford, 1998), 63.

[86] See D. Napthine and W. A. Speck, 'Clergymen and Conflict', in W. J. Shiels (ed.), *Studies in Church History* (Oxford, 1983), 231–51. See also Ch. 7, below, pp. 290–4.

[87] See e.g. Charles Bulkley, *The Nature and Necessity of National Reformation. A Sermon Preached at the Barbican, Feb 6, 1756* (1756), esp. pp. 30–1; Joseph Greenhill, *A SERMON Preached on the SUNDAY Preceding the FAST DAY, February 11, 1757, in Preparation to the FAST* (1757), 7.

[88] Quoted in *Scots Mag.* (1758), 129.

biography of the life of James Gardiner, who fell in valiant and bloody circumstances in the uniform of his country at the Battle of Prestonpans.[89] The only Protestant religious group unable to embrace and promote martial values were the pacificist Quakers. During the Seven Years War, in London and in Dublin, the premises of Quakers, who kept their shops open on these occasions, were attacked for their failure to mark days of fasting and thanksgiving and celebrations of military victories.[90]

The character and content of debates about war and foreign affairs were shaped, therefore, by a potent assemblage of prejudice, prior convictions, and deep-rooted political and religious traditions. These lent them (and popular attitudes) an extreme and essentially volatile character. The course of debate about war and diplomacy, and conceptions of British national identity, were also shaped very closely by a very widely based and intense preoccupation with French international goals and ambition. It was, in fact, the changing conditions of Anglo-French rivalry which appear to have been primarily responsible for the main shift which took place in debates about war and foreign affairs in this period—the growing emphasis on trade and empire as the most important spheres of competition between the two powers. Writers were not slow to expatiate on the economic potential of colonies and empire in this period. There were also a number of advocates of further territorial expansion overseas as the means to increase trade and prosperity. One such was Arthur Dobbs of Carrickfergus, who in 1752 became governor of North Carolina. Dobbs was an enthusiast for imperial expansion in North America and in the north Pacific. His empire was a widening arc of trading power, Protestantism, and political liberty.[91] In 1762, he was advocating imperial expansion in Spanish America.[92] He was also, interestingly, a rare Irish supporter of incorporating union between Britain and Ireland, largely as a means of strengthening British power and the nation's capacity to resist French power and aggression.[93] Voices like Dobbs were unusual, however.[94] Most Britons appear to have been made aware of the importance and potential of North America because of the course of war and the unfolding French threat to existing British colonies and interests there. In 1757, one pamphleteer

[89] Philip Doddridge, *Some Remarkable Passages in the Life of Col. James Gardiner, who was slain at the Battle of Prestonpans, Sept. 21, 1745* (1747).

[90] See *Scots Mag.* (1756), 97. The *Monitor* printed an attack on the Quakers for their failure to participate in the general fast of 6 February 1756 in its issue for 14 February and again on 20 February 1756. On 28 August 1759, the Dublin Meeting of the Society of Friends published 'A Brief Apology in Behalf of People called Quakers, for their Conduct and Opinion during Publick Rejoicings' (*Belfast Newsletter*, 31 July 1759). See also *Gent. Mag.*, 26 (1756), 89, 116–17; 27 (1757), 220–2; 29 (1759), 92; *Lond. Ev. P.*, 6–8 Sept. 1759.

[91] See D. Clarke, *Arthur Dobbs* (1958); D. Helen Rankin and E. Charles Nelson (eds.), *Curious in Everything: The Career of Arthur Dobbs* (1990).

[92] Black, *America or Europe?*, 182–3.

[93] PRONI, D 2092/1/8 (Castleward Papers), fo. 97: Dobbs to Justice Ward, 16 Apr. 1754.

[94] Another who may have shared similar views is the hack writer on trade and maritime issues, John Campbell. See esp. his *Candid and Impartial Considerations on the Nature of the Sugar Trade* (1763).

complained: 'however important . . . our concerns in America may be, it must be owned that the whole nation has been very neglectful of them, 'till the French opened our eyes about them, and made us take notice of them, whether we would or not.'[95] The level and intensity of press interest in North America was also determined very largely by the course of military and diplomatic conflict there. As Ian Steele has noted: 'Although cosmopolitan in content, English provincial newspapers accorded space to colonial events only when British military adventures . . . happened to be colonial.'[96] Contemporary writers on foreign affairs also tended to emphasize strategic motivations for British activity overseas first and economic motivations second. Putting it slightly differently, the developing conflict in and for America in the early 1750s was seen as having its roots in European power politics and the traditional French aspiration to 'universal monarchy'. It was also viewed as a war of defence; the goal was the security of Britain's existing North American colonies not the acquisition of new ones. More fundamentally, it was a war to ensure the survival of Britain's 'empire of the seas'.

MERCHANTS, PROFITS, AND WAR

Reactions to war and international rivalry were—as in any other period—underpinned by powerful material interests, and an array of private hopes for enrichment or equally fears of economic ruin, as well as by ideology and perceptions of the issues at stake in war. Throughout Britain and Ireland, large areas of contemporary economic life were very closely affected by the changing conditions of war and international rivalry. Perhaps the clearest example—and certainly one of the most important—is overseas trade, which in England and Wales had grown rapidly during the years of Walpolian peace in the 1720s and 1730s, and which in Scotland and Ireland began to grow strongly from the later 1740s. Insofar as it is possible to make generalizations, merchants' attitudes towards war appear to have been finely balanced, their support depending very closely on the ways in which the changing course of war affected conditions of trade and its future prospects; profit tended to come before patriotism.

For merchants, war meant risk and uncertainty, as well as opportunities. The main risks were disruption, the loss of ships and goods, and the loss of markets. On the other side of the coin, war might, as in the case of the Seven Years War or the later stages of the War of the Austrian Succession, bring about the destruction of enemy trade, as well as the prospect of future profits in new markets created by territorial aggrandisement.[97] War could also bring

---

[95] *The Contest Between Great Britain and France* (1757), p. ix.

[96] I. K. Steele, *The Atlantic Community, 1675–1740: An Exploration of Communication and Community* (New York, 1986), 141.

[97] See esp. the comments in Nicholas Rogers, *Whigs and Cities: Popular Politics in the Age of Walpole and Pitt* (Oxford, 1989), 111–13, which emphasize the opportunities for profits created by the Seven Years

about rich rewards from privateering ventures against enemy trade and shipping.[98]

At the start of war, merchants faced the twin problems of embargoes on trade and impressment as the British navy desperately sought manpower. In peacetime, the numbers of seamen mustered were low, a reflection of the desire for economy on the part of ministers, which, in turn, reflected political pressures on them. In 1739–40, following the outbreak of war against Spain and spreading conflict in Europe, the demands of naval recruitment were very keenly felt by merchants.[99] At the beginning of the Seven Years War, the navy's demand for seamen grew even more sharply.[100] A proportion of the men enlisted were volunteers, attracted through a system of bounties financed by the Treasury, and sometimes supplemented by local authorities. There were never sufficient volunteers, however, and this, together with fierce competition for manpower from the merchant marine and privateers, compelled resort to the press gangs. The battle between the merchants and seamen, on the one hand, and press gangs, on the other, was unremitting, frequently descending into violence.[101] Incoming ships were particularly vulnerable, and crews in port often conducted themselves as no less than armed troops to deter the press gangs. It was also not uncommon for seamen to hide, with the connivance of merchants and ships' captains, from the press gang. Some groups and trades—for example, apprentices, fishermen, the keelmen of the north east, those involved in the coal and coasting trades—were normally protected, but in a period of a 'hot press'—such as occurred in the spring of 1756 and again in 1759—all protections lapsed.[102] Even when such conditions did not apply, protections might not have the desired effect.[103] In the Seven Years War, the press was considerably extended—in the 1740s it had been

War for important and often vocal sectors of the mercantile community. For reports of mercantile satisfaction in the final phases of the previous war, see e.g. BL, Add. MS 35407, fos. 97–8: Thomas Birch to Philip Yorke, 31 Oct. 1747.

[98] See esp. David J. Starkey, *British Privateering Enterprise in the Eighteenth Century* (Exeter, 1990). Investment in privateering was broad-based, involving most sections of the mercantile and financial communities, as well as members of the landed classes.

[99] For contemporary comment on this, see CRO (Carlisle), D/Lons/W2/1/10.

[100] *Commons Journals*, 27 (1754–7), 844. See also S. F. Gradish, *The Manning of the Navy during the Seven Years' War* (1980), 212.

[101] See esp. Rogers, *Crowds, Culture and Politics in Georgian Britain*, ch. 3. See also *Lond. Ev. P.*, 15–18 Sept. 1759 for para. on battle between crew of the Eagle, a Bristol vessel, and a press gang in Cardiff, which led to the retreat of the press gang, leaving one man dead and four dangerously injured. For attitudes towards the press gang among seamen, see also Ralph Davis, *The Rise of the English Shipping Industry* (1962), 321–2.

[102] See Rogers, *Crowds, Culture and Politics in Georgian Britain*, ch. 3.

[103] See e.g. CRO (Carlisle), D/Lons/W2/1/109: Lowther to John Spedding, 19 Apr. 1748. For a very illuminating study of similar tensions at the end of the eighteenth century, see Philip Woodfine, '"Proper Objects of the Press": Naval Impressment and Habeas Corpus in the French Revolutionary Wars', in Keith Dockray and Keith Laybourn (eds.), *The Representation and Reality of War: The British Experience, Essays in Honour of David Wright* (Stroud, 1999), 39–60. I am grateful to Philip Woodfine for bringing this piece to my attention.

concentrated on the eastern and southern shores of England—reflecting the increased demand for seamen, and the periodically acute shortages of manpower for the navy.[104] Embargoes—imposed to facilitate impressment or, in several cases, to prevent trading with enemy powers—could be equally damaging, interrupting access to markets abroad, and leaving ships lying idle in ports. Merchants also complained that they merely served to allow foreign ships to capture the carrying trade.

There were several attempts during this period to find alternatives to impressment, and frequent paper schemes to create a naval reserve.[105] In 1740, a bill to introduce a register of seamen to facilitate recruitment, supported by the Walpole ministry, was met by a storm of outrage, not least from merchants themselves. In 1749, plans to create a naval reserve were briefly debated by ministers and the Admiralty and in Parliament, but dropped, almost certainly because of the cost. The Free British Fishery Society, formed in the same year, also won support because it was hoped that it would significantly increase the pool of seamen available for recruitment to the navy in wartime.[106] In 1758, George Grenville also sponsored the passage of an act through Parliament designed to aid recruitment by improving the system of payment to sailors in the navy.[107] In the same year, an abortive bill to create a registry of seamen was introduced into the Commons. This too raised opposition from many merchants.[108] Local authorities in many ports also, as referred to above, instituted a system of bounties in wartime to attract volunteers to enlist in the navy. This was especially common in the early years of the Seven Years War, and was often presented in the press as evidence of patriotic spirit. There were other motives, however, notably the prevention of disruption to local merchants, and equally importantly for local authorities, popular disorder and riots caused by the activities of the press gang. Scotland was generally excepted from the press before 1755. It is no accident that a system of bounties was widely adopted amongst burghs in that year, when the press was, under the direction of Captain John Ferguson, extended to Scottish shores. In Edinburgh in 1756, the actions of Ferguson's men triggered a major riot.[109]

---

[104] See Gradish, *The Manning of the Navy*, 56–7.

[105] See e.g. *A Proposal for the Encouragement of Seamen to Serve in the Navy, for Preventing Desertion, Supporting their Families, and the Easier Government of His Majesty's Ships* (1758).

[106] See Ch. 6, below, pp. 254–5.

[107] 31 Geo II, c 10. The act was first passed by the Commons in 1757, but rejected by the Lords. For details of the act, which was supported reluctantly by Newcastle and his allies in 1758, see Gradish, *The Manning of the British Navy*, ch. 4.

[108] Gradish, *The Manning of the British Navy*, 108.

[109] See Rogers, *Crowds, Culture and Politics in Georgian Britain*, 100. See also BL, Add. MS 32864 (Newcastle Papers), fo. 91: Corbyn Morris to Newcastle, 30 Mar. 1756, Edinburgh. Morris noted that 'a very large mob' had assaulted Ferguson's house 'whom, if they could have seized, they wou'd have serv'd as Captn Porteous was!' All Ferguson's windows had been broken, and the mob only dispersed through the intervention of soldiers from the Castle to assist the Town Guard. Eighteen of the ringleaders had been seized and were presently confined in the Tolbooth. Porteous, a captain of the Town Guard, was famously lynched and hanged by the Edinburgh mob in 1736. For the bounties, which were

If merchants and the state competed for manpower in wartime, war also brought the threat of enemy privateers. In 1738–9, Walpole had argued that war against Spain would lead to large losses for British merchants owing to the vulnerability of their vessels to the predations of Spanish privateers. In the event, he was proved right, and the substantial losses of merchants were one reason why mercantile opinion was so hostile to Walpolian rule in its final years.[110] Ministers were fully aware of the problem and its potential political repercussions, and naval vessels were regularly deployed in wartime to protect and convoy British trade. Naval bases were also established in Jamaica and the Leeward Islands to protect ships involved in the colonial trades.[111] The issue of proper protection was politically very sensitive, and the mercantile community vocal in its demands for naval support. During the War of the Austrian Succession, two separate bills were introduced into Parliament—in 1742 and again in 1746—in an attempt to legislate for fuller protection for trade, reflecting the poor performance of the navy before 1747.[112] In 1756, the formation of the Devonshire–Pitt administration led to the suggestion that control of convoys and the deployment of cruisers be placed under the direction of a committee of merchants.[113] MPs for ports made regular requests for naval protection during the wars, as did the Convention of Royal Burghs on behalf of Scottish merchants.[114] In some cases, on request from merchants in a port, the admiralty hired and armed a ship to cruise neighbouring waters, which was then manned at the expense of the merchants.[115] It was never possible, however, to provide full protection since the strategic demands on the navy were too great.[116] In 1744, the entry of France into the War of the Austrian Succession immediately meant that French privateers were menacing British shipping in the Channel and the North Sea. French privateers also cruised off the Capes of Virginia from Cape Breton ports, hence the enthusiasm of many

offered by many of the royal burghs, see *Scots Mag.* (1755), esp. 154, 267. Several also advanced money to wives of sailors and their families to encourage enlistment.

[110] In 1741 alone, 107 vessels were lost to Spanish privateers (Starkey, *British Privateering Enterprise*, 119).

[111] For a general discussion, see Daniel A. Baugh, 'Maritime Strength and Atlantic Commerce: The Uses of "a Grand Marine Empire" ', in Lawrence Stone (ed.), *An Imperial State at War: Britain from 1689–1815* (1994), 185–223.

[112] Sheila Lambert (ed.), *Sessional Papers of the Eighteenth Century*, viii, *George II, Bills 1742–7* (Wilmington, Del., 1975), 61–7, 313–19. For the 1746 attempt, see Bodl., MS Don c 107, fos. 256, 259, 262–3. Losses in the War of the Austrian Succession were heavy—3,238 vessels in total. The total number of enemy vessels captured or sunk was 3,434 (John Brewer, *The Sinews of Power: War, Money and the English State 1688–1783* (1989), 198).

[113] *Newcastle Courant*, 13 Nov. 1756, para. under 'London' heading.

[114] *Extracts From the Records of the Convention of the Royal Burghs of Scotland, 1738–59* (Edinburgh, 1905), 132–3, 160–2, 173–4, 188, 219–21, 223, 227, 252–4, 531, 539–40; Bodl., MS Don c 112 (Tucker Papers), fos. 67, 77. See also Patrick Crowhurst, *The Defence of British Trade 1689–1815* (1977).

[115] This happened, for example, at Whitehaven in both major wars of the period, and in Bristol during the Seven Years War.

[116] For a detailed discussion of the impact of war and enemy privateering on Scottish merchants, see Eric J Graham, 'The Impact of Mercantilism and War on the Scottish Marine, 1651–1791', Ph.D. thesis (Strathclyde University, 1998), 147–84.

merchants for the island's capture in 1745 and their eagerness not to see it returned to France at any peace settlement.[117] French privateers also had considerable success cruising off Scottish north east ports until the very end of the war. Bristol's merchants were particularly adversely affected by French privateering between 1744 and 1748, allowing Liverpool to gain a greater share of the Africa and Caribbean trades.[118] In the Seven Years War, the navy had much better success in protecting British shipping. In 1756, large numbers of naval vessels were dispersed to protect merchant shipping, a reflection of the political sensitivity of the question; later in the war naval power was deployed more strategically in blockading French Channel ports and other-wise in offensive operations against French colonies overseas. Yet even in this war there were notable failures. In 1759–60, the famous Captain Thurot was to terrify the northern ports of Britain and Ireland in 1759–60. Professor Devine has recently emphasized the threat during the Seven Years War to Glasgow tobacco traders from French privateers operating in the Clyde estuary and off the west coast of Britain.[119] In March 1757, the Convention of Royal Burghs received a letter from merchants operating on the east coast of Britain between Peterhead and the Humber estuary, claiming that more ships had been taken since July of last year by French privateers than during four years of the last war.[120] Bristol merchants again suffered very significantly from the depredations of French and Spanish privateers, which was one factor in a higher incidence of bankruptcy among Bristol merchants than at any other time in the century.[121]

Shipping costs climbed in wartime. One cause was higher wages as demand and competition for the services of seamen increased; waiting for convoys also meant longer shipping times. The costs of marine insurance also rose, espe-cially when privateers were known to be operating in certain seas. In the Chesapeake trade, for example, insurance rates surged temporarily from May 1744, and again in early 1745 and 1748.[122] In the months before a war was declared, underwriters often refused to insure vessels because they feared they might be seized in foreign ports when war was proclaimed. In wartime, the conditions of trade were, in sum, even more than usually hazardous, even if for some they could bring large gains.

[117] On 27 July, soon after news of the island's capture reached London, Thomas Birch reported: 'Our merchants universally consider it as more than an equivalent for the loss of Flanders, & talk of procuring an Act of Parliament next session to annex it for ever to the Crown of Great Britain' (BL, Add. MS 35396 (Hardwicke Papers), fos. 298–9). *Wye's Newsletter* reported on 23 July that over 200 guineas had been collected by merchants in the city to celebrate the capture of the island (repr. in *Norwich Gazette*, 27 July 1745).

[118] Kenneth Morgan, *Bristol and the Atlantic Trade in the Eighteenth Century* (Cambridge, 1993), 20–1.

[119] T. M. Devine, 'The Golden Age of Tobacco', in id. and Gordon Jackson (eds.), *Glasgow*, i, *Beginnings to 1830* (Manchester, 1995), 145.

[120] *Extracts from the Records of the Convention*, 539–40.

[121] Morgan, *Bristol and the Atlantic Trade*, 21.

[122] Crowhurst, *The Defence of British Trade*, 153.

Investment and involvement in overseas trade were far from the sole preserve of merchants, but rather extended across the ranks of the middling sort and up into those of the landed classes.[123] A substantial and increasing proportion of manufacturing was also dependent on access to overseas markets. The Birmingham metal trades and the potteries of Staffordshire exported large quantities of products to colonial and European markets. The growing Scottish linen industry exported coarse linen to Caribbean markets. Other regions and towns grew prosperous on the back of provisioning British forces abroad. In Ireland, Cork became a major source of supply of provisions to the British navy, a role which had substantial repercussions for the development of commercial agriculture in its rural hinterland. Elsewhere—for example, East Anglia—significant quantities of corn were exported to foreign markets. In 1748, the profits of East Anglian farmers and landowners were placed under threat when an embargo was placed on exports of corn to France. Overall, the effect of the War of the Austrian Succession seems to have been to depress British overseas trade, with the end of the war producing a surge in exports.[124] In the Seven Years War, British overseas trade continued to expand rapidly, at least before the end of the war, a major reason why it won greater popular support than the previous war.[125]

If trade was much affected by the conditions of war, so too was the availability of public and private credit—on which merchants, tradesmen, manufacturers, and shopkeepers all depended heavily.[126] In 1745 and 1761, there were full-blown crises in public credit, caused by, respectively, the Jacobite Rebellion and the declaration of war against Spain.[127] In 1748, a government loan narrowly avoided disaster.[128] Julian Hoppit has suggested that these crises were largely confined to public credit, reflecting a separation between networks of private and public borrowing, a separation which was to break down in the later eighteenth century.[129] On the other hand, what the state of public credit did indicate very closely was confidence in the security of the state and conduct of war, and a loss of confidence could easily affect other sectors of the economy. These factors added additional unpredictability to an economy already plagued by regular short-term fluctuations. Rising demands for public borrowing could also squeeze private credit, as occurred in the final stages of the Seven Years War, leading to business failures.[130] For those,

[123] Wilson, 'Empire, Trade and Popular Politics', 102; Brewer, *Sinews of Power*, 193–4.

[124] 1744–5 saw a trade recession. The Jacobite Rebellion had a very disruptive impact in this context.

[125] Ralph Davies, 'English Overseas Trade 1700–1774', *Economic History Review*, 2nd ser., 15 (1962), 285–303.

[126] J. Brewer, 'Commercialization and Politics'; Julian Hoppit, *Risk and Failure in English Business, 1700–1800* (Cambridge, 1987).

[127] Julian Hoppit, 'Financial Crises in Eighteenth-Century England', *Economic History Review*, 2nd ser., 39 (1986), 39–58.

[128] Dickson, *The Financial Revolution*, 227–8.

[129] Hoppit, 'Financial Crises'.

[130] See Sir Lewis Namier, *The Structure of Politics at the Accession of George III*, 2nd edn. (1957), 171.

however, who had capital to invest in public stocks, the terms of investment became very favourable after 1759, as Newcastle sought to secure ever greater loans to finance Britain's massive war effort.

War also brought about substantial increases in taxation to finance public borrowing. Country gentry, strongly represented in the Tory ranks in this period, were usually quick to complain about the burden of increased land tax during wartime and the failure to reduce it sufficiently quickly after war ended, although their resentment was also fuelled by the perception, referred to earlier, that the 'monied interest' did very well in wartime. Pelham's decision to keep the land tax at 4 shillings in the pound in 1749 and 3 shillings in the pound between 1750 and 1753, in order to expedite his restructuring and consolidation of the national debt, attracted predictable criticism from some Tories and landed gentry, although others saw it as essential to post-war reconstruction and putting Britain in a condition to face further conflict in the not-too-distant future.[131] With their attachment to economy, and in particular low rates of the land tax, Tory country gentry were always awkward supporters of a bellicose patriotism, as their increasing political restiveness in the Seven Years War from 1758 to 1759 demonstrated. As the costs of war mounted, so their support for Pitt frayed, although attempts were made to shore it up with measures such as the Freeholders Act of 1758, which disfranchised copyholders in county elections.

The reality, nevertheless, was that taxation fell increasingly heavily on trade and consumption, rather than on land or income.[132] High taxes would also have to continue after war ended to pay the interest on a much increased national debt. This was seen as potentially undermining the competitiveness of British manufactured exports by inflating prices and the cost of labour. It was a line of argument which had strengthened in the course of opposition to Walpole's excise scheme in the early 1730s. During the middle decades of the century, several writers—including Josiah Tucker—argued that the only way of alleviating the burden of taxation on trade and those who lived by trade, and raising sufficient revenue to fund the expenses of government in war, was to tax 'luxuries' more systematically.[133] In the mid-1740s, Matthew Decker put

[131] See Walpole, *Memoirs of King George II*, i. 21, 147. On 16 February 1751, William Grant reported to the Lord Advocate in Scotland: 'You are this year, & probably hereafter during peace, to pay 3 Sh. Land Tax on this principle, to be fund to reduce gradualy the great National debt, & be provided for an evil day when that comes, & to avert it by appearing to be provided—this seemed so salutary that several of the usual Minority voted with us—& ye Division in the Committee was 43 to 160 (NLS, MS 5076 (Erskine Murray Papers), fo. 182).

[132] Langford, *Public Life and the Propertied Englishman*, ch. 5. See also J. V. Beckett, 'Land Tax or Excise: The Levying of Taxation in Seventeenth- and Eighteenth-Century England', *EHR* 100 (1985), 287–306.

[133] Josiah Tucker, *A Brief Essay on the Advantages and Disadvantages which Respectively Attend France and Great Britain, with Regrad to Trade*, 3rd edn. (1753), 129–33, 150–68; *Proposals for Carrying on the War with Vigour* (1757). The luxuries Tucker had in mind were china service; silver plate; jewels; two-wheeled chaises; packs of hounds; men servants in livery; saddle horses; port; gold and silver in dress; plays and diversions; pictures and prints; tea and coffee; and card playing.

forward the idea of a tax on houses as the sole means of raising revenue; it was an idea which was to be put forward again in 1756 as a way of shifting the burden of taxation away from the economically productive and the poor towards the 'man of fortune'.[134] Other favourites were taxes on places and pensions held from government or on public diversions. The aim was to 'oblige those who live in splendour and magnificence to pay something for their pleasure and ostentation'.[135] In December 1746, another writer urged the raising of supply within the year—a regular Patriot demand—thereby obviating the need for public borrowing, and for taxes on trade and the poor to pay the interest on the national debt. The same individual argued that the money could be raised through reform of the land tax to ensure that its burden fell evenly across the country.[136]

Government fiscal policy reflected sensitivity about imposing new or additional taxes on what were regarded as 'necessities'—although this did not include beer and ales; there was also a growing tendency to favour taxes on luxuries or on items the possession of which could be seen as a proxy for income. During the War of the Austrian Succession, new or additional taxes were laid on, amongst other things, spirits; imported French and other wines; windows; and coaches.[137] The tax on coaches was a new departure in that it was 'the first tax aimed at property by taking an article of expenditure as prima facie evidence of the possession of means'.[138] In the next war, items or individuals which or who were subject to new or raised taxes included silver plate of over a certain amount in value owned by individuals and corporations; cards and dice; retailers of beer and exciseable liquors; newspapers, advertisements, licences, and deeds; retailers of wine; coal exported; salaries, fees, and perquisites of offices and employments held from government, pensions, and gratuities; houses; houses with a certain number of windows or lights; retailers of gold and silver plate; malt; spirituous liquors; and strong beer and ale. The rate of customs duties was also increased by 5 per cent in 1748 and again by a further 5 per cent in 1759.

[134] Matthew Decker, *Serious Considerations on the Several High Duties which the Nation in General, as well as its TRADE in particular Labours Under*, 2nd edn. (1744). This pamphlet was in its sixth edition by 1748. Decker's proposal was repeated by the author of *An Essay on Ways and Means for Raising Money to Support the Present War* (1756). Decker argued that 'the most wealthy, and most substantial Part of any Nation should bear the greatest Part of the Burthen'. He envisaged excluding 500,000 houses inhabited by the poorest, taxing the rest according to rental value. This would allow Britain, he argued, to raise enough revenue during the year not to add to the national debt through borrowing. He also envisaged the dismantling of elaborate customs and excise regulations and duties on trade; instead Britain would become a free port.

[135] *Westminster Journal*, 5 Mar. 1746.

[136] *General London Evening Mercury*, 4 Dec. 1746. For a similar recommendation, see *Craftsman*, 31 Jan., 14 Feb. 1747.

[137] See Dickson, *The Financial Revolution*, 218–19.

[138] Stephen Dowell, *A History of Taxation and Taxes in England: From the Earliest Times to the Present Day* ii, *Taxation from the Civil War to the Present Day* (1965 repr. [1st edn., 1884]), 118. The duty was annual and was charged on the number of carriages kept. Stage coaches, post-chaises, and hackney carriages were exempted.

Fiscal policy was a political minefield, raising difficult issues about who should bear the burden of financing the state and British arms overseas and how. This was quite apart from uncertainty about the practicality and equity of certain taxes.[139] There were attacks on the plate tax of 1756 for falling unduly heavily on the 'middle state of the nation'.[140] There were also fears that it might extend the reach of the dreaded exciseman into the private home.[141] Attempts to increase duties on sugar were defeated by the powerful West India lobby in 1743—a significant defeat for Pelham—and again in 1758. In 1748, Henry Fox sought to defend the increase in the rate of customs duties against potential criticism that it would depress commerce by arguing that it was better—or at least more practical and politically acceptable—than any alternative, such as increasing the land tax or imposing new or increased excises.[142] In 1747, Pelham shrank from the task of reforming the land tax, and this considerably constrained the fiscal options thereafter. As the tax burden grew in this period—the new taxes raised during the War of the Austrian Succession remained after it ended—so too did the conviction that the spread and burden of taxation threatened national prosperity.

It might be tempting to discount the contemporary fears on these issues, since public borrowing was to grow exponentially in later wars in the eighteenth century. Yet the developments in public finance in this period were unprecedented, and their impact needs to be judged accordingly. The growth in public expenditure during the Seven Years War was particularly marked, with annual average expenditure reaching a total of £18,036,142 compared to £8,778,900 in the previous war. The annual sums borrowed also climbed remorselessly, leaving the national debt in 1763 at £132,600,000. In 1748, it had stood at £76,100,000.[143] In the final stages of the Seven Years War, fears about the deleterious impact of taxation on commerce were frequently used as an argument for holding on to colonies captured from France and Spain at any peace; only the accession of wealth this would bring would enable Britain to meet the fiscal burdens left by enormous wartime borrowing and expenditure.[144] (The same argument had also been widely used in 1747–8.) Apprehensions about declining prosperity—or its prospect—and the burden which high rates of taxation laid on the economy, also, as we will see in a later Chapter (chapter 7), lay behind rising apprehension in this period about the

---

[139] See esp. the discussion of various proposals for new taxes in 1757 at BL, Add. MS 32875, fos. 340–57, which highlights the many political constraints on fiscal policy.

[140] *Monitor*, 27 Mar. 1756. Significant amendments had to be made to the tax before it gained parliamentary approval. These had the effect raising the threshold at which plate became liable for taxation and limiting the liability of plate at the upper end.

[141] See the petition of the City of London against the plate tax (*Commons Journals*, xxvii (1754–7), 535).

[142] Dowell, *History of Taxation*, 119–23.

[143] Figures quoted from Brewer, *Sinews of Power*, 30 Table 2.1.

[144] See e.g. *Considerations on the Approaching Peace*, 3rd edn. (1762), 31; *A Letter to His Grace the Duke of N——, On the Present Crisis in the Affairs of Great Britain* (1761).

level of the poor rates. Looking ahead slightly to the years after 1763, it is also the context in which taxing America to pay for the increased costs of defending the British empire in North America became not merely politically desirable, but perhaps inevitable.[145] More generally, the incidence and burden of taxation was another important factor behind the political salience of the conduct of war and foreign policy amongst the propertied classes; it was also another of the reasons why attitudes towards the state and the politics and personnel of the Hanoverian regime were very strongly influenced by perceptions of British fortunes and activity overseas.

PATRIOTIC SPIRIT

Ministerial conduct of the Seven Years War was, unlike in the previous war, eventually to win political and patriotic support across Britain and indeed parts of Ireland. Many of the ideological, religious, and economic reasons for this should be apparent from the discussion above. The support of sections of the merchant community, for example, reflected the continuing buoyancy of British overseas trade during the war, and the ability of the British navy to inflict very substantial damage on French overseas trade after 1758. West India merchants and planters, for example, watched their profits in the sugar trade soar as the French sugar trade collapsed under the impact of the capture of the major French sugar-producing Caribbean colonies, notably Guadeloupe.

Broad-based political and popular support for the ministerial conduct of the Seven Years War from 1757 to 1758 did not mean an absence of argument or division. As Marie Peters has shown very clearly in her authoritative account of the course of press debate surrounding the war, issues arising from the conduct of the war continued to cause controversy even in 1759–60, when political and public opinions were most strongly united behind the ministry.[146] Many of these issues concerned the question of the strategy which Britain should adopt towards the main theatres of the war—Europe and America. Particularly controversial in this respect was increasing British support, from 1757, for Frederick the Great and the German army of observation under Prince Ferdinand of Brunswick.[147] On the Patriot and Tory side, it was the rise of Pitt to political pre-eminence in government from 1756 to 1757, and his ability to continue to act as a beacon for Patriot hopes and aspirations, which helped the opposition to reconcile itself to supporting Britain's cause in the war, although this also reflected the sense that, unlike the previous war, this

---

[145] See the comment in Elijah H. Gould, *The Persistence of Empire: British Political Culture in the Age of the American Revolution* (Chapel Hill, NC and London, 2000), 118–19. See also Nancy F. Koehn, *The Power of Commerce: Economy and Governance in the First British Empire* (Ithaca, NY and London, 1994), ch. 5.

[146] Peters, *Pitt and Popularity*.

[147] Ibid., chs. 2 and 3. See *The Honest Grief of a Tory Expressed in A Genuine Letter to the Monitor* (1759), for the continuing sensitivity of this issue in 1759.

was a war begun and fought for the 'national' interest—namely, trade and the defence of Britain's 'empire of the seas'. Pitt, rightly or wrongly, was credited with responsibility for the victories of British forces after 1758, which served, in turn, to begin to allay many of the fears and anxieties about the condition of society and contemporary morals which had reached a climateric of intensity in England and Wales in 1756–7. After 1759, and the defeat of the final Franco-Jacobite invasion threat of the mid-eighteenth century, these victories also held out the promise of enabling Britain to ensure that French ambitions would not in the future continue to threaten British trade, prosperity, and security.

The upsurge of support for the war effort from the later 1750s reflected several other factors. In 1757–8, much opinion became reconciled, albeit temporarily, to a major financial and military commitment to Europe because Britain's main ally—Frederick the Great—could be portrayed as a patriotic hero. The interest in his campaigns was enormous, at times overwhelming coverage of the war in North America. In Ireland and Scotland, he gained particular popularity. In both the Irish and Scottish press, the coverage of his campaigns was generally much greater than that of the colonial theatres of war.[148] As was noted earlier in this chapter, in 1757 and 1758 his birthday was widely celebrated throughout Britain and Ireland. In Dublin, a Prussian club was formed in 1758, which dined in the Phoenix Tavern. Signs of Frederick's popularity were everywhere. Horace Walpole was to write to one of his regular correspondents: 'It is incredible how popular he is here (London)'. He also noted that even the 'lowest of the people' were 'perfectly acquainted with him'.[149]

How do we explain this upsurge of enthusiasm for Frederick the Great? As Eda Sagarra has noted in a short article on his 'image' in eighteenth-century Dublin, very relevant was the state of the war in 1757.[150] The course of the war in Europe in that year was, as emphasized at the beginning of this chapter, disastrous for Britain, and for Frederick. It was Frederick's stunning victories over the French in the winter of 1757, at Rossbach (5 November) and Leuthen (one month later), which stabilized the situation and enabled British ministers to induce George II to repudiate the Treaty of Neutrality reached between the French and the Duke of Cumberland after the defeat of Hastenbeck and to rebuild the British-financed German army of observation under a new commander, Prince Ferdinand of Brunswick. The popularity of Frederick was, however, more than an enthusiasm bred of desperation, and of a feeling that Frederick had rescued Britain from imminent calamity. As Sagarra has also emphasized, crucial to his appeal was a confessional dimension. Again

---

[148] A conclusion which is based on a close reading of several of the Irish and Scottish papers for these years.
[149] Quoted in Sagarra, 'Frederick II', 54.
[150] Ibid.

and again in the profusion of panegyrics to him published in the press, Frederick was portrayed as the saviour of Protestant liberties not just in Britain but in Europe. He was also depicted as a 'providential hero' whose victories, indeed his survival, was a direct consequence of God's favour. Contemporary accounts of his campaigns emphasized his religious convictions, as, for example, manifested in the prayers in which he led his soldiers before battle.[151] In Glasgow, one minister, preaching a sermon on the occasion of a thanksgiving for victory in the battle of Rossbach, entitled it, 'The Voice of Rejoicing in the Tabernacles of the Righteous'. By 1758, the sermon had been printed in six editions.[152] In 1745–6, Cumberland had been portrayed in similar terms, as the avenging hero of Protestantism against the forces of international Catholicism, represented by the Young Pretender and his French supporters. It was a message which may have had particular attraction for the Irish Protestants, for whom the notion of a 'Protestant interest' continued to have far more immediate relevance and resonance than in England and Wales. Presbyterian Scotland was also more than usually susceptible to the notion of the cause of Protestantism which transcended national boundaries. This reflected its recent history of emergence from persecution; the early-Hanoverian Church of Scotland was also a proselytizing church, north of the Tay, in the Highlands and in North America.[153] Such tendencies were not absent in England and Wales, although they were probably less powerful in the Anglican church. Anti-Catholic feeling was intense and very deep rooted south of the border, as well as north and west of it.[154] There was also enough evidence of continuing persecution of Protestants in France and on the continent to sustain a sense that the religious conflicts of an earlier era had not yet completely disappeared.[155] Protestant Dissenters in England and Wales may also have had a marked disposition to see the course of international rivalry in religious terms, although evidence for this is currently limited. The Lancashire dissenter and doctor, Richard Kay, certainly saw the conflict against France in the War of the Austrian Succession in confessional terms.[156] We should, however, be careful about not exaggerating the importance of confessional identities and feelings in shaping the course of debate and reac-

---

[151] See e.g. *Belfast Newsletter*, 28 Aug. 1761.

[152] Sagarra, 'Frederick II', 53.

[153] See the comments in W. R. Ward, *The Protestant Evangelical Awakening* (Cambridge, 1992), 324–5.

[154] See esp. Colin Haydon, *Anti-Catholicism in Eighteenth-Century England, c.1714–80: A Political and Social Study* (Manchester, 1993).

[155] For contemporary awareness of renewed persecution of French Protestants, see *An Historical Memorial of the Proceedings against the Protestants in France, from 1744 to 1751* (1752); Isaac Maddox, *The Duty of Wisdom of Remembering Past Dangers and Deliverances: A Thanksgiving Sermon for the Suppression of the Late Unnatural Rebellion . . . 9 October 1746*, 4th edn., with new preface (1756), esp. pp. xv–xxiii; *Two Discourses Occasioned by the Cruel Oppression of the Protestants in France* (1756); *Scots Mag.* (1754), 149; ibid. (1755), 69; Jean Marteilhe, *The Memoirs of a Protestant Condemned to the Galleys of France for his Religion* (2 vols., 1758).

[156] *The Diary of Richard Kay, 1716–51 of Baldingstone near Bury: A Lancashire Doctor*, ed. Frank Brockbank and F. Kenworthy, Publications of the Chetham Society, 3rd ser., 16 (Manchester, 1968), 101, 124, 128.

tions to the Seven Years War. The projection of Frederick as a military and religious hero was relatively short-lived; it did not last in Britain much beyond 1759, although in Ireland it may have persisted slightly longer. The tone of press debate about war and foreign affairs was predominantly secular.

In Scotland, enthusiasm for the Seven Years War also reflected how far it allowed the Scots to demonstrate the extent to which they had put the events of 1745–6, and the taint of disloyalty which these left, behind them. The background to this is explored in greater detail in the next chapter. Suffice to say here that the Scottish press and burghs (as was emphasized earlier) were enthusiastic in their celebrations of British victories overseas. The fact that from 1757 new Highland regiments were raised to fight in the war, and subsequently showed conspicuous bravery in colonial campaigns across the globe, only served to diminish further the spectre of recent Scottish disloyalty. Scottish newspapers were filled with letters commenting with pride on Highland bravery and courage, this time in support of the Hanoverian regime abroad rather than the Catholic Stuart dynasty on British soil.[157] Military valour had long been a staple element of Scottish national identity; in the 1750s the process of transforming it into a crucial element of a North British identity was underway, a process which would be resumed, with even greater effect, in later eighteenth-century wars.

The press throughout Britain and Ireland, therefore, reflected, and helped to reinforce, an upsurge of patriotic sentiment created by the circumstances of the Seven Years War. Patriotic spirit in both major wars of the period was most visible at moments when Britain or Ireland were threatened with invasion—in 1743–4, 1745, 1756, and 1759. The full range of defensive loyalism in these years is too great to document here in any detail, and its extent, especially with respect to 1745–6, has yet to be revealed fully. During late 1745, it included issuing loyal addresses; raising loyal subscriptions to support recruitment to the armed forces, provide soldiers with clothes, and mobilize loyal volunteer forces; raising loyal volunteer companies from tenants and workforces; providing horses and transport for the army moving north to suppress the rebellion; disseminating loyal propaganda; and numerous demonstrations of loyal spirit.[158] Liverpool's merchants and citizens raised a volunteer company to defend their town in 1745 and again in 1759.[159] In 1756, nobility and gentry in each county came together, under a plan agreed between the Duke of Cumberland and Lord Gower, to use their influence to raise men for new regular regiments for home defence.[160] In 1759–61, the embodiment of

---

[157] See e.g. *Scots Mag.* (1759), 553; *Edinburgh Chronicle*, 31 Mar. 1759.

[158] But see the wealth of information in, esp. Speck, *The Butcher*, chs. 3 and 4. See also Colley, *Britons*, 80–5; Gould, *The Persistence of Empire*, 24–8; Bob Harris, ' "A Great Palladium of our Liberties": The British Press and the 'Forty-Five', *Historical Research*, 68 (1995), 67–87. For Scotland and Ireland, see respectively Ch. 5, below, pp. 150–9 and ch. 6, pp. 232–4.

[159] See *Gent. Mag.*, 29 (1759), 547.

[160] BL, Add. MS 32863 (Newcastle Papers), fo. 109; Walpole, *Memoirs of King George II*, ii. 150.

the militia in many English counties, and the establishment of militia camps, became the focus for patriotic spectacle and demonstrations. The initial reviews of the county militias in the summer of 1759 could last anything up to a week, and involved exercises, often on open spaces outside of important towns, which attracted numerous spectators. During the week of the camp, balls and assemblies also took place for the officers and their ladies.[161] In several counties the militia also attracted gentlemen and other volunteers.[162] In Lincolnshire in the same year, several tradesmen set on foot an association and put themselves to learning military exercises, being determined to join either the militia or regular forces in the event of a French invasion; in Newcastle a 'great number of young gentlemen' were learning the 'Prussian exercise' with a view to joining regular forces if the occasion arose.[163] The march on Belfast of the militia companies of Antrim, Down and Armagh in early 1760 on the news of Thurot's landing at Carrickfergus became a major demonstration of the defensive loyalism of the north of Ireland.[164]

The Seven Years War stimulated other patriotic activities beyond a purely defensive patriotism. We have already seen how widely and regularly major military victories were celebrated from 1757 in towns and cities across Britain and Ireland. In 1756, many amongst the landed and urban elites in England and Scotland sought to encourage enlistment in the army through the provision of bounties or payments to wives and families who would be left without a breadwinner.[165] There was widespread support throughout Britain for the Marine Society, formed in 1756, which sought to train up young orphan boys for service in the navy. It was a support which, as is further emphasized in Chapter 7, spread right across the upper and middling ranks, and far beyond London. In Dublin in 1758, a separate Irish branch of the Society was established.[166] The Troop Society was established in 1759 in London, devoted to supporting the widows and orphans of soldiers killed on action in Germany. Between its establishment and the end of May 1760, the Society raised over £7,000 through subscriptions. Supporters included many London merchants. Collective subscriptions flowed in from coal traders; Dover, Bridport, Lancaster, Leeds, Exeter, and Bath; a tradesmen's club in Liverpool; the City

[161] See the decription of the activities surrounding the Wiltshire militia camp at Devizes in the first week of June 1759 in the *Lond. Ev. P.*, 14 June 1759.

[162] J. R. Western, *The English Militia in the Eighteenth Century* (London and Toronto, 1965), 154–61.

[163] *Edinburgh Chronicle*, 9 Aug. 1759. For a similar development in Tenterden in Kent, see *Lond. Ev. P.*, 25–7 Sept. 1759.

[164] The events were described at the time in a diary in the *Belfast Newsletter*. This was the source which Henry Joy used in his later manuscript history of Belfast (Linenhall Library, Belfast, Joy MS 4, pp. 104–53). See also A. T. Q. Stewart, *A Deeper Silence: The Hidden Origins of the United Irishmen* (Belfast, 1998), ch. 2.

[165] *Scots Mag.* (1756), 195; BL, Add. MS 32864, fos. 2–3, 22, 62–3, 279–80.

[166] For the Marine Society in Dublin, see *Universal Advertiser*, 15 Apr., 9 May, 13 May, 16 May, 24 June 1758. See also *Belfast Newsletter*, 30 Mar. 1759, for a list of subscribers to the society. See also Ch. 7, below, pp. 312–13.

incorporations; friendly societies and freemason's lodges; clubs, including 'sundry societies and clubs at Sheffield'; the Quakers of Newcastle; and even the young ladies of one boarding school in Bristol.[167] Local authorities throughout England and Scotland also once again provided bounties to encourage enlistment into regiments which had been left understrength through losses at the Battle of Minden. The effort was led by the City of London. The nobility, gentry, and others in Middlesex and West-minster subscribed over £4,726 as a voluntary contribution to be distributed in bounties and rewards to able-bodied men who enlisted in the army. The magistrates of Glasgow offered 2 guineas to every men who enlisted in British regiments in Germany before 1 November. At the end of the war, these men, if they survived, were to be admitted as burgesses without payment of a fee or reward. A similar bounty was offered by the magistrates of nearby Paisley to those who enlisted in Major Craufford's royal volunteers.[168]

The patriotic spirit of the Seven Years War cut across party and partisan political divisions, as it had done during the Jacobite Rebellion of 1745–6 and during the years of peace between the two mid-eighteenth-century wars. In the north east, the efforts of landed gentry to support recruitment to the army in 1756 included leading Whig and Tory peers and gentry.[169] In 1759, officers in the English militia also included members of both parties. It also cut across religious divisions, again as it had done in 1745–6. In Edinburgh in 1759, the evangelical George Whitefield preached the duty of opposition to Catholic France and of support for the Hanoverian and Protestant Succession.[170] Dissenters were some of the regime's staunchest supporters, identifying the cause of Protestantism and religious toleration with the regime's survival and displaying a degree of positive identification with the Hanoverian monarchy which was unusual amongst members of the established Church.[171]

[167] *An Account of the Society for the Encouragement of the British Troops, in Germany and North America* (1760).
[168] CLRO, Journals of the Court of Common Council, 62 (1759–61), fos. 32–4, 113–16; *Edinburgh Chronicle*, 15–18, 22–5 Sept., 2–4 Oct. 1759. See also *Scots Mag.* (1759), 443, 490–1; *Gent. Mag.*, 29 (1759), 390, 439, 493.
[169] *Newcastle Courant*, 3, 10, 17 Apr. 1756.
[170] *Edinburgh Chronicle*, 11–16 Aug. 1759.
[171] This is best approached through dissenting sermons. See e.g. James Hancox, *The Safety of a Good Prince* (1744). Hancox was newly arrived as minister of the Old Meeting House in Dudley in the West Midlands. The sermon was preached in 1743 on the occasion of George II's return from the conti-nent. Hancox expressed relief at the preservation of the King during the summer's campaigning on the continent and at the battle of Dettingen. He also reminded his hearers, in this context, that 'there are persons now living who remember the time when such an Assembly as this durst not come together for the Worship of God' (p. 22). After a final parallel between the return of George II to these domin-ions and the 'Return of the great King of Kings from Heaven to his lower world', the congregation sang a hymn specially composed for the occasion (p. 32):

Sing Britons with triumphant Voice
With Shouts of Joy in God rejoice
Each heart be glad and Sorrow cease,
Since George our King's returned in Peace.

The existence of this sermon was brought to my attention by Albert Cumberland.

During the '45, London's dissenters were amongst the first to offer support to the regime.[172] In Scotland, Seceders from the Church of Scotland were forward in demonstrating their support for the regime, as indeed—as we will see in Chapter 5 below—was the established Presbyterian church. In Ireland in the Seven Years War, even the Catholic Church, if not the majority of Catholics, sought to demonstrate its support for Dublin Castle and the Hanoverian regime in 1756 and, more visibly, in 1759–60.[173] In 1745, the Reverend Alexander Macleane, a Presbyterian minister in Monaghan, counselled his flock to put aside their differences with established authority until the crisis of the Jacobite Rebellion was over.[174] In the 1750s, Ireland's Patriots also ostentaciously and loudly declared their loyalty to the Hanoverian regime and to the cause of Britain overseas, as they did to so much else, in large numbers of toasts.[175] The Freeholders Society, an important Patriot organization which met in Dublin in the later 1750s when the Irish Parliament was in session, also advertised the willingness of its members to 'enter into and act in any military service, which our most gracious sovereign shall require of us, in any part of this kingdom or of Great Britain, during the present war, and arm ourselves and our protestant tenants at our own expence . . . '.[176]

However, it is important to recognize some of the limitations of the wartime patriotism of this period. How much of it signified positive enthusiasm for the Hanoverian regime and its politics is a moot point; what it did certainly indicate in 1745–6 and again in 1756 and 1759 was intense opposition to France and to the Stuart pretenders to the thrones of Britain and Ireland. Patriotism also tended, as in subsequent wars during the 'long eighteenth century', to be most forthcoming when it least interfered with the lives and civilian interests of people, except perhaps in periods of particular crisis. Much that was portrayed as evidence of patriotism was happily consistent with other motives. The case of local authorities providing bounties for naval recruits has already been referred to. In 1756, the *London Evening Post* called on cities and counties to enter into subscriptions to build and operate privateering vessels. The Yorkshire Society in London, a society of gentlemen with Yorkshire

---

[172] *Newcastle Courant*, 14 Sept. 1745, which included a report from *Wye's Newsletter* of 5 September to the effect that the Dissenting deputies had met and agreed to keep in pay several thousand men in the event of an insurrection. For the loyal efforts of Dissenting ministers in Northampton, see HMC, *Calendar of General Correspondence of Philip Doddridge, D.D.* (1979), 1096, 1099, 1113.

[173] See esp. *Catholic Ireland in the Eighteenth Century: Collected Essays of Maureen Wall*, ed. Gerard O'Brien (Dublin, 1989), esp. ch. 6.

[174] I. R. McBride, *Scripture Politics: Ulster Presbyterians and Irish Radicalism in the Late Eighteenth Century* (Oxford, 1998), 96.

[175] Thus, for example, the Independent Freeholders of County Cavan, meeting at Cavan on 25 February 1754, made the following toast: 'May the Subjects of Great Britain be as loyal to his Majesty, as the protestant Subjects of Ireland'. Other Patriot clubs commonly toasted the 'Wooden Walls of Great Britain'.

[176] *Gent. Mag.*, 26 (1756), 369.

connections, did just this.[177] The main impetus behind privateering, however, was profit. The largest privateering concerns were, in essence, highly capitalized businesses, drawing together the interests of London financiers and merchants and seamen in the capital and elsewhere. Merchants fitted out privateers in largest numbers when opportunities for normal trade were limited and it made sense to divert energies and money into capturing enemy ships and trade.[178] Volunteering, such as occurred in Liverpool in 1745–6 and 1759, meant service during the duration of a crisis, and maintaining strong control over the terms of that service. As Elijah Gould has recently emphasized, there were also many who exercised their right to do very little or nothing, or at least nothing that involved them doing anything other than contributing money or celebrating Hanoverian political anniversaries.[179] During the '45, efforts to raise volunteer companies often ran into difficulties. It was often easier to gain pledges of financial support for loyal subscriptions than individuals to join the volunteer companies. A considerable number of people argued that support for recruitment to the regular army would be a more effective response; it was also, unsurprisingly, easier to rally support for subscriptions and volunteer companies in regions or places which were directly threatened by the rebellion or by the threat of invasion from France.[180]

The history of the militia reveals most clearly the constraints which surrounded the patriotic spirit of the mid-eighteenth century.[181] Promoted as a patriotic body—at least by the opposition press and opposition politicians—and designed to defend Britain against invasion scares, Whig and Tory gentry showed little initial enthusiasm for it. Neither did the people who would have to fill the rank and file. Newcastle and the old corps had opposed it from the beginning, seeing it as incompatible with the commercial society Britain had become; national defence was the proper remit of the regular army.[182]

[177] *Newcastle Courant*, 11 Sept. 1756. The involvement of similar bodies in privateering was to become much more common in later eighteenth-century wars.

[178] See Starkey, *British Privateering Enterprise*. See also Morgan, *Bristol and the Atlantic Trade*, esp. ch. 5, for comment on the rush of privateering in Bristol in both wars owing to difficulties in normal trade and the adverse repercussions this had on Bristol following the war.

[179] Gould, *The Persistence of Empire*, 24–7.

[180] Ibid., 27. See Avon Public Library, Bristol, Southwell Papers, vol. 9 for letters which provide a revealing insight into the debates, arguments, and problems surrounding the loyal subscription in Bristol and attempts to raise a regiment of loyal volunteers. See also Lancashire County Record Office, DDK 1741/7, for letters of Lord Derby describing similar debates and arguments concerning raising a loyal volunteer force in Lancashire. For the argument that associations should be directed towards strengthening the national effort to suppress the rebellion, see *Old England Journal*, 26 Oct. 1745; *Newcastle Gazette*, 27 Nov. 1745; *General Evening Post*, 14 Nov. 1745; *General Advertiser*, 12 Oct., 17 Oct., 25 Oct., 28 Oct. 1745; *Westminster Journal*, 9 Dec. 1745; *General Evening Post*, 12–15 Oct., 5–7 Nov., 12–14 Nov., 14–16 Nov., 16–19 Nov. 1745; *The Folly and Danger of the Present Associations Demonstrated* (1745). In London, the parish of St Martin's in the Fields sought to meet this objection by creating a subscription to raise troops for the army.

[181] See esp. Gould, *The Persistence of Empire*, ch. 3. Gould's book appeared after early drafts of this chapter. His views are consistent with the basic thrust of the argument being presented here.

[182] Western, *The Militia* (pt. 2).

Attempts to embody and appoint officers to the militia in 1757–8 became embroiled in disputes about party and personal advantage and influence. In fact, the overriding impression the sources create is that the militia was more an embarrassment to county gentry than anything else; subscriptions to encourage recruitment to the regular army were much less bother. In 1757, as we saw in an earlier chapter, attempts to implement the Militia act provoked intense popular protests in many counties. Underlying these was the perception that the financial and personal costs of service in the militia fell disproportionately heavily on the middling and lower ranks; the militia was patriotic service enforced by the landed classes on the poorer classes and at the latter's expense. There were also strong fears that militia units would be posted abroad. The protests only provided a further reason for county elites to stall on implementation of the act. As John Western wrote in his classic study of the English militia, it 'might well have died the natural death so ardently wished for by Newcastle and his friends had there not been the reappearance of danger which it was meant to oppose.'[183]

By 1759, some of these grievances had been met through amendments to the Militia Act in 1758. The families of militiamen on service, for example, were to be supported through the county rates. The country was also denuded of regular forces because of the ministry's aggressive military strategy overseas. In such circumstances, the militia could be portrayed as a vital, if supplementary, arm of national defence. Even then the politics behind its extension and deployment were messy, and some ostensibly patriotic support for it was motivated by personal or political interest. The Prince of Wales and Bute sought to identify Leicester House with the militia because they feared that the Duke of Cumberland might be brought out of retirement to bolster the defence of Britain. The gentry also quickly began to complain, once the invasion crisis was over, about the cost of maintaining the families of militiamen on service. Faced with the prospect of compulsory service, many potential rank and file members joined charitable or collective subscriptions to purchase a substitute. Others sought to avoid service using other means, such as appealing to the courts about shortcomings in the way in which militia ballots had been conducted.[184] In 1759 and 1761, there were renewed riots in Huntingdonshire; there was also a 'rebellion' in the Devon militia in 1759.[185] At Hexham in the north east an attempt in 1761 to ballot the militia led to between twenty-one and fifty people being killed, and many wounded, in clashes between colliers, protesting about the ballot, and a party of the Yorkshire militia sent to prevent disturbances.[186] The basic problem was how

---

[183] Ibid., 154.

[184] *Gent. Mag.*, 29 (1759), 438.

[185] For a contemporary account of the mutiny in the Devon militia, see BL, Egerton MS 3444, fos. 246–7.

[186] John Stevenson, *Popular Disturbances in England 1700–1832*, 2nd edn. (1992), 48. See also BL, Egerton MS 3436, fos. 381–2.

to devise a system which imposed least burden on the landed elites and indeed other ranks in society, which was consistent with military efficiency, and which reflected the sort of society England was becoming—both landed and hierarchical *and* commercial. In Scotland, a campaign between 1759 and 1762 to revive the Scottish militia came unstuck precisely because of these contradictions, and the unhappy experience of the revived militia south of the border.[187]

Wartime patriotism in this period can, therefore, appear less impressive when viewed at close quarters, although this is generally true of patriotism through the ages. Yet it was not unimportant because of this; rather it was a further dimension of political activity which serves to highlight how far war and a heightened sense of international rivalry in this period acted as politicizing experiences across a broad cross-section of society. The immediate stimulus to the widespread, public agitation for a reformed Scottish militia was the invasion scare of 1759, which, as south of the border, had found the country short of regular forces. What forces there were had had to be drawn together around Edinburgh to defend the Scottish capital, leaving much of the rest of Scotland exposed to the enemy. The only Scottish force raised during the crisis was the Argyll and Sutherland militias and several volunteer forces in north-east burghs. It was a similar picture in Ireland. When Thurot landed at Carrickfergus in Ireland in early 1760, most of the British army in Ireland was stationed away from the north; the Irish militia was also in a state of disarray. Many of the men of Ulster who marched to Belfast in 1760 were armed with pitchforks and scythes.[188] In the aftermath of the invasion, which ended in the defeat and capture by British naval ships of the French vessels carrying Thurot and his forces—Thurot was killed in the fight, his body washing up on Scottish shores some weeks later—the grand jury of Down and the gentlemen of Armagh produced addresses critical of Dublin Castle for their weakness and ill-preparedness of the administration exposed by Thurot's raid.[189] From 1759, Pitt and the adminstration in London were also forced to concede the necessity of raising forces in Ulster to strengthen the military establishment in Ireland. They were also forced to rely on northern gentry and nobility to recruit these forces for them.[190] In this way, the circumstances of the Seven Years War emphasized how far the cause and security of Britain had come to depend on the efforts of all the nations from which it was made up, and on the willingness of British subjects to see advantage, personal and national, in supporting its security at home and activities overseas.

The transformation of Britain's military and international standing between the beginning and end of the mid-eighteenth century was profound.

---

[187] John Robertson, *The Militia Issue and the Scottish Enlightenment* (Edinburgh, 1985).

[188] For provision of arms in 1759, see PRONI, T 1060/5/3323: Bedford to Pitt, 25 Dec. 1759.

[189] *Belfast Newsletter*, 1 Apr., 18 Apr. 1760. See also Ch. 5, below, pp. 231–2.

[190] For the proposals, and the government's responses to them, see PRONI, T 1060/5 & 6.

It was also one which many in Britain had not yet fully come to terms with in 1763. This was partly because this transformation was so unforeseen and unexpected. But it was also a consequence of how far attitudes and debate continued to be influenced by the preoccupation with French power and ambition. Symptomatic of this was the terms in which the prospect of peace with France were debated from 1759 to 1762. Many came to argue that Britain should enforce a draconian peace on the French in order to destroy their capacity to threaten British interests overseas and in Europe. A concern with 'security' also led a significant body of opinion to argue that while the retention of Canada promised fewer economic benefits than Guadeloupe or other West Indian islands seized from France, it would disable France from ever again seeking to undermine Britain's colonies in North America. As one pamphleteer declared: 'The only way to deal with the French nation is not to permit them to have an inch of ground near any of our North American settlements. In a word, it is the only way we can act with safety to ourselves ...'[191] Several commentators raised the issue of Louisiana in this context, which remained in French hands, and there were calls for an expedition to seize it from the French.[192] Another argued that Britain should keep Cape Breton rather than Canada as the cheaper, more effective way of securing its North American colonies; they also stressed the economic and strategic value of the Cape Breton fisheries.[193] Even in defeat, France was still seen as ambitious and naturally threatening to British and European interests.[194]

The more astute argued that to remove France from North America would be to remove an important constraint on Britons in North America seeking political independence from the mother country.[195] One writer also saw clearly the self-deception behind the argument for 'security':

To desire the Enemy's whole country, upon no other principle, but that otherwise you cannot secure your own, is turning the Idea of mere Defence into the most dangerous of all Principles. It is leaving no medium between Safety and Conquest.[196]

Others sought to reconcile long-standing conceptions of Britain as a pacific power uninterested in territorial aggrandisement with self-serving visions of

---

[191] *Considerations on the Approaching Peace*, 3rd edn. (1762), 24. See also *The Interest of Great Britain Considered with Regard to her Colonies* (1760), 13, 19–20; Philip Lawson, ' "The Irishman's Prize" ', 575–84.

[192] See e.g. *Reflections on the Present Posture of our Affairs in North America* (1760).

[193] *General Reflections Occasioned by the Letter Addressed to Two Great Men and the Remarks on that Letter* (1760).

[194] See *Considerations on the Approaching Peace*, 32; *A Letter . . . addressed to Two Great Men* (1760); *A Letter to a Member of the Honourable House of Commons, on the Present Important Crisis of National Affairs* (1762), esp. p. 29; Joseph Massie, *An Historical Account of the Naval Power of France* (1762); *A Letter from a Member of Parliament in Town, to his Friend in the Country, upon the Three Great Objects of Present Attention, Peace, Parties, and Resignations* (1763). For the views of one Pittite, see George Heathcote, *A Letter to the Right Honourable the Lord Mayor . . . of the City of London . . . From an Old Servant* (1762).

[195] See e.g. *The Reasons for Keeping Guadeloupe at a Peace, Preferable to Canada, Explained in Five Letters from a Gentlemen in Guadeloupe to his Friend in London* (1760), 8; *Remarks on the Letter Addressed to Two Great Men* (1761), 31

[196] *Remarks on the Letter Addressed to Two Great Men*, 13.

the humanity of British rule overseas; the implicit contrast here was with the cruelty and ignoble nature of the French and Spanish empires.[197]

In 1763, Britons were giddy with excitement about the scale of the military defeat recently inflicted on France, and the prospect of a secure and prosperous future unthreatened by French designs and international ambition. There were some who were beginning to be concerned that the military spirit created by the war was at odds with Britain's commercial identity.[198] One writer called on the nobility to lay aside their 'military trappings', warning that unless they did so Britain would see 'the System of military Subordination extending itself throughout the kingdom, universal Dependence upon Government influencing every Rank of Men, and the Spirit, nay the very Form of the Constitution destroyed.'[199] There were other shadows on the horizon—the size of the national debt, which had climbed massively since the last war, the need to introduce greater economy and efficiency into administration, the state of popular morals, the burden of tax on trade, even the possible restiveness of the North American colonies freed from the French threat.[200] Yet these were problems which were not yet pressing or which might be managed. Contemporaries also saw the military successes of the final years of the war in terms of a revival or vindication of public virtue and honour, as proof that a commercial society such as Britain in this period could still produce brave and selfless patriots and military heroes. Throughout Britain, testimonies to British military valour began to proliferate. The most famous example was the patriotic apotheosis of General Wolfe, who lost his life in the assault on Quebec in 1759.[201] The commemoration of Wolfe and his exploits in verse and visual art, also demonstrated how a discourse of sentimentalism, which was growing in influence in this period, served further to disguise the grimmer realities of war from its enthusiasts at home, and to construct warfare as a drama of national character and individual valour.[202] Yet Wolfe was only the brightest in the patriotic firmament of the Seven Years War, and only one among many whose deeds were celebrated and commemorated. Near Carnwarth, a little way outside of Edinburgh, a monument was erected to Alexander Lockhart, who, aged 18, had died at the Battle of Minden. The

---

[197] See e.g. *A Political Analysis of the War*, 2nd edn. (1762), 82, where the author writes: 'Are the noble, generous, humane capitulations we have every where given to the vanquish'd, the freedom, ease and liberty they enjoy under the British government . . .'

[198] See *A Letter to the Right Hon Earl of B——, On a Late Important Resignation, and its Probable Consequences* (1761); *A Letter to Two Great Men*, esp. pp. 46–7; Josiah Tucker, *The Case for Going to War, For the Sake of Procuring, Enlarging and Securing of Trade, Considered in a New Light* (1763).

[199] *A Letter Addressed to Two Great Men, On the Prospect of Peace; and on the Terms necessary to be insisted upon in the Negotiation* (London and Edinburgh, 1760), 46–7.

[200] For a balanced statement of the prospects in and promise of 1763, see *Propositions for Improving the Manufactures, Agriculture and Commerce of Great Britain* (1763).

[201] See e.g. the 'postscript' in the *Lond. Ev. P.*, 25–7 Oct. 1759 on the 'conquest of Quebec'.

[202] See the comments in David H. Solkin, *Painting For Money: The Visual Arts and the Public Sphere in Eighteenth-Century England* (New Haven, Conn. and London, 1993), ch. 5.

significance of this is only increased by the fact that Lockhart's grandfather was George Lockhart, who had been a leading Scottish Jacobite in the two decades or so which followed the Union of 1707.[203] Beyond this, however, few had begun to ponder the significance of the much-expanded agglomeration of territories, with its heterogeneous native populations, which Britain now ruled over, or indeed how they would be governed in Britain's interests. When they did begin to do so, in the years after the Peace of Paris, they would come to view empire and the impact of empire on their society and politics with a marked ambivalence. Many would also continue to cleave to the notion that the British empire was an 'empire of the seas', and not a territorial empire. Indeed, in the final stages of the next major war Britain was involved in—the War of American Independence—it was a conception of national identity which would offer succour to a nation bewildered by its apparently sudden fall from the peak of national greatness in 1763.[204]

[203] *Edinburgh Chronicle*, 15–18 Sept. 1759.
[204] See reactions to the naval victory over the French at the battle of the Saints in 1782, which was seen as confirmation that Britain's 'empire of the seas' remained intact. See e.g. *Public Advertiser*, 29, 30 May 1782. See also John Sinclair, *Thoughts on the Naval Strength of the British Empire* (1782); James Anderson, *The Interest of Great Britain with Regard to the American Colonies Considered* (1782).

CHAPTER FOUR

Scotland: Expunging the Memory of the '45

In the Pelham papers in the Newcastle (Clumber) manuscripts in Nottingham University Library is a memorandum entitled 'Some Considerations on the *Present* State of the Highlands of Scotland, Tending to shew What may be Expected to Happen—If France shall think fit, to Risk a Few Batallions, with some Arms & Money, And a Small Quantity of Meal—to feed the Common Highlanders, who are Starving—To be Landed on the Western Coast'.[1] The memorandum dates from the autumn of 1746, that is several months after the Highland army of 'Bonnie Prince Charlie' had been cut down on Drumossie Moor and before the sending away of British troops to the continent to resume the fight against France. Since Culloden, the British army had conducted a campaign of retribution against the disaffected clans which has recently been described as 'genocidal'.[2] Jacobite neighbourhoods had been subjected to, first, terroristic attack and, then, the calculated destruction of crops, livestock, and property. The memorandum represented a contribution to discussions about the prudence of denuding Scotland of troops at this point. The author counselled caution, emphasizing the vulnerability of the Highlands and the rebellious disposition of the Highlanders, despite the presence and actions of the military. The threat was not simply a Scottish one:

Should the Troops . . . Abandon the North; and Place themselves on the South side of the Forth—The Possession which the Rebels might Gain, of so great a tract of Country, twould Give this Attempt too much Reputation, & might Encourage Numbers, who have not yet pulled off the Mask, in Both Nations [i.e. England and Scotland], to declare themselves;—especially if France should Cause a Distraction of our Force, by any Attempts on Our Coast.

The author was convinced that the French would, given the cheapness and ease of such tactics, promote such a disturbance were the Duke of Cumberland and British troops to be transferred to the continent.

The memorandum serves as a powerful reminder that Culloden is not the end of the Jacobite story in Scotland and Britain. The '45 saw the final destruction of genuine military and political prospects for a Stuart restora-

---

[1] NUL, NeC 1865.
[2] Allan I. Macinnes, *Clanship, Commerce and the House of Stuart, 1603–1788* (East Linton, 1996), 211–17.

tion—it even perhaps exposed their already terminal condition—yet this is a judgement which is more easily made in retrospect.[3] Ministers, politicians, and supporters of the Hanoverian regime saw things differently at the time. For them, the '45 appeared to demonstrate—all too alarmingly—the continuing fragility of Hanoverian rule in Scotland and, therefore, Britain. The Duke of Cumberland declared simply, 'I tremble for fear that this vile spot may still be the ruin of this island and our family'.[4] Conditions in the Highlands remained disordered and unstable for some years following the suppression of the rebellion; Jacobite conspiracy and plotting continued; and the hopes of the disaffected in the Highlands and in Lowland Scotland rose and fell according to international developments and the stories told by Jacobite leaders and agents and Scots officers 'lurking' in the glens and straths. International conditions were also full of menace and unpredictability. Until 1748 and the end of the War of the Austrian Succession, France—as the author of the memorandum quoted from above recognized—offered the Jacobites the greatest hopes of military and diplomatic support for their cause. Even after 1748, international politics was, as was emphasized in the previous chapter, marked by intense diplomatic rivalry and recurrent fears of renewed European war. In the later 1740s and early 1750s, these were briefly focused on the Baltic. Prussia also emerged by 1753 as an unpredictable and hostile force in international diplomacy. The Jacobites were known to have good connections in Frederick the Great's Berlin, primarily through the Earl Marischal.

Against this background, it was widely believed that an effective solution to disaffection in the Highlands needed at last to be found. If it were not, the survival and future prosperity of the Hanoverian regime, Protestant religion, and trade would remain in doubt. The Highlander was to be transformed from a slavish, violent plunderer into an industrious, loyal subject. This was to be achieved through a combination of intimidation, exemplary 'justice', and social engineering. Amid the bleak, forbidding, unwelcoming terrain of the Highlands—'Britain's Siberia', as one contemporary put it[5]—commercial society was to be brought into being. The strategy was one of internal colonization or, as the colonizers happily saw it, liberation, through capitalism.

If commerce was the means of transforming Highland society, it was also the principal vehicle for the expression of a British patriotism in mid-eighteenth-century Scotland. The '45 produced a strong patriotic reaction in Scotland, providing the crucial impetus to a historic transformation in feelings and attitudes towards Scotland's place within the Union. In the later

[3] For recent views of the 'Forty-Five and the gravity of the threat it posed to the Hanoverian regime in Britain, see ibid.; W. A. Speck, *The Butcher: The Duke of Cumberland and the Suppression of the '45*, 2nd edn. (Gwynedd, 1995); Jeremy Black, *Culloden and the '45* (Stroud, 1990); Eveline Cruickshanks, *Political Untouchables: The Tories and the '45* (1979); Paul Kleber Monod, *Jacobitism and the English People, 1688–1788* (Cambridge, 1989); Bruce Lenman, *The Jacobite Risings in Britain, 1689–1746*, 2nd edn. (Aberdeen, 1995).
[4] Quot. in Annette M. Smith, *Jacobite Estates of the 'Forty-Five* (Edinburgh, 1982), 1.
[5] PRO, SP 54/37/31.

eighteenth century, Scots were to prove fiercely loyal subjects of the British crown, contributing disproportionately in terms of population to armed mobilizations and offering the staunchest support for British arms abroad. This period looks forward to this development. It was a shift in emotions and outlook which was, to some extent, forced on the Scots by the perception in England, hardened by the '45, that all Scots were disloyal and Jacobites at heart if not in deed. It was also a reflection, however, of currents of opinion and feeling that were sharpened by the rebellion and its aftermath. Many Scots competed to demonstrate their commitment to the Union and Scotland's place within Britain. Loyalty became the touchstone of politics. The often clumsy interventions in Scottish politics and administration of English ministers and officials in the later 1740s and early 1750s served both to complicate and underpin this process. Factional battles and struggles also continued, yet significantly these often involved disputes or allegations about loyalty.[6] When the Seven Years War broke out, the stage was set for the Scots to 'wipe away the stain' of their recent history.[7]

'LOYAL SCOTLAND' AND THE '45

While the outlines of a loyal Scotland came into sharper definition after the Jacobite Rebellion of 1745–6, they were clearly discernable during the crisis itself. The existence of this body of loyal Scots has tended to be overlooked in recent years. Rather, it has been assumed that most Scots who were not committed to rebellion reacted to the invasion with either indifference or passivity.[8] No doubt, many did respond in this way, including some sympathetic to the Jacobite cause, those who failed, as the author of the memorandum quoted from above put it, to 'pull off the mask'. As in towns and communities in northern England, the '45 created much disruption and panic.[9] The burgh authorities in Perth, for example, fled on the arrival of

---

[6] By the later 1740s, the squadrone faction, opponents of the Argathelians (followers of the Duke of Argyll), had all but broken down as a coherent force. This development was accelerated by efforts to broaden the governing interest in Scotland from 1746 to include loyal Whigs who were not members of Argyll's faction. Apart from the Argathelians, Scottish politics was dominated by interests often focused on individuals or families. See J. S. Shaw, *The Political History of Eighteenth-Century Scotland* (1999); Richard Scott, 'The Politics and Administration of Scotland, 1725–1748', Ph.D. thesis (Edinburgh University, 1981).

[7] A point strongly made by Alexander Murdoch in his *'The People Above': Politics and Administration in Mid-Eighteenth-Century Scotland* (Edinburgh, 1980), esp. p. 91.

[8] See esp. B. P. Lenman, 'A Client Society: Scotland between the '15 and the '45', in Jeremy Black (ed.), *Britain in the Age of Walpole* (1984), 93; Daniel Szechi and David Hayton, 'John Bull's Other Kingdoms: The English Government of Scotland and Ireland', in Clyve Jones (ed.), *Britain in the First Age of Party: 1680–1750: Essays Presented to Geoffrey Holmes* (1987), 256. It is perhaps worth noting that Lenman places rather different emphasis on the lack of support for Jacobitism during the '45 in his *The Jacobite Risings in Britain*, esp. p. 257.

[9] See esp. R. C. Jarvis, *Collected Papers on the Jacobite Risings* (2 vols., 1971).

Jacobite forces. The crisis also exposed chaos and ineptitude amongst officials in Scotland, although this also reflected divisions and suspicions amongst them. Just as in England, there was uncertainty about the legal position when it came to raising forces to meet the rebels. Civilians had little or no active military tradition to draw on and no training. There was also a lack of arms. Unlike in many parts of England, loyal activities also had to take place in the shadow or even in the presence of Jacobite forces.

Volunteer forces were, nevertheless, raised from the inhabitants of several important Scottish burghs—namely, Edinburgh, Glasgow, Paisley, Kilmarnock, Stirling, Renfrew, Perth, and Linlithgow.[10] On 17 November 1745, Mary Campbell wrote from Stirling: 'there has not been such a spirit of loyalty among almost the whole Burgess of many years. John Finlayson our friend is at the head of about 300 well look'd well Affected men.'[11] The disposition to raise volunteer forces was particularly strong, unsurprisingly perhaps, in the Whig Presbyterian strongholds of the south-west and west of Scotland. In late September, after the battle of Prestonpans, the Moderator of the Provincial Synod of Dumfries wrote to the Marquis of Tweeddale, since 1742 Secretary of State for Scotland: 'People are ready to take up arms *but* require proper Authority & necessary arms'.[12] Another individual, writing of the loyalty of the western counties of Scotland, declared in the same period:

I'm fully persuaded that between four and six thousand volunteers might be soon raised, in ye Counties of Renfrew, Clidsdale, and Air, and ye towns therein . . . If those men were raised and armed, under such leaders as they had any confidence in, they woud freely venture their lives, in defence of ye government.[13]

Seceders from the Church of Scotland seem to have been particularly keen to offer their services. In early December, there was a report that Seceders in Nithsdale and Galloway had joined some of the 'lowest people' in Dumfries and gone to Lockerbie and carried off part of the Jacobite army's baggage.[14] Lord Home reported in the same month that one hundred Seceders were prepared to join volunteer forces mobilizing to defend the pass at Stirling at

---

[10] The mobilization of volunteers in Edinburgh is described in the 'Memorial to His Royal Highness', Royal Archives, Windsor Castle, Cumberland Papers [RACP] (microfilm copy in the Cambridge University Library), Box 21/141–3; 'Memorial Stating the facts relative to the Conduct of the Toun of Glasgow during the present Rebellion, with proper Vouchers', RACP, Box 21/157–61; 'Memoriall for the Soldiers Volunteers serving in the Perth Independent Company under the Command of Capt James Campbell, 1746', Perth and Kinross Archives, A. K. Bell Public Library, Perth, B59/30/77; NLS, MS 16608 (Saltoun MS), fo. 2: list of Linlithgow volunteers; NLS, MS 16609 (Saltoun MS), fos. 77–8: Lord Home to Andrew Fletcher, 2 Dec. 1745 (for Paisley volunteers); NLS, MS 16609, fos. 86–7: Lord Home to Fletcher, 9 Dec 1745 (for Renfrew volunteers); NLS, MS 16609, fo. 164: Magistrates of Kilmarnock, n.d.
[11] NLS, MS 16605 (Saltoun MS), fo. 196.
[12] NLS, MS 7072 (Tweeddale MS), fo. 28.
[13] NUL, NeC 2204.
[14] NLS, MS 16604 (Saltoun MS), fos. 76–7.

their own expense.[15] A few weeks later, a captain of the militia from Stranraer reported: 'We are talking of raising volunteers, & nothing Hinders but want of Directors . . . the Country here seems all Hearty & takes it amiss that they have not an opportunity to rise in Defence of the present Govern[ment] . . .'.[16] In Kirkudbright, men were raised and exercised in several parishes.[17] Associations were formed in Renfrewshire, Clydesdale, and Stirling County.[18] In December, Duncan Forbes, Lord President of the Court of Session, wrote of expectations of help to prevent rebels crossing the Forth from Linlithgow and Kilsyth as well as Glasgow and Stirling.[19] Men were also mobilized into companies in and around Hamilton.[20]

As was the case south of the border, there was much uncertainty about the legal position in respect of volunteering and a fair amount of chaos. Thanks to the diligence of Lord Provost Andrew Cochrane in writing letters explaining and defending the conduct of its magistrates and citizens, events in Glasgow, which compiled an impressive record of loyal activity during the crisis, are relatively well documented. On 10 September, Cochrane wrote that the inhabitants of the city had been having several meetings to discuss how best to respond to the growing Jacobite menace. He emphasized, like many others at the time, the lack of direction from above; he also laid particular emphasis on the feelings in the city that their wealth made its inhabitants particularly vulnerable to depredations on the part of the Jacobite army. There was also a lack of military knowledge and experience amongst Glaswegians, as well as the fear that nothing effective could be done before the Jacobites were upon them.[21] It appears that an application was made to the Lord Justice Clerk for authority to raise forces and for arms.[22] In the event, nothing was done until the Jacobites had left Edinburgh towards the end of October. With Edinburgh having been secured by troops detached from Marshal Wade's forces, and with a second Jacobite army mobilizing around Perth, a new decision was taken to raise forces in the city. These were to be commanded by the Earl of Home. Six hundred troops were raised in nine days. This force was dispatched to guard the pass at Stirling, while a further force, also of 600, was raised for the defence of the town. With the retreat of the Jacobite army from England, the Glasgow regiment was marched to Edinburgh. It later fought at the battle of Falkirk, where one officer and eighteen privates were killed and three officers and around twenty men taken

---

[15] NLS, MS 16609, fos. 86–7.
[16] NLS, MS 16604, fo. 127.
[17] NLS, MS 16606, fos. 168–9.
[18] NLS, MS 16607, fos. 40–1, 122.
[19] Ibid., fo. 241.
[20] NLS, MS 16609, fo. 207.
[21] NLS, MS 16606, fos. 87–8.
[22] The warrants are mentioned by Tweeddale in a letter to Andrew Fletcher of 12 Sept. 1745 at NLS, MS 16608, fo. 219.

prisoner.[23] Leading men in counties and burghs looked to Lord Milton, the Lord Justice Clerk, for guidance about what was legal in respect of raising men in late 1745. Some despaired of making an effective defence. The JPs and commissioners of supply in Dumfries met in early September and declared that they were in no condition to attempt anything in their defence. The commissioners of supply also posed a series of questions: could they be supplied with arms from the public and on what terms; could the county legally 'gather together with such Arms as they have & Rendezvous, for which they shew the great Ardor'.[24] Warrants were sent to the magistrates of Glasgow and Aberdeen in early September to levy arms and men for their own defence. In Aberdeen, lists were taken up of all fencibles between the ages of 16 and 60, and the Provost declared that they intended to call regular musters. He also remarked, however, that he was unsure about the legal position and only possessed arms for about a third of the men.[25] In October, Fletcher was also arguing for raising forces in various counties—Berwickshire, East Lothian, Midlothian, Roxburghshire, and Dumfriesshire—although there was concern in London about the prudence of this measure.[26] From Paisley, there were complaints in early December that the many applications which had been made for authority to raise forces had to date been ignored.[27]

The military significance of the volunteer companies was small. Military resistance on the part of volunteers tended to dissolve on the appearance of Jacobite forces. Most of the Edinburgh volunteers raised before Prestonpans disbanded and gave up their arms before the battle, although about one hundred did join Cope's forces on the battlefield.[28] In Glasgow, fears about the potential consequences of raising volunteers and the threat from Highland forces were not easily lessened. The view was expressed that only the deployment of regular forces at Stirling would allay these anxieties.[29] In Stirling in December, once the regular troops were withdrawn to Edinburgh, and with the main Jacobite army in Glasgow, and other forces quartered around Perth, the defence of the town was left to the garrison at Stirling Castle and the Stirlingshire and Stirling volunteers. The town capitulated to Jacobite forces in early January without making any military resistance.[30] This led, as in other similar cases in Scotland and England, to allegations of disaffection. These were unfair, and ignore the military realities, the poor state of the defences in many towns, and, more importantly, the way in which panic could easily undercut loyal feelings and determination in the face of the much feared

[23] RACP, Box 21/157–61.
[24] NLS, MS 16607, fo. 81.
[25] NLS, MS 16610 (Saltoun MS), fo. 267.
[26] See NLS, MS 16609, fos. 32–5: Andrew Fletcher to Newcastle, 12 Oct. 1745.
[27] NLS, MS 16609, fos. 77–8.
[28] Speck, *The Butcher*, 47.
[29] NLS, 16606, fo. 203.
[30] John Brims, 'The Jacobites in Stirling', *Scottish Local History*, 36 (1996), 28–33.

Highland Jacobite army.[31] Moreover, the existence of lowland volunteers, militarily ineffective as they may have been, did serve to show, as several people argued at the time, that a Scottish commitment to the Hanoverian regime was not absent in 1745–6, particularly in traditionally Whig, Presbyterian regions.

It was a commitment which was revealed in several other ways. The full extent of this activity is difficult to recover as the sources are very patchy.[32] Linda Colley lists six loyal addresses from Scotland issued between September and mid-December (Glasgow, Edinburgh, Stirling, Dumfriesshire, Kirkudbright, and Ayr).[33] Parishioners in Lesmahagow seized an individual in Highland dress in November who was carrying letters.[34] In Dumfries, a subscription was raised for procuring men to enlist in the British army.[35] In early December, Sir Robert Dickson wrote that four hundred men from the parish of Inveresk were ready, on twelve hours' notice, to march to Edinburgh and take up arms for the defence of the city.[36] Just how many individuals and burgh officers provided intelligence and transport for the British army during the crisis we will never know, but a significant number did. The Provost and magistrates of Aberdeen made efforts to collect intelligence about rebel movements, which they then communicated to Lord Findlater and Forbes, the Lord President.[37] Throughout much of Scotland, individuals and groups engaged in minor, although sometimes costly in terms of their repercussions, acts of loyalty. The *Glasgow Journal* appears to have acted as an important loyal voice during the crisis, which led John Murray, the Young Pretender's secretary, to write in his master's name to the Lord Provost in late October:

Whereas many scurrilous and false reflections on our army as well as a number of Groundless reports are maliciously insert in the Glasgow Journal and particularly in the Journal of the twenty first inst. we therefor order and require you to search for seize and secure the person of the publisher of that newspaper entitled the Glasgow Journal whom you are to detain in secure custody untill our further orders; And you are hereafter carefully and diligently to inspect all news of other papers published at Glasgow that no reflections or reports be published there . . .[38]

---

[31] Scare stories about the brutality of the Highlanders were circulating widely in late 1745, many of them deliberately fostered as anti-Jacobite propaganda. Ironically, one effect of these may have been to underpin panic in many communities which found themselves under occupation by the Jacobite army or who lay on its route or possible route southwards.

[32] No copies of the two Glasgow papers, the *Glasgow Courant* and the *Glasgow Journal*, survive for late 1745, while the Edinburgh press was divided in its political allegiance. The *Scots Magazine* and English papers, which reprinted private letters from Scotland during the crisis, do contain a limited amount of relevant material. Otherwise, we are reliant on activities and events being reported in correspondence, most of which was more concerned (understandably) with the movements of rebel forces than conditions and feelings in the localities.

[33] Linda Colley, *Britons: Forging the Nation, 1707–1837* (New Haven, Conn. and London, 1992), 376–7.

[34] NLS, MS 16607, fo. 3.

[35] NLS, MS 16606, fos. 168–9.

[36] NLS, 16607, fo. 24.

[37] RACP, Box 21/132–3.

[38] NLS, MS 7073 (Tweeddale MS), fo. 5.

In Aberdeen in November, James Chalmers, who was printing news sheets—the precursor to the establishment in 1748 of the *Aberdeen Journal*—had his type and presses attacked by Jacobites, which suggests that he was printing material hostile to their cause. Chalmers had been forced to jump from a window in his house to escape the Jacobites, straining his leg in the act.[39]

Ministers of the Church of Scotland formed an impressive loyal phalanx during the rebellion, a fact of no small importance in a country in which the clergy retained greater importance in the mobilization of popular opinion than south of the border. The Commission of the General Assembly called in the second week of November for presbyteries and synods to call days of fasting 'as may best suit their several circumstances'. They also drew up and had printed in early December 'A Seasonable Warning to the People Concerning the Danger of Popery and Subversion of our happy Constitution in Church & State'. This was to be read out in pulpits with suitable 'Exhortations' to loyalty.[40] The Presbytery of Edinburgh had called a fast as early as the end of August.[41] Other presbyteries and synods followed suit, not waiting for the direction of the Commission. The minutes for the Presbytery of Forfar noted on 11 December that the proclamation for a fast had not arrived, but that they were determined 'to see such occasion observed.'[42] Fasts were held at intervals throughout the crisis.[43] The Synod of Glasgow and Ayr had drawn up its own 'Memorial and Admonition' for reading out in pulpits at the beginning of October.[44] The Commission and lesser bodies of the Church also issued loyal resolutions and addresses. Many ministers refused to be intimidated or cowed by Jacobite soldiers. In early September, a detachment of 200 rebel soldiers entered Dundee to proclaim the Pretender, and search for arms and ammunition. The magistrates pointedly remained in the town. The ministers went to their churches on Sunday and prayed for King George II.[45] In Highland parishes, several ministers acted as spies, sending intelligence about rebel movements to the authorities in Edinburgh, a role some of their number continued to play after 1746.[46] Throughout Lowland Scotland, a significant number continued, like their Dundee counterparts, to pray for George II and the royal family during services. In Dundee in December, by

[39] 'Extracts from the Diary of the Rev John Bisset, Minister at Aberdeen, 1745–6', *Miscellany of the Spalding Club*, 1 (1891), 355.
[40] NAS, CH1/3/24 (Records of the Commission of the General Assembly, 1739–48), fos. 402–3, 406–14.
[41] NAS, CH2/121/15, fos. 372, 374–6.
[42] NAS, CH2/159/2 (Minutes of the Presbtery of Forfar, 1743–8). The Presbytery of Dunfermline appointed a day of fasting on 1 Nov. (CH2/105/7, fos. 5–11), while the Presbytery of Paisley appointed one on 1 Oct. (CH2/294/9 (Minute Book of the Presbytery of Paisley, 1735–)).
[43] A fast was called by royal proclamation for 18 December 1745. The Commission of the General Assembly called further fasts on 20 January and 13 March 1746.
[44] NAS, CH2/464/3, fos. 355–9.
[45] NLS, MS 7071 (Tweeddale MS), fos. 107–8.
[46] See RACP, Box 21/412, for comment on the role of clergy in Caithness during the crisis. See also below, p. 165.

then under the control of Jacobite forces, it was decided that no public preaching would take place as long as ministers were forbidden to pray for George II.[47] In Aberdeen, ministers gathered together to pray 'against the trouble of Israel' during the Jacobite occupation of the town.[48] The synod of Aberdeen also recommended to all its members to 'pray *nomination* for King George'.[49] Presbyterian ministers were also obstructing Jacobite recruitment with some success in and around Aberdeen in October 1745.[50] Edinburgh ministers actively supported the raising of loyal volunteers in the capital in November.[51] It is doubtful, however, that many went as far in their loyalty as the Revd Mr Davidson of the parish of Navar in Angus between Glen Clova and Glen Esk. In 1746, Davidson assembled around sixty of his parishioners, who, supporting themselves at their own expense, sought to guard the passes in the lower parts of Angus.[52]

After the crisis had passed, the loyalty of the ministers was frequently proclaimed by the General Assembly, and widely acknowledged by others. In May 1748, General Bland, then commander of the British forces in Scotland, wrote to one minister in Nether Banchory in the north east: 'The Steadiness of the Clergy dur:g the Late unnatural Rebellion, & the great Zeal they shew'd dur:g the Late progress of it, wou'd make me stretch any Power to serve them . . .'.[53] Some ministers were subject to harassment from rebels and disappointed Jacobites in the months and years after 1746, further testimony to the importance and visibility of the loyal role which they had played. Ministers in and around Aberdeen were victims of a rash of violent robberies.[54] In the parish of Cortachy and Clova, the Rev William Brown was harried from his position as minister because of antipathy created by his activities during the crisis. In the autumn of 1746, the Earl of Albermarle and Lieutenant General Huske wrote to the Duke of Cumberland on Brown's behalf. The petition described Brown's services during the rebellion, which included relieving prisoners held by the Jacobites at Glamis Castle, and corresponding with officers stationed in the neighbourhood of his parish. He also conducted the military party which had apprehended the killers of an individual who had been murdered for his efforts to aid the prisoners at Glamis. This had apparently

---

[47] Dundee Archives and Record Centre, CH1/212/2, Dundee General Session Minutes, 1716–1756, 21 Dec., 28 Dec. 1745, 16 Jan. 1746.

[48] Prayer meetings appear to have been common throughout Scotland and were encouraged by the Commission of the General Assembly. In Edinburgh, ministers were meeting almost daily for prayers from November until the suppression of the rebellion (NAS, CH2/121/15). For similar meetings in Glasgow and the west, see NAS, CH2/464/3.

[49] 'Extracts from the Diary of the Rev John Bisset', 349.

[50] *Miscellany of the Spalding Club*, 1 (1891), 403, 410.

[51] NAS, CH2/121/15, fo. 385.

[52] RACP, Box 44/230.

[53] NLS, MS 304, fo. 71. See also John Campbell, *A Full and Particular Description of the Highlands of Scotland* (1752), 41.

[54] NAS, CH1/3/24, fos. 466–7, 499. See also below, pp. 178–9.

rendered Brown 'extreamly odious and obnoxious to the Rebels & disaffected in that country'. Brown was recommended for presentation to the parish of Fordoun in Mearns.[55] Brown remained at Cortachy until 1747 when he was finally allowed by the Presbytery of Forfar to demit his office. During this time, he appears to have been subject to a campaign of hostile rumours—some concerning an illegitimate child; he even claimed that threats had been made on his life.[56]

Several ministers did fall below the standard of loyal conduct expected from them; however, they were a tiny minority. Thomas Man, minister of Dunkeld, was suspended between May and November 1747 while his conduct in late 1745 was investigated. Man's behaviour appears to have been that of someone who allowed prudence to outweigh loyalty to George II rather than simple disaffection. Faced with leading Jacobites from occupying forces in his congregation, he omitted to pray for the royal family. James Ker, minister of the parish of Duns, was accused of entertaining rebels in early 1746; he was also absent from his parish during the crisis.[57]

The Church also played a prominent part in combating disaffection in the aftermath of the crisis. Efforts were made to ensure that no official of the Church who had shown disloyalty during the '45 remained in post thereafter. Schoolmasters, as educators of the young, were subject to particular scrutiny.[58] Ministers were also used to collect information about disaffection in their parishes.[59] In 1747, the Commission of the General Assembly responded to the general pardon passed in that year by ordering ministers to be 'at all pains in dealing with these People [returned rebels] in order to Extirpate out of their minds the seeds of Disloyalty and reconcile them to the present Government of which they have so lately experienced great clemencie'.[60] In 1749, the General Assembly agreed that ministers should deliver quarterly sermons on the 'Principles of Reformation and Revolution', although some appear to have seen this as unnecessary.[61] There was also renewed debate about the role of the Church as a proselytising force in disaffected regions, with a view

[55] PRO, SP 54/36/16B.

[56] NAS, CH1/1/51, fos. 442–5; BL, Egerton MS 3433, fos. 196–7. Brown subsequently settled in Utrecht as minister of the English congregation there. In 1756, he was presented to the Professorship of Ecclesiastical History at St Andrew's University. This produced a protest from the Presbytery of St Andrew's about Brown's fitness for office, and an attempt to block Brown's appointment, an attempt upheld by the relevant synod. The General Assembly dismissed the process, however, thereby enabling Brown to take up his post.

[57] For Ker, see NAS, CH1/3/26 (Records of the Commission of the General Assembly, 1748–57), fo. 82; for Man, see CH1/3/24 (Records of the Commission of the General Assembly, 1739–48), fos. 483–93.

[58] NAS, CH1/1/45 (Records of the General Assembly, 1746–9), fos. 78–9.

[59] In June 1746, the Lord Justice Clerk wrote to ministers to draw up lists of parishioners who had supported the rebellion. For one presbytery's difficulties in responding to this request, see NAS, CH2/159/2 (Minutes of the Presbytery of Forfar, 1743–8), fos. 107, 120–1, 122–3.

[60] NAS, CH1/3/24, fo. 506.

[61] NAS, CH1/1/45, fos. 503–5.

crystalizing that rather than continuing to support itinerant ministers and catechists in large Highland parishes, the royal bounty to support missionary activity in the Highlands should be used to create new, smaller parishes.[62]

Loyal Scots found other opportunities during the rebellion to demonstrate their attachment to the Hanoverian regime. This activity was, moreover, not confined to the west and south west of the country. Events in Aberdeen in late 1745 and early 1746 are described in some detail in the diary of a local minister, the Revd John Bisset. Bisset was an opponent of the Union with England, but loyal to the Hanoverian and Protestant Succession. On 24 October, he noted that the drum beats of Jacobite recruiting parties in the town were being greeted by cries from boys in town of 'God save King George'. The Jacobite governor of the city tried to prevent celebration of the King's birthday on 30 October. The attempt was unsuccessful, and the usual bonfires were spontaneouly lit in the streets, which rang with loyal cries. On 20 January, Prince Frederick's birthday, 'young people' rang the college and church bells. As on 30 October, there were also bonfires and loyal cries.[63] This loyal crowd, in which the youth of the town seems to have played a large role, was opposed by a Jacobite one. The latter created its own counter-theatre of Stuart 'loyal' celebration during the same months.[64]

Celebrations of George II's birthday, a major calendrical occasion in early-Hanoverian Scotland, were not confined to Aberdeen in 1745.[65] With its well-established (and well-understood) forms of public celebration, the Monarch's birthday provided an excellent opportunity for loyal Scots publicly to demonstrate their repugnance for the Jacobites and their commitment to George II and his rule. In Dundee and Perth, loyal inhabitants used the occasion to attack occupying Jacobite soldiers.[66] In Perth, the moving forces behind the demonstrations were the maltmen and trades lads. They seem to have decided to conduct the normal festivities of the day despite the fact that the town was under Jacobite control. Events culminated in clashes with Jacobite soldiers guarding arms stored in the council house. An attack on the council house led to the death of one loyal weaver, George Gorrie, and four of the attackers being wounded. When Jacobite reinforcements entered Perth on the following day, many of the loyal mob fled. A substantial number of them made their way to Stirling Castle where they enrolled in a loyal volunteer regiment—General Blakeney's Company of Perthmen. They appear to have seen little action, apart from digging fortifications around the castle. Nor did they

---

[62] The debates about the erection of new parishes can be followed in the records of the General Assembly and that body's Commission.

[63] 'Extracts from the Diary of the Rev John Bisset', 352–3, 369–70.

[64] Ibid., 361, 370.

[65] For a fuller discussion of these celebrations, and of the significance of the King's birthday in the Scottish political calendar, see Bob Harris and Christopher A. Whatley, ' "To Solemnize his Majesty's Birthday"; New Perspectives on Loyalism in George II's Britain', *History*, 83 (1998), 397–419.

[66] Events in Dundee are described in Annette Smith, 'Dundee and the '45', in Lesley Scott-Moncrieff (ed.), *The '45: To Gather an Image Whole* (Edinburgh, 1988), 99–112. For Perth, see *Scots Mag.*, 7 (1745), 492.

receive much financial support, and in 1746 they were forced to issue a memorial to Blakeney complaining about their treatment.[67] The loyalty of the
Perthmen was not repaid, and the coda to this story is a miserable one. In a
memorandum drawn up a few years later, the widow and children of George
Gorrie were alleged to be starving; William Robinson, a maltster disabled by
the attack on the council house, was living on 'common charity'; Robert
Gardiner, who led the attack, had been forced to leave the town for four
months afterwards, and was now 'in the most miserable circumstances'.[68]

The view that all Scots were rebels or potential rebels, which was current
in England during and in the immediate aftermath of the rising, was, therefore, a false one, as some Scots protested at the time. Murray Pittock has
recently talked of Lowland displays of loyalty having to await the 'distancing'
of Jacobitism in the 1740s and 1750s.[69] He has also sought to draw attention to the level of Jacobite support in the Lowlands. Given the fluidity of
Jacobite forces, the high rate of turnover of men, any estimate of numbers is
necessarily tentative. Nevertheless, the second Jacobite army which mobilized around Perth in December 1745 probably included a few thousand
Lowlanders.[70] An extremely conservative estimate of Lowlanders in arms to
defend the Hanoverian regime would be around 3,000. The existence of this
loyal Scotland in 1745–6 was to have some significance for years after the crisis,
serving to expose further the political fault lines which ran through Scottish
society, notably (but not exclusively) between Presbyterian and Episcopalian.
Yet in another sense, it counted for little. The task of distancing Scotland from
the events of 1745–6, of extinguishing the Jacobite threat and the taint of
disloyalty from the Scottish body politic had to begin anew.

EXTINGUISHING THE TAINT OF DISLOYALTY

The obstacles which stood in the way of establishing the loyalty of the Scots
in the aftermath of the '45 were considerable. They included the anti-Scottish
prejudices of English ministers, politicians, and military men, stoked to new
heights by the rebellion. The Duke of Cumberland's loathing of Scotland and
the Scots—recall the reference to the country as this 'vile spot' quoted
earlier—is well known. It was also significant because of Cumberland's continuing influence on Scottish politics and ministerial policy towards Scotland
after 1746.[71] William Keppel, Earl of Albermarle, who commanded British
forces in North Britain following Cumberland's departure for the continent at

[67] Perth and Kinross Archives, A. K. Bell Public Library, Perth, B59/30/77.
[68] RACP, Box 44/230.
[69] Murray G. H. Pittock, *The Myth of the Jacobite Clans* (Edinburgh, 1995), 10.
[70] See NLS, MS 3733 (Campbell Letters), fos. 46, 47.
[71] This was at its greatest between 1746 and 1748. For which, see B. F. Jewell, 'The Legislation
Relating to Scotland after the Forty-Five', Ph.D. thesis (University of North Carolina, 1975) [microfilm
copy in the NLS]. See also Murdoch, '*The People Above*'.

the end of the summer of 1746, also despised the Scots, thinking them universally disaffected or self-interested. He was desperate to follow Cumberland quickly to the continent, where he sensed (wrongly as it turned out) the opportunities for advancement and military glory lay. In early January 1747, he summed up his feelings for the country and its inhabitants: 'I neither like ye Country, ye Inhabitants or ye air'.[72] Similar sorts of attitudes, although less marked, were displayed by General Humphrey Bland, his successor who was to serve as commander of forces in Scotland between 1747 and 1751 and again between 1753 and 1756. In early February 1748, Bland offered Newcastle the following sketch of Scottish character: 'A Rapacious low cunning is the characteristick of the People of this Country. It is their Chief, or rather their only study, and to Gain Riches, they will sacrifice their Friends, Relations, and their oaths even to the Best of Princes.'[73] A common complaint, levelled particularly against the judges of the Court of Session, was that they were 'Highland' sympathizers because of their slowness in expediting punitive legal measures against rebel clan leaders and their estates.[74] The 3rd Duke of Argyll, the leading Scottish political figure of the period, sought to shield Scotland from some of the more clumsy interventions of English ministers, a role which was misunderstood or viewed with impatience in some circles south of the border. For a short time after 1754, following the death of Henry Pelham, who was a conciliatory influence on Anglo-Scottish political relations in the 1740s and 1750s, the Duke of Newcastle sought, with limited success, to create a stronger group of so-called 'King's friends' in Scottish administration to secure (as he saw it) greater compliance with English rule and ambition.[75] The English were also suspicious of tight connections which bound the relatively small Scottish political community together.

Disagreements amongst Scots about how best to treat Jacobites, suspected Jacobites, and the Highlands after 1746 added another layer of difficulty to the task of undermining English suspicions of the Scots. Loyal Scots were divided between those who, on the one hand, looked for severity in punishment and treatment of the rebels and suspected rebels, and those who, on the other, counselled moderation. Lord Edlin, an English baron of the exchequer, wrote to Pelham in late 1751: 'One sett of the King's friends here think proper to take the part of great moderation and lenity to all that were concerned in or favoured the late Rebellion . . . The others are keen Whigs and shew great zeal against the Jacobites . . .'[76]. As will be further emphasized below, some of the punitive legislation against the Highlands and disaffected Scots passed in the aftermath of the rebellion aroused the opposition of leading Scottish

---

[72] NUL, NeC 1770: Albermarle to Pelham, 17 Jan. 1747.

[73] PRO, SP 54/38/25A. See also Lenman, *The Jacobite Risings in Britain*, 269.

[74] For Cumberland's similar judgement of Duncan Forbes of Culloden for counselling moderation in 1746, see Lenman, *The Jacobite Risings in Britain*, 264.

[75] Murdoch, '*The People Above*', esp. chs. 2 and 3.

[76] NUL, NeC 1885/2: Edlin to Pelham, 23 Nov. 1751.

politicians. Argyll and his supporters, for example, opposed the abolition of private jurisdictions in 1747.[77] The attempt to outlaw Highland dress was also seen as needlessly provocative and likely to prove counter-productive by a section of Scottish Whig opinion, which included Lord Milton, Argyll's man of business in Edinburgh.[78]

Distancing Scotland from the taint of disloyalty also involved confronting the problem of a recalcitrant Jacobite interest in Scottish politics, as well as frequent allegations about the health and vigour of this interest. The idea that calm and peace rapidly descended on Scottish politics after the '45, and that this was reflected in the accelerating pace of improvement in Scotland in the mid-eighteenth century, is a common misreading of Scottish and British history in this period. A Jacobite interest, or amalgam of interests, remained deeply rooted in Scottish society, as most Scots were aware. It also appears to have remained remarkably confident in the face of the defeat of the Young Pretender and the onslaught against some of its props, for example non-juring meeting houses and ministers, after 1746. In Edinburgh in 1746, there was a 'surprizing, audacious and impudent' attempt to celebrate the Young Pretender's birthday, an attempt foiled only by deploying infantry troops in the Cannongate, and dragoons on the links at Leith. Guards were also posted on roads leading from Leith into the capital, and detachments of troops attended magistrates who visited the houses of the disaffected and those who were suspected of disaffection.[79] Accusations were frequently made that the disaffected were flourishing in Scotland after the '45.[80] Jacobites and Jacobite sympathisers fought a rearguard action against punishment in the courts. Some soldiers found themselves the subject of lawsuits brought against them for damages allegedly inflicted on the plaintiffs during and the immediate aftermath of the rebellion.[81] False claims were entered against the forfeited estates, a source of endless delay and complication. Cameron of Fassifern was to be banished from Scotland in 1755 for just such a tactic. In disaffected regions and communities, those who had displayed conspicuous loyalty could easily find themselves ostracized or worse. One of the saddest cases, if true, was that of Alexander Hay. Hay joined the British army during the rebellion, but by so doing allegedly lost his friends and business in Banffshire. After the rebellion, efforts were made to provide for him in the linen industry, but these came to nothing. No longer able to maintain himself, Hay, now 'out of his senses', was put into gaol.[82] As we will see below, non juring ministers and their

---

[77] See below, pp. 168–9.

[78] J. S. Shaw, *The Management of Scottish Society 1707–1764: Peers, Nobles, Lawyers, Edinburgh Agents and English Influences* (Edinburgh, 1983), 197.

[79] PRO, SP 54/34/55A–C.

[80] See e.g. the anonymous reports sent by 'P.O.' to Henry Pelham (NUL, NeC 1842–58).

[81] NUL, NeC 2079: 'Abuses or Neglects in the general Management of Scotland, since the Rebellion, 1752'. This mentions five lawsuits against soldiers.

[82] RACP, Box 44/270.

congregations appear to have regrouped with considerable speed after the intimidation levelled against them by Cumberland and his forces. (Many Episcopalian meeting houses were put to fire or destroyed in 1746.) They also quickly found ways of flouting or circumventing the law which sought to prevent their meeting or to force them to pray for the royal family.

Quite a few Scots also interpreted the acquittal of the former Lord Provost of Edinburgh, Archibald Stewart, as a notable victory for the Jacobites and their sympathizers.[83] Stewart was charged with negligence and obstructing efforts to defend the city against the rebel army, and prevent its occupation, in late 1745: charges Stewart strongly refuted. There were hopes (even expectations) amongst leading legal officers that Stewart would be convicted. The Lord Provost, George Drummond, scribbled a note on the evening of the 31 October—on hearing 'dark hints' that the jury were going to acquit his predecessor—'On Monday, I reckon we shall see the Jacobites triumphing at the cross'. On 3 November, both Edinburgh newspapers carried notices of a celebration to be held to mark Stewart's acquittal. Lord Milton, the Lord Justice Clerk, wrote to the Duke of Newcastle, in London: 'The unsuccessful issue whereof [of the trial] gives me great pain. The Behaviour of the Jacobites & their deluded partizans on this occasion has been most insolent and does not abate as your Grace will see by the paragraph in the inclosed news paper.' Milton also had a meeting with General Bland and Drummond where it was agreed to maintain a close watch on proceedings, and, in the event of any illegality, to prosecute with 'the utmost rigour of the law'.[84] Under direction from Milton, Drummond and the Edinburgh magistrates also succeeded in preventing the planned celebration. They also arrested the printer of a poem published to mark the occasion.[85] By contrast, the relative success of Scottish legal officers in proceeding against rebels excepted from the Act of Indemnity in 1747 was viewed as a major success. In October 1748, William Grant wrote, somewhat anxiously, to Pelham: 'I hope the success that has been in finding Bills against so many of the Rebels will be well received in England & elsewhere.' Another contemporary described the trials against the rebels as 'a Thunderbolt on the Jacobites & a verry [sic] seasonable one'.[86]

Claims of disloyalty in post-rebellion Scotland were, nevertheless, not always what they seemed and on closer investigation could dwindle into

[83] See NUL, NeC 1942: Earl of Morton to Pelham, 14 July 1747; NeC 1849/2: 'P.O.' to Pelham, 16 Nov. 1747; NAS, GD 248/572/8 (Seafield Papers), fo. 1: Lord Hardwicke to Lord Findlater, 25 Aug. 1747; GD 248/572/21, fo. 1: Findlater to Hardwicke, 19 Sept. 1747.

[84] PRO, SP 54/37/19A.

[85] PRO, SP 54/37/22A and 27. The poem is to be found at SP 54/37/17 and is entitled 'A Poem Compos'd the Second of November, 1747 The Day the Honourable ARCHIBALD STUART, Esq: was assoilzed from his Second TRIAL'. What particularly alarmed the authorities about the poem was the bitter attack on Cumberland and British military savagery contained in the opening verses.

[86] NUL, NeC 1968: William Grant to Pelham, 18 Oct. 1748; NUL, NeC 1858/1: 'P.O.' to Pelham, 17 Nov. 1748.

relative insignificance. Charges of Jacobitism were common currency in Scotland after 1746, as indeed they had been before. Thomas Hay of Hunting-don, for example, had to endure a major investigation into allegations that he was tainted with disloyalty before being appointed to the Court of Session in 1754, a charge that almost certainly came from a group of politicians around the Earl of Hopetoun unhappy about his elevation.[87] Few were exempt from imputations of disloyalty. Lord Milton, who played a crucial part in suppress-ing the rebellion from Scotland, was the subject of just such a denunciation a few years after the crisis.[88] George Drummond, who had led one of the Edinburgh volunteer companies in the '45 and who led the effort to secure the Scottish capital's government for loyal whigs after the rebellion, was also accused of being sympathetic to Jacobites, if not worse.[89] Whig loyalists who felt their own claims were being advanced too slowly, or who were suspicious of those who had links with suspected Jacobites, found it all too easy to make spurious allegations about allegiances.[90]

Relatively few allegations of disloyalty survived close examination. Some individuals were expelled from their positions in the revenue service in 1746, and a handful were removed in 1752 following further allegations about Jacobite office holding initiated by the Duke of Bedford, influenced by Cumberland, in the House of Lords debate on the Annexation bill. What impresses about the response to these allegations is the thoroughness with which they were investigated, and how many were dismissed as false or partial. In the aftermath of the rebellion, seven excise officers, twenty-one customs officers, and seventeen officials in the salt department were dismissed.[91] In 1752, the enquiries drew in officials in the revenue services, sheriff deputes, officers in the army, ministers of the Church, and local magistrates. The amount of paperwork generated was formidable. A draft copy of the eventual report submitted by Pelham to George II runs to twenty-five sections, each

[87] Murdoch, 'The People Above', 54.
[88] RACP, Box 44/231.
[89] James Mackay, *The Spirit of Loyalty, and of Rebellion, During some Late Troubles, Detected, in the Conduct of the Commissioners of Excise in Scotland: And of an officer, who distinguished himself in Behalf of the Government* (1755), esp. p. 21.
[90] One of the most determined was James Mackay, an excise officer at Tain in the northern Highlands. Mackay was to be dismissed from his position in 1752, for making allegations of disaffec-tion against fellow officers and two of the commissioners of the excise in Edinburgh. Mackay, who had played a notably loyal part during the rebellion, promptly took himself to London, where he bombarded ministers with petitions against his treatment and arguing that he had information about disaffection within the excise service. He also threatened to take his accusations to the Dukes of Bedford and Cumberland, at this point raising their own allegations about the administration of Scotland. It was perhaps to forestall this that Pelham provided him with money and directed him to return to Edinburgh to make some investigations. Relations with the excise commissioners were under-standably strained, and nothing much resulted. In 1754, on Pelham's death, he received no further support from ministers, prompting him in 1755 to publish his case and his allegations in a pamphlet. In 1756, he petitioned the Treasury for reimbursement of expenses, claiming that he was a 'ruined' man. See PRO, T1/351/38 and 39; 353/56/ 355/7.
[91] NUL, NeC 2156.

section comprising four sides.[92] It resulted in several further dismissals. In total, it seems that the original charges made by Bedford and his allies led to one dismissal from the customs services and two from the excise services. Four allegations against revenue officers were found to be groundless. A susbsequent general enquiry led to three further dismissals from the customs administration. Fourteen revenue officers were, however, cleared of any imputations of disloyalty. Some of the allegations made in 1752 look as if they were calculated to cause trouble and embarassment rather than anything else. For example, Colin Campbell of Glenure and Robert Campbell of Barcaldine, highlanders who were appointed factors on the forfeited estates, were alleged to be Jacobites. In this case, there may actually have been some substance to the allegations, but the real point was that the issue of appointing highlanders as factors on these estates was politically very sensitive.[93] In 1752, it was Campbell of Glenure who was famously assassinated because he was turning Jacobites out of their tenancies on the forfeited estates of Charles Stewart of Ardshiel. The Earl of Breadalbane saw the manner of his death as ample refutation of the tenacious rumours of Glenure's disaffection.[94] It was easy in the aftermath of the '45, with anxiety about disloyalty raised, and politicians in England ready to make political capital out of them, to throw allegations of disaffection about, although this was nothing new in Scottish politics. As George Vaughan put it: 'Calling a Jacobite has made many a mans fortune in my time, there certainly are such in Scotland, and in England, but I believe many yt [that] is called so, may with as much justice be call'd son of a whore.'[95]

The campaign to destroy Jacobitism and the taint of disloyalty after the '45 had, therefore, to take place against a background of a Scotland divided about how best to deal with the Jacobite threat and very uncertain about the favour or at least good will of English ministers, politicians, and public opinion. At times, Scotland was treated, especially by English military officers, as a conquered country. There was an intolerance of the compromises and evasions that most divided communities indulge in for the sake of relative peace and harmony. To the military and other English officials in Scotland, things tended to be viewed in starkly simple terms. They expected enthusiastic

[92] The draft is to be found at NUL, NeC 2224.

[93] Young Glengarry alleged that he had regularly met Campbell of Glenure at the Buck Club in Edinburgh, where they had 'always' drunk the Pretender's health (NUL, NeC 2,086/1: 'Narrative and Information from Alexander Macdonald of Glengarry'). See also Angus Stewart, 'The Last Chief: Dougal Stewart of Appin (died 1764)', *Scottish Historical Review*, 76 (1997), 219. As Stewart notes, Campbell of Glenure had suffered because of the policy on the Argyll estates of introducing from 1737 commercial bidding for tenancies. Ironically, this had the effect of alienating traditional tacksmen such as Campbell of Glenure, who found themselves outbid by Jacobites.

[94] Stewart, 'The Last Chief', 219. Breadalbane's recommendation had been instrumental in Glenure's appointment, whch may explain his reaction.

[95] NLS, MS 5078 (Erskine Murray Correspondence), fo. 80: George Vaughan to Charles Areskine, 30 July 1754.

cooperation in the implementation of punitive legislation; if this was not forthcoming it indicated culpable negligence or more probably disloyalty. Yet the military and England perspectives were not simply a produce of bigotry, an over-heated imagination, or plain ignorance. They also reflected the perception or fear that the disaffected clans continued to represent the greatest menace to peace on British soil.

DEFEATING HIGHLAND JACOBITISM

Ministers in London and their colleagues in Edinburgh were, as referred to at the start of this chapter, far from assuming that the spirit of disaffection in the Highlands had collapsed after Culloden. Ministers, officials, and military officers maintained a very close watch on the region, testimony to their concern. The intelligence network that was created or improvised comprised military officers stationed in the Highlands, ministers of the Church, itinerant ministers of the Scottish Society for the Promotion of Christian Knowledge (SSPCK), and revenue officers.[96] Letters were regularly intercepted by the post office, and customs officers directed to search incoming ships for mail and attainted rebels seeking to return to Scotland. In late 1746, the Lord Justice Clerk employed one Patrick Campbell, who had undertaken a similar role during the rebellion, to travel through the Highlands collecting intelligence.[97] At around the same time, Albermarle was assuring Newcastle that he had procured 'proper people' among the clans to collect information.[98] These individuals appear to have created their own networks of informers.[99] Military officers also created their own networks of informers in their localities and were expected to report back regularly to the commander in chief of British forces in Scotland. Not all were successful. In April 1747, Lieutenant General William Blakeney wrote from Inverness about his difficulties in securing good intelligence despite assurances of secrecy and offers of monetary reward.[100] In December 1747, General Bland had an officer sent to Mull to make enquiries about reports that a ship had landed there. This individual was

[96] Bits of it can be pieced together from various sources. Especially illuminating are the letter books of successive commanders of British forces stationed in Scotland (NLS, MS 304–9). There is, however, no work on the mid-eighteenth century comparable to Paul Fritz's *The English Ministers and Jacobitism between the Rebellions of 1715 and 1745* (Toronto, 1975). There is also relevant material in the Erskine Murray papers in the National Library of Scotland, the papers of the Earl of Holderness in the British Library, and the Cumberland papers at Windsor. There was also a lively international market for military and political intelligence in this period.

[97] PRO, SP 54/34/42C, 43A.

[98] PRO, SP 54/34/13A.

[99] See e.g. PRO, SP 54/37/136, where Ensign James Stewart, one of Albermarle's informants, describes securing the services of a former officer in the rebel Appin regiment and of a minister in Lochaber.

[100] PRO, SP 54/36/10.

also to see whether the officer stationed there had neglected his duty and if so to arrest him. A month later, Bland was writing to another military officer in the Highlands about his dissatisfaction with the reports about conditions and activities in the area of his command that he was sending back to Edinburgh.[101]

Ministers in the south had their own sources of intelligence in Scotland and on the continent, where the activities and movements of attainted rebels were carefully scrutinized. An important figure in this context was Richard Wolters, resident in Rotterdam. Wolters also had a Paris correspondent who reported on Jacobite relations with the French Court; he also had correspondents in Liège, Brussels, and Emden.[102] It was through Wolters that efforts to watch French ports were intensified in 1755–6.[103] It was also through Wolters that ministers sought details on the common practice of Scottish recruits to Dutch regiments deserting once on the continent and joining French regiments.[104] Leading officials in Edinburgh were frequently called on to pursue enquiries in Scotland about information that had come into the hands of ministers in London. In April 1749, the Duke of Newcastle wrote to Charles Areskine, the Lord Justice Clerk, about a report that the Young Pretender had left Avignon in France to go to Scotland. Areskine was asked to discover the truth of this report and take appropriate action if the report was substantiated in conjunction with General Churchill.[105] There were also several former rebels and clansmen willing to offer information. The most famous example is 'Pickle', Young Glengarry, who kept ministers informed about the Elibank plot (1751–3). As was mentioned in an earlier chapter, it was information provided by 'Pickle' which enabled the seizure of Archibald Cameron, brother of Cameron of Lochiel, near Inversnaid in 1753. Another to offer information was the slippery James Drummond, reprobate son of Rob Roy Macgregor, although no enthusiasm for this was shown by politicians and officers in Scotland. Drummond faced a charge of assisting in the abduction and rape of a 19-year-old widow and heiress, and was looking to squirm his way out of conviction and hanging. Another who appears to have passed information to the military was Cameron of Gleneves.[106]

Official concern about the Highlands fluctuated according to international

---

[101] NLS, MS 304, fo. 9: Bland to Governor Campbell, 22 Dec. 1747; fo. 27: Bland to Governor Campbell, 25 Jan. 1748.

[102] See BL, Egerton MS 3465 and 3466.

[103] Wolters arranged new correspondents at Brest, Furnes, and Dunkirk.

[104] One estimate put the number of such deserters at 600 a year. BL, Egerton MS 3466, fos. 152–3. The practice reflected efforts to prevent Scots officers in French regiments recruiting in the aftermath of the '45.

[105] NLS, MS 5076 (Erskine Murray Correspondence), fo. 89: Newcastle to Areskine, 7 Apr. 1749.

[106] For Macgregor, see NUL, NeC 1992, where General Churchill writes (on 21 Dec. 1751): 'I was Extreamly glad to keep free of negotiating, in which I know, there was no truth or credite to be got .' See also NLS, MS 308, fo. 34. For Cameron of Gleneves, see MS 308, fos. 63, 158–9; RACP, Box 44/194.

circumstances and reports about rebel activity. In 1747, concern intensified at the beginning and end of the year. The latter was a response to Jacobite excitement caused by the fall of Bergen-op-Zoom to the French; at the beginning of the year, ministers were inundated with reports about hopes for a French invasion in the spring. In October 1752, the Lord Justice Clerk emphasized the enormous importance of possible foreign assistance in a letter to the Earl of Holdernesse, then secretary of state:

> I dare say the Jacobites abroad are constantly forming and offering wild schemes at Rome, and may lay stress upon ane insurrection here—but unless we were to be overpower'd from the continent, all any attempt here cou'd produce to them, wou'd be a new offering of the Pretenders friends head and necks, to the Ax and Gibbett.[107]

Ministers and officials fully recognized that in watching the disaffected clans they were entering a world of rumour and misinformation. As one contemporary put it in 1747: 'We have too much imaginary News amongst us . . .'[108] Reports were, nevertheless, carefully followed up and acted upon, even when there was little conviction that they were true. In 1749, for example, Newcastle was sceptical about reports of the Young Pretender heading for Scotland, but, as we have seen, he still wrote to the Lord Justice Clerk to take appropriate action. In the spring of 1753, when reports of arms being landed in the western isles from the continent were current, as part of the rumours stimulated by the presence of Archie Cameron and Lochgarry in Scotland, an intelligence gathering force was sent round the islands on board a customs sloop under Ensign James Small.[109] Small was followed, in turn, by Captain John Ferguson, who visited the islands of Barra, the Uists, Harris, Long Island (present-day Lewis), Canna, Eigg and Rum, and all harbours on Skye. Where his sloop had been unable to enter, Ferguson had sent boats to land and collect information.[110] Even after the exposure of the Elibank Plot, and the capture of Archie Cameron, ministers, officials, and the military did not let their guards drop. Concern revived at the outbreak of the Seven Years War and especially in 1756 and again in 1759 when Britain faced invasion threats from one or both of the Bourbon powers, France and Spain.[111] As late as 1760, Charles Areskine, the Lord Justice Clerk, was advocating keeping a prudent

---

[107] BL, Egerton MS 3433, fos. 58–9.

[108] NLS, MS 16642 (Saltoun MS), fos. 30–1: Donald Campbell to Lord Milton, Inverary, 27 Feb. 1747.

[109] See NAS, RH 2/4/377, fos. 19–20. Small's report is at RACP, Box 45/15.

[110] NAS, RH 2/4/377, fos. 49–51: Ferguson to John Cleveland, 30 Mar. 1753. Ferguson had initially been placed in command of a vessel in 1747 following receipt of reports of continued Jacobite activity in the Highlands (NLS, MS 16641 (Saltoun MS), fos. 141–2, 149–50, 151–2).

[111] In 1756, a ship was again used to visit the western isles to collect intelligence (NLS, MS 5079, fo. 41). In May 1759, General Beauclerk wrote to Areskine, the Lord Justice Clerk, that he had set officers to watch strangers and suspected persons and give the earliest notice of the 'least appearance of Turbulence or Caballing'. He also recommended stationing a frigate or cruiser on the north west coast (NAS, RH 2/4/381, fo. 218: Beauclerk to Areskine, 22 May 1759).

watch on the Highlands whatever the appearance of peace and stability there. As he wrote, with disarming candour:

I hope there is no danger, from that quarter [the Highlands] which by the late levys [of Highlanders into the British army], has been very salutarily thin'd but as mischief, unforseen, unexpectedly spring out of the dust, we are never to dismiss our Guards.[112]

It is in the light of this continuing anxiety about the possibilities of disturbance in the Highlands, especially up until the early 1750s, that, along with the other factors discussed above, we must view the development of ways of trying finally to pacify the disaffected clans and regions of the Highlands. It also helps explain why there was such a determination to succeed, at least initially.

The outlines of official policy were put in place before the rebellion was over. As early as January 1746, the issue was considered by the ministers and by March the ministry were committed to a programme of systematic reform.[113] Most of the proposals resulted in legislation between 1746 and 1747. Acts for disarming the Highlands and suppressing non-juring meeting houses were passed in August 1746. In June 1747, an act was passed abolishing ward holding in Scotland, a form of tenure by which the tenant could be called out for military service. Passage of legislation abolishing private jurisdictions proved more complicated and difficult. This was because of the amount of opposition north of the border. Several loyal Scottish peers were owners of private regalities; indeed the greatest owner was Argyll. To some, their abolition appeared, therefore, to punish the innocent alongside the guilty. It was also politically contentious because it contravened the terms of the Union of 1707, which had explicitly safeguarded private jurisdictions as a sop to the Scottish landowning classes. One pamphleteer argued that the precedent set by their abolition threatened all property rights in Scotland. It also represented a significant breach in the fabric of the constitution.[114] Argyll and other Scots, including the judges of the Court of Session, expressed their opposition to this measure through sullen non-cooperation and silent opposition in Parliament.[115] From Edinburgh, Milton refused to offer advice on such a 'delicate' matter.[116] To ministers, however, and their supporters, private jurisdictions were a deformation of justice, a relic of a barbaric past. Planting Whig justice in the Highlands was, as we will see, a major plank in the campaign of exemplary civilizing imposed on the region after 1746. The English

[112] NAS, RH 2/4/382, fo. 487.

[113] For a good survey of developments, on which the following paragraph is based, see Speck, *The Butcher*, esp. pp. 171–7. See also NLS, MS 17528 (Saltoun MS), fos. 181–4: 'Sketch of Regulations proposed to be made in Scotland with HRH the Duke's Remarks thereupon'.

[114] *Observations Upon a Bill, entitled, An Act for Taking Away, and Abolishing the Heriditable Jurisdictions in that Part of Great Britain called Scotland* (Edinburgh, 1747), 14–15.

[115] For contemporary comment on this, see RACP, Box 22/275: Chesterfield to Cumberland, 22 May 1747. See also Scott, 'The Politics and Administration of Scotland', 529.

[116] Shaw, *The Management of Scottish Society*, 169.

model of justice represented security of property and person, and constituted a crucial support for the growth of industry and commerce. To this extent, Scots were being denied the benefits of important liberties enjoyed south of the border. As one contemporary wrote, the private jurisdictions were a form of 'Egyptian slavery' and a 'shame and disgrace to our constitution'.[117] The government did not completely ignore Scottish objections, and in certain respects the bill was watered down before it passed into law. Regalities were abolished and their jurisdictions vested in the King's courts, and heritable sheriffdoms were also abolished or annexed to the Crown. In the future, all Scottish sheriffs were to be appointed by the Crown and to hold their offices at the King's pleasure. Baronial courts survived and with at least some of their powers intact. The package of measures was completed with an act vesting property forfeit from attainted rebels in the Crown.

The most significant element of the campaign to subjugate the disaffected clans did not depend, however, on new legislative enactments, although it did require financial support from the British parliament. This was the maintenance of sufficient military force in Scotland and the Highlands to prevent further disturbances. There was nothing new about this prescription, and efforts had been made to facilitate this in the aftermath of the 'Fifteen through the construction of new garrisons—Ruthven (1719–22), Fort Augustus (1718–21), Glenelg or Bernera (1720–3) and Inversnaid (1718–20). Between 1725 and 1737, the government had also, under the influence of Marshal Wade, sponsored a major programme of road and bridge building. In 1745, however, the Jacobite army found a British military presence in Scotland that was short on numbers and, in various respects, poorly prepared to meet the threat the Jacobites posed.[118] After 1746, there was general agreement that only the better and stronger deployment of regular forces in the Highlands could ensure peace in the region. Force was to be the ultimate authority which held the disaffected clans and neighbourhoods within the Union until disaffection was damped down or eradicated. In this context, there was concern about drafting of regiments from Scotland to the continent in 1746 and again in 1747 when two regiments were transported to the United Provinces to defend Zealand.[119] Bland also managed to argue successfully in 1748 for a temporary reprieve during the winter of 1748–9 for five additional Highland companies.[120] After 1749, seven foot regiments and three regiments of dragoons were used systematically to police disaffected areas in the Highlands and islands of north-west Scotland. Military fortifications were also surveyed and

---

[117] *An Ample Disquisition into the Nature of Regalities and other Heredable [sic] Jurisdictions, in that Part of Great Britain call'd Scotland* (1747), preface.

[118] Speck, *The Butcher*, ch. 2.

[119] NUL, NeC 1865; RACP, Box 22/2: Chesterfield to Cumberland, 1 May 1747. For Bland's comments on the lack of adequate manpower with which to police the Highlands in early 1748, see NLS, MS 304, fo. 22.

[120] NLS, MS 304, fos. 114, 117.

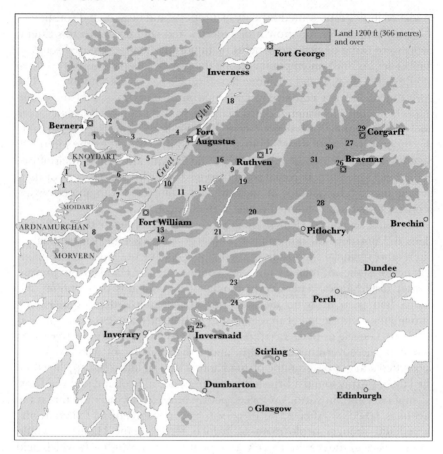

MAP 1. Troop Deployment in the Highlands, Summer 1749

Keppoch and Derribeg have not been identified. Keppoch is described as being south of the chain—i.e. south of the Great Glen. The troops, who numbered 429 in total, were divided into three commands. Throughout Scotland, there were seven infantry regiments—stationed at Fort William, Inverness, Aberdeen, Montrose, Perth, Edinburgh, and Glasgow—and three regiments of dragoons. The latter were stationed up and down the coasts to help customs officers combat smuggling. Parties of troops from Perth were also posted at Crief and Dunkeld.

	Location	From	No		Location	From	No
1	Loch Hourn, Knoydart, Morar, Arissig	Bernera	25	17	Ruthven	Ardersier	9
2	Head of Glen Shiel	Bernera	7	18	Loch Ruthven	Ardersier	4
3	Strath Clunie	Fort Augustus	13	19	Dalwhinnie	Fort Augustus	5
4	Head and centre of Glen Moriston	Fort Augustus	17	20	Dalnacardoch	Perth	7
5	Between Lock Quoich and Loch Garry	Fort Augustus	9	21	Head of Loch Kannoch	Perth	18
6	Head of Loch Arkaig	Fort William	19	22	Derribeg	Perth	7
7	Glenfinnan and head of Loch Eile	Fort William	11	23	Killin	Perth	5
8	Strontian	Fort William	15	24	Braes of Balquidder and Montieth	Stirling	23
	Moving patrol	Fort William	23	25	Inversnald	Stirling	34
9	Laggan	Fort Augustus	13		Moving patrol	Perth & Stirling	33
10	Nine Mile Bridge (Spean Bridge)	Fort William	5	26	Braemar	Aberdeen	24
11	High Bridge (Roy Bridge)	Fort William	6	27	Duburgh (head of River Cairn)	Aberdeen	9
12	Glen Coe	Fort William	9	28	Spittal of Glenshee	Aberdeen	5
13	Head of Loch Leven	Fort William	5	29	Corgaff	Aberdeen	22
14	Keppoch*	Fort William	15	30	Inch Rory (head of River Avon)	Aberdeen	5
15	Head of Glen Spean	Fort Augustus	5	31	Ribbalach Laggan (head of River Dee)	Aberdeen	6
16	Garvy More (Garvamore)	Fort Augustus	7		Moving patrol	Aberdeen	9

either rebuilt or strengthened. Several new fortifications—Corgarff, Braemar —were garrisoned (see Map 1). It was, however, Fort George, situated on Ardersier Point near Inverness, and designed in 1747 by military engineer William Skinner, that was both symbol and demonstration of the extension of Hanoverian power into the Highlands in this period. Built under the direction of the Adam family between 1748 and 1767, it was to cost the state over £100,000.[121] By the time it was complete, it had already outlived its military purpose. In 1748, however, circumstances had seemed very different. Wade's programme of road and bridge construction was also resumed after 1746. The motivation for this was not solely a military one. There was also recognition (or hope) that opening up the Highlands to traffic in goods, persons, and ideas from the south would promote change in the region.[122]

If the acts referred to above, and the extension and strengthening of the military presence in the region, laid the basis of the assault on Highland disaffection, this assault was broadened and the emphasis shifted in certain respects in the years after 1746. The main impetus for this came from the Scottish political classes. Ministers in London were never short of advice about how to deal with the 'Highland problem', and in the months and years which followed the rising they were bombarded with plans and proposals from north of the border. The authors included leading Scottish officials and politicians— Lords Milton, Tinwald, Elchies, and Deskford, the Earl of Findlater, Lord Advocate William Grant, and Duncan Forbes of Culloden—Scottish military men such as John McVicar, a former captain in Lord John Murray's regiment and Captain Molesworth of Guise's regiment, and several who remain anonymous.[123] There was much borrowing from and between different plans; they also restated policies which had been proposed or partially implemented during the past 150 years of efforts to 'civilize' the Highlander. Thus, education in English and the elimination of the Gaelic language, conversion to the Presbyterian faith through the division and erection of new parishes, the funding of charity schools (a scheme particularly promoted by Lord Deskford), the apprenticeship of Highland children in lowland Scotland and England, colonization of the Highlands by outsiders, the planting of industry and improved agriculture, the provision of speedy, impartial, and strict justice,

---

[121] Chris Tabraham and Doreen Grove, *Fortress Scotland and the Jacobites* (1995), 93–100.

[122] NAS, GD 124/15/1569 (Mar and Kellie MS), fo. 15: 'Memorial concerning the Highlands of Scotland, and the Borders of South & North Britain'.

[123] BL, Add. MS, 35858 (Hardwicke Papers): John McVicar, 'A Scheme for Civilizing the Clans in the North of Scotland'; NLS, MS 2970 (Culloden Papers), fos. 143–5: Duncan Forbes, 'Some Thoughts concerning the Highlands of Scotland' (this was actually written before the rebellion); *Enquiry into the Causes of the Late Rebellion* (1746); Charles Stanford Terry (ed.), *The Albermarle Papers . . . with an appendix of letters from Andrew Fletcher, Lord Justice Clerk, to the Duke of Newcastle, 1746–48* (2 vols., Aberdeen, 1902), ii. 479; BL, Add. MS 35477 (Hardwicke Papers), fos. 89–95: 'Report by David Bruce, one of the surveyors of the Forfeited Estates in Scotland'; RACP, Box 44/148: 'Suggestions for Civilizing the Highlands, 1751'; RACP, Box 44/213: 'Observations on Improvements in the Highlands'; NLS, MS 16640, fos. 187–8: 'Memoriall concerning the Disaffected Highlands'; ibid., fos. 189–90: 'Proposals for Improving and Preventing Rebellion in the Highlands of North Britain'; NAS, GD 248/1071/16, 248/641/1 and 2 (Seafield Papers).

as well as the construction of forts and roads and more intensive deployment of regular troops, were all urged on ministers. Some of the proposals were remarkable in their scope, ambition, impracticality (one memorialist was suggesting the removal of Highlanders who refused to be 'industrious' south of the Forth), and financial implications, a major reason why policy as enacted and implemented tended to be modest by comparison. Lord Milton called in 1748 for the purchase of a chain of estates in the Highlands between Inverness and the west coast on which to plant colonies of lowlanders and outsiders and to encourage the development of commercial agriculture and manufacturing.[124] A shrewd critic of some of the weaknesses likely to attend the exploitation of the annexed estates—the author referred to the small rental income likely to accrue from them—called for a fund of between £8,000 and 10,000 a year to be used to encourage the growth of manufacturing in commercial colonies of Chelsea pensioners and other new inhabitants sited on the edges of region notorious for thieving. The specific locations mentioned were Rannoch, Glen Roy, and Glen Spean, parts of Glengarry's estate near Fort Augustus, and the lands of the Grants of Glenmoriston. The scheme's geographical logic was clearly spelt out:

The inhabitants of all these Lands are Thieves, and the Lands themselves run from North to South, through the Middle of the Highlands, and are the furthest to the East of any Countries remarkable for thieving—so that if honest inhabitants were settled there, it would cut off the passage from the western thieves, to the Low Countries, on the East Coast, where they commonly go for their prey.

The author also advised the acquisition of part of Glencoe to form a barrier between Argyllshire and bands of Highland thieves.[125] Several memorialists, including Milton, also called for the expulsion of the chiefs and tacksmen from disaffected estates.[126]

Whatever the favoured solution (or solutions), contemporaries tended to view the 'Highland problem' from the same perspective. Influenced by emergent Enlightenment thinking and the tenets of commercial Whiggism, they adopted a sociological frame of analysis. Disaffection was seen as stemming from the nature of clan society and not religion or political motivation. Some expressed this in loosely historical terms, seeing in Highland society the lineaments of classical barbarian civilizations as described by French philosophes such as Buffon and Montesquieu.[127] The language of others was more direct and simple. Clanship was viewed as a structure of oppression, its relationships and conditions standing in stark contrast to those of modern commercial society. John McVicar talked of a system of 'sordid subordination' and of the 'exorbitant and lawless power' of the clan chief.[128] Poverty and violence were

---

[124] For this, see Shaw, *The Management of Scottish Society*, 171–7.
[125] NAS, GD 248/654/1: 'On the Subject of Civilizing the Highlands, 1748'.
[126] See n. 123, above.
[127] NAS, GD 248/654/1.
[128] BL, Add. MS 35858.

products of oppression, as was the prevalence of cattle theft in the Highlands. Clan leaders deliberately imposed a system of poverty and insecurity on their followers. Other facets of Highland culture, such as Highland dress and the use of arms, were potent expressions of this reality. The fundamental answer followed directly from the depiction of clanship. The clansmen had to be freed from the tyranny of the clan leaders and tacksmen, and Highland society reconstructed to bring it into line with modern commercial principles.

The influence of Scottish opinion on policy was most clearly evident in the Annexation Act, eventually passed in 1752. The plan which acted as a model for the act was probably produced by Milton, Elchies, and Bland with Tinwald acting as critic.[129] The act itself was in several respects a less ambitious measure than some of the proposals which lay behind it. For example, no provision was made for purchasing estates such as recommended by Milton. What it did do was permanently annex thirteen forfeited estates from outlawed rebels to the Crown.[130] (The act actually named fourteen estates but that of Alexander MacDonald of Keppoch was found not to be forfeited.) These were to be, in the first place, standing testimony of the grave penalties of active rebellion in Scotland. After the '15, the forfeited estates had been sold, a policy which had allowed several disaffected families to regain control of their patrimonies. Permanent annexation to the Crown left no hope of restoration of estates to outlawed families or their relatives, or appeared to do so in 1752. (De-annexation actually took place in 1784.) The forfeited estates were also to become laboratories of social engineering. Clanship on them was to be eradicated through tenurial reform and encouragement of progressive agriculture, commerce and industry. This policy was to be guided by a board of commissioners overseeing factors appointed to manage the estates. It was also a line of policy strongly promoted by other Scottish bodies, politicians and landowners.[131]

THE IMPLEMENTATION OF POLICY

Passing acts and concocted plans and schemes for planting commerce and industry in the Highlands was one thing; ensuring they were fully implemented and had the desired effects was another thing entirely. The record of efforts to transform and thereby pacify the Highlands after 1746 is, in fact, a very mixed one. In many cases, ambition in conception was not matched by consistency and efficacy in implementation. In some cases, policies were ill suited to local conditions. The attention to detail and degree of oversight which were required by many of these policies was greater than ministers and officials in London and Edinburgh could provide. With the slide into renewed conflict and war with France from the mid-1750s, other priorities also intervened to deflect

[129] Smith, *Jacobite Estates of the Forty Five*, 20.
[130] These are listed ibid., 23.
[131] See below.

the attention of ministers away from Scotland. For these reasons, historians have tended to be sceptical about the effects of the campaign of exemplary civilizing in the Highlands after the '45.[132]

In order to draw up a proper balance sheet of successes and failures, we need to separate out different elements of the campaign. We also need to be clear about what criteria are being used to assess effectiveness. Government-sponsored initiatives may have played only a small role in destroying the clan system—this probably imploded, weakened by the political convulsions of the seventeenth and eighteenth centuries and spreading commercialism amongst clan leaders, rather than being deliberately destroyed by intervention from without—yet the disaffected clans were subdued after the '45 and some order brought to the region. Jacobites and former rebel clansmen also found themselves remorselessly harried in disaffected areas.

The role of the military in Scotland and the Highlands after 1746 was crucial and had various dimensions. It encompassed harassment of Jacobites; collection of intelligence; enforcing the bans on Highland dress and the carrying of arms; a major assault on cattle theft; as well as ensuring the peace of the region. All presented significant challenges and difficulties; all also depended on the quality, commitment, and morale of military officers and private soldiers posted in often unfamiliar and hostile country. Not surprisingly, they were hardly welcomed in disaffected regions, and there were frequent problems concerning supply of food, fuel, and goods to troop detachments and the provision of shelter.[133] Desertion was strictly dealt with, which suggests that the command was very sensitive to the dislike amongst the rank and file of service in the Highlands.[134] It was also necessary for officers to develop a familiarity with Highland society, and the rivalries and tensions which afflicted different areas and clans. Knowledge was a major weapon in the war against the clans and in the extension of state power in the region. This was not simply a matter of gathering intelligence; it was also a question of mapping accurately the region, a task undertaken by Lieutenant Colonel David Watson between 1745 and 1750.

The role of the military was also politically delicate. Military–civilian relations were a troublesome matter in eighteenth-century Britain, a reflection in part of the value placed on liberty in contemporary political culture, a deep-rooted suspicion of standing armies, but perhaps more importantly the potential for friction (or worse) with local communities when soldiers were quartered upon them. During the final stages of the rebellion and in its immediate aftermath, the military, motivated by revenge, and licensed by a thirst for violence amongst its commanders, indulged in a period of bloodletting, plunder, and harassment in parts of Lowland as well as Highland Scot-

---

[132] For a recent view, see Macinnes, *Clanship, Commerce and the House of Stuart*, ch. 8.

[133] See e.g. RACP, Box 45/9: letter from Capt Barlow, Inverness, 20 Jan. 1753.

[134] In 1754, Bland was recommending that deserters be given a chance to throw a dice for death or lesser punishment. The deserter who threw the lowest number was to be shot (NLS, MS 305, fo. 40).

land.[135] Thereafter, conscious of the political sensitivities surrounding its role and behaviour, the army appears to have sought to display, on most occasions at least, moderation and respect for the forms and rule of law. On the other hand, their presence in many towns and communities was far from popular and relations between them and locals were frequently hostile, and this could lead to episodes of disorder or violence involving military personnel. The sentiments of the Stirling citizens who damned a party of soldiers singing loyal songs in a tavern in 1748 as 'Rascals and Scoundrels' and 'English Bougars' before assaulting them were probably shared by many Scots.[136] The military could also step over the line of legality, although how often this occurred is impossible to say. In late 1748, General Bland commented on a captain commanding troops in Strontian, then afflicted with an upsurge in banditry, who wished to give orders to burn the houses of those who harboured thieves and deserters. Bland's reaction was that of a sympathetic parent faced with an errant, but fundamentally benign, child. Munro's 'error' was to be excused if not condoned 'as he thinks it woud tend to the good of the community'. In the same year, Bland expressed enthusiasm about an individual who had been shot dead trying to escape from a party of soldiers who had seized him for concealing or carrying arms. His comments show how easy it was for some to continue to view the Highlander as not deserving of the usual protections of the law: 'To men it is ridiculous to talk of law to a parcel of savages, who never observed any but lived at large, prey:g on every thing that came their way like many Lyons & Tygers.' Some years later, Bland argued, 'Where Diseases become Desperate remedies must be applied, or no cure can be effected.'[137] In 1755, troops were illegally cantoned on the Clan Macpherson in Badenoch in an attempt to flush out the elusive Cluny Macpherson. Bland declared that it was important that the officers and soldiers for this duty were carefully selected so as 'to avoid, as much as possible, irregularities of all kinds'.[138] Military commanders and officers were aware of the political constraints under which they operated, even if they sometimes strained under them or slightly beyond them; equally importantly, so too were their political masters back in London.

The relationship between civilian authorities in Scotland and the military was also one which contained great potential for friction. This was partly, as we will see below, a consequence of how far the military felt it lacked the

---

[135] The military appear to have harassed (or worse) disaffected individuals and families in the north east of Scotland. One narrative of events, by William Lascelles, last Constable of Broadsea, and a Jacobite Episcopalian and follower of Lord Pitsligo, claims that around four people were killed in Buchan by Lord Cobham's dragoons. The same source also refers to living through a 'rain [*sic*] of terror' (David Fraser, *The Christian Watt Papers* (Collieston, 1988), p. 9). John Brims has also noted harassment and plunder of communities suspected of Jacobitism around Strathallan (Brims, 'The Jacobites in Stirling', 32).

[136] Quoted in Brims, 'The Jacobites in Stirling', 32.

[137] NLS, MS 304, fo. 113: Bland to Capt Forbes, 22 Nov. 1748.

[138] NLS, MS 305, fos. 101–2: Bland to Lord George Beauclerk, 26 June 1755.

cooperation of these authorities in enforcing punitive legislation after 1746. The military were also used, however, to maintain a check on these authorities. In 1747, Bland was calling on his officers to report to him about how diligent magistrates were in executing laws against papists, non jurors, and unlawful meetings.[139] In December in the same year, Bland received reports about the Provost of Linlithgow releasing on bail a man accused of uttering seditious words against the royal family without an order from the Lord Justice Clerk or the Lord Advocate in Edinburgh. The Lord Provost was forced to write a grovelling letter of apology and explanation to Bland. As far as Bland was concerned, it was simply further illustration of what he called the 'supiness of the civil power' in Scotland.[140]

All major pieces of punitive legislation passed in the aftermath of the rebellion proved difficult to enforce and several served to create tension between the military and magistrates. It was widely recognized, by the military themselves, that great efforts were made to evade the terms of the disarming act, as had happened when similar acts were passed in 1716 and 1725.[141] In 1746, as after the earlier acts, large numbers of arms were undoubtedly hidden or buried, and the arms that were handed in were old or defective.[142] In that year, Cumberland had argued for annual searches for arms, and punishment by death or transportation for those found carrying or concealing them. In the event, no provision was made for such searches, and punishment was, in the first instance, the imposition of a fine. Provision for licensing the carrying of arms by gentry and their servants made enforcement of the law more difficult, particularly since these provisions appear to have been widely abused. In October 1751, General Churchill wrote to James Wolfe, future hero of Abrahams Heights, then posted at Inverness, that licences were being given 'to almost every petty laird in the Highlands'. He also suggested that licences were being given to persons under 'fictitious characters, such as Horsekeepers, Goatkeepers'. Wolfe was directed to gather information about rental values and oaths from the collector of land tax and the local sheriff as a preliminary to eliminating abuses in the system of licensing.[143] Cooperation from civilian authorities was often not forthcoming. It appears that many sheriff deputes and their substitutes doubted that they possessed the authority to issue warrants for searches for arms when information about their existence was forthcoming, while JPs were reluctant to do so.[144] One way in which this problem was partly overcome was to make military officers of various

[139] NLS, MS 304, fo. 7.

[140] NLS, MS 304, fo. 6: Bland to Capt Hamilton commanding at Linlithgow, 12 Dec. 1747; NLS, MS 304, fo. 10: Lord Provost of Linlithgow to Bland, 22 Dec. 1747.

[141] See e.g. NUL, NeC 1861/7: 'Short Account of the Rise of Disaffection in Scotland & the Remedies pointed to prevent it for the Future'.

[142] See e.g. NUL, NeC 1765: John Huske to Cumberland, 16 June 1746, Fort Augustus.

[143] NLS, MS 308, fos. 31–2.

[144] See RACP, Box 44/148 for the unreliability of JPs and the need to ensure that sheriff deputies were not compromised by local attachments.

garrisons justices of the peace, a measure which would have been unthinkable south of the border.

Lack of cooperation, as the military saw it, from civilian authorities was also evident in efforts to suppress Highland dress. Local JPs and other officers of the law frequently refused to commit offenders brought in by the military, much to the irritation of officers and command of the military. Captain Hughes wrote from his station at the head of Loch Rannoch in August 1749 that the local sheriff depute had been dismissing individuals taken before him for wearing Highland dress. Later that month, the same official acted in an even more provocative manner, as Hughes reported it. Hughes had sent his corporal to seize men wearing Plaid trousers at Killin. The corporal had duly done this, and was conducting the two offenders to Hughes when he was met by the sheriff and what was described in the report as 'a mob'. The rest of the story is best told in Hughes' words:

[the sheriff then] peremptorily ordered the soldiers at their Peril to dismiss them [the two prisoners] immediately or that he would that instant order them all to Prison, at the same time abusing them greatly for molesting people in a dress he thought proper to tolerate. He likewise told them in the hearing of the mob, that if they continued to apprehend the inhabitants, they were to expect whatever usage their Resentment might suggest to them.

Intimidated, the soldiers released their prisoners. Hughes reported the consequence: 'the People Insult & Triumph, and while their sheriff protects them make a Jest of Military Power'.[145] No doubt, as the incident just referred to makes clear, part of the reason for non-cooperation was opposition to overly stringent enforcement of the measure, which was seen as needlessly provocative. There were also persistent problems in defining what constituted Highland dress. Highlanders sought to evade the terms and spirit of the act by experimenting with new styles of dress. The sheriff-substitute in Killin had been faced with a decision about a dress that was, in the words of his superior, the Sheriff of Perthshire, 'neither Highland or Lowland', but 'resembling a sailors dress'.[146] There were other reasons for the dilatory behaviour of civilian authorities. The disincentives to rigour were manifold. Sheriffs reportedly lacked great weight or standing in localities. Opposition to the laws was also widely based; implementing them risked earning the odium of their neighbours. There was no shortage of lawyers seeking to frustrate efforts to implement the measures. Moreover, there was no financial incentive for sheriffs to act, only financial costs and much trouble. There was also no special provision made for the costs of holding offenders in prison before commitment to trial or to finance the costs of prosecution.

The act to suppress non juring meeting houses affected Lowland areas and burghs as well as the Highlands. What appears to have happened is that some non-juring Episcopalians very rapidly resumed public meetings for worship

[145] RACP, Box 43/307.   [146] BL, Egerton MS 3433, fos. 132–3.

after the rebellion and the harassment and destruction of meeting houses in some areas, particularly the north east, by Cumberland's army. The Duke of Gordon wrote to the Duke of Newcastle in late 1747: 'The Nonjurors and their Followers meet now in as Publick a manner as ever.'[147] The act was in two parts. Episcopalian ministers had to qualify themselves by taking oaths of allegiance to the Crown. They also had to pray for George by name. Anyone who went to an Episcopalian service disallowed under the terms of the act was to be deprived of their civil rights and subject to a fine of £5. If the fine was unpaid, the defendant faced six months imprisonment. Episcopalian ministers and their congregations sought to evade the terms of the law by conducting services in private houses with doors and windows open.[148] The Duke of Argyll also reported that in Edinburgh the spirit if not the terms of the act were being flouted by outbursts of sneezing and coughing amongst congregations when ministers were praying for George II by name.[149] On the whole, however, it appears that many magistrates did seek to enforce the law to suppress non-juring meeting houses faithfully. The problem was the ability of non-juring Episcopalians to exploit loopholes in the law, or evade its purpose. In November 1747, the sheriff of Aberdeen responded to criticism that he had allowed preachers whose meeting houses were burnt down during the rebellion to resume their office by declaring that 'the preachers pretend to have conform'd to the Law, and have Lawyers opinions that they have done so.' He also asked for guidance about what actions he could take in response that were 'legall and proper'.[150]

If the presence of the military ensured that significant efforts were at least made to enforce the punitive legislation passed after the rebellion, the soldiers' most important task was to secure the peace and relative stability of the Highlands. This was evident in initial instructions issued to Bland in October 1747. Bland was to distribute his forces in order to 'secure the Publick Peace & Tranquility'; he was also to redeploy his forces according to any intelligence he might receive about designs or plans amongst the disaffected clans to make any 'fresh disturbance' in the Highlands.[151] As Allan Macinnes has emphasized recently, the months and years after the rebellion saw an upsurge of banditry by rebel clansmen and demobbed soldiers in Lochaber and Rannoch, and throughout the mountainous districts of the southern and central Highlands.[152] The Lowland fringe of the Highlands, particularly Aberdeenshire, was also afflicted with raiding and depredations from the

---

[147] NLS, MS 16646, fos. 77–8: Duke of Gordon to Newcastle, 5 Oct. 1747. See also NLS, MS 16645, fos. 7–8: John Forbes to Milton, 17 Mar. 1747, Deer Manse, for the reconstruction of meeting houses in the north east.

[148] NLS, MS 17528, fo. 44: copy of part of letter from George Miller, deputy sheriff of Perth, to Milton, 14 Dec. 1747.

[149] BL, Add. MS 35447, fos. 295–6.

[150] NLS, MS 16646, fos. 112–13.

[151] NLS, MS 307, fos. 103–4.

[152] Macinnes, *Clanship, Commerce and the House of Stuart*, 214.

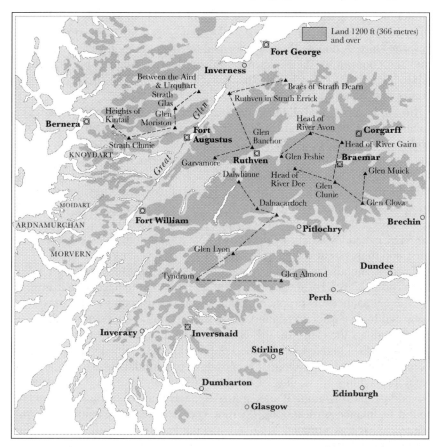

MAP 2. Cantonment of Troops to Prevent Raids from the Highlands, winter 1748–9

In the winter of 1748–9, the five additional companies of Lord John Murray and Lord Loudon were stationed in a series of chains to prevent raids from parties of disaffected Highlanders on exposed parts of Invernesshire, Banff, Aberdeen, and Mearns. The chain for covering north of the River Ness and Ross and Sutherland is the most difficult to reconstruct. Troops were stationed at places called Curravachie, Kinlochbanchaven, Tinaiouse, and Glenluack. I have been unable to locate these.

Highlands.[153] The response of the military was, in the first place, intrusive cantonment of troops during the summer months in disaffected areas and throwing a chain of troops round Lowland fringes subject to Highland raiding in the winter months. In the summer of 1749, around 450 soldiers were deployed at various points throughout the Highlands (see Map 1). In the

[153] See NAS, JC 11/13, Justiciary Court, Processes, May 1748–Oct. 1749, for a series of prosecutions for violent robberies in and around Aberdeen in 1748. In April 1749, 3 individuals, including the minister of Durris, were petitioning against the release on bail of one of the alleged perpetrators, a Robert Reid, for fear of him doing them 'bodily harm'.

winter of 1748–9, the additional companies of Lord John Murray and the Earl of Loudon were quartered at various locations (see Map 2) to cover parts of Invernesshire. A double chain was formed to cover the south side of the Spey and the counties of Banff, Aberdeenshire, Mearns, Angus, and Perthshire, while the northern Highlands, Ross, and Sutherland, were also protected by strategically placed troops.

Secondly, substantial efforts were made to bring cattle thieves to justice. The military saw the assault on cattle theft as a crucial part of their role and the wider programme of civilizing the Highlands. This reflected assumptions about the importance of cattle theft to the economy of violence in the Highlands, as it was seen from the outside at least. Cattle theft served to maintain the martial traditions of the clans; it constituted a training in endurance, mobility, and violent conduct. In 1754, Bland described suppressing cattle theft as the only sound 'Foundation' on which the 'superstructure' of improvement could be raised.[154] Two years previously, General Churchill described it as the 'first and most essential step to be taken Towards civilizing the Highlands'.[155] Officers in the affected regions sought to cultivate informers to secure notorious cattle thieves. For some years, their efforts appear to have been frustrated by the reluctance of people to bring prosecutions against thieves, or for witnesses to give evidence against defendants. It was also recognized that attitudes amongst the clans towards cattle theft were unhelpful—to the military, that is—a fact highlighted by the continued practice in the Highlands of compounding for cattle theft.[156] Proposals were periodically made to simplify legal procedures in dealing with cattle thieves to expedite prosecutions. Several people, including Bland, argued strongly that public money should be found to finance prosecutions.[157] From 1752, soldiers were stationed in the winter, as well as summer, in areas particularly afflicted with thieving—the head of Loch Arkaig, Strontian, and Laggan Achadrom.[158] A list also appears to have been compiled by 1753 for the commander of British forces in Scotland of the most notorious cattle thieves in the Highlands.[159]

The result of all these actions was that, by the early 1750s, the military appear to been having some success in suppressing cattle theft and in bringing the most notorious thieves to book. Indicative of this success was the successful prosecution for murder and theft of 'Serjeant Mor Cameron' in 1753.[160] Cameron, a deserter from the British army, led a party of around twenty bandits or thieves in and around Rannoch Moor. In 1752, he appears to have

[154] NUL, NeC 2220: Bland to Pelham, 5 Feb. 1754.

[155] NLS, MS 309, fos. 3–4.

[156] See esp. NAS, GD 248/654/1; NLS, MS 308, fos. 140–1.

[157] BL, Add. MS 32734, fos. 142–3; PRO, T1/355/33–4; BL Add MS, 35858: John McVicar, 'A Scheme for Civilizing the Clans in the North of Scotland'. See also PRO, T1, 355/33.

[158] NLS, MS 307, fos. 162–3, 174.

[159] NLS, MS 309, fo. 55, where reference is made to a list in the possession of General Churchill of all the notorious thieves with their social standing.

[160] NAS, JC 11/14, Justiciary Court, Processes, May 1753–Apr. 1754. On 8 October, Cameron was found guilty of murder and theft and sentenced to hang in chains 'in terrorum'.

realized that the net was closing in around him as he sought to come to terms with the authorities.[161] He was seized in April 1753, apparently with the help of Angus Cameron, brother of Cameron of Gleneves.[162] In 1754, public money was provided to defray the costs of prosecutions of cattle thieves, and, with the help of informers, greater numbers of thieves were secured.[163] Not all were hanged; some were banished and some were enlisted in the army.[164] Where the military appear, however, to have been less successful is in prosecuting someone of higher social status for compounding for cattle theft.[165]

The final main task performed by the military was harrying and detecting Jacobites and attainted rebels who returned to Scotland after the flight of the Young Pretender and many of his leading supporters at the end of the summer of 1746. Skulking rebels could count on shelter and support from their clansmen and help in frustrating the efforts of the military to seize them. In the north-east—outside of the Highlands—Lord Pitsligo evaded capture for some years after the rebellion. Great care was required when attempting to seize rebels, and efforts were made to disguise the purpose of expeditions to do this. In some cases, secrecy was not maintained, and attempted seizures were fruitless. For example, in 1751, Archie Cameron's wife was closely watched in the hope that she would have in her possession incriminating correspondence from France to rebels in Scotland. When she was seized, nothing of significance was found, a fact which was put down to information being leaked about military intentions through the customs service.[166] Some rebels also proved specially elusive, notably Cluny Macpherson, who controlled the French treasure landed off Loch Arkaig in the summer of 1746. On the other hand, these rebels had to keep moving to avoid capture. Before he was seized near Inversnaid, Archie Cameron had been forced, because of military pursuit, to leave Lochaber, Sunart, and Ardnamurchan.[167] Even where the military were unable to capture a rebel known to be present in the Highlands, they could apply pressure to make communication and cooperation between the disaffected clans very difficult. In October 1752, Churchill wrote to one of his officers that while it was unlikely that Lochgarry could be seized, given his knowledge of the country and friends, life could be made very difficult for him by conducting general searches.[168] Had any concerted effort

---

[161] NLS, MS 307, fos. 162–3.

[162] NLS, MS 309, fos. 70–1. It was reported that soldiers had been withdrawn from the area, while the Serjeant had been got drunk by Cameron. He was then captured by the military.

[163] See esp. NLS, MS 305, fos. 225–6: Bland to George Ross, 31 July 1756. This letter refers to the sum of £500 which had been provided by the Treasury for defraying the costs of 'suppressing theft, detecting thieves, murderers and other lawless persons in the Highlands'. This fund was now exhausted and further expenses of £274 12s. 10½d. had been incurred.

[164] NLS, MS 305, fos. 225–6. This refers to cattle thieves being hanged, transported, several being enlisted in the fleet, some being forced to flee the country, and several being allowed to enlist in the army.

[165] NLS, MS 309, fos. 13, 171.

[166] RACP, Box 44/192: copy of a letter from General Churchill to Newcastle, 24 Oct. 1751.

[167] NLS, MS 309, fos. 83–4.

[168] Ibid., fo. 6: Churchill to Governor Leighton, 26 Oct. 1752.

been made to prepare or even engineer a rising after 1746, it seems inconceivable that the military would not have quickly gained knowledge of it and been able to suppress it at origin. In late 1752, Archie Cameron and Lochgarry were sent to Scotland on the back of an 'expedient lie'—namely, that Prussia was committed to supporting a rising. The capture of Dr Cameron exposed the hollowness of the desperate optimism which prevailed amongst the disaffected clans in early 1753. After 1753, they did not even have this to comfort themselves with.

A semblance of order was, therefore, slowly imposed on disaffected clans and regions. The sight of the redcoat must have become a grimly familiar one in such regions. Following reports of disaffection and disorder, troops were also stationed in the summer in the western isles from 1754.[169] The presence of troops acted as a deterrent to law breaking, as well as the activities of Jacobite agents, attainted rebels, and Catholic priests and missionaries, about whom there was recurrent concern. Beneath all the talk of civilizing and planting commerce was recognition that *force majeure* was the ultimate basis of Hanoverian rule in the region. This was reflected in the anxiety of Bland and others to see exemplary justice imposed on those who sought to disturb the peace or to defy authority. The disaffected clans were to be cowed not only through the presence and proximity of soldiers, but also by the sight of the corpses of their heroes suspended in chains in their parishes of origin. It was a calculus of power that was most dramatically demonstrated in the responses to the murder of Campbell of Glenure in May 1752. Glenure was factor on the forfeited estates of Ardsheal, Callart, and part of Lochiel. His murder was seen as a calculated gesture of contempt for Hanoverian power and ambition in the region, which required an immediate and effective response from the government. Every effort was put into discovering and capturing the perpetrator. A reward of £100 was offered for their capture. The Lord Advocate and Solicitor General, William Grant, attended the 'state trial' of James Stewart of the Glens, as an accessory to the murder, at Inverary.[170] Stewart, who went to his death protesting his innocence (his dying speech was printed and dispersed after his execution), was hanged and his corpse hung up in chains in Appin country; a party of one officer and thirty men were stationed in the area to ensure that no one cut him down.[171]

If a strained peace was imposed on the disaffected parts of the Highlands after 1746, the longer-term solution to securing the region was, as we have seen, to be through the reconstruction of Highland society and the encouragement of the practice and habit of industry in the region. The bringing of order to the region, and compelling respect for the law, as opposed to clan leaders and loyalties, was inextricably bound up with this ambition. Creating

[169] BL, Add. MS 35448 (Hardwicke Papers), fos. 57–8.
[170] BL, Add. MS 35447, fo. 301.
[171] *Scots Mag.* (1755), 512–13.

security of property and person were viewed as essential prerequisites of destroying clanship. As one anonymous memorial writer asserted in 1752:

Theft & Robbery, in time of Peace, and Rebellion in War, was the profession of these People; and the Interest of their Chieftains consisted in keeping this up, & preventing of Industry. By stationing the Troops properly in, the Highlands, Thieving has been prevented, and that way of their Bread being prevented, they must necessarily begin to be industrious; which the Circulation of the Pay of the Troops encourages, at the same time that they find their Property secured by the Troops.[172]

The abolition of private jurisdictions was also part and parcel of this aim. A persistent concern about the quality and presence of justice in the Highlands after 1748 was the paucity of officers of the law in disaffected areas and the distance of many parts from these officers and the courts. Inverness-shire was a major worry in this respect, and the creation of more sheriff substitutes in this county and in other disaffected areas was, at various times, urged on ministers and officials in Edinburgh.[173] Annette Smith has noted that in 1755 in a questionnaire sent to factors to obtain a fuller picture of social conditions, the commissioners of the forfeited estates were much more concerned about the provision of law and order than education or religious instruction. The Board asked their factors detailed questions about the presence of Justices of the Peace, the proximity of prisons, and the distance of estates from Sheriff Substitutes, and all this before mentioning churches and schools.[174] The rule of law was to be imposed on the Highlands as a preliminary to the encouragement of industry.

The full tale of limited achievement, obstruction, and misadventure with regard to commercial experiments in the Highlands after 1746 is beyond the scope of this chapter and, in any case, would take us well beyond the mid-eighteenth century. In the later 1740s and 1750s, attention was focused mainly on the annexed estates, the deployment after 1753 of a subsidy to encourage linen manufacture in the Highlands, and efforts to encourage exploitation of the fisheries. The story of the management of the annexed estates has been told in great detail by Annette Smith.[175] What emerges from her account is how difficult ministers and officials in Edinburgh found it to overcome complex legal problems involved in annexation: for example, the settling of claims on the estates and the compensation of those holding superiorities on them. This last issue dragged on for years after 1752. Five estates and two parts of estates affected by the act remained under the control of the Barons of the Scottish Exchequer, where they had been since 1748, until 1770. In other

---

[172] NUL, NeC 2,082: 'Measures taken by the Military, since the Rebellion, & the Effects thereof, 1752'.

[173] See e.g. BL, Add. MS 35858; BL, Add. MS 35477, fos. 87–8; NLS, MS 304, fos. 145, 163; RACP, Box 44/148: 'Suggestions for Civilizing the Highlands, 1751'; NAS, GD 248/651/1: 'Causes of Ye Present Disorderly State of the Highlands of Scotland'.

[174] Smith, *Jacobite Estates of the Forty-Five*, 33.

[175] Ibid.

words, it took fifteen years to complete negotiations with the relevant subject superiors and until the Crown could take over complete control of the estates. Pelham's anxiety to reduce public expenditure after 1748 was also felt strongly. Basically, rental income from the estates was left to finance improvements and reforms, always a limited source given other calls on it, for example, the costs of administration. Delay and obstruction characterized direction from the centre, to an extent that seems remarkable. The Treasury omitted to respond to the plans of the commissioners between 1755 and 1760, and this understandably diminished the enthusiasm of any commissioners to attend meetings in Edinburgh. Surveyors and factors faced different, but equally formidable problems on the ground, including non-cooperation, evasiveness, and open hostility on the part of local clansmen. Factors were also expected to undertake a huge range of tasks under a system of remuneration that left their salaries vulnerable to the vagaries of climate and the harvest. (Factors' salaries comprised 5 per cent of rents, a large element of which was made up of barley and oats.) More fundamentally, the plans developed by the commissioners were beyond the capacity of the most enlightened and committed bureaucracy (which the management and officers of forfeited estates were not) to implement successfully. They envisaged large-scale changes to tenurial arrangements, as well as to forms of farming which had developed over many generations. These could not be introduced quickly and would take time to embed themselves in society. The schemes to instruct and plant manufacturing, meanwhile, came up against the obstacles of lack of skills, poor communications, and distance from markets.

The spearhead of efforts to encourage manufacturing was to be linen. As has been noted elsewhere, a large amount of energy was expended after 1746 in trying to expand linen manufacturing in the Highlands. Along with the Board of Commissioners of the Annexed Estates, the Trustees for the Improvement of Manufacturing and Fisheries, several private landowners made great efforts to encourage the linen industry in the Highlands after the rebellion, notably the Earl of Morton in the Orkneys, and the Duke of Argyll in Bute and Argyllshire.[176] The Trustees supported the provision of spinning schools and the distribution of wheels and reels to manufacturers. They also subsidized the heckling of flax at Logierait in Perthshire and at Inverness to enable spinning to be extended further into the central Highlands. They lobbied officials in Edinburgh and ministers at Westminster for public money to reinforce these efforts.[177] In 1753, they were rewarded when Parliament voted an annual subsidy or bounty of £9000 for nine years 'For Encouraging and Improving the

---

[176] Alastair J. Durie, *The Scottish Linen Industry in the Eighteenth Century* (Edinburgh, 1979), 88–9.

[177] See the annual reports of the Trustees. A run of these for this period can be found in the Moses Supplementary Collection of the Convention of Royal Burghs material in the Edinburgh City Archives at SL 30/248. The Trustees were spending any surplus funds after 1746 on encouragement of the linen industry in the Highlands. Other Scottish politicians and officials were also recommending similar schemes. For this, see NAS, GD 248/572/21, fos. 4–5.

Linen Manufacture in the Highlands of Scotland'.[178] Following the solicitation of proposals about how best to use the money—The Trustees received forty-one of these—it was decided to set up four manufacturing stations, at Loch Carron, Loch Broom, Glenmoriston, and Glenelg. The modern authority on the eighteenth-century Scottish linen industry suggests that in retrospect this decision represented 'a tragic error'.[179] Costs of construction were high; difficulties of transporting flax to them great; and the natives viewed them with suspicion. The stations acted as a steady drain on funds, irrespective of who controlled them. (They were transferred from the Trustees to the Commissioners of the Annexed Estates in 1762.) Moreover, no success was achieved in establishing weaving, a male employment. The only progress was in encouraging spinning, a female one. Given the underlying aims of extending linen manufacturing in the region, this was a considerable disappointment.

The other great hope for providing employment and encouraging the habits of industry in the Highlands was fishing, particularly for herring. Attempts from 1727 by the Trustees to promote the herring fishery had come to little or nothing, failing by the mid-1730s.[180] Sir John Clerk of Penicuick, who had been witness to these earlier efforts, was sceptical about the likely success of further ventures in the later 1740s and early 1750s.[181] Yet his was a relatively isolated voice. Optimism after the rebellion about the potential of the fisheries as a source of employment and means of nurturing the values and habits of industry in the Highlands was very strong. One commentator emphasized what today would be called the multiplier effects of properly exploiting the fisheries: 'their [the Highlanders] land would by this means become finely manur'd, houses would be built, gardens planted, their families would be well fed and cloath'd, and affluence flourish in every corner of their now waste and neglected countrey . . .'.[182] It appears an attempt was made to launch a Scottish fishery after 1746, with the support of leading Scottish and British landowners and politicians.[183] This attempt was quickly overtaken in 1748 by proposals for the creation of a body called the Free British Fishery Society. The Society was widely supported by all shades of Scottish opinion. When the bill to establish it passed the Commons, in March 1750, Andrew Fletcher wrote to Lord Milton:

upon the whole this is certainly the most beneficial Bill for Scotland and if properly carried into execution will contribute more towards promoting Industry and civilizing the Highlands, than all the Bills which have hitherto pass'd for that purpose.[184]

---

[178] The occasion of this subsidy was the temporary ending of the bounty on linen exports in 1754.

[179] Durie, *The Scottish Linen Industry*, 90.

[180] Bob Harris, 'The Scottish Herring Fisheries and the Prosperity of the Nation, c.1660–1760', *Scottish Historical Review*, 79 (2000), 39–60.

[181] 'Clerk of Penicuick's Memoirs', *Publications of the Scottish Historical Society*, 13 (1892), 220.

[182] *An Ample Disquisition into the Nature of Regalities and other Heredable Jurisdictions*, 35.

[183] This is discussed in Bob Harris, 'Patriotic Commerce and National Revival: The Free British Fishery Society and British Politics (c.1749–58)', *EHR*, 114 (1999), 291–2.

[184] NLS, MS 16515 (Saltoun MS), fos. 210–11.

The relatively brief (and not very successful), but important history of the Fishery Society is told in detail in Chapter 6. Here, what needs to be emphasized is how far plans failed to take proper cognizance of the nature of the problems which faced the development of the herring industry in Scotland.[185] Attention was focused instead, as were previous plans, on capturing the deep-sea herring industry from the Dutch. This involved supporting the building and employment of decked fishing busses, an activity which required substantial capital. In Scotland, substantial support for the scheme was forthcoming, and outchambers were formed in 1749 in Edinburgh, Glasgow, Montrose, Inverness, and in 1751 in Campbeltown on the coast of Argyllshire. But the sort of fishing that most Highlanders engaged in was small boat fishing off the coast, in the firths and on the sea lochs. No initial support was given to this, although some attention was given to it in a report drawn up by the group of merchants who were behind the formation of the Society.[186] There was also no attempt initially to grapple with the very difficult issue of the salt laws, a major impediment to establishing a successful fishing industry in Scotland. The whole question of the salt laws was raised in the mid-1750s by the Convention of the Royal Burghs and the case was put before the Treasury and ministers in London, as well as Parliament. The result was the Scottish Fisheries Act of 1756, which sought to amend and simplify the salt laws as they applied to fish curing. It also sought to suppress restrictions and imposts levied on fishing by Highland landowners. This was a further facet of attacking the feudal obstructions to industry and commerce in Scotland after the '45.

PATRIOTISM AND COMMERCE

The enthusiasm with which landowners, merchants, and politicians in Scotland greeted projects such as the development of the forfeited estates, the extension of linen manufacturing to the Highlands, and the establishment of the Free British Fishery Society was as much motivated by patriotism as economic calculation. After the rebellion, the relationship between commerce and patriotism, already a strong one in post-Union Scotland, was further strengthened. Commerce and commercial projects seemed to provide the proper outlet for the expression of patriotic feeling. The subjugation or civilizing of the Highlands was easily portrayed as beneficial to Scotland and the British state. Transforming the Highlander from a disturber of stability into a servant of the British state and economy represented an urgent patriotic duty.

Patriotic commerce in mid-eighteenth-century Scotland—or commercial patriotism, as it might perhaps better be called—was not focused solely on the Highlands. In Lowland Scotland, its clearest expression came in the determi-

---

[185] For a detailed discussion, see Harris, 'The Scottish Herring Fisheries and the Prosperity of the Nation'.

[186] See BL, Add. MS 15154 (Minute Books of the Free British Fishery Society), fos. 6–7.

nation in the early 1750s of George Drummond and his allies, who included many leading Scottish politicians, landowners, and members of the intelligentsia, to recreate Edinburgh as the capital of a prosperous, patriotic, and commercial country. After the 'Forty-Five, Drummond led a concerted and successful political campaign to secure the government of Scotland's capital in the hands of loyal Whigs, by which was meant those untainted with Jacobite or Jacobite associations. In 1746, Drummond and his allies were elected to all the key posts on the Council, despite opposition from supporters of Archibald Stewart and those who in the later 1730s and early 1740s had supported a Patriot political platform. There were scrupulous efforts to ensure that only those well-affected to the regime were allowed to vote. Ironically, one tactic adopted by the opposition was an attempt to blacken the names of some of Drummond's friends as Jacobites. Drummond was also opposed on the grounds of his being recommended from London.[187] At the 1747 general election, Drummond's candidature was unsuccessful, partly because he failed to gain full support from the Duke of Argyll. Edinburgh's new MP was one of the Trades' Deacons, James Kerr, who, like Drummond, had led one of the volunteer companies in the city raised during the rebellion. As Lord Provost, Drummond worked closely with the Lord Justice Clerk, and General Bland, to keep a close eye on Jacobite activity in the city; he also made efforts to suppress non-juror meeting houses. He was a leading figure in the so-called Revolution Club, which originally met to celebrate the birthday of William III, and which became a major vehicle of Whig loyalism in the city in the aftermath of the '45, ostentatiously celebrating Hanoverian royal anniversaries.

The plans to improve Edinburgh were an expression of the same political drive—to demonstrate the capital's loyalty. They were contained in the *Proposals for carrying on certain Public Works in the City of Edinburgh*, which were put before the Convention of Royal Burghs in 1752 by Sir Gilbert Elliot. As an expression of North British patriotism in the mid-eighteenth century, it is a compelling document. This is as much for what it does not say as what it does. The question of Jacobitism and the taint of disloyalty, which still hung over the city in the later 1740s and early 1750s, were simply dismissed in the statement 'now that the rage of faction is abated'. The *Proposals* encapsulated both the assimilationist and the competitive urges which underpinned North British patriotism, as well as the sense of movement and progress in Scottish society and economy from the 1740s. They also contained a loyal, but far from submissive, reading of Scottish history. The Union marked the origins of Scottish national revival after the wasted years, national rivalries, and divisions of the seventeenth century. The source of the revival was the manners of the great; the Scottish landowning classes were to lead their country into a new history of commerce and prosperity. A new phase in this history started with

[187] PRO, SP 54/34/32A–D, 36.

1746, and the suppression of the rebellion. There had been a 'revolution' in trade and manufacturing: 'Husbandry, manufactures, general commerce, and the increase of useful people, are become the objects of univeral attention.' The sources of this progress were, it was argued, to be found in the activities of the improving landowning classes and nobility.

The planned improvements were designed to expedite and strengthen the advance of commerce. Bridges at the north and south ends of the city, an aristocratic suburb across the north loch, and new public buildings in the old town—a merchant exchange and new buildings for the courts of justice, royal burghs, town council and its officers, as well as the Advocates Library—were to regenerate the Scottish capital as both a model of and competitor to London. It was a self-consciously modernizing, national project. As the *Proposals* declared: 'A nation cannot at this time be considerable, unless it be opulent. Wealth is only to be obtained by trade and commerce, and these are only carried on to advantage in populous cities.' The landowning classes were to be enticed back to the capital, where they were to provide the wealth, manners, and leadership of the modern Scotland. An improved Edinburgh was also to be the wellspring of further economic progress, both example to and powerhouse of the national economy. The vision was of general prosperity, 'industry and opulence'.

In the summer of 1752, Drummond wrote to the Earl of Holdernesse, one the secretaries of state, for support for the improvements. He also wrote to the Mayor of London. In the second of these letters, in which he enclosed a copy of the *Proposals*, he asserted that they related to a 'city, which had for many years, the name of a metropolis, but . . . had had little else'. Noting that Scotland was beginning to recognize the advantages of union with England, he also urged the Lord Mayor to support the proposals as they might lead to Edinburgh becoming a 'trading place' and thus 'usefull to our common countrey'.[188] In the same year, John Adam designed the new Merchant Exchange to be located in the heart of the Old Town. Building commenced in 1753, with the foundation stone being laid in a grand ceremony, appropriately, by Drummond.[189] It has recently been described as 'one of the most ambitious building projects ever seen there [in the Scottish capital]'.[190] The Royal Burghs gave £1,500 in 1753 to support the new public buildings in the capital.[191] In September of that year, the Duke of Argyll wrote to Pelham about the enthusiasm for the project, and advising him about how much financial support the government should make available:

The scheme is very popular & is certainly for the public benefit, it has been encouraged by individuals, boards & courts of Judicature, The Earls of Morton & Hopetoun

---

[188] BL, Egerton MS 3434, fos. 50, 52.

[189] *Scots Mag.* (1753), 425–30.

[190] Miles Glendinning, Ranald MacInnes, and Aonghus MacKechnie, *A History of Scottish Architecture: From the Renaissance to the Present Day* (Edinburgh, 1996), 170.

[191] *Extracts From the Convention of Royal Burghs, 1738–59*, 397–9, 422.

have subscribed £100 each; the duke of Athol & I £200 each, & great numbers of people of rank have subscribed in different proportions.

Argyll recommended that the Crown provide an annual sum of £500 for four years, which it duly did.[192]

The outbreak of the Seven Years War found, therefore, a Scotland, or elements of it, looking forward. The memory of the '45, and the hostility which it created south of the border towards Scotland and all things Scots, was dimmed but not destroyed. Relative peace and stability had been imposed on the disaffected parts of the Highlands as a result primarily of military occupation and subjugation, but also the bankruptcy, from 1753, of Jacobite hopes for revival of their cause. In 1754, General Bland saw a big difference in conditions in the Highlands in this context from when he had first been appointed commander of British forces in Scotland in 1747.[193] Ministerial confidence in this new-found stability was to become clearer during the war. In 1756 and again in 1759, Britain and Scotland faced major invasion threats from France. On both occasions, the response, so far as the Highlands is concerned, was prudent but limited. As we have seen above, officials in Edinburgh and military officers in Scotland were instructed to maintain a close watch on conditions in the Highlands. Suggestions were also made, in 1756 and 1759 respectively, that militia forces be raised to police disaffected forfeited estates and leading Jacobite sympathizers in the Highlands be taken up by the military.[194] Neither suggestion was taken up. Nor were additional regular forces moved into Scotland. Moreover, officers and politicians in Scotland were unable, in both 1756 and 1759, to find any evidence of Jacobite plotting or activity in the Highlands.[195] The contrast with the later 1740s, and indeed the early 1750s, was striking.

As was shown in Chapter 3, the Seven Years War served to arouse the patriotic spirit and enthusiasm of people throughout Britain and parts of Ireland. People in Scotland as well as England invested considerable hopes in the actions of British military forces overseas. Even the much despised Highlander began the process of rehabilitation in English and Lowland Scots' minds because of their recruitment, from 1757, into British military forces and valiant exploits particularly in colonial military theatres. Support for the war throughout Scotland was widespread and vocal, and was expressed through defensive loyalism in the face of invasion scares in 1756 and 1759, a force in which the Church of Scotland was again to the fore in promoting, as well as in the loyal addresses on the capture of overseas colonies and popular celebrations of the military victories of Britain and her allies.[196] Scottish overseas

---

[192] NUL, NeC 2,211: Argyll to Pelham, 30 Sept. 1753.

[193] NAS, RH 2/4/378, fos. 65–6: Bland to Earl of Holdernesse, 4 June 1754.

[194] NLS, MS 5127, fos. 111–13, 119–21; NAS, RH 2/4/381, fos. 314–15: Lord George Beauclerk to Earl of Holdernesse, 25 Oct. 1759; RH 2/4/381, fos. 327–8: Holderness to Beauclerk, 1 Nov. 1759.

[195] NAS, RH 2/4/390, fos. 28, 50, 121; RH 2/4/381, fos. 216, 218, 286, 329, 339.

[196] See ch. 3, above, pp. 137–8, 139–40.

trade grew strongly during the war. The war was also ostensibly fought to protect British commerce and markets in North America and the West Indies, markets which were increasingly vital to the growing linen industry. In 1756, the claim was even made that formerly disaffected parts of the Highlands shared in the general hostility to the French.[197] In Lowland burghs, this hostility drew sustenance from the same sources which had propelled elements within these communities to display their opposition to the Young Pretender in 1745–6, most importantly religion. As was emphasized in Chapter 3, the Seven Years War was not just perceived as being a war about commerce and power, it was also a war for the protection of British liberties and the survival of the Protestant religion in Britain and indeed in Europe.

The sense of participation in a common British enterprise created by the Seven Years War did not eliminate national rivalries or prejudices between the Scots and the English. This was to be shown only too clearly in the final stages and immediate aftermath of the war with English reactions to the rise to political pre-eminence of the Earl of Bute, the much-detested favourite of the new King, George III. Unscrupulous politicians like John Wilkes found it only too easy to stir up the deeply entrenched scotophobia of some sections of English opinion. Linda Colley has also emphasized how far the success of many Scots in achieving promotion in the army in the mid-eighteenth century helped to create fears about an influx of Scottish parasites seeking preferment in England and British institutions after the end of the war.[198] In some ways, the war also served to raise difficult questions about the nature of the British state and the ideological forces which bound it together. These questions were posed most clearly in 1759, when Scots found themselves exposed to the small French naval squadron led by Admiral Thurot. Against this background, an agitation was, as we saw in an earlier chapter, launched to revive the Scottish militia. The major supporters of this campaign were those who Richard Sher has labelled the moderate literati: key figures in Scotland's Enlightenment.[199] Many of the promoters of the Scottish militia were also the same individuals who lay behind the proposals for the improvement of Edinburgh in the early 1750s. To the thinkers of the Enlightenment, the militia represented a vehicle for reviving the moral condition of the Scottish nation, for reconciling her commercial progress with the perpetuation of public spirit and virtue amongst her citizens. In this respect, it was part of a wider British campaign for militia reform. Yet, with Scotland's exclusion from the Militia Act of 1757, it also came to represent Scotland's full status as a partner within the Union, or rather the apparent denial of that fact. It became the vehicle to express Scotland's distinctive nationalism, particularly her martial history, albeit within a Union context.

---

[197] NAS, RH 2/4/380, fo. 50.
[198] Colley, *Britons*, 117–32.
[199] Richard B. Sher, *Church and University in the Scottish Enlightenment* (Edinburgh, 1985).

Charles Townshend's visit to Edinburgh in the winter of 1759—Townshend had been a key architect of English militia reform—represented the high point of hopes of securing a Scottish militia, and for a few weeks the Scottish capital was awash with talk of national revival. Ministers in London, however, showed no willingness, perhaps understandably given recent history, to arm the Scots or indeed to revive martial traditions amongst the Scottish population. The most that they would do is permit the embodiment of the Argyllshire and Sutherland fencible regiments, regiments which had been raised during the '45. The militia agitation was renewed in 1762, with a similar lack of success. In 1762, there were also signs that it received less than committed support, if not opposition, from important sections of opinion north of the border. Opponents of the militia (David Hume was one) always argued that it was an anachronism and detrimental to commercial and manufacturing activity. The drain on manpower in Scotland to fight the war helped to diminish enthusiasm for a scheme which would have deprived farmers, merchants, and manufacturers of labour at certain times of the year. As an instrument of Scottish national revival, the militia campaign was, therefore, an abortive one, although it re-emerged again during the War of American Independence. It was also a campaign which served to expose some of the contradictions and tensions within North British patriotism in Scotland (and indeed throughout Britain) in the mid-eighteenth century and beyond. For the moderate literati who supported the campaign, the militia was a means of recalling a bellicose national past in a way which was compatible with the Union and combating the debilitating moral and social effects of commerce and the division of labour on Scottish society. It was also a further means of ensuring landed leadership of the Scottish political community. Patriotic commerce, however—so enthusiastically embraced by most sections of the Scottish political elite after the '45—promised to eliminate the impress of a violent, unstable, impoverished Scottish past and replace it with a prosperous and peaceful present and future.

CHAPTER FIVE

'True English Genius':
Patriots and Patriot Clubs
in Ireland

On 21 May 1754, Isaac Drury, a Justice of the Peace in Dublin, penned a sorry letter to Lord George Sackville, Chief Secretary to the then Lord Lieutenant of Ireland, the Duke of Dorset. Dorset had just left Ireland; it had been Drury's role—and misfortune, as it turned out—to try to ensure that Dorset's departure was marked with suitable displays of gratitude from the people of Dublin. Drury described what had occurred:

I attended his grace to the lower end of Ringsend with upwards of ten thousand manufacturers and tradesmen. I also had the north wall lined by many thousands. I sent a vast number of men to the Castle who attended his grace to College Green, where I met his grace with the greatest sight of tradesmen ever seen on the like occasion.[1]

According to Drury, this crowd had displayed nothing but enthusiasm for the Duke and his government of Ireland.[2]

This was not the sum of Drury's efforts. On 13 May, a large crowd of 'many thousands' had assembled in the Liberties, the centre of the textile industry in the capital, with the intention of seeing Dorset off in a rather different manner, or, as Drury rather coyly and tellingly put it, 'in a manner they liked'. The crowd which Drury had brought into existence prevented this. A paragraph in the *Belfast Newsletter* partly confirms his claims. According to this paragraph, on that day (13 May), 2,000 individuals had marched from the Liberties with green boughs in their hats to the Earl of Kildare's grand *palazzo* erected in the 1740s, Kildare House (subsequently Leinster House), in front of which they made 'repeated huzzas'; they then went and did the same in front of a series of other houses.[3] Dorset had, moreover, been detained in the Irish capital for several days by contrary winds. During this time, Drury had expended a substantial sum (£150) to maintain his crowd and ensure that they

---

[1] Repr. in James Walton, *The King's Business: Letters on the Administration of Ireland 1740–1761, from the Papers of Sir Robert Wilmot* (New York, 1996), 90–2.

[2] For a contemporary account which broadly confirms Drury's, see HMC, *Report on the Manuscripts of Mr Stopford-Sackville of Drayton House, Northamptonshire* (2 vols., 1904–10), i. 209.

[3] *Belfast Newsletter*, 14 May 1754.

did not return to work. He also asserted that he had been forced to spend all this time amongst them as there had been strong efforts taken to defeat his purposes.

Drury's actions earnt him the fierce enmity of a substantial section of the Dublin populace. He had subsequently been forced to place a city guard outside his house as the 'city mob' were threatening to pull it down. The city jury were currently preparing to present him for his actions in marching through the city at the head of a crowd.[4] 'I am', he whined, 'so highly threatened and abused that I find it not safe to go through the city, as I am abused by the mob there and meet insults too great to bear from some of the better sort of people'. What made this worse was that he had, as yet, received no compensation from the administration for his expenses and efforts.

Drury's actions also made him the object of an attack in a contemporary pamphlet, which placed a rather different construction on what had happened. Drury was depicted as having led a 'drunken and armed Mob' through the Liberties and down to the quays 'to the great Terror of his Majesty's peacable and liege Subjects'. He had also 'for several weeks, daily entertain[ed] many Hundreds of his Associates in Drunkeness and Riot and had several publick Houses open for their free Entertainment.' According to this pamphlet, Drury had performed the same function on a similar occasion in the previous year.[5]

Drury's letter, and the pamphlet quoted from above, are relatively unusual in providing such a clear picture of the degree of manipulation which could lie behind popular interventions in politics throughout the British Isles in this period, realities not always evident in newspaper reports of such events. It also, however, illuminates equally well the highly theatrical element of the Lord Lieutenant's rule in Ireland in the eighteenth century. Dublin Castle was the site of sometimes extravagant splendour, especially on the monarch's birthday, and Lord Lieutenants tended to cultivate a grand, vice-regal style in public.[6] Both the formal entry and departure of the Lord Lieutenant into and from the kingdom were normally marked by elaborate public ritual. Dorset appears to have been particularly enthusiastic about this aspect of the Lord Lieutenant's role. In 1751, he had a new coach built in Paris, at the cost of around £890, which he used to carry himself to his customary address to Parliament at the opening of the parliamentary session of that year. Considerable sums were also spent refurbishing the Castle in advance of his arrival.[7] The normal rituals

---

[4] In the event, the Lord Mayor took examinations and issued a warrant for Drury's arrest for inciting riot. In July, a bill of indictment was found against Drury on this charge. See HMC, *Stopford-Sackville*, i. 210, 212, 215, 217.

[5] *A Letter to the Right Honourable James, Earl of Kildare, on the Present Posture of Affairs* (Dublin, 1754), 23–7.

[6] See the comments in S. J. Connolly, *Religion, Law and Power: The Making of Protestant Ireland 1660–1760* (Oxford, 1992), 133–4.

[7] See Declan O'Donovan, 'The Money Bill Dispute of 1753', in Thomas Bartlett and David Hayton (eds.), *Penal Era and Golden Age: Essays on Irish History 1690–1800* (Belfast, 1979), 77–8.

attending rule in Ireland took on, nevertheless, more than usual significance in 1754. This was because, as Drury's letter also begins to indicate, the political struggles of the elites had spilled out on to the streets of Dublin and even beyond the capital. On one side were Dorset and the administration, joined by adherents of the Primate of Ireland, Archbishop Stone of Armagh, and the Earl of Bessborough; on the other side were a group who became known as the Patriots, led by Speaker Henry Boyle, and including factions led by the Earl of Kildare and that of the Gores led by the Prime Serjeant Anthony Malone and Teller of the Exchequer Nathaniel Clements. Boyle also received support from MPs instinctively suspicious of the government. For a period of several years, Ireland's leading politicians fought to demonstrate their popularity, and to have this represented not just in the behaviour of the crowd but in the pages of the press. The longer-term effects on Irish political life were substantial and are easily underestimated. As several other historians have noted, the 1750s marked a significant phase in the politicization of Irish public opinion, and the opening up of Irish politics to greater public scrutiny and influence.[8] Other symptoms of the same underlying transformation in the nature of political life were the strengthening of the forces of Patriotism and independence both inside and outside the Irish Parliament. The rules of the political game in Ireland were changed irrevocably.

This chapter begins with a brief description of the crisis which overtook Irish politics in late 1753—the so-called money bill dispute. The parliamentary and ministerial elements of this affair have been well covered elsewhere.[9] The main emphasis here is on why what was in essence a factional struggle about power and influence appeared to raise such sensitive issues in Irish politics, and how its reverberations were felt throughout the country and far down the social scale. In other words, what this chapter seeks to explore is the broader politicization of Irish politics in this crisis and in the years which followed. This necessarily leads us into wider questions about changing attitudes and political and economic conditions in mid-eighteenth-century Ireland.

THE MONEY BILL DISPUTE: BACKGROUND AND NATURE

The money bill dispute reached a climacteric on 17 December 1753 when the Irish House of Commons rejected by 122 votes to 117 a money bill which had

---

[8] See esp. ibid.; Thomas Bartlett, *The Fall and Rise of the Irish Nation: The Catholic Question 1690–1830* (Dublin, 1992), esp. ch. 3; Connolly, *Religion, Law and Power*, ch 3; Jacqueline Hill, *From Patriots to Unionists: Dublin Civic Politics and Irish Protestant Patriotism, 1660–1840* (Oxford, 1997); Eoin Magennis, 'Politics and Government in Ireland During the Seven Years War, 1756–1763', Ph.D. thesis (Belfast University, 1996).

[9] See O'Donovan, 'The Money Bill Dispute'; Robert E. Burns, *Irish Parliamentary Politics in the Eighteenth Century*, ii, *1730–60* (Washington, DC, 1990); J. L. McCracken, 'The Conflict between the Irish Administration and Parliament, 1753–6', *Irish Historical Studies* (1942–3), 159–79.

been returned in altered form by the English Privy Council in London. The Privy Council had introduced an explicit reference in the amended bill to the King's 'prior consent' in the use of surplus funds in the Irish Exchequer for paying off some of the principal of the national debt. To understand what was at stake it is necessary to understand something of the complexities of the Irish revenue. Briefly, the costs of Irish government, which included the often controversial pensions on the Irish establishment, were funded from two sources—the 'hereditary' revenue, a combination of common law levying rights and taxes voted to the monarch for life, and the additional duties on alcohol, tobacco, and other goods, voted to the monarch every two years. Other monies were raised through borrowing, the interest payments being secured by specific funds voted by Parliament. In most years, the funds from the hereditary and additional duties were not in surplus—in other words, revenue did not exceed expenditure. But in 1749, 1751, and 1753, they were. This raised the issue of who should decide how this surplus was disposed of. Dublin Castle argued that since the funds had been entrusted to the monarch for disposal, and through him the executive, so the King's 'prior consent' was needed before the Parliament could allocate money from the surplus to specific ends. The executive remained, nevertheless, accountable to Parliament for its use of the funds. Opponents of 'prior consent' argued that Parliament had an equal right to a say in their disposal; a money bill which sought to allocate these funds to an identified purpose did not, therefore, require the monarch's 'previous consent'. To acknowledge this was to detract from the powers of the Parliament and its necessary control over the purse of government.

It is important to be clear at the outset that the money bill which was defeated in 1753 pertained only to the disposal of the surplus on the revenue. A money bill which raised the funds necessary to the continuance of government was passed. Following the defeat of 17 December, the Parliament was quickly adjourned for the Christmas recess on 22 December. On 28 December, a public letter was sent from the Earl of Holdernesse, one of the two secretaries of state in London, which announced that it was the King's pleasure that Parliament should not sit again that session, and that several office-holders who had opposed the bill be stripped for their positions and pensions—namely, Prime Serjeant Anthony Malone, Thomas Carter, Master of the Rolls, Michael O'Brien Dilkes, and Bellingham Boyle, the Speaker's nephew. On 5 February, Parliament was prorogued. Owing to this, several important bills were lost, including one pertaining to the increasingly powerful and important linen industry. To opponents of the Castle, this further symbolized the alleged violation, if not worse, of national interests by Dorset and the arch villain in this episode, Archbishop Stone.[10] In April, Boyle lost his

[10] See esp. William Bruce, *Some Facts and Observations Relative to the Fate of the Late Linen Bill, last Session of Parliament in this Kingdom* (Dublin, 1753).

sinecure as Chancellor of the Exchequer, while Sir Richard Cox, another leading member of the opposition, was dismissed from his post of Collector of the Customs for the port of Cork.

Dorset and the administration's stance on the money bill—to insist on the passage of the amended bill—was strongly supported at Court and amongst ministers in London. (Attitudes regarding how to resolve the crisis were more ambivalent and freighted with tensions and recriminations between Dorset, Sackville, Stone, and London.) Ministers informed Dorset and the Castle that they should use their full endeavours to have the bill passed. There was also, as referred to above, support expressed for the dismissals of several office holders who had opposed 'prior consent'. Even more telling was the reception given to the Earl of Kildare, who travelled to St James's in late 1753 to present the case of the opposition to George II. James Fitzgerald, twentieth Earl of Kildare was Ireland's foremost peer, and a man of prickly self-regard. In May 1753, he had presented his King with a memorial on disputes in Ireland, which had prompted a severe response in the form of a letter from Holdernesse to the Irish Lord Chancellor, Lord Newport, expressing London's full support for Dorset and his administration.[11] Kildare's mission in early 1754 was portrayed in the Irish press as a heroic journey in defence of national liberties and was probably conceived in such terms.[12] Bishop Synge of Elphin caught the temper of the enterprise very well, together with the extent to which it grew from Kildare's personality, writing just two days after the peer was reported to have left Dublin: 'It is not a measure either concerted or approved of. But if Wilful will do it, he cannot be controlled.'[13] Kildare's embassy was mock-heroic. George II refused to have anything to do with him, and Kildare was saved from humiliation at Court by the advice to desist of his brother-in-law, Henry Fox. This did not seem to matter, however, to the Dublin populace, or at least a part of it, and the peer was fêted as a hero on his return to the Irish capital in February.[14]

Meanwhile, the battle for political supremacy and popularity had been fully joined by, on the one hand, Dublin Castle and the Lord Primate and, on the other, the Patriots. On the Patriot side, this involved political celebrations and dinners in Dublin and many places beyond the capital; addresses and resolutions of congratulations to MPs who had voted against the money bill on 17 December; a contagion of pamphleteering and argument in the press; and the formation of so-called Patriot clubs, especially (but not exclusively)

---

[11] As Robert Burns has noted, these were quickly printed in pamphlet form and widely circulated in Ireland (*Irish Parliamentary Politics*, 147).

[12] See e.g. *A Second Letter to a Person of Distinction from a Gentleman in the Country* (Dublin, 1753), 30–1. (This pamphlet also reprinted Kildare's memorial to George II.) A letter from 'An Irishman' printed in the *Universal Advertiser* of 3 Jan. 1754 compared Kildare to the English Tory MP Sir John Philipps, who was, as the author put, 'Advocate of the People' on the matter of access to Richmond Park.

[13] Synge to Lord Limerick, 24 Dec. 1753, quoted in O'Donovan, 'The Money Bill Dispute', 65.

[14] BL, Add. MS 32734 (Newcastle Papers), fo. 131: Sackville to Newcastle, 11 Feb. 1754.

in the province of Ulster. Dublin Castle responded with several meetings and addresses of its own; a concerted defence of its position in the press; and a major attempt to rally opinion around Dorset and the administration focused on his action to underpin public credit, under severe stress in the spring of 1754. It was these events which provided the background to Dorset's carefully staged exit from Dublin in May 1754.

If the money bill dispute quickly assumed a significant popular dimension, it was in origin and at bottom a fierce struggle for political supremacy. The tussle went back to 1747, when the ambitious Stone had been appointed to the archbishopric. It ended with Boyle returning to influence and a peerage in 1756 and Stone's subsequent return to favour at the Castle in February 1758, following a period out in the political cold, the price of an accommodation reached between the Castle, Boyle, and John Ponsonby, head of the Bessborough interest, arranged by the Marquis of Hartington, who in 1755 had replaced Dorset as Lord Lieutenant.[15] A striking, although sometimes unremarked, feature of the dispute is that Dorset and Stone gained the support of several MPs who were from 1755 to 1756 to make notable reputations for themselves as Patriots—Edmund Sexton Pery, elected to Parliament for Limerick in 1751, William Brownlow, victorious in a bitterly contested by-election in County Armagh in 1753, and Robert French, elected as MP for Galway later in the same year. Part of the reason for this was that Boyle's actions could without great difficulty be seen as factious; it was also possible to portray the goal of breaking his interest as undermining the hold of faction on Irish politics.[16]

An important way in which the conditions of Irish politics differed from those in England and Wales was the fairly rapid disappearance of party divisions after 1714.[17] Thereafter, the main structures in Irish politics were political interests centred on individuals or families. Political control was imposed from the Castle by alliance with so-called undertakers, who were heads of important political interests. Undertakers had been present in Irish politics from the early 1690s, but after 1725 this function was usually monopolized by one person, up until 1729 by William Connolly, and from of 1733 by Henry Boyle.[18] The undertaker parlayed political support, in the form of the votes of MPs, for patronage from the executive. They were not, however, simply servants of an executive appointed from London, and their authority was not unconditional, as a recent study of the famous Wood's halfpence affair

---

[15] The best guide to these developments is Eoin Magennis, 'Politics and Government in Ireland During the Seven Years War'.

[16] See esp. E. S. Pery, *A Letter to his Grace, the Duke of Bedford* (Dublin, 1757). Pery's pamphlet represented an offer of support to Bedford, as newly appointed Lord Lieutenant, if he acted to curb faction.

[17] Connolly, *Religion, Law, and Power*, ch. 3; David Hayton, 'Walpole and Ireland', in Jeremy Black (ed.), *Britain in the Age of Walpole* (1984), 95–114.

[18] David Hayton, 'The Beginnings of the "Undertaker System" ', in Bartlett and id., *Penal Era and Golden Age*, 32–54.

of the 1720s has emphasized.[19] Boyle did, on occasion, seek to put off administration proposals. He was not, for example, prepared to support relief for Protestant dissenters from the Test Act in the early 1730s. And in 1748, he successfully urged Dublin Castle to drop proposals to augment the army on the Irish establishment from 12,000 to 18,000.[20] The leverage and political control of the undertaker was also dependent on the position and authority of the Lord Lieutenant relative both to other political interests in Ireland and, as crucially, ministers and the Court in London. As Robert Burns has argued, it was Lord Harrington's lack of political support at St James's and amongst ministers which enabled Boyle to assume such domination of Irish politics between 1747 and 1750.[21] Between 1757 and 1760, the power of the undertakers was increased by the Duke of Bedford's relative lack of support at St James', a consequence of the Duke of Cumberland's political and military eclipse at the beginning of that period.[22]

From the end of 1751, Boyle's political influence was under increasingly clear threat from Stone. Stone was receiving support from Dorset and Lord George Sackville for what was presented, by Stone at least, and occasionally by Sackville, as a project to break the power of Boyle and the undertakers in Irish politics and restore control to Dublin Castle and London. Boyle's response was to seek to repel this challenge by demonstrating his power in the Commons. During the session of 1752–3, he and his allies had succeeded in passing a series of resolutions critical of the management of monies voted for building and reconstruction of military barracks by the Surveyor General, Arthur Jones Nevill; they had also begun a vicious whispering campaign against Stone.[23] The factious motivation of Boyle was widely recognized at the time. The fact that he was to come to terms with Dublin Castle in 1756 threatened to undermine completely the reputation of Patriotism in Ireland and appeared to underline the self-interested nature of his opposition. Boyle (or Shannon as he became) was, in this context, widely compared to William Pulteney, the 'great betrayer' in mid-century English Patriot politics.

The vote of 17 December 1753 was the climax of a series of divisions in the parliamentary session which opened on 9 October of that year in which Boyle and his allies tested the ability of the administration to rally support without the Speaker's aid. The first major success for Boyle and his supporters in the same session came on 23 November when they were victorious on a motion

---

[19] Patrick McNally, 'Wood's Halfpence, Carteret, and the government of Ireland, 1723–6', *Irish Historical Studies*, 30 (1997), 354–76.

[20] PRONI, T 3019/1151.

[21] Burns, *Irish Parliamentary Politics*, esp. Appendix, pp. 324–7. Harrington was singled out for particular reproach by George II for his role in the resignation of old corps ministers in 1746, designed to force the King to dispense with reliance on Lord Granville. The office of Lord Lieutenant might be seen as part of his punishment.

[22] Magennis, 'Politics and Government'.

[23] Burns, *Irish Parliamentary Politics*, esp. pp. 120–54.

to expel Nevill from Parliament. Declan O'Donovan has argued that Boyle was still at this late stage playing a balancing game, resisting the entreaties of Kildare and Anthony Malone for more aggressive tactics, and there is evidence that he and some of his allies were looking for a compromise on the issue of 'prior consent'. This would have taken the form of glossing over the question of who had authority to dispose of the surplus—in other words, both sides opting to avoid outright confrontation. What appears to have changed Boyle's attitude was a vote on 10 December. On that day, Boyle and his supporters narrowly lost (120 votes to 119) a division on an election petition for the county of Armagh. Stone had given his full and vigorous support to the victorious candidate, William Brownlow, referred to above. As O'Donovan writes:

Given that the Irish Speakership was an active office and that control of the issue of contested elections in the Commons was one of the great buttresses of its political influence, Boyle had now reached the stage where his immediate objective must be to defeat his opponents whatever the large consequences.[24]

The money bill dispute was seized on by Boyle, influenced also by the mounting evidence of popular support for opposition to the Castle—which included, significantly, pressure from constituents on MPs—as an issue with which to harass Dorset and the Lord Primate.[25]

What needs explaining, therefore, is how what was essentially a struggle over power and influence developed into a major political crisis which had repercussions far beyond the Irish Parliament and Dublin Castle. Any full explanation needs to encompass ideology and identity in mid-eighteenth-century Irish politics; the development of new techniques and instruments for popularizing politics; and several deeper-lying trends in Irish society. Put slightly differently, the question is how Boyle and his allies managed to 'create' a sense of crisis in Irish politics between 1753 and 1755.

PATRIOTISM AND POPULARITY

Boyle's achievement in late 1753 was to re-fashion himself as Ireland's pre-eminent Patriot. The development of Patriotism in Ireland has been much studied in recent years, and there is no need here to go over this ground in great detail.[26] Nevertheless, several basic points can usefully be made. First, it

---

[24] O'Donovan, 'The Money Bill Dispute', 60. See also PRONI, T 3228/1/59: John Ryder, Archbishop of Tuam to Dudley Ryder, 18 Dec 1753, where Ryder remarked: 'The truth is, the Court having prevailed in a late important question, in which they had the majority by one vote only, the Speaker and his party, knowing the popularity they should gain if they prevailed in this, were determined to go through with it . . .'

[25] PRONI, T 3019/2227: George Sackville to Thomas Wilmot, 18 Dec. 1753.

[26] See the useful summary in Patrick McNally, *Parties, Patriots and Undertakers: Parliamentary Politics in Early-Hanoverian Ireland* (Dublin, 1997), ch. 8.

was a body of argument and perceptions which was already strongly present in Irish politics by the mid-eighteenth century. Indeed, as recently as 1748–50 there had been a major efflorescence of Patriot argument under the inspiration and the pen of the apothecary and Dublin politician, Charles Lucas.[27] Lucas' influence as a precursor to the money bill crisis is something we will return to. Secondly, as in England and Wales, Patriotism was a notably broad ideological stream, one that could easily contain several distinctive but related viewpoints. Henry Brooke, for example, developed a line of Patriot argument in 1749 which had very marked religious emphases; others wrote in a more secular vein.[28] Similarly, it could contain a Lucas, who rejected outright the right of Westminster to make laws for Ireland, and several Patriot writers and politicians in the 1750s who were more circumspect on this point.[29]

Thirdly, Patriotism in Ireland shared many elements and sources with English Patriotism.[30] It was, therefore, characterized by a suspicion of executive influence and the bribery and corruption which were seen as accompanying this. Similarly, it lionized 'independent, resolute, landed men' as the primary representatives and protector's of the nation's interest;[31] it also looked to public virtue and public spirit, allied to a truculent and suspicious public informed by a 'free press', as guarantors of liberty; and it also portrayed Parliament and especially the Commons as the principal theatre of the struggle for liberty. A precondition of liberty was a free, independent Commons, which meant, it was increasingly argued in this period, a Commons that was also accountable to the 'people' and an electorate that was free of influence and landlord control.[32]

The Patriot cause in Ireland, as in England and Wales, also looked beyond national boundaries; it was the struggle of liberty against tyranny and corruption.[33] Patriots and Patriot argument moved easily back and forth across the St George's Channel. Henry Brooke, referred to above, was in the later 1730s one of several Patriot writers—poets and playwrights—who clustered round the Court of Prince Frederick at Leicester House. His play 'Gustavus Vasa', written in 1738, was one of the first to be suppressed under the Theatrical Licensing Act of 1737. This reflected the fact that it could fairly

---

[27] Hill, *From Patriots to Unionists*, ch. 3.

[28] Brooke, *A First [to Tenth] Letter from the Farmer to the Free and Independent Electors of the City of Dublin* (Dublin, 1749).

[29] A point emphasized by J. G. McCoy, 'Local Political Culture in the Hanoverian Empire: The Case of Ireland, 1714–1760', D.Phil. thesis (Oxford University, 1993), esp. pp. 243–54.

[30] This has been clearly emphasized by Jacqueline Hill (see Hill, *From Patriots to Unionists* ch. 3). For Patriotism in England in this period, see Ch. 2, above.

[31] *Hezekiah Oldbottom to the Adviser of the People of Ireland* (Dublin, 1755), 10–11.

[32] For this point, see below, pp. 224–5. See also *Dedication on Dedication: or the Second Dedication to his Grace the D[uke] of D[orset]* (1753).

[33] For a general discussion of this point, which places Patriotism in a wider European context, see J. T. Leersen, 'Anglo-Irish Patriotism and its European Context: Notes towards a Reassessment', *Eighteenth-Century Ireland*, 3 (1988), 7–24.

easily be interpreted (almost certainly wrongly) as Jacobite in inspiration and meaning, concerning as it did the intervention of a prince from abroad as the saviour of Swedish liberty.[34] In 1749, Brooke lent powerful and prolific polemical support to the cause of Charles Lucas and Patriotism in Dublin. He depicted the struggle underway in Dublin as having far more than purely national importance. In Brooke's eyes, the Patriot flame has now passed from England to Ireland. As Brooke counselled Lucas' supporters or potential supporters:

it is here, and here alone, where the life of ESSENTIAL LIBERTY seems at length to revive; where VIRTUE seems to prepare here SEAT and her HABITATION; That while the *American*, *African*, and *Asian* worlds, groan under universal *Bondage*; while most of *Europe* hath bowed to the *Yoke*; while those few Nations, who boast *remaining Freedom*, are enslaved by their Appetites, and prepared for outward chains by inward Depravity; while even in *Britain*, the Terms LIBERTY and PATRIOTISM are secretly ridiculed as *chimerical*, as Topics of speculation rather than Reality; it is to *Ireland* alone, as to the *Heart*, where the *Animal Spirits*, the *Vital Heat* of *Political Nature* appear to make their Retreat; from hence I trust to re-expand, to inform their accustomed channels, and carry Life *and* health anew throughout the whole system.[35]

Pamphlets and newspaper essays first published in London—Patriot or other—were regularly reprinted in Ireland. Through the press, and in a multiplicity of other ways, the two political cultures were umbilically linked. Irish newspapers depended largely on the pacquet boats from England and the London newspapers they carried for their contents.[36] In the later 1750s, essays from the London Patriot paper, the *Monitor*, were frequently reprinted in the Irish press.[37] English essay papers and periodicals—for example, the *London Chronicle*—were reprinted in Irish editions. Such was the expectation that pamphlets originally published in London would appear in Dublin that in 1751 the Duke of Newcastle wrote to Dorset asking his officials to prevent publication of *The Case of Alexander Murray*, which had been voted a seditious libel by the Commons and which resulted in the publisher, one William Owen, facing trial for seditious libel.[38] When Charles Lucas fled from Ireland in 1749, and the condemnation of the Commons, his destination was London. Once in London, he appears to have written paragraphs on his cause and fate for the leading opposition tri-weekly paper, the *London Evening Post*. He also published

[34] M. J. W. Scott, *James Thomson, Anglo-Scot* (Athens, Ga., 1998), 288; James Sambrook, *James Thomson 1700–1748: A Life* (Oxford, 1991), 191; John Loftus, *The Politics of Drama in Augustan England* (Oxford, 1963), 150.

[35] Brooke, *An Occasional Letter from the Farmer to the Free-Men of Dublin* (Dublin, 1749), 4–5.

[36] See esp. Robert Munter, *The History of the Irish Newspaper 1685–1760* (Cambridge, 1967), 95–6.

[37] See e.g. *Belfast Newsletter*, 12 Jan., 6 Feb., 13 Mar., 1 May, 19 Oct., 13 Nov. 1759; *Cork Evening Post*, 24 Nov. 1757.

[38] PRONI, T 3019/1752: Newcastle to Dorset, 12 July 1751; T 3019/1759: Waite to Wilmot, 23 July 1753.

a pamphlet defending himself and his cause. Officials of the Irish government recognized that these would inevitably find ther way back to Ireland. There were also calls from Dublin to have Lucas prosecuted in England for his pamphlet.[39] In 1752, Lord George Sackville sought to take advantage of the same circuit of communication by having paragraphs favourable to Dublin Castle appear in English newspapers, knowing that a few weeks later they would reappear in the Dublin press.[40]

Patriotism was not, therefore, essentially nationalist; if anything it tended to produce a cosmopolitan outlook. As a vehicle for Irish national sentiment, or rather Irish Protestant nationalism, it was also compromised in other ways. It was frequently argued, following William Molyneux, that Irish liberty was at least as old as English liberty. Yet, again following Molyneux, it was also argued that the history of Irish liberty was of a part with the history of English liberty, that it shared the same genealogy and heroes.[41] English liberties had been transplanted into Ireland, along with English colonists; the story of liberty was the story of the English in Ireland. Others argued, however, that the Irish constitution was of recent vintage, a copy of the English constitution lacking deep roots. As one writer put it in 1753: 'We have not root of our own, and are only grafted on another stock; and if left to abide where at first we took Growth, many live and flourish; but will languish and die, if our situation be changed.'[42] The Patriot defence of liberty represented the 'true English genius' or even, although more rarely, the 'true British genius'.[43] Indeed, from one perspective, what was at stake in the money bill dispute was who better represented the 'true English interest', or so it was portrayed.[44] It was also an extension of the struggle against Stuart tyranny which had consumed seventeenth-century English politics. A typical toast amongst the Irish Patriots of the mid-1750s was to 'the Exclusionists' and the Whig martyrs of 1683, Sydney and Russell.[45]

Irish Patriotism was, nevertheless, also shaped by a series of developments which could easily lend it a proto-nationalist or at least anti-English cast. At

---

[39] PRONI, T 3019/1497: Edward Weston to Wilmot, 26 Feb. 1750; T 3019/1498: Sir John Cope to Wilmot, 27 Feb. 1750; T 3019/6455/207: Weston to Wilmot, 10 Feb. 1750; T 3019/6455/222.

[40] PRONI, T 3019/1905: Waite to Wilmot, 26 May 1752; 1907: Waite to Wilmot, 28 May 1752. See also 1981: Sackville to Wilmot, 8 Oct. 1752.

[41] For Molyneux, see Jacqueline Hill, 'Ireland Without Union: Molyneux and his Legacy', in John Robertson (ed.), *A Union for Empire* (Cambridge, 1995), 271–96.

[42] *A Letter to a Member of the H[ouse] of C[ommon]s of I[relan]d on the Present Crisis of Affairs in that Kingdom* (London, 1753), 5–6. See also Samuel Blacker's (an Armagh JP and supporter of the Patriots in 1753), comments that he 'shall always be friends of the late Revolution [i.e. 1688–9], a time when our happy constitution was begot' (PRONI, D1606 (Gosford Papers)/1/16).

[43] The phrase 'true British genius' was used in *The Conduct of a Certain Member of Parliament, During the Last Session* (Dublin, 1755), 6.

[44] This is how it was represented, for example, by the author of the Patriot pamphlet *An Answer to a Late Pamphlet intituled A Free and Candid Enquiry, Addressed to the Representatives &c of the Kingdom* (Dublin, 1753), 31.

[45] See Appendix 2, below.

one level, this was a function of the arrangements by which Ireland was governed for much of the eighteenth century.[46] The executive in Ireland, the Lord Lieutenant and the Chief Secretary, were appointed from London; they were also responsible to London and not to the Irish Parliament. The latter was a subordinate body. Under the fifteenth-century Poynings Law, ultimate legislative power rested with the English Privy Council. The practice evolved, none the less, of the Irish Parliament originating the 'heads of bills' in the eighteenth century. These were referred first to the Irish Privy Council and then to London. They could be dropped by either, but if accepted were embodied into legislation by the English Privy Council and passed back to Dublin for parliamentary ratification. In 1720, moreover, the Declaratory Act had declared the sovereignty of Westminster over the Irish Parliament and vested the right of legal appeal in the British House of Lords. The practical implications of this act were never realized, since the British Parliament resisted legislating for Irish internal affairs. What it did, nevertheless, was symbolize Ireland's predicament as a dependent Kingdom.[47] So too did legislation passed by Westminster protecting English economic interests from Irish competition, most notoriously the Woollen Act of 1699 which denied Irish woollen goods access to English markets. (There were several calls for the repeal of this act from British writers on economic affairs in this period as part of an attempt to prevent Irish wool being smuggled to Britain's major enemy, France.[48])

Dependency has a twofold effect on Irish Patriot argument. In the first place, the threat to liberty was easily represented as an English one, identified as it was with Dublin Castle, and through the Castle, with London. Secondly, in focusing on Parliament as the cynosure of liberty, Patriotism naturally served to direct people's attentions to threats to the independence of Parliament and Irish MPs, which included the legislation which compromised its sovereignty. It is no accident that the 1750s saw renewed debate in Ireland about Poynings Law.[49] What was being called for was the full development of English liberty in Ireland, not independence. As one contemporary put it in 1754, the question was '[w]hether the present Inhabitants of Ireland, who are

[46] These are well described by Connolly, *Religion, Law, and Power*, ch. 3.

[47] For the significance of the Declaratory Act, see esp. David Hayton, 'British Ministers and the Irish Question 1714–1725', in Stephen Taylor, Richard Connors, and Clyve Jones (eds.), *Hanoverian Britain and Empire: Essays in Memory of Philip Lawson* (Woodbridge, 1998), 37–64; D. W. Hayton, 'The Stanhope/Sunderland Ministry and the Repudiation of Irish Parliamentary Independence', *EHR* 113 (1998), 610–36.

[48] See Ch. 6, below, p. 239.

[49] See esp. *A Clear and Reasonable Answer to that Disingenuous Pamphlet, call'd Considerations on the late Bill for Payment of the Remainder of the National Debt* (Dublin, 1754), which called the law a 'fraud' and also counselled: 'An oppression . . . insisted upon by virtue of this law, should be vigorously opposed by all the sons of liberty in I[relan]d, who should sooner resign their P[arliamen]t, than be like so many [?] Adjectives in it, and their Edicts less decisive, and of less Force, than a petty Act of Vestry, for the Regulation of a petty Parish' (pp. 24–5).

really English, ought not to enjoy all the privileges of Englishmen.'[50] There was no questioning of Westminster's and London's control over foreign and imperial policy or of its conduct of the war.

Patriotism also expressed the 'cause of Ireland' in other ways. Political patriotism in Ireland, as described above, drew strength from, and overlapped significantly with, a form of non-partisan patriotism which looked to the promotion of the good of the 'nation' or well-being of the public. There are clear parallels here with the improving patriotism of Scotland, which as we saw in the previous chapter gathered strength from the mid-1720s and flowered from the later 1740s. As in Scotland, against a background of perceptions of serious economic weakness and debility, this form of patriotism looked primarily to economic progress and improvement as the means of national revival. In Ireland, it was also linked, even more closely than in Scotland, to the strengthening of Protestantism, a reflection of the confessional wars which continued to rage in Ireland in this period, and the peculiarly acute fears which a Catholic majority implanted in the minds of the Protestant ascendancy.[51] The twin aims were powerfully combined in the establishment of the so-called Charter Schools from 1734, which sought converts amongst young Catholics to Protestantism and industry. By 1741, fifteen schools had opened, and others were either being built or planned; in the subsequent decade, their further development was supported by financial subventions from Parliament.[52] But the most famous early eighteenth-century improving foundation in Ireland was the Dublin Society, established in 1731. Founded against the background of a mood of acute pessimism about Irish economic conditions, the goal and purpose of the Society was to promote Irish economic development and prosperity through import substitution. (In this, its aims were basically similar to the Board of Trustees for the Improvement of Manufactures and Fisheries in Scotland and, slighty later, the Society for the Promotion of Arts, Manufactures and Commerce in England and Wales.) In its early phases, the Society sought to encourage the dissemination of information about new techniques and technologies, and was one of the first bodies in Irish society to exploit systematically the growing power of the press.[53] The 1740s and 1750s saw further activity in the same vein, provoked initially by the dire effects of famine and disease in 1741. (This may have claimed around 250,000 lives.) There was a strengthening campaign to promote tillage at the expense of pastoral farming through the agency of farmers' clubs formed at the county level. This was seen as the means to

[50] *Patriot Queries, Occasioned by a Late Libel entitled, Queries to the People of Ireland* (Dublin, 1754), 3.

[51] There is a useful discussion of this type of patriotism in J. G. McCoy, 'Local Political Culture'.

[52] Kenneth Milne, *The Irish Charter Schools, 1730–1830* (Dublin, 1997), 21.

[53] I owe this point to a presentation on the Society given by Dr David Dickson at the Tenth International Congress on the Enlightenment held in Dublin, 21–31 July 1999. Between 1736 and 1750, the Society published an annual essay in *Faulkener's Dublin Journal*.

reverse the drain of population out of the kingdom, as well as specie to pay for imports of grain. Premiums were also provided at the local level to stimulate further progress in the linen industry. Linen manufacturing was viewed as the means to plant Protestant tenants in predominantly Catholic parts of Ireland, and also to 'civilize' the Papists. In 1757, one writer eulogized, in the context of arguing that Catholics should be admitted to this expanding world of economic improvement:

Meer Conquerors, stimulated by the lust of power, wild Ambition, Revenge or Avarice, but inattentive to the ways of Heaven, and the salutary Maxims of Religion; have ever been Visitations, or Instruments of God's Wrath, against Rebellious Man; not Blessings and Heroes. To erect Churches and Cities; to plant, cultivate and improve the land; to nurture Science; cherish Art; encourage Industry; reward Invention; promote Manufactures; extend Commerce; and above all, to establish true Religious worship; are the benign offices of an Angel.[54]

Parliament voted increasing amounts of money to finance the costs of improving transport, especially the construction of navigable waterways and canals. Limerick, for example, benefited susbtantially from this; between 1755 and 1761, grants of £11,000 were made for building the Plassey canal into the city, and £8,000 for a new bridge and other city improvements.[55] Parliament also passed several important pieces of legislation designed to expedite economic improvement in various areas, including an act in 1757 which provided bounty payments on the land carriage of corn to Dublin, designed to encourage greater grain production in Ireland, as well as to ensure that the capital was well provided with the staple.

During the 1740s and 1750s, against the background of a marked acceleration in economic activity in 1747–52, the Dublin Society continued to extend its activities, also raising its profile as a national institution. In 1740, it introduced a premium system to encourage the development of craft skills and experimentation in agriculture. In 1746, it received its first public funding, and in the same year it established its first drawing schools with the aim of improving design in manufacturing. In 1750, its rising status was endorsed by the grant of a royal charter.[56] Four years later, a subscription was raised to fund prizes for drawing. In 1761, it attracted regular parliamentary funding. The same period also saw the establishment of a host of philanthropic foundations, including most famously the Dublin Lying-in-Hospital, begun in 1751. Thomas Sheridan, father of the playwright and Whig politician, Richard Brinsley Sheridan, battled unsuccessfully to reform the Dublin stage in the

---

[54] *The Protestant Interest, Considered Relative to the Operation of the Popery Acts in Ireland* (Dublin, 1757), 41. See also Richard Cox, *A Letter from Sir Richard Cox to Thomas Prior, Esq* (Dublin, 1749).

[55] David Dickson, 'Large-scale Developers and the Growth of Eighteenth-century Irish Cities', in P. Butel and L. M. Cullen (eds.), *Cities and Merchants: French and Irish Perspectives on Urban Development, 1500–1900* (Dublin, 1984), 118.

[56] PRONI, T 1060/3/2738.

name of national cultural improvement. Ironically perhaps, one of the reasons for his failure was that he, or his theatre in Smock-Alley at least, became caught up in the money bill dispute.[57] He also promoted the foundation in 1757 of the Hibernian Society, which sought to improve education in Ireland as a means for producing a more virtuous, refined elite.[58] Through this society, Ireland was not only to educate its own elite in Ireland—rather than at Eton, Westminster, and Oxford—but to show the rest of Britain how to improve command of rhetoric and oratory in the English language. As Sheridan extolled: 'Let it be the Glory, let it be the Boast of this Country, that of the *British* dominions, IRELAND first led the way, in an institution best calculated to revive the ancient Honour of these Realms . . .'[59]

Improving patriotism gained support from across the political spectrum. Initial subscribers to the Hibernian Society, for example, included people who had lined up on either side of the money bill dispute.[60] Nevertheless, it also provided a prism through which a sense of Irish national interest could be defined. The two ideologies—improving patriotism and political patriotism—were overlapping but not coterminous. Arthur Dobbs of Carrickfergus, a leading economic improver of the 1730s and 1740s, saw empire and union as the means to Irish prosperity and happiness, not the greater independence of the Irish Commons.[61] The notion of improvement helped to focus attention more strongly on what was seen as debilitating Irish economic prospects. This included the absenteeism of a large section of the Irish elite, and luxury and the importation of foreign manufactures and goods to feed the luxurious habits of the elites. As in England and Scotland, it also served to frame a series of oppositions—between luxury and virtue, industry and idleness, commerce and manufacturing and luxury. Much of Charles Lucas' writings of the later 1740s, in his addresses to the citizens of Dublin and in his periodical, the *Censor*, reflected these binaries, framing them within an overtly political and opposition construction of patriotism. In 1753, a pamphlet calling on Irish MPs to attend Parliament and their duty recommended the introduction of new laws to curtail luxury.[62] As in England in this period, gaming became a

---

[57] E. K. Sheldon, *Thomas Sheridan of Smock Alley* (Princeton, NJ, 1967). Sheridan, manager of the Royal Theatre in Smock Alley, Dublin, forbade one of his actors, West Digges, to give an encore of part of the prologue to James Millar's play *Mahomet the Imposter* on 2 March 1754. This provoked a riot in the theatre, and made Sheridan the target of popular fury. It also caused him to leave Ireland for two years.

[58] For a brief discussion of the Hibernian Society, see James Kelly, *Henry Flood: Patriots and Politics in Eighteenth-Century Ireland* (Dublin, 1998), 35–7.

[59] Sheridan, *An Oration, Pronounced before a Numerous Body of the Nobility and Gentry, Assembled at the Musick Hall in Fishamble Street, Tuesday, 6th December 1757* (Dublin, 1757), 31.

[60] The subscribers are listed in *The Proceedings of the Hibernian Society, Drawn up by their Order* (Dublin, 1758). Among the politicians were Sir Arthur Gore, Thomas Adderley, Charles Gardiner, Kean O'Hara, Hercules Longford Rowley, William Brownlow, and William Scott.

[61] For Dobbs, see Ch. 3, above, p. 125.

[62] *A Letter of Advice to I——sh Members* (Dublin, 1753), which noted that luxury 'is now spread amongst all Degrees of People' (p. 5). For a later exposition of the same theme, see *Hints Relative to some*

significant source of concern in this context, and in 1757, prompted by Patriot MPs, Parliament passed an anti-gaming statute.[63]

It is against this ideological background that Boyle's apotheosis as a Patriot hero can begin to be understood. The Speaker was certainly helped in this by his character and disposition. In 1733, before his election as Speaker, he was described by one contemporary as 'a country gentleman of great good nature and probity'. He also had a rather understated parliamentary style, eschewing great oratorical set pieces.[64] In Patriot pamphlets between 1754 and 1756, he was portrayed as 'honest Roger', the embodiment of the independent country gentleman. He was a man of 'moderate fortunes', 'little ambitions', and 'less art'; his interest was the 'natural' interest of Ireland.[65] Archbishop Stone represented his antithesis. He was portrayed as an English-born ecclesiastic of low birth, who revelled in sensual appetites and desires. He was the personification of 'upstart power' plotting to undermine the natural ruling order.[66] The attacks on Stone in the opposition press were deeply personal, and show that the Patriots of this period were quite happy to descend to scandal-mongering to further their goals. Much was made of his supposed sexual tastes—for young boys. One particularly savage pamphlet intoned mockingly: 'We thank thee for thy exemplification of *Pederasty* and Endeavours to stop the future Growth of the human species, and consequently of those public spirited mortals that opposed thee . . .'[67] No doubt, this was partly inspired by homophobia, and was designed to stir up the homophobic prejudices of the Dublin crowd, in which it succeeded admirably.[68] Yet it was a form of attack which worked on other levels. As Kathleen Wilson has emphasized in an English context, Patriotism was a masculinist discourse; it celebrated and valorized manliness.[69] Stone's sexual appetites represented a symbol of his lack of

Laws that May be for the Interest of Ireland to have Enacted. In a Letter to a Member of Parliament (Dublin, 1759), esp. pp. 9–11.

[63] As in England, claims were made that gaming was reaching new heights in Dublin. See e.g. *Universal Advertiser*, 3 Feb. 1753.

[64] Connolly, *Religion, Law, and Power*, 95.

[65] See esp. *An Answer to a Late Pamphlet, intituled A Free and Candid Inquiry, Addressed to the Representatives &c of this Kingdom* (Dublin, 1753), pp. 8–9.

[66] See e.g. *Patriot Queries*, 5; *A Letter from a Prime Sejeant to a High Priest* (Dublin, 1754); *The Patriot*, 22 Nov.; 29 Nov.; 6 Dec. 1753. (*The Patriot* was a serial publication which appeared weekly for seven numbers from 25 Oct. 1753.)

[67] *A New Litany For the People of I[re]l[an]d, or a General Supplication to Caiphas, the High Priest, Pope ENOTS the First* (Dublin, 1754), 7. See also *An Address from the Influenc'd Electors of the County and City of Galway to the D[uke] of D[orset], L[ord] G[eorge], and the P[rimate]* (1754), which included the spoof Patriot toast, 'May the Head of the C[hur]ch never get into a S[co]tch Man's Arse again.'

[68] Dudley Ryder, the Solicitor General in London, reported in his diary for 9 January 1754 the following information he had received from his brother, John, archbishop of Tuam: 'He says the Lord Primate is afraid of being assassinated, the Irish are so excessively angry with him, and abuse him publickly by turning up their children's backsides and saying what a fine pair of buttocks they are . . .' (PRONI, T 3228/1/61).

[69] Kathleen Wilson, 'Empire of Virtue: The Imperial Project and Hanoverian Culture c.1720–1785', in Lawrence Stone (ed.), *An Imperial State at War: Britain from 1689–1815* (1994), 128–64.

political virtue, of his corruption and of the unnatural in politics as well as in personal life. He was, one writer disparagingly commented, hiding behind the 'petticoats' of ecclesiastical office.[70] Stone was also pilloried as the Laud of mid-century politics, a figure of ecclesiastical ambition and tyranny. (Another frequent historical analogy was with Cardinal Wolsey.) It was an association, and line of attack, calculated to appeal especially to traditional Presbyterian anti-clerical sentiment. It is also one of the factors which helps to explain how Presbyterians, in Dublin and in the north, were drawn into supporting the Patriot side in the money bill dispute.[71]

If Boyle came to be represented and seen as the embodiment of Patriot interest and virtue, there is still the question of why contemporaries thought so much was at stake in the money bill dispute. At one level, the issues raised by 'prior consent' were rather abstract and not easily clarified. Much argument took the form of picking over of recent precedents, 1749 and 1751, or of densely presented constitutional principles, especially when aimed at the 'thinking people'.[72] At another level, however, Patriot propaganda and argument succeeded in infusing the issue with a significance far beyond its immediate importance. Some of this was achieved by blatant scare tactics, such as the claim by William Howard, MP for Doneraile, that were the principle of 'prior consent' to be endorsed by the Commons 'the money might be carried to Hanover'.[73] Yet, as was recognized at the time by Castle officials, the issue was a 'delicate' one.[74] This was because of the importance which was attached to the Irish Parliament as guardian of Irish liberties and the national interest. From one perspective, the history of Patriotism in Ireland in the eighteenth century is the history of growing status and influence of the Irish Parliament after 1692. By the mid-eighteenth century, the Irish Commons had acquired the right to initiate all money bills, with the exception of the supply bill drawn up by the Irish Privy Council as a cause for calling a new parliament. In 1760, following the death of George II, even this exception was to be a source of controversy, as Irish privy counsellors struggled to evade the burden of unpopularity by originating such a bill.[75] Control of money was the major means by which the Commons could exert leverage over and seek to control the executive; to remove this would be to remove the essential prop of liberty.

The issue of 'prior consent' was also very rapidly placed in a wider context. Repulsing the executive on this occasion was to display the vigilance necessary

---

[70] *An Answer to a Late Pamphlet*, 38.

[71] A Patriot celebration in Enniskillen on 17 December 1754 included, for example, the toast 'No Protestant Priestcraft' (*Universal Advertiser*, 24 Dec. 1754).

[72] The phrase was used in this context by John Ryder, archbishop of Tuam (PRONI, T 3228/1/64).

[73] Burns, *Irish Parliamentary Politics*, 171. Archbishop Ryder wrote on 18 December that the issue 'appears to have been debated with no other view but to gain popularity to the leaders of the opposition . . .' (PRONI, T 3228/1/59).

[74] PRONI, T 3019/1444: Edward Weston to Wilmot, 2 Dec. 1749.

[75] Burns, *Irish Parliamentary Politics*, ch. 8.

to the defence of freedom. The Irish constitution was, it was argued, distinctively susceptible to the ambitions of unscrupulous ministers who used corrupt methods to achieve their goals. This was a consequence of the fragility of this constitution, but also the fact that Irish cries regarding the violation of their liberties would not easily be heard by an absent monarch in London. As one Patriot urged: 'In this Kingdom it [freedom] is very tender, and requires continued Care and Cherishment'.[76] As the political conflict developed in 1754–5, Patriot propagandists and politicians did not, moveover, shy away from raising expectations and fears even further. The spectre of union, and the suppression of the Irish Parliament and subjugation to a dominant English interest, were explicitly raised in several pamphlets as the ultimate goals of Dublin Castle and London. In 1751, Lord Hillsborough's floating of the idea of union as a means to strengthen Ireland's standing and economy, and also to create a greater Britain, had been received with scorn in Ireland; Ireland did not want to become another Scotland, forgotten, miserable, and marginal to the interests of Westminster.[77] In 1753, in the context of the money bill dispute, one writer talked of the 'most monstrous, detestable, and pernicious [plan] that ever was formed against the Happiness of a Kingdom.'[78] What was at stake was national prosperity and liberty. Imprecise but powerful notions of revival were very much in the air. One pamphleteer talked of a 'great and happy Reformation'; others hinted at the complete defeat of corruption, the flowering of liberty and growth of trade and prosperity.[79] It was precisely this sense of anticipation, of possible national revival, which Charles O'Connor sought to exploit in one of his appeals for the liberalization of penal laws affecting Catholics in the mid-1750s.[80] It is only

---

[76] *The Conduct of a Certain Member of Parliament*, 21.

[77] Lord Hillsborough, *A Proposal for Uniting the Kingdoms of Great Britain and Ireland* (London and Dublin, 1751); *An Answer to the Late Proposal For Uniting the Kingdom of Great Britain and Ireland* (Dublin, 1751); *An Humble Address to the Nobility, Gentry and Freeholders, of the Kingdom of Ireland* (Dublin, 1751); Nicholas Archdall, *An Alarum to the People of Great Britain and Ireland: In Answer to a Late Proposal for Uniting these Kingdoms* (Dublin, 1751). See also *The R[o]y[a]l Mistake, or a Catechism for the I[ri]sh Parliament* (London, 1753), 12, for hostility to the notion of union and negative representation of Scotland's fate under the incorporating union of 1707. One irony is that Scotland was in precisely this period beginning to reap clear economic benefits from union with England.

[78] *A Letter to a Person of Distinction in Town, From a Gentleman in the Country. Containing Some Remarks on a Late Pamphlet intitled A Free and Candid Inquiry &c* (Dublin, 1753), 17–19, 47. See also *A Second Letter to a Person of Distinction from a Gentleman in the Country* (Dublin, 1753), which refers to the 'Junto scheme' formed 'on the other side' (p. 27); *Common Sense: in a Letter to a Friend* (Dublin, 1755), which instructs readers that 'a more suddenly decisive stroke was ultimately resolved on, and ripe for introduction' (p. 4); *Faction's Overthrow: or More Fair Warning, and Good Advice, to the Nobility, Gentry and Commonalty of Ireland* (Dublin, 1755), 10. In 1755, these warnings may have been partly stimulated by the appearance of a pamphlet advocating union, *Policy and Justice: An Essay being a Proposal for Augmenting the Power, and Wealth of Great-Britain, by Uniting Ireland* (Dublin, 1755).

[79] See e.g. *The Review: Being A Short Account of the Doctrine, Arguments, and Tendency, of the Writings Offered to the Publick, by the C[our]t Advocates, since Last September* (Dublin, 1754), 51; *The Conduct of a Certain Member of Parliament*, 42–3.

[80] O'Connor, *Seasonable Thoughts Relating to our Civil and Ecclesiastical Constitution* (Dublin, 1753).

against this background of heightened expectations and hopes too that we can understand the widespread revulsion and keen sense of betrayal felt at Boyle's accommodation with Dublin Castle in 1756 and elevation to the peerage. As one contemporary wrote, Boyle, once adored, had brought 'his grey head with infamy to the grave'.[81] Michael Ward simply wrote: 'A compleater scheme to ruin ye Patriots I can not imagine . . .'[82]

If the Patriot's message was skilfully constructed, drawing strength from a well-established tradition of argument, but also from a potent discourse of national improvement, its successful dissemination and publicization was achieved by a variety of means. The years 1753–6 were marked by an eruption of political pamphleteering and propaganda. Thomas Adderley, the Earl of Charlemont's uncle, and himself alienated by the populist tactics employed by the Patriots, noted in 1754 that the government had been 'without mercy . . . pelted with libels'; he also noted that certain pamphlets had been 'with some industry dispersed through the kingdom'.[83] One contemporary catalogue of political pamphlets 'written in Defence of the Principles and Proceedings of the Patriots of Ireland' between 1751 and 1755 lists thirty-six separate items. This, however, considerably underestimates the upsurge in pamphleteering. In 1753 alone, around sixty pamphlets were published relating to the money bill dispute; in 1754, the figure rose to around seventy-five, before falling back to around forty in the following year.[84] It is not just, however, the volume of propaganda produced by the Patriots which stands out, but the range, as well as the efforts to ensure that it circulated as widely as possible. In volume and energy, and in scope, this effort was unprecedented in Irish politics since the Glorious Revolution. Pamphlets included detailed, closely argued accounts of the original dispute, elaborate allegorical representations of Irish and British politics, as well as more populist forms of propaganda designed to widen the audience for the Patriot message, including dialogues, ballads, and verse.[85]

Important pamphlets also appear to have been distributed throughout Ireland, not just in Dublin, as Adderley's comments quoted above suggest. Demand for Patriot propaganda was substantial, as indicated by, amongst other things, multiple editions of individual works. *Common Sense: in a Letter to*

---

[81] Robert Maxwell to Bernard Ward, 13 Mar. 1756, quoted in Connolly, *Religion, Law, and Power*, 97.

[82] PRONI, D 2092/1/8, 126: Ward, 9 Mar. 1756.

[83] HMC, *Charlemont MSS*, i. 192, 196.

[84] These are rough estimates based on data from the Eighteenth-Century Short-Title Catalogue. The approximation arises because of difficulties about categorizing various items and the publication of variant editions of items.

[85] More populist forms of propaganda, issued by opponents and supporters of the Patriots, also included a flurry of pamphlets comprising politically loaded questions, or 'queries'. See e.g. *A Second Number of Queries Relative to the Present Crisis of Affairs, Humbly Addressed to all True Patriots* (Dublin, 1753); *Patriot Queries, Occasioned By a Late Libel entitled, Queries to the People of Ireland* (Dublin, 1754); *Queries to the Querist: or a Series of 141 Queries, in Vindication of the Conduct and Character of the Patriots of Ireland* (Dublin, 1754). I intend to publish a full analysis of the pamphlets produced by the crisis in due course.

a Friend (Dublin, 1754), a reply to an influential defence of the administration's position by Christopher Robinson, went through, for example, four editions. A pamphlet containing the major documents created by the crisis was published by one enterprising printer, while in 1756 all the major Patriot pamphlets produced in the last three years were collected together and reprinted in a two-volume work entitled the *Patriot Miscellany*.[86] Other forms of printed propaganda produced included several division lists, as well as a version of an address from gentlemen and traders in Dublin to Boyle 'elegantly printed on imperial paper for framing and glazing'.[87] Engraved prints of Boyle were also produced in late 1753.[88]

The politicization of the press extended to newspapers. The modern historian of the early Irish press, Robert Munter, has argued that the crisis represented a crucial phase in the political maturation of Irish newspapers. 'By 1750', he writes, 'newspapers were beginning to make themselves felt in the political sphere as organs of public instructions and persuasion.'[89] The Lucas affair played a crucial role in this context, with Lucas' own paper, the *Censor*—which Lucas self-consciously modelled on the English opposition paper, the *Craftsman*—leading the way in the advent of new, overtly political journals. In the mid-1750s, important supporters of the Patriot cause in the press included the *Universal Advertiser*, founded in 1753, and the *Belfast Newsletter*, first published in 1737 and one of the first successful newspapers in Ireland to be produced outside of the capital. Both papers carried many paragraphs and articles supportive of the Patriot cause. The *Universal Advertiser*, published in Dublin by Lawrence Dunn, was at the very heart of the Patriot propaganda effort, a fact recognized by Dublin Castle in 1754 when its circulation through the post office was stopped. Other arrangements were quickly made for the dissemination of the paper outside Dublin, a reflection of the importance which it was felt to have within Patriot circles.[90] In 1754, the paper was also on sale in Belfast.[91] One reader suggested that the print run for an edition was 5,000.[92] If true, this was a substantial figure not just in an Irish but in a contemporary British context. (Munter suggests that the average circulation of an Irish newspaper before 1760 was between 400 and 800, with the very

---

[86] *The Cabinet: Containing A Collection of Curious Papers relative to the Present Political Contests in Ireland: some of which are now first published* (Dublin, 1754).

[87] *A List of Members of the H[ouse] of C[ommon]s of Ireland who voted on the Question Previous to the Expulsion of Arthur Jones Nevill, Esq, Late Engineer and Surveyor-General of that Kingdom* (London, 1753). A division list of the 122 MPs who had opposed the money bill on 17 December was separately published under the motto 'Liberty and Prosperity'. There was also one printed in *An Address From the Independent Electors of the County of Westmeath to Anthony Malone, Esq* (London, 1754), 14–20.

[88] *Universal Advertiser*, 27 Nov. 1753.

[89] Munter, *Irish Newspapers*, 170–85.

[90] See *Universal Advertiser*, 5 Mar. 1754. This announced that a subscription had been opened in several counties to carry the paper from Dublin on the day of publication, with the free use of servants and horse being offered.

[91] *Belfast Newsletter*, 10 Sept. 1754.

[92] *Universal Advertiser*, 28 May 1754.

largest circulations not exceeding 2,000.[93]) Articles and other material from the *Universal Advertiser* were, as often occurred in the case of influential papers in the London press, also reprinted in pamphlet form.[94]

At the height of the dispute (in 1754) every issue of the *Universal Advertiser* was full of notices and paragraphs describing Patriot celebrations and meetings. The paper served not just to publicize these occasions, but also to link together Patriots in different parts of the country; it gave their demonstrations more than purely local significance. This was crucial to their impact, as was witheringly noted by Edmund Sexton Pery in 1757, when he referred to 'the facetious invention of conveying satyr in Toasts, of which such wonderful use was then made, by publishing them in the Newspapers, and dispersing them through the K[ingdo]m.'[95] The *Universal Advertiser* almost certainly had the countenance of major Patriot politicians. By the spring of 1755, by which time Boyle and others had begun to negotiate for an accommodation with Dublin Castle, Sir Richard Cox, author of several important Patriot pamphlets on the money bill dispute, was reported to be overseeing the paper, if not contributing to it. Lord Chancellor Bowes also remarked on 'how greedily' the paper was being 'received and attended to through the country'.[96]

An incident which took place in early 1754 illustrates just how sensitive press reportage of political activities was to become during the crisis. On 16 February, a meeting was held at the Tholsel, Dublin, of nobility, gentlemen, and merchants from Ulster who supported the Patriot cause. The chair was taken by the Earl of Kildare. A central feature of the meeting, as for many other Patriot gatherings in this period—as we will see further below—was the drinking of large numbers of political toasts expressive of the politics of the occasion. Reports of the dinner were carried in several newspapers. George Faulkener, printer and publisher of *Faulkener's Dublin Journal*, which supported Dorset and the administration, inserted a paragraph claiming that a toast had been drunk on the occasion to the Duke of Dorset. This version of events was strongly rejected by the Patriots. Lord Carrick, the Speaker's son-in-law, visited Faulkener, and insisted that he insert a notice denying any such toast had been drunk in the next issue of his paper. This was not the end of the matter, however. The Lord Mayor and Sheriffs of Dublin, who had been present at the meeting, were ordered to attend the Privy Council. John Ryder, archbishop of Tuam, described what happened in a letter to his brother, Dudley Ryder, Solicitor General, in London:

the Chancellor then complained to them in Council of these Libellous papers and advertisements, and told them of their duty in discovering the authors, and particu-

[93] Munter, *Irish Newspapers*, 87–8.
[94] *The Universal Advertiser. Containing A Collection of Essays, Moral, Political and Entertaining: Together with Addresses from Several Corporate and other Bodies in Ireland, to their Representatives in Parliament, in relation to their conduct on the 23d of November and 17th of December 1753* (Dublin, 1754).
[95] Pery, *A Letter to His Grace the Duke of Bedford*, 17–18.
[96] PRONI, T 3019/2624: John Bowes to Wilmot, 31 May 1755.

larly told them they shocked humanity, and mentioned the accounts of the healths in the advertisement, vizt. Becket's fate to all turbulent priests; and it was then proposed and agreed to that a proclamation should be published suppressing libels.[97]

The proclamation was issued on 22 February.

Dublin Castle also sought other ways to combat the Patriot's press campaign. We have already seen that the circulation through the post of the *Universal Advertiser* was stopped. It appears that the country-wide circulation of papers favourable to the administration—*Faulkener's Dublin Journal* and the *Dublin Gazette*—may have been supported by the administration, although a general problem here is that evidence for some aspects of official intervention in the press in this period, such as this one, comes from hostile sources.[98] The administration also sponsored pamphlets defending its position. The first of these, *Considerations on a Late Bill*, was published in January 1754. Its author was Christopher Robinson, one of His Majesty's Counsel in Ireland, who was to write several pamphlets during the crisis.[99] On 24 January, Thomas Waite, an official in Dublin Castle, wrote that the pamphlet had been extremely well received. One thousand five hundred had been printed, and around 200 had been circulated to different parts of Ireland. The remainder had been sold by the printer. A second edition of 1,000 was to be printed, and a substantial number sent into the country through the post. Arrangements were also in train to have an edition published in London.[100] It seems likely that other pamphlets supportive of the administration were treated similarly. One Patriot correspondent from Cork in early February 1754 referred to an item of administration propaganda being 'hawked thro' streets'.[101] Several of the pro-administration tracts were clearly aimed at the artisan and shopkeeping classes, reflecting directly the apprehension that politics was consuming the attention of substantial sections of the middling and even the lower sort.[102] Correspondence between Thomas Waite and Sir Robert Wilmot provides further evidence of the anxiety of the administration to see its case supported in the press, and of the perception that the ongoing battle for popularity was an important one. In early February, Waite noted that the Patriots had been

---

[97]   PRONI, T 3228/1/65.

[98]   *Universal Advertiser*, 20 May 1754. For other hostile comment on court propaganda efforts, see *The Review: Being A Short Account of the Doctrine, Arguments, and Tendency, of the Writings Offered to the Publick, by C[our]t Advocates, since Last September* (Dublin, 1754).

[99]   *An Answer to a Part of Pamphlet, intitled, the Proceedings of the Honourable House of Commons of Ireland, in rejecting the altered Money Bill* (Dublin, 1754); *Remarks on a Pamphlet entitled, Considerations on the Late Bill for Paying the National Debt* (Dublin, 1754); *A Supplement to the Remarks . . .* (Dublin, 1754).

[100]   PRONI, T 3019/2259: Waite to Wilmot, 19 Jan. 1754; 2264: Waite to Wilmot, 22 Jan. 1754; 2266: Waite to Wilmot, 24 June 1754. The *Universal Advertiser* printed a letter from Dingle in its issue for 2 February 1754 which referred to the pamphlet being supplied locally from the post office.

[101]   *Universal Advertiser*, 9 Feb. 1754. The item was probably *The Honest Man's Apology to the Country for his Conduct* (Dublin, 1754). This was written by Eaton Stannard, who became Prime Serjeant in succession to Anthony Malone, dismissed for his role in the money bill dispute.

[102]   See esp. *The Weaver's Letter to the Tradesmen and Manufacturers of Ireland* (Dublin, 1754).

put out by celebrations of Lord George Sackville's birthday which coincided with the return of Kildare to Ireland from his ill-fated mission to St James's. Waite urged Wilmot to have paragraphs describing these celebrations, which had appeared in the *Dublin Gazette*, placed in the English capital's evening posts, knowing that they would return in that form to Ireland in a few weeks time.[103]

If the upsurge of political commentary in the press in the mid-1750s is striking, equally important is how far the Patriots contrived other ways of sustaining the high political temperature, especially in 1754–5. To some extent, innovation was forced upon them. This was because the Irish Parliament only sat once every two years. Having prorogued the Parliament early in 1754, and having secured the passage of a money bill to raise the funds for the normal expenses of government, the administration had no need to call a new session before 1755. The energy and enterprise of the Patriots were, nevertheless, striking. As one contemporary observed in November 1754: 'Our Patriots, as they call themselves, do everything that can be done with impunity to irritate the people against the government, in order to prepare them for the work of the next session of Parliament.'[104]

The main means used by the Patriots to excite the 'people' were fivefold: political celebrations; meetings and dinners; addresses to MPs; the granting of freedoms to MPs and the Speaker; and the formation of political clubs. To some extent, these methods built directly on the Patriot politics of Lucas and his supporters in Dublin in the later 1740s. Lucas had used civic institutions, notably the Dublin guilds, to mobilize support for himself and his cause. The first extra-parliamentary body in Irish politics, the Dublin Free Citizens, started in 1750.[105] All these elements were present in the 1750s, and Dublin's Patriots, including the Free Citizens and many guilds, provided fulsome support to Boyle and his allies.[106] The Free Citizens may have represented the tip of an iceberg of organized Patriotism in the Irish capital. One report referred to 300 Patriot clubs assembled in the city in 1754 to celebrate the anniversary of the defeat of the money bill in the previous year.[107] The Free Citizens continued to meet at regular intervals throughout the mid- to later 1750s several times a year, including on 17 December and 10 November, George II's birthday.[108]

Elements of the Dublin crowd also supported Boyle and other Patriots at various points. Indeed, they were an important and very visible actor in the

[103] PRONI, T 3019/2272: Waite to Wilmot, 11 Feb. 1754. See also T 3019/2280 and 2389 for further evidence of administration concern about the press.

[104] PRONI, T 3228/1/68: John Ryder to Dudley Ryder, 30 Nov. 1754.

[105] Hill, *From Patriots to Unionists*, 114.

[106] Ibid., 117. Six guilds issued addresses in support of the Patriot cause. They also conferred honorary freedoms on leading opposition figures. See Appendix 1, 'Irish Patriot Addresses, 1754', below.

[107] *Universal Advertiser*, 21 Dec. 1754.

[108] Notices of their meetings appear regularly in the *Universal Advertiser*.

crisis. Just a few examples of their intervention will suffice to give an indication of their vigour in this period. On 27 November 1753, 4,000 attended Boyle on his journey home from the Commons. After the vote of 17 December, a crowd carried Boyle home. One report also referred to 1,000 bonfires in the streets on that evening.[109] Thomas Adderley wrote: 'the populace upon this defeat were quite mad with joy, the town was illuminated everywhere, and nothing but rejoicings for two days after were to be heard in the streets'. Apparently, Lord George Sackville slunk home the 'back way' to avoid being mobbed.[110] In 1756, Boyle was to be burnt in effigy in Dublin, and Malone had the mob at his door.[111]

No doubt, a considerable amount of this crowd activity was organized or at least encouraged from above. Patriot meetings in Dublin, of which there were a significant number in 1754 especially, commonly involved bonfires and gifts of ale to the populace. One hostile pamphlet in 1754 referred to the 'extraordinary arts avowedly made use of, to inflame the lower multitude.'[112] O'Donovan has argued that straitened economic conditions in 1753–4 provide a strong explanation of the success of the Patriot campaign in the mid-1750s.[113] They may also help to account further for some of the anti-English sentiments manifested by the populace, for example, stopping passers-by in 1754 and asking them if they supported the 'English' or the 'Irish'.[114] Dubliners had, however, showed themselves amply capable of organizing themselves in other spheres by this date. Rioting was endemic in Dublin, and battles between the Protestant Liberty Boys and the Catholic mob were a recurring, and to those in office troubling, feature of city life.[115] Forestallers and profiteers, those who threatened the independence and livelihoods of Dublin's artisans and workers, all could find themselves subject to protest and, on occasion, physical attack.[116] Print culture reached far down the social scale. One writer remarked in 1753:

There is not a cobler now, who would not rather have it said, that he had made a fine Harangue at one of the meetings of the sons of liberty (as they are termed) than that he had made a Handsome Earning by his Day's Labour for his famishing family.[117]

There are indications that having been conjured into existence by the Patriots, the latter lost control of the crowd. A significant obstacle in the negotiation of

[109] *Belfast Newsletter*, 27 Nov.; 22 Dec. 1753.

[110] HMC, *Charlemont MSS*, i. 191: Adderley to Charlemont, 29 Dec. 1753.

[111] See PRONI, D 2092/1/8, 119. See also PRONI, T 3019/2775: Henry Seymour Conway to Wilmot, 6 Mar. 1756.

[112] *A Letter to the Tradesmen, Farmers, and Rest of the Good People of Ireland* (Dublin, 1754), 20.

[113] O'Donovan, 'The Money Bill Dispute', 74–8.

[114] Kelly, *Henry Flood*, 68.

[115] Patrick Fagan, 'The Dublin Catholic Mob (1700–1750)', *Eighteenth-Century Ireland*, 4 (1989), 133–42.

[116] See Jim Smyth, *Men of No Property: Irish Radicals and Popular Politics in the Later Eighteenth Century* (1992), ch. 6: Connolly, *Religion, Law and Power*, 219–20.

[117] *A Letter upon Libels* (Dublin, 1753), 6–7.

an accommodation between Dublin Castle, from 1755 headed by a new Lord Lieutenant, Lord Hartington, and Boyle and the other Patriots expelled from office in 1754 was the latter's fear of the reaction of the crowd. Anthony Malone was mobbed at the door of his house by a crowd demanding whether he was going to take government office. Perhaps unsurprisingly, he asked the Duke of Devonshire (as Hartington became following the death of his father) to keep quiet about his restoration as Chancellor. Thomas Carter also denied any knowledge of the negotiations.[118] As we will see later, many Irish politicians in the later 1750s and early 1760s displayed a notable timidity when it came to dealing with 'popular' issues. The famous 1759 anti-union riot—when a crowd anxious that a proposal for union was about to be introduced into the Irish Parliament occupied the Commons and staged an unruly demonstration—marked the culmination of a process of politicization which had entered a crucial phase in the mid-1750s. As several contemporaries judged, the riot was best understood in terms of the effects which the money bill dispute had had on politics and the populace.[119]

If the Patriots were in Dublin building on firm foundations in contriving a popular style of politics, they nevertheless managed to innovate in this context in several crucial ways. This fact becomes much clearer once the focus of our attention shifts to include areas and places beyond the capital.

The most notable of the innovations was the meeting at which numerous political toasts were drunk. Notices about these meetings and long lists of the toasts were then placed in several newspapers. Thus, for example, the Patriot Club of Antrim inserted a notice about its meeting of 17 December 1754 in the *Universal Advertiser*, the *Belfast Newsletter*, and the *Dublin Journal*.[120] On several occasions in early 1754, the *Universal Advertiser* had to produce additional, 'extraordinary' issues, so numerous were these notices.[121] Several notices about meetings had to be reprinted in the paper on popular demand, for example, one describing a meeting of nobility, gentlemen, and merchants of Leinster, which was convened in Dublin on 9 March 1754.[122] A typical meeting could produce around forty toasts, many of them highly charged politically, others laying claim to a flourishing tradition of Irish Whig loyalty. Edmund Sexton Pery alleged that the inventor of this tactic was Anthony Malone, seen by several, including Henry Pelham in London, as the malign spirit behind the agitation, although this may have simply reflected suspicions about him because he was a Catholic convert.[123] A possible precedent was an English

---

[118] Magennis, 'Politics and Government', 119–20.

[119] For the riot, and contemporary views about it, see Sean Murphy, 'The Dublin Anti-Union Riot of 3 December 1759', in G. O'Brien (ed.), *Parliament, Politics and People* (Dublin, 1989), 49–68; Smyth, *Men of No Property*; Magennis, 'Politics and Government', 200–4.

[120] *Universal Advertiser*, 21 Dec. 1754.

[121] Ibid., 7 Jan., 17 Jan. 1754.

[122] Ibid., 12 Mar., 14 Mar. 1754.

[123] Pery, *A Letter to His Grace the Duke of Bedford*, 17–18.

extra-parliamentary body, the Westminster Society of Independent Electors, formed in Westminster in 1741 to fight the Patriot cause in the general election of that year and at a subsequent by-election in the following year. The Westminster Independents held annual dinners throughout the 1740s, to commemorate the struggles of 1741–2, which were usually hosted by opposition MPs. At these meetings, politically sensitive toasts were drunk and subsequently publicized in the press.[124]

Whatever the origins, it was a tactic which rapidly caught the imagination of the Patriots. Dublin was the scene of many such meetings, with Patriots assembling on a county or provincial basis. Similar meetings also took place in many other places in these years, especially in Ulster. That this tactic was viewed as very effective has already been partly demonstrated above, by the concern of Dublin Castle about the inflammatory content of some of the toasts. Imitation being the sincerest form of flattery, it is also striking that Dublin Castle officials and supporters sought to arrange similar events in the spring of 1754 to demonstrate support for Dorset. In early February what were described as the nobility and gentlemen of the north met in Dublin for a dinner, and their toasts included 'Shame and Disappointment to Mock Patriots'.[125] In Kilkenny in late January, the 'principal gentlemen' of that city met at the house of John Blount on the birthday of the Earl of Bessborough, who was governor of the county. Toasts were drunk on that occasion to Dorset, Lord George Sackville, the Primate, and also the 'true Friends of the Constitution in Church and State'.[126] But considerably the most important of these meetings took place at the Tholsel in Dublin in March, when a 'polite and grand entertainment' was arranged for Dorset to thank him for his recent support for public credit. The toasts drunk on this occasion included: 'All the true Patriots of Ireland'; 'Liberty without Licentiousness'; 'That Moderation and good Manners may always prevail over Violence and Scurrility'. Also included were several toasts to Irish economic improvement, the fortunes of British arms overseas, and to Irish manufactures.[127] One of the features of Dorset's Lord Lieutenancy, and one which again indicates how strong and pervasive the cause of the Irish economy was in this period, was his and the Duchess's very public support for national manufactures.[128]

Apart from meetings and toasts, the Patriots and their supporters organized popular celebrations of political victories, notably 17 December 1753 and its anniversary; addresses to MPs expressing support for the Patriot cause;

[124] See e.g. *Gent. Mag.*, 15 (1745), 107. See also Ch. 1, above, pp. 53–4.

[125] *Faulkener's Dublin Journal*, 5 Feb. 1754. See also PRONI, T 3019/2273: Lord George Sackville to [ ] Maxwell, 11 Feb. 1754. Sackville noted: 'There will be more people of property than ever were known at any meeting. We hope to have 70 members of the 2 houses of Parliament.'

[126] *Faulkener's Dublin Journal*, 9 Feb. 1754.

[127] Ibid., 16 Mar. 1754.

[128] Ibid., 1 Dec. 1753, which reported that the Duke and Duchess had been dressed in clothes made from Irish cloth at a Castle entertainment staged for the birthday of the Princess of Wales.

MPs were also fêted on their progress from Dublin to their seats in the Spring of 1754. From the Summer and Autumn of 1754, we also begin to see the formation of Patriot Clubs.

Several important points emerge from close analysis of all these activities. First, they enabled the Patriots to maintain opinion at least throughout 1754, and in the north for longer, in a state of heightened mobilization and anticipation.[129] A closer look at just two places will illustrate this—Cork in the south-west and Newry in County Armagh. Cork, like many other Atlantic ports in the eighteenth century, was an expanding city—it was the second largest port in Ireland after Dublin—enjoying the benefits of the colonial trades, and the provision trade, especially salt beef, and butter. It was dominated socially and economically by a merchant community with close links to local landowning families.[130] Sir Richard Cox, a leading figure in the Patriot opposition of these years, had held the locally important and lucrative office of Collector of the Customs, before he was dismissed from it for his opposition to the administration in late 1753.[131] Cork also fell within the ambit of Boyle's electoral influence. The round of Patriot celebrations and events began on 30 November 1753 with rejoicings on the occasion of the vote to expel Nevill from the Commons. It was quickly followed by another celebration of the vote of 17 December. In February 1754, the 'truly free and independent freeholders, freemen, merchants and inhabitants' met to address their MPs and express their enthusiasm for the Patriot cause. On 18 May, the merchants of the Cork dined with Cox. About a month later, the 'Friends of Virtue and their Country' met to agree to present Boyle with their acknowledgement of his services to the country in a gold box. An address and gold box were duly presented to Boyle in the city on 28 July. On 17 December 1754, the 'Friends of Liberty and the Constitution' met to celebrate the anniversary of the famous vote of the previous year. There were also celebrations on this occasion throughout the city. In April 1755, the city saw celebrations on the announcement that Dorset was to quit his office as Lord Lieutenant. In September of that year, various Patriot MPs were entertained by a 'numerous body of gentlemen of the city and county'. Finally, on 17 December of that year, the anniversary of the vote of 1753 was again commemorated.[132]

Newry lay at one corner of the developing 'linen triangle' in Ulster, an area bounded by Dungannon and Lisburn. The Newry canal, opened in 1742, was

---

[129] In February 1755, Sir Dudley Ryder reported remarks of Dorset in his diary to the effect that 'the spirit of the Irish is a good deal quieted, except in the North, where they are going to keep up the spirits . . .' (PRONI, T 3228/1/68).

[130] See Angela Fahy, 'Residence, Workplace and Patterns of Change: Cork 1787–1863', in Butel and Cullen, *Cities and Merchants*, 41–2.

[131] Cox wrote several important pamphlets in these years, including *The Proceedings of the Honourable House of Commons of Ireland, in Rejecting the Altered Money Bill, on December 17, 1753, Vindicated* (Dublin, 1754).

[132] *Universal Advertiser*, 4 Dec. 1753; 1 Jan., 23 Feb., 14 May, 6 July, 6 Aug., 3 Dec., 28 Dec. 1754; 15 Apr., 23 Sept., 30 Dec. 1755.

the first major inland navigation in the British Isles, opening an important line of communication to Dublin and stimulating substantial development in the port and neighbouring region. Until the 1770s, Newry and Belfast competed for economic pre-eminence in Ulster. The pattern of Patriot activity in Newry was broadly similar to that in Cork, although, as was common in the north, it persisted for longer. It began on 15 December 1753, when the 'principal inhabitants' addressed the local MPs who had supported the Patriot cause. On 2 March 1754, Bernard Ward, MP for County Down, was joyously received in the town. The events were described in the *Belfast Newsletter* of 12 March:

On Wednesday last the Principal Inhabitants of this Town, fully sensible of the their high Obligations to Bernard Ward, Esq; the truly Patriot Representative of this County, who, in conjunction with the other worthy Members of the House of Commons, made so glorious a Stand for the Privileges of their Country the 17th of December last, met him about 6 miles from hence, on his Way to the Country; and after an elegant Entertainment provided on the Occasion at the King's Head, they drank the following Toasts. The King; the Royal Family and Protestant Succession; the Duke and the Army; The Glorious and Immortal Memory of King William; The Earl of Kildare and Liberty; The Speaker of the House of Commons and his Friends; Prosperity to Ireland; The 4 displaced Members; May the true Friends of Great Britain and Ireland ever be united in Affection as they are in Interest; May we never want a Ward of Principles and Spirit of the present to represent the County of Down ... Plenty of Ale was given to the Populace, and the Evening concluded with Bonefires, Illuminations, &c.&c.&c.

On 17 December 1754, the Independent Club of the County of Armagh, almost certainly the precursor of the Patriot Club of Armagh, met in the town. On 1 January 1755, the Patriot Club of Newry was founded, with an initial membership of fifty. It met again on 1 July, anniversary of the Battle of the Boyne. In August 1755, a reception for the Earl of Charlemont was held. The Patriot Club of Newry continued to meet in 1757 and 1758. In December 1760, in anticipation of the general election which followed the death of George II, a body calling itself the Independent Electors of the Borough of Newry met to issue resolutions pertaining to the imminent election.[133]

Patriot celebrations were often elaborate, carefully staged events; they also involved, or sought to do so, a sizeable cross-section of the local population. The receptions mounted in different places across Ulster of the heroes of the vote of 17 December 1753 in the Spring of 1754 are particularly striking in this regard. One of the most elaborate took place in Londonderry in late March. William Scot, recorder of the city, and a local MP, was met five miles from the city by what were described in one report as 'a great Number of the principal Gentlemen, Freemen and Inhabitants' of the city. The party formed into ranks, and on arrival at the city gates, it was met by the trades incorporations,

---

[133] Ibid., 18 Dec. 1753; 5 Mar., 7 Dec., 24 Dec. 1754; 11 Jan., 26 Aug. 1755; 25 June 1757; 1 July 1758; 22 Dec. 1760.

dressed in their 'formalities' and attended by a musical band and 'several' hundred inhabitants. They then, together, processed to the Town Hall where they were received by the Lord Mayor and several aldermen and burgesses. Ships in the river fired their guns in salute. The party was then entertained by the Mayor in the Town House. They also drank a series of toasts. Each toast to the royal family was marked by a seven-gun salute from the balcony of the building, and all the rest by a three-gun salute. As on other days of public celebration, the flag was displayed on the steeple of the town church; bells rang 'incessantly'; ships displayed their colours; the Town Hall and many other buildings in the city were illuminated; and the evening concluded with bonfires and other 'demonstrations of joy'.[134] It was a scene repeated in other towns and cities. In Enniskillen later that year, on 17 December, the corporation and gentlemen of the neighbourhood met. The bells were rung, houses were illuminated, and the inhabitants assembled under arms, firing three vollies in honour of the day.[135] Events a year earlier in Strabane were described in a paragraph which appeared in the *Universal Advertiser* of 26 December: 'There was the greatest Assembly of the burgesses and inhabitants of the loyal Borough, at the Town Hall, that ever was known, except when they rejoyced for the Glorious Victory obtained against the enemies of his sacred Majesty, at Culloden Muire.' Reports of such celebrations were partisan and readily susceptible to exaggeration. What cannot be easily dismissed, however, is the success with which Patriot supporters appropriated the usual rituals of public celebrations—the processions, bell ringing, bonfires, and illuminations—together with the consistent efforts made to demonstrate popular endorsement of the Patriot cause. Through such celebrations, groups well below the social elites in a number of towns and cities, especially in the north, were also drawn into the money bill dispute.

The full scope and incidence of Patriot activities throughout Ireland between 1753–5 is indicated in Maps 3 and 4. What stands out is the heavy concentration of activity in Ulster and to a lesser extent in Leinster, a pattern which was to be repeated during the years of volunteering in the later 1770s and early 1780s.[136] The addresses to MPs flowed from the beginning of January 1754. By the end of that year, a total of thirty-four had emerged from outside the capital, and a further ten from groups or bodies within it.[137] Beyond Dublin, the addresses were issued by, variously, corporations, the sheriff and grand jury at assize meetings, and in several cases by what were described as the 'inhabitants' or the 'independent freeholders, burgesses

---

[134] *Belfast Newsletter*, 30 Mar. 1754.

[135] *Universal Advertiser*, 24 Dec. 1754.

[136] See esp. A. T. Q. Stewart, *A Deeper Silence: The Hidden Origins of the United Irishmen* (Belfast, 1993); P. D. H. Smyth, 'The Volunteer Movement in Ulster: Background and Development, 1745–85', Ph.D. thesis (Queen's University, Belfast, 1974).

[137] The addresses are listed in Appendix 1, below.

and freemen'. The Belfast address to Speaker Boyle was signed by 125 'free and independent inhabitants'; from Enniskillen, the addressees were 'the Independent Electors of the Antient, Loyal and ever Memorable Town of Inniskillen'; Bernard Ward, MP for County Down, was the recipient of an address from the 'inhabitants of Downpatrick and independent freeholders in the neighbourhood of the borough'. Addresses from Carrickfergus were issued, separately, by the corporation and the incorporated traders. Several of these addresses, while commending the Patriot spirit of their MPs, also emphasized the accountability of MPs to their constituents and their determination to support only candidates in the future elections who displayed Patriot principles.[138] The address from the 'independent Electors of the County of Westmeath'—to Anthony Malone—even raised the possibility that because of the disproportionate representation of small boroughs in the Irish Commons, a majority in parliament might not represent the 'sentiments, either of the better sort of People, or of the Majority of the Nation'. The address also declared: 'Every Member, Sir, is supposed to speak the sentiments of his constituents, and that member who does not, is a Betrayer of his Country, and unworthy to represent the meanest of the Hottentots.'[139]

Dublin Castle (or its supporters) appear to have attempted to engineer several counter addresses in 1754. A few were forthcoming in the context of the Duke of Dorset's actions to shore up public credit in the Spring. In March, the merchants and traders of Dublin issued such an address; there was also one forthcoming from the merchants and traders of Cork.[140] There were claims made in the *Universal Advertiser* that attempts to procure similar addresses in Belfast and Wexford had failed.[141] Several other pro-Dorset meetings were, nevertheless, engineered in different parts of the country—Waterford, Mullingar, Letterkenny, and Wexford—during the rest of the year.[142]

Patriot Clubs, meanwhile, were formed in several counties, cities, and towns. In Ulster, county Patriot Clubs were formed in five of the nine counties—Antrim, Down, Tyrone, Armagh, and Londonderry. There were also Patriot Clubs in Newry, Downpatrick, and Killyleagh in Down; Monaghan (town); Antrim (town); and Letterkenny in Donegal. Leinster saw Patriot Clubs formed in counties Louth, Meath, Westmeath, and in King's and Queen's counties, in Dublin, and the city of Kilkenny. In Munster, Patriot Clubs were founded in Cork and Kinsale. In some cases, these clubs were short-lived. The Independent Club of the County of Armagh was scheduled to meet in Portadown on 16 April 1755, but no such meeting took place. A successful

---

[138] See e.g. the address from the burgesses and gentlemen of Strabane to one of their MPs, William Hamilton (*Universal Advertiser*, 3 Jan. 1754).

[139] This address was separately published as *An Address From the Independent Electors of the County of Westmeath to Anthony Malone, Esq* (London, 1754).

[140] *Faulkener's Dublin Journal*, 9 Mar., 23 Mar. 1754.

[141] *Universal Advertiser*, 21 Mar., 9 Apr. 1754.

[142] *Faulkener's Dublin Journal*, 23 Mar., 6 Apr., 2 Nov., 19 Nov. 1754.

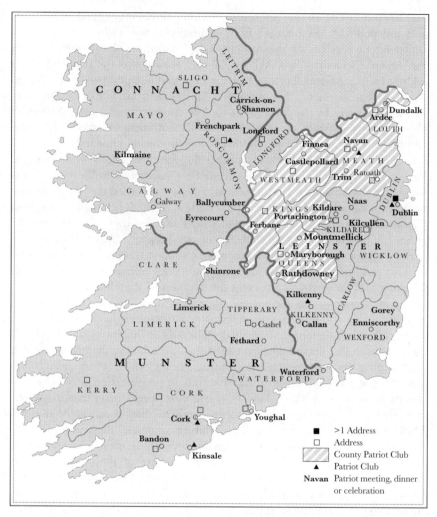

MAP 3. Patriot Activity in Leinster, Munster, and Connacht, 1753–6

attempt to relaunch the club was held in Newry on 1 August.[143] In other cases, the influence of local patrons can be clearly discerned. The borough of Kilkenny, for example, formed part of Boyle's own electoral interest. In several cases, their formation appears to have been closely linked to electoral contests. In Navan, electoral contests from local office and for the borough's parliamentary representation in 1754 and 1755 respectively provided an independent

---

[143] *Universal Advertiser*, 5 Aug. 1755.

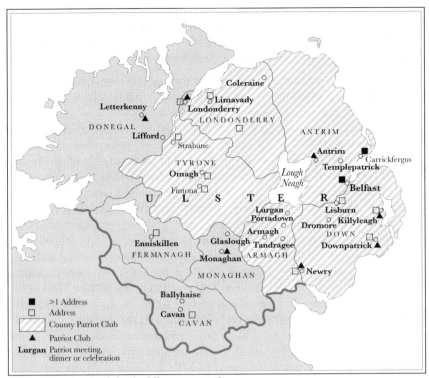

MAP 4. Patriot Activity in Ulster, 1753–6

stimulus to local Patriot organization.[144] In the later 1750s, by-election contests caused by the death of the sitting MP could lead to the formation of Patriot Clubs or continued activity by existing clubs. In County Louth, the immediate stimulus to the formation of a Patriot Club in 1755 appears to have been to support the candidature of Thomas Tippling in a by-election. In 1756, the Independent Gentlemen of the County of Louth opened a subscription to fund silver medals to be presented to the freemen and freeholders who voted for Tippling.[145] Yet even if the impetus behind these clubs, and indeed much if not most Patriot activity came from the existing political elite, what is important is how split this elite was in 1753–5 at the local as well as the national levels. Lord Chancellor Bowes wrote to Edmund Sexton Pery in March 1755 from Wexford: 'I am now on circuit and in a town where resentment runs so high that they will not eat together even at an assizes'.[146] Thomas Adderley wrote in January 1755:

Were these disputes confined to the chiefs of the parties it would be of little or none avail; but unfortunately the poor country is involved in them; it is split into divisions

---

[144] See PRONI, T 3019/2402 and 2408. See also *Universal Advertiser*, 9 July, 27 July, 20 Aug., 21 Sept. 1754.

[145] *Universal Advertiser*, 10 Jan. 1756.

[146] PRONI, T 3087 (Emly Papers)/1/10: Bowes to Pery, 18 Mar. 1755.

that the artificers have neglected their trades; . . . the union of families has been dissolved, and perhaps may never be cemented again; brother against brother, uncle against nephew, have entered the lists; people who have for a long course of years lived happily together fly from each other as from a plague.[147]

So sharp were the political fissures running through the elites that spaces were opened up for groups who were not normally participants in national political debate, at least in any organized or very visible way.

   Membership of Patriot Clubs was not notably large in size, typically fewer than a hundred. It is perhaps significant how often these clubs met in the houses of members.[148] Forty-Five were present at the formation of the Patriot Club of Downpatrick in November 1755.[149] Membership appears to have largely comprised freeholders and the more prosperous merchants. Neverthe-less, in Antrim it appears that in 1755 three distinct Patriot Clubs had been formed by tradesmen and other inhabitants.[150] The clubs also sponsored cele-brations for the local populace in various places. Perhaps more importantly, they also gave institutional form to a new sort of politics of independence, a politics which survived the 'betrayal' of Shannon and other Patriot notables in 1756, at least in the north. This was expressed in many of their resolutions, which spoke of the need to maintain a vigilant watch on the activities of MPs to ensure their accountability. Several also expressed the intention to exercise their votes independently and in accordance with the behaviour of MPs at the next general election.[151] There is a strong parallel here with the opposition campaign of constituency instructions to MPs in England, Wales and Scot-land in 1740 on the issue of a place bill, and its connection to the general election that was due in 1741.[152] The violently contested Armagh by-election of 1753 was portrayed by several writers as marking a new departure in this context, a model of what could be achieved.[153] As was referred to earlier, this saw a contested return, with the Patriot candidate, Francis Caulfield, failing to overturn the result in his favour on petition to the Commons. William Brownlow, the victorious candidate, spent over £5,000 in securing his seat, much of this going on entertainment for the freeholders. It was also an elec-tion in which the press, in the form of both newspapers and election literature, played a full role. Through the press, voters in Armagh were reminded of the

---

[147] HMC, *Charlemont MSS*, i. 198: Adderley to Charlemont, 7 Jan. 1755.

[148] For example, the Patriot Club of Antrim met on 11 June 1755 at the house of a Mr Curry. Sixty-three were present on this occasion (*Universal Advertiser*, 17 June 1755).

[149] Ibid., 15 Nov. 1755.

[150] *Belfast Newsletter*, 21 Jan. 1755.

[151] See *Universal Advertiser*, 11 Jan. 1755 for the resolutions of the Patriot Club of Newry, which included 'May the Freemen and Freeholders of the Ireland always exert their constitutional Right of judging the conduct of their Representatives'.

[152] For this, see Nicholas Rogers, *Whigs and Cities: Popular Politics in the Age of Walpole and Pitt* (Oxford, 1989), 249.

[153] *Patriot Queries*, 15. I am very grateful to Eoin Magennis for allowing me to read his paper 'Patriotism, Popery and Politics: The Armagh By-election of 1753' in advance of publication.

high duty of an MP and, by implication, the importance of the trust vested in them as voters. They were urged, therefore, to exercise their vote independently of landlord influence and bribery.[154]

In certain places, Patriot activity also became connected with local struggles in borough politics. In England, similar sorts of linkages and relationships emerge very clearly in the context of the Wilkite movement of the later 1760s and early 1770s. Detailed local study is needed to substantiate this for places in Ireland outside of Dublin, but it is a set of circumstances which can certainly be discerned in Navan and Kinsale.[155]

THE MONEY BILL DISPUTE: REPERCUSSIONS AND SIGNIFICANCE

If the Patriots, then, devised new ways of mobilizing popular support for their cause, and maintaining pressure on Dublin Castle, the significance of the money bill dispute remains somewhat elusive. Boyle's betrayal in 1756 did undoubtedly produce much public indignation and disillusionment with the Patriot cause. In this sense, the episode could appear to have significance only in terms of rivalry amongst leading politicians. At the time, however, and in the years which followed, several people saw deeper meanings in it, apart from the simple fact of challenge to the rule of the Castle and, through it, London and a period of turbulence in Irish politics. The reaction of London was fairly typical of ministerial attitudes towards Ireland throughout the century—a pattern of initial concern caused by the crisis in relations between Dublin and London, followed by an equally rapid detachment from events once conditions settled down. Confronted with often conflicting reports from Dublin, ministers struggled to make sense of what was going on in Ireland in the mid-1750s. There was some apprehension, fuelled primarily by correspondence from Stone, that Ireland's Patriots aimed at independence, although this was a conclusion which was rejected by Pelham and other ministers on more considered reflection. Instead, politicians in London saw it largely as a factional struggle, a judgement which they were confirmed in by the eventual accommodation of differences between the various sides and political interests reached in 1756.[156] Paradoxically perhaps, Stone's later behaviour in 1757,

[154] *A Letter from A Free Citizen of Dublin to a Freeholder in the County of Armagh* (Dublin, 1753) [2 edns.]; *A Second Letter From A Free Citizen to a Freeholder in the County of Armagh* (Dublin, 1753); *A Third Letter from a Free Citizen to a Freeholder of the County of Armagh* (Dublin, 1753); *A Fourth Letter From a Free Citizen of Dublin, to a Freeholder of the County of Armagh* (Dublin, 1753); *A Fifth Letter from a Free Citizen of Dublin, to a Freeholder of the County of Armagh* (Dublin, 1753). A pamphlet supporting the administration, *A Free and Candid Enquiry humbly addressed to the representatives of the several counties and boroughs of Ireland* (Dublin, 1753), was apparently dispersed throughout the county (*Universal Advertiser*, 3 July 1753).

[155] For Navan, see p. 222, above. For Kinsale, see esp. *Universal Advertiser*, 7 Oct. 1755. For an example of a local study, see Eamon O'Flaherty, 'Urban Politics and Municipal Reform in Limerick, 1723–62', *Eighteenth-Century Ireland*, 6 (1991), 105–20.

[156] A point emphasized by Burns, *Irish Parliamentary Politics*, 219.

when he posed as a Patriot to level his way back into favour with the Castle, only deepened cynicism in London about the motives behind opposition in Ireland. Ministers also had other things to worry about by 1755, notably the imminent renewal of conflict with France. Hartington was sent to Dublin in 1755 to settle the differences of Irish politicians and to allow London to forget Ireland, except as a source of finance and manpower for the ensuing war.

Nevertheless, if ministers wanted no better than to view Ireland with indifference—or as a source of patronage, money, and manpower—we do see from this period accumulating evidence of deepening concern about the governability of Ireland, and the need to wrest influence back into the hands of the executive. Such views were not continuously expressed, but from the mid-1750s they become more common. Henry Pelham was in 1754 discussing the desirability of bringing Ireland within the scope of the Riot Act, as an answer to the ease with which crowds could apparently be raised by politicians in Dublin. It was a view repeated by others in the aftermath of the anti-Union riot of 1759.[157] At several points in the mid- to later 1750s—for example 1757–8—there was talk of the desirability of appointing a deputy Lord Lieutenant to rule when the Lord Lieutenant was absent in England in place of the usual Lords Justices. This was partly motivated by short-term factors, the difficulties of arranging the appointment of Lord Justices without alienating one or other important factions. There was also little support from London at this stage.[158] In March 1756, John Ryder had 'much conversation . . . about union and management of Ireland' with Charles Yorke, younger son of the Lord Chancellor and a future Attorney General.[159] It has been argued that there was a plan to break the dominance of the factions in Irish politics under the Duke of Bedford from 1757.[160] This may have been briefly entertained as a strategy—and Bedford certainly complained to London of the 'spirit of faction' and of 'vain popularity' in Irish politics[161]—but it became one of simply not favouring any one faction. As further evidence of Irish 'independence' mounted, at the end of the decade and into the early 1760s, attitudes in London began, moreover, to harden further. The road to the appointment of a resident Lord Lieutenant, which occurred in 1767, was not an uncomplicated one, but the context which made it a desirable change in the way Ireland was ruled, in the eyes of London and its agents at least, was already by the end of the Seven Years War becoming visible.[162]

---

[157] For Pelham and the Riot Act, see PRONI, T 3228/1/65.

[158] Magennis, 'Politics and Government', 167.

[159] PRONI, T 3228/1/74.

[160] J. C. D. Clark, 'Whigs, Politics and Parliamentary Precedent: The English Management of Irish Politics 1754–56', *HJ* 21 (1978), 275–301.

[161] See PRONI, T 1060/4/415.

[162] For the issue of a resident Lord Lieutenant, see Thomas Bartlett, 'The Townshend vice-royalty', in id. and Hayton, *Penal Era and Golden Age*, 88–112. See also Martyn J. Powell, 'The Reform of the Undertaker System: Anglo-Irish Politics, 1750–67', *Irish Historical Studies*, 21 (1998), 19–36.

The growing, if intermittently expressed, concern about the problem of governing Ireland reflected deeper-lying changes in the conditions of Irish politics. Looking back from the vantage point of the 1780s, the Earl of Charlemont famously depicted the money bill dispute as a crucial moment in the political education of Protestant opinion in Ireland, a view with which Henry Joy, the Belfast printer and historian, was to concur. As Joy wrote:

In consequence of the noble opposition made by the Rt Hon.ble Mr Boyle, Speaker of the Irish House of Commons, with 125 members of the same—a number of 'Patriot Clubs' started up in different parts of the kingdom, some of them in the Towns and others in the Country. In some, all Tradesmen were enrolled; and the People at large were by these means warmed in the Cause of Liberty, and taught to know their own consequence as Electors and Members of the state.[163]

Joy's assessment of electoral behaviour was a fair one. Several by-elections in the late 1750s saw the formation of bodies of independent electors, for example, the Real and Independent Freemen of the Borough of Athlone, who flickered into existence in 1759, or the continued activity of established Patriot Clubs.[164] It was, however, at the general election of 1761 that the politics of independence, which had taken root in 1753–6, became much more visible. The strength of this politics should not be exaggerated; the interests of major electoral patrons—Shannon in Munster, Ponsonby in Leinster, and Stone in parts of Armagh—were not easily overthrown. Yet, as Eoin Magennis has recently emphasized, in counties and boroughs without a dominant patron, contests did take place, involving independent campaigns.[165] In Cork, for example, which as we saw earlier, was a site of sustained Patriot agitation in the mid-1750s, John Hely Hutchison and Sir John Freke ran a successful popular campaign. The Cork merchants, who in the mid-1750s had showered praise on Boyle and Cox, also paid Hely Hutchison's election expenses. In County Tipperary, Thomas Matthew was supported by independent clubs in Clonmel and Cashel. In Kilkenny, candidates in the 'independent interest' stood, although they were defeated. Ulster also, perhaps unsurprisingly given the strength of Patriotism there in the 1750s, saw considerable electoral activity, with contests in three counties (Armagh, Antrim, and Cavan) and two boroughs (Newry and Carrickfergus), as well as considerable activity falling short of a contest in Londonderry. The Patriot Clubs in Antrim and Armagh had still been active in 1757–8, while in Down the Patriot Club was reactivated in September 1760.[166] In Newry and County Antrim, Patriot candidates were unsuccessful, although in Antrim John O'Neill garnered substantial popular support. But in the other contests Patriot candidates were victorious. Finally,

---

[163] HMC, *Charlemont MSS*, i; Belfast, Linenhall Library, Joy MS 4, fos. 96–7.
[164] *Universal Advertiser*, 10 Jan., 21 Apr., 21 Aug. 1759; 30 Aug., 10 Sept., 13 Sept., 26 Sept., 15 Oct., 18 Oct., 25 Oct. 1757.
[165] Magennis, 'Politics and Government', esp. pp. 238–46.
[166] See notices in the *Universal Advertiser* and the *Belfast Newsletter*.

in Dublin, the Free Citizens managed to secure the election of their returning hero back from exile in England, Charles Lucas, behind James Grattan, recorder of the city.[167]

The election of 1761 was characterized by several other features, which again indicate the transformations which were taking place in Irish politics. In the first place, the press played a much more significant role than in previous elections, reflecting its growing political maturity and importance in political life.[168] In Ulster, election notices from candidates and paragraphs reporting on electoral activity were prominently displayed in the *Belfast Newsletter*. These frequently declared the independent stance of candidates such as John O'Neill in Antrim.[169] Secondly, an ongoing campaign for a septennial act for Ireland became closely intertwined in the election, with significant numbers of candidates pledging themselves to support the cause of shorter parliaments.[170] This campaign, and its prominence in the elections, reflects how far the events in the mid-1750s had directed people's attention to the desirability of securing a parliament more accountable to popular opinion. In 1757, a freeholders' society had been formed in Dublin which was to meet every two weeks while Parliament was in session. It also stimulated a series of articles in the *Universal Advertiser* in which the need for the accountability of MPs was reiterated, along with the imperative of Ireland assuming complete control over its financial affairs, including the granting of pensions. Calls were also made for shorter parliaments, as well as for the provision of salaries for MPs.[171] In the event, Ireland had to wait until 1767 for the passage of the Octennial Act, although a septennial bill did pass in the first session of the new Parliament, only to be dropped in London.[172]

The growing vitality of the politics of independence was evident in other areas of Irish political life from the later 1750s. In 1755–6 a new Patriot opposition emerged in the Commons in which leading roles were taken by Edmund Sexton Pery, William Brownlow, and Robert French. This opposition harried the administration in the Commons, campaigning on a series of popular issues such as place and septennial bills, a bill to reform the Dublin corporation, and pensions on the Irish establishment. They also successfully proposed legislation to ensure that the food market was better supplied, and that tillage was encouraged. What stands out about the role of these individuals in this period is how far they were able to have an influence out of the proportion to

---

[167] See Hill, *From Patriots to Unionists*, 124–6.

[168] This point is emphasized by David Dickson, *New Foundations: Ireland 1660–1800* (Dublin, 1987), 128.

[169] *Belfast Newsletter*, 13 Jan., 20 Jan., 10 Mar., 20 Mar., 10 Apr., 17 Apr., 12 May, 15 May, 22 May, 29 May 1761.

[170] See esp. Magennis, 'Politics and Government', 238.

[171] *Universal Advertiser*, 19 Feb., 26 Feb., 12 Mar., 26 Mar., 2 Apr., 9 Apr., 16 Apr., 23 Apr., 30 Apr., 7 May, 14 May, 21 May, 5 July, 16 July, 19 Oct. 1757.

[172] See James Kelly, 'Parliamentary Reform in Irish Politics 1760–90', in David Dickson, Daire Keogh, and Kevin Whelan (eds.), *The United Irishmen* (Dublin, 1993), 74–87.

their small numbers.[173] This partly reflected their skill as parliamentary operators. In 1757, to cite just one example of this, Robert French, MP for Galway, managed to engineer the appointment of a permanent Commons committee to investigate the fate of all bills. This was designed to shed light on the role of the Irish Privy Council, with an eye to reforming Poynings Law. Before 1758, Patriot success also reflected continuing divisions amongst important factions in Irish politics. In 1757, Archbishop Stone used the issue of Irish pensions to put pressure on the Duke of Bedford to readmit him to a position of influence at Dublin Castle, a tactic which proved to be successful, but which also, as referred to earlier, only deepened cynicism in London about the motives of Irish politicians in opposition. But the impact of this Patriot opposition also reflected the general timidity and evasiveness of many Irish politicians when faced with popular issues in this period. As was mentioned above, in the 1761–2 session, a septennial bill was passed, only to be dropped by the Privy Council in London. Irish MPs were not prepared to be seen to oppose the measure outright. (They had also sought to weaken the measure through a series of amendments.) As the Earl of Halifax, Bedford's successor as Lord Lieutenant in 1761, had written in December of that year, 'I have great reason to believe that many of the principal members in the House of Commons would be glad to find them [i.e. the bill] rejected by any hands but their own.'[174] In 1760, an act was passed reforming the Dublin corporation, a long-standing goal of Lucas and the Dublin Patriots. As Magennis writes: 'This piece of legislation was an example of the undertakers accepting a measure that they had long resisted'.[175] The election of 1761, moreover, saw a further accession of talent to the ranks of the parliamentary Patriots, with the entry into the Commons of John Hely Hutchison, Henry Flood, and also Charles Lucas. In the 1760s, Patriot MPs such as Flood were to enjoy an even higher profile than, say, Edmund Sexton Pery in the later 1750s.[176]

There is one final perspective from which the events in Irish politics in this period need to be viewed. Several Patriot writers sought, however sketchily, to place the money bill dispute in the context of the broader development of Irish society and the Irish polity since 1688. What they appear to have apprehended or sensed is that it was an important moment in Ireland's, or at least Protestant Ireland's maturing as a nation. As one of them declared during the dispute:

A Little Time will shew, whether Madness or Reason shall prevail, and whether the Endeavours of the Needy and Profligate shall be able to reduce to a State of Wretchedness and abject Dependence, a People just emerging from Poverty to Wealth,

---

[173] This is emphasized in Magennis, 'Politics and Government'.
[174] PRONI, T 1060/6/194: Halifax to Pitt, 4 Dec. 1761.
[175] Magennis, 'Politics and Government', 210.
[176] See esp. Kelly, *Henry Flood*.

and from Contempt to Veneration; or Whether the righteous Guardian of their Property, and every Thing valuable, to whom they have entrusted themselves and their Posterity, shall be able to resist the Torrent of Corruption that has been breaking in upon them, and reserve their Country for better Times and a happier Fate.[177]

By the 1750s, following the notable and severe setback of famine in 1741, confidence about the kingdom's economic prospects was beginning to strengthen.[178] Signs of economic growth and development were strongly present, albeit they were unevenly distributed across the country. In Ulster, the linen industry was developing rapidly, as John Willes, appointed Chief Baron of the Irish Court of Exchequer in 1757, noted in his letter to the Earl of Warwick in the later 1750s;[179] while in the south-west the Atlantic and provisioning trades, directed through Cork, were stimulating growth in the port's hinterland. On the other hand, the Irish economy in certain respects continued to remain fragile and susceptible to short-term setbacks. In 1756 and 1757 there was considerable dearth and social tension in Ireland, as in England and Wales; there were also banking crises in 1754–5 and again in 1759–60.[180]

Changing attitudes may also, however, have reflected how far external events interacted with changing perceptions of domestic tensions to 'tip the balance' in favour of increasing assurance amongst the Protestant communities of Ireland.[181] The shift in mood was complex, and uneven, and is necessarily hard to document with any degree of completeness. Fear and anxiety amongst the Protestants of Ireland was not quickly or completely eliminated, as several commentators have recently emphasized.[182] The Catholic majority had been politically and socially quiescent for a number of decades, at least before the outbreak of the Whiteboy agrarian disturbances in Munster in 1762; they had also remained so during the scare of the Jacobite Rebellion of 1745–6; but if the Protestant elites could feel a fair degree of confidence about the disposition of their Catholic counterparts, uncertainty and concern about the mentality of the Catholic lower orders remained. It was partly for this reason that public expressions of loyalty on the part of propertied Catholics, especially evident in the second half of the 1750s, appear to have had a limited impact on attitudes amongst Protestants.[183] In 1756, Samuel Blacker wrote to the Earl of Charlemont from Tandragee in Armagh:

---

[177] *A Letter to a Member of the H[ous]e of C[ommon]s of I[relan]d*, 22.

[178] Connolly, *Religion, Law and Power*, 57.

[179] See James Kelly (ed.), *The Letters of Lord Chief Baron Edward Willes to the Earl of Warwick 1757–62: An Account of Ireland in the Mid Eighteenth Century* (Aberystwyth, 1988).

[180] See id., *Henry Flood*, 67–8.

[181] Magennis, 'Politics and Government', 63.

[182] See e.g. Thomas Bartlett, *The Fall and Rise of the Irish Nation*, esp. chs. 4 and 5; Connolly, *Religion, Law and Power*, esp. ch. 6; C. D. A. Leighton, *Catholicism in a Protestant Kingdom: A Study of the Irish Ancien Regime* (Dublin, 1994).

[183] For Catholic loyalism, see Maureen Wall, *Catholic Ireland in the Eighteenth Century: Collected Essays of Maureen Wall*, ed. Gerard O'Brien (Dublin, 1989).

If Ireland is to be attacked, it will be by our lurking enemies at home, who are bred up with the notion of eternal salvation by the utter annihilation of Protestants. It is against these home enemies we are to arm. But I'm sorry to say they are well acquainted with the use of arms and are as great in number, even in the north, as the Protestants.[184]

John Ryder reported in May of the previous year from Tuam in Galway: 'The Popish gentlemen do not conceal from us their fear that the populace, of which 99 in 100 are Papists, would not be restrained from any violence on the landing of a foreign force.'[185]

Ireland was vulnerable, or felt itself to be so, as Ryder's comments underline, to invasion from a foreign, Catholic power. Following the outbreak of the war against Spain in 1739 this again became an intermittently important element in the country's politics. It is worth noting in this context that Ireland's military capability in this period was limited. The militia was in disarray as a fighting force; and the army in Ireland was, in years of war, regularly denuded of numbers to fight Britain's enemies abroad.[186] This practice became a source of tension at various times between Dublin and London. The Duke of Bedford expressed clear irritation about this to Pitt, especially in 1759 when Britain was menaced by the mobilization of a massive French invasion force.[187] The paucity of troops in Ireland also meant that those that were deployed were concentrated in several places, in particular away from the north and towards the south-west, where any invasion force was expected to land.[188] It also forced the ministry to accept offers from leading Protestants in the north to raise troops from 1759. Before that date, with the exception of 1745–6, regiments on the Irish establishment were recruited in Britain. This was because of very deeply-entrenched anxieties about inadvertently arming Catholics, and a desire not to weaken Ulster's Protestant and manufacturing population.

The sense of vulnerability, and the panic which this could induce, was felt at various times during the mid-eighteenth century—in 1740, 1744, 1745, 1755, and again in 1759–60. During the '45, erroneous reports that Jacobite rebels were collecting boats together for passage across the Irish Channel caused temporary alarm in Ulster.[189] Even the relatively minor landing of Francis

---

[184] HMC, *Charlemont MSS*, i. 251: Blacker to Charlemont, 3 Apr. 1756.

[185] PRONI, T 3228/1/68: John Ryder to Sir Dudley Ryder, 20 May 1755. For similar comments by Ryder almost exactly a year later, see T 3228/1/75.

[186] Smyth, 'The Volunteer Movement in Ulster', 25–36.

[187] See e.g. PRONI, T 1060/6/40–7: Bedford to Pitt, 30 Nov. 1759.

[188] For contemporary assessments of the defensibility of Ireland against invasion, which tended to stress the low number of regular forces, the poor state of the militia, and the need to strengthen defences in the south west, see e.g. PRONI, T 3019/239: Duke of Devonshire to Henry Bilson Legge, 1740; T 3158 (Chatsworth MS)/169: report by Lord Molesworth on state of Irish fortifications, 17 Dec. 1740; T 1060/2/62–5: Harrington to Newcastle, 5 Oct. 1747; T 2915 (Lord Lieutenancy Papers of the Duke of Bedford, 1757–61)/1/1: Lord Rothes to Bedford, 1 Jan. 1757; T 2915/8/10: Bedford to Pitt, 29 Aug. 1759.

[189] See esp. PRONI, D 2092/1/7, fos. 13–14: William McCartney to Michael Ward, Belfast, 28 Oct. 1745; fos. 49–50: Charles Brett to Ward, Bangor, 4 Jan. 1746.

Thurot at Carrickfergus in early 1760 set off termors of concern among northern Protestants. Thurot came with only three ships and 600 men; it was, moreover, a force divided amongst itself and in poor condition following months at sea.[190] There were, on the other hand, few regular troops in either Carrickfergus or north east Ulster at the start of the scare. Co-existing, however, with these occasional panics was also a burgeoning sense of pride in the loyalty of the Irish kingdom to the Hanoverian and Protestant Succession in this period, and in their contribution to Britain's struggle against France and its other enemies. This may have been especially important amongst the Presbyterians, whose loyalty was, as late as the '45, viewed with suspicion by many Anglicans in Ireland.

The '45 may have marked a crucial moment in the flowering of this mood of proud loyalism and the emotions which accompanied it. The loyal response amongst Protestants to the crisis has not been studied in great detail, and there were certainly some contemporaries who questioned its promptitude and vigour.[191] As in England and Scotland, the initial confusion and complacency of ministers was mirrored in a general lack of public concern during the early stages of the rising. Nevertheless, as the crisis unfolded, the upsurge of loyal sentiment and demonstration gathered momentum. It was also not led from Dublin Castle, where Chesterfield entertained, at least in the eyes of some, a remarkable sang-froid.[192] The Irish Parliament offered to raise 4,000 additional troops to defend Ireland for the duration of the crisis, but this idea was quashed by Chesterfield and the administration.[193] Through addresses— between September and December, forty loyal addresses were issued (see Map 5)—a militia array, and loyal associations, different parts of the kingdom expressed their loyalty in a noisy and very visible fashion.[194] Some sense of the prevailing mood, and its intensity, is communicated by events in Bangor. There, twenty men had undergone two weeks' training under arms, and were anxious to have this extended. It was why they wished this which is perhaps so telling—partly to prove their loyalty, but also to demonstrate it to the surrounding region. To these ends, they urged:

there was no place that could more easily raise them [a company], or was more willing & loyal and that they could not but grieve when they went into any of the neigh-

---

[190] Marcus Beresford, 'Francois Thurot and the French Attack at Carrickfergus, 1759–60', *Irish Sword*, 10 (1970–2), 255–74.

[191] See e.g. *A View of the Grievances of Ireland. By a True Patriot* (Dublin, 1745). See also PRONI, T 3228/1/14: John Bowes to Sir Dudley Ryder, 5 Oct. 1745.

[192] See Connolly, *Religion, Law and Power*, 257.

[193] See PRONI, T 3019/711: John Ryder to Wilmot, 20 Dec. 1745.

[194] Associations were entered into by Protestants in Counties Antrim and Down, King's County in Leinster, and the Irish peers. For the association in County Down, see PRONI, D 2092/1/6/267. On 16 October 1745, the Earl of Chesterfield noted that the Antrim association was being carried from parish to parish 'where I am credibly informed it is almost universally adopted by the subscription of the Protestant inhabitants' (PRONI, T 1060/1/2521). The Earls of Kildare and Clanrickard, and Edward Southwell offered to raise regiments during the crisis (T 1060/1/2488).

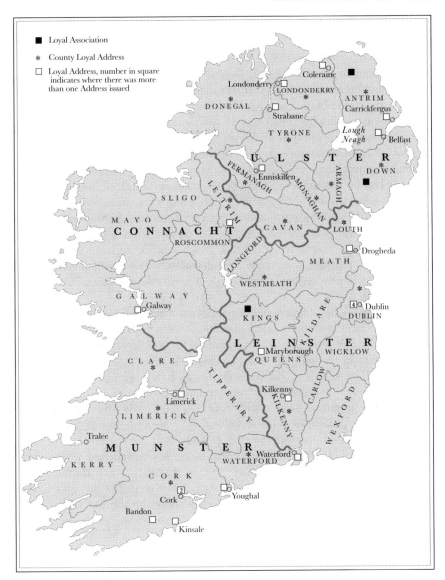

MAP 5. Irish Loyal Addresses, September–December 1745

Source: PRONI, T 1060/1. Between 6 September and the end of December, Ireland produced forty loyal addresses. These were issued by county elites, corporations, clergy (Lord Bishop and Clergy resident in Kilkenny), and educational institutions (Trinity College, Dublin, Scholars of the Diocesan School, Cork). There were also addresses issued by the merchants and traders of Dublin; the Protestant Dissenters of Ireland; the Protestant Inhabitants of County Waterford; and the legal profession. In January 1746, further addresses were forthcoming from the county elite of Galway and from the Corporation of Tralee in Kerry.

bouring towns, they were obliged either to submit themselves to the scoffs of the people or quarelling . . .[195]

There is some evidence that it was the Presbyterians who led the way in demonstrating loyalty throughout Down.[196] The celebrations of the crushing of the Jacobite army at Culloden were vociferous and widespread, and the anniversary of the battle continued to be celebrated in Ireland with an intensity that was unmatched elsewhere in the British Isles. Pride in their loyalty was commonly expressed by Irish Protestants, and, as James Kelly has noted, the cult of Hanoverian monarchy flourished in this period, alongside a cult of Williamite anniversaries.[197] A minor, but very telling, reflection of this was the fact that Dublin was the only of the British capitals (or indeed major cities and towns) to boast a statue of George II. Erected in 1754, and designed by John Van Nost, the statue was situated at the very centre of St Stephen's Green. Significantly, the pedestal had had to be moved from an earlier position because it would have made the statue insufficiently conspicuous. Positioned where it was, and given its scale and elevation, views along several grand streets in the improving and increasingly elegant eastern side of the capital converged on it.[198]

The connections between the impact of war and international rivalry in this period and domestic political conditions were not direct ones, although there was a weak reflection of the agitation for a Scottish militia in Ireland in the later 1750s. A common Patriot toast in the mid-1750s was for reform of the militia. The events of Thurot's landing, when large numbers of Ulster Protestants had converged on Belfast, but had lacked regular arms to defend the city, also provoked some criticism of Dublin Castle and calls, amongst some, for the militia to be rendered effective.[199] Nevertheless, if fear was not removed from Irish politics in this period—and very negative attitudes towards the Catholic majority remained stubbornly entrenched—the experience of the mid-eighteenth century, and of the wars which dominated it, posed very clearly the issue of Ireland's place in and contribution to the British state and empire, and the degree to which it shared in the fate of the other kingdoms from which this state was formed. It may also have taught many Protestants to prize more greatly their loyalty and support for the Hanoverian monarchy. Patriot writers in the 1750s emphasized Ireland's value to the Hanoverian regime and British state and its contribution to British power and prosperity. In the case of many communities in Ulster, it also reinvigorated

---

[195] PRONI, D 2092/1/7, 49–50: Charles Brett to Michael Ward, Bangor, 4 Jan. 1746.

[196] See the hints to this effect in PRONI, D 2092/1/7, 93–4: Bernard Ward to Michael Ward [ ] Oct 1745.

[197] James Kelly, 'The Glorious and Immortal Memory: Commemoration and Protestant Identity 1660–1800', *Royal Irish Academy Proceedings*, 94 (1994), 25–52.

[198] Edward McParland, 'A Note on George II and St Stephen's Green', *Eighteenth-Century Ireland*, 2 (1987), 187–95.

[199] Smyth, 'The Volunteer Movement in Ulster', 35.

deep-seated memories about the Williamite wars of 1689–91 and defeat of the Jacobites, of a loyalty forged and proved in the most threatening of circumstances. As James Kelly in particular has emphasized, the period saw a proliferation of Aughrim and Boyne societies, in which veterans of these battles paraded on anniversaries of these momentous battles.[200] There was also much pride in the military contribution which Irishmen made to Britain's cause in the period's wars. In this sense, it was one further factor which promoted greater assurance amongst the Protestants of Ireland, and a greater willingness to test the limits of their dependence. It also, moveover, served to intensify sensitivies to the all-too-frequent disparagement of the Irish and Ireland by the English.[201] It was the conjunction of these attitudes and sensitivities which was also in coming decades to encourage the Protestant Irish to begin to assume a more self-consciously Irish rather than simply loyal Whig identity.

[200] Kelly, 'The Glorious and Immortal Memory'.

[201] The importance of this disparagement in shaping identities in Ireland in the first half of the eighteenth century has been emphasized by David Hayton in 'Anglo-Irish Attitudes: Changing Perceptions of National Identity Among the Protestant Ascendancy in Ireland, ca. 1690–1750', *Studies in Eighteenth-Century Culture*, 17 (1987), 145–57.

CHAPTER SIX

Trade and the National Interest

In 1751, William Hogarth produced two companion prints, *Gin Lane* and *Beer Street*. A response to the passage of the Gin Act, both were intended as popular prints, employing a heavier line than was usual with Hogarth and selling at a relatively cheap price.[1] Their purpose was reformative; they were 'calculated to reform some reigning Vices peculiar to the lower Class of people'. *Gin Lane* is the better known of the two. In it, Hogarth depicts the hideous, denaturing effects on the lower orders of consumption of spirituous liquors. A man and a dog are fighting for a bone; a diseased drunken mother drops her baby in order to take a pinch of snuff. Other characters are starving to death or fighting or insensible to the horrors which are enveloping them. The only prosperous characters are the pawnbroker, the distiller, and the undertaker. *Beer Street*, by contrast, is a vision of an ideal England, an England rendered wealthy and happy by industry and honest labour. An emaciated Frenchman is being hoisted into the air by a fat and jolly blacksmith. The pawnbroker now trades behind closed doors. A newspaper on a table shows a speech by the King to Parliament in which he recommends 'the Advancement of Our Commerce, and cultivating the Arts of Peace'. Two fisherwomen, their baskets replete with fish, sit reading a poem by John Lockman entitled 'A New Ballad on the Herring Fishery'. In the background, on a housetop, workmen are celebrating the King's birthday, as indicated by the flag on the church steeple.[2]

By including the newspaper and the figures of the fisherwomen, Hogarth was deliberately connecting his vision of a robust, healthy England with a contemporary patriotic goal—the promotion of prosperity through commerce. His perspective was turned in on society; commerce and hard work were to revitalize and reform a society disfigured by gin and idleness. Many contemporaries shared Hogarth's anxieties about a labouring class afflicted by the twin viruses of idleness and disorder. They also worried about a population seemingly destroying itself through disease. The labouring classes were not fulfilling their role—to work hard and to reproduce. The basis of

---

[1] *Hogarth's Graphic Works: Compiled with a Commentary by Ronald Paulson* (1989), 145–9, 367–71.
[2] The 'royal' parish of St Martin's hoisted the flag on this day.

economic strength and military power—a growing, industrious population—was being undermined.

It was contemporary conditions of diplomacy and international relations which made this alarming. Against a background of fragile and uneasy peace with France, the condition of society appeared to threaten the security of the state. Commerce was readily seen as providing a solution, and not just because it, or the employment which it would create, held out the prospect of a reformed and healthy labouring class. In the eyes of contemporaries, commerce also brought prosperity and security in the form of money and maritime power. Britons in this period were convinced, as we saw in Chapter 3, that they possessed a maritime empire, an empire resting on the pillars of global trade, overseas colonies, and naval power. It was, however, precisely this network of connections and influence which was under threat after 1748 from France. The herring, as we will see, became a somewhat unlikely weapon in the battle against French ambitions, as well as in the campaign for the regeneration of British society. John Lockman, dubbed the 'Herring Poet' by contemporaries, was secretary to the Free British Fishery Society, a body founded in 1749 to encourage and oversee British participation in deep-sea fishing for herring.

This chapter begins by looking briefly at debates about commerce and the promotion of commerce and manufactures during the 1740s and 1750s. The growing fears of contemporaries about the strength of French commercial competition and progress since 1713 are emphasized. The chapter then goes on to explore activities and initiatives to strengthen several branches of commerce and industry undertaken by politicians, merchants, and the public in response to these fears. These were heavily concentrated in the period 1748-*c.*1754, in other words during years of peace which divided the two main mid-eighteenth-century wars. As we will see in this and the following chapter, in what was a pattern common throughout eighteenth-century Europe, peace naturally turned the attention of ministers and others to domestic matters. It was also a pattern which was to be repeated after 1763 at the end of the Seven Years War, as well as, even more importantly, following the end of the War of American Independence. In 1783, as in the later 1740s, it was the perception of international vulnerability, and the depth of the challenge to vital British interests from France, which lent urgency to domestic and economic policy and reform.

Efforts to promote British commerce after 1748 were diverse, encompassing legislation, ministerial initiatives, and the foundation of several important extra-parliamentary bodies. Apprehension about French economic progress focused attention on the issue of how best to promote commerce. Some expressed strong admiration in this context for the achievements of the centralized French state. There were also calls for a more rational approach to government in several spheres. Here again the policies and activities of continental rulers—for example, Frederick the Great—acted as inspiration and reproach. The political constraints, however, on any extension of central power remained very potent. William Thornton, the independent Whig MP for York, exclaimed in 1751 against what he saw as a growing tendency towards French terminology, the adoption of new powers by the state, and talk of establishing police forces, portraying this as an insidious threat to English liberties.[3] In England it was voluntary initiatives which were to prove most successful in gaining widespread support. These initiatives worked to encourage private energies and enterprise; they were also symptomatic of a growing body of opinion which viewed restraints on economic activity —monopolies, charters, even apprenticeship regulations—as counter-productive. As Josiah Tucker argued, the surest way to increase national wealth was 'a prudent direction of Self-Love'.[4] The state did have a role to play in this context, a role which supported and complemented that of the voluntary bodies. New and strategic branches of commerce and manufacturing were to be nurtured through protection from foreign competition, and financial support in the form of bounties. There was also no dilution in the commitment (or at least aspiration) to close regulation of the economic development of the colonies. Against a background of revived mercantilism in Europe—and thus the prospect of shrinking markets there for British goods—and a keen sense of the economic threat from France, perceptions of the economic value and potential of the colonies, and their importance to British prosperity and security, were only further enhanced. Contemporaries looked to the colonies for the production of raw materials usually imported from European countries. Some years later, as tensions between the North American colonies and Britain mounted, Benjamin Franklin was to exclaim (in marginalia he wrote on his copy of a pamphlet by Josiah Tucker): 'Buy your Indigo, Pitch, Silk and Tobacco where you please, and let us buy our Manufactures where we please. I fancy we shall be the Gainers. I am sick of these forced Obligations.'[5]

Most of the measures undertaken to promote commerce also represented, therefore, an extension of existing policy and of mercantilist principles with a long genealogy. Their political significance—which, as we will see, was considerable—derived, however, from the context in which they were proposed. The task which many Britons saw facing them after 1748 was how to put their country in a condition to combat a France pursuing very actively a strategy of military revival and commercial and territorial expansion which aimed at undermining Britain's mastery of the seas and which would, if not opposed, ultimately threaten her independence and freedom. Promoting

[3] *Parl. Hist.*, xxvi. 731–2.
[4] Josiah Tucker, *Elements of Commerce* (1755).
[5] Quoted in D. G. C. Allan, 'The Society for the Encouragement of Arts, Manufactures and Commerce: Organization, Membership and objectives in the First Three Decades, 1755–84', Ph.D. thesis (London University, 1979), 195.

commerce and the industry of the lower sort represented vital ways of responding to this challenge.

The principal geographical focus of the chapter is England and to a lesser extent Scotland. Scotland is included so far as it participated in British-wide initiatives. Scottish political elites were no less committed than their English contemporaries to the promotion of commerce in this period; if anything, they were more committed. Yet, the promotion of commerce in Scotland carried a set of distinctive meanings in this period, as we saw in Chapter 4. The integration of Ireland into the economy of Britain and her empire had hardly begun by the mid-eighteenth century. Irish commerce was set about by restraints imposed from London. These were, as is well known, periodically the source of considerable grievance in Ireland.[6] Interestingly, there were calls in our period for the full economic integration of Ireland into the British economy and empire as part of a programme of strengthening British commercial and military power. Integration was one means of preventing the export of Irish wool to France and thus weakening the French woollen industry.[7] This was not practical politics, however, given the inevitable resistance of vested interests faced with the threat of new competition from Irish manufactures. It also assumed a generosity of vision and spirit that was far from present. As one contemporary warned:

To raise these People [the Irish and the Scots] therefore from their Barbarism, to throw ourselves gradually into the same state again; to rival our Growth, drain off our Numbers, and dissipate our Strength, is too high a strain of Heroism.[8]

There were isolated concessions made to Irish trade in our period. The prohibition on the export of cattle and cattle products into Britain was lifted in 1759. Irish linen was further helped in 1743 by the imposition of a new bounty on its re-export from England. Conditions surrounding the export of raw wool to England were further relaxed in 1753. Yet these were not real liberalizations, but measures which either did not threaten major British economic interests or which were justified by English economic circumstances.[9]

THE CAUSE OF COMMERCE: PERCEPTIONS AND ANALYSES

Perceptions of the condition and importance of commerce were very closely shaped by, as indicated above, an intense sense of rivalry and competition with France. It is well known that British overseas trade was relatively buoyant in

---

[6] See also Ch. 5, above, pp. 203.

[7] See Josiah Tucker, *A Brief Essay on the Advantages and Disadvantages which Respectively Attend France and Great Britain, with Regard to Trade*, 3rd edn. (1753), esp. pp. 59–62. Another who recommended allowing Ireland to export woollen goods to Britain was the Tory MP for Colchester, Charles Gray (*Considerations on Several Proposals Lately Made for the Better Maintenance of the Poor* (1751), 18–20).

[8] *Reflections on Various Subjects Relating to Arts and Commerce; Particularly, The Consequences of Admitting Foreign Artists on Easier Terms* (1752), 50–1.

[9] See esp. Louis Cullen, *Anglo-Irish Trade 1660–1800* (Manchester, 1968).

the early Hanoverian period, continuing to grow, albeit at a less impressive rate than in the later seventeenth century. It is also well established that the main causes of the further expansion of trade in the mid-eighteenth century were the colonial and re-export trades.[10] Trade patterns were shifting, with mainland Europe becoming relatively less important as a market for British products, while the North American market grew very rapidly, albeit from a much lower base. The rate of growth of overseas trade picked up significantly from the later 1740s, largely owing to the influence of North American markets, but also to the colonial re-export trades. It was this shifting pattern of trade, and the growing importance of North America as a destination for British exports, which served to strengthen the awareness in Britain of the interdependencies between various branches of overseas trade, and between Britain and her colonies, and of their role in prospects for future prosperity. It also underlined the contribution made by the North American colonies to British power and plenty. 'The American colonies', one writer declared in 1757, 'are now become a great source of that wealth, by which this Nation maintains itself, and is respected by others'.[11]

If overseas trade remained on an upward trajectory in this period, espe-cially from the later 1740s, contemporary assessments of its prospects were, nevertheless, frequently coloured by anxiety and very often strong pessimism. Trade may have promised a golden future; the rule of law and British liber-ties may have in theory provided the ideal soil for success in manufacturing and commerce; but it was a prospect which appeared remote for much of the period. Since 1713, French trade had grown more rapidly than British; its expansion also threatened important branches of British trade. Most alarm-ingly, the French had succeeded in poaching a greater part of the entrepot trade in Caribbean produce from English merchants, developing a large and rapidly expanding re-export trade to northern Europe.[12] The intensity and effects of French competition were stressed in several important economic lobbying campaigns from at least the later 1720s, and throughout the later 1730s and 1740s—for example, the campaign for a universal registry of wool to prevent the smuggling of wool to France, seen as contributing powerfully to the rapid strides being made by the French in what was traditionally Britain's foremost industry and export.[13] In 1743, the monopoly of the Levant Company was weakened by Parliament, under pressure from Bristol and Liverpool merchants amongst others, again in part as a response to growing

[10] Ralph Davies, 'English Overseas Trade 1700–1774', *Economic History Review*, 2nd ser., 15 (1962), 285–303.

[11] John Mitchell, *The Contest in America Between Great Britain and France* (1757), p. v.

[12] See François Crouzet, 'England and France in the Eighteenth Century: A Comparative Analysis of Two Economic Growths', in his *Britain Ascendant: Comparative Studies in Franco-British Economic History* (Cambridge, 1990), 17–20.

[13] Joshua Gee's *Trade and Navigation of Great Britain Considered*, first published in 1728, was the earliest comprehensive statement of mercantile anxiety about French commercial progress since 1713. For the campaign by the wool lobby, see Michael Jubb, 'Economic Policy and Economic Development', in Jeremy Black (ed.), *Britain in the Age of Walpole* (1984), 125–7.

supremacy of the French in what had formerly been a successful and very remunerative branch of British overseas trade.[14] The powerful sugar lobby had long complained about growing French competition in the West Indian sugar trades.[15] The arguments deployed by these groups and lobbies were, in Michael Jubb's words, 'the product of sectional interest masquerading as patriotism'.[16] Their cumulative effect, however, was significant. By the end of the 1730s, fears about the French commercial, as well as diplomatic, challenge to Britain's standing were pervasive.

It was the outbreak of general war in Europe in 1740 which compelled more general attention to the issue of French commercial competition. As early as 1743, when the main theatre of the war was in Germany and on the continent, George Burrington, a former governor of North Carolina, published an important pamphlet urging British destruction of French trade and capture of French colonies as a response to French commercial expansion and the threat this created.[17] The capture by the British navy and British colonial forces of the island of Cape Breton in the mouth of the St Lawrence river from the French in July 1745 turned popular and political attention decisively towards the sources and extent of growing French commercial power. Against a background of military failure and disappointment on the continent, this success was greeted with a frenzy of enthusiasm.[18] It also produced a wave of pamphlets and items in the press emphasizing both the importance of the conquest and the gravity of the commercial challenge from France. The author of one pamphlet, *The Present State of the British and French Trade to Africa and America Consider'd and Compar'd* (1745), declared bluntly:

The Design of this Treatise is to shew the Advantages the *French* have gain'd over the English in several Branches of Commerce since the Peace of Utrecht, which is so astonishing as to require the most serious Attention at this Juncture.[19]

French control of Cape Breton was represented as the greatest source of the expansion since 1713 of French overseas and colonial trade; it was also portrayed as the key to Canada and access to the Newfoundland fisheries, widely seen as a great nursery of seamen and, therefore, source of maritime strength.[20] Considerable attention was also devoted to the skill and determination with which the French state was pursuing commercial expansion, a

[14] The monopoly was completely removed in 1753. For the Levant trade, see Ralph Davies, *Aleppo and Devonshire Square: English Traders in the Levant in the 18th Century* (1967).

[15] See R. B. Sheridan, 'The Molasses Act and the Market Strategy of the British Sugar Planters', *Journal of Economic History*, 17 (1957), 62–83.

[16] Jubb, 'Economic Policy and Economic Development', 127.

[17] Burrington, *Seasonable Considerations on the Expediency of a War with France* (London, 1743). Burrington expressed similar views in the *Champion* (24 Oct., 3 Nov. 1741, 30 Jan., 4 Feb., 11 Feb. 1742) and later in the *Lond. Ev. P.* (25–7 Mar. 1755).

[18] See esp. Robert (Bob) Harris, *A Patriot Press: National Politics and the London Press in the 1740s* (Oxford, 1993), 189–91, 222–8.

[19] *The Present State*, p. i.

[20] See esp. Robert Auchmuty, *The Importance of Cape Breton Consider'd, in a Letter from an Inhabitant of New England* (1746); William Bollan, *The Importance and Advantages of Cape Breton, Truly Stated and Impartially*

theme in public debate which, as we will see, became ever more insistent in the following decade. The spectre of France wresting from Britain some of her colonies, as well as her trade, and gaining the much prized 'empire of the seas', was also raised.[21] Calls for Cape Breton to be retained were mounted almost as soon as it capture became known in England, and popular enthusiasm for its retention became an important factor in British diplomatic policy in the final stages of the war and an impediment to negotiation of peace between Britain and France.[22] Growing naval control and supremacy in the later stages of the war, especially after the major naval victories by Admirals Hawke and Anson off Cape Finistere in 1747, led to strengthening calls for the complete destruction of French trade and the further captures of French colonies. This would have the effect, it was argued, of not simply undermining French commerce and power, it would help Britain to recover much more rapidly from the fiscal burden under which she would be left labouring when the war ended.[23]

Discussions about the relative prospects for British and French overseas trade intensified after the Peace of Aix-la-Chapelle. This was a consequence of the course of diplomacy and international rivalry between the two powers, and perceptions of this, which were explored in Chapter 3. As we saw in that chapter, unfolding diplomatic disputes about the status of the so-called neutral islands in the Caribbean (St Lucia and Tobago), territorial boundaries in North America, control of the Africa trade, and conflict and hostility between the British and French East India Companies, created a rising conviction in Britain of vulnerability to French diplomatic and commercial ambition. This was reinforced by the perception that peace would be shortlived. French naval reconstruction after 1748, together with their actions in North America and other colonial theatres, were interpreted as a major bid by Louis XV's France to seize control of the seas from Britain, to secure maritime and colonial supremacy as a prelude to destroying finally British opposition to their long-standing ambition of establishing French hegemony in Europe. Concerns about the increase in the national debt caused by borrowing during the war, and the incidence and burden of taxes levied to pay the interest on it, were also widely articulated in the later 1740s. Britain's financial position was portrayed by opposition commentators as parlous, and several did not hesitate to talk of national bankruptcy.[24] There were strong calls for retrenchment and economy. The weight of indirect taxes falling on trade and manufacturing was also seen as a depressing prospect for growth of British trade, even though the

Considered (1746); *The Great Importance of Cape Breton Demonstrated and Exemplified* (1746). See also Harris, *Patriot Press*, 189–91.

[21] *The Present State*, 4.
[22] Richard Lodge, *Studies in Eighteenth-Century Diplomacy 1740–1748* (1930).
[23] Harris, *Patriot Press*, 218–53.
[24] See *Considerations upon a Reduction of the Land Tax (1749); The Necessity of Lowering Interest and Continuing Taxes Demonstrated* (1750); *Remembrancer*, 24 Mar., 30 Dec. 1749; *Westminster Journal*, 1 July 1749; *The Groans and Miseries of Great Britain Modestly Stated* (Edinburgh, 1748).

end of the war coincided with a major upsurge in trade overseas. Contemporaries were also aware that the other major states in Europe, apart from France—Austria, Prussia, Spain, and Denmark—were undertaking ambitious administrative and commercial reform programmes after the destructive influence of the recent war. In 1752, to cite just one example, Frederick II's plan for an East India Company aroused the concern of many merchants and others in London. 'Everybody here', wrote the Duke of Newcastle, 'and, particularly the trading people of all kinds, are most zealous for taking all possible measures for discouraging, at once, the new Emden Company, as far as the Law of Nations will justify us in so doing'.[25] Britain's efforts to promote their commerce after 1748 are, as referred to at the start of this chapter, properly seen in the context of these wider European developments.

Against a background of continuing anxiety about French diplomatic and international aims, Anglo-French disputes about the status of colonial possessions, and the efforts of other European powers to strengthen their national commerce and manufactures, several writers sought to assess the health of British overseas trade and manufacturing; they also made various proposals about how best to promote their growth. These writers included Josiah Tucker, the future Dean of Gloucester. Tucker wrote several important pamphlets in the later 1740s and early 1750s defending unpopular bills to secure the general naturalization of foreign Protestants and the even more disliked Jewish Naturalization Act.[26] In 1749, the first edition of his *A Brief Essay on the Advantages and Disadvantages which respectively attend France and Great Britain, with Regard to Trade* appeared. One index of the importance of this last work is that by 1755 it had gone into its fourth edition. A separate Scottish edition was also published in Glasgow in the same year.

In this lengthy pamphlet, which ran to around 170 pages, Tucker identified several major threats to the future health of British trade, most notably the insubordination and inflexibility of labour, the large numbers of the poor, the debauched and declining state of the population, the nature and burden of taxation, and the continuing existence of monopolies in overseas trade. The most striking feature of his proposals—one which was echoed strongly in many contemporary pamphlets on economic and social issues—was his authoritarian and often hostile attitude towards the labouring poor. Habits of industry and virtuous behaviour needed to be re-instilled in them if British trade was to grow and prosper. Tucker identified electioneering as a major source of corruption and insubordination amongst the lower orders. As he wrote:

The want also of subordination just now complained of, is mostly to be imputed to the same cause [electioneering], as it sets them above controll, frees them from all

---

[25] Quoted in Black, *America or Europe?*, 128.

[26] Tucker, *Reflections on the Expediency of a Law For the Naturalization of Foreign Protestants*, Part I (1751); id., *Reflections on the Expediency of a Law for the Naturalization of Foreign Protestants*, Part II (1752); id., *A Letter to a Friend concerning Naturalizations* (1753); id., *A Second Letter to a Friend Concerning Naturalizations* (1753).

Restraint, and brings down the Rich to pay their Court to them, contrary to the just and proper order of society.[27]

He proposed restricting the franchise to £20 of modern rent for a freeholder and £200 stock in trade for the tradesman. This would, he argued, ensure proper subordination in society; eliminate the disruption to manufacturing caused by elections; it would also enable the laws against idleness and immorality to be properly enforced. The vote, meanwhile, would again become a source of honour and a reward for industry. He also recommended the creation of courts of guardians of the morals of the poor in all manufacturing places. These courts were to be given extensive powers over popular leisure and conduct.[28]

Tucker urged the need for reform and action in several other areas. These included the system of taxation (the incidence of taxation was to be shifted from trade on to luxuries); regulation of the quality of British goods (he wanted to see public inspection of exports); the commercial and fiscal relationship with Ireland (he was a proponent of liberalization and full integration of the two economies); policy towards the colonies (he sought greater encouragement of production and export from the colonies of important raw materials); and smuggling (he advocated the creation of a new police for the prevention of smuggling and the establishment of bonded warehouses to reduce customs fraud). He also expressed great concern about mortality levels in the capital. This concern became a pressing one in this period; the bills of mortality for London were showing Britain's vast capital city eating up its population faster than its natural rate of growth.[29] Some drew the conclusion that the national population was falling.[30] Several important charitable bodies were founded in the mid-eighteenth century to combat the problem—pre-eminently, Thomas Coram's famous Foundling Hospital, established in 1740.[31] Tucker advocated a tax on bachelors and widowers of a certain age as a means of encouraging marriage and greater fertility.[32] In 1751, abortive legislation was introduced into Parliament to grant privileges to poor married persons, to promote marriage

---

[27] Tucker, *Brief Essay*, 37.

[28] Ibid., 55.

[29] See esp. *Observations on the Bills of Mortality of London* (1751).

[30] See D. V. Glass, *Numbering the People: The Eighteenth-Century Population Controversy and the Development of Census and Vital Statistics in Britain* (Farnborough, 1973).

[31] See Ruth McClure, *Coram's Children* (New Haven, Conn., 1981); Donna T. Andrew, *Philanthropy and Police: London Charity in the Eighteenth Century* (Princeton, NJ, 1989), 98–102. Other metropolitan charities which sought directly to tackle the problem of a declining population were the British Lying-in Hospital and the City Lying-in Hospital, both founded in the later 1750s. The growing number of provincial hospitals also sought, amongst other things, to save lives of the labouring poor.

[32] Tucker, *Brief Essay*, 129–31. See also *Propositions for Improving the Manufactures, Agriculture and Commerce of Great Britain* (1763), 74–9, for a similar proposal. The author of *Populousness with Oeconomy. The Wealth and Strength of a Kingdom* (1759) recommended the provision of family allowances as a means of promoting greater fertility amongst the poor (p. 27).

and the 'Encrease of his Majesty's Subjects'.[33] The passage of the Gin Act in the same year was also partly motivated by concern about a declining population.[34] Between 1756 and 1760, Parliament voted for the same reason an annual grant of £100,000 to the Foundling Hospital on condition that it admit all infants brought to it under two months of age. A direct, causal connection between, on the one hand, the size and condition of the population and, on the other, economic and military strength was treated as axiomatic in this period, and only began to be questioned in the 1770s.[35] Tucker supported a general naturalization partly because he saw it as another means of reforming the labouring classes, of exposing them to the stimulus of competition and good habits and skills of foreign workers. He also saw it as another way of boosting the country's crucial economic resource—its population.[36]

Tucker's emphasis on the importance of the quality and price of British labour for future commercial growth was a common one. Contemporaries recognized that labour costs were relatively high in England. Some saw this as an inevitable consequence of the development of a commercial society. The implications were only partially grasped, however. Assumptions that low wages were *the* crucial factor in the competitiveness of British exports, as well as a vital spur to industry and thrift amongst the lower orders, were only just beginning to be challenged.[37] Most contemporaries continued to call for the reimposition of habits of industry on a labouring class that was perceived to be breaking free of traditional restraints. 'To hold the lower orders to industry, and guard the morals of the Poor, on whom all Nations must rely for Increase and Defence, is', one contemporary wrote, 'the truest Patriotism.'[38]

Powerful expressions of concern about French commercial progress and ambition in this period also came from the pens of William Douglass, Henry McCulloh, John Campbell, and Malachy Postlethwayt, as well as an array of anonymous writers.[39] Postlethwayt was the most influential of these. Unlike Tucker—who has been seen as prefiguring some of the laissez-faire ideas

---

[33] *Commons Journals*, xxvi. 61. See also R. T. Connors, 'Pelham, Parliament and Public Policy, 1746–1754', Ph.D. thesis (Cambridge University, 1993), 230–2.

[34] See Ch. 7, below, pp. 297–9.

[35] See esp. Andrew, *Philanthropy and Police*, 22–5.

[36] Tucker, *Reflections on the Expediency of a Law For the Naturalization of Foreign Protestants*, Part II (1752), esp. p. 19.

[37] See A. W. Coats, 'The Relief of Poverty: Attitudes to Labour and Economic Change in England, 1660–1782', *International Review of Social History*, 21 (1976), 98–115.

[38] *Reflections on Various Subjects Relating to Arts and Commerce*, 62–3.

[39] See William Douglass, *A Summary, Historical and Political, of the First Planting, Progressive Improvements, and Present State of the British Settlements in North America* (1749–50); Henry McCulloh, *A Miscellaneous Essay Concerning the Course pursued by Great Britain in the Affairs of her Colonies* (1755); id., *The Wisdom and Policy of the French in the Construction of the Great Offices* (1755); John Campbell, *The Present State of Europe; explaining the interests, connections, political and commercial views of its several powers, comprehending also, a clear and concise history of each country, so far as to shew the nature of their present constitutions*, 4th edn. (London, 1753). 1755 also saw the publication of the sixth edition of Joshua Gee's *Trade and Navigation of Great Britain Considered*.

associated with Adam Smith—there was no element of originality to his views.[40] What his influence does underline, however, is how far mercantilist assumptions continued to shape very closely the terms of debate about trade and the economy in this period. In several works published in the middle years of the 1750s, Postlethwayt constructed a stark picture of a French state ambitiously and successfully expanding their commerce, empire, and maritime power.[41] Their goal was to create a 'universal empire', to achieve global commercial supremacy, and to expel Britain from North America as a prelude to domination of Europe or 'universal monarchy'. In *A Short State of the Progress of the French Trade and Navigation*, published in 1756, Postlethwayt itemized the powerful advantages which he saw France as possessing in the battle for prosperity and international power. These included the extent of her dominions and population, which gave her the potential to carry commerce 'to a pitch, equal, if not superior to that of Great Britain'. A combination of relatively cheap labour and the range of her manufactures made such an outcome close to inevitable. France also boasted a system of commercial policy ideally suited to increase their 'wealth, and their mercantile shipping, and consequently the royal maritime power, to an equality with those of Great Britain'. Postlethwayt's litany of doom and pessimism did not end there. If the rate of commercial progress since 1713 were sustained, France would soon achieve parity of naval and maritime strength with Britain. French ports and coasts were also as well positioned for trade and navigation as those of Britain. Britain's naval supremacy was, consequently, precarious and under great threat. As Postlethwayt wrote:

If it should so fall out, that the naval power of Spain should be united to that of France, and both act in concert against us, with the full exertion of their whole maritime strength, and Great Britain should have not foreign naval power to join her, the combat by sea may at least be precarious, if such united Fleets might not prove an invincible armada.[42]

Since the Peace of Utrecht, France had rivalled Britain in the Newfoundland fisheries, the herring fisheries, the sugar trades, and the African trades. Elsewhere in the same pamphlet, Postlethwayt described the manifold achievements of French commercial policy and manufacturing. These included, amongst other things, the Toulon dockyards; the Lyons woollen industry; the size and ingenuity of her population; the silk and glass industries; the health of her West Indian colonies of Guadeloupe and Dominica; the strength of her

---

[40] The Tucker of the 1740s and 1750s was hardly, however, a proto-liberal in economic matters. Apart from his opposition to monopolies and charters, which was increasingly widely shared, he was not a critic of the mercantilist state. Indeed, in some ways, what he was calling for was a more effective and efficient mercantilism.

[41] Malachy Postlethwayt, *The Universal Dictionary of Trade and Commerce* (2 vols., 1751–5); id., *Great Britain's True System* (1757); id., *Great Britain's Commercial Interest Explained and Improved* (2 vols., 1757).

[42] Id., *A Short State*, 75.

commercial position in India and at Wydah on the African coast.[43] The warning was explicit: Britain must respond to the threat posed by French commercial progress and ambition; at stake was not only her own trade and future prosperity, but her very existence as an independent power. As Postlethwayt urged, 'it certainly becomes us to think of every Measure that can contribute to enable us to stem the Torrent of their [French] Commercial Rivalship.'[44]

PARLIAMENT, NOVA SCOTIA, AND THE FISHERIES

Anxieties and views such as those expressed by Postlethwayt, Tucker, and others form an essential part of the context for the promotion of initiatives in the later 1740s and 1750s to support British commerce and maritime strength. They also helped to determine the high levels of public support for several of these. The initiatives were, as referred to at the beginning of this chapter, diverse, and it would be easy to exaggerate their coherence. They were, nevertheless, linked by common or similar aims and the involvement of overlapping groups and individuals. Many MPs, for example, were closely involved with the voluntary initiatives, as well as shaping and supporting relevant legislation. There was no overall coordination. Extra-parliamentary initiatives relied heavily on the ambition and vision of small numbers of individuals, as well as the support of a broader cross-section of society. Legislation was also closely shaped by individual initiative and by lobbying by economic groups and interested parties. (This was something which was true of all eighteenth-century economic and social policy.) Ministerial efforts, led by, first, Pelham and then after 1754 his brother, the Duke of Newcastle, were primarily focused on reducing the national debt, the pursuit of economy in national finances, and reducing the land tax to as low a rate as possible. Through the King's speeches to Parliament, however, they did seek to create a general political context conducive to such initiatives.[45] In March 1750, Pelham explained—in words which reflected his unease about his brother's continental diplomacy—his goals and hopes for the nation to the Earl of Holdernesse, then ambassador to the United Provinces:

It is with pleasure to me to reflect that a foundation is laid [by his debt reduction scheme] for the recovery of the country; if you on the other side of the water will keep us out of difficultys and jarring interests on the continent, and in turn our thoughts to the improvement of our trade, domestick economy and the lessening of the Publick debt those that come after me, may possibly see Great Britain in a condition to take that share in the common cause of Europe as becomes her dignity and with her interest, but we must have quiet, and our Allys must have it too . . .[46]

---

[43] Ibid., 2–61.
[44] Ibid., *Great Britain's True System*, 261.
[45] *Commons Journals*, xxv. 889–90, 891; xxvi. 3, 530.
[46] BL, Egerton MS 3413, fos. 72–3.

Individual ministers and ministerial supporters also played important roles in securing the passage of relevant legislation. They can also be found supporting bodies such as the Marine Society and the Free British Fishery. Parliament, meanwhile, represented an important focus for contemporary discussion about commercial issues; the press was another.

After 1748, legislation was passed or parliamentary attention devoted to a wide range of measures which aimed at promoting or protecting British trade and manufactures. This activity included passage of legislation to prohibit the import and sale in Britain of French cambrics (acts were passed in 1748 and 1759 amending an earlier act passed in 1745); an act 'for the more effectual preventing the importation and wear of foreign embroidery, and of gold and silver thread lace, or other work made of gold and silver wire manufactured in foreign parts' (1749); acts to stimulate the manufacture or production of bar iron and pot and pearl ashes (1750) and growth of silk (1755) in the North American colonies; the provision of bounties (1749, 1750) and other measures designed to promote the whale and herring fishing industries; parliamentary and ministerial support from 1749 for the settlement of Nova Scotia in North America; legislation to dissolve monopolies in the Levant (1744, 1753) and Africa trades (1750) and a major parliamentary enquiry into the monopoly on trade to Canada of the Hudson's Bay Company (1749); an effort to make more effective legislation to prevent the emigration of British craftsmen and industrial skills and knowledge (1749). It also included abortive bills to achieve a general naturalization of foreign Protestants (1747, 1748, and 1751) and the Jewish Naturalization Act, rapidly repealed following its passage in 1753. Taxation policy also continued to be used to promote the production and import of strategic and raw materials from the colonies. This list does not include legislation specifically aimed at promoting commerce in the Scottish Highlands as part of a wider programme of reconstruction in the area after the Jacobite Rebellion.[47] There was also legislation or abortive legislation which sought to tackle outstanding problems such as smuggling and fraud in the tobacco trades (1751); to promote marriage and increased fertility amongst the labouring classes (1751), referred to earlier; and to reform the poor law and promote habits of industry amongst the poor (1752). Reform of the calendar (1752), an abortive proposal for a census of population (1753), and parliamentary committees on and resolutions about weights and measures (1758, 1760) and laws on trade and commerce (1751) were further symptoms of a wider concern with expediting trade and manufacturing and the sinews of national power, as well as a general disposition towards moderate and cautious reform.

In many cases, this legislation and parliamentary activity was, as mentioned above, the result of, or involved much, lobbying by interested parties and individuals. The settlement of Nova Scotia was first suggested to the Board of

---

[47] For which, see Ch. 4, above.

Trade in 1748 by Otis Little, an American merchant.[48] The driving force
behind the proposals in 1753 for a national census was Corbyn Morris, a
customs official with close links to the ministry.[49] Morris was the author of
Observations on the Past Growth and the Present State of the City of London (1751), which
raised fears about the destruction of the population in the capital. Morris
envisaged the census as providing information to Parliament from which it
could make more considered decisions about whether, and how far, to support
for schemes which sought to reduce mortality. Thomas Potter, who introduced
the measure in the Commons, had a wider vision of its utility. He saw in it
possibilities for better ascertaining the collective strength of the nation, and
for making more informed decisions about emigration and mobilization of
manpower in wartime. He also saw it, or the information it would furnish, as
a remedy for the 'political and civil ailments of the internal part of the constitution'. Here he had in mind principally public relief of the poor, which, as
we will see in the next chapter, attracted much discussion in this period. The
initial stimulus to parliamentary consideration of the fisheries appears, as
we will see below, to have been a petition to the Commons from the York
Buildings Company, although there were plans and proposals to develop the
Scottish fisheries circulating since the end of the '45.[50] The assaults on the
remaining monopolies in overseas trade were driven by major lobbying
campaigns on the part of interested merchants and communities.[51] Legislation to promote the growth of silk in the North American colonies was a
response to concern amongst silk manufacturers about new barriers to the
supply of raw silk from Spain and Italy.[52] The two Commons select committee
reports of 1758 and 1759 into weights and measures appear to have been the
private initiative of Lord Carysfort, an Irish peer and minor office holder.[53]

Argument or debate about this legislation was also, for the most part, non
partisan. The removal of duties on the importation of pig and bar iron from
the colonies in 1750 set forgemasters against those in the cutlery, nail, and
other iron-working trades, as the issue had done in the past.[54] The Cambric

[48] W. S. McNutt, *The Atlantic Provinces: The Emergence of Colonial Society 1712–1867* (Toronto, 1965), 37, 53–4.
[49] The following discussion draws heavily on Connors, 'Pelham, Parliament, and Public Policy', 241–6. For Morris, see also Ch. 1, above, p. 29.
[50] For the fishery, see below pp. 25.
[51] K. G. Davies, *The Royal Africa Company* (London, 1957); Ralph Davies, *Aleppo and Devonshire Square*. See also *Commons Journals*, xxv and xxvi, for petitions from manufacturing communities and mercan-tile groups against the monopolies of the Royal Africa, Levant, and Hudson's Bay companies.
[52] *Commons Journals*, xxv. 928, 996–7.
[53] Julian Hoppit, 'Reforming Britain's Weights and Measures', *EHR* (1993), 94. The resolutions of the 1758 and 1759 committees were repeated in the Commons in 1760. Two bills were then introduced on the subject, but too late to succeed. The same thing happened five years later. Hoppit concludes that this fate was indicative of the general lack of government support for reform in this sphere, although Newcastle did meet the expenses of Carysfoot's committees.
[54] Diplomatic tensions in the Baltic were again threatening supplies of pig and bar iron from Sweden and Russia in 1750, which formed the crucial background to the passage of the act. For earlier disputes on this issue, see Jubb, 'Economic Policy and Economic Development', 129–30.

Acts created considerable and protracted opposition amongst linen traders in different parts of Britain. The issue was not the aim of the legislation—to prohibit French cloth from the British market—but its practical operation and effects.[55] The failure of several legislative proposals designed to promote British economic strength to gain parliamentary support—for example, the bill to promote marriage amongst the lower orders, as well as a number of pieces of legislation designed to improve the operation of the poor laws—is also not easily explicable in terms of partisan politics.[56]

There were exceptions to this general pattern. The main opponent in the Commons to the proposed census was William Thornton, a major force in opposition politics in the early 1750s. Thornton argued that his major enemies were 'place men and tax masters' and that he would be doing his constituents a disservice were he 'to concur to increase the knowledge or power of either'.[57] Despite Thornton's rhetoric, and his sniping opposition in committee, the proposal passed a third reading in a thinly attended house; it did not, however, gain the support of the Lords. How far the peers shared Thornton's apprehensions about the political menace supposedly inherent in the proposal is not known; whatever the case, Newcastle saw no purpose in expending political capital on pushing further for its passage. Opposition to repeated attempts, in 1747, 1748, and 1751 to gain support for bills to offer a general naturalization for foreign Protestants and for the Jewish Naturalization Act (1753) was even more evidently partisan in source and inspiration. The issue of a general naturalization, raising as it did the issue of the position and strength of the Anglican Church in society, divided Whigs from Tories. In 1747, a major opponent outside Parliament was Sir John Philipps, the leading Tory who had declined to stand again for parliament at the recent general election, who sought to exploit popular xenophobia and fears about cultural betrayal amongst the upper ranks to defeat the bill.[58] Fears about the effects of a general naturalization on wages—it was believed it would lead to their lowering—also fuelled popular opposition. In 1747 and again in 1751, when a further attempt was made to pass

[55] The act forbade the importation (except for re-export), wearing, and selling of cambric. The measure was circumvented by smuggling or entering the linen to the customs as fabric of a lower quality, a practice which legitimate linen traders argued was almost impossible to detect. Linen traders from London and elsewhere petitioned parliament in 1750 and 1753 against the act, arguing that it was ineffective and damaging to legitimate trade. In 1753, several MPs closely linked to the City—Sir John Barnard, William Calvert, William Beckford—and the Tory MP for Preston, Nicholas Fazakerly, representing the linen traders of the north west, supported a motion to repeal the acts. Rather than repealing what one periodical called 'a phanatical piece of anti-gallicanism' (*Scots Mag.*, 22 (1760), 240), Parliament chose instead to try and improve the legislation on two occasions—1748 and 1759. The traders argued that the prohibition simply forced up the price of German fine linens imported in place of the cambrics. Enforcement of the act also depended on informers, which was another source of its unpopularity and ineffectiveness.

[56] For poor law reform, see ch. 7, below, pp. 309–11.

[57] Quoted in Connors, 'Parliament, Pelham and Public Policy', 242–3.

[58] See *A Letter to Sir John Phillips, Bart Occasion'd by a Bill brought into Parliament to Naturalize Foreign Protestants* (1747).

such a bill, the City of London petitioned Parliament against the bills.[59] Opposition to the Jewish Naturalization Act was, in large part, factious in origin, as some contemporaries emphasized. Yet it was also fed by the revival of traditional Tory values, attitudes, and emotions. In several places outside London, lesser clergymen, who saw in it a threat to the standing of the Church of England, formed an important element of opposition to the measure.[60]

Of the various measures taken to promote commerce in the aftermath of the peace of 1748, two stand out in terms of their political importance and of the intensity of the hopes which were invested in them. These are the settlement of Halifax in Nova Scotia from 1749 and the encouragement of the British fisheries, alluded to at the beginning of the chapter. Both policies were a response in part to the problem of absorbing demobilized soldiers following the end of the war. The demobilizations of 1748 reduced the army from 50,000 to 18,850 and the navy from 51,550 to 17,000. Recognizing the potential social dislocation this was likely to cause, Parliament supported several measures designed to aid the reintegration of these soldiers into society, of which these policies were the most ambitious.[61]

The plan to settle Nova Scotia was strongly supported by Board of Trade under the Earl of Halifax, and by other ministers. The settlement was designed to act as a barrier against further French encroachment in North America and a source of commercial expansion, as well as furnishing the means of subsistence to demobilized soldiers. Some, such as Otis Little and William Shirley, Governor of Massachusetts, argued that its development was crucial to Britain's position in North America and her maritime strength.[62] Little, an American merchant from Massachussets, and who came to London to lobby the ministry to adopt the plan, was the author of the most important contemporary pamphlet published in its support—*The State of Trade in the Northern Colonies Consider'd* (1748). Little argued that it would more than compensate for the loss of Cape Breton at the recent peace, emphasizing its potential contribution to supporting British exploitation of the rich North American fisheries.[63] Former soldiers and sailors were offered free passage, land, and tools to induce them to settle in the colony. Letters home from the early settlers described the rapid progress of the settlement at Halifax and the natural bounty of the land and rivers and surrounding seas.[64] Ministers lent strong diplomatic support to the colony, especially in 1750 when fears about

[59] *Commons Journals*, xxv. 269–70; xxvi. 53.

[60] For a fuller discussion, see Ch. 1 above, pp. 49–50.

[61] See Connors, 'Pelham, Parliament and Public Policy', 278. A statute was passed (22 Geo II, c 44) exempting soldiers and sailors from having to complete apprenticeships before entering trades.

[62] Otis Little, *The State of Trade in the North Colonies Consider'd; with an Account of their Produce and a Particular Description of Nova Scotia* (1748). For Shirley, see Jeremy Black, *America or Europe? British Foreign Policy, 1739–63* (1998), 68.

[63] Little, *The State of Trade*, 78–80.

[64] See e.g. *Gen. Mag.*, 15 (1750), 42.

French threats to the new British settlement at Halifax were at their strongest. The Earl of Albermarle, Britain's ambassador in Paris, pressed French ministers about the actions of their colonists and colonial officials in Nova Scotia, and in July 1750, following what was seen as an unsatisfactory response from the French, they assured the colony's governor, Edward Cornwallis, that he would receive further military support if the French sought to reinforce their colonies from Europe. In March of the following year, they decided to station permanently two ships of war off the coast of the colony. The source of this proposal was Halifax's Board of Trade, and it was supported by all except Bedford, Sandwich, and Marlborough.[65] Parliament, meanwhile, voted around £450,000 between 1749 and 1754 to maintain the colony.[66]

The settlement of Nova Scotia helped to focus contemporary anxieties and hopes about the future of Britain's empire in North America. Many in Britain and the British colonies in North America were convinced that France was attempting to strangle the British seaboard colonies by erecting a chain of strongholds between Louisiana and the Mississippi delta in the south and Quebec and Canada in the north. At the same time, the desirability of better exploiting the colonies as markets for British goods and as sources of raw materials for British manufacturing was commonly and insistently urged. Empire held out the promise of expanding markets, while contemporary Europe was witnessing a new wave of aggressive mercantilism, thereby diminishing opportunities for British exports. The development of the commercial potential of the colonies was, in short, another aspect of a specifically British response to the contemporary efforts to promote overseas commerce by various European powers. The petitions submitted to Parliament in 1749 calling for the removal of monopoly of the Hudson's Bay Company reflect the magnetic power that colonial markets had on merchants and manufacturers, particularly in the woollen and metal trades, searching for new profits and markets.[67] The criticisms levelled against the company were long-standing—

[65] BL, Add. MS 32870, fos. 175, 222–3. The opposition of Bedford and Sandwich reflected the divided state of the ministry in the spring of 1751. See also T. R. Clayton, 'The Duke of Newcastle, the Earl of Halifax, and the American Origins of the Seven Years' War'. *HJ* 24 (1981), 583–4.

[66] *British Parliamentary Papers, Accounts and Papers*, xxv. 121–31, quoted in Connors, 'Pelham, Parliament and Public Policy', 281.

[67] Petitions calling for the dismantling of the monopoly were issued by: the merchants and traders of London; the merchants of Great Yarmouth; the principal traders and inhabitants of Wolverhampton; the traders and inhabitants of Stockport; the inhabitants of the borough of Wigan; the gentlemen, merchants, traders, and others involved in the woollen manufactures in Wakefield; the master, wardens, searchers, assistants, and commonalty of the company of cutlers in Hallamshire; the mayor, recorder, aldermen, merchants, and inhabitants of the city of Carlisle; the inhabitants of Whitehaven; the master, wardens, assistants, and commonalty of the Society of Merchants Adventurers in the city of Bristol; the inhabitants of Kendal; the mayor, aldermen, and other inhabitants of the borough of Appulby; the merchants of Lancaster; the traders and inhabitants of the town of Manchester; the subscribers, principal traders, and inhabitants of the town of Nottingham; the principal merchants and traders of Birmingham; the inhabitants of the borough of Derby; the merchants and other inhabitants of the town of Liverpool; the merchants and clothiers of Leeds; the trading inhabitants of Chester. (*Commons Journals*, xxv. 810, 817, 820, 822, 824, 825, 826–7, 827–8, 830, 833, 845, 850).

the failure to find the north-west passage to India and the East and to colonize any part of the Canadian wastelands which fell within its monopoly and to exploit fully the economic potential of trade with its native inhabitants. Yet they gained force from the international context in which they were revived. As the merchants and traders of London urged:

That most of the neighbouring Nations of Europe by prohibiting or discouraging our Manufactures, make it necessary that all proper Encouragement should be given towards increasing our colonies, and Extension of our Trade and Navigation.[68]

Unlike the Levant and Africa companies, however, the Hudson's Bay Company survived the concerted attack on its status.

If colonial markets and colonial trade appeared to represent a major source of potential growth in this period, exploiting the fisheries after 1749 was of even greater political moment. In what is one of the more unremarked (and perhaps unlikely) features of this period, promoting various elements of the fishing industry came to function, for several years following the Peace of Aix-la-Chapelle, as a lightening conductor for many of the hopes and anxieties which contemporaries held about the future of their nation after the end of the war.[69] The notion of seeking to exploit the fisheries more fully was not in itself new, although as a response to the pressures created by demobilization it was innovative. Since the later sixteenth century the vision of a flourishing British fishery creating prosperity, maritime power, and security had resurfaced at regular intervals. The seventeenth century had seen several attempts at realizing this vision, and efforts to promote the fisheries continued in the early part of the eighteenth century, north and south of the border, although with very limited results. Plans and proposals had continued to appear throughout the 1730s and into the early 1740s. In late 1745, as the Jacobite army retreated from Derby, they were revived in the press.[70]

Several factors explain why such proposals were revived in 1749, apart from the concern about the disruptive effects of demobilization. The first, and the most important, was anxiety about the efforts of the French to rebuild their naval power following the defeats inflicted on it by the British navy in the final stages of the War of the Austrian Succession. As we saw in Chapter 3, these efforts were anxiously watched and commented on in the press. They were also fully commented on in debates in the Commons in 1750, 1751, and 1752 on the number of seamen to be kept under pay in that year. In each of these

---

[68] Ibid., xxv. 850.

[69] Historians who have commented on the significance of the scheme include Paul Langford (*A Polite and Commercial People: England 1727–1783* (Oxford, 1989), 178) and Richard Connors ('Pelham, Parliament and Public Policy', 276–80).

[70] *Old England Journal*, 21, 28 Dec. 1745; *Westminster Journal*, 24 May 1746. For a full discussion, see Bob Harris, 'Patriotic Commerce and National Revival: The Free British Fishery Society and British Politics (c.1749–58)', *EHR* 114 (1999), 285–313; id., 'Scotland's Herring Fisheries and the Prosperity of the Nation, c.1660–1760', *Scottish Historical Review*, 79 (2000), 39–60.

years, several MPs argued that this number was too few. Lord Barrington, one of the Lords of the Admiralty, complained in 1751, when opposition to the navy estimates included Pitt the Elder, then secretary at war, George Lyttleton and the Grenvilles:

I know I shall be told of the late great preparations of the French, and their diligent application to the increase of the marine; and I confess, that of late we have been by our Gazette pretty much amused of these accounts . . .

Such accounts were, he declared, 'phantoms which are dressed up by our newspapers'.[71]

The widespread, intense concern about French efforts to rebuild her navy was reflected directly in the content of many of the plans for developing the fisheries in circulation in 1749–50. These included a series of proposals to expedite the manning of the British navy, and provide an alternative to the much-disliked impressment, including a register of the seamen engaged in fishing, placing charity boys on fishing busses as a training in seamanship—thereby anticipating the operations of the Marine Society—and imposing an obligation on the fishing busses to provide manpower to the navy in times of war.[72] The first, abortive bill to support the herring industry, introduced into the Commons towards the end of the 1748–9 parliamentary session, included clauses which would have created a naval reserve.[73] These may have been dropped in the second, successful bill—passed in 1750 in the next parliamentary session—because of ministerial plans for creating such a reserve briefly floated in 1749. In October 1748, Newcastle had written from Hanover about discussions he had been having with George II about how to balance the need for retrenchment and economy after the end of the war with the maintenance of naval superiority over the French. Ministers were directed, along with the Admiralty, to consider how best to achieve this.[74] In January 1749, Lord Anson, the First Lord of the Admiralty, sent Newcastle the resulting proposal. This involved maintaining a reserve of seamen on a bounty of £10 a year. These seamen were to be ready to serve when called to do so. Were they to refuse, they were liable not only to forfeit the bounty, but to be punished as deserters. The plan was for a reserve of 3,000 to be retained in 1749; this was to be increased in the following year to 10,000.[75] In 1749, ministers duly

---

[71] *Parl. Hist.* xiv (1813), 831. In 1750, Sir Peter Warren, Lord Baltimore, Vernon, and Sir John Rushout called for additional seamen to be taken into pay. In 1751, the opposition included Pitt, Lyttleton, the Grenvilles, and eight other ministerial supporters, as well as Tories and supporters of Leicester House. In 1752, it was William Beckford and William Thornton who called for an increase.

[72] See esp. *Plans and Proposals Transmitted to the Committee on the British Fishery. By Several Hands* (1758). See also n. 78, below.

[73] *House of Commons Sessional Papers of the Eighteenth Century*, ix, *George II Bills 1748–1754* (1975), esp. 206–7.

[74] BL, Add. MS 35410 (Hardwicke Papers), fos. 29–30: Newcastle to Hardwicke, 12/23 Oct. 1748.

[75] BL, Add. MS 32718 (Newcastle Papers), fo. 19.

explored before the Commons the possibility of creating a voluntary reserve of 3,000 seamen. There was some opposition, notably from Lord Egmont, who saw in it, as he did in most things, a scheme to extend ministerial power. He also argued that it was impractical. Nevertheless, a proposal of City MP Sir John Barnard's to establish a committee of the whole house to consider the matter was adopted. Eventually, a resolution supportive of the plan was agreed to by the house.[76] No further action was taken, however, and the scheme was quietly dropped. Despite strong support from Newcastle and Hardwicke, here, as in other areas, Pelham's drive for economy after 1748 appears to have triumphed.[77]

Exploitation of the fisheries also seemed to hold out other strong advantages in the later 1740s and early 1750s. Not least, it created the prospect of solving, or helping to solve, many of the economic and social problems which appeared to face Britain following the end of the war.[78] Commercial growth, and the wealth this would create, were needed to combat international commercial rivalry and to help repay the national debt and thereby reduce taxes. There was great optimism expressed about the scale of wealth and employment that proper exploitation of especially the herring fisheries would generate. In the summer of 1749, the press was circulating a figure of 78,000 for those who would gain some form of employment.[79] A witness to the parliamentary committee on the British fisheries set up in 1749 produced the figure of 100,000.[80] Henry Fielding, meanwhile, told Thomas Wilson in December 1750: 'The new manufacture of Herring Netts would employ 200,000 men, women and children. The charity schooles as well as the parish poor may all be enclosed in this scheme.'[81] This employment would serve not only to help absorb demobilized sailors and soldiers, but also to inculcate habits of industry amongst a labouring class that, as is emphasized earlier in this chapter and elsewhere in the present work, was perceived to be becoming dangerously infected by idleness and disorder. One commentator declared: 'Should the National Undertaking of the Fishery flourish properly,

---

[76] *Commons Journals*, xxv. 846, 867.

[77] This is suggested in a letter from Newcastle to Hardwicke where Newcastle notes, 'But money is wanting for this as well as other necessary Expences; and I hear, *The Treasury*, complain, That the Expence of the Fleet *only* for the ensuing Year, amounts to 3 shillings in the Pound Land Tax . . .' (BL, Add. MS 32719 (Newcastle Papers), fo. 151: Newcastle to Hardwicke, 2, 6, 10 Sept. 1749).

[78] See *Considerations Upon the White Herring and Cod Fisheries* (1749); *The Wealth of Great Britain in the Ocean Exemplified, from Materials Laid before the Committee of the House of Commons, Appointed to Examine into the State of the British Fisheries* (1749); *A Letter to a Member of Parliament, Concerning the Free British Fisheries* (1749); *The Fisheries Revived: or, Britain's Hidden Treasure Discovered* (1750); *England's Path to Wealth and Honour: In a Dialogue between an Englishman and a Dutchman. To which is added Articles relating to the Dutch Herring Fishery* (1750); *The Vast Importance of the Herring Fishery to these Kingdoms* (1749); *The British Fishery Recommended to Parliament* (Edinburgh, 1749).

[79] *General Evening Post*, 24 Aug. 1749.

[80] *Commons Journals*, xxv. 871.

[81] C. L. S. Linnell (ed.), *The Diaries of Thomas Wilson, D.D.* (1964), 258.

it may greatly lessen, if not totally annihilate the Poors Rates'.[82] It would, therefore, relieve the landed interest and the economy of this burden.

The fisheries also represented, or were portrayed as so doing, a means of healing some of the major divisions and fault lines in British society and the British state which had been exposed in the course of the recently ended war. In this context, one such division stood out—that which separated the Scottish Highlands from the rest of Britain. The effort to develop the fisheries was portrayed as an important plank in the attempt, after 1746, to reconstruct the Highlands along modern, commercial lines. Owing to a fortunate combination of geography and natural abundance, the fisheries appeared to the an ideal vehicle for transforming the Highlander from a state of savage barbarism into the embodiment of industry and contentment. The keynote to the whole project was unity in search of fish, profits, and greater national security. One writer argued that it would serve to 'twist' the landed, monied, and trading interests into 'one strong cord'. The fishery was promoted not by a spirit of 'Party' or of 'Faction', but one of 'Activity and Industry'.[83] All major economic, social, and political interests could come together in support of the project and its goals.

The initial parliamentary impetus to the campaign to promote the fisheries came in February 1749 when the York Buildings Company, the speculative and by 1749 debt-ridden company which purchased and sought to exploit Scottish estates forfeited after the 'Fifteen, submitted a petition to the House of Commons complaining about not being allowed to export Scottish goods and in particular fish to foreign countries. It also asked for a renewal of a bounty on whale fishing, arguing that such a move would 'greatly tend to the Encouragement and Increase of the Trade and Navigation of these Kingdoms'.[84] In response, a Commons committee was established to consider the state of the British fishery. Several members of this committee were to play a vital role in the promotion of the British herring fishing industry in the later 1740s—notably General James Edward Oglethorpe, Edward Vernon, Sir Richard Lloyd, and Stephen Theodore Janssen. The committee examined whether and how best to promote the whale fishery and the herring and cod fisheries. It also had referred to it a petition from the inhabitants of Westminster complaining about the price of fish and recommending the creation of a free market for fish in Westminster to bring down prices and to stimulate employment for fishermen.[85] The deliberations and several reports of the committee, which strongly favoured measures to exploit the fisheries, led to separate bills being introduced to promote the whale fishery, to establish a new fish market in Westminster, and to promote the herring industry.[86]

---

[82] *Penny London Post*, 29 Apr.–1 May 1750.
[83] *Considerations Upon the White Herring and Cod Fisheries*, 9, 42–3.
[84] *Commons Journals*, xxv. 724–5.
[85] Ibid., xxv. 785.
[86] For the committee reports, see ibid., xxv. 808–9, 829, 871.

The first two resulted in legislation; the bill to promote the herring fishery was lost due to lack of parliamentary time. Yet the momentum behind this last measure was not lost, and it received powerful support from the press in the second half of 1749 and on the eve of the new parliamentary session.[87] In January 1750, a group of merchants and traders met at the King's Arms Tavern in London and established a committee to draw up plans to submit to Parliament.[88] This group was to be eventually reformed as the Free British Fishery Society. The second, successful bill was introduced towards the beginning of the new parliamentary session.

Political backing for the promotion of the fisheries was, as for the settlement of Nova Scotia, widely based, although Sir James Lowther argued that his fellow MPs were slow to perceive the value of the scheme. Lowther maintained that it was largely owing to his efforts that the Commons was made aware of the contribution which exploitation of the fisheries would make to British prosperity and naval security. As he wrote in June 1749: 'People are hugely pleas'd with the Bills for incouraging the Fishery, & the prospect of carrying it on much further next year, which they look upon as very much owing to me.'[89] Whatever the truth was—Lowther was prone to trumpet his own achievements and importance in London in his correspondence to his estate steward in Whitehaven, John Spedding— politicians from across the political spectrum lent their weight to the relevant legislation or to the Free British Fishery Society after its establishment in 1750. Many of these individuals had long-standing interests in philanthropic and social issues, or a concern with trade and commercial questions. Lowther, who sat on the committee which drew up the first abortive bill to promote the herring fisheries, and who sat on the council of the Free British Fishery Society, was an independent Whig whose concern with trade was displayed not just in Parliament, but also in his native Cumberland and in the town of Whitehaven.[90] He was troubled in a general way in the later 1740s about British commercial prospects, and anxious that the ministry was not doing enough to improve these.[91] He also saw in the Free British Fishery Society possibilities for expanding local wealth in Whitehaven, as well as solving the long-standing problem of how to mobilize seamen for naval service in time of war without adversely affecting trade. Like many others involved in trade, the desperate experiences of impressment suffered by traders and merchants during the early years of the

[87] For details on this, see Harris, 'Patriotic Commerce and National Revival', 292–3.

[88] BL, Add. MS 15154 (Minute Books of the Free British Fishery Society), fos. 1–5.

[89] CRO (Carlisle), D/Lons/W2/1/110: Lowther to John Spedding, 15 June 1749.

[90] See esp. J. V. Beckett, *Coal and Tobacco: The Lowthers and the Economic Development of West Cumberland, 1660–1760* (Cambridge, 1981).

[91] On 22 April 1749, Lowther declared: 'As Nothing is like to be done to help the publick credit nor nothing to purpose about Trade, & every thing is turn'd to Jobbs Luxury & Corruption, Nothing but miracles can save the Nation' (CRO (Carlisle), D/Lons/W2/1/110).

war against Spain and the War of the Austrian Succession would have been easily recalled by Lowther when thinking about the benefits of the scheme.[92] He also had long-standing philanthropic interests. (In the early 1750s, he was a strong supporter of plans to encourage the poor and the labouring classes to adopt herring soup in their diets.[93]) Vernon, who sat on the committee which drew up the second, successful bill to promote the herring fisheries and who was a leading, if often destructive, influence in the early years of the Free British Fishery Society, saw his particular role in politics as being to defend the interests, as he saw then, of the bulwark of English liberties—the navy— and of the seamen who manned her ships. He was also a governor of St Bartholomew's Hospital and in the 1760s was to play a significant role in the workhouse movement in East Anglia.[94] Oglethorpe, a Tory of sorts, had long-standing philanthropic interests, serving with Vernon on the famous 1729 Gaols committee. He played a key role in the early history of Georgia, that near-Utopian philanthropic experiment of the mid-1730s. He was also virulently anti-French.[95] Lloyd, a leading lawyer on the ministerial benches—he opened the case against the slippery Jacobite Lord Lovat in 1747—was an expert on the poor laws and legal matters. Also on the committee which drafted the second bill were several politicians with close links to Leicester House—Sir John Cust, Chauncy Townshend, and Lord Baltimore. Leicester House was keen to identify itself with the scheme and its aims. Several leading ministers also lent their political weight to the passage of the relevant legislation, including Pelham and Newcastle.[96] The Duke of Argyll, the linchpin of ministerial management in Scotland, was also a strong supporter not just of the herring fishery but also of efforts to exploit the Greenland whale fishery. Argyll financed the construction of buildings which were leased to the Campbeltown chamber of the fishery, and also interceded with Pelham and the Treasury on behalf of Scottish merchants and shipmasters involved in the fishery on the 'dark and intricate' business of the salt laws.[97] Other Scottish Whig politicians who were not part of the Argathelian faction also strongly backed promotion of the fisheries inside and outside Parliament, including Alexander Hume Campbell.[98]

---

[92] See Ch. 3, pp. 127.

[93] CRO (Carlisle), D/Lons/W2/1/114, esp. Lowther to Spedding, 4 Nov. 1752.

[94] For Vernon, see esp. Gerald Jordan and Nicholas Rogers, 'Admirals as Heroes: Patriotism and Liberty in Hanoverian England', *JBS* 28 (1989), 201–24; Kathleen Wilson, 'Empire, Trade and Popular Politics in Mid-Hanoverian Britain: The Case of Admiral Vernon', *Past and Present*, cxxi (1988), 79–109; Paul Langford, *Public Life and the Propertied Englishman, 1689–1789* (Oxford, 1991), 240–1.

[95] L. F. Church, *Oglethorpe: A Study of Philanthropy in England and Georgia* (1932); Rodney M. Baine, *The Publications of James Edward Oglethorpe: Forward by Phinizy Spalding* (Athens, Ga. and London, 1994).

[96] See the comments in the *Edinburgh Evening Courant*, 27 Mar, 10 Apr. 1750. The progress of the bill through Parliament is also described in James Solas Dodd, *An Essay Towards the Natural History of the Herring* (1752). In 1750 and 1751, the Earl of Holdernesse also interceded with the Dutch authorities on the Society's behalf (BL, Egerton MS 3413, fos. 343, 345–6, 376–7).

[97] NLS, MS 17,578 (Saltoun Papers), fos. 40–1, 94.

[98] See *Edinburgh Evening Courant*, 27 Mar. 1750.

The composition of the Council of the Free British Fishery Society presents a similar picture.[99] The first president was Slingsby Bethell, MP for London between 1747 and 1758, and a member of the Fishmongers' Company. Elected Alderman of Walbrook Ward in place of the fierce opposition Whig George Heathcote in 1749, he was another opposition Whig and merchant who had extensive charitable interests. Another Vice President, Stephen Theodore Janssen, was also an opposition Whig, alderman, and City MP. He was also an important figure in the Laudable Society of Anti-Gallicans, one of several anti-French societies established in 1746 which, as well as stirring nationalist sentiment through meetings and publications, promoted English manufactures.[100] Janssen was, as we have seen, on the parliamentary committee which drew up and introduced the first bill to promote the herring fishery. Several Tory MPs were members of the Council (Sir Walter Blackett, Nathaniel Curzon, Charles Gray, Velters Cornewall, William Northey, Francis Gwynn), as were several MPs with links to Leicester House (Roger Handasyde, George Bubb Dodington), and some firm supporters of the ministry (Sir Bourchier Wrey and Richard Onslow). In the early 1750s, other independent opposition politicians joined the Society, including the Earl of Shaftesbury and William and Richard Beckford. William was responsible for searching new markets for the Society's herrings in the West Indies. Elected to the Council in 1752, he also challenged Janssen (unsuccessfully) for the vice president's office a year later.[101]

Beyond the ambit of Parliament, support encompassed important mercantile groups and interests—London merchants, representatives of the major London financial interests and merchant companies, the Convention of Royal Burghs in Scotland—local politicians in areas which had something to gain from supporting fishing—Edinburgh and Glasgow burgh councils, Southwold borough council—all aspects and levels of the press, and a broad measure of popular support. The Convention of Royal Burghs addressed the King in July 1749, referring to the 'opening of new views for the improvement of the British fisheries, which may prove an inexhaustible treasure, a certain source of strength to the navy, and wealth to the nation'.[102] The Edinburgh Burgh

---

[99] See also Appendix 3, 'The Free British Fishery Society', below.

[100] For the Anti-Gallicans, see esp. Linda Colley, *Britons: Forging the Nation 1707–1837* (New Haven, Conn. and London, 1992), 88–90. There would appear to have been as many as four different Anti-Gallican societies. The societies expressed, in their most extreme form, the widespread mid-century fears about French commercial expansion and the corrupting influence of French manners and luxury goods on English society. See e.g. *A Sermon Preached before the Several Associations of the Laudable Order of Anti-Gallicans, at Bow Church in Cheapside, On Friday, May 24, 1751. By Richard King, MA* (1751); *A Sermon Preached in the Church of Greenwich in Kent, on Wednesday the 29th of May, 1754, Before the Laudable Association of Anti-Gallicans, Established at Greenwich. By John Butley* (1754).

[101] See Thomas Cole, *A Plan for the Better Carrying on the British White Herring Fishery, Humbly Offered to the Consideration of William Beckford Esq* (1754), 1; BL, Add. MS 15155, fos. 52–3; BL, Add. MS 15154, fos. 140, 163–5. In 1755, William and his brother, Richard, bought up large amounts of stock in the Society from defaulters.

[102] *Extracts from the Records of the Convention of the Royal Burghs in Scotland, 1738–59* (Edinburgh, 1905), 319–20.

Council, then under firm Whig control, voted to confer the freedom of the city on the main parliamentary architects of the Society—Vernon, Ogle-thorpe, Lowther, and Janssen—as well as on two other important parliamentary champions of the fishery—William Belchier and Alexander Hume Campbell.[103] Support could be self-interested, as well as patriotic or philanthropic in motivation; involvement in the whale and herring industry appeared, after 1750, to offer easy profits and returns on investment. Sir John Anstruther of Elie, chief promotor of the short-lived Anstruther Whale Fishing Company, founded in 1752, wrote, 'I am assured that there can be nothing but a trifle lost were the ship unsuccessful, the bounty given by the government being so considerable.'[104] Monied men and merchants who invested in the Free British Fishery Company in 1750 were likewise looking for easy returns on their investment at a time when rates of return on public stocks were declining. Hamburg merchants, such as Francis Craisteyn, also had a specific interest in that it was through Hamburg that herrings reached important continental markets.[105]

Of the three strands in the promotion of the fisheries, the most important in terms of scale and organization, as well as popular hopes invested in it, was support for the herring industry. The relevant act established financial incentives in the form of bounty payments on busses employed in the industry and interest on capital invested in it through subscription to a new fishery company—the Free British Fishery Society.[106] The early phases of the Society, which was incorporated by Royal charter in that year, were marked by relative success and great, although not universal, optimism.[107] The gainsayers were a small minority, however. Subscribers readily came forward with promises of capital; officers and council members were elected; and a governor, the Prince of Wales, was found and invested in office.[108] Outchambers, meanwhile, were formed in Edinburgh, Glasgow, Montrose, Inverness, Whitehaven, Liverpool, and Newcastle; in 1751, a further outchamber was established at Campbeltown.[109] In the first year, the Society built and prepared four fishing busses for participation in the fishery; by 1754, it was operating forty. Charity schools, parishes, and the Foundling Hospital put children to work making

[103] *Edinburgh Evening Courant*, 19 Apr. 1750; *Whitehall Evening Post*, 30 June–3 July 1750. Glasgow Burgh Council also conferred the freedom of the city on William Belchier.

[104] NAS, GD 26/12/648/1 (Leven and Melville Papers), 29 Nov. 1756.

[105] Craisteyn also, however, had extensive philanthropic interests. He was, for example, a governor of the Smallpox Hospital; he was also later to be on the committee of the Marine Society.

[106] *Public and General Acts*, 1749, xxxiii. 459–60.

[107] Thomas Wilson noted in September 1750, 'Some people think it will not do because they can't transfer their stocks nor can ever sell so cheap as the Dutch' (*Diary of Thomas Wilson*, 250).

[108] The subscribers are listed in BL, Add. MS 15154, fos. 8–9. The Society initially approached George II to become governor, but he declined partly because ministers were suspicious about the body's links to Leicester House.

[109] Any number of persons together subscribing £10,000 to the Society could form themselves into local fishing chambers or outchambers, and organize their own trade under the protection of the parent body.

nets.[110] The press, in London, Scotland, and across the provinces, was very active in commenting on the state of the fisheries and efforts to exploit them.[111] Ballads and songs, including a number by the 'Herring Poet', John Lockman, the secretary of the Society, were published celebrating important phases in the early history of the Free British Fishery Society.[112] Other patriotic bodies—for example, the Laudable Society of Anti-Gallicans and, later, the Society for the Encouragement of Arts, Manufactures and Commerce—also lent their support to different elements of the promotion of the fishing industry. According to Lowther, popular support in London actually strengthened in the early 1750s, a support which reflected awareness of the contemporary efforts that foreign states were making to encourage their commerce.[113]

The hopes on which the Society was launched were relatively quickly exposed as having been wildly optimistic. The success of the first year, widely trumpeted in the press, flattered to deceive, and problems arose thereafter. In 1753, the Society was forced to petition Parliament for a change in the regulations governing the conduct of the Society and the eligibility of busses for bounty payments.[114] Far from spreading prosperity and creating employment, the fishery never proved profitable, and by 1755 the Society was desperately looking for economies. In 1756, it was claimed that in every year losses had never been less than £3,000; in one year they had climbed to £14,000.[115] In 1756, the Council of the Society was forced to debate whether to continue.[116] In the following year, they appealed to the Treasury to increase the bounty payment on ships involved in the fishery by another 20s. per ton, an appeal that was granted by Parliament. This did not presage new success, however. The opening stages of the Seven Years War brought disruption through impressment and privateering. In 1759, the decision was taken to employ only five busses and one supply ship. Other busses were to be sold or rented to the Admiralty and other concerns.[117] The Society limped on into the 1760s, but momentum was never recovered.

[110] Progress can be followed in the records of the society (esp. BL, Add. MS 15154). Council members Richard Baker and John Vaughan were made governors of the Foundling Hospital. Vernon and Oglethorpe were already governors.

[111] See e.g. *Whitehall Evening Post*, 28–30 June; 30 June–3 July; 5–7 July; 17–19 July; 26–8 July; 11–13 Sept.; 29 Sept.–2 Oct.; 22–4 Nov.; *General Evening Post*, 13–16 Oct.; 18–20 Oct.; 24–7 Nov.; *Edinburgh Evening Courant*, 14 June; 6 Aug.; 21 Aug.; 27 Aug.; 30 Aug.; 20 Sept.; 15 Oct.; *Caledonian Mercury*, 28 June; 28 July; 2 Aug.; 18 Aug.; 23 Aug.; 6 Sept. 1750.

[112] *Whitehall Evening Post*, 26–9 May; 5–7 July; 13–16 Oct. 1750; *Caledonian Mercury*, 22 Jan. 1750.

[113] On 25 November 1752, Lowther wrote: 'People are growing more & more fond of the Herring Fishery not only on acct of its breeding & employing so many Seamen, but as they perceive so many branches of our Trade are declining, most other Kingdoms in Europe are increasing their Woollen Manufactures to the great prejudice of ours tis felt already in Yorkshire & the West of Engld the Princes abroad incourage the Manufactures & the People can work cheaper & support their Family wth less wages than is done here, we have not the advantage so much in any Trade as the Herring Fishery it being on our Coast . . .' (CRO (Carlisle), D/Lons/W2/1/114).

[114] *Commons Journals*, xxvi. 612. All the changes asked for were granted by Parliament.

[115] *Commons Journals*, xxvii. 742.

[116] BL, Add. MS 15159, fos. 97–8.

[117] BL, Add. MS 15160, fo. 40.

Why did the Society fail to meet the heady expectations which had attended its establishment? Some of the problems it encountered stemmed from the relative speed with which it was formed. A memorial drawn up in 1751 referred to 'hasty deliberation'.[118] Contemporaries had been transfixed by Dutch practice and success in deep-sea herring fishing from busses, partly because they conceived of the scheme as a major means to strengthen the country's maritime power. (The busses were also required to stay at sea for protracted periods to be eligible for the bounty payments for the same reason.[119]) As the son of the Sir John Clerk of Penicuick later remembered:

Having constantly in our view the success with which the Dutch had so long carried on the Herring Fishery, it was reasonable to conclude, that the same success would surely attend us, were we carefully to copy and follow out a similar mode.[120]

One consequence of this preoccupation was the imposition of overly restrictive conditions on buss masters, some of which had to be loosened in 1753.[121] Very little concerted thought was given to how best to encourage Scottish participation in the industry.[122] This was not simply the fault of the Englishmen involved; initial Scottish support for the Society had been equally enthusiastic and uncritical. On 20 February 1750, *The Edinburgh Evening Courant* noted of the bill which had established the Society, 'a more important bill, for the Benefit of these Nations, has not perhaps at any time passed the House'. Andrew Fletcher wrote in similar terms to Lord Milton on 22 March:

upon the whole this is certainly the most beneficial Bill for Scotland and if properly carried into execution will contribute more towards promoting Industry and civilizing the Highlands, than all the Bills which have hitherto pass'd for that purpose.[123]

The particular demands of Scottish conditions were largely, although not completed, overlooked until the mid-1750s.[124] Small boat and inshore fishing on the firths and in the coastal waters and lochs of the north west predominated north of the border, not the deep sea fishing favoured by the projectors of the Society. Complex regulations surrounding the use of the salt—a result in part of a deliberate attempt to protect Scottish salt manufacturers at the

---

[118] NLS, MS 15578, fos. 14–22: Memorial on the Protection of the Coast Fishery in Scotland, 27 Feb. 1751.

[119] See later comments in John Knox, *Observations on the Northern Fisheries with a Discourse on the Expediency of Establishing Fishing Stations, or Small Towns, in the Highlands of Scotland, and the Hebride Islands* (1786), 92–3.

[120] *Reports of the Committee of the House of Commons*, x. 148.

[121] See n. 117, above.

[122] For much more detailed discussion of this, see Harris, 'Scotland's Herring Fisheries'.

[123] NLS, MS 16515 (Saltoun Papers), fos. 210–11.

[124] The report of the committee established by the merchants who went on to become the Free British Fishery Society and which was submitted to Parliament in February 1750 included several passages which bore on Scottish conditions and problems concerning the fisheries. See BL, Add. MS 15154, fos. 6–7.

time of the Union—also acted a formidable impediment to the export of Scottish herrings.[125] Many Scottish fishermen were also oppressed by the imposition of certain feudal levies and exactions by Scottish landowners. In 1753, Archibald MacDonald of Barisdale, an attainted rebel, was captured off Loch Hourn, where he had been exacting a due called 'Saturday's catch' on local fishermen. He claimed that this was widely levied by heritors on the loch side to compensate them for wood cut by the fishermen and also for maintaining order amongst them.[126] An effort was made to grapple with these problems in the form of the Scottish Fisheries Act of 1756.[127] The problem of the salt laws, however, was too difficult to admit of an easy solution, as those involved in the establishment and early history of the British Fisheries Society, founded in 1786 after another major war, the War of American Independence, were to discover.[128] The change to bounty payments on herring busses in 1757 also signalled the abandonment in Scotland of trying to emulate the Dutch in deep-sea herring fishing. The terms of eligibility were loosened to allow inshore fishing, and this was to provide the spur to a significant rise in herring fishing on Clydeside following the end of the Seven Years War.[129]

The structure and mode of operations of the Society also created its own set of difficulties. The Society contracted with manufacturers and traders to supply the equipment it needed. Control of costs was very loose in the early years. The Society blamed this in part on the requirement, established by the act under which it was formed, that it spend £100,000 of its capital in 18 months. As a parliamentary committee later reported: 'This led them into great and hasty contracts, and Persons knowing the obligations they lay under, took Advantage of their Necessity.'[130] Repeated complaints were made about the quality of nets supplied. The Society lacked the necessary expertise to avoid many problems. Too many busses were built. There was also a shortage of skilled labour to draw on. The early busses were copied from Dutch designs, and advice sought from Dutch fishermen. Danish fishermen were also contracted, at considerable expense, to crew the early busses.[131]

[125] See Christopher A. Whatley, *The Scottish Salt Industry 1570–1850: An Economic and Social History* (Aberdeen, 1987), ch. 4. Much can also be learnt from two later eighteenth-century pamphlets on the salt industry: John Girvin, *The Impolicy of Prohibiting the Exportation of Rock Salt from England to Scotland, To be Refined here, Illustrated* (1799); 9th Earl of Dundonald, *The Present State of the Manufacture of Salt Explained* (1785).

[126] PRO, SP 54/43/32 and 67.

[127] The campaign for greater attention to Scottish conditions and problems was led by the Convention of Royal Burghs. The passage of the Scottish Fisheries Act was also financed by the Convention.

[128] See Jean Dunlop, *The British Fisheries Society, 1786–1893* (Edinburgh, 1978), 115–19.

[129] Ibid., 10–11. See also Frank Bigwood, 'A Database of Sources for Scottish West Coast Fishing and Trading Enterprises 1750–1800', *Scottish Archives*, 3 (1997), 95–103.

[130] *Commons Journals*, xxvii. 742.

[131] Ibid. See also BL, Add. MS 15154. Another source of seamen was Orkney, their recruitment being arranged by the Earl of Morton.

Lack of expertise and haste also left the Society prey to graft and peculation. In 1753, the Society's accountant had to be dismissed. At the same time,
there were also bitter disputes amongst the Society's members arising from
accusations of peculation and malpractice by an agent of the Society at
Southwold.[132] These appear to have set the difficult and intemperate Vernon
against most of the rest of the Council. Vernon and his allies were ousted from
the Council and Society in 1754, which led to a brief upsurge of renewed optimism about prospects for the Society.[133] The underlying problem, however,
had not been tackled. Responsibility for oversight and supervision fell on the
shoulders of a small number of individuals, such as the successive Vice
Presidents, Stephen Theodore Janssen and Slingsby Bethell. They and other
members of the Council were forced to visit Southwold annually to maintain
a check on the Society's agents and preparations for that year's fishing.[134] The
burdens this imposed were unrealistic, and by 1754 proposals were being aired
for a major change in the way the Society operated.[135] No longer would it
contract for materials and men, but this role and responsibility would be
devolved on to the masters and captains of the busses. Nothing came of these
proposals.

If these problems had not been enough to undermine the fortunes of the
Society, it was also a victim of circumstances over which its members could
have no control and which could not have been foreseen at its inception. From
1752, it faced new competition from the Swedish fishery. The cause was an
unpredictable shift in the movements of herring shoals on to the Swedish
coast. The result was that British-caught herrings found themselves squeezed
out of Baltic and several European markets.[136] The reappearance of great
shoals of herrings in and around the Firth of Clyde during the early 1750s also
further diverted interests in that region away from deep sea fishing from busses
towards inshore fishing from small open boats.

The picture of limited achievements, if not failure, was repeated in the case
of the Greenland whale industry and the Westminster fish market. The Act
for 'the further encouragement and enlargement of the Whale Fishery'
extended two existing acts. It was drafted by Lloyd, Oglethorpe, Vernon, and
Sir Peter Warren, a popular admiral and ministerial MP for Westminster.
The most important element of the act was the provision for seven years of
an increased bounty on ships of 200 tons involved in the industry.[137] Earlier

---

[132] BL, Add. MS 15154, esp. fos. 63–4.

[133] See CRO (Carlisle), D/Lons/W2/116, Lowther to Spedding, 30 Nov. 1754; BL, Add. MS 15155,
fos. 122–4.

[134] The *Scots Magazine* reported in 1755 that Bethell had 'declined [his] own business to attend that
of the company' (*Scots Mag.* (1755), 153).

[135] See esp. Thomas Cole, *A Plan*.

[136] Knox, *Observations on the Northern Fisheries*, 28. The Society also faced fierce competition in
European markets from the Dutch who lowered their prices to undersell British caught herrings.

[137] *Public and General Acts*, 1748, xxxii. 915–22. As with the herring busses, the bounty on tonnage was
an attempt to offset the substantial capital costs of building and fitting out a whaling vessel. One

bounties in 1734 and 1740 had not been sufficient to stimulate growth in the industry. The act also offered foreign Protestants the opportunity of naturalization if they served in the British whale fishery. In Scotland and England, the increased financial incentive led to the establishment and significant increase respectively of Greenland whaling industries. Organized in the form of several limited liability companies, the Scottish industry drew on the energies, money, and hopes of major politicians, their landed allies, merchants, and tradesmen.[138] In 1753, when Parliament was considering the extension of the bounty, the *Scots Magazine* printed copies of the relevant legislation.[139] In 1751, there was one Scottish vessel operating in the whale trade, from Leith. In the following year, it was joined by ships from Dunbar, Bo'ness, Glasgow, and Campbeltown. In July 1753, George Drummond reported from Edinburgh, with an eye no doubt on the following year's general election: 'The Town is very happy at present by the arrival of three of their whale ships—Scotland have 12 ships in the Trade, from East Coast this year, whereof 6 belong to Edinburgh.'[140] Early involvement on the west coast was not sustained—two west coast whalers, the 'Campbeltown' and the 'Argyle' were put up for sale as early as 1752. The modern historian of the eighteenth-century Scottish whaling industry has passed a very negative judgement on those involved. Early Scottish whalers appear to have lacked the basic skills to kill and retain whales; nor did they see fit to hire experienced harpooners from elsewhere. Ships very often came home 'clean'—that is having failed to make a catch—simply staying in Artic waters for long enough to meet the requirements of bounty payment. The vast majority of all Scottish voyages also depended on the bounty for any profit.[141] In 1749, witnesses before the Commons committee on the British fisheries stated that only two ships were currently employed in the whaling trade in London, and that this poor representation reflected a lack of skilled men. In 1753, there were twenty-six whalers operating out of London, and twenty-three from outports in England and Scotland. According to one estimate, this represented 14,700 tonnes of

contemporary estimate put the value of the fitted out whaling ship at over £5,000. Once this cost had been met, however, the tonnage bounty 'nearly' covered the costs of the voyage. PRO, T1/353/99: 'The Case of the Merchants and Others Concerned in the Whale Fishery'.

[138] The owners of two whalers, the 'Argyle' and 'Campbeltown' are listed in NLS, MS 17578, fo. 27. They included the Duke of Argyle, Lord Milton, George Walker, a major figure in the Scottish fisheries, agent at sea of the Free British Fishery Society and member of the council of the Society, Richard Taunton, a Southampton merchant who again played a significant role in the early history of the Free British Fishery Society, James Stewart, a writer in Edinburgh, two Argyllshire landowners and promoters of the linen industry in that county, Alexander McMillan of Dunmore and David Campbell of Dunloskin, as well as a number of Glasgow merchants.

[139] *Scots Mag.* (1753), 361, 417; (1755), 284–8, 358.

[140] NUL, Newcastle (Clumber) Papers, Nec 2,025. PRO, T1/351/86. Other Scottish ports involved by 1753 were Aberdeen and Dundee.

[141] Gordon Jackson, 'Government Bounties and the Establishment of the Scottish Whaling Trade, 1750–1800', in John Butt and J. T. Ward (eds.), *Scottish Themes* (Edinburgh, 1976), 46–66.

shipping, and employment for 2,156 seamen.[142] In 1757, a substantial number of whaling vessels were taken into service by the Admiralty as armed transports.

The establishment of the Westminster fish market, meanwhile, underlines the strong philanthropic element that was present throughout the promotion of the fisheries. It also reflects the readiness of Parliament and MPs in this period to intervene in markets for foodstuffs in ways designed to limit or eliminate what was seen as the deleterious influence of 'middlemen'—those who intervened between producer and consumer and who 'artificially' inflated prices to generate excessive profits. (In 1749 and again in 1757, Parliament passed legislation respectively renewing and reforming the assize of bread, under which the sale of bread was regulated.) The committee's report on the fish market argued that middlemen were inflating the prices of fish and that they also were depriving fishermen of gains that would otherwise encourage greater numbers to engage in the industry.[143] The subsequent act sought to restrict forestalling in the fish market, as well as appointing trustees to oversee the construction and operation of a fish market on land set aside near Westminster bridge. The trustees included many MPs who were closely involved in the Free British Fishery Society, such as Lloyd, Oglethorpe, Vernon, Sir Bourchier Wrey, the ministerial MP for Barnstaple who visited Hamburg in 1752 on behalf of the Society, and George Bubb Dodington, a leading figure in the febrile and unstable politics of Leicester House.[144] They were directed to deliver yearly accounts and ordered not to accept profits arising from their role in the fish market. There were early difficulties in establishing the market, including frictions with the trustees of Westminster bridge, and arguments amongst the trustees. The legislation establishing the market also needed to be amended and strengthened in the following year. As Thomas Wilson, one of the trustees, noted in January 1750: 'Complain[t]s haveing [*sic*] been made of the Fishmongers and combining against the Market, we met again and are to apply for a new Bill to make the last stronger . . .'. Towards the end of that year, Wilson was again reporting problems with the market and the high price of fish.[145] That the trustees and market continued to experience difficulties in the following years is suggested by the need for further legislation in 1756 and 1760, and petitions from fishmongers complaining about the operation of the acts in 1758 and 1760.[146] Support for the aims of the market remained strong, nevertheless.[147]

---

[142] PRO, T1/353/99.

[143] *Commons Journals*, xxv. 808–9.

[144] *Public and General Acts*, 1748, xxxii. 976.

[145] *Diary of Thomas Wilson*, 225, 254.

[146] 29 Geo II, c39; 33 Geo II, c27; *Commons Journals*, xxviii. 84, 729. See also PRO, T1/392/24–31, for proposals about how to rectify the problems with the operation of the market.

[147] This was channelled in part through the Society for the Encouragement of Arts, Manufactures and Commerce. In November 1761, a member of the Society, John Blake, an East India trader, put

SOCIETIES AND COMMERCE

The fears, hopes, and goals which had brought about the establishment of the Free British Fishery Society did not die with its declining fortunes in the mid-1750s. Indeed, many of them were simply transferred in 1756 to the Marine Society. Some of the individuals who sat on the Council of the Free British Fishery also sat on the Council of the later society—for example, William Belchier, William Bowden, Sir James Creed, Francis Craisteyn, the Earl of Shaftesbury, and John Tucker. There was also significant overlap in respect of subscribers to the two societies, perhaps unsurprisingly since both drew heavily for support on the enthusiasm and purses of metropolitan merchants and financiers.[148]

The Marine Society, which is examined further in the next chapter, sought to strengthen British maritime power in the face of fears about challenges from France. These fears rose to new heights in 1756 with the loss of Minorca to the French. Merchants also had to contend again with the effects of impressment as demand for manpower rose to unprecedented heights from the navy, which may have stimulated some of their support for the Society and its aims. The Society for the Encouragement of Arts, Manufactures and Commerce, the other great patriotic foundation of the mid-1750s, had as its principal goal the direct support of British manufactures and commerce. A similar society was founded a year later in Edinburgh (in 1755) by members of the newly established Select Society.[149] The Society shared several of the aims of the Free British Fishery Society and the Marine Society, as well as complementing the purposes of much of the legislation on commercial matters referred to earlier. As its modern historian, D. G. C. Allan has shown, its origins were relatively minor, depending on the enthusiasm and initiative of a select group of individuals, notably William Shipley, the son of a London stationer and provincial drawing master, whose conception it was.[150] Perhaps

forward a plan for supplying the markets of London and Westminster with fish from distant sea ports and rivers by land carriage. Blake was given £2,000 to bring into execution the design of his land carriages for fish. A premium was also granted in May 1762 for the best models of these carriages to be built. Parliamentary support was also sought and successfully achieved. An act was passed in that year which lessened the tolls paid by such carriages on turnpikes; which protected fishermen from impressment, and which laid the liberty of buying and selling fish open to every person, whether they had been brought up in the trade or not. Blake was provided with a further £1,500 in May 1762, for which he had to give 'proper security'. He was also voted the thanks of the Society at an extraordinary meeting and unanimously voted the gold medal of the Society. This was inscribed with the words 'To John Blake Esq' and within a laurel wreath 'Fish Monopoly Restrained'. The Society also set aside £500 to be distributed in premiums for the encouragement of the turbot fishery. The potential stimulus to British naval power and security was emphasized.

[148] The subscribers to the Marine Society between 1756 and 1759 are listed in Jonas Hanway, *An Account of the Marine Society* (1759). See also Appendix 3, below.

[149] See *Scots Mag.* (1755), 126–30.

[150] D. G. C. Allan, *William Shipley, Founder of the Royal Society of Arts* (1979); id., 'The Society for the Encouragement of Arts, Manufactures and Commerce'. See also Derek Hudson and Kenneth W. Luckhurst, *The Royal Society of the Arts 1754–1954* (1954).

oddly, Shipley appears to have conceived of the idea initially unaware or un-influenced by the Dublin Society, which had similar aims and used similar methods, and which, as was referred to in an earlier chapter, had been estab-lished as long ago as 1731.[151] Shipley received crucial support at an early stage from two noble patrons, Lords Folkestone and Romney.[152] It was not until 1755, by which time it had constituted itself as a formal body and, equally importantly, started to publicize through the press its activities and existence more successfully, that membership started to grow substantially. From 1756, the society grew rapidly.[153] Two years later, Tobias Smollett could claim, extravagantly:

In a word, this society is so numerous, the contributions so considerable, the plan so judiciously laid, and executed with such discretion and spirit, as to promise much more effectual and extensive advantage to the public than ever accrued from all the boasted academies of Christendom.[154]

Its Scottish counterpart appears to have been less successful, although it could claim the support of many of the major politicians in mid-eighteenth-century Scotland.[155] In July 1755, it petitioned the Convention of Royal Burghs for financial support arguing that its funds were not as great as 'what might be deemed necessary for carrying on so noble and benevolent a design'. The Convention donated 100 guineas to the Society. In 1757, the Society was again informing the Convention that its funds were precarious. On this occa-sion, the Convention recommended to the burghs to 'contribute gentilely' to its funds. A year later, the Convention was informed that its funds still 'fell far short of those of the 2 neighbouring kingdoms'. The Convention duly donated 50 guineas.[156]

The English and Scottish societies pursued similar goals—the encourage-ment of native manufactures and commerce—and through similar means —the payment of premiums. The Scots provided honorary rewards to those whose achievements were in the fine arts. South of the border, honorific reward—in the form of a gold medal—was reserved to members of the upper ranks. Each year lists of premiums were advertised in the press, as was the

[151] Although Samuel Madden did write to Shipley in 1757 offering his advice about how to promote his new society (Allan, *William Shipley*, 16–17). The Board of Trustees for the Improvement of Manufactures and Fisheries in Scotland offered another potential precedent for using premiums or financial incentives to promote economic activity, although again this seems not to have had any influ-ence on the foundation of the Society.

[152] See esp. *A Concise Account*, 17–26. Another eminent supporter was Isaac Maddox, Bishop of Worcester. Maddox was also a supporter of the Free British Fishery Society.

[153] Allan, 'The Society', 50.

[154] Tobias Smollett, *History of England* (6 vols., 1758–65, 1805), v. 448–9.

[155] See the list of original managers in the *Scots Mag.* (1755), 128. They included the Duke of Hamilton, Lord Deskford, Lord Kames, George Drummond, Andrew Pringle, Gilbert Elliot, Alexander Wedderburn, and Patrick Duff.

[156] *Extracts from the Records of the Convention of the Royal Burghs*, 494, 496, 553, 555, 575, 579.

award of these premiums. In 1755, the Society for the Encouragement of the Arts justified the premiums on the grounds that all other countries in Europe were 'attempting manufactures and striving to gain a superiority in commerce'.[157] In other words, its premiums and activities substituted for the role that the state undertook in other countries. As we have seen at various points throughout this chapter, an awareness of the contemporary efforts in several European countries to stimulate overseas trade and domestic manufacturing provided an important motivation for similar efforts in Britain. At the same time, there was little support for any major extension of the role of the state in this sphere; self-interest chanelled and stimulated by the state and voluntary bodies was the means better suited to a free and commercial society such as Britain.

The two societies gave their support to a broad range of industries and activities, although unsurprisingly, given its importance as a growth point in the Scottish economy, the linen and textiles industries loomed very large in the thinking of the Edinburgh body. The English society showed an overriding concern with improving the balance of trade, and nurturing domestic manufactures to a point where they could compete with their foreign rivals. The members of both societies also gave concerted early encouragement to instruction and achievement in drawing and design. This was a field in which the French excelled and which was seen as underpinning the success of many of their luxury trades. In 1744, Matthew Decker had, in a widely read tract on trade, asserted the 'need to establish a drawing school at public expense and not suffer the French to be the only people of taste and invention . . .'.[158] In 1752, the establishment of a public academy of the arts was recommended for the same reason.[159] Both societies also acted as important forums for debates and lobbying on issues relating to the economy and economic improvement. The Edinburgh Society, for example, sponsored considerable discussion about the laws on the maintenance of roads and highways.

Another persistent concern of the English Society was social problems, in particular those which were seen as arising from the un- and underemployment of the poor. As one writer declared, early premiums had been designed to help introduce

such manufactures as may employ great numbers of the poor, which seems the only way of lessening the swarms of thieves and beggars throughout the kingdom, and relieving parishes from the burden they labour under, in maintaining their numerous poor, as well as rendering multitudes of the unemployed lower class of people useful to the community and happy in themselves.[160]

---

[157] Quoted in Allan, 'The Society', 130.

[158] Decker, *Essay on the Decline of Foreign Trade* (Dublin, 1749), 181, quoted in Iain Pears, *The Discovery of Painting: The Growth of Interest in the Arts in England, 1680–1768* (1988), 155.

[159] *Reflections on Various Subjects Relating to Arts and Commerce.*

[160] *A Concise Account*, 17.

As we have already seen in this chapter, and as is further demonstrated in the next chapter, the notion that provision of employment and hard work was the solution to poverty was revived very strongly in this period, spurred in large part by fears about the relative costs of English labour and the independence or idleness and insubordination of the labouring classes.

Other issues which engaged the attention of the English society in the 1750s included the actions of forestallers in the grain and other food markets.[161] The immediate stimulus to this concern was waves of food rioting in 1756 and 1757 caused by poor harvests and steeply rising grain prices. This concern emphasizes again the extent to which paternalistic assumptions about the economy and access to essential foodstuffs remained deeply entrenched amongst the ruling elites and political classes. Henry Baker, a prominent figure in the Society, was probably going rather further than most, however, when, in response to a grain riot in Norfolk in 1757, he complained of engrossers who were withholding grain from the market in a time of shortage, declaring, 'though I am an Enemy to all Riots could the mob act with Distinction, and take only from such Engrossers, I think they would do no great harm, or deserve any considerable punishment.'[162] Premiums were also used by the Society to encourage the cultivation of timber, a crucial resource for the economy and the navy. Parliament acted to support this goal by passing legislation to facilitate the planting of trees in 1758.[163] Members also looked to the empire and the colonies as a powerful motor of commercial growth and potentially rich source of crucial raw materials, especially for the textiles industries. Thus, through its premiums and lobbying, it supported the cultivation in the North American colonies of, amongst other things, silk, hemp, olive and cinnamon trees, and aloes.[164] Again these efforts were, in some cases, supported by parliamentary legislation.[165]

Finally, the English society became closely involved in efforts to establish an academy of the arts.[166] Proposals for an academy similar to that which oversaw painting in France were closely associated with a group of artists—including Francis Hayman, Francois Roubiliac, Thomas Hudson, and the young Thomas Gainsborough—who frequented Old Slaughter's Coffee House near St Martin's Lane. (A notable opponent of the idea was William Hogarth, although he shared strongly in the nationalistic feelings which lay behind it.[167]) In 1749, Jonathan Gwyn produced an important pamphlet

---

[161] Allan, 'The Society', 127.

[162] Ibid.

[163] *Commons Journals*, xxviii. 379, 574–5. Edward Wade, a member of the Society, was the author of *Proposal for Improving and Adorning the Island of Great Britain* (1755).

[164] *A Concise Account*, 62–3.

[165] See p. 248, above.

[166] The following paragraph relies heavily on Iain Pears, *The Discovery of Painting*, 119–32; and Brian Allen, *Francis Hayman* (1987), 4–6.

[167] See David Bindman, *Hogarth* (1981), 149–50.

arguing the case for an academy entitled *An Essay on Design, including Proposals for Erecting a Public Academy*. As referred to above, the case was restated and strongly linked to Britain's commercial fortunes in a pamphlet published in 1752. Before his death in 1751, it was hoped that the Prince of Wales would support the foundation of a formal academy organized along French lines.[168] In 1753, a printed circular was distributed from the St Martin's Lane Academy designed to produce support for 'a public academy for improvement of painting, sculpture and architecture'. Three years later, the sculptor Henry Cheere, another frequenter of Old Slaughter's, put forward a similar proposal to the Society for the Encouragement of the Arts. In 1757, Francis Hayman joined the Society and led a committee of artists in negotiations with the Society in the hope of gaining their support for the establishment of a royal academy, but with no success. The Society did, however, lend its premises in the Strand in 1760 for an annual exhibition of the work of the group of artists led by Hayman. Almost immediately problems arose between the Society and the artists. The source of these problems is not fully clear, but they may have stemmed from different perceptions between the Society and the artists about the function and role of art and artists. Influenced by their founder Shipley, the Society's idea of the importance of art was closely shaped by its perceived contribution to commerce and the luxury trades. The artists, however, saw their function and status differently, and were keen to emphasize their distance from commercial and narrowly utilitarian conceptions of their role.

There was an echo of these developments north of the border with the foundation in the mid-1750s of the Foulis Academy for Sculpture and Painting. The Foulis brothers, Andrew and Robert, were key figures in the development of an Enlightenment print culture in Glasgow. Robert Foulis appears to have developed the idea for an academy in the later 1730s when visiting France. As he later wrote:

We had opportunities of observing the influence of invention in Drawing & Modelling on many manufactures. And 'tis obvious that whatever nation had the lead in fashions must previously have invention of drawing diffus'd, otherwise they can never rise above copying their neighbours.[169]

The idea was only revived more than a decade later. The academy was supported by several leading Glasgow merchants—notably Archibald Ingram and his brother in law, John Glassford. Ingram was, like Glassford, a highly successful tobacco trader and a principal developer of the Pollokshaws Printfield Company, which was an innovator in the field of calico printing. He was also an evangelical, and like many west coast evangelicals saw no

---

[168] See Christine Gerrard, *The Patriot Opposition to Walpole: Politics, Poetry, and National Myth, 1725–1742* (Oxford, 1994), 57.

[169] Quoted in *Notices and Documents Illustrative of the Literary History of Glasgow, During the Greater Part of Last Century* (Glasgow, 1831), 17.

contradiction between the values of strict religion, commerce, and liberty.[170] The University, meanwhile, provided a gallery for paintings and works produced in it. In 1759, the Foulis' decided further to promote native arts by arranging a subscription to purchase works of art. The productions of these artists were to be exhibited in Robert Fleming's shop in Edinburgh and the Glasgow gallery. Subscribers were to be allowed to choose items to the value of the sum they had subscribed.[171] The Foulis Academy emphasizes again how closely linked promotion of the arts and promotion of trade and commerce were in the eyes of many contemporaries in this period. In Edinburgh, the Board of Trustees created a publicly funded design school in 1760, the first in Britain.[172] In Ireland, as we saw in an earlier chapter, the Dublin Society established drawing schools in 1746, and in 1754, raised a subscription to fund prizes for drawing.[173]

Commerce and commercial questions exercised a strong hold over public debate and the political imagination in Britain in the mid-eighteenth century. In Scotland, the increasing pace of commercial and economic activity, and the commitment of politicians, landowners, and merchants to the patriotic promotion of commerce, and economic improvement more generally, deepened, a process reinforced by the political reverberations set off by the Jacobite Rebellion of 1745–6.[174] Britain's fortunes and prosperity, even her very survival, seemed to be ever more closely linked to commerce. Britain was a commercial society in which trade was the principal national interest, or so many contemporaries argued. Linda Colley has recently talked of a 'cult of commerce' in Britain in this period.[175] Trade and conceptions of the national interest were on sharply converging paths. One contemporary announced, 'we have almost introduced a new criterion of virtue and vice, regarding not more their moral Differences, than their influence on Trade'.[176] Behind this convergence lay mercantilist assumptions about the sources of national prosperity, the particular constellation of diplomatic and international forces and developments in this period, and a confluence of concerns and assumptions about the influence on society of commerce and the employment which it created. War and rivalry with France, and before the end of the 1750s a pervasive sense of anxiety about the future, propelled the issue of prospects for British commerce and trade, and her 'empire of the seas', to the forefront

---

[170] Ned C. Landsman, 'Liberty, Piety and Patronage: The Social Context of Contested Clerical Calls in Eighteenth-Century Glasgow', in Andrew Hook and Richard B. Sher (eds.), *The Glasgow Enlightenment* (1995), 216.
[171] *Scots Mag.* (1759), 46–7.
[172] J. Mason, 'The Edinburgh School of Design', *Book of the Old Edinburgh Club*, 27 (1949), 67–96.
[173] See Ch. 5, p. 205, above.
[174] For this, see Ch. 4, above.
[175] Colley, *Britons*, 56.
[176] *Reflections on Various Subjects Relating to Arts and Commerce*, 33–4.

of debate. The pursuit of profit was portrayed as a patriotic act. The conditions of diplomacy and international relations served also to concentrate minds on the relative health of the economy and the country's essential economic and military resource—its population. Contemporaries looked for what Isaac Maddox, Bishop of Worcester, was to call 'diffusive economy' in poor relief and philanthropy.[177] Images of an idle, unruly labouring class drunk on relative prosperity and freedom haunted much discussion. They also sought solutions that would transform the labouring ranks into diligent, docile toilers, as well as relieving the landed classes of the burden of escalating poor rates.

The patriotic promotion of commerce and manufactures furnished, as Colley and others have emphasized, vehicles for merchants, bankers, some professionals, and tradesmen to achieve greater political respectability and status.[178] It is possible to detect in this a challenge, albeit implicit rather than explicit, to a political order which was, in certain respects, becoming increasingly closed in this period. Bodies such as the Free British Fishery Society, the Marine Society, and the Society for the Encouragement of the Arts were organized as subscriber democracies. These bodies also emphasized openness and accountability in their operations and finances. In 1753, the Council of the Free British Fishery Society ordered that every proprietor (or susbscriber) of £300 and above was at liberty to inspect the accounts of the Society on the first Tuesday of every month from 10a.m. to 3p.m.[179] Publicity through the press was intrinsic to their being and their operations. Their very establishment, moreover, reflected perceived shortcomings on the part of the British state. Compared to the French state, and other European states—for example, the Prussia of Frederick the Great—state support for British commerce and manufacturing was viewed in this period by many people as weak and disorganized. The value of commerce and the promotion of commerce in this period were also easily contrasted with the debilitating influence of luxury and the giddiness and insubstantiality of fashion which seemed to consume the time and energy of the social elites who frequented London's West End.

Yet support for the promotion of commerce in this period was not simply or even perhaps primarily fed by opposition to or dissatisfaction with the political and indeed social status quo, at least not in any simple way. Many of the individuals and bodies who supported the Free British Fishery, the Society for the Encouragement of the Arts, and the Marine Society were far from alienated from the mid-century state. As emphasized above, these individuals included representatives of the 'monied interest' and the big financial and merchant companies whose fortunes were inextricably intertwined with those

---

[177] Maddox, *The Duty and Advantages of Encouraging Public Infirmaries, preached before the President and Governors of the London Infirmary, 25 March 1743*, 3rd edn. (1743), 13.

[178] Colley, *Britons*, 85–106. See also Kathleen Wilson, 'Urban Culture and Political Activism in Hanoverian England: The Example of Voluntary Hospitals', in Eckhart Hellmuth (ed.), *The Transformation of Political Culture: England and Germany in the Late Eighteenth Century* (Oxford, 1990), 165–84.

[179] BL, Add. MS 15155, fo. 12.

of the state and the Treasury. The report to Parliament of the committee of merchants who later became the Free British Fishery Society was signed by men such as Sir James Creed, MP and East India merchant, George Wombwell, East India Company director and government contractor, and John Bance, director of the East India Company and the Bank of England.[180] Many members of the landed classes and titled nobility gave their support to these bodies, although they were a minority of the total membership. The modern historian of the Society for the Encouragement of the Arts has concluded, based on a close examination of the position in 1764, that general membership reflected 'the whole spectrum of upper, middle, and lower middle class ranks and occupations'. By 1758, members included most of the leading members of the ministry—the First Lord of the Treasury, the Duke of Newcastle, the Chancellor of the Exchequer, Henry Bilson Legge, the two Secretaries of State, William Pitt and Lord Holdernesse, the First Lord of the Admiralty, Lord Anson, and the Attorney General, Charles Pratt, as well as other representatives of the titled nobility.[181] If those who actually ran the Society were of a lower social rank, what united them, apart from their common commitment to the aims of the Society, and often a particular interest in certain aspects of the Society's business, appears to have been their aspiration for respectability. Along with broader moral and religious concerns, their view of society was conservative; they wanted to shore up or reimpose strict hierarchy in society, to restore the lower orders to subordination and compliance. Landed and non-landed members of the propertied class closed ranks in seeking to reform the habits of the labouring classes and the poor. The non-landed members were men who adopted the title 'esquire', who were proud of the respectability of the Society and its membership which included many of the great. The landed and political elites may not have predominated numerically, but their support was crucial and very visible.

Support for British commerce and manufactures and maritime power in this period emanated from many parts of the political and social elite. Lord Townshend endowed a prize at Cambridge University in 1754 for the best essay in any given year on a nominated commercial issue or topic. Most members of the royal family identified themselves with the cause of commerce, albeit to differing degrees. Frederick, Prince of Wales was only the most ostentatious about this, resuming a role as a friend of trade that he had adopted whilst in opposition in the later 1730s. His investiture as Governor of the Free British Fishery Society was a carefully staged piece of political theatre, emphasizing his support for British commerce.[182] In the summer of 1750, he went on a progress through the west country which again was

---

[180] See Appendix 3, below.

[181] Allan, 'The Society', 63, 94.

[182] An occasion fully described in the *Caledonian Mercury*, 1 Nov. 1750. In December 1750, the Prince was presented with the freedom of the Fishmonger's Company in a gold box with the company's arms engraved on it. He was also presented with a poem by John Lockman.

designed to emphasize his support for native manufactures and commerce. In August, the Prince visited Portsmouth, where he inspected the dock and ship-yard and fortifications, and Southampton. At this last place, the town clerk announced:

It must fill the Heart of every true lover of his Country with the utmost sensible Pleasure, to behold your Royal Highnesses, in whom are united all the Graces that form and adorn the Character of a true Patriot Prince and most amiable Princess, whose great Regard for the Welfare and Happiness of these Nations, and particularly the Trade thereof, has rendered you the Delight and Admiration of Mankind, and will ever attract the just Esteem of this and every Trading Town and City in this Kingdom.[183]

In 1749, George II gave £1,000 to managers of the fisheries on the coast of Scotland.[184] Along with the future George III and the Princess Dowager of Wales, he also made the largest individual contribution to the funds of the Marine Society.[185] The Duke of Cumberland, meanwhile, supported an effort to establish an English rival to the great Gobelins and Chaillot carpet factories in France.[186]

The cult of commerce appeared, therefore, to carry all before it in this period. Yet it did so partly because of contingent factors, notably the perception, reality, and nature of the threat from France. In changed circumstances, deep-rooted tensions between mercantile activity and patriotism (or conceptions of the national interest) would become more apparent. The notion of 'a commercial interest' was, in any case, simply a convenient political fiction. The mercantile community was divided into many competing interests and groups. Merchants pursued their own narrow self-interest, or so it was commonly argued, and with much justification. Attitudes towards commerce, moreover, remained more ambivalent than is often recognized. Many contemporaries, as is revealed elsewhere in this book, worried about the repercussions of commercial progress for the moral condition, unity, and military strength of Britain. Under changed circumstances, such as those which pertained after 1763, when the French threat seemed much diminished, the influence of trade and empire on society would come to seem less benign and positive. Patriotic championing of commerce, moreover, posed little serious threat to landed political leadership. Tensions between landed stewardship of the national interest and the commercial nation were relatively minor, whatever opposition propagandists might claim. As we will see in the final chapters, the elites were subject to some pointed criticism from opposition sources on social and cultural grounds, primarily as sources of moral and political corruption and

---

[183] *Whitehall Evening Post*, 18–21 Aug. 1750.
[184] *Caledonian Mercury*, 31 July 1749.
[185] See Hanway, *An Account*.
[186] The attempt is described briefly in the *Scots Mag.* (1754), 399.

agents of cultural betrayal. Significantly, however, one of the only issues in this period which threatened to divide the landed and commercial or manufacturing interests, the prohibition on distilling from grain between 1757–60, was dealt with by Parliament in a way which sought to satisfy both major interests. Under the impact in part of petitioning from manufacturing interests and communities, MPs voted to raise the duties on spirituous liquors at the same time as lifting the prohibition on distilling. The landed political elite knew that commerce mattered, and were prepared to commit money and manpower to supporting it and protecting British markets overseas. A parliament dominated by landed representatives was receptive to commercial lobbying and passing legislation to protect and nurture British economic and trading interests. The legislation on commercial matters passed in this period is testimony to this, as is the serious consideration which Parliament gave to trade and commercial issues more generally. The record of Parliament and of ministers could always be criticized. Sir James Lowther was, for example, very censorious about ministerial actions in the later 1740s and early 1750s, condemning them for not taking a bolder stance on fiscal retrenchment and reform. Lowther, however, was particularly exercised by customs fraud in the tobacco industry in Scotland, and wanted the Treasury and ministers to lower duties as a major part of the solution. Lowther also favoured more rapid reductions in tax as part of the programme of economy and debt reduction to be pursued at the end of the war.[187] More generally, contemporaries might look to the bold reforms being pursued on the continent and measure progress in Britain less favourably. Several issues were raised but never tackled—for example, the debt laws, widely perceived to be unfair and an obstacle to commerce, and the standardization of weights and measures. Yet all this merely highlights the generally cautious and piecemeal nature of reform in this period. It also fails to acknowledge the weight of the political and practical constraints under which Pelham, other ministers and MPs were operating. Modern historians have tended to praise Pelham's management of the national debt after 1748 and emphasized the skill and nerve with which he executed a reduction in interest on it and a subsequent consolidation of national stocks.[188] Pelham had also learnt his political skills at the feet of Sir Robert Walpole. He sought to balance the interests of trade and land; he also recognized, as did those who joined or followed him in high ministerial office, that major reforms threatened the conciliatory, albeit unexciting, political strategy Whig oligarchy had marked out as most likely to promote its continued political supremacy, as well as the stability and peace of the nation. From 1754, ministers, the Treasury, the other departments of government, and Parliament were, furthermore, faced with the enormous and urgent task of mobilizing manpower and

[187] CRO (Carlisle), D/Lons/W2/1/111 and 112.

[188] See esp. Lucy Sutherland, 'Sampson Gideon and the Reduction of Interest, 1749–50', in Aubrey Newman (ed.), *Politics and Finance in the Eighteenth Century: Lucy Sutherland*, (1984), 399–413.

resources for a new war against France, a war which would be fought across the globe and which would place unprecedented demands on British society and financial power. Large-scale schemes to promote commerce, and further reform, would have to wait for this new war to end.[189]

[189] A good illustration is the failure of the Treasury to respond to any of the plans submitted to them by the Commissioners of the Forfeited estates in Scotland in the second half of the 1750s (see Ch. 4, pp. 184, above).

CHAPTER SEVEN

Morals and the Nation

The crowd which assembled on 3 October 1750 to witness the hanging of highwayman James Maclaine was an unusually large one for such occasions. 'Almost infinite' in size, one London newspaper reported that 'There was the greatest concourse of People at Tyburn ever known at any Execution'.[1] The condemned man was not, in any simple sense, a popular criminal hero, although he was handsome and as such much fawned over, at a safe distance, by the ladies of the town. He also provided a temporary attraction for the London population. According to Horace Walpole, 3,000 went to see him on the first Sunday after his condemnation.[2] It was, however, a sombre crowd that watched his final progress towards death, and Maclaine had no wish to cheat the Tyburn tree of its monitory purpose; he travelled to his place of execution in an open cart and in a state of religious devotion.

What we know about Maclaine is owing to two pamphlets published soon after his death. The most important of these, *An Account of the Behaviour of Mr James Maclaine, From the Time of his Condemnation to the Day of his Execution* (1750), was written by the Revd Dr Allen, the clergyman who attended Maclaine in his final days. According to Allen, it was 'drawn up and published at the earnest Desire of Mr Maclaine himself'.[3] It rapidly went through four editions, and was extracted in at least one London newspaper.[4] A separate edition was also published in Dublin. The author of the second pamphlet, *A Compleat History of James Maclean, The Gentleman Highwayman* (1750), is unknown, but the motive for writing it was declared in the opening pages. Concerned, like many contemporaries, that executions were losing their deterrent force, that their purpose was being subverted by an irreverent, unruly crowd and the 'mock heroics' of the condemned, the author sought to reinforce the lessons of Maclaine's life (and death) through the written word.[5] Neither pamphlet was, therefore, a simple recitation of fact. Both were carefully constructed moral

---

[1] *Penny London Post*, 3–5 Oct. 1750.

[2] Walpole, *Correspondence*, xx. 199. See also the mock-satirical *A Petition to the Right Hon Mr ——, in Favour of Mr Maclean. By a Lady* (1750).

[3] *An Account*, 1.

[4] *Penny London Post*, 24–6 Oct.; 26–9 Oct.; 29–31 Oct.; 31 Oct.–2 Nov.; 2–5 Nov.; 5–7 Nov.; 7–9 Nov. 1750.

[5] *A Compleat History*, esp. pp. 1–4.

narratives; they were attempts to impose pattern and meaning on a life for an explicitly exemplary purpose.

The story they tell is of a life wrecked by an addiction to pleasure and to cutting a figure in fashionable society. 'My Love of Pleasure, and of a gay Appearance has undone me', Maclaine confesses at one point in Allen's account.[6] Maclaine is portrayed as an anti-hero, a cowardly man led astray by keeping 'low company' and tormented by his conscience. Responsibility for his fate was also his alone. Born into a 'genteel' Scottish Presbyterian family, he was provided with a 'decent and pious' education, the source of an inexpungable conscience. Furnished with these early advantages, he had every 'rational prospect of Prosperity and temporal happiness'.[7] When he was still young, his family emigrated to Ireland where his father took up a position as the minister of a Dissenting congregation in Monaghan. Maclaine was educated to follow a mercantile career, and provision was made for him to be sent to Rotterdam to work in the accounting house of a Scots merchant. Before the latter part of this scheme could come to fruition, however, his father died. It was the wealth that Maclaine inherited from his father which sowed the seeds of his extravagance and eventual ruin.

Using his inheritance, Maclaine decided to equip himself with the 'gayest dress' which Monaghan could provide, together with a 'fine' gelding. His major pastime became 'gallenting all the Farmers' daughters within 10 miles to all fairs and publick meetings'. Deaf to all advice from his family, he decided to go to Dublin with the aim of making his fortune by ensnaring an heiress. This plan only led to him getting into disreputable company and exhausting the remains of his fortune. It was a pattern which would be repeated.

On his return to Monaghan, Maclaine was shunned by his family. With no other obvious means of supporting himself, he was forced to take a job as a servant to a gentleman en route to England. It was a position that his vanity rebelled against, and which he lost after only a few months. Following another period of service, which ended when Maclaine was accused of stealing from the household, his former master financed his passage to London. (The 'bewitching pleasures of London' were to play a significant part in Maclaine's downfall.) Maclaine soon found himself a position as the kept lover of the Irish mistress of a nobleman. It was in this woman's arms that Maclaine's cowardice first fully became apparent. Disturbed 'making warm Return of Gratitude' to her by the arrival of the nobleman, the latter proceeded to give Maclaine a severe beating. This was despite the fact that Maclaine was much stronger than his assailant and equally well armed. His mistress being turned upon the town by the peer, Maclaine quickly found himself a new one.

A few months later, tiring of such dependency, Maclaine decided to reactivate his earlier plan—to secure an independent fortune by capturing an

[6] *An Account*, 12.
[7] *A Compleat History*, 5.

heiress. He was no more successful, however, than he had previously been in Dublin. Following the failure of his hopes, he threw himself on the charity of his family, who furnished him with money to travel to Jamaica to seek his fortune there in business. The scheme's attraction did not last long; instead Maclaine chose to marry the daughter of an innkeeper and dealer in horses who brought with her a fortune of £500. With this, he set up as a grocer in London. Predictably, the business did not flourish, the profits being continually sacrificed to his love of pleasure and finery.

It was following his wife's death several years later, that Maclaine finally met his nemesis, an Irish surgeon and apothecary by the name of Plunket. With Plunket, Maclaine embarked on a career of again attempting to ensnare an heiress, and highway robbery. The two men devised a scheme to entrap an heiress with a fortune of £10,000. It involved Maclaine disguising himself as a 'fine beau'. The scheme was foiled when Maclaine became embroiled in a dispute in a pleasure garden with an apothecary, and his real identity was exposed by a half-pay officer who had known him in former guise as a footman. There was one final opportunity for Maclaine to redeem himself. His friends raised a subscription of sixty guineas for him to go to Jamaica. But before he left, Maclaine went to a masquerade and took to the gaming table; a small win was followed by a much more conclusive loss.

It was Plunket who now put forward the idea of becoming a highwayman, and Maclaine's final months of freedom were spent in a cycle of robbing and trying to resurrect the plan of winning a fortune through ensnaring a heiress. Maclaine's career as a highwayman was as unheroic as the rest of his life. Such was his cowardice that he would neither utter a word nor hold a pistol during the robberies. Having been caught, Maclaine tried to save himself by confessing and turning over his accomplice. In court, he sought to retract his confession; the jury, unaffected, found him guilty.

Maclaine's last days were spent in repentance and religious devotion. Whilst in gaol, he received a series of letters from his brother, pastor of the English congregation at the Hague, severely admonishing him for his wickedness and impressing upon him that now he could only seek repentance and forgiveness in God. Maclaine was portrayed as being in a state of religious crisis; he had returned to the faith in which he had been brought up and educated, a faith that had left its mark throughout his wayward life. Maclaine had, according to Allen at least, also been indifferent towards his own death at the end, occupying his final night in prayer and devotion with another inmate of the gaol. There was time was for one final act of contrition. From his cell on the morning of his execution, he wrote a letter to a friend counselling him to lead a religious and virtuous life and to avoid 'Fondness for the Gaitie [*sic*] of life' He also expressed happiness about his approaching death and the judgment which awaited him.

Why should we pay any attention to Maclaine and his unhappy end?

Criminals and criminal trials regularly furnished part of the constantly changing drama that was eighteenth-century London life. Yet Maclaine, or the representations of Maclaine that survive, do have a deeper importance. His life (and death) served to dramatize anxieties and fears about the condition of society that many people felt at the time. It furnished a repertoire of images and words which confirmed contemporary assumptions about the roots of much crime. His addiction to pleasure and to the dress and appurtenances of gentle status tempted him into a life of crime. Pleasure entrapped him, enveloping him in its insidious folds; it led him to associate with criminals, as well as free-thinkers and atheists. His story also highlighted the dangers to property and rank posed by a world where display and manners were increasingly the mark of gentle status. His story also forms a small part of an unfolding campaign in England to regulate public entertainments more stringently, to reimpose order and regularity on a society in which social boundaries were perceived to be dissolving under the impact of economic change and the popularity of new forms of leisure, and to eliminate what was widely viewed as a major cause of crime.[8] Finally, in his stricken conscience, Maclaine could be seen as demonstrating, albeit belatedly, that religion was the best prophylactic against immorality and crime and fears which these created amongst the propertied classes. Just how significant these lessons were for contemporaries in the early 1750s and indeed for most of the mid-eighteenth century will become clear during the rest of this chapter.

I have also chosen to begin with Maclaine's story because his life and the uses that were made of it help to alert us to a very important fact about Britain in the mid-eighteenth century—that it was a period which saw periodically intense debate about morals and social manners and diverse, episodic but cumulatively impressive efforts to reform these. This was true of Scotland as well as England, although different religious and political contexts and inheritances inevitably lent divergent shape and content to these debates and responses. There was, in short, a mid-eighteenth-century movement for moral and social reform, or perhaps more accurately a series of strong impulses towards these things. It is a facet of the period which has received limited attention from historians and this neglect has helped a series of misperceptions about the mid-eighteenth century to take hold.[9] These include the idea

---

[8] See, as well as the two pamphlets on Maclaine's life cited above, *A Letter to the Honourable House of Commons Relating to the Present Situation of Affairs* (1750).

[9] Historians who have begun to recognize its importance are John Beattie, *Crime and the Courts in England, 1660–1800* (Oxford, 1986), esp. ch. 10; Nicholas Rogers, 'Confronting the Crime Wave: The Debate over Social Reform and Regulation, 1749–1753', in Lee Davison, Tim Hitchcock, Tim Keirn, and Robert B. Shoemaker (eds.), *Stilling the Grumbling Hive: The Response to Social and Economic Problems in England, 1689–1750* (Stroud, 1992), 77–120; Richard Connors, ' "The Grand Inquest of the Nation": Parliamentary Committees and Social Policy in Mid-Eighteenth-Century England', *Parliamentary History*, 14 (1995), 285–313. Tim Hitchcock has also recently written, 'There was from around 1740 to

that it was a period which witnessed little interest in social reform.[10] Equally dangerous and misleading is the notion that it was a period marked by religious torpor: that having emerged from the fractious debates and fervour of the early eighteenth century, clergymen, ministers, and their lay supporters had lapsed into a content indifference, too focused on dry theological speculation to campaign to reform society's morals or perhaps too diverted by the growing pleasures of this world. Linked to this (mis)perception is a tendency to portray politics and public debate in this period as largely uninfluenced by religion and religious concerns. Yet, as this chapter will show, the reality was more complex. One of the salient features of public debate in this period was the entanglement of religious, commercial, political, and social issues. To separate them too starkly is to risk making distinctions which would have meant little to contemporaries. Where morals was being discussed religion followed closely. Indeed, for many, the degeneration of morals and manners was primarily a religious problem.

MORALS IN THE MID-EIGHTEENTH CENTURY: PERCEPTIONS AND BACKGROUND

The notion that society was irreligious and immoral was commonly expressed in this period. In 1740, one individual talked of the 'total disregard to Virtue, which reigns amongst us in this degenerate Age'.[11] A few years later, John Warden of the Edinburgh Canongate Church complained of the prevalence of infidelity, profanity, and the fashionableness of vice in the Scottish capital.[12] In 1750, Sir James Lowther, independent Whig MP for Cumberland, was writing of the 'people of fashion' in London being 'prodigiously given to gaming even on the L[or]ds day' and of the 'meaner folks' being 'desperately wicked'. On 19 December in the same year, Lowther was telling Thomas Wilson that Britain was 'undone as a Nation, or shall be in a few years under the heels of France thanks to the excess of Gaming and Diversions of all kinds'.[13] Lowther was an old man who had just had his leg amputated for gout (without the aid of an anaesthetic), which may account for his pessimism. Yet his sense that society had fallen into new depths of degeneracy was widely shared. In a sermon given in 1757, Thomas Scott commented on

the late 1750s what might accurately be described as a crisis of social policy' (id., 'Demography and the Culture of Sex', in Jeremy Black (ed.), *Culture and Society in Britain 1660–1800* (Manchester, 1997), 77).

[10] The same point has been made by a number of other historians. See n. 9 above. See also Joanna Innes, 'Parliament and the Shaping of Eighteenth-Century English Social Policy', *TRHS*, 40 (1990), 63–92.

[11] *A [Serious] Address to the Electors of Great Britain* (1740), 8.

[12] John Warden, *The Happiness of Britain Illustrated. In a Sermon* (Edinburgh, 1749).

[13] CRO (Carlisle), D/Lons/W2/1/112, Sir James Lowther to John Spedding, 22 Dec. 1750; C. S. L. Linnell (ed.), *The Diaries of Thomas Wilson, DD* (1964), 258.

'the numerous, repeated well-supported complaints of the vast increase, within a few years, of infidelity, or popery, of enthusiasm, of luxury, of all sorts of vices, in the higher, middle, and in the lowest class of our people'.[14] John Witherspoon, a minister in Paisley at this point, appears to have felt that Britain was in an age of luxury, and that this portended terminal national decline.[15] Towards the end of our period, in 1761, Thomas Cole declared: 'An ostentacious extravagance is continually displaying itself in every part of this voluptuous city [i.e. London], and amongst all ranks and conditions of men.'[16] The widely held conception was, in short, of a society which was sinking under the combined inundations of irreligion, immorality, and the love of pleasure.

As Joanna Innes has recently commented, 'concern about the corrupt state of contemporary morals formed a persistent theme in English thought, engaging the attention of people at many different social levels throughout the eighteenth century.'[17] The 1690s saw a crescendo of debate and anxiety about morals.[18] In the mid-1730s, the so-called 'gin craze' provided a focus for similar concerns; the colony of Georgia was also founded in 1733 as an experiment in forming a virtuous society in contradistinction to the corruption of London and Walpole's England.[19] In these activities and debates, we can discern common threads—in the form of individuals, reforming alliances, and perceptions—which connect the first eighteenth-century wave of reform with the debates and responses of the mid-century. The Country opposition to Walpole also reflected a strong feeling that Walpolian rule was undermining the moral health of society, a feeling which had in the mid- to later 1730s led to a strong strain of pessimism about the possibility of moral and political

[14] Quoted in D. Napthine and W. A. Speck, 'Clergymen and Conflict 1660–1763', in W. J. Shiels (ed.), *Studies in Church History* (Oxford, 1983), 239.

[15] John Witherspoon, *A Serious Enquiry into the Nature and Effects of the Stage. Being an Attempt to Show, That Contributing to the Support of a Public Theatre, is Inconsistent with the Character of a Christian* (Glasgow, 1757).

[16] Thomas Cole, *Discourses on Luxury, Infidelity, and Enthusiasm* (1761), 11.

[17] Joanna Innes, 'Politics and Morals: The Reformation of Manners Movement in Later Eighteenth-Century England', in Eckhart Hellmuth (ed.), *The Transformation of Political Culture: England and Germany in the Late Eighteenth Century* (Oxford, 1990), 58.

[18] T. C. Curtis and W. A. Speck, 'The Societies for the Reformation of Manners: A Case Study in the Theory and Practice of Moral Reform', *Literature and History*, 3 (1980), 45–64; T. B. Isaacs, 'Moral Crime, Moral Reform and the State in Early Eighteenth Century England: A Study of Piety and Politics', Ph.D. thesis (University of Rochester, 1979); id., 'The Anglican Hierarchy and the Reformation of Manners, 1688–1738', *Journal of Ecclesiastical History*, 33 (1982), 391–411; A. G. Craig, 'The Movement for the Reformation of Manners, 1688–1715', Ph.D. thesis (Edinburgh University, 1980); David Hayton, 'Moral Reform and Country Politics in the Late Seventeenth Century House of Commons', *Past and Present*, 128 (1990), 48–91; R. B. Shoemaker, 'Reforming the City: The Reformation of Manners Campaign in London, 1690–1738', in Lee Davison, *et. al., Stilling the Grumbling Hive*, 99–120; id., *Prosecution and Punishment: Petty Crime and the Law in London and Rural Middlesex, c.1660–1720* (Cambridge, 1991), ch. 9; D. W. R. Bahlman, *The Moral Revolution of 1688* (New Haven, Conn., 1957).

[19] See Harvey H. Jackson and Phinizy Spalding (eds.), *Forty Years of Diversity: Essays on Colonial Georgia* (Athens, Ga., 1984).

reform and renewal.[20] What was striking about the mid-century, certainly in England, was, nevertheless, the frequency and clarity with which a general sense of degeneracy of manners was expressed, especially from the later 1740s. There was also a hardening of a perception that corruption and luxury had spread throughout society, including amongst the lower orders.[21] As one writer in the *London Evening Post* put it in 1753: '[I]t now seems a Point of Notoriety, that the Lowest of the People are now as universally and as thoroughly corrupt as the greatest in other countries.'[22]

How do we explain this new upsurge of anxiety about morals? As Peter Borsay has argued in a different context, as far as England is concerned it was at one level a symptom or consequence of an improvement in general standards of living which began in the later seventeenth century and which was, for some, to end during the later 1750s.[23] A combination of a stable population and a run of good harvests, especially in the 1730s and 1740s (1740 was a notable exception), almost certainly led to a rise in real wages for a broad cross-section of the English labouring classes. The major increases in real and disposable incomes were amongst the middling ranks and skilled labouring classes, two groups unusually well represented in metropolitan society. This was the background to significant developments in the provision of commercial leisure and entertainment, especially but not exclusively in London and its environs, referred to below. It may also have promoted changes in habits of consumption quite well down the social scale. Some contemporaries, who viewed such changes with alarm, represented this as a contagion of social emulation. Thomas Cole, quoted above, talked of 'an emulous endeavour to outvie each other in all the elegant accommodations of life' as 'the main ambition of the vast majority' and as the 'almost universal passion of the age'. Novelist Henry Fielding saw this facet of behaviour as a defining characteristic of a social revolution wrought by the expansion of trade. Trade has, he wrote in 1751, 'given a new Face to the whole Nation.'[24]

The position north of the border was different in several important respects. Real wage levels appear in general to have remained flat until the later 1760s, and lagged considerably behind those found in England.[25] Economic growth in Scotland in the early decades of the eighteenth century was also more patchy and had shallower roots.[26] The wages of Edinburgh

---

[20] H. T. Dickinson, *Liberty and Property: Political Ideology in Eighteenth-Century Britain* (1977), ch. 5; Isaac Kramnick, *Bolingbroke and His Circle: The Politics of Nostalgia in the Age of Walpole* (Cambridge, Mass., 1968).

[21] See John Sekora, *Luxury: The Concept in Western Thought, from Eden to Smollett* (Baltimore, 1977).

[22] *Lond. Ev. P.*, 11–13 Jan. 1753.

[23] Peter Borsay, *The English Urban Renaissance: Culture and Society in the Provincial Town, 1660–1770* (1989), 303.

[24] Cole, *Discourse on Luxury*, 11; Henry Fielding, *An Enquiry into the Late Increase of Robbers and Related Writings*, ed. Marvin Zirker (Oxford, 1988), 71.

[25] A. J. S. Gibson and T. C. Smout, *Prices, Food and Wages in Scotland, 1550–1780* (Cambridge, 1995).

[26] See C. A. Whatley, *The Industrial Revolution in Scotland* (Cambridge, 1997), ch. 2.

builders reflect these trends, remaining static until the 1740s.[27] Nevertheless, as Rab Houston has shown, there is evidence of growing inequalities of wealth in Edinburgh manifesting themselves in rising consumption of luxury goods and products, for example, fruit, from the 1690s through to the early 1760s.[28] From the 1740s, moreover, the notion of Scotland as a rapidly developing, increasingly prosperous, commercial society—with all the repercussions that had for social relations, manners, and morals—was articulated with ever-increasing insistence and clarity.[29]

The central decades of the century also coincided with an expansionary phase in public, commercial entertainments in and around London. This development cannot be documented with precision, but what evidence there is points strongly in this direction. One writer referred in 1751 to the 'Number of Publick Places of Diversion, which have for some Years past so greatly increased in or near' to London.[30] The Middlesex justices wrote to the Duke of Newcastle in similar terms in 1744.[31] The most visible aspect of growth in this sphere, and certainly the most important in influencing contemporary perceptions, was the rise and spread of the pleasure gardens.[32] The two most fashionable and notorious were Vauxhall, south of the Thames, and Ranelagh, in Chelsea. Jonathan Tyers obtained the lease for Vauxhall in 1728 and altered and improved gardens were opened in 1732. The famous rotunda at Ranelagh was erected in 1741, and the public were first admitted to the gardens in April 1742.[33] Ranelagh's popularity was immediate and sustained, as indicated in the letters of Horace Walpole.[34] On 26 April 1749, the gardens hosted the first of the famous Jubilee masquerade balls in the Venetian taste. Tyers' response to the rise of Ranelagh was a major programme of improvements to his gardens from the later 1740s, a programme which had been largely completed by 1751.[35] In May 1751, one evening at

[27] L. Cullen, A. Gibson, and T. C. Smout, 'Wages and Comparative Development in Ireland and Scotland, 1565–1780', in R. Mitchison and P. Roebuck (eds.), *Economy and Society in Scotland and Ireland 1500–1939* (Edinburgh, 1988).

[28] R. A. Houston, 'The Economy of Edinburgh 1694–1763: The Evidence of the Common Good', in S. J. Conolly, R. A. Houston and R. J. Morris (eds.), *Conflict, Identity and Economic Development: Ireland and Scotland, 1600–1939* (Preston, 1995), 45–63.

[29] See Ch. 4, above.

[30] *Penny London Post*, 1–4 Feb. 1751.

[31] GLRO, MJ/OC/5, fos. 46–7.

[32] Much of the following section is based on information provided in Warwick Wroth, *The London Pleasure Gardens of the Eighteenth Century* (repr. 1979; 1st edn., 1896).

[33] See *Gent. Mag.*, 12 (1742), 412.

[34] Walpole was initially decidedly unimpressed by Ranelagh, although he acknowledged on 26 May 1742, two days after it officially opened, that it was attracting 'everybody that loves eating, drinking, staring or crowding' (Walpole, *Correspondence*, xxxvii. 434). By the summer of 1744, however, he was telling Henry Seymour Conway, 'you must be informed that every night constantly I go to Ranelagh, which has totally beat Vauxhall. Nobody goes anywhere else; everybody goes there' (Walpole, *Correspondence*, xxxvii. 164).

[35] Brian Allen, 'The Landscape', in T. J. Edelstein and Brian Allen, *Vauxhall Gardens* (New Haven, Conn., 1983), 19–22.

Vauxhall saw between 7,000 and 8,000 present; this represented, according to one contemporary, the 'greatest concentration of persons of distinction ever known'.[36]

Ranelagh especially was strongly attacked for encouraging lewdness and immorality.[37] (Under Tyers' careful management and promotion of his gardens, in which poet John Lockman played a considerable role, Vauxhall escaped some of the hostility which Ranelagh attracted.[38]) The pleasure gardens were also places where there was much gaming, and, as we will see below, a major effort was made in the early 1750s to remove gamesters from the gardens. Contemporaries were also very aware that the crowds which collected at them were socially very mixed. Henry Fielding complained: 'Nobleman and his Taylor, the Lady of Quality and her Tirewoman, meet together and form one common Assembly.'[39]

With their fanciful architectural features, their deliberate appeal to the senses, the pleasure gardens were readily seen as stimulating unsuitable passions and desires.[40] The gardens acted in this context as a powerful focus for contemporary anxieties, greatly sharpened by the perception of the military and diplomatic threat created by an expansionist and ambitious French state, about the impact of polite culture and entertainment on sexual identities. As was emphasized in Chapter 3, the figure of the effeminate fop was commonly encountered in social criticism in this period. John Brown's *Estimate of the Manners and Principles of the Times*, first published in 1757, is perhaps the best-known articulation of contemporary anxiety about 'effeminization'.[41] Yet it was simply one of many. In early December 1749, for example, a leading contributor to the *London Evening Post* urged readers to:

Behold the gewgaw Butterfly, the Beau, who looks like a Girl, and smells like a Civet Cat, whose very Words are Female, and his Gesture of doubtful Gender, who plumes himself upon his Taylor's Art, and, like a Peacock, proudly spreads his gaudy Feathers; whose utmost Knowledge is the newest Modes, and highest Ambition the most admired Dress; . . .[42]

---

[36] *General Advertiser*, 22 May 1751.

[37] See e.g. *The Ranelagh Religion Displayed* (1750).

[38] See esp. David H. Solkin, *Painting For Money: The Visual Arts and the Public Sphere in Eighteenth-Century England* (New Haven, Conn. and London, 1993), ch. 4.

[39] Fielding, *An Enquiry into the Late Increase of Robbers*, ed. Zirker, 82. A tirewoman was a lady's maid.

[40] For a contemporary description of Ranelagh, see *Gent. Mag.*, 12 (1742), 419. See also Walpole, *Correspondence*, xx. 46–7, for Horace's description of the Jubilee masquerade in the Venetian manner in 1749.

[41] Brown argued that the 'character of the Age and nation' was 'by no means that of abandoned Wickedness and Profligacy' but rather of 'vain, luxurious and selfish effeminacy'. 'The Sexes' he observed, 'have now little other apparent Distinction, beyond that of Person and Dress: Their peculiar and characteristic Manners are confounded and lost: the one Sex having advanced into Boldness, as the other has sunk into Effeminacy' (Brown, *Estimate of the Principles and Manners of the Times* (1757), 26, 51).

[42] Repr. in *Edinburgh Evening Courant*, 4 Dec. 1749.

Women, meanwhile, were portrayed as gaining, through the sorts of entertainment on offer at Vauxhall and Ranelagh, an inappropriate visibility and freedom; they were also, because of their new devotion to pleasure, neglecting their domestic and maternal responsibilities. 'The *Oeconomist* and the *Housewife* are characters quite forgot, or if ever *remember'd*, are subjects of *Modern Ridicule*', one writer declared in 1754.[43] Ranelagh and Vauxhall were public diversions where 'all Distinctions of Quality, Fortune, and Sex, were confounded'.[44]

The rise of Ranelagh, and Vauxhall's continuing popularity, far from exhaust the growth and vitality of London pleasure gardens in this period. Indeed, what needs to be emphasized is how much investment and improvement there was exclusive of Ranelagh and Vauxhall. There is not space here to provide details of all the developments, and a few examples will have to suffice.[45] Marylebone Gardens, which dates from 1738 as a place of entertainment, was enlarged in 1753.[46] Cuper's Gardens in Lambeth was improved under Ephraim Evans between 1738 and 1740 and went on to flourish under the management of his widow between 1741 and 1759. These were fashionable places of resort; they provided the sorts of entertainment and places to congregate and walk which Ranelagh and Vauxhall offered. There was, however, a proliferation of gardens and places of entertainment aimed at less elevated patrons. In 1745, the proprietor of the Mulberry Garden in Clerkenwell made an appeal to 'the honest sons of trade and industry after the fatigues of a well-spent day'. In 1756, Joseph Barras, proprietor of Bowling Green House, near to the Foundling Hospital, announced that he had greatly altered and fitted up his establishment in a 'genteel manner'. Around London, there appear to have developed a whole series of resorts or places of diversion for the middling and lower ranks. The Parish of St James, Clerkenwell included within its boundaries Sadlers Wells, New Wells, Lord Cobham's, and Sir John Oldcastle's. New Wells opened in 1737; Sir John Oldcastle's Tavern and Garden was open between 1744 and 1746. In 1744, the inhabitants of the parish petitioned the Middlesex Justices against these places, complaining that each of them was 'capable of receiving four or five hundreds of loose idle & disorderly persons ... together every Evening'.[47] There were also a vast number of inns in and around London providing games such as skittles and gambling of one sort or another.

If economic factors, and developments in commercial entertainment and leisure are essential parts of the background to contemporary concern about luxury and immorality, a further crucial factor was crime, or rather

[43] *Lond. Ev. P.*, 4–7 Sept. 1754.
[44] *An Account of the Behaviour of Mr James Maclaine*, 29.
[45] Most of the information in the following paragraph is derived from Wroth's *The London Pleasure Gardens*.
[46] See esp. Mollie Sands, *The Eighteenth-Century Pleasure Gardens of Marylebone, 1737–1777* (1987).
[47] GLRO, MJ/OC/5, fo. 38.

perceptions of this. It is no accident that one peak of concern about immorality coincided with a crime wave which followed the end of the War of the Austrian Succession. It was a pattern prefigured by a smaller crime wave that took place in England in the mid-1740s.[48] Crime sharpened fears about morals because of contemporary diagnoses of the causes of crime. It was widely believed that the roots of criminal behaviour and activity were idleness or an inappropriate addiction to pleasure amongst the lower orders. As a parliamentary committee on felonies appointed in February 1751 reported, the cause of crime was the 'habit of idleness, in which the lower People have been bred from their youth.'[49] The criminal personality was one in which the passions were dominant; it was these which impelled or lured members of the lower orders into a life of crime as they sought to assuage their addiction to pleasure. In this period, as we will see below, gaming became a particular source of concern, precisely because it seemed to exemplify this explanation for crime. It highlighted crime's supposed psychological roots, the ways in which the lower orders were driven to commit crimes to feed unsuitable habits or aspirations. It will be recalled that James Maclaine was led into crime because he failed to be 'content' in the 'humbler' station he was 'designed to fit'.

The other very important fact about the crime wave after 1748 was the immediate threat it posed (or appeared to pose) to the property and persons of the propertied classes. As John Beattie and Douglas Hay have shown in studies of Surrey and Staffordshire respectively, property crime climbed steeply after 1748, a consequence of the demobilization of soldiers and sailors following the end of the war.[50] Beattie emphasizes the seriousness of the crime wave, with indictments of property offences in Surrey reaching a mid-century peak in 1751. Anecdotal evidence suggests that the pattern was similar elsewhere in England. One magistrate wrote from Nottingham in July 1751,'I never knew the Country so full of Rogues in my life. I have committed three Highwaymen to Goal [*sic*] who will all be found guilty and I hope will be executed.'[51] In January of the previous year, the *Penny London Post* reprinted a letter from Gosport, which reported, 'Robberies are grown so frequent in and near this Town, that it is not safe to be out after it is dark.'[52] It was, however, through the press and their own experiences that most contemporaries viewed crime. The metropolitan press, lacking after 1748 a war to generate copy for its pages, became consumed with reporting this crime, creating in the process a vision of London and the roads around London beset with dangers to

[48] See Ruth Paley, 'Thief Takers in London in the Age of the McDaniel Gang, c.1745–1754', in Douglas Hay and Francis Snyder (eds.), *Policing and Prosecution in Britain 1750–1850* (Oxford, 1989), 301–41.

[49] *Commons Journals*, xxvi (1750–4), 190.

[50] Beattie, *Crime and the Courts in England*, 219–35; Douglas Hay, 'War, Dearth and Theft in the Eighteenth Century: The Record of the English Courts', *Past and Present*, 95 (1982), 117–60.

[51] BL, Add. MS 32724 (Newcastle Papers), fos. 498–9.

[52] *Penny London Post*, 17–19 Jan. 1750.

individuals of substance and thus further contributing to the panic.[53] Several papers—the *Whitehall Evening Post*, James Ralph's *Remembrancer*, and Fielding's *Covent Garden Journal*—developed special sections dealing with robberies. Through the reports of incidents of crime and assault carried on its pages, the press provided the raw materials, the images, and events, which allowed to readers to identify their interest in combating the threat which crime posed to individuals of wealth and standing. The sense of panic was created through repetition, the relentless accumulation in the pages of newspapers of incidents where persons of standing and wealth were either robbed or attacked. The dangers were real as well as imagined, however, and they were dramatically underlined by the hazards of travel around London in this period. Highwaymen were operating on most major roads to and from the capital, and it was the number and violence of the gangs of robbers which were particularly frightening to contemporaries.

The scale and nature of the contemporary response to the crime wave underlines just how important it was in shaping perceptions and emotions in this period. It included creative and important developments in policing in London, associated with Henry and John Fielding, the issuing of proclamations offering rewards for the discovery and prosecution of highway robbers, and the unprecedented creation of a parliamentary committee in 1751 to investigate the law on felonies and find ways of suppressing the crimes which had recently grown to such a height.[54] This committee was preceded and accompanied by a wealth of discussion about policing the lower orders, including the operations of the poor law, and the sufficiency of current judicial and penal policy. This discussion and the resolutions this committee produced indicate how far the crime wave acted to raise concern about popular morals and behaviour. Much emphasis was placed on idleness and the pursuit of pleasure as well-springs of crime.[55] Meanwhile, at parochial and vestry level in and around London, there were many initiatives to improve policing, including subscriptions for extraordinary guards on roads or to finance rewards for the taking of housebreakers and robbers and for the detection of gaming and bawdy houses.[56] There was also an upsurge in the numbers of statutes passed by Parliament which aimed at improving the arrangements for the watch and lighting in different parts of London.[57]

[53] For a suggestive exploration of how newspaper reporting in the eighteenth century may have shaped public perceptions of crime, see Peter King, 'Newspaper Reporting, Prosecution Practice and Perceptions of Urban Crimes: The Colchester Crime Wave of 1765', *Continuity and Change*, 2 (1987), 423–54.

[54] See esp. J. Styles, 'Sir John Fielding and the Problem of Criminal Investigation in Eighteenth-Century England', *TRHS*, 33 (1983), 127–49; Beattie, *Crime and the Courts*, ch. 10.

[55] Two of the Felonies Committee's resolutions referred specifically to popular entertainments, including gaming, as causes of the crime wave. *Commons Journals*, xxvi (1750–4), 190.

[56] See e.g. *Penny London Post*, 31 Jan.–2 Feb.; 7–11 Nov. 1751.

[57] See Elaine Reynolds, *Before the Bobbies: The Night Watch and Police Reform in Metropolitan London, 1720–1830* (Basingstoke, 1998), ch. 2.

Another important factor which aroused concern about the state of the nation's morals was perceptions of Britain's international standing and circumstances. The prominence and nature of the latter were explored in detail in Chapter 3. Suffice it to say here that, against a background of continual war and international rivalry, and pressing international threats to vital British interests, their influence on attitudes towards and feelings about the condition of society was substantial and, at certain moments—for example, in the summer and autumn of 1756 following the loss of Minorca—critical. As we also saw in Chapter 3, there was a marked disposition throughout many parts of society to interpret the changing course and conditions of war and diplomacy in terms of domestic factors.

Behind this disposition lay another significant cause of rising concern about moral and social reform in this period. This was the revival, under the impact of war from 1739, the trauma of the Jacobite Rebellion of 1745–6 and the London and Lisbon earthquakes of 1750 and 1755 respectively, of a sense of an active providence. Weighing the importance of this is extremely difficult, yet it needs to be attempted because most accounts of this period tend to pass over it very quickly, if indeed it is acknowledged at all. The tendency to see the destiny of the nation as governed by a God who intervened in the course of human history was very actively promoted by all elements of the Anglican church and the Church of Scotland, most Dissenters, and the state in this period. The jeremiad was also very strongly embedded in both the Anglican and Presbyterian traditions.[58] Most years of war saw proclamations of days of national fasting or thanksgiving.[59] The forms of prayer followed on such days, together with the sermons delivered by clergymen and ministers, contained a common set of assumptions. Of these, the most important was the existence of a covenant between God and his 'chosen' people, the English or Scots, or increasingly in this period the British.[60] Britons were encouraged to see themselves as 'elect nation' occupying a similar position in God's favour to the Jewish nation in the Old Testament, and to see war as a special sphere for providential interventions. 'Victory', as one clergyman counselled, 'doth not always attend the wisest Counsels, nor the best concerted Schemes, nor the greatest Armaments; nor doth that side which boasteth most, or is in human Estimation the most powerful, always prevail and triumph . . .'[61] Just as the Jewish nation had forfeited God's protection through their disregard for his

---

[58] Napthine and Speck, 'Clergymen and Conflict'; Richard B. Sher, 'Witherspoon's "Dominion of Providence" and the Scottish Jeremiad Tradition', in id. and Jeffrey R. Smitten (eds.), *Scotland and America in the Age of the Enlightenment* (Princeton, NJ, 1990), 46–64.

[59] In Scotland, fasts were proclaimed by the General Assembly and other lesser bodies of the Church, as well as by proclamation. The Anti-Burghers and some elements of the Burgher Seceding congregations refused to acknowledge the authority of the state in this sphere, but did hold fasts on days chosen by themselves. See *Scots Mag.* (1756), 102–5.

[60] For the growing tendency of Scottish ministers to refer to Britain as the 'nation', see Sher, 'Witherspoon's "Dominion" ', 50.

[61] *A Sermon Preached in the Parish Church of St Mary, Lambeth, upon April 11, 1744 . . . by John Denne, D.D., Rector of the said Parish, and Archdeacon of Rochester* (1744), 13.

injunctions, so a similar fate awaited the British people if they neglected to reform their morals. Thus, Obadiah Hughes declared in 1742: 'GOD has made Great Britain very much to resemble his ancient people; and I wish with all my soul, we had not made ourselves so much like to them in another respect.'[62]

In England, it was the London and Lisbon earthquakes which prompted the most impressive efforts from clergymen to recall their flocks to their religious and moral duty. On 2 April 1750, following the second London earthquake, Horace Walpole wrote to his regular correspondent, Horace Mann:

> Showers of sermons and exhortations. Secker, the Jesuitical Bishop Oxford began the mode. He heard the women were all going out of town to avoid the next earthquake, and so for fear of losing the Easter Offerings he set . . . to advise them to await God's good pleasure . . . But what is more astounding Sherlock (Sarum) who has much better sense, and much less of the Popish confessor, had been running a race with him with old ladies and has written a Pastoral Letter, of which 10,000 were sold in two days. You never read so imprudent, so absurd a piece. The earthquake which has done no hurt, in a country where earthquakes ever did any, is sent, according to the Bishop, to punish bawdy prints, bawdy books . . . gaming, drinking etc.[63]

As a Deist, Walpole could perhaps afford to affect disdain; David Hume was similarly and equally unsurprisingly sceptical, seeing the clergy's efforts as crudely opportunistic.[64] The demand for Sherlock's letter, for which he received the thanks of the Mayor and Aldermen of the City and the Middlesex justices, is, however, a better indication of the depth of the panic. Other clergymen preached similar messages, and for a few weeks at least were received with close attention.[65] On 30 March, Thomas Wilson recorded in his diary, 'People seem to be mightily affected. God grant that they my continue so.'[66]

The panic created by the London earthquakes of 1750 was, however, short-lived. When a third earthquake, which a lunatic trooper prophesied for the night of 4 April or morning of the 5th and which would destroy London, failed to take place, the sense of panic and alarm dissipated quickly. The Middlesex Justices, Thomas Wilson and others—including the Prince of Wales—however, still mounted a campaign, albeit the outcome was unsuccessful, to prevent a masquerade ball taking place at Ranelagh on 25 April.[67] An entry in the order book of the Middlesex sessions for 26 April records that

---

[62] Obadiah Hughes, *Obedience to God the Best Security Against Our Enemies: A Fast Sermon Preached in Maid Lane, in Southwark, Nov. 10, 1742* (1742), 31.

[63] Walpole, *Correspondence*, xx. 133–4. See also William Briggs to John Wesley, 5 Apr. 1750, in *The Works of John Wesley*, xxvi, *Letters II, 1740–1755*, ed. Frank Baker (Oxford, 1982), 414–17.

[64] See T. D. Kendrick, *The Lisbon Earthquake* (1956), 20.

[65] See also William Stukeley's *The Philosophy of Earthquakes, Natural and Religious, Or an Inquiry into their Cause, and their Purpose* (1750), in which Stukeley advocated elecricity as the natural cause of earthquakes, but also emphasized their divine purpose. Stukeley ended the pamphlet by calling for a reformation of manners.

[66] Linnell (ed.), *The Diaries of Thomas Wilson*, 234.

[67] Ibid., 236.

a 'great concourse of people' had attended, including gamesters and disorderly persons. The High Constables of Holborn and Westminster were ordered to make enquiries about the latter and to submit a report to the Justices on 8 May. A committee of justices was also appointed to suppress gaming and other disorders at the assemblies at Ranelagh.[68]

The call for reform of morals which followed the Lisbon earthquake was significantly greater in scale and had a substantially greater impact, partly because it followed the earlier panic, but also because it coincided with the outbreak and early military setbacks of the Seven Years War. The government called a day of national fasting for the earthquake and outbreak of war on 6 February 1756. The response from the clergy was impressive, and England's presses were kept busy with the production of a huge number of fast sermons, itself an indication of how deeply contemporaries were affected.[69] Several were printed in more than one edition. John Thomas, the Bishop of Lincoln's sermon before the House of Lords in Westminster Abbey appeared in a second edition, while John Wesley's *Serious Thoughts Occasion'd by the Late Earthquake at Lisbon*, published in 1755, went through at least five. The fast day appears to have been widely and seriously observed. Sir Roger Newdigate, Tory MP for Oxford University, in London for the parliamentary session, recorded in his diary for 6 February, 'all ye churches crowded'.[70] John Wesley commented in his journals, with more than a modicum of satisfaction, 'The fast day was a glorious day such as London has scarce seen since the Restoration. Every church in the City was more than full and a solemn seriousness sat on every face'.[71] Quakers in Lombard Street who kept open their businesses had their windows broken by the crowd, while the Bishop of London and Archbishop of Canterbury managed to get a masquerade stopped at the Haymarket Theatre towards the end of January.

The mood was evidently a brittle one. The clergy were also preaching a message which belies the emphasis in some textbooks on a decorous and dry theology which supposedly overtook the English clergy in the eighteenth century. The destruction of Lisbon and loss of over 30,000 lives made graphically clear the dangers of failure to reform immediately. As one clergyman urged: 'Tomorrow's sun may never rise upon us; this night may plunge us into the sleep of death . . .'[72] Charles Bulkley was echoing a common message when he observed, 'It looks, indeed, like a great and mighty effort of provi-

---

[68] GLRO, MJ/OC/5, fos. 195–8. Philip Doddridge also noted in a letter to his wife at this time that 'since the Earthquakes the King has forbid any playing at Court on Sunday Nights' (HMC, *Calendar of Correspondence of Philip Doddridge, D.D. (1702–51)* (1979), 335).

[69] The Eighteenth-Century Short-Title Catalogue (STC) includes around forty such sermons.

[70] Warwickshire County Record Office, CR 136 A 587 (Diary of Sir Roger Newdigate, 1756), entry for 6 February.

[71] *The Works of John Wesley*, xxi, *Journals and Diaries, iv (1755–65)*, ed. W. R. Ward and R. P. Heitzenrater (Nashville, Tenn., 1992), 41.

[72] Thomas Hunter, quoted in Kendrick, *The Lisbon Earthquake*, 153.

dence, intended to call not this or that particular nation only, but the whole human race to consideration and amendment.'[73] A year later, John Milner asked of the Lisbon earthquake:

Don't these shocks seem to be struggles and pangs of nature, preceding some change in its constitution? Or rather, is not this the voice of heaven: the thunder of the Almighty, to awaken the secure, to appall the guilty, and raise in the world an expectation of some grand Revolution approaching?[74]

Several clergymen and contemporaries found such preaching dangerously close to 'enthusiasm'. The *Critical Review* referred critically to a spate of sermonizing 'ad captum vulgus'.[75] William Romaine and William Jones were described by the same writer as 'visionaries of the age'. Romaine was one of a number of individuals who made 'simultaneous, but independent' conversions to 'vital' religion in this period, the most famous being John Wesley and George Whitefield.[76]

Paul Langford has written that the War of American Independence was 'the first war of the age in which the Church could plausibly sustain a campaign based on the assertion that the Lord had a controversy with his chosen people of modern Israel.'[77] One cannot fault clergy and ministers, however, for trying very hard in this regard in the 1740s and 1750s, and with considerable help from circumstances. The rise of Methodism from the late 1730s; the dire winter, harvest failures, and food shortages of 1740–1; the cattle plague, which afflicted England from the mid-1740s; the London and Lisbon earthquakes; the harvest failures, food shortages and widespread rioting of 1756–7; all were, quite apart from the tensions and threats created by war and heightened international rivalry with France, significant sources of alarm. It was the accumulation of problems that reinforced the sense of a society under stress and challenge. To interpret crises in terms of an active God was a reflex deeply rooted in society, as events during the Jacobite Rebellion of 1745–6 also revealed. As the threat from the rebellion reached its climax in late November and early December 1745, a day of national fasting was called for 18 December. Even before then, the Commission of the General Assembly of the Church of Scotland had issued a recommendation to presbyteries to appoint days of fasting within their bounds 'as may best suit their several circumstances'.[78] According to John Wesley, on 18 December 'such a solemnity and seriousness

[73] Bulkley, *The Nature and Necessity of National Reformation. A Sermon Preached at the Barbican, Feb 6, 1756. Being the Day appointed for a General Fast* (1756), 6.

[74] Milner, *Signs of the Times. In Two Discourses Delivered at Peckham in Surrey. On the General Fast, February 11, 1757* (1757), 31.

[75] *Critical Review*, 4 (1757), 199.

[76] J. C. D. Clark, *English Society 1688–1832* (Cambridge, 1985), 243 n. 140.

[77] Paul Langford, 'The English Clergy and the American Revolution', in Hellmuth (ed.), *The Transformation of Political Culture*, 292.

[78] NAS, CH1/3/24 (Records of the Commission of the General Assembly, 1739–48), fos. 402–3.

everywhere appeared as had not been lately seen in England'.[79] The clerk to the Presbytery of Forfar recorded in the presbytery minutes for 11 December: 'No copies of proclamation for a national fast come to hand, but determined to see such occasion observed.'[80] Further days of fasting and humiliation were held in Scotland throughout early 1746, when the country was still menaced by the retreating Jacobite army. Members of the Edinburgh Presbytery were meeting each afternoon for prayers in this period.[81] Tracts were widely distributed in London calling on people to solicit God's protection. The Lord Mayor of London distributed papers amongst the capital's trained bands dissuading them from cursing and swearing. *An Earnest Exhortation to Serious Repentance* was given at every church door, in and about London, to every person who came out, and copies were also left at the door of every householder who was not present at church.[82] As the threat lifted, and the Jacobite army retreated into Scotland to be finally crushed on Culloden Moor in April 1746, the tendency to see the Rebellion as an instance of divine warning and punishment continued. Hugh Blair, preaching before the General Assembly of the Church of Scotland on 18 May 1746, just over a month after Culloden, declared that the '45 had been a divine warning to enable the British to acknowledge their sinfulness and return to the paths of true religion and virtue.[83] As we will see later, the General Assembly launched a campaign against vice and immorality in the aftermath of the crisis. James Burgh, a Scot by birth, but at this stage a Dissenting schoolmaster in Stoke Newington, published his *Britain's Remembrancer, or, The Danger Not Over*, which rapidly went through a number of editions and was also extracted in various newspapers and magazines.[84] Burgh recreated the vision of tyranny, popery, and persecution that had terrified many Britons in late 1745. Emphasizing the narrow escape which their nation had experienced, and setting the rebellion in a firmly providential framework, Burgh called forthrightly for a reformation of manners.

In early 1746, Parliament lent some support to such calls. On 31 January it was ordered that leave be given to bring in a bill to prevent profane cursing and swearing.[85] The sponsors of this bill, Thomas Carew, Humphrey Sydenham, Edward Gibbon, and Sir John Philipps, were all Tories. There is

[79] *The Works of John Wesley*, xx, *Journals and Diaries*, iii *(1743–54)*, ed. W. R. Ward and R. P. Heitzenrater (Nashville, Tenn., 1991), 108.
[80] NAS, CH2/159/2 (Minute Book of the Presbytery of Forfar, 1743–8), 82–3.
[81] NAS, CH2/121/15 (Minute Book of the Presbytery of Edinburgh, 1742–6), fos. 376, 382, 385, 400–1, 402, 403, 405.
[82] *Works of John Wesley*, xx. 108–9.
[83] Hugh Blair, *The Wrath of Man Praising Man* (Edinburgh, 1746).
[84] Bob Harris, ' "American Idols": Empire, War and the Middling Ranks in Mid-Eighteenth-Century Britain', *Past and Present*, 150 (1996), 121. Burgh later claimed that the pamphlet had gone through between six and eight editions in London, and sold between 10,000 and 12,000 copies in Scotland and Ireland (Burgh, *Youth's Friendly Monitor* (1754), p. iv).
[85] *Commons Journals*, xxv (1745–50), 49.

no evidence that it met with serious opposition in either house, and the bill became 'The Profane Oaths Act'.[86]

There is one final factor which helped to focus public attention on morals and to broaden debate on this topic—the successive political betrayals of opposition politicians in the 1740s, beginning with, and pre-eminently, that of William Pulteney and his fellow opposition Whigs in 1742. As we saw in Chapter 2, the failure of opposition politicians who entered the ministry to live up to the ideals and goals they espoused when out of office created intense disillusionment with national politics and politicians. Politics became in the later 1740s and early 1750s a less important focus of public discussion, with magazines and periodicals which concentrated on literary and social matters or contemporary manners proliferating from the later 1740s. This was the context in which the novels of Richardson, Fielding, and Smollett, with their overt moral purpose, were conceived and flourished. The Jewish Naturalization Act of 1753 and the Marriage Act of the same year also helped to bring moral and religious issues to the fore in public debate. An array of writers stepped forward to lambast the ministry and parliament which had passed these bills, and to flay contemporary social mores and habits. Both pieces of legislation were portrayed as symptomatic of the love of money and lack of respect for religion which supposedly characterized society.[87] They also led to a call from Tories and several churchmen in England for a return to the Church and its disciplines.

REFORMING MORALS (I): PARLIAMENT, MAGISTRATES, THE LAW

Concern about morals had, therefore, several sources in Britain in the 1740s and 1750s. The recurrent sense of moral and social degeneration led to widespread and at moments intense debate about how best to respond. It also provoked a range of legislative and other initiatives to reform morals. These were largely uncoordinated, and what unity they did possess reflected the common assumptions underpinning them, their shared or overlapping aims, and the fact that they often drew on the energies of the same groups or individuals. As Richard Connors has recently emphasized, in England a series of parliamentary committees served as a powerful focus for debate in the early 1750s.[88] North of the border, the various bodies of the Church of Scotland provided the dominant forum for action and debate.

---

[86] The preamble to the Act read: 'Forasmuch as the horrid, impious and execrable vices of profane cursing and swearing (so highly displeasing to Almighty God, and loathsome and offensive to every Christian) are become so frequent and notorious that, unless speedily and effectually punished, they may justly provoke the divine vengeance to increase the many calamities these nations now labour under . . ..'

[87] See Ch. 2, above, pp. 82–3.

[88] Connors, ' "The Grand Inquest of the Nation" '.

In England, it was widely asserted that an urgent task was to re-establish the morals and improve the manners of the lower orders. Many proposals in this context focused on the legal system—how to secure greater numbers of prosecutions and thus enhance the deterrent effects of the law—and on systems of policing society. The parliamentary committee on felonies of 1751, referred to earlier, produced a series of resolutions, several of which resulted in legislation. One piece of failed legislation its members sponsored would have provided for punishment by hard labour in the dockyards. This would have enabled judges to pass sentences for felonies more proportionate to the crimes committed, something which was increasingly urged as a way of underpinning the power and effectiveness of the law.[89] The Murder Act of 1752 sought, meanwhile, to shore up the horror of executions by providing for murderers to be hanged two days after sentencing, and if necessary in chains, and by giving the Surgeon's Company the right to dissect and anatomize the corpses of those sentenced to hang at Tyburn. There were also attempts to reinforce the forces of order in the capital and the effectiveness of the law in punishing property crime. These efforts were closely associated with Henry Fielding, who was appointed to the benches of Westminster and Middlesex in 1748, and, following his death in 1754, with his half brother, John. In 1749, Fielding submitted a plan for an ambitious new law to revitalize and strengthen the watch and constables in Westminster to Lord Chancellor Hardwicke.[90] Nothing came of this, but in 1753, he submitted another plan, this time to the Duke of Newcastle, then secretary of state for the northern department.[91] It was under this plan that a system of salaried runners or police in Westminster was established.[92]

Other plans had similar goals. Joshua Fitzsimmonds recommended the establishment of a system of neighbourhood scrutiny of morals and behaviour to be overseen by the clergy.[93] Other calls were made for much tighter licensing of alehouses and of the retailing of gin or spirituous liquors, the suppression of popular entertainments, begging, and popular disorder, the trade in pornographic literature and 'obscene' prints, prostitution, sabbath breaking, and other moral crimes.[94]

[89] Beattie, *Crime and the Courts*, 554–9.

[90] The bill is reproduced in Martin C. Battenstin with Ruth R. Battenstin, *Henry Fielding: A Life* (1993), Appendix I, pp. 706–11.

[91] The plan is reproduced in John Fielding, *An Account of the Origins and Effects of a Police* (1758).

[92] For a more detailed examination of these efforts, see J. Styles, 'Sir John Fielding and the Problem of Criminal Investigation'. See also Sir Leon Radzinowicz, *History of the English Criminal Law and its Administration from 1750* (4 vols., 1948–68), iii. 29–62. The Disorderly Houses Act was the first statute in the eighteenth century to provide for court award of subventions to meet prosecution costs. A further statute in 1754 included provision for meeting the costs of poor witnesses testifying at criminal trials. In 1756, an act regarding the duties and appointment of constables in Westminster was also passed.

[93] Joshua Fitzsimmonds, *Free and Candid Disquisitions on the Nature and Execution of the Laws of England* (1751), 49–50. See also, for a similar proposal, *Lond. Ev. P.*, 19–21 Dec. 1751.

[94] See, *inter alia*, *Reflexions on Gaming; and Observations on the Laws relating thereto* (n.d., 1750?); *A Letter to the Honourable House of Commons Relating to the Present Situation of Affairs* (1750); Saunders Welch,

The story of the legislative and magisterial responses to all these proposals cannot be fully told here. More research is needed about especially magisterial strategy and tactics, and on patterns of prosecution for misdemeanour offences. The following assessment is necessarily tentative, although the outlines are stated with a fair measure of confidence. The picture which begins to emerge is of a series of responses which are, when seen in their totality, impressive in range and intensity, if uneven and, in some cases, limited in effect. Proposals which did not challenge the existing basis of government and authority in society, in particular the discretionary power of local elites, were also, as in other periods in the eighteenth century, much more likely to succeed; most pieces of legislation also represented an extension of well-established principles of governance or social regulation.

Tighter regulation of popular consumption of alcohol was achieved, in the first place, through the Gin Act of 1751. Earlier attempts to suppress or regulate the gin trade, in 1729 and 1736, had proved unworkable and had had only a very limited impact on its growth.[95] The regulatory regime was even relaxed in 1743 as a revenue raising measure necessitated by war.[96] Renewed pressure for stricter controls came, in part, because of information, collected by constables, about the numbers of gin shops within the Bills of Mortality and the number of convictions for retailing without a licence in 1749.[97] It also came from an new campaign for tighter regulation led by Isaac Maddox, Bishop of Worcester. His spittal sermon of April 1750, *The Expediency of Preventive Wisdom*, preached before the Lord Mayor, Aldermen, and governors of the various London hospitals, summed up a terrifying vision of the population being destroyed by gin and of society fast losing its capacity to control the lower orders. This sermon was published in 1751. Meanwhile, the introduction and extracts from Maddox's sermon were reprinted in the same year in a pamphlet entitled *An Epistle to the Right Honourable the Lord Mayor, Aldermen and Common Council, of the City of London*. Both sermon and pamphlet went through several editions. The pamphlet was also sold at a reduced charge of half a guinea

---

Observations on the Office of Constable with Cautions for the More Safe Execution of that Duty (1754); id., *A Proposal to Render Effectual a Plan, to Remove the Nuisance of Common Prostitutes From the Streets of the Metropolis* (1758); Henry Fielding, *An Enquiry into the Causes of the Late Increase of Robbers* (1751); Joshua Fitzsimmonds, *Free and Candid Disquisitions on the Nature and Execution of the Laws of England, Both in Civil and Criminal Affairs* (1751); John Fielding, *A Plan for Preventing Robberies within Twenty Miles of London* (1755); id., *An Account of the Origins and Effects of a Police* (1758); *Serious Thoughts in Regard to Public Disorders, with Several Proposals for Remedying the Same; Particularly in Respect to Gaming, Public Houses, Pawnbrokers, and Receivers of Stolen Goods* (1751); *The Vices of the Cities of London and Westminster Trac'd from their Original* (1751); *A Scheme Offered to the Consideration of the Publick; which if Countenanced & Encouraged, will not only Promote and Invigorate the Execution of the Laws now Extant, against the Breaking and Profaning of the Christian Sabbath or Lord's Day* (1752).

[95] Lee Davison, 'Experiments in the Social Regulation of Industry: Gin Legislation, 1729–1751', in Davison, *et. al.*, *Stilling the Grumbling Hive*, 25–48; P. A. Clark, 'The "Mother Gin" controversy in Early Eighteenth-century England', *TRHS*, 5th ser., 39 (1988), 63–84; M.D. George, *London Life in the Eighteenth Century* (1966 edn.), 42–3.

[96] Davison, 'Gin Legislation', 44.

[97] Paul Langford, *A Polite and Commercial People: England 1727–1783* (Oxford, 1989), 149.

for twenty-five copies to facilitate wider distribution.[98] The thanks of the Common Council of the City of London were voted to Maddox in February 1751, at the same time as a petition to Parliament was drawn up calling for much tighter restraints on the trade. The petition was submitted to Parliament on 4 March and provided the immediate stimulus to the parliamentary campaign to introduce new regulatory legislation. The City's petition was followed by sixteen others, six of them from parishes in Westminster.[99] The content of the petitions provides a good illustration of how religious and 'prudential' concerns became very closely intertwined in contemporary debates about reforming manners, with several of them laying emphasis on the threat which spirituous liquors presented to labour discipline as well as morals and religion.[100] The threat to discipline amongst the workforce had also been raised by Maddox, and was emphasized by several other writers.[101] An interesting feature of the resulting legislation is that Henry Pelham, usually notoriously reluctant on such matters, was prepared to forego revenue in imposing tighter regulations on the trade. The contrast with 1743 was marked, when the needs of the Exchequer triumphed over the desirability of doing just this, much to the concern and against the opposition of the bench of bishops.[102] Nor was there opposition to the act from distillers. Davison emphasizes, no doubt correctly, the influence of the contemporary crime wave in this context, and the fears which it aroused.[103] The timing of the passage of the bill is especially relevant here; it coincided with the discussions of the felonies committee.[104] Against a background of widespread alarm amongst the propertied classes about social control, the 'moral' case against gin seemed unanswerable. Another important factor was growing concern that the British population was declining, another alarming symptom of national decline.[105]

---

[98] Sir James Lowther wrote to his agent in Carlisle on 16 February 1751: 'My good friend the Ld Bp of Worcester having preach'd a most excellent sermon & printed that & other papers (to show the miserable effects of drinking spirituous liquors) for w.ch his Ldp is hugely commended, I have sent of the first part of it this Post to Dr Brownrig & you may give him the inclos'd wch is the remainder, if the Dr & Mr Sewel & You think it wil do good, I wil send a good many of them to you by the Carrier to be given among the Gentlemen & Clergy to make use of them among their Neighbours' (CRO (Carlisle), D/Lons/W2/1/113, Sir James Lowther to John Spedding, 16 Feb. 1751). Other important pamphlets in the campaign included Josiah Tucker, *The Impartial Enquiry into the Benefits and Damages . . . from the Present Very Great Use of Low-Priced Spirituous Liquors* (1751); Fielding, *An Enquiry into the Causes of the Late Increase of Robbers*. William Hogarth's prints 'Gin Lane' and 'Beer Street' and his print series 'The Four Stages of Cruelty' were also published in cheap versions to add a visual element to the unfolding campaign.

[99] The petitions are listed in Connors, ' "The Grand Inquest of the Nation" ', 304 n. 87.

[100] See e.g. the petition from Norwich (*Commons Journals*, xxvi (1750–4), 88).

[101] See e.g. *General Advertiser*, 30 Apr. 1751.

[102] For the bishops' opposition to the Gin Act of 1743, see Stephen Taylor, 'Church and State in the Mid Eighteenth Century: The Newcastle Years 1742–1762', Ph.D. thesis (Cambridge University, 1987), 174–5.

[103] Davison, 'Gin Legislation', 43.

[104] For the close relationship between the felonies committee and the Gin Act, see Connors, ' "The Grand Inquest of the Nation" ', 303.

[105] See Ch. 6, above, pp. 00.

Gin retailers were not the only members of the drink trade to find themselves subject, or potentially subject, to tighter regulation. As the Webbs emphasized at the beginning of this century, the ten years after 1743 saw a series of changes to licensing legislation designed to make judicial oversight and control of licensing of alehouses much more effective. As they comment: 'From 1753 onwards . . . the justices had in their uncontrolled discretion to grant or refuse a licence, and in the existing penalties against unlicensed sellers, an almost unlimited power of confining the drink traffic within legitimate bounds.'[106]

Other legislation focused on regulating or suppressing popular entertainments, especially in London. Gaming was a particular source of concern. Contemporaries were alarmed by the extent of gaming and the degree to which it was consuming the passions and time of people from groups below the elites. Like the pleasure gardens, it was also seen as activity that promoted a dangerous intermingling of the ranks and of young people and criminals. Whether this period actually saw an increase in gaming amongst the lower or middling orders is impossible to judge. The perception, nevertheless, that gaming was reaching new and unprecedented levels was widely held. One contemporary asserted, 'the Misfortune is, that the Itch of Gaming does not confine itself to the Gentry, it has caught the Mob . . .'[107] The *Gray's Inn Journal* of 10 March 1753 described gambling as 'the grand business of the Nation'. Thomas Wilson saw 'Gin and Gaming' as the main sources corrupting the Common People and undermining their 'Industry and Sobriety'.[108]

Magisterial and legislative efforts to suppress gaming were, like so many other responses to social problems in this period, nothing new. Since the Tudor period, important anti-gaming statutes had periodically been passed.[109] The early 1720s had also seen a major campaign against gaming houses by Westminster magistrates.[110] New statutes against gaming were passed in 1738, 1739, 1740, and 1744, while important measures to clamp down on gaming were also included in legislation passed in 1752 and 1757.[111] The Disorderly Houses Act of 1752 included clauses designed to make it easier to prosecute

---

[106] S. Webb and B. Webb, *The History of Liquor Licensing in England* (1903), 42.

[107] *The Vices of the Cities of London and Westminster*, 24.

[108] Linnell (ed.), *The Diaries of Thomas Wilson*, 260.

[109] See esp. *Reflexions on Gaming; and Observations on the Laws relating thereto* (1751), *passim*.

[110] Shoemaker, 'Reforming the City', 113.

[111] The relevant acts are 12 Geo 2. c.28 (An Act for the more effectual preventing of excessive and deceitful Gaming); 13 Geo 2. c.19 (An Act . . . for amending an Act made in the last Session of Parliament, intituled 'An Act for the more effectual preventing of excessive and deceitful gaming'); 18 Geo 2. c.34 (An Act to explain, amend and make more effectual the Laws in being to prevent excessive and deceitful Gaming . . .); 19 Geo 2. c.? (An Act to restrain and prevent the excessive Increase of Horse Races, and for amending an Act, made in the last Session of Parliament, intituled 'An Act for the more effectual preventing of excessive and deceitful Gaming); 25 Geo. 2. c. 36 (An Act for better preventing Thefts and Robberies, and for regulating Places of Publick Entertainment, and punishing Persons keeping disorderly Houses); An Act for the more effectual Punishment of Cheats; and for the futher preventing of the Embezzlement of Goods and Apparel, by those who are entrusted with them; and for preventing Gaming in Publick Houses. In 1759, Gabriel Hanger also introduced an

keepers of gaming houses. Five years later, legislation was passed against publicans who permitted journeymen, labourers, servants, or apprentices to game in their houses.[112]

The targets of the Disorderly Houses Act extended more broadly than simply gaming. The act was also an attempt to facilitate the suppression and regulation of, as the title suggests, disorderly houses and bawdy houses. In October 1750, a Grand Jury presentment to the quarter sessions of the City had complained about the negligence of constables in presenting disorderly houses as a cause of their 'manifest increase'. A few months later a Middlesex Grand Jury made a similar point to the Court of King's Bench and also called for prosecution to be changed from indictment to the summary method.[113] In May 1751, the vestry of St Mary's, Whitechapel announced that it would defray the costs of prosecuting disorderly houses in Goodman's Fields, an area of London particularly associated with disorder.[114] Meanwhile, at the beginning of 1752, either Henry Fielding or his clerk, Joshua Brogden, highlighted in the *Covent Garden Journal* the difficulties involved in prosecution for keeping bawdy houses.[115] Such prosecutions were said usually to take a year and cost above £50. This was because the plaintiff had the right to move a writ of *certiorari* transferring the case from a lower court to the King's bench. By so doing, they also gained the ability to delay prosecution and further add to the prosecutor's costs. Under the new Act, a reward of 10 guineas was allowed to any two inhabitants for information leading to the prosecution of keepers of disorderly and bawdy houses. The right to remove the case to a higher court by writ of *certiorari* was also removed.

The Disorderly Houses Act also sought to regulate places of public entertainment. Under its terms, any person living within London or Westminster or in a twenty-mile radius of these places and keeping a room, garden, house, or other place for public dancing, music, or other entertainment had to get a licence from magistrates sitting at the previous Michaelmas quarter sessions.

To have any effect, this and other legislation aimed at preventing immorality obviously had to be matched by efforts by magistrates and lesser officers of the law to implement it. This was fully recognized by ministers in 1754, although with little conviction that they possessed a solution to the challenge this posed. In late 1753, when alarm about violent crime was intense, they studied precedents from the reigns of William III, Queen Ann,

---

unsuccessful bill into Parliament to amend and make more effective an act of 1739 against the increase of horse races and to amend the act of 1757 to make it apply to horse racing.

[112] The author of this piece of legislation was Sir John Fielding. See BL, Add. MS 32876 (Newcastle Papers), fos. 274–5, where Fielding refers to the 'bill which I drew against cheats and for punishing Gaming in publick places'.

[113] *Whitehall Evening Post*, 20–3 Oct. 1750; *Penny London Post*, 13–15 Feb. 1751.

[114] *Whitehall Evening Post*, 23–25 May 1751.

[115] *Covent Garden Journal*, 25 Jan. 1752.

George I, and the present King for issuing proclamations and orders for punishing profaneness and immorality and for apprehending street robbers and highwaymen. They decided to revive a practice from William III's reign of calling the judges before the King before they went on circuit to encourage their support for the proclamation and to urge them impress upon magistrates in the country the need to enforce laws against vice and immorality. The meeting took place on 28 February 1754, and Hardwicke's speech to the judges is preserved in his papers.[116] A copy of Hardwicke's address was sent by the Duke of Newcastle to JPs in Middlesex and Westminster.[117] A decision was also taken to issue a new proclamation against vice and immorality, and the support of the bench of bishops was sought for this. The only demur came from Archbishop Thomas Herring, who questioned the timing.[118] He was also concerned about it appearing as if it had been suggested to the King in Council by the episcopal bench. His concerns reflected a strange effort in February in the Lords by Isaac Maddox to have a Lords committee appointed to take into consideration the state of the nation's morals. The attempt is described in a letter from William Lorimer to Ludovick Grant, MP for Inverness burghs:

Your friend Bishop Maddox got the h. of Peers yesterday to attend to a Motion he was to make, to consider the present State of Religion & Morality in Engl.d & to find out proper Remedys. There was accordingly a very full house both of Peers & Commoners of all kinds & the Bishop gave them a Long Sermon of an hour and a half describing the several Instances of Immorality & setting forth the Several Sources . . .[119]

Maddox appears to have had no initial proposal or motion; he also acted alone, without discussion or coordination with other members of the episcopacy. He was answered by the Duke of Newcastle who argued that there were already sufficient laws on the statute book to remedy the problems he had raised, if these were properly enforced. Maddox responded by making a motion for a committee to be established to consider the 'proper ways & means for Reformation'. He also proposed a second motion for a day of fasting 'for our many sins'. Both were defeated, and Maddox had to be satisfied with entering a protest into the Lords Journals.[120]

What evidence is there that magistrates took notice of the judges, or sought to use the extensive powers available to them to reform popular morals? The Webbs argued that the new licensing legislation of this period was not

---

[116] BL, Add. MS 35870 (Hardwicke Papers), fos. 241–3. Hardwicke had earlier expressed doubts about whether reviving the proclamation against immorality and profaneness would have much effect, although he did acknowledge that it might have a good appearance. See PRO, SP 36/153/11. I owe this reference to Joanna Innes.

[117] BL, Add. MS 32734, fos. 166–7, 186, 398–9, 400–2.

[118] BL, Add. MS 35599 (Hardwicke Papers), fos. 158–9: Archbishop Herring to Hardwicke, 3 Mar. 1754.

[119] NAS, GD 248/49/1 (Seafield Papers), item 66: William Lorimer to Grant, 9 Feb. 1754.

[120] *Lords Journals*, xxviii (1754–6), 202.

matched by greater magisterial efforts to restrict the sale of alcohol or to enforce laws against tippling or drinking during divine service. The contrast they drew was with events thirty years later when a new campaign to reform manners was launched, which included widespread and sustained attempts to exercise tighter control on alehouse licensing. The contrast with the mid-century can be drawn too starkly, however. Peter Clark has noted a decline in licences granted in southern counties from this period.[121] On 21 April 1757, the Middlesex justices issued an order for keepers of public houses not to suffer individuals to continue drinking and tippling in their houses during divine services on Sundays.[122] There were also changes to licensing policy designed at least to prevent any further increase in alehouses in and around London. As we will see below, there was also a drive not to renew licences for alehouses which allowed forms of gaming such as skittles to take place in them.[123] The overall impact of such directions was probably limited. In the 1760s, John Fielding was still complaining about the profusion of alehouses in the capital, arguing that their great number acted as encouragement to continue gaming within them as a way of attracting custom. He also drew strong attention to one part of the alcohol trades which continued to flourish beyond magisterial oversight—the wine trade.[124]

A similar picture—of sporadic activity and successes, but limited results overall—emerges with respect to attempts to suppress and regulate gaming. Joshua Fitzsimmonds suggested in 1751 that the multiplicity of anti-gaming statutes was one reason for their ineffectiveness.[125] As far as the mid-century statutes are concerned, there are other reasons why their impact was less than their architects anticipated. The statutes of the later 1730s and early 1740s sought to suppress specific, named games. As particular games were outlawed by name—or by description—so new games were devised which circumvented the prohibitions. Ironically, one effect of this merely seems to have been to make gaming even more accessible. One game which had been suppressed, 'pharoah', had been too difficult to be 'quickly mastered by the vulgar'. This was not true of its successors—'rowley powley', 'E and O', and 'G and S'—said to be 'games learnt in a minute'.[126] The number of prosecutions in Middlesex by indictment for keeping gaming houses or for various gaming offences in the mid-century is relatively small.[127] This may reflect the cost of such prosecutions. John Fielding later claimed that his brother, Henry,

---

[121] Peter Clark, *The English Alehouse: A Social History 1200–1830* (1983), 254–60.

[122] GLRO, MJ/OC/6, fo. 119.

[123] GLRO, MJ/OC/5, fos. 227, 234–5, 253; CLRO, Repertories of Court of Aldermen, 155 (1750–1), 437–8.

[124] Wine licences were issued by excise officials. Sir John Fielding, *Extracts from Such of the Penal Laws as Particularly Relate to the Peace and Good Order of this Metropolis* (1768), 414.

[125] Fitzsimmonds, *Free and Candid Disquisitions*, 14.

[126] *The Vices of the Cities of London and Westminster*, 25.

[127] This conclusion is reached from examination of indictments between 1740 and 1760 listed in the Process Register of Indictments for the Middlesex sessions (GLRO, MJ/SBP/14–16).

had some success in entrapping gamesters who sought to cheat the elites of some of their wealth in London's pleasure gardens.[128] The press also contains reports of the concerted efforts in the early 1750s to suppress gaming houses within Westminster, an effort closely associated with Henry Fielding and another active Westminster magistrate of the period, Thomas Lediard.[129] Neither was gaming amongst the propertied classes immune to regulation, or calls for tighter regulation. We have already seen that in 1750 the Middlesex bench acted to suppress gaming at assemblies at Ranelagh. The early 1750s saw similar efforts to suppress or reduce gaming at Bath and Tunbridge Wells, notable spa towns and places of elite leisure. In June 1751, the Kent justices, consciously following the example of Fielding in Westminster, decided to suppress the 'E and O' and 'G and S' tables at Tunbridge Wells.[130] The Bath corporation played a significant role in securing the 1744 Act against gaming. In 1751, the Lords of Regency also wrote to the mayor of Bath to suppress the 'E and O' tables in his jurisdiction.[131]

How often the Disorderly Houses Act was used to regulate other commercial and public entertainments is difficult to say given the current state of research. Several pleasure gardens appear to have lost their music licences after 1752. Cuper's Gardens lost theirs in 1752 and became a tea room, while Marylebone Gardens and Ranelagh were refused licences in 1754.[132] In 1755 a prosecution was started in the City of London against one Benjamin Wilton and his wife for keeping a public dancing house in Cursitor's Street, off Chancery Lane, without a licence.[133] Magistrates and officers of the law also possessed powers under the Theatrical Licensing Act of 1737 to act against places offering certain types of entertainment. Fielding sought on a number of occasions to suppress dramatic productions by apprentices in Westminster.[134] The Middlesex Justices also invoked powers under the same act in the early 1740s against a number of establishments—Goodman's Fields, Sadler's Wells, New Wells in Goodman's Fields, and New Wells in Clerkenwell, as well as the proprietors of several booths in Moorfields.[135] In 1744, orders were also issued against performers of interludes, plays, or farces at Bartholomew and Southwark fairs. These were renewed in 1750 and 1751, and,

---

[128] John Fielding, *An Account of the Origin and Effects of a Police*, 28.

[129] See e.g. *Whitehall Evening Post*, 22 May, 5 June 1751.

[130] *General Evening Post*, 20–3 June 1751; *General Advertiser*, 21 June, 12 Aug. 1751.

[131] *General Evening Post*, 20–3 June 1751. Peter Borsay suggests that there is evidence from Bath and York that gambling legislation was 'far from ineffective' (Borsay, *English Urban Renaissance*, 304). It seems probable, however, that efforts to control or regulate gaming were overwhelmed by the demand of visitors for these entertainments.

[132] Wroth, *London Pleasure Gardens*, 9–10, 210. Wroth also notes, however, that entertainments of the old kind were revived in Cuper's Gardens in 1755 under the disguise of private subscription concerts.

[133] CLRO, Repertories of the Court of Aldermen, 159 (1754–5), fo. 732.

[134] *Covent Garden Journal*, 4 Apr.; 11 Apr.; 15 Aug. 1752.

[135] CLRO, Repertories of the Court of Aldermen, 145 (1740–1), fos. 46, 392, 420; 146 (1741–2), fos 237, 264, 265, 277–8, 288–9, 290, 318.

in the case of Bartholomew fair, again eleven years later.[136] In early 1752, the Court of Aldermen received complaints against one Potier, a dancing master, who had allegedly staged plays or dramatic entertainments at his house near Bow Lane, and about similar activities at Castle Taven in Paternoster Row. The Court ordered the Lord Mayor to contact the offenders and forbid such performances; he was also to warn that those who offended against the law in this respect would be subject to prosecution.[137]

The Westminster and Middlesex benches also mounted repeated attempts to suppress popular fairs, which were viewed as major sources of disorder, as well as serving to lure the young from the path of industry and virtue. Efforts to suppress the fairs began in 1743, during an upsurge of concern about property crime in the capital, and were renewed in 1750 and for several years thereafter.[138] That these achieved some success, at least in the short term, is suggested by remarks made in 1754 by Saunders Welch, constable for High Holborn and later a magistrate and an important figure in debates about policing the capital in this period:

> Those who viewed the debauchery, excesses and immoralities of the numerous fairs about town, a few years since, saw them the bane of the youth of both sexes, and a great cause of robberies. The suppression of those sinks of vice and idleness, was ardently wished for by every good mind, and happily effected by the steady resolution of the magistrates of this county [Middlesex].[139]

Renewed efforts at the suppression of Bartholomew and Southwark fairs between 1760 and 1762 indicate, however, that what success there was was relatively short-lived. Suppressing Bartholomew Fair proved to be beyond the legal powers of the City magistrates, but orders against performing interludes and other forms of dramatic entertainment at the fair were reissued.[140]

There were also renewed efforts to stamp down on disorderly houses within the metropolitan area. The City magistrates sought to encourage the prosecution of keepers of disorderly houses by calling on wardmotes to make presentations, as well as defraying the costs of prosecution.[141] In 1755, for example, Daniel Stebbin was presented by the Grand Jury at the Old Bailey. Stebbin was alleged to keep an 'ill gov'd Alehouse' at the Fleet Ditch called the Shepherd and Goat.[142] In Westminster, Henry Fielding appears to have sought to facilitate similar prosecutions by establishing a system of anonymous

---

[136] CLRO, Repertories of the Court of Aldermen, 148 (1743–4), fos. 359, 379; 154 (1749–50), fos. 154, 388–90; 150 (1750–1), fos. 428, 431; Journals of the Court of Aldermen, 62 (1759–61), fos. 340–5.

[137] CLRO, Repertories of the Court of Aldermen, 156 (1751–2), fos. 179, 194–5.

[138] The fairs involved were, as well as Bartholomew and Southwark fairs: Totteham Court fair; Welch fair in Clerkenwell; Mile End fair; May fair in the parish of St George's, Hanover Square; Paddington fair; Bow or Goose Green fair; Acton fair; and Sharking fair in Kensington.

[139] Welch, *Observations on the Office of Constable*, 26–7.

[140] CLRO, Journals of the Court of Aldermen, 62 (1759–61), fos. 180, 260–5, 336–40, 340–5.

[141] Ibid., 154 (1749–50), fos. 83–4.

[142] Ibid., 160 (1755–6), fo. 465.

informing against disorderly and bawdy houses.[143] Such was the general hostility towards informing in this period, it is likely that this was a factor which impeded action being taken against a significant number of offenders.

Prosecutions in Middlesex for keeping bawdy houses appear to have been notably rare, and the impact of the Act on levels of prostitution short-lived.[144] There is no easy explanation for this, except perhaps the difficulties involved in proceeding by information and indictment. It is also likely that some bawdy house keepers were prosecuted for keeping disorderly houses. Concern about prostitution was substantial and continued to be expressed after 1752. This was one aspect of a wider concern about cleansing the street, about imposing order and reasserting respect for rank and property. Saunders Welch predicted in 1758 that if nothing was done by Parliament to restrain the numbers of prostitutes in the capital, 'an universal debauchery will . . . spread among our youth'.[145] From 1757, prostitutes or street walkers were also, as we will see below, major targets of the activities of reforming constables and informers connected with a revived reformation of manners society in the capital. Attitudes towards prostitution were becoming more ambivalent. While prostitutes were widely seen as a nuisance, symbolizing the degradation and hazards of urban life, there was a growing view which saw them as victims of economic necessity and manipulation on the part of bawdy house keepers. It was this latter perception which lay behind the campaign for and foundation in 1758 of the Magdalen Hospital for Fallen Women, a reformatory rather than punitive institution.[146]

Action against gaming and popular entertainments needs to be seen as part of a broader drive to eliminate a culture of criminality and disorder in London. The major impetus came in the early 1750s, but many aspects of it were foreshadowed in an earlier campaign in the mid-1740s.[147] The catalyst on both occasions was concern about levels of crime in the capital. In October 1744, the Middlesex JPs sent a letter to the Duke of Newcastle which laid down an agenda for action which anticipates most of the strategies adopted in the following decade.[148] In the 1750s, attempts were made to police more effectively parts of the capital which attracted a criminal underworld, in

[143] John Fielding, *An Account of the Origin and Effects of a Police*, 30.

[144] See Tony Henderson, *Disorderly Women in Eighteenth-Century London: Prostitution and Social Control in the Metropolis, 1730–1830* (1999), esp. pp. 93–5.

[145] Welch, *A Proposal*, 17.

[146] S. Nash, 'Prostitution and Charity: The Magdalen Hospital, a Case Study', *Journal of Social History*, 17 (1974), 617–28. In 1762, the directors of the Magdalen Hospital were able to boast that of 390 women admitted, 119 had been placed in service with reputable families or to trades. The women were taught, in short, 'every . . . Necessary to make them useful members of the community' (William Dodd, *A Sermon on Job, xxix, ver. 11–13. Preached at the Anniversary Meeting of the Governors of the Magdalen Charity, on Thursday, March 18, 1762* (1762)).

[147] This can be followed in the order books of the Middlesex sessions and in the repertories of the Court of Aldermen.

[148] GLRO, MJ/OC/5, fos. 46–7.

particular the open fields around London, such as Moorfields. In early July 1750, justices in Southwark and Newington issued warrants for the apprehension of idle and disorderly people who used to 'loiter all day about Locke Fields'. These individuals were to be whipped and committed to bridewell for a period of hard labour.[149] Another repeated target for magisterial action was cock throwing and gaming conducted from wheel barrows.[150] It was a subculture of excitement and diversion which appears to have been particularly attractive to apprentices and the young, for which reason magistrates were particularly keen to see it suppressed. This was the world of, as Saunders Welch described it, the 'inferior gamblers'. It was these 'Wretches [who] first teach the art of gaming, and with these, the first foundation of ruin . . . to thousands'.[151] In addition to magisterial orders to constables to take action to suppress this world of plebeian gaming, information was also printed in the press about various of the cheats and frauds commonly practised by the sharpers and charlatans who infested the streets of the capital, lying in wait for the gullible.[152] In 1752, the Middlesex sessions took the decision to recommend that magistrates did not grant licences to individuals who keep skittle grounds or allow gaming in alehouses.[153] This was, as referred to above, followed in 1757 by legislation against alehouse keepers who allowed gaming amongst apprentices and journeymen on their premises.

Apart from the Profane Oaths Act (1746), there was only one new law passed to police or to suppress what might be described as moral crimes. It was not a major piece of legislation, but rather an attempt to make a piece of existing legislation more effective. The law—An Act to Amend and Strengthen an Act against Perjury and Subornation of Perjury—passed in 1750, did deal, nevertheless, with a crime that was the subject of considerable debate and concern, especially in the 1750s. A major source of this concern was the proliferation of oaths required under particularly revenue legislation, which were said to invite perjury.[154] Under the new legislation, plaintiffs no longer had the right to remove their indictment by writ of *certiorari* into the King's Bench, which we have already seen was a means by which a case could be delayed and rendered more costly to the prosecutor. Two contemporary pamphlets claim that the change to the law was ineffective in encouraging higher numbers of prosecutions for perjury or encouragement of perjury.[155] Saunders Welch also implied in 1754 that the law against perjury was not being enforced strictly.[156]

[149] *Penny London Post*, 2–4 July 1750.
[150] See e.g. CLRO, Repertories of the Court of Aldermen, 154 (1749–50), fos. 81–3.
[151] Welch, *Observations on the Office of Constable*, 23.
[152] See e.g. *General Advertiser*, 2, 3 July 1751.
[153] GLRO, MJ/OC/5, fo. 253.
[154] Bob Harris, 'The "London Evening Post" and Mid Eighteenth-century British Politics', *EHR* (1995), 1147.
[155] *A Treatise Concerning Oaths and Perjury* (1750); Charles Jones, *Some Methods Proposed* (1752).
[156] Welch, *Observations on the Office of Constable*, 23–4.

The fact that so little legislation was passed in this period concerning moral crimes does not reflect lack of concern about these; rather it reflected the raft of such laws already on the statute book. Complaints were made that such laws were very infrequently enforced.[157] Justices in the metropolitan area were, on a number of occasions, enjoined to do otherwise. In 1750, the Court of Aldermen declared that neglect on the part of lesser officers was leading to moral offences being commited with impunity. The Court also stated its resolution to see the law put into execution. Offences specifically mentioned were sabbath breaking, profane swearing and cursing, keeping lewd houses, gaming houses, or houses of 'ill fame', publication and selling of profane or obscene books, prints, and pictures. Copies of this resolution were sent to all aldermen, beadles, constables, householders, and inhabitants of the wards of the City. They were also printed in the daily papers.[158] The judges, as referred to earlier, also took a similar message with them on circuit in 1754.[159]

There is some, albeit limited, evidence that such measures did result in an upsurge in judicial activity. Sabbath breaking amongst especially butchers and other tradesmen was periodically punished in Middlesex during the mid-century.[160] Ruth Paley has also noted a rise in punishment of sabbath breakers in the early 1750s by the Hackney JP, Henry Norris.[161] There were also periodic orders in the City to enforce laws against sabbath breaking.[162]

There was also a separate initiative in 1757 to revive the reformation of manners societies. These had emerged in London and elsewhere in the 1690s, but had disappeared by the later 1730s.[163] Much about the attempt remains shrouded in mystery, and we are largely reliant on a single source for our knowledge of it—an account of the society by John Wesley published in 1765 along with a sermon given by him before it two years earlier.[164] The bulk of the membership appears to have comprised followers of Wesley and George Whitefield, and Dissenters, although it did also include some members of the Church.[165] The initial impetus came from a desire amongst members of a

[157] See e.g. *The Deity's Delay in Punishing the Guilty Considered, on the Principles of Reason* (1751); *The Vices of the Cities of London and Westminster*, 9.

[158] CLRO, Repertories of the Court of Aldermen, 154 (1749–50), fos. 235–41.

[159] See above, pp. 00.

[160] W. B. Whitaker, *The Eighteenth Century Sunday: A Study of Sunday Observance from 1677 to 1837* (1940), esp. p. 111.

[161] Ruth Paley (ed.), *Justice in Eighteenth-Century Hackney: The Justicing Notebook of Henry Norris and the Hackney Petty Sessions* (London Records Society, 1991), p. xxvi.

[162] CLRO, Repertories of the Court of Aldermen, 154 (1749–50), fos. 235–41; 166 (1761–2), fo. 289.

[163] On their decline, see esp. Curtis and Speck, 'The Societies for the Reformation of Manners'.

[164] Wesley, *A Sermon Preached before the Society for Reformation of Manners on Sunday, January 30, 1763* (1765). I am also grateful to Joanna Innes for letting me read her unpublished paper 'William Payne of Bell Yard, Carpenter, c.1718–1782: The Life and Times of a London Informing Constable', which contains relevant information.

[165] A hostile cartoon of 1763 entitled 'Dr Squintum's Exaltation or the Reformation' emphasizes the link, in contemporary eyes, between the revived society and the Methodists, depicting Whitefield as the presiding spirit. See Innes, 'William Payne of Bell Yard', 26–8.

religious society to do something about sabbath breaking in Moorfields. Six of their number waited on John Fielding, at this stage a magistrate in Westminster, for advice about how to proceed. The society delivered petitions on the subject to the Middlesex and Westminster benches, both of which apparently encouraged them to take further action. They also informed clergy and ministers, as well as several people of 'eminent rank' of their design. They had printed and dispersed several thousand copies of instructions to constables informing them of their duties in respect of policing behaviour on the Sabbath, as well as tracts against sabbath breaking which they distributed throughout London. In 1758, they began informing against individuals breaking the Sabbath. They started with those selling on Sundays and then moved on to those tippling in alehouses, which exposed them to considerable and unsurprising hostility not just from drinkers but also from alehouse keepers and landlords. They also sought to enforce the laws against gaming, profane swearing, and prostitution. Wesley claimed that in their drive against the last, they had caused to be detected, prosecuted, and suppressed a large number of bawdy houses. Between August 1757 and August 1762, the revived society claimed responsibility for 4,596 prosecutions for moral offences. Between August 1762 and 1765, the number rose to 10,588. The bulk of these were for sabbath breaking and for prostitution and keeping a disorderly house.[166]

The number of prosecutions was a misleading guide to the health of the society. There was considerable hostility to its activities, manifested both in criticism in the press—the reformers were depicted as hypocritical bullies— and in attacks on its informers. Already by 1764, there were signs that it was running into serious financial difficulties; in that year, it appealed to Wesley and his supporters for financial support.[167] This was not forthcoming, and in 1765 it effectively fell into abeyance. What precipitated its demise were the costs of fighting a case of perjury against a witness from an earlier trial against one of its members for wrongful prosecution.[168] In this earlier case (in 1763), Charles Pratt, later Lord Camden, had refused to set aside as excessive costs of £300 awarded against a reforming constable for assaulting and wrongfully imprisoning the keeper of a supposed brothel. There is a parallel here with the earlier Society for the Reformation of Manners (SRM), the fortunes of which were crucially affected at various stages by both favourable and unhelpful judicial decisions.[169] Pratt appears to have been happy to have an opportunity to show his 'dislike' towards the reformers. In so doing he may

---

[166] Wesley, *A Sermon*, 10.

[167] *The Works of John Wesley*, xxi, *Journals and Diaries*, iv *1755–65*, ed. W. P. Ward and R. P. Heitzenvater (Nashville, Tenn., 1993), 493–4.

[168] *The Works of John Wesley*, xxii, *Journals and Diaries*, v *1765–75*, 30 n. 27, where the editors note that in the 1771 appendix to the sermon Wesley preached in 1763 before the SRM, he comments, 'After this Society had subsisted several years and done unspeakable good, it was wholly destroyed by a verdict given against it in the King's Bench, with three hundred pounds damages.'

[169] See esp. Shoemaker, *Prosecution and Punishment*, ch. 9.

well have reflected a much wider body of opinion which saw their activities as incompatible with the principles of justice—flexibility and discrimination—inscribed in the legal system. He also reflected unease at the power being assumed by zealous men from the lower orders.[170]

REFORMING MORALS (2): INDUSTRY AND VIRTUE

Punishment, repression, better regulation, and policing represented only one side of the coin in the contemporary campaign to combat popular immorality; the other was represented by attempts to furnish work for and to re-instil habits of industry and virtue amongst the lower orders. This was the 'preventive wisdom' of which Maddox spoke in his famous sermon of 1750. It was in this context that debates about crime and immorality were very closely intertwined with proposals for reform of the poor laws and with philanthropy. It was here too that the gloomy assessments of British commercial prospects and economic rivalry with France which were explored in the previous chapter were influential. Fears about French economic competition and progress focused attention on the economic, as well as social and moral, effects of poverty and idleness amongst the labouring classes, and on the inadequacies of existing mechanisms for relieving the poor.

As Joanna Innes has emphasized, against a background of rising concern about idleness amongst the labouring classes, the early 1750s saw considerable hostility expressed towards public provision for the needy poor.[171] In 1744, Sir Matthew Decker called the poor rates 'a tax on the industrious'.[172] There was also a growing feeling that the poor laws, as currently administered, by neglecting to provide employment for the poor, and through their relative generosity, were having negative effects on popular morals and industry. In early 1752, two bills aimed at reforming the poor laws were introduced into the Commons. The more ambitious of these, the brain-child of the Earl of Hillsborough, sought to replace the existing system of relief with multi-purpose hospitals to accommodate and reform the poor at county level financed by a county rate. These hospitals would provide relief to children, the disabled, the aged, and the sick, but to 'no other kind of people whatsoever'. The second bill, associated with Sir Richard Lloyd, sought the rescue and reform of pauper children, a recurring aim of social reform and philanthropic endeavour in this period. It would have allowed the establishment of corporations to do this at

---

[170] These points are forcefully made by Joanna Innes in her unpublished paper 'William Payne of Bell Yard'.

[171] Joanna Innes, 'The "Mixed Economy of Welfare" in Early Modern England: Assessment of the Options from Hale to Malthus (*c*.1683–1803), in Martin Daunton (ed.), *Charity, Self-Interest and Welfare in the English Past* (1996), 139–80.

[172] Decker, *Essay on the Causes of the Decline in Foreign Trade* (1744), quot. Innes, 'The "Mixed Economy of Welfare" ', 158.

the level of the hundred—a subdivision of the county—which would have been financed by private subscriptions as well as public sources. They would also have left most of the existing system of relief unchanged, but in the expectation that it would, in the future, only deal with the genuinely impotent. Both bills were informed by similar criticisms of the existing system of relief— namely, that it was expensive and inefficient and self-defeating.

Both were also defeated at the committee stage. The reasons why cannot be established with certainty since reports of the committee discussions have not survived. Thomas Alcock claimed that their passage was suspended so that, during the recess of Parliament, 'the Matter might be more thoroughly canvassed and considered'.[173] Using principally several pamphlets on the subject published at the time, one by Charles Gray, Tory MP for Colchester, the chairman of the committee which drew up the poor children's bill, Nicholas Rogers suggests that parliamentary opinion was far from convinced that they would achieve their goals—economical and effective relief of the poor and the instilling of habits of industry and virtue. Not all were persuaded that removing responsibility for the operation of public relief from smaller to bigger units would necessarily be accompanied by frugal, sensible management, quite apart from possible libertarian objections.[174] The reforms were also criticized on the grounds that they proposed public provision in areas currently catered for by voluntary charities.[175] Gray argued instead for measures to revive and make more representative the county benches of JPs— by representative he meant the inclusion of Tories as well as Whigs, as well as ensuring that members of the landed elites performed their duty in this context rather than leaving people of lower standing to assume the responsibility. Gray portrayed his revived bench exercising close supervision of the operation of the poor laws. He also put forward proposals for reform of poor relief in Westminster and outparishes in the capital. Significantly, however, he envisaged his reformed system operating on the basis of small, traditional units.[176] The argument was one about means—how best to create an orderly and industrious labouring class.

The reforming vision which underpinned discussions of the operation of the poor laws tended to be harsh. Thomas Alcock advocated a withering away of public provision for the poor.[177] As an interim measure, however, he proposed establishing hospitals for the impotent, workhouses for the able, and houses of correction for the work-shy. The idea that large workhouses were the most promising means of reform persisted throughout the decade, partly because of undiminished concern about the operation of the existing system of public poor relief, but also because contemporaries managed to convince themselves so

[173] Quot. Fielding, *An Enquiry into the Late Increase of Robbers*, ed. Zirker, 264 n. 7.

[174] Rogers, 'Confronting the Crime Wave', 90–1.

[175] Innes, 'The "Mixed Economy of Welfare" ', 160.

[176] Gray, *Considerations on Several Proposals Lately Made for the Better Maintenance of the Poor* (1751), esp. pp. 12–14, 24–5. Gray was also a supporter of the settlement laws, which he saw as promoting social order.

[177] Thomas Alcock, *Observations on the Defects of the Poor Laws* (1752).

thoroughly that the provision of work represented the best solution to contemporary social and economic ills. In the later 1750s, there was a new attempt to gain parliamentary support for a scheme whereby county funds would be started for the maintenance of workhouses. Around the same time, Joseph Massie advocated the creation of houses of industry to serve more than one parish.[178] In these houses, the poor would be put to work, but on terms which did not carry reproach. This reflected Massie's conviction that behind the higher levels of crime in the capital lay an inability on the part of many people to find work, as well as the inability of a poor law system devised for a simpler society to meet new pressures created by change. But Massie, like Fielding, was also convinced that the poor had become infected by the contagion of luxury and immorality. He also sought, therefore, the establishment of a separate house of confinement and correction. This would provide punishment in the form of 'Hard Labour and Hard Fare' for the idle and refractory, as well as for persons suspected of robbery. As John Beattie has emphasized, Massie was also another advocate of lesser, proportionate punishments for petty offenders.[179] This was partly because existing, severer punishments deterred prosecutions, but also because this would enable such offenders to be rescued for society. Britain needed its population—to bolster its prosperity and international power—but it needed a population which was industrious and disciplined.

The conviction that work and religious instruction represented the best means of reforming the labouring classes informed much philanthropic activity. To contemporaries, public relief and philanthropy were interlinking elements in strategies of governance. By furnishing work and inculcating habits of industry, so charitable bodies could help to reduce poverty, criminality, and disorder amongst the lower orders. As the Society for the Promotion of Arts, Manufactures and Commerce suggested in 1758, 'the readiest way perhaps of reforming Habits of vice, is to remove those of idleness, itself the greatest political vice'.[180] Charity was potentially more discriminating and economical than public relief; correctly deployed it could also staunch poverty and idleness at source and thus alleviate the burden on the poor rates. The text accompanying the 1738 'Plan and Elevation of the Bath Infirmary conjured a picture of future patients restored 'from misery to ease, from impotence to strength, and from beggary to want, to a capacity of getting an honest livelihood, and comfortable subsistence.'[181]

[178] Massie, *A Plan for the Establishment of Charity Houses for Exposed or Deserted Women and Girls and for Penitent Prostitutes . . . Considerations relating to the Poor and the Poor's Law of England: wherein the great increase of unemployed Poor and of Thieves and Prostitutes, are shown to be immediately owing to the severity as well as defects of our Poor's Laws; and to be primarily caused by the Monopolizing of Farms and the Inclosure of Common Lands* (1758).

[179] Beattie, *Crime and the Courts*, 553.

[180] *Rules and Orders of the Society instituted at London for the Encouragement of arts, manufactures and commerce* (1758), 2.

[181] Quot. in Anne Borsay, *Medicine and Charity in Georgian Bath: A Social History of the General Infirmary, c.1739–1830* (Aldershot, 1999), 212.

The middle decades of the century, as Donna Andrew has recently emphasized, saw a 'remarkable flowering of charitable activity', itself a further symptom of the pervasiveness of contemporary anxieties about prevailing moral and social conditions.[182] Of twenty-four provincial hospitals founded between 1735 and 1783, nine were founded in the 1740s and 1750s.[183] The list of London philanthropic bodies established in this period is even more striking and includes the Foundling Hospital; the Lying-in Hospital for Delivering Poor Married Women; the General Lying-in Hospital; the Marine Society; the Magdalen Hospital for Penitent Prostitutes, referred to earlier; and the Asylum for Orphaned Girls.[184] In Scotland, infirmaries were established or expanded in Edinburgh and Aberdeen. Subscribers to these charities ran into thousands, especially if we include institutional subscriptions. Andrew has emphasized how far this activity was motivated by mercantilist goals, in particular a concern about boosting the nation's population, a crucial resource in the contemporary struggle against the French. She has also emphasized how far the metropolitan or national charities depended on the enthusiasm, concerns, energies, and purses of a network of largely metropolitan merchants.[185] They also grew from the nexus of concerns, assumptions, and feelings which we have been exploring above. The provincial infirmary movement was not just designed to mend the bodies of patients, but to reform their manners as well. As Mary Fisell has written:

> Like the workhouse, the hospital would help to rid the streets of the idle and disorderly, and England's special relationship to providence would thus be apparent to all. Inside the Infirmary, the poor were removed from the bad influences of their friends and neighbours . . . Bristol patients were exposed to daily prayers, and forbidden to gamble and swear. Other provincial infirmaries's wards were adorned with Biblical texts painted on the walls.[186]

Charity was to be frugal and carefully directed; it was reformatory in purpose. Sir James Lowther wrote, in the context of the establishment of the Free British Fishery Society, a body which was discussed in detail in the previous chapter, of 'honest labour & industry' being the 'best charitys'.[187]

The Marine Society, founded in 1756, exemplified the character of much philanthropy.[188] It sought to rescue a vulnerable and potentially disorderly

[182] Donna T. Andrew, *Philanthropy and Police: London Charity in the Eighteenth Century* (Princeton, NJ 1989), 74.

[183] York (1740); Exeter (1741); Northampton (1743); Liverpool (1745); Shrewsbury (1745); Worcester (1746); Newcastle (1751); Gloucester (1755); Chester (1755).

[184] One estimate puts the number of voluntary hospitals founded in London between 1740 and 1760 at 12 (Beattie, *Crime and the Courts*, 542).

[185] Andrew, *Philanthropy and Police*, chs. 3 and 4.

[186] Mary E. Fissell, 'Charity Universal? Institutions and Moral Reform in Eighteenth-Century Bristol', in Lee Davison, *et al.*, *Stilling the Grumbling Hive*, 129. See also Borsay, *Medicine and Charity in Georgian Bath.*

[187] CRO, W/Lons/W2/1/114: Lowther to Spedding, 21 Apr. 1752.

[188] For the marine society, see Andrew, *Philanthropy and Police*, 109–15. See also Stephen James Taylor, *Jonas Hanway: Founder of the Marine Society* (1985).

section of the population—pauper children—and render them useful members of society, in this case as future manpower for the navy. It had its origins in a subscription established in February 1756 to provide clothes for 'friendless and deserted' boys to join the navy. According to John Fielding, the previous year had seen the transportation of gangs of friendless boys between 14 and 18 years old, presumably for petty larceny and related offences.[189] There was also a perception that these boys, like their female counterparts who became prostitutes at even younger ages, were victims of economic necessity and therefore particularly deserving of charity. Jonas Hanway, merchant and indefatigable philanthropist, was the guiding hand behind this and several other charities in this period. He talked of the objects of the charity as 'children whose parents have not only left them in extreme poverty, but totally friendless, and exposed to all the complicated miseries which are most disgraceful to human nature'.[190] His Marine Society represented a union of patriotism and Christian benevolence. It was a vehicle for improving the military readiness and capacity of the state; it was also a means for restoring Britain's proper relationship with God and re-establishing the morals of the population. As Hanway declared: 'There certainly is a God, and he as certainly rewards and punishes nations, in collective bodies, as well as private men!' Charity also represented an appropriate response to the evils created by commercial progress and prosperity:

If we are not more evil than our fathers were, some evils have become epidemical amongst us. An inordinate desire of money, blended with strong habits of expence and dissipation, have prevailed very much, and it is hard to say which of these have been most closely followed by want of public love.[191]

For Hanway, as for many others, patriotism and religion were synonymous. A proper sense of God's majesty would recall society to its duties and restore to it public spirit and martial valour. It would, in Hanway's phrase, instil disdain for 'unmanly joys'. The fact that Britain's international circumstances were, in 1756, precarious and threatening only made support for initiatives such as the Marine Society more urgent.

SCOTLAND'S MORALS

To what degree did Scotland see similar efforts to reform morals in this period? It was mainly through the lesser courts of the Church that moral discipline was enforced on the population north of the border, although JPs and burgh and sheriff courts also had a potentially significant role to

---

[189] Fielding, *An Account of the Origins and Effects of a Police*, 42–3.
[190] Hanway, *An Account of the Marine Society*, 12.
[191] Ibid., 29.

play.[192] The Convention of Royal Burghs also lobbied Edinburgh's MP, James Ker and the Lord Advocate in 1749 and 1755 respectively, at the behest of Glasgow's burgh authorities, about legislation on licensing of alehouses and sale of alcohol.[193] The background to the latter request was almost certainly an upsurge of concern about violent crime in and around Glasgow and Edinburgh in the winter of 1753–4.[194] The response from magistrates and the local elites was vigorous. In Edinburgh, several general searches were made for suspects; rewards were offered for the apprehension of robbers; victims of crime were encouraged to come forward and give notice that a crime had been committed to the clerk's office at Edinburgh. In Glasgow, a prosecution society called the Glasgow Friendly Society was founded in 1754.[195]

It has been argued that the kirk session—the principal disciplinary body of the Church of Scotland—was retreating from actively pursuing moral offences other than adultery in urban society from the 1730s, although whether this means that the influence of the church on morals was weakening is unclear.[196] A recent study of Edinburgh has also painted a picture of a church in the Scottish capital with declining ability and ambition from the middle of the century to enforce strict moral conduct on the population.[197] Presbyteries, synods, and the General Assembly of the Kirk continued, nevertheless, throughout this period to urge strict observance of the sabbath and moral behaviour.[198] Such actions are perhaps unsurprising, given the strong representation of ministers from the popular wing of the church in many lesser bodies of the Kirk.

More noteworthy, however, are a series of systematic campaigns of moral reform instigated within the Kirk in the 1740s and 1750s. The first occurred in 1742–3, and was organized by the Edinburgh Presbytery.[199] It coincided with renewed opposition in the Scottish capital to the establishment of a theatre there. It also appears to have been linked to an attempt from 1740 to revive the reformation of manners societies in Edinburgh and throughout the rest of Scotland.[200] The meetings of the revived society were poorly attended, and

[192] For the division of legal responsibilities between different courts, see esp. Stephen J. Davies, 'The Courts and the Scottish Legal System 1600–1747: The Case of Stirlingshire', in V. A. C. Gatrell, B. Lenman, and G. Parker (eds.), *Crime and the Law: The Social History of Crime in Western Europe since 1500* (1980), 120–54. See also Leah Leneman and Rosalind Mitchison, *Sin in the City: Sexuality and Social Control in Urban Scotland 1660–1780* (Edinburgh, 1998), chs. 2 and 3.

[193] *Extracts from the Records of the Convention of the Royal Burghs of Scotland, 1738–59* (Edinburgh, 1905), 307, 331, 490, 492.

[194] *Scots Mag.* (1753), 627; (1754), 46–7.

[195] Ibid. (1754), 548; (1755), 55. By the beginning of 1755, membership of the society numbered 100.

[196] Leah Leneman, ' "Prophaning" the Lord's Day—Sabbath Breach in Early Modern Scotland', *History*, 241 (1989), 217–31. A slightly different interpretation is offered in Leneman and Rosalind Mitchison, *Sin in the City*, ch. 3, where the authors suggest that observance of Sabbath was becoming 'internalized' by most sections of the population.

[197] Rab Houston, *Social Change in the Age of the Enlightenment: Edinburgh 1660–1760* (Oxford, 1994), esp. pp. 195–214. Houston does note the limited nature of cultural liberalization before the 1770s.

[198] See e.g. NAS, CH2/521/18, fos. 57, 273–4.

[199] NAS, CH2/121/14, fos. 440–1; CH2/121/15, fos. 6, 27–31.

[200] NLS, MS 1954, Minutes of the Edinburgh Reformation of Manners Society, 1740–5; *The Narrative and Resolution, with the Rules of the Society for the Reformation of Manners* (Edinburgh, 1742).

a great deal of its energies were taken up with attempting to sustain, through prayer meetings and publicity in the press, the contemporary religious revival in Cambuslang and in other parts of Scotland, as well as in England and the North American colonies.[201] What its resolutions did reflect, however, was a heightened sense of providential judgment. Its members included the famous popular minister, John Erskine's father and grandfather, other ruling elders from the popular wing of the church, and several members of the Edinburgh burgh council. Initial ambitions for a full-scale revival of the SRM in Scotland went unrealized, although it, or the Presbystery, does appear to have gained some support for renewed moral reform from the capital's authorities in 1742.[202] Elsewhere, the Provincial Synod of Galloway inaugurated its own campaign of renewed moral discipline in 1751. This involved a lengthy overture to ministers, as well as the provision of a summary of laws against vice and immorality which were to be read out in the pulpits within its bounds.[203]

That such an effort should have taken place in the south-west, with its Covenanting heritage, is perhaps understandable. The General Assembly of the Kirk, while the shadow of the Jacobite Rebellion still hung heavy over Scotland, launched a similar campaign, however, throughout the body of the Church in 1746. Following the defeat of the rebellion, and apparently spurred by the passage of the Profane Oaths Act, the General Assembly agreed to revive earlier acts of the Assembly against profaneness and immorality, and sponsor a series of recommendations to inspire greater efforts at moral discipline from kirk sessions, presbyteries and synods, as well as ordinary church members. It followed a similar campaign conducted by the Synod of Glasgow and Ayr, which appears to have involved religious societies in Glasgow and its environs.[204] The Commission of the General Assembly was instructed to inspect the recent act against profane swearing and other earlier acts for similar purposes and draw up their own proper act against vice and immorality, as well as pointing out expedients for promoting 'true religion and Godliness'. The result was a summary of relevant legislation which was to be sent to all ministers to be read out in the pulpits.[205] Seven years later, the Assembly issued a new act against the

---

[201] Houston has described the minutes of the society in the 1740s as giving 'the impression more of a religious discussion group than a body of dynamic campaigners' (Houston, *Social Change*, 199).

[202] See Edinburgh City Archives, Convention of Royal Burghs, Moses Collection, Supplementary Bundles 16/2: *Acts of the Town Council of the City of Edinburgh for Supression of Vice and Immorality, made since the Happy Revolution, especially since the Year 1700* (Edinburgh, 1742). I am grateful to Professor C. A. Whatley for this reference.

[203] NAS, CH2/165/4 (Register Book of the Synod of Galloway 1747–1784), fo. 53.

[204] NAS, CH2/464/3 (Register of the Synod of Glasgow and Air), fos. 363–3. See also NAS, CH2/171/11 (Records of the Presbytery of Glasgow), 28 Oct. 1746.

[205] NAS, CH1/3/24 (Records of the Commission of the General Assembly, 1739–48), fos. 439, 444; CH1/1/45 (Records of the General Assembly, 1746–9), fos. 78, 79, 444.

profanation of the Sabbath.[206] This episodic activity represented a revival of more than ordinary concern in the General Assembly about morals last manifested briefly, in 1734, and before than in 1722, and, more importantly, during the crisis-ridden decade of the 1690s.[207]

RELIGION AND MORALS

So far, we have discussed mid-century efforts to re-establish morals in terms of a diverse series of legislative, magisterial, voluntary, and, in the case of Scotland, clerical responses. There was significant overlap between them, in terms of goals, as has been emphasized at various points above, and in terms of personnel. Henry Fielding, architect of several important reforms to the police, and author of an important pamphlet on reform of the poor law, was a supporter and promoter of the new metropolitan charities. Many MPs who sat on committees considering proposals for and bills designed to achieve social reform were donors to these charities. Several important figures in reform debates and activities also had a long-standing involvement in moral or social and philanthropic causes, emphasizing the continuity with earlier upsurges of moral and social concern. These individuals included William Hay, Thomas Wilson, Sir James Lowther, James Edward Oglethorpe, Sir Richard Lloyd, and Isaac Maddox. Oglethorpe had been involved in prison reform since the later 1720s; he had also been the chief promoter of the colony of Georgia, serving as its first governor; in the early 1750s he promoted a successful rebuilding of the King's Bench prison.[208] Enthusiasm for projects which sought, amongst other things, to reverse moral decline, to restore order and stability to society, to promote commercial and military strength, cut across partisan allegiances.[209] This is not to say, however, that there were not tensions or differences in emphasis, underlying the apparent unity of concern. The Jacobite paper, the *True Briton*, of which Oglethorpe was a supporter, was strongly critical of Fielding and his proposal for multi-purpose hospitals to reform the poor, presenting the latter as symptomatic of the oppressive nature of Pelham's England.[210] As we saw above, several proposals, including those which aimed at reconstructing the system of public poor relief, proved too radical for the majority of MPs.

Some of these tensions also emerge when we look more closely at attitudes

[206] NAS, CH1/3/26 (Records of the Commission of the General Assembly, 1748–57), fo. 370.

[207] *Acts of the General Assembly of the Church of Scotland 1638–1842* (Edinburgh, 1843). I hope to write in more detail about this topic at a later date.

[208] Amos Ascbach Ettinger, *James Edward Oglethorpe: Imperial Idealist* (Oxford, 1936); Henry Bruce, *Life of General Oglethorpe* (New York, 1890); *Oglethorpe. A Brief Biography*, ed. Phinizy Spalding (Macon, Ga., 1989).

[209] See the comments on this in a parliamentary context in Connors, ' "The Grand Inquest of the Nation" ', 292–4.

[210] *True Briton*, 21 Mar. 1753.

towards the relationship between religion and morals. Many, and not just churchmen and ministers, argued that the revival of the influence of religion represented the only genuinely effective solution to moral decline. The arguments were long-standing ones, and had been frequently articulated during the reformation of manners movement of the 1690s. Conscience and religion served to create good, orderly citizens; they provided the cement of society in a way in which the law, concerned only with outward actions, could not.[211] The perception that irreligion represented a major threat was widely held. One writer expressed a desire and hope to see the revival of 'a golden age of virtue' and 'Religion, pure, rational and uncorrupted' flourish. The same writer counselled his readers: 'the Cause of God and Religion demand your support. Infidelity and scepticism are every Day prevailing more and more, and even Atheists dare defend their Blasphemy.'[212] Comments such as this were commonplace in this period. Thomas Hayter described 'vice and immorality' as an 'intestine plague, that lurks in the bowels, and prey upon the vitals of a state'. He also declared that the sole remedy was the influence of 'true religion', by which he meant unaffected piety as opposed to the raptures of 'enthusiasm'.[213]

The emphasis on religion inevitably brought into clearer focus the role of the Churches and their perceived inadequacies. In Scotland, divisions between the moderates, coming to prominence in the General Assembly at this time, and the more numerous popular party focused on, amongst other things, attitudes towards moral discipline and the style and content of preaching on morals and religious duty.[214] In England, criticism was expressed of the Anglican clergy for its worldliness and inattention to its religious duty, and not just by supporters of John Wesley. Thomas Sherlock's pastoral letter of 1750, in which he lambasted contemporary morals, provoked several responses critical of the clergy.[215] There were also calls in the press for Convocation—the legislative body of the Church—to be reconvened as part of a wider campaign to restore the health and influence of the Church and combat irreligion and immorality. These appeared in 1753–4 in the influential tri-weekly evening paper, the *London Evening Post* and several years later in the Tory-Patriot weekly, the *Monitor*.[216] The timing is significant. The Jewish Naturalization Act, passed in 1753, aroused a storm of protest from particu-

---

[211] For a striking statement of this position, see William Romaine, *A Method for Preventing the Frequency of Robberies and Murders* (1754), esp. p. 21.

[212] *A Letter to the Honourable House of Commons Relating to the Present Situation of Affairs* (1750), 13, 25–6.

[213] Hayter, *A Sermon Preached in the Parish Church of Christ Church, London, on Thursday May the 1st: Being the Time of the Yearly Meeting of the Children Educated in the Charity Schools in and about the Cities of London and Westminster* (1755), 43–5.

[214] See J. R. McIntosh, *Church and Theology in Enlightenment Scotland: The Popular Party, 1740–1800* (East Linton, 1998).

[215] *Modest Remarks upon the Bishop of London's Letter* (1750); *A Serious Expostulation with . . . the Bishop of London* (1750); *An Address to the Public Occasioned by the Bishop of London's Letter* (1750).

[216] Harris, 'The "London Evening Post" ', 1143–5.

larly the lower clergy, who portrayed this very limited measure of religious liberalization as a major threat to the Church. The Act revived a strain of Tory Churchmanship and ideology that had lain dormant for a considerable number of years. It also stimulated a further round of criticisms of the Church under Whig stewardship.[217] There was, however, no enthusiasm for major reforms of the Church amongst the bench of bishops and probably many clergymen, something which reflected in part the rise of a Whig Anglicanism in the Church and the perception that any major reform might create political controversy that was destructive and damaging rather than helpful to the Church.[218] Instead the emphasis was placed on pastoral care and activism and supporting the efforts of the secular power in fighting immorality and irreligion.

The clergy's other major function in this sphere was exhortation. As Stephen Taylor has emphasized, and as should have started to become apparent earlier, the Anglican clergy were not slow in this period to condemn immorality and irreligion.[219] The same was true of ministers of the Church of Scotland, especially evangelical ministers, such as, in the west, John Gillies and, even more famously, John Witherspoon and, in the north-east, John Willison. Indeed, contemporary sermons fully reflected the general perception that immorality and irreligion were pressing problems. Unlike in earlier periods, there was little dispute that the secular power should play an active role in combating these. The change is exemplified by Edmund Gibson, Bishop of London. In the 1720s, protective of the power and authority of the Church independent of the state, he had been a leading critic of secular intervention in policing moral crimes. By the early 1740s, however, he had changed his mind.[220] Clergymen also urged reform through personal reformation, especially amongst the upper ranks, whose behaviour set the example and tone for the rest of society. As Taylor has written of episcopal sermons in this period:

the rich and powerful were more liable to fault [in the eyes of the bishops] since their position in society gave them additional obligation. It was the duty of 'Persons of higher ranks' to use their 'eminent stations' to set 'Examples of Piety and Virtue'.[221]

The bishops and many of their clergy, and indeed several laymen, argued that reform amongst of the upper ranks would be the most effective method of curing immorality and irreligion amongst the lower orders.[222] Taylor argues that the emphasis in many sermons on moral duty has misled some historians,

---

[217] T. W. Perry, *Public Opinion, Propaganda and Politics in Eighteenth-Century England* (Camb., Mass., 1962). See also *A Guide to the Knowlege of the Rights and Privileges of Englishmen . . .* (1757) for one of the most severe Tory-Patriot attacks on Whig stewardship of the Church in this period.

[218] See esp. Stephen Taylor, 'Whigs, Bishops and America: The Politics of Church Reform in Mid-Eighteenth-Century England', *HJ* 36 (1993), 331–56.

[219] Taylor, 'Church and State', esp. pp. 140–5.

[220] Ibid., 143.

[221] Ibid., 144–5.

leading them to portray the Church in this period as increasingly closely shaped in its theology and conduct by requirements of the secular state. But it was its sense of spiritual responsibility that led it to emphasise morals at the expence of doctrine. It was, writes Taylor, a 'conscious reaction to the swelling tide of immorality and irreligion, which many feared was threatening to engulf the nation'.[223]

The perception that society was in a state of incipient collapse, or terminal decline, that the bases of national power were unravelling, was one which kept resurfacing in eighteenth-century Britain. The twin threats of luxury and corruption provided a nagging counterpoint to the urge to celebrate economic and commercial progress, the spread of politeness and religious toleration, freedom, and, increasingly important, Britain's status as a transoceanic power. Concern in the mid-eighteenth century about immorality and social degeneration might, therefore, seem less remarkable or indeed important. Yet such a conclusion would be wrong. In the first place, moral reform, or the urge to moral reform, had distinctive forms and meanings in this period. Luxury and corruption were porous terms or concepts; they did not have single meanings but rather multiple ones which shifted and changed over time and between different writers. Secondly, the later 1740s and 1750s, were, like the 1690s and the 1780s, a period in which moral anxieties were greatly prominent.

The sources of these anxieties were, as we have seen, various. What gave particular shape and content to them was, however, the coincidence of concerns about levels of crime and popular disorder, national decline and weakness, a revival of a sense of an active providence, and a perception that important changes were taking place in society, changes which stemmed from the ever-increasing forces of commercialization and prosperity in society. Henry Fielding articulated the latter with perhaps the greatest clarity in his social pamphlets of the early 1750s. But it also informed the thinking and writing of other important writers and voices in the period. As Donna Andrew has written of Jonas Hanway:

What gives much of the writing of this period [the central decades of the century] a sense of immediacy and urgency was the feeling that Hanway shared with his contemporaries of imminent and important changes in the political and social structure of the nation.[224]

The responses of contemporaries to this sense of fundamental change were contradictory and ambiguous. Britain's emergence as a 'commercial society'

---

[222] See e.g. Thomas Hayter, *A Sermon Preached in the Parish Church of Christ Church, London, on Thursday May the 1st, 1755: Being the Time of the Yearly Meeting of the Children Educated in the Charity Schools in and about the Cities of London and Westminster* (1755).

[223] Taylor, 'Church and State', 145.

[224] Andrew, *Philanthropy and Police*, 96.

was not simply a source of celebration and national self-congratulation. Many worried that addiction to pleasure and money was dissolving traditional social bonds, that virtue, morality, and religion were being undermined, with potentially alarming consequences for the future integrity of society and social order, and for Britain's commercial and international power and standing. In the face of this challenge, they sought ways of reconciling the tensions this created, or ways to reconstitute society along familiar, hierarchical lines. For wealthy members of the middling ranks, philanthropy not only sought to promote national, mercantilist goals, it also served to allow these individuals to exhibit the ways in which their wealth could be turned to ends which strengthened the moral basis of society and which recreated a 'natural' social order. Obituaries of wealthy men of upper middling rank disclose this very clearly. In 1750, the *Scots Magazine* carried an obituary for Gerard Van Neck. Van Neck, a leading London merchant, supposedly left a fortune of £24,000. Ten thousand pounds of this he left to relatives, friends, and to various charities; the remainder went to his brother, Joshua, with the advice 'Ever to prefer justice and honour to profit and lucre, and a good repute to desire of riches'.[225]

Most legislation and magisterial action dealt, as we have seen, with vice in low places. This reflected the 'prudential' factors which lay behind it—the desire to create a more secure and orderly environment for the property and persons of the wealthy, or at least comparatively wealthy, and to revive the economy and overseas commerce. Vice in high places was not immune to severe criticism, however. Some, like Fielding, argued that only vice amongst the lower orders was susceptible to legislative and magisterial action; Fielding used satire and wit against the upper ranks.[226] Others argued that reform of the upper ranks was crucial to the wider process of social and moral reform. 'Estimate Brown' adopted precisely this position, arguing, 'For the blind Force or weight of an ungoverned multitude can have no steady or rational Effect, unless some leading mind rouse it into Action, and point it to its proper End.'[227] The values which informed this critique of upper-class immorality have been presented elsewhere as 'middle class'.[228] Social criticism of the upper ranks was often cast in an anti-aristocratic mould, or focused on behaviour, for example, the Grand Tour, or sexual libertinism, which was identified closely with the nobility or more often denizens of the fashionable world of West End London society. The nobility or 'great ones' were in danger of forfeiting respect by deviating from behaviour that was appropriate to individuals of their rank. There was, nevertheless, no hostility to rank per se or

---

[225] *Scots Mag.*, 12 (1750), 399.

[226] Battestin and Battestin, *Henry Fielding*, 542–6.

[227] Brown, *Estimate*, 25.

[228] Gerald Newman, *The Rise of English Nationalism: A Cultural History, 1740–1830* (1987), esp. pp. 63–84.

indeed to social hierarchy. Rather the upper ranks were being called to return to their traditional, paternalist function and role in society, to reestablish the bonds of trust and re-assume the benevolent leadership of society. They had the crucial role to play in helping to 'create the social framework within which a more virtuous society might henceforth take shape'.[229]

Contrary to what Nicholas Rogers has recently asserted, the framework for debates about social policy and morals was not exclusively or even perhaps predominantly secular in the mid-eighteenth century.[230] Nor was its confined to secular media. Religious sentiments, perceptions, and language reinforced secular political language about corruption, as well as the languages of social reform or political arithmetic. This became much more apparent in public and press discussion in the 1750s, especially after 1753. The shift can be followed in the contents of the *London Evening Post*. In the 1750s, the leading writer in the paper, the pseudonymous 'Britannicus', was arguing for political reform as the means to wider moral and religious reform.[231] The *Monitor*, a leading Tory-Patriot essay paper launched in 1755, expressed similar views, or at least was susceptible to similar readings. As Joanna Innes has noted, Thomas Turner, the Sussex shopkeeper, was struck by the paper's efforts 'to point out the only way to restore the nation to its former strength and dignity, which is by suppressing vice and encouraging virtue and merit'.[232] Clergymen and others also had ample opportunity in this period to draw the attention of Britons to the relationship between national fortunes and God's favour. The notion of Britain as an 'elect nation' was a tenacious and powerful strand in national feeling in this period. This imparted a strong sense of destiny to conceptions of national identity. But it also carried a threat: the ominous shadow of God's wrathful judgment fell sporadically and heavily in the Britain of this period.

What, finally, about the forms and content of the mid-century reformation of manners movement? Martin Ingram has recently written that simple notions of continuity and change are 'hardly adequate for understanding the history of the reformation of manners'. More appropriate, he suggests, are 'musical metaphors invoking ideas of theme, variation, transposition and transformation'.[233] Much about the drive to reform society and its moral health in this period recalls the better-known regulatory drive of the 1690s. There is a similar range and diversity of motives, aspirations, and initiatives. The reasons for its failure, or limited impact, were also similar—the failure to win consistent support from the gentry and upper ranks and the cooperation of many of the lesser officers of the law. Many members of the elites paid lip

[229] The phrase is Joanna Innes ('Politics and Morals', 66).
[230] Rogers, 'Confronting the Crime Wave', 93.
[231] Harris, 'The "London Evening Post" ', 1143.
[232] Innes, 'Politics and Morals', 111 n. 136.
[233] Ingram, 'Reformation of Manners in Early Modern England', in Paul Griffiths, Adam Fox, and Steve Hindle (eds.), *The Experience of Authority in Early Modern England* (1996), 68–9.

service to the need for reform, but gave little active support. In 1752, James Burgh launched, together with Stephen Hales, a plan for a Grand Association of Prominent Persons. This association was to support a periodical designed to inculcate 'virtue and truth'. The plan failed, and Burgh was left to write a series of articles defending revealed religion for the *General Evening Post*.[234] The ideological context is also more similar than several historians have recently recognized. Yet important shifts in cultural, economic, and religious contexts had taken place and these inevitably lent it shades of difference. Its agenda was set by problems specific to the period—for example, the crime wave after 1748, commercial and economic rivalry with France. In England, it was also a movement or series of initiatives that were shaped more closely by magisterial intervention and concerns and parliamentary debate and legislation. In this sense, as Richard Connors has written, it was more pragmatic and the emotions underpinning it less intense than those of the 1690s.[235] This is, however, a matter of degree, as Connors recognizes, and the mid-century movement was not without idealism. Hanway talked of tracing 'out some footsteps of the Golden Age'.[236] To find the spiritual tone and content of the mid-century movement, we need to look to the remarkable effloresence of philanthropic initiatives and to the exhortatory efforts of the clergy and widespread hopes of 'national revival' entertained amongst the opposition.

The reformation of manners in the mid-century was also strongly centred on London and its environs, although, as we have seen, it did not lack echoes outside of the metropolis. These were, however, less strong than those of the 1690s or indeed what they were to be in the 1780s, when networks of reforming associations spread throughout provincial society. What may partly explain the scarcity of reforming societies in the mid-eighteenth century was the Evangelical Revival from the later 1730s. Methodism and evangelicalism may have worked to deflect reforming energies away from broader reforming plans and bodies towards the sustaining and support of conversion to 'vital' religion. It is striking, for example, that the revived Edinburgh reformation of manners society devoted most attention to publicizing the evangelical awakening in Scotland and North America, and in building and sustaining connections between evangelical congregations and ministers.[237] Methodism looked to individuals to change their own lives. The evangelical clergyman, William Romaine, argued in 1754 that only a renewed sense of God's majesty and judgment could provide an effective remedy to popular licence and criminality. James Hervey, rector of Weston-Favell in Northamptonshire, was another who saw 'vital religion' as the 'means of safety' in a 'time of

---

[234] Carla H. Hay, *James Burgh: Spokesman for Reform in Hanoverian England* (Washington, DC, 1979).
[235] Connors, ' "The Grand Inquest of the Nation" ', 307.
[236] Hanway, *An Account of the Marine Society*, 18.
[237] NLS, MS 1954.

danger'.[238] Two days after the fast day of 6 February 1756, Thomas Turner, whose diaries reveal what Henry Rack has called in a different context a 'diffused puritan and high church piety', drew up a detailed regimen to achieve his own personal reformation.[239] On the other hand, as we saw earlier, supporters of Wesley and Whitefield were prominent in the revival of the SRM in London in 1757. In Bristol, the newspaper printer and Methodist Felix Farley urged enforcement of the Profane Oaths Act as part of a wider drive towards the reformation of manners.[240] The number of Methodists and evangelical congregations was, however, relatively small in the mid-century and cannot, therefore, provide a full explanation for the absence of reforming societies in the provinces. Perhaps what was really lacking was a single event, or series of events, which could have served to focus the diverse reforming energies of the period into a coordinated, nationwide campaign. In the 1690s, this was provided by the crisis of the Revolution and subsequent wars of British succession (the Williamite wars in Ireland, the Highland war of 1689–92, and the Nine Years War); in the 1780s, a similar role was performed by defeat in the War of American Independence and the loss of the thirteen North American colonies. In 1756–7, the military setbacks of the early phases of Seven Years War, coming on top of the Lisbon earthquake, and coinciding with widespread riot and popular disorder and acute ministerial instability, began to create conditions in which such a movement might have begun to take shape. The sense of gloom and crisis, which reached a climax of intensity in the autumn of 1757, began to lift, however, in the following year. In 1758–9, gloom turned into excitement as British armies achieved victories across the globe. Against this background, the idea that God might have an argument with his chosen people, and that there might be something fundamentally wrong with British society and government, suddenly became much more difficult to sustain.

---

[238] Romaine, *A Method for Preventing the Frequency of Robberies and Murders* (1754); Hervey, *The Time of Danger, and the Means of Safety: To Which is Added, the Way of Holiness. Being the Substance of Three Sermons, Preached on the Late Public Fast Days* (1757), quoted in the *Critical Review*, 4 (1757), 196.

[239] Henry D. Rack, *Reasonable Enthusiast: John Wesley and the Rise of Methodism* (1989), 22; *The Diary of Thomas Turner 1754–65*, ed. David Vaisey (Oxford, 1984), 25–6.

[240] *Felix Farley's Bristol Journal*, 5 July; 12 July; 13 Sept.; 20 Sept.; 4 Oct. 1746; 25 Nov.–2 Dec. 1752. In the issue of 4 Oct. 1746, the back page of the paper comprised an item entitled *Considerations drawn from the past National Dangers and our Rescue, by the ever memorable Victory at Culloden*, which called for a national reformation of manners. This item was also printed separately on fine paper priced 9d. for a dozen to be given away. On 13 September, a copy of the Profane Oaths Act had been printed on the front page of the paper. Such was the demand for this that three additional (or 'extraordinary') editions had been printed.

Conclusion

The accession of George III was greeted enthusiastically. The Dissenter Andrew Kippis told his congregation that their new king had 'come to the Crown at a time when it is not only firmly established, but adorned with peculiar circumstances of prosperity and honour'. Kippis also extolled the nation George III was to govern:

he is supreme governor of a nation so large, powerful, and prosperous; a nation which abounds in wealth, agriculture, manufactures, and commerce; which is distinguished for science, literature, taste, and politeness; which possesses ample territories in the remotest parts of the globe; which is the unrivalled mistress of the seas, holds the chief place among the seats of Europe, and is the most illustrious seat of civil and religious liberty that ever existed.[1]

The new king promised a new era of national harmony and reconciliation; many of his subjects were keen to be convinced that they were witnessing a moment of historic change.

The anticipation was sustained for most of the first year of the reign, although several discordant notes were quick to make themselves heard. The King's favourite and guide, the Earl of Bute, was, barely a month into the new reign, arousing suspicion and hostility amongst some of the London crowd.[2] Coronation day (22 September 1761) was, nevertheless, elaborately celebrated throughout the British Isles.[3]

Diverse hopes and expectations lay behind the patriotic harmony of 1760–1. Tories wished for the reinstatement of the natural rulership of land, and a revival of religion and royal support for the Church of England. One Patriot pamphleteer depicted George III as liberating Britain from the 'dark and arbitrary influence' which had supposedly characterized Whig rule under George II. The Whig-Tory division would disappear; Britain was now, in any case, a 'nation of Whigs'; the salient issue was whether Britain would continue to be governed by the 'narrow maxims of faction'. An independent Parliament composed of landed gentry would inaugurate a programme of economy and reform.[4]

---

[1] Kippis, *Observations Upon the Coronation. A Sermon Preached at the Chapel in Long Ditch, Westminster on Sept 20, 1761* (1761), 7, 11–12.

[2] See PRONI, Shannon Papers, 2707/A1/12/20A, for a report of this dating from November 1760.

[3] For the celebrations in Dublin, which were particularly grand, see *Belfast Newsletter*, 29 Sept 1761. The Dundee burgh authorities secured the services of Neil Gow, the foremost fiddler of his time, for their coronation ball (Dundee Archives and Records Centre, Dundee Burgh, Treasurers' Account Books, 1760–1).

[4] *Seasonable Hints From an Honest Man on the Present Important Crisis of a New Reign and a New Parliament* (1761).

For others the revival of public virtue, led by the Court, was seen in terms of the values of modesty, economy, and strict religious observance, and the defeat of the luxury and political corruption which had been associated, in some minds, with Whig oligarchy. The Presbyterian-owned *Belfast Newsletter* printed a letter from London in January 1761 which noted with approval the religious duty and example set by the new King, as well as his adherence to domestic values and duty. The former had been recently demonstrated by his disapproval of gaming; he had publicly rebuked several 'ladies of quality' for playing cards on Sundays.[5] Kippis declared that George III was 'universally allowed to have uncomon attachment to religion and virtue', also observing, 'We may, therefore, rationally expect that, thro' the benevolence of Heaven, his felicity will not be shaken: for the way of piety and righteousness is the surest way to divine protection and favour.'[6] A few years earlier, another writer had conjured a vision of George presiding over a regime characterized by concern for public welfare—to be demonstrated through the provision of workhouses, public granaries, and public libraries; justice— to be achieved through reform of the law to make it simpler, quicker, and less costly; rational administration—portrayed in terms of lifting burdens on the poor and the productive and a continuous, close scrutiny of servants of the state; virtue—to be created through Princely example and through careful custodianship of the Church; and, finally, a proper respect for social hierarchy.[7] A revived public spirit was to be the basis for reform and progress, as well as for the restoration of the natural social order overturned by the corrupt ambitions and 'low-born' agents of Whig rule.

That many of these hopes were to unravel with great rapidity in the early 1760s is well known.[8] The process by which the optimism of the beginning of the reign was destroyed was to exercise a very important influence on the pattern of politics in subsequent decades. The history of parliamentary reform, for example, can only be fully understood in this context. Many of the underlying structures of British politics also began a period of rapid and fundamental change, which again distances this world from the one we have been exploring. Since the later 1730s, the junior Court had between 1737 and 1742 and again between 1747 and 1751 provided a focus for opposition, and acted as a lightening conductor for alienation from the politics and personnel of the Hanoverian regime. Given the capacity of Jacobitism to appeal to alienated metropolitan politicians and Whigs, such as George Heathcote, it may have performed a similar function. Under George III, similar lightening conductors did not exist, and this was an important part of the context in

---

[5] *Belfast Newsletter*, 27 Jan. 1761.

[6] Kippis, *Observations upon the Coronation*, 12.

[7] *The Ghost of Ernest, Great Grandfather of Her Royal Highness, the Princess Dowager of Wales. With Some Account of his Life* (1757).

[8] See the discussion in Paul Langford, *A Polite and Commercial People: England 1727–1783* (Oxford, 1989), 340–57.

which support for parliamentary reform grew and party was reinvented by Burke and the Rockingham Whigs as justification for their opposition to the government. The 'Country Interest' of the early-Hanoverian period had embraced parliamentary and extra-parliamentary elements, as well as metropolitan politicians and country gentlemen. Similar sorts of alliances continued to appear in the new reign; Wilkite politics is perhaps best seen as the final phase of the old Country platform.[9] Nevertheless, the relations between extra-parliamentary and parliamentary politics were from the early 1760s marked by greater distance and mutual suspicion. This, in turn, reflected, on the one hand, the rising ambitions and hopes of some extra-parliamentary politicians and opinion and, on the other, the changed conditions of parliamentary and ministerial politics under George III. With the end of the proscription of Tories from office, the essential conservatism of most parliamentary opinion became more evident.

The reconciliation of Tories to the Hanoverian regime also brought about the final destruction of the old party divisions which had underpinned political life since the 1680s. Contemporaries still sought to understand the kaleidoscopic politics of the 1760s in terms of Whig and Tory labels, but this was a language which had been forged to describe a political world which had passed.[10] At a national level, Toryism in the 1740s and 1750s had already ceased to be a major force, functioning largely as an important component of successive 'Country' oppositions and of a politics of patriotic regeneration. Tories did, nevertheless, retain a distinctive identity into the final years of George II's reign; and Whig-Tory loyalties continued to divide landed and indeed parts of urban society across England and Wales. Not the least important explanation for this is how long the Jacobite threat continued to haunt contemporaries, and thus underpin the hostile stereotypes which helped to sustain party identities. One of the main effects of the '45, in this context, was to cause many Whigs to relearn the crux of their political faith—the need to support the Hanoverian and Protestant Succession. Also crucial was the looming mid-century threat from French military power; as late as 1759, the French Court looked to an invasion in support of the Jacobites to rescue their military position in Canada and India. It was certainly possible to argue before 1760 that party identities were moribund—or should have been so—but, significantly, this was usually in the context of warning about their damaging influence.[11]

[9] See esp. John Money, 'The Masonic Moment; Or, Ritual, Replica and Credit: John Wilkes, the Macaroni Parson, and the Making of the Middle-Class Mind', *JBS* (1993), 358–95. See also Peter D. G. Thomas, *John Wilkes: A Friend to Liberty* (Oxford, 1996).

[10] For a convenient and authoritative summary, see Ian R. Christie, 'The Changing Nature of Parliamentary Politics 1742–1789', in Jeremy Black (ed.), *British Politics and Society from Walpole to Pitt 1742–1789* (1990), 101–22.

[11] See e.g. *The Country Gentleman's Advice to his Son, on his Coming of Age, with Regard to his Political Conduct* (1755). The author argued that the issues which had divided Whigs and Tories had been superseded

In Scotland, the accession of George III had a less marked impact, if only because the final destruction of Jacobitism as a serious political and military option was a much more important transition. In retrospect, it is easy to see Culloden as the turning point here, however tempting it may be to dwell on the course of the rebellion itself. Yet, as Chapter 4 sought to demonstrate, in many ways, the historic importance of the '45 in Scotland is what happened after Cumberland's crushing victory. The final phase of Jacobite history awaits its modern historian; when this history is written, however, it will in part be a story of the processes by which Jacobite hopes did not die in 1746, but lived on, however precariously, into the early 1750s. There was a mood of sullen alienation and desperation amongst many of these clans after the '45, which readily fed on rumours about renewed risings and a return of the Young Pretender to Scottish shores. When Archie Cameron was executed in 1753, some contemporaries saw this an unduly savage punishment and likely to prove counterproductive. Surely, they argued, Britain could now afford to be lenient.[12] Ministers knew otherwise, or at least thought they did.

The accession of a new King was enthusiastically greeted north of the border. Many north of the border were impressed by George III's declaration when he met his Privy Council for the first time at Carlton House that he had been born a 'Briton', pointedly not an Englishman. Sir Alexander Grant told his constituents in Forres in 1761: 'Gentlemen, we live at a glorious period of time, which yields us happy prospects, under the rule and protection of a young sovereign, who is justly celebrated; so trained up in virtue and accomplishments, that he is an ornament to humanity, as well as a blessing to his people.'[13] Since 1745, Scots believed that their countrymen, including many Highlanders, had proved beyond doubt their loyalty and value as 'Britons'. They were also looking with increasing confidence to a future of commercial prosperity and development, and national revival, as part of Britain's expanding 'empire of the seas'. The ideological streams which fed this outlook can be traced back through the early Hanoverian period and into the later seventeenth century. In the later 1740s and 1750s, partly stimulated by legislative support, the pace of economic activity in Scotland markedly quickened, as did the rate of formation of new commercial ventures. Against this background, the relationship between commerce and conceptions of national identity took on added ideological weight. The recreation of Edinburgh from the early 1750s as the loyal capital of North Britain was one facet of these wider shifts. One parody of the famous *Proposals* of 1752 satirized what the author saw as the sense of provincial inferiority which infused them, by

by a new set of issues relating to whether 'our affairs are well or ill administered' (pp. 22–3). He also put forward various well-worn arguments against party as a corrupting force in society. At the same time, however, as calling for political unanimity and moderation, he also acknowledged the continuing existence of Whig–Tory divisions. 'Party rage' and 'party clubs' were a major threat to the improvement of public reason; they also served to benefit the few at the expense of the many.

[12] See e.g. *Scots Mag.* (1753), 279–81; *London Daily Advertiser*, 6 June 1753.
[13] *Belfast Newsletter*, 9 May 1761.

recommending the erection of a large new public lavatory: 'In a word, *London* is opulent and beautiful, because it abounds in *necessary-houses*; *Edinburgh*, from being deprived of these conveniences, is poor, and wallowing in mire'.[14] It was a palpable hit, but what it omitted was the equally strong sense that an improved Edinburgh might even exceed London as both a polite and commercial capital, that it could avoid the 'luxury and vice' which London had become famous for.[15]

Ireland presents us with a superficially similar picture. As with Scotland, the change of monarch had a less dramatic impact than in England and Wales, although it did mean calling a general election in 1761, the first since 1727. Patriotism was an important feature of Irish Protestant society and politics in the early Hanoverian period. But from the mid-1750s, it gained new political force, and began to change the rules of Irish political life. An important part of the background to this was quickening economic growth from the later 1740s which, as in Scotland, created greater confidence in the country's economic prospects. Economic improvement was a cause which won more and more adherents amongst the landed and urban elites, symbolized by the continuing development and official support for the activities of the Dublin Society, and by the proliferation of farmers' societies in the mid-1750s, which sought to encourage greater manuring and tillage through payment of premiums to improving farmers. There was no necessary convergence between Patriot politics and economic improvement, but the latter readily reinforced the former.

It was, however, the Money Bill crisis which acted as the principal stimulus to Patriotism as a political force, and which also worked to politicize Irish public opinion in ways which were explored in Chapter 5. A rapidly politically maturing press played a crucial role in this. Divisions amongst the political elites also created spaces in which elements quite low down the social scale entered the political arena in very visible ways. Dublin Castle fully recognized this, and a notable element of the crisis is the administration's sponsorship of pamphlets squarely aimed at a popular readership. John Gast wrote in the persona of a Haberdasher—'in the plain words of a man like yourselves', as he declared to his putative readers. He also observed that: 'Even the most diligent of our Journeymen are borne away by the Phrenzy of the Times.'[16] Another pro-administration pamphlet was written in the form of a dialogue,

---

[14] *Proposals for Carrying on a Certain Public Work in the City of Edinburgh* (Edinburgh, 1752). This has been attributed to Sir David Dalrymple. I am grateful to Prof. Charles McKean for drawing my attention to this source.

[15] The superiority of morals and manners in Scotland as a component of a 'North-British' identity in eighteenth-century Scotland has been highlighted by Colin Kidd ('North Britishness and the Nature of Eighteenth Century British Patriotisms', *HJ* 39 (1996), 361–82. See also John Dwyer and Alexander Murdoch, 'Manners, Morals and the Rise of Henry Dundas, 1770–1784', in Roger Mason, John Dwyer, and Alexander Murdoch (eds.), *New Perspectives on the Politics and Culture of Early Modern Scotland* (Edinburgh, 1992), 210–48.

[16] Gast, *The Haberdasher's Letter to the Tradesmen, Farmers and the Rest of the Good People of Ireland* (Dublin, 1754), 6, 8.

and sold at the relatively low price of 2*d*.[17] Under the impact of the Money
Bill crisis, Presbyterians also emerged as a more important, and independent
force in Irish political life. The author of the dialogue referred to above
claimed that the Patriots had gained their support by telling them they would
get the Test Act repealed.[18] The growing restiveness of the Presbyterians in
the later 1750s, evident in their opposition, amongst other things, to tithe
farming, was linked by several writers to the events of 1753.[19] The mid-century
wars may have helped to reinforce these developments. The course of the war
was very closely followed in Ireland, and British victories were enthusiastically
celebrated. There was also pride in, or at least marked consciousness of,
Ireland's support for the cause of 'Britain' in the war. In 1747, a memorial on
the Irish economy written in the hand of Henry Boyle argued that Ireland's
contribution to Britain's military effort was deserving of greater reward in
respect of London's attitude towards the regulation of Irish trade. Noting the
drain of money out of Ireland to support three Irish regiments stationed in
England, the memorial urged:

No other mother country in the world receives so much advantage from any dependent province or its colonies as England does from Ireland, for which reason Ireland
should be treated in the most favourable manner in all the brances of its trade since
whatever they gain is sure to centre in England.[20]

Protestant Ireland was also proud of its staunch loyalty to the Hanoverian
regime during the mid-century. In 1745, Presbyterians in several counties in
Ulster appear to have been at the fore in the defensive loyalism stimulated by
the Jacobite invasion of Scotland. The defensive loyalism of these years also
served to recall, and revive memories of, a defensive loyalism forged in the
more threatening times of the Jacobite wars of 1689–91.

What did not change in Ireland is equally important. While there was
some liberalization in attitudes towards Catholicism in this period, it was a
process led by successive Lord Lieutenants (Chesterfield, Bedford, Halifax) and
Dublin Castle.[21] The attitudes of most Protestants towards Catholicism appear
to have remained deeply suspicious and hostile. The confessional outlook of
Irish Protestants explains why the cult of Frederick the Great as 'Protestant
hero' was so enthusiastically embraced in Ireland in the Seven Years War. The
Dublin guilds who had offered such visible support to Charles Lucas and the
Patriots in the later 1740s and 1750s, and whose members loudly celebrated

[17] *A Dialogue Between Dick —— And Tom ——, Esqs; Relating to the Present Divisions in I[relan]d* (Dublin, 1754).
[18] *A Dialogue*, 11.
[19] *Farewell to the Duke of Bedford* (1758); *A Letter to the People of Ireland on the Subject of Tithes* (1758).
[20] PRONI, 2707/A1/12/3.
[21] See *Catholic Ireland in the Eighteenth Century: Collected Essays of Maureen Wall*, ed. Gerard O'Brien (Dublin, 1989), esp. chs. 5 and 6. See also Thomas Bartlett, *The Fall and Rise of the Irish Nation: The Catholic Question 1690–1830* (Dublin, 1992), chs. 3–5.

Frederick's birthday in 1757 and 1758, in the 1760s pursued, under Lucas's leadership, a battle to have reimposed quarterage payments on Catholic merchants and traders. In 1762, there was a proposal from Lord Trimelston, a Catholic peer, to raise Catholic regiments for the King's service.[22] Spain had declared war on Britain in January 1762, reviving fears of invasion in Ireland, and exposing once again shortages of military manpower in the Kingdom. Halifax took up the proposal with enthusiasm, although it was decided that the regiments should serve in Catholic Portugal, and there were elaborate attempts to construct safeguards around the mobilization and arming of these regiments—to ensure that arms were not distributed to Catholics who might remain or return quickly to Ireland. The proposal was, however, sunk by an anti-popery storm which broke out in 1762, caused by agrarian rioting in Munster—the Whiteboy disturbances.[23] Official accounts of these disturbances, which emphasized economic causes—the effects of enclosure and the level of tithe payments—did not persuade local Protestants or indeed the Irish House of Commons. They saw the disturbances as a 'popish conspiracy'. The *Belfast Newsletter* carried reports of Spanish friars spreading sedition and Frenchmen in the port of Brest talking of an insurrection.[24] The Catholic Church and propertied Catholics might have increasingly in this period demonstrated their loyalty to Dublin Castle and the Hanoverian regime, and as a force for order. But did they express the views of the majority of Catholics? This was the question on which many Protestants remained sceptical.

To emphasize the distance between the political world of the mid-century and that which immediately followed it, at least in the politics of England and Wales, is not to overlook important continuities, as has been already suggested above. These were particularly evident in the extra-parliamentary arena. John Wilkes and his supporters in the 1760s were building on substantial foundations, in terms of rhetoric, ideology, platform, and tactics. John Brewer has emphasized the ways in which Wilkes and his supporters drew on clubs and associations which formed a crucial aspect of urban middling society.[25] In the 1750s, many of these clubs subscribed to the Marine Society and the Troop Society, and in doing so very visibly—the subscriptions were publicized in the press—connected themselves to issues of national political importance. The Anti-Gallican associations, formed in 1746, espoused a hostility towards the 'Great' and a sense of the self-worth of the commercial middling ranks which was to reappear under Wilkes' influence. The fact that, under the impact of the course of war and international rivalry with the French, commerce

[22] Bartlett, *The Fall and Rise of the Irish Nation*, 57–9.
[23] See e.g. the attack on the proposal mounted in *Some REASONS Against Raising an Army of Roman Catholicks in IRELAND in a Letter to a Member of Parliament* (Dublin, 1762).
[24] Eoin Magennis, 'Government and Politics in Ireland During the Seven Years War, 1756–1763', Ph.D. thesis (Belfast, 1996), 266.
[25] John Brewer, 'The Number 45: A Wilkite Political Symbol', in S. B. Baxter (ed.), *England's Rise to Greatness, 1660–1763* (Berkeley, Calif., 1983), 349–80.

came to be so insistently portrayed as the national interest in the 1740s and 1750s created a series of political contexts which, while not overtly hostile to landed rule, helped some of the middling ranks to develop a stronger sense of their own political importance. In the mid-1750s, a world of honest commerce and industry (which included the middling sort in the rural economy) was readily contrasted with a world of elite pleasure and dissolution, as well as the corrupt politics of Whig oligarchy with which it was, supposedly, intimately linked.[26]

The liberty of the press was also already very well established by the mid-century, as ideology and in practice. Politicians of all stripes supported the 'liberty of the press'. Ministers were wary of using their powers to police the press and tended to avoid prosecutions. Those they did attempt were very carefully chosen, and usually the provocation was extreme. As the Attorney General told the court in the trial of John Shebbeare in 1758: 'I have learned that moderation from my predecessors to let the common cry of scriblers sleep in peace'.[27] The press continued to be closely watched, and important prosecutions took place.[28] Ministerial efforts at policing the content of the press had, nevertheless, limited effects. In 1743–4 and again in the mid-1750s, the press contained savage and deeply disaffected attacks on the Hanoverian regime and the Anglo-Hanoverian union. In the mid-1750s particularly, there was a violence in press comment on politics which was rarely matched in the eighteenth century. There was a sense amongst ministers that the press was becoming more outspoken in its attacks on them, and that little could be done to alter this. In 1757, Lord Holdernesse wrote to Sir Lionel Pilkington, then struggling with anti-militia riots in the East Riding in Yorkshire:

I entirely agree in opinion with you that the unbounded licentiousness of the News Writers is a great cause of the ungovernable spirit which unfortunately appears among all the Common People. But it is easier to see the Evil than to chalk out the Remedy & to find the true Bounds between the usefull Liberty of the Press & the Abuse that is made of it . . .[29]

There was also a seam of popular political literature, especially in the 1750s—ballads, posters, prints—which adopted a tone of mocking irreverence which was to characterize much political ephemera in subsequent decades.

[26] See e.g. *Useful Remarks on Privateering. Addressed to the Laudable Association of Anti-Gallicans* (1756), esp. p. 1.

[27] BL, Add. MS 36202 (Hardwicke Papers), fo. 270.

[28] BL, Add. MS 32879, fo. 133: John Ibbut to Newcastle, 11 Apr. 1758. Ibbut was a messenger of the press, an office he had filled for forty years. His job was to buy pamphlets and newspapers published in London for use as evidence in press prosecutions. His bills, submitted every three months, were certified by the Treasury Solicitor and subsequently paid from the Treasury. The occasion of the letter was that the current Treasury Solicitor, Philip Carteret Webb, was not signing Ibbut's bills with the regularity of his predecessors. Ibbut urged the need for payment to resume if he was to be saved from ruin and if he was to be able to 'carry on his service as usual'.

[29] BL, Egerton 3436, fos. 178–90

As John Brewer emphasized some years ago, it was during the middle of the century that the press came of age in British society, helping to sustain an extra-parliamentary political culture of considerable depth and geographical extent.[30] Kathleen Wilson and H. T. Dickinson have made substantially the same point, although they have emphasized the importance of final years of opposition to Walpole in this context.[31] It was part of a wider flowering of print culture—embracing book publication, selling and ownership, press advertising, provincial printing, the establishment of libraries, the growth of coffee houses in provincial cities and towns—which expanded rapidly in Britain from the 1740s and which was closely linked to a strengthening provincial urban culture.[32] As has been emphasized at various points in this book, two decades of war and continuous international rivalry after 1739 stimulated an often intense demand for news and comment on Britain's fortunes overseas. It has recently been argued that historians have overestimated the influence of war and national political controversies on the growth of the press across the eighteenth century.[33] In the mid-century, however, the impact of war would be difficult to exaggerate, and contemporaries were well aware of the connection. In 1764, one estimate put the number of London newspapers being sent into the provinces through the post office as not less than 15,000 in peacetime; in war, they suggested the figure would rise to 21,000.[34] The growing centrality of the press, especially the newspaper, to public life in this period, and not just politics, remains to be fully documented. Yet what is striking is how many bodies came to rely on publicity through the press for their operations, bodies such as the Society for the Improvement of Arts, Commerce and Manufactures and the Edinburgh Society for Improvement.[35] The growth of organized philanthropy, which was such a pronounced feature of the mid-century, relied heavily and in a number of ways on publicity in the press, as Anne Borsay has recently stressed in her examination of the Bath Infirmary.[36] Sensitivity to the importance of publicity in the press was not new to this period, but the number of bodies and institutions systematically exploiting it grew. Groups of workers were becoming more adept at ensuring

---

[30] John Brewer, *Party Ideology and Popular Politics at the Accession of George III* (Cambridge, 1976), ch. 8.

[31] Kathleen Wilson, *The Sense of the People: Politics, Culture and Imperialism in England, 1715–1785* (Cambridge, 1995), esp. ch. 1; H. T. Dickinson, *The Politics of the People in Eighteenth-Century Britain* (1994), ch. 6.

[32] The literature on this is huge, but there is general agreement that the 1740s and 1750s represented a watershed. Thomas Munck's recent figures on book publication in London, Dublin, Glasgow, and Edinburgh, derived from the STC, underline the fact that this was the general pattern of growth (*The Enlightenment: A Comparative Social History 1721–1794* (2000), 91–2).

[33] Hannah Barker, *Newspapers, Politics and English Society 1695–1855* (1999), 36–7.

[34] PRO, T1/431/103.

[35] Peter Clark has recently emphasized the importance of the press in the flowering of associational life in Britain in the eighteenth century (*British Clubs and Societies 1580–1800: The Origins of an Associational World* (Oxford, 2000)).

[36] Anne Borsay, *Medicine and Charity in Georgian Bath: A Social History of the General Infirmary, c1739–1830* (Aldershot and Brookfield, V.t, 1999), esp. pp. 42–5.

their case was articulated in the press as an important aspect of labour disputes.[37] Even more striking is the use of the press by various religious groups. The evangelical religious awakening of the early 1740s was a transoceanic development, stretching from Britain to the new world in America. Evangelicals deliberately used the press to provide a 'synoptic, even cosmic, view of the revival as a whole'.[38] In the process, they showed very clearly how the mid-century press could be used to create widely extended circuits of communication, thereby also expanding the realm of the imagination far beyond the boundaries of locality and even nation.

The mid-century political world was, then, one of considerable depth and significance, especially when we move the focus away from the battles of politicians for office and power which tend to dominate traditional perceptions of the politics of this period. It was also a world of much uncertainty. Political stability did not mean tranquillity, or an absence of apprehension. John Cannon has recently argued that the notion of political stability does, nevertheless, continue to have relevance to early-Hanoverian politics, and that historians should be wary of passing over too quickly the very real difference in the mood of politics between the later seventeenth and early eighteenth centuries and the middle of the latter century.[39] As Cannon himself points out, much depends on how we define stability. It is possible to argue, nevertheless, that the surface calm of political life for much of the final years of George II's reign is potentially very misleading. One of the most important themes in political life in this period was a sense of mounting vulnerability to French international ambition and military power. This interacted with, and framed, a whole series of other anxieties about the capacity of British society and the Hanoverian regime to resist the French threat. Some of the fears about French power and ambition seem exaggerated in retrospect, and there was an element of paranoia about them. In 1756, in the context of the invasion scare of the early months of that year, Lord Tyrawly was anxious that French servants, dancing masters, and hairdressers should be moved out of London, since, in his eyes, they represented a French fifth column at the heart of the British state.[40] Contemporaries were captive of their own preconceptions about the French state, and French international interests. Fears of the French also, however, reflected the course of war and international rivalry. The War of the Austrian Succession was notable by the abrupt fluctuations in military and diplomatic fortunes of the participating powers. The course of

---

[37] See e.g. Keith Wrightson and David Levine, *The Making of an Industrial Society: Whickham, 1560–1765* (Oxford, 1991), 375–427.

[38] W. R. Ward, *The Protestant Evangelical Awakening* (Cambridge, 1992), 336. See also Michael J. Crawford, *Seasons of Grace: Colonial New England's Revival Tradition in its British Context* (New York, 1991); NLS, MS 1954, Minutes of the Edinburgh Reformation of Manners Society, 1740–5.

[39] John Cannon, *Samuel Johnson and the Politics of Hanoverian England* (Oxford, 1994), 255–6.

[40] BL, Egerton MS 3444, fos. 64–70: 'Some Considerations humbly offered to HRH the Duke by Lord Tyrawly, Feb 1756'.

the Seven Years War was, in some respects, more straightforward, although here what deserves special emphasis is the startling reversal of British military fortunes, as contemporaries saw it, from 1758. When it arrived, success in the war was also a much closer run thing than it can be made to seem in retrospect.[41]

Attitudes towards Anglo-French rivalry were unstable and contradictory. It was possible to celebrate the unique freedoms and security of property created by Britain's constitution and the unexampled stimulus this provided to commercial expansion and ever-increasing prosperity. At the same time, however, there was a growing fear—certainly before the latter phases of the Seven Years War—that rapid French commercial expansion since 1713 would destroy the basis of British prosperity and security. In the early 1750s, there was also anxious praise for the role of the centralized French state in the spheres of colonial government and commercial matters. This sat uneasily alongside a growing conviction that restrictions on commerce, such as monopolies, were impeding commercial growth.[42] Contemporaries celebrated the benevolence and public spirit of Britons in giving to organized philanthropy. Yet they also looked for reassurance about the state of society in the face of fears that rapid commercialization was dissolving the habits, values, and order on which the cohesion, liberties, and future of the nation depended. The Revd John Brown identified 'honour' as one of the defining features of French society, contrasting this with what he saw, like many others, as the crude materialism of English society and its absorption in the twin delusions of money and pleasure. It was a comparison which led one critic to exclaim: 'The meanest Briton would wish to live free under all the ills which Dr Brown describes, rather than be a Frenchman and a slave.'[43] The 'luxury' of the poor was a central anxiety of the age. The growing conviction that the population was declining; waves of protests about food prices in 1756–7, unprecented in scale and number; the anti-militia riots of 1757, which manifested a disturbing 'levelling spirit' amongst the lower orders; and major labour disputes in the west country woollen industry in 1756; all these things only reinforced the widespread concern about the condition of the labouring poor—the ultimate basis of British power and prosperity. Others, meanwhile, faced with evidence

---

[41] See the analysis offered in R. Middleton, *The Bells of Victory: The Pitt–Newcastle Ministry and the Conduct of the Seven Years' War, 1757–1762* (Cambridge, 1985).

[42] The liberalization of economic life was as yet limited and uneven. Yet the trend was becoming increasingly evident, although contemporary tendencies in this context were often contradictory. This is highlighted by the Westminster fish market, which, as we saw in Chapter 6, was created under legislation passed in 1749. The market was an open one in order to undermine monopolies and, thus, improve the supply and lower the price of fish in the market. At the same time, however, increasingly elaborate regulations were imposed on supplying and selling in the market to defeat the efforts of fishmongers to manipulate supply and prices. There is a good account of the fish market and the problems it encountered in the *Gentleman's Magazine* (1760), 256–8.

[43] *The Real Character of the Age, in a Letter to the Rev. Dr Brown, Occasioned by his Estimate of the Manners and Principles of the Times* (1757), quoted in the *Critical Review* (1757), 532–5.

of British failure in war and alienated from the politics and personnel of the Hanoverian regime, looked to political reform to cleanse society of corruption and to revitalize public spirit. What was singular was not the specific worries, or in many cases the responses to them, but the ways in which the international context coloured how people saw them, and imparted an urgency to responding to them.

A second major theme was the sharp convergence between conceptions of the national interest and commerce from the later 1740s. The sense that Britain was rapidly changing under the impact of commerce, and that commerce represented the national interest, substantially strengthened in this period. French expansionist activities overseas also helped to clarify conceptions of the global reach of British power and interests, and awareness of the crucial role which North America had come to play in Britain's 'empire of the seas'. An increasingly important strand in public debate concerned institutional and legal reforms designed to promote commercial growth and meet the needs of a commercial society. Debates about fiscal policy were driven by a perception of the dangers of imposing high rates of taxation on trade and manufacturing. In 1757, one adviser to the Duke of Newcastle talked of seeking a 'Regulating standard for Taxes in a commercial state'.[44] Commerce was a cause which transcended political divisions, hence the breadth of enthusiasm for initiatives such as the Free British Fishery Society. William Tindal later noted of the bill which established the Society (passed in 1750): 'It is incredible with what ardour the news of this Bill passing, was received by the public'.[45] Commerce was invested with enormous transformatory potential, as well as being viewed as a source of prosperity and national security and greatness. In the 1750s, it was complex of meanings which found expression in John Dyer's georgic *The Fleece* (1757), which traced, in minute detail, the production of wool and manufacture of textiles and their export throughout Britain's expanding maritime empire. There is a potent sense in Dyer's poem of the expansive potential of commerce, of a trading world stretching across the globe, creating peace, harmony, and prosperity in its wake.

Alexander Murdoch has suggested that in the eighteenth century being British came to be defined in increasingly secular terms, partly because of the growth of commerce and the meanings which were attached to it.[46] Yet commerce was portrayed in ambivalent, often contradictory terms, and we need to be very careful about how we conceive of the influence of the contemporary 'cult of commerce' on the language and imagery of political discourse. In the first place, one of the reasons why commerce was so readily projected as the national interest was that there was no perceived tension between this and the continued hegemony and rule of the landed classes in society. The

---

[44] BL, Add. MS 32875, fo. 349.
[45] *Parl. Hist.*, xiv. 763.
[46] Alexander Murdoch, *British History 1660–1832: National Identity and Local Culture* (1998), 65.

conviction that only landownership provided the personality and outlook suited to political leadership also remained very strongly present. Landed gentry had a fixed interest in the nation; they also had the independence and education to conceive of a national interest which subsumed, and might conflict with, the myriad of particular interests which comprised the nation. How to make commerce or commercial society 'virtuous' was also a central problem of the period. It was a problem heightened by two decades of continuous war and international rivalry.

Various answers were forthcoming. One of these was to contrast a world of elite leisure and moral dissolution with that of commerce and the industrious, moral middling ranks—to portray it as essentially a problem of the manners and morals of the upper ranks. Conceived in such terms, the solution was simple—to reform the morals and manners of the elites. Parliament, meanwhile, passed several pieces of legislation which aimed to undermine the 'luxury' of the poor, and to improve the 'policing' of society. At the level of the individual behaviour and motivation, the philanthropic enthusiasm and disposition of London merchants have been well noted in recent years.[47] It is dangerous for any period in the past to advance one factor as the principal motivation behind charitable activity. Nevertheless, it seems very likely that this was so marked because it was a way of demonstrating 'public virtue' and that the pursuit of profit did not necessarily undermine a capacity to support the public good. In John Money's words, it helped the middling ranks form 'their own sense of moral responsibility in a society which they themselves were changing irrevocably'.[48] It also represented a means of shoring up social hierarchy, or so it was believed.[49] Merchants and other members of the middling sort were not meekly following the lead of the landed classes in wishing for this; social order and peace were very much in their own interest.

The language used to describe Britain's international interests was also less straightforward than might, at first sight, appear. Concern about commerce and commercial growth certainly figured significantly in debates about war and foreign affairs. Considerations of national prosperity and national security were also usually viewed as inseparable, but it was security which was, in the last resort, viewed as most important. Notions of national honour and glory also heavily coloured attitudes towards war. As Philip Lawson has emphasized, there was an evident need to clothe British actions overseas in a more dignified language than one concerned only solely with commercial

---

[47] Donna T. Andrew, *Philanthropy and Police: London Charity in the Eighteenth Century* (Princeton, NJ, 1989).

[48] Money, 'The Masonic Moment', 361.

[49] This was an important theme in charity sermons in this period. See e.g. *A Sermon Preached at the Cathedral of Glocester [sic] At the Opening of the Infirmary, on Thursday, August 14, 1755. By the Honourable and Reverend George Talbot, Minister of Temple-Guiting* (1755); *A Sermon Preached at the Parish Church of St Anne Westminster, on Thursday, April the 29th, 1752 Before the Governors of the Middlesex Hospital. By John Thomas, LL.D.* (1752).

and material interests.⁵⁰ This, in turn, was a symptom of the underlying complexity of attitudes towards the relationship between commerce and the national interest, and of the different ways in which widespread and often intense concerns about morals and public virtue pressed hard on debates about war and international affairs.

The health and progress of society also continued to be viewed in religious as well as secular terms. It is a fact which is easily overlooked, especially if we view political culture largely through the prism of contemporary newspapers and pamphlets. These usually, but far from always, portrayed politics and public life from secular perspectives. Yet taking a broader view, what stands out about this period, and indeed others in the eighteenth century, is the way in which secular and religious viewpoints and languages were frequently mutually reinforcing and overlapping if not inseparable. Britain's Protestant identity—which went unquestioned before the early 1770s—was inextricably intertwined with its libertarian and developing commercial identity. Just as Popery and tyranny were co-joined in the contemporary imagination, so were Protestantism, liberty, property, and commercial progress. It was a relationship that was made most explicit in this period in Ireland and Scotland. To transform the Catholic Irish into loyal British subjects meant converting them to industry *and* Protestantism; amongst the disaffected clans in the Highlands, it meant conversion to industry *and* Presbyterianism. The language of virtue and public spirit should also be seen in more than secular terms, as has been emphasized at various points in this book. Indeed, one of the reasons why it exercised such a tenacious hold on contemporary perceptions was that it could be so easily interpreted in religious terms. To many, the only proper basis for true public virtue was religious conviction. Secular and religious conceptions of national fortunes in war could also easily be reconciled through the notion of the providential ordering of history and the history of the British nation in particular. It is this intertwining of perspectives which further helps to explain why war had such a huge impact on contemporary attitudes and perceptions, and why the temper of public opinion was so changeable and so closely influenced by the shifting conditions of war and diplomacy. Fear and optimistism vied for supremacy in the 1740s and 1750s, often within the same mind. The challenge for any historian is to understand the problems, prejudices, ideologies, contradictions, and tensions which produced this state, and which made reviving the nation appear to be such an urgent task to many contemporaries until, with the accession of George III, it appeared—for a short time at least—as if Britain stood on the threshold of a new era of national prosperity, security, and harmony.

⁵⁰ Philip Lawson, ' "Arts and Empire Equally Extend": Tradition, Prejudice and Assumption in the Eighteenth-Century Press Coverage of Empire', in id., *A Taste for Empire and Glory: Studies in British Overseas Expansion, 1660–1800* (Aldershot and Brookville, Vt., 1997), 140.

Appendix 1.
Irish Patriot Addresses, 1754

Place	From	Source
Strabane	burgesses and other gentlemen	*Universal Advertiser*, 1 January
Newry	gentlemen, freemen, and freeholders	*Universal Advertiser*, 5 January
Longford		*Universal Advertiser*, 5 January
Killileagh		*Universal Advertiser*, 8 January
Navan	freeholders of Meath	*Universal Advertiser*, 19 January
Lisburn	inhabitants	*Universal Advertiser*, 19 January
Roscommon	gentlemen of county (met in Dublin)	*Universal Advertiser*, 22 January
Maryborough	corporation	*Universal Advertiser*, 28 January
Portarlington		*Universal Advertiser*, 29 January
Newtonlemevady		*Belfast Newsletter*, 1 March
Downpatrick	borough and freeholders in neighbourhood	*Universal Advertiser*, 2 February
Downpatrick	inhabitants and independent freeholders	*Belfast Newsletter*, 12 February
Carrickfergus	corporation	*Universal Advertiser*, 5 February
Carrickfergus	incorporated societies	*Universal Advertiser*, 5 February
Carrickfergus	court and grand jury	*Belfast Newsletter*, 29 January
Belfast	free and independent inhabitants to Boyle	*Universal Advertiser*, 5 February
Belfast	free and independent inhabitants to Bernard Ward and Arthur Upton	*Universal Advertiser*, 5 February
Cork	JPs, etc. to Boyle and Hyde	*Universal Advertiser*, 7 February
Cork	truly free and independent freeholders, freemen, merchants, and inhabitants to MPs	*Universal Advertiser*, 23 February
Cashel	mayor and citizens	*Universal Advertiser*, 12 February
Waterford	county	*Universal Advertiser*, 16 February
Rotoath		*Universal Advertiser*, 23 February
Youghall	corporation	*Universal Advertiser*, 2 March
Cavan	independent freeholders, burgesses, and freemen	*Universal Advertiser*, 5 March
Ardee (County Louth)	resolution of thanks to MPs	*Universal Advertiser*, 9 March

Sligo	principal gentlemen of county	*Universal Advertiser*, 26 March
Londonderry	assizes	*Universal Advertiser*, 16 April
Londonderry	mayor and corporation to MP for Coleraine	*Belfast Newsletter*, 1 March
Fintona	freeholders of manor to William Hamilton, MP for Strabane	*Universal Advertiser*, 16 April
Longford	sheriff and grand jury	*Universal Advertiser*, 27 April
Kildare	gentlemen and freeholders	*Universal Advertiser*, 27 April
Westmeath	gentlemen and freeholders (assizes)	*Universal Advertiser*, 4 May
Kerry	principal gentlemen and freeholders (Tralee)	*Universal Advertiser*, 11 May
King's County	gentlemen and freeholders (Clara)	*Universal Advertiser*, 11 May
Enniskillen	corporation, address to Boyle	*Universal Advertiser*, 25 June
Cork	High Sheriff, grand jury, and freeholders (assizes)	*Universal Advertiser*, 5 October
Bandon		*Universal Advertiser*, 30 December

Dublin
Corporation of Hosiers
merchants and tradesmen
Corporation of Taylors
Corporation of Coopers
Corporation of Butchers
Guild of Merchants
Corporation of Tallow Chandlers
Corporation of Shoemakers
Grand Jury of Commissioner of Oyer and Terminer
Principal citizens, address to Samuel Cooke

Appendix 2.
Irish Patriot Toasts

The following toasts were drunk at a meeting of the independent freeholders of the County of Cavan, and of the burgesses and freemen of the Borough of Cavan, held in Cavan on 25 February 1754. They are entirely typical in their emphasis of loyalty, and claim to true Whig identity, of the volleys of toasts drunk by Patriots in Ireland in the mid-1750s.[1]

The King
The Prince of Wales
The Princess Dowager of Wales and all the Royal Family
The Duke and the Army
The Glorious Memory of King William
Prosperity to Ireland
May the Crown of Great Britain be perpetuated in the Illustrious House of Hanover
Prosperity to the County of Kildare and the Governor of it
The Speaker of the House of the Commons and the Majority of the 17th of December 1753
May the Misrepresenter be truly Represented
Lord Kildare and Success to all his Endeavours
May we never want a Kildare or a Boyle, to assert our Loyalty, and defend our Liberty
May the Commons of Ireland ever preserve the spirit they showed in the last sessions
The Beaver's fate to the D—— of N——
The honest Patriot Members of the County of Kildare
May the enemies of Ireland never pocket the Bread of it
The nine Gores
May the Commons of Ireland ever hold the Purse of the Nation
The Four Martyrs
Liberty and Property
The Friends of Ireland in the British Parliament
A Speedy Exportation to the Enemies of Ireland, without a Draw back

[1] Source: *Belfast Newsletter*, 9 Mar. 1754.

Liberty to those, that dare support it, and Slavery to those, that lie down to be kicked

The Author of the Vindication of the Proceeding of the House of Commons in rejecting the Money Bill, and Shame to the Libellers against it

The two Strangers at the C——e

May the Lovers of the Memory of King William always have it in their power to support the Hanoverian Succession

Confusion to the Schemes of those that assume the Names of Whigs and act on Tory Principles

All those who were honest in the Worst of Times, and dare continue so

May the Lovers of Liberty never want Power of Property in Ireland

May all high Priests, that have the Ambition of Wolsey, meet with the fate of Laud

May Liberty, and Loyalty ever go Hand in Hand together

Disappointment to those, who would build their Fortunes on the Country's Ruin

The P—— S—— Picture frame to the Enemies of Ireland

Dissention among, and Disappointment to, the Enemies of Ireland, especially to those, Who are the Growth of it

The Friends of Ireland in the Irish Parliament

May all antipatriot Lawyers carry empty Bags into the Four-Courts, and Empty Purses out

May all bad Men in Power be as Humber as they are now insolent

May the Misrepresenter fall into as much Disgrace, as those He has turn'd out, have gain'd Honour

May Loyalty to the House of Hanover always inspire, the Resolutions of the Parliament of Ireland

A high Wind, a lee Shore, and a leaky Vessel to the Enemies of Ireland

May the Subjects of Great Britain be as loyal to his Majesty, as the protestant Subjects of Ireland

The Memory of the Exclusioners

The Duke of Cumberland, and the 16th of April 1746

May Hemp bind those, that Honour can not

Appendix 3.
The Free British Fishery Society

Name[1]	Status/occupation	Amount
Earl of Galway	peer	£5,000
Slingsby Bethell	merchant/Alderman of City of London/MP	£1,000
Velters Cornewall	gentleman/MP	£1,000
Sir Nathaniel Curzon	gentleman/MP	£1,000
Roger Handasyde	Army/MP	£1,000
Sir John Hinde Cotton	gentleman/MP	£2,000
Thomas Fonnereau	merchant/contractor/MP	£500
Richard Gildart	merchant/Director of East India Company/MP	£?
Francis Gwynn	gentleman/MP	£?
Paul Humphry	gentleman/MP	£500
Stephen Theodore Janssen	merchant/Alderman of the City of London/MP	£2,000
Sir James Lowther	gentleman/MP	£500
William Northey	gentleman/MP	£1,000
Richard Onslow	Army/MP	£1,000
Edward Vernon	Navy/MP	£2,000
Sir Cyril Wich	merchant/MP	£2,000
Sir Bourchier Wrey	gentleman/MP	£2,000
Francis Gosling	merchant/Alderman of the City of London	£500
Sir Samuel Pennant	merchant/Alderman of the City of London	£2,000
Claud Alexander	merchant	£500
John Baldero	banker/broker	£1,000
Richard Baker	merchant/contractor/Director of East India Company	£2,000

[1] Source: BL, Add. MSS 15154–5 (Minute Books of the Free British Fishery Society). For many of the merchants the source gives an address, which allowed individuals to be identified with some certainty using trade directories searchable in the 'Biography Database, 1680–1830', published on CD-ROM by Avero Publications, Newcastle. Where identification is uncertain—usually owing to the name being a common one—this is indicated by a question mark. There are a further 34 subscribers I have not been able to identify.

John Bance	merchant/Director of Bank of England and South Sea Company	£2,000
William Bowden	merchant	£5,000
Robert Cady	merchant [?]	£1,000
Samuel Child	merchant	£1,000
Samuel Clark[e?]	merchant	£3,000
Richard Clay	merchant	£500
Michael Wilkins Conway	seaman/Navy	£2,000
Thomas Cooper	warehouseman	£700
Abraham Craisteyn	merchant/financier	£2,000
Francis Craisteyn	merchant/financier	£2,000
Robert Crammond	merchant	£10,000 plus £21,500 for 'sundry others'
James Crockatt	merchant	£1,000
William Davis	merchant [?]	£10,000
Deneusville and Schuman	merchants	£5,000
Robert Dinwiddie	gentleman/colonial governor	£1,000
Andrew Drummond	banker/contractor	£2,000
George Dunbar	Navy [?]	£2,000
Laurence Dundas	merchant/Army contractor	£1,000
John Edwards	merchant/Director of South Sea Company	£2,000
Peter Fearon	merchant	£500
Jonathan Forward	merchant	£1,000
Jeffrey French	gent/MP from 1754	£2,000
Charles Gibbon	Commissioner of the Lottery and court officer [?]	£500
Francis Grant	merchant/agent for Royal Burghs	£2,500
Alexander Grant	merchant	£2,000
Grieg and Campbell	ships chandlers	£1,000
John Harrison	merchant [?]	£500
Abraham James Hillhouse	merchant	£1,000
Roger Hogg	merchant/broker	£2,000
William Horsley	writer on trade/journalist	£1,000
William James	merchant [?]	£1,000
William Janssen	gentleman/holder of sinecure office in West Indies	£1,000
Alexander Johnson	merchant	£2,000
Claud Johnson	merchant	£1,000
Ambrose Kent	broker [?]	£500
Robert Laing	merchant	£500
Thomas Law	merchant	£1,000
John Lidderdale	merchant	£2,000
Thomas McKenzie and Co.	merchants, Dingwall	£500
Patrick and Robert Macky	merchants	£5,000

Mr Mackraby	haberdasher [?]	£100
Hutchison Mure	merchant	£2000
Herman Verelst	collector of duties payable by act for making free fishmarket in Westminster	£500
John Pattoun	merchant	£3,000
Thomas Penn	gentleman/proprietor of Colony of Pennsylvania [?]	£500
Jonathan Perrie	merchant [?]	£2,000
James Riddell	merchant	£1,000
Robert Scott	merchant	£2,000
Peter Simond	merchant	£2,000
George Spence	merchant	£2,000
Capt George Steevens	merchant	£1,000
Archibald Stewart	merchant	£2,000
Walter Stirling	merchant [?]	£500
Jonathan Sydenham	merchant	£1,000
Richard Taunton	ship owner	£5,000
Peter Taylor	merchant	£1,000
William Vaughan	merchant	£500
Francis Wilson	merchant	£500
Robert Wilson	merchant	£500
John Woodbridge	coopers	£1,000

ORIGINAL MEMBERS

Name	Status/occupation
William Belchier	banker/MP/ministerial Whig
Slingsby Bethell	Alderman/MP/opposition Whig
Sir Walter Blackett	gentleman/MP/Tory
Velters Cornewall	gentleman/MP/Tory
Sir Nathaniel Curzon	gentleman/MP/Tory
George Bubb Dodington	gentleman/MP/Leicester House
Thomas Fonnereau	merchant/contractor/MP/ministerial Whig
Richard Gildart	merchant/Director of East India Company/MP
Charles Gray	gentleman/MP/Tory
Francis Gwynn	gentleman/MP/Tory
Roger Handasyd	Army Officer/MP/Leicester House
Paul Humphry	gentleman/MP/opposition Whig [?]
Stephen Theodore Janssen	Alderman/MP/opposition Whig
Sir Richard Lloyd	lawyer/MP/ministerial Whig
Sir James Lowther	gentleman/MP/independent Whig
William Northey	gentleman/MP/Tory

[2] Source: *His Majesty's Royal Charter . . . For Incorporating the Society of the Free British Fishery* (1750).

James Edward Oglethorpe	gentleman/MP/independent
Richard Onslow	Army Officer/MP/ministerial Whig
Edward Stephenson	merchant/former MP/opposition Whig
William Thornton	gentleman/MP/independent Whig
Edward Vernon	Naval Officer/MP/independent Whig
Sir Cyril Wich	gentleman/MP
William Willy	gentleman/MP/opposition Whig
Sir Bourchier Wrey	gentleman/MP/ministerial Whig
Arthur Beardsley	merchant
Michael Beecher	Bristol merchant
Samuel Clarke	merchant
Robert Cady	merchant [?]
Theodore Cock	?
Michael Wilkins Conway	seaman/merchant
Francis Craisteyn	merchant/financier
Robert Crammond	merchant
Thomas Curtis	merchant
William Davis	merchant [?]
Peter Delme	banker/Director of Bank of England
Deneuville and Schuman	merchants
Andrew Drummond	banker/contractor
George Dunbar	Navy [?]
Laurence Dundas	contractor
John Edwards	Director of South Sea Company
Jeffrey Friensh [French?]	elected MP for Bedford in 1754
John Hardman	Liverpool merchant (MP for Liverpool, 1754–5)
Richard Hogg	merchant [?]
Edward Ironside	Alderman/banker
Robert Macky	merchant
Michael Miller	Bristol merchant
Hutchison Mure	merchant
John Pattoun	merchant
Joseph Percival	?
Jonathan Perrie	merchant [?]
Thomas Salisbury	Judge of the Admiralty Court [?]
Robert Scott	merchant/Alderman
Peter Simond	merchant
George Spence	merchant
John Spooner	merchant
Capt George Steevens	merchant
Richard Taunton	shipowner
George Walker	shipmaster, commander of Royal Family Privateers in War of the Austrian Succession
Jonathan Watson	?
William Whitaker	merchant/Alderman
Taylor White	lawyer/judge [?]

COMMITTEE ELECTED TO CONSIDER PROPOSALS AND
PLAN TO BE SUBMITTED TO PARLIAMENT, 1749

Name	Status/occupation
George Arnold	merchant/former Alderman of the City of London/Sheriff of London, 1740–51
John Bance	merchant/Director of East India Company and Bank of England
William Bowden	merchant
Sir James Creed	merchant/MP
James Crockatt	merchant
Mr Wilkins Conway	seaman/merchant
Robert Crammond	merchant
John Edwards	Director of South Sea Company
Rowland Frye	merchant
Thomas Godfrey	Merchant/Director of South Sea Company of London Assurance Company
Thomas Hyam	merchant
Edward Ironside	banker/Alderman of the City of London
Robert Jones	Director of East India Company [?]
Claude Johnson	merchant
Ralph Knox	dir of Royal Exchange Assurance Company
Nicholas Magens	dir of London Assurance Company
Robert Macky	merchant
Peter Thomas	Director of Bank of England
Thomas Winterbottom	merchant/Alderman of the City of London/ Director of Bank of England
George Wombwell	merchant/Director of East India Company

ORIGINAL COUNCIL, 1749

Name	Status/occupation
Slingsby Bethell, President	MP/opposition Whig/Alderman of the City of London
Stephen Theodore Janssen, Vice President	MP/opposition Whig/Alderman of the City of London
Richard Baker	merchant/contractor/Director of Bank of England and South Sea Company
Robert Bootle	merchant/Director of East India Company
William Bowden	merchant
Michael Wilkins Conway	seaman/merchant
Velters Cornewall	MP/Tory
Francis Craisteyn	merchant/financier
Robert Crammond	merchant
Sir Nathaniel Curzon	MP/Tory

William Davis	merchant [?]
George Bubb Dodington	MP/Leicester House
Andrew Drummond	banker/contractor
George Dunbar	Navy [?]
John Edwards	Director of South Sea Company
Francis Gwynn	MP/Tory
Roger Handasyd	Army Officer/MP/Leicester House
Roger Hogg	merchant
Claud Johnson	merchant
John Lidderdale	merchant
William Northey	MP/Tory
James Edward Oglethorpe	MP/independent
Charles Raymond	merchant
Simon Rogers	?
George Steevens	merchant
John Turner	merchant
John Vaughan	Navy [?]
Edward Vernon	Navy/MP/independent Whig
Jonathan Watson	?
Sir Bourchier Wrey	MP/ministerial Whig

COUNCIL MEMBERS, 1753

Name	Status/occupation	Number of votes
Earl of Shaftesbury	peer/Tory	181
Nathaniel Curzon	MP/Tory	181
Sir Bourchier Wrey	MP/ministerial Whig	181
Sir Richard Hoare	banker	181
Sir James Creed	MP/merchant/future Director of Marine Society	181
Francis Craisteyn	merchant/financier	181
George Bowes	MP/independent Whig	181
William Beckford	MP/Tory/merchant/Alderman of the City of London	181
George Bubb Dodington	MP	181
Andrew Drummond	banker/contractor	181
John Edwards	Director of South Sea Company	181
Roger Handasyde	Army Officer/MP	181
William Northey	MP/Tory	181
John Tucker	MP/Whig	181
John Vaughan	Navy [?]	181
Sir Walter Blackett	MP/Tory	180
Velters Cornewall	MP/Tory	179
Capt. Thomas Collett	Navy	179
Capt. Charles Raymond	merchant	179

John Lidderdale	merchant	178
Capt. John Hallett	?	177
Robert Bootle	merchant/Director of East India Company	175
Francis Treg[a]gle	?	111
William Sloane	?	101
William Swinburn	?	101
John Bennet	merchant	101
Thomas Gordon	merchant	99
Edward Godfrey	?	98
William Watson	merchant	96
Solomon Ashley	merchant	85
Capt. Samuel Hough	?	84
John March	merchant	84
Henry Savage	merchant/Director of East India Company	84
Samuel Jones	merchant [?]	83
Capt. Michael Wilkins Conway	seaman/merchant	82
Lewis Way	banker	77

Bibliography

UNPUBLISHED PRIMARY SOURCES

A. K. Bell Public Library, Perth

Material Relating to Jacobites
Perth Burgh, miscellaneous

Avon Public Library, Bristol

Southwell Papers

Bodleian Library, Oxford

Dashwood Papers
Johnson Ballads
Tucker Papers

British Library

Add. MS 26238, correspondence of George Osborne relating to the *True Briton*
Egerton MS (Holdernesse Papers)
Egmont Papers
Hardwicke Papers
Holland House Papers
Kings MS 433
Minute Books of the Free British Fishery Society
Newcastle Papers

Cambridge University Library

Cholmondeley Houghton Papers
Cumberland Papers (microfilm)
Madden Collection

Corporation of London Record Office, Guildhall

Journals of the Court of Common Council
Repertories of the Court of Aldermen

Cumberland Record Office, Carlisle

Lonsdale Papers

Dundee Archives and Records Centre

Dundee Burgh Treasurers' Account Books
Dundee General Session Minutes

Edinburgh City Archives

Moses Collection, miscellaneous papers of the Convention of Royal Burghs

Greater London Record Office

Middlesex sessions books
Process register of indictments

Lancashire Record Office, Preston

DDK 1741/7

Linenhall Library, Belfast

Joy Papers

Public Record Office

Entry Books, Criminal (SP 44)
George II (SP 36)
King's Bench Papers, (KB 1, KB 33)
State Papers Domestic
State Papers Scotland (SP 54)
Treasury Board Papers (T 1)
Treasury Solicitors Papers (TS 11)

Public Record Office of Northern Ireland

Bedford Papers, official and personal correspondence of the Duke of Bedford, Lord
    Lieutenant, 1757–61
Carberry Papers
Castleward Papers, personal and estate papers of the Ward family, County Down
Chatsworth Papers
Emly Papers
Harrowby Papers, Irish correspondence of Sir Dudley Ryder

Shannon Papers, personal and official papers of Henry Boyle, first Earl of Shannon
State Papers Ireland
Wilmot Papers

National Archives of Scotland, Edinburgh

Church of Scotland, Records of the General Assembly; Records of the Commission
   of the General Assembly; Records of the Presbytery of Edinburgh; Records of the
   Presbtery of Perth; Records of the Presbtery of Dunfermline; Minute Book of the
   Presbytery of Paisley; Records of the Presbtery of Forfar; Records of the Synod of
   Glasgow and Ayr; Register Book of the Synod of Galloway
Clerk of Penicuick Papers
Grant of Monymusk Papers
Mar and Kellie Papers
Records of the Board of Trustees for Fisheries and Manufactures
Seafield Papers
State Papers Scotland

National Library of Scotland

Culloden Papers
Erskine Murray Papers
Letter Book of Andrew Lumisden
Letter Books of Generals Bland and Churchill
Minutes of the Edinburgh Reformation of Manners Society, 1740–5
Saltoun Papers
Yester Papers

Nottingham University Library

Newcastle (Clumber) Papers

Shropshire Records and Research Unit

Bridgnorth Borough, Bailiffs' and Chamberlains' Accounts

University of St Andrew's Archives

St Andrew's Burgh Records, supplementary papers

Warwickshire Record Office

Newdigate Papers
Sanderson-Miller Papers

NEWSPAPERS AND PERIODICALS

England and Wales

London

British Magazine
Champion
Common Sense, or, the Englishman's Journal
Con-Test
Covent Garden Journal
Craftsman
Critical Review
Daily Advertiser
Daily Gazetteer
Daily Post
General Advertiser
General Evening Post
General London Evening Mercury
Gentleman's Magazine
Grand Magazine
Gray's Inn Journal
Jacobites Journal
London Chronicle
London Courant, or, New Advertiser
London Daily Post and General Advertiser
London Evening Post
London Gazette
London Magazine
Mitre and Crown
Monitor, or the British Freeholder
Monthly Review
National Journal, or the Country Gazette
Penny London Post
Protestor, on Behalf of the People
Remembrancer
Old England, or the Constitutional Journal
St James's Evening Post
Test
True Briton
True Patriot
Westminster Journal, or the New Weekly Miscellany
Whitehall Evening Post

Provincial

Bristol Journal
Country Advertiser (Bristol)

Derby Mercury
Felix Farley's Bristol Journal
Henry's Reading Journal, or Weekly Review
Ipswich Journal
Jackson's Oxford Journal
Kentish Post, or Canterbury News Letter
Manchester Magazine
Newcastle Courant
Newcastle Gazette
Newcastle Journal
Northampton Mercury
Preston Weekly Journal
Reading Mercury, or Weekly Post
True British Courant or Preston Journal

Scotland

Aberdeen Journal
Caledonian Mercury
Edinburgh Chronicle
Edinburgh Evening Courant
Glasgow Courant
Glasgow Journal
Scots Magazine

Ireland

Belfast Newsletter
The Censor, or the Citizen's Journal
Cork Gazette
Dublin Gazette
Faulkener's Dublin Journal
The Freeman's Journal
Universal Advertiser

PUBLISHED

Primary Sources

'An Account of the Life and Writings of Dr John Shebbeare', *The European Magazine* (Aug. 1788), 83–7, 167–8, 244–5.
Bolingbroke's Political Writings: The Conservative Enlightenment, ed. Bernard Cottret (1997).
The British Linen Company, 1745–1775, ed. A. J. Durie, *Publications of the Scottish History Society*, 5th ser., 9 (Edinburgh, 1996).
Clerk of Penicuik Memoirs, 1676–1755, *Publications of the Scottish Record Society*, 13 (1892).

The Correspondence of the Dukes of Richmond and Newcastle, 1724–1750, ed. T. J. McCann (Lewes, 1984).

The Diaries of Thomas Wilson, DD, ed. C. L. S. Linnell (1964).

The Diary of Richard Kay, 1716–51 of Baldinstone near Bury: A Lancashire Doctor, ed. Frank Brockbank and F. Kenworthy, Publications of the Chetham Society, 3rd ser., 16 (Manchester, 1968).

The Diary of Thomas Turner 1754–65, ed. David Vaisey (Oxford, 1984).

'Extracts from the Diary of the Rev John Bisset, Minister at Aberdeen, 1745–6', *The Miscellany of the Spalding Club*, i (Aberdeen, 1891),.

Extracts from the Records of the Convention of Royal Burghs of Scotland, 1711–38 (Edinburgh, 1885).

Extracts from the Records of the Convention of Royal Burghs of Scotland, 1738–59 (Edinburgh, 1905).

Fielding, Henry, *An Inquiry into the Late Increase of Robbers and Related Writings*, ed. Malvin Zirker (Oxford, 1988).

Glover, Richard, *Memoirs of a Celebrated Literary and Political Character from the Resignation of Sir Robert Walpole, in 1742, to the Establishment of Lord Chatham's Second Administration, in 1757, containing Strictures on some of the most Distinguished men of that Time* (1873).

Henry Fox, First Lord Holland. His Family and Relations, ed. Earl of Ilchester (1920).

Hogarth's Graphic Works: Compiled with a Commentary by Ronald Paulson (1989).

Hume, David *Essays: Moral, Political and Literary* (Oxford, 1963).

Journals of the House of Commons

Journals of the House of Lords

Justice in Eighteenth-Century Hackney: The Justicing Notebook of Henry Norris and the Hackney Petty Sessions, ed. Ruth Paley (London Records Society, 1991).

'A Leicester House Political Diary 1742–3', ed. R. Harris, *Camden Miscellany*, xxxi, 4th Ser., 44 (1992), 375–411.

'Leicester House Politics, 1750–60, From the Papers of John, Second Earl of Egmont', ed. Aubrey Newman, *Camden Miscellany*, xxiii, 4th Ser. (1967), 85–228.

The Letters of Lord Chief Baron Edward Willes to the Earl of Warwick 1757–62: An Account of Ireland in the Mid Eighteenth Century (Aberystwyth, 1988).

Letters to Henry Fox, Lord Holland, with a few Addressed to his Brother, Stephen, Earl of Ilchester, ed. Earl of Ilchester (1915).

The Memoirs and Speeches of James, 2nd Earl Waldegrave, 1742–1763, ed. J. C. D. Clark (Cambridge, 1988).

Notices and Documents Illustrative of the Literary History of Glasgow, During the Greater Part of Last Century (Glasgow, 1831).

'The Opening of the Radcliffe Library in 1749', *Bodleian Library Quarterly*, i (1915), 165–72.

The Parliamentary History of England from the Earliest Period to the Year 1803, ed. William Cobbett and J. Wright (36 vols., 1806–20).

The Political Journal of George Bubb Dodington, ed. John Carswell and Lewis A. Dralle (Oxford, 1965).

Royal Commission on Historical Manuscripts (HMC), *Charlemont MS*, vol i.

—— *Correspondence of Philip Doddridge, D.D. (1702–51)*.

—— *Egmont Diary*, iii.

—— *Polwarth MS*.

—— *Stopford-Sackville MS.*

—— *Trevor MS.*

Sessional Papers of the Eighteenth Century, viii, *George II, Bills 1742–7*, ed Sheila Lambert (Wilmington, Del., 1975).

Thompson, Captain Edward, *The Poems and Miscellaneous Compositions of Paul Whitehead with Explanatory Notes on his Writings and Life* (1777).

Tory and Whig: The Parliamentary Papers of Edward Harley, Third Earl of Oxford and William Hay, MP for Seaford, 1716–1753, ed. Stephen Taylor and Clyve Jones (Bury St Edmunds, 1998).

Walpole, Horace, *Memoirs of the Reign of King George II*, ed. John Brooke (3 vols., New Haven, Conn. and London, 1985)

—— *The Yale Edition of Horace Walpole's Correspondence*, ed. W.S. Lewis, *et al.* (34 vols., New Haven, Conn., 1937–70).

Walton, James, *The King's Business: Letters on the Adminstration of Ireland, 1740–1761, from the Papers of Sir Robert Wilmot* (New York, 1996).

Watt, Christian, *The Christian Watt Papers*, ed. David Fraser (Collieston, 1988).

Wesley, John, *The Works of John Wesley*, xx–xxii, ed. W. R. Ward and R. P. Heitzenrater (Nashville, Tenn., 1991–3).

—— *The Works of John Wesley*, xxvi, *Letters II, 1740–1755*, ed. Frank Baker (Oxford, 1982).

Yorke, Philip C., *The Life and Correspondence of Philip Yorke, Earl of Hardwicke* (3 vols., Cambridge, 1913).

Pamphlets, Broadside, Sermons

Arranged chronologically. Publication is in London unless otherwise stated.

England and Wales

Hales, Stephen, *A Friendly Admonition to the Drinkers of Brandy, and other Distilled Spirituous Liquors* (1734).

Wilson, Thomas, *Spirituous Liquors the Bane of the Nation* (1736).

An Impartial Enquiry into the Reasonableness and Necessity of a Bill for Reducing and Limiting the Number of Places in the House of Commons (1739).

Some Useful Observations on the Consequences of War with Spain (1739).

The Consequence of Trade, as to the Wealth and Strength of our Nation (1740).

An Enquiry into the Melancholy Circumstances of Great Britain (1740?).

A Letter to a Member of Parliament Concerning the Present State of Affairs at Home and Abroad (1740).

The Livery Man: Or Plain Thoughts on Public Affairs (1740).

Lord Marchmont, *A Serious Exhortation to the Electors of Great Britain* (1740).

Morrell, T., *The Surest Grounds for Hopes of Success in War. A Sermon, Preached at Kew Chapel, on January 9, 1739–40. Being the Day Appointed for a General Fast* (1740).

Partington, John, *The Right Improvment of a Publick Fast. A Sermon, Occasioned by the Late Declaration of War against Spain, Preached at Founders Hall, January 9, 1739/40* (1740).

A Serious Address to the Electors of Great Britain (1740?).

Bentley, William, *The Lord's Mark, the Saint's Protection of all Times: A Sermon Preached on the 4th of February; Being the Day Appointed for His Majesty's Proclamatioin for a General Fast, On Occasion of the Present War with Spain, in Crispin Street, Spittalfields* (1741)

Clarke, Reuben, *A Sermon Preach'd Before the Honourable House of Commons, at St Margaret's, Westminster, on Wednesday, Feb. 4, 1740–1, Being the Day Appointed by his Majesty's Proclamation for a General Fast, on Occasion of the Present War with Spain* (1741).

An Essay on the Ways and Means For Improving the Inland Navigation and Increasing the Number of Sailors in Great Britain (1741).

Great Britain's Memorial: A Collection of Instructions etc. to the Members of Parliament, Part I (1741).

The Groans of Germany: Or, an Enquiry of a Protestant German into the Original Cause of the Present Distractions of the Empire (1741).

Campbell, John, *The Case of the Opposition Impartially Stated* (1742).

Great Britain's Memorial . . . Part II (1742).

Hughes, Obadiah, *Obedience to God the Best Security Against Our Enemies: A Fast Sermon Preached in Maid Lane, in Southwark, Nov. 10, 1742* (1742).

A Key to the Business of the Present S[essio]n (1742).

A Letter to a Member of this New Parliament From a True Lover of the Liberties of the People (1742).

Middleton, Conyers, *The History of the Life of Marcus Tullius Cicero, 2 vols (1742)*

The New Ministry. Containing a Collection of all the Satyrical Poems, Songs, &c since the Beginning of 1742 (1742).

A Poem (1742).

A Second Letter to a Member of Parliament Concerning the Present State of Affairs (1741).

Stukeley, William, *National Judgements the Consequence of a National Profanation of the Sabbath* (1742).

Beef and Butt Beer, against Mum and Pumpernickle (1743).

BRITAIN'S Triumph, or Monsieur Defeated [ballad] (1743).

Bumper to Old England, Huzza. A New Drinking Song (1743).

Burrington, George, *Seasonable Considerations on the Expediency of a War with France* (1743).

A Letter to a Great Man in France (1743).

Maddox, Isaac, *The Duty and Advantages of Encouraging Publick Infirmaries. Preached Before the President and Governors of the London Infirmary, 25 March 1743* 3rd edn. (1743).

A New Bloody Ballad on the Bloody Battle of Dettingen. Printed in BLOODY CHARACTERS (1743).

A New Song on the Sharp and Bloody Battle of Dettingen (1743).

Old England's Te Deum (1743).

Stennett, Joseph, *A Sermon Preach'd in Little Wild Street, the 17th of July, 1743. Being the Day Appointed, By their Excellencies the Lord Justices, For Returning Thanks to Almighty God, For the Late Glorious Victory Obtained by His Majesty at Dettingen* (1743).

A True Dialogue between a Trooper and Serjeant (1743).

The YELLOW SASH, or H——R BESHIT. An Excellent New Ballad (1743).

An Address to the People of Great Britain (1744).

Considerations on the Politics of France (1744).

Decker, Matthew, *Essays on the Causes of the Decline in Foreign Trade* (1744).

—— Decker, Matthew, *Serious Considerations on the Several High Duties which the Nation in General, as well as its TRADE in particular Labours Under*, 2nd edn. (1744).

Denne, John, *A Sermon Preached in the Parish Church of St Mary, Lambeth, upon April 11, 1744 . . . by John Denne, D.D., Rector of the Said Parish, and Archdeacon of Rochester* (1744).

French Perfidy Illustrated in General, But Particularly in the Present Intended Invasion and the State of Dunkirk (1744).

French Snakes in British Clover (1744).

Hancox, James, *The Safety of a Good Prince* (1744).

The Jubilade—an Ode (1744).

A Letter to a Friend Concerning the Electorate of Hanover (1744).

The Manifesto of a Certain Power (1744).

The Political Views of the Court of France, Shewing the Perfidious Conduct of the French (1744).

Warning to the Whigs, and to Well-Affected Tories (1744).

Wilson, Bernard, *A Sermon Preached at Newark, Nottinghamshire, On Wednesday April 11, 1744. Being the Day Appointed by Majesty's Royal Proclamation for a General Fast* (1744).

Amory, Thomas, *The Prayer of King Jehosophat Considered and Aplied to the State of the Nation: In a Sermon Preached at Taunton, December 18, 1745. On Occasion of the Publick Fast* (1745).

Arrowsmith, E., *God's Judgement Considered, as to the Nature and End that Should be Made Use of Them. A Sermon Preach'd at the Parish Church of St Olave, Hart Street, on the 17th of December, 1745. Being the Fast Day on Account of the War* (1745).

Christmas Chat: Or, Observations on the Late Change at Court (1745).

Considerations Addressed to the Publick (1745).

Considerations on the State of the British Fisheries in America (1745).

The Court Bargain (1745).

The Folly and Danger of the Present Associations Demonstrated (1745).

A Letter to a Certain Foreign Minister; in which the Grounds of the Present War are Truly Stated (1745).

Lisle, Samuel, *A Sermon Preached Before the House of Lords in the Abby Church of Westminster, On Wednesday, Dec 18, Being the Day Appointed by His Majesty's Royal Proclamation for a General Fast* (1745).

Miscellaneous Thoughts, Moral and Political, Upon the Vices and Follies of the Present Age (1745).

Place Book For the Year Seventeen-Hundred, Forty-Five. A New Court Ballad (1745).

The Present State of the British and French Trade to Africa and America Consider'd and Compar'd (1745).

Remarks Occasion'd by the Plain Reasoner (1745).

Auchmuty, Robert, *The Importance of Cape Breton Consider'd, in a Letter from an Inhabitant of New England* (1746).

Bollan, William, *The Importance and Advantages of Cape Breton, Truly Stated and Impartially Considered* (1746).

The Great Importance of Cape Breton Demonstrated and Exemplified (1746).

Hargreaves, Robert, *Unanimity and Public Spirit, Recommended in Two Sermons. The First Preach'd September the 22d, 1745, the Sunday before the Association at York. The Second Preached December the 18th, 1745, The Fast Day* (York, 1746).

The Present Conduct of Great Britain (1746).

The SEQUEL of ARMS and the MAN: A New Historical BALLAD (1746).

Squire, Samuel, *The Important Question Discussed: Or A Serious and Impartial Enquiry into the True Interest of England with respect to the Continent* (1746).

A True Copy of the Paper read by Mr James Bradshaw and delivered by him to the Sheriff of Surry just before his Execution at Kennington Common on Friday, November the 28th 1746 (1746)

A True Copy of the Papers, Wrote by Arthur Lord Balmerino, Thomas Syddal, David Morgan, George Fletcher, John Berwick, Thomas Deacon, Thomas Chadwick, James Dawson and Andrew Blyde, and delivered to the Sheriffs by them at the Places of their Execution (1746).

Tucker, Josiah, *Hospitals and Infirmaries, Considered as Schools of Christian Education for the Adult Poor, and as Means Conducive Towards a National Reformation in the Common People* (Bristol, 1746).

The UNEMBARRASSED COUNTENANCE. A NEW BALLAD (1746).

An Ample Disquisition into the Nature of Regalities and other Heredable Jurisdictions, in that Part of Great Britain call'd Scotland (1747).

An Authentic Journal of the Remarkable and Bloody Siege of Bergen-op-Zoom by the French (1747).

Burgh, James, *Thoughts on Education* (1747).

Doddridge, Philip, *Some Remarkable Passages in the Life of Col. James Gardiner, who was slain at the Battle of Prestonpans, Sept. 21, 1745* (1747).

Fielding, Henry, *A Dialogue between a Gentleman of London and an Honest Alderman of the Country Party* (1747).

The History, Rise and Progress of Patriotism drawn from a Close Observation of the Conduct of our Late Illustrious Patriots (London and Dublin, 1747).

A Letter to Sir John Philipps, Bart, Occasion'd by a Bill brought into Parliament to Naturalize Foreign Protestants (1747).

The Lord's Lamentation; or The Whittington Defeat [ballad] (1747).

The Ordinary of Newgate's Account of the Behaviour, Dying Words, and Confession, Birth, Parentage, and Education of the Several Malefactors that were Executed at Westminster on Friday Last, for the Horrid Crimes of B[ribery] and C[orruption]. To which is annexed Mr P[elha]m's Speech Immediately before the Execution (1747).

Plot or No Plot or, Sir W—— m and his Spy Foil'd. A New Ballad (1747).

Ranelagh House: A Satire in Prose (1747).

Tit for Tat, A Sea Kick, for a Land Cuff [ballad] (1747).

A Collection of Declarations, Proclamations and other Valuable Papers. Published by Authority at Edinburgh, in the Years 1745 and 1746 (repr. 1748).

An Essay upon Publick Credit. In a Letter to a Friend Occasioned by the Fall of Stocks (1748).

The Importance of the Liberty of the Press . . . Being Six Papers, Publish'd in the OLD ENGLAND . . . (1748).

A Letter to a Noble Negotiator Abroad, on the Present Prospects of a Speedy Peace (1748).

Little, Otis, *The State of Trade in the Northern Colonies Consider'd; with an Account of their Produce and a Particular Description of Nova Scotia* (1748).

The State of the Nation for the Year 1747 and Respecting 1748. Inscrib'd to a Member of Parliament (1748).

The State of the Nation, with a General Balance of the Publick Accounts (1748).

Walpole, Horace, *Three Letters to the Whigs, Occasion'd by the Letter to the Tories* (1748).

Considerations Upon a Reduction of the Land Tax (1749).

Considerations Upon the White Herring and Cod Fisheries (1749).

Conybeare, John, *Sermon Preach'd Before the Honourable House of Commons on Tuesday, April 25th, 1749. Being the Day of Thanksgiving for the General Peace* (1749).

A Dialogue between Thomas Jones, A Life Guard Man and John Smith, Late Serjeant in the First Regiment of Foot Guards Just Returned from Flanders (1749).

Douglass, William, *A Summary, Historical and Political, of the First Planting, Progressive Improvements, and Present State of the British Settlements in North America* (1749–50).

Egmont, John, 2nd Earl of, *An Examination of the Principles and an Enquiry into the Conduct of the Two B[rothe]rs* (1749).

A Letter to a Member of Parliament, Concerning the Free British Fisheries (1749).

Manchester Vindicated: Being a Compleat Collection of Papers Lately Published in Defence of that Town, in the Chester Courant (Chester, 1749).

A Short Dissertation upon that Species of Misgovernment called Oligarchy (1749).

A Short State of the Countries and Trade of North America. Claimed by the Hudson's Bay Company (1749).

The Vast Importance of the Herring Fishery to these Kingdoms (1749).

The Wealth of Great Britain in the Ocean Exemplified, from Materials Laid before the Committee of the House of Commons, Appointed to Examine into the State of the British Fisheries (1749).

The World in Disguise: or Masks All (1749).

An Address to the Public Occasioned by the Bishop of London's Letter (1750).

Dr Allen, *An Account of the Behaviour of Mr James Maclaine, From the Time of his Condemnation to the Day of his Execution* (1750).

The Best and Most Approved Method of Curing White Herrings and all Kinds of White Fish (1750).

Campbell, John, *The Present State of Europe. Explaining the Interests, Connections, Political and Commercial Views of its Several Powers* (1750; 4th edn., 1753).

The Chester Miscellany. Being a Collection of Several Pieces, both in Prose and Verse, which were in the Chester Courant from January 1745, to May 1750 (Chester and London, 1750).

A Compleat History of James Maclean, The Gentleman Highwayman (1750).

A Copy of a Letter wrote to a Member of Parliament (1750).

Dame Ranelagh's Remonstrance in Behalf of Herself and Her Sisters (1750).

England's Path to Wealth and Honour: In a Dialogue between an Englishman and a Dutchman. To which is added Articles relating to the Dutch Herring Fishery (1750).

An Exact and Authentic Account of the Greatest White Herring Fishery in Scotland (1750).

The Fisheries Revived: or, Britain's Hidden Treasure Discovered (1750).

Hales, Stephen, *Some Considerations on the Causes of Earthquakes* (1750).

A Letter to a Member of Parliament, Concerning the Free British Fisheries (1750).

A Letter to the Honourable House of Commons Relating to the Present Situation of Affairs (1750).

Modest Remarks upon the Bishop of London's Letter (1750).

A Petition to the Right Hon Mr ——, in Favour of Mr Maclean. By a Lady (1750).

The Necessity of Lowering Interest and Continuing Taxes Demonstrated (1750).

Stukeley, William, *The Philosophy of Earthquakes, Natural and Religious Or and Inquiry into their Cause, and their Purpose* (1750).

A Treatise Concering Oaths and Perjury (1750).

An Apology for the Robin Hood Society (1751).

Constitutional Queries, Earnestly Recommended to the Serious Consideration of Every True Briton (1751).

The Deity's Delay in Punishing the Guilty Considered, on the Principles of Reason (1751).

Fitzsimmonds, Joshua, *Free and Candid Disquisitions on the Nature and Execution of the Laws of England, Both in Civil and Criminal Affairs* (1751).

Genuine and Authentic Memoirs of the Stated Speakers of the Robin Hood Society (1751).

Gray, Charles, *Considerations on Several Proposals Lately Made for the Better Maintenance of the Poor* (1751).

Hooke, Andrew, *An Essay on the National Debt, and National Capital*, 2nd edn. (1751).

King, Richard, *A Sermon Preached before the Several Associations of the Laudable Order of Anti-Gallicans, At Bow Church in Cheapside, On Friday, May 24, 1751* (1751).

Maddox, Isaac, *An Epistle to the Right Honourable the Lord Mayor, Aldermen and Common Council, of the City of London*, 2nd edn. (1751).

Observations on the Bills of Mortality of London (1751).

Postlethwayt, Malachy, *The Universal Dictionary of Trade and Commerce* (2 vols., 1751–5).

Serious Thoughts in Regard to Public Disorders, with Several Proposals for Remedying the Same; Particularly in Respect to Gaming, Public Houses, Pawnbrokers, and Receivers of Stolen Goods (1751).

A Small Collection of Valuable Tracts Relating to the Herring Fishery (1751).

Two Historical Accounts of the Making of the New Forest in Hampshire, by King William the Conqueror; And Richmond New Park in Surry (1751).

Tucker, Josiah, *The Impartial Enquiry into the Benefits and Damages . . . from the Present Very Great Use of Low-Priced Spirituous Liquors* (1751).

—— *Reflections on the Expediency of a Law For the Naturalization of Foreign Protestants*, Part I (1751).

Whitehead, Paul, *The Case of the Hon Alexander Murray in an appeal to the people of Great Britain* (1751).

Alcock, Thomas, *Observations on the Defects of the Poor Laws* (1752).

A Brief Account of the Martyrdom of K. Charles I of Blessed Memory (Chester, 1752).

Campbell, John, *A Full and Particular Description of the Highlands of Scotland* (1752).

Dodd, James Solas, *An Essay Towards the Natural History of the Herring (1752)*

An Historical Memorial of the Proceedings against the Protestants in France, from 1744 to 1751 (1752).

Reflections on Various Subjects Relating to Arts and Commerce; Particularly, The Consequences of Admitting Foreign Artists on Easier Terms (1752).

A Scheme Offered to the Consideration of the Publick; which if Countenanced & Encouraged, will not only Promote and Invigorate the Execution of the Laws now Extant, against the Breaking and Profaning of the Christian Sabbath or Lord's Day (1752).

Thomas, John, *A Sermon Preached at the Parish Church of St Anne Westminster, on Thursday, April the 29th, 1752, Before the Governors of the Middlesex Hospital* (1752).

The Trial of John Peter Zenger, of New York, Printer (1752).

Tucker, Josiah, *Reflection on the Expediency of a Law For the Naturalizaton of Foreign Protestants*, Part II (1752).

An Address to the Friends of Great Britain (1753).

The Advantages of the Revolution Illustrated, By a View of the Present State of Great Britain (1753).

Considerations on the Bill to Permit Persons Professing the Jewish Religion to be Naturalized by Parliament (1753).

Copy of what Dir Archibald Cameron Intended to have delivered to the Sheriff of Middlesex at the Place of Execution—with A Letter to his Son in France (1753).

Further Considerations on the Act . . . (1753).

The Impartial Observer: Being a Modest Reply To What has lately been Published Relating to the Intended Naturalization of the Jews (1753).

A Letter to a Member of Parliament on the Registering and Numbering of the People of Great Britain (1753).

The Life of Dr Archibald Cameron, Brother to Donald Cameron of Lochiel, Chief of their Clan (1753).

A Proposal Humbly Offered to the Legislature of this Kingdom For the Re-establishment of Christianity (1753).

A Sermon Preached at the Parish Church of St George, Hanover Square, Sunday, October 28 1753. By the Rev Mr Winstanley, Rector of Llanwenarth in Monmouthshire (1753).

Tucker, Josiah, *A Brief Essay on the Advantages and Disadvantages which Respectively Attend France and Great Britain, with Regard to Trade*, 3rd edn. (1753); 4th edn. (Glasgow, 1755).

—— *A Letter to a Friend Concerning Naturalizations* (1753).

—— *A Second Letter to a Friend Concerning Naturalizations* (1753).

Advice to the Freeholders of Kent (Maidstone[?], 1754).

Advice to the Freeholders of Kent. A New Ballad (Maidstone [?], 1754).

Burgh, James, *Youth's Friendly Monitor* (1754).

Butley, John, *A Sermon Preached in the Church of Greenwich in Kent, on Wednesday the 29th of May, 1754, Before the Laudable Association of Anti-Gallicans, Established at Greenwich* (1754).

Cole, Thomas, *A Plan for the Better Carrying on the British White Herring Fishery, Humbly Offered to the Consideration of William Beckford Esq* (1754).

The Country Gentleman's Advice to his Son, on his Coming of Age, with Regard to his Political Conduct (1755).

Hales, Stephen, *A Friendly Admonition to the Drinkers of Gin, Brandy, and other Distilled Liquors*, 5th edn. (1754).

The Kentish Candidates (Maidstone [?], 1754).

Lediard, Thomas, *A Charge Delivered to the Grand Jury, at the Sessions of Peace held for the City and Liberty of Westminster, 16 October 1754* (1754).

A Letter to the Author of Some Considerations on the Act to Prevent Clandestine Marriages (1754).

Old Nick to the Liverymen of London (1754).

The Oxf–rd Election [ballad] (Oxford, 1754).

The Oxford Rag-Plot: or, A Rag-a-Muffin Song of Tag, Rag, and Bob-tail (Oxford, 1754).

Peckard, Peter, *A Sermon on the Nature and Extent of Civil and Religious Liberty* (1754).

Shebbeare, John, *The Marriage Act. A Novel containing a Series of Interesting Adventures* (1754).

Some Considerations on the Act to Prevent Clandestine Marriages in a Letter from a Gentleman of the Temple To the Lord B——p of L—— (1754).

Stennett, Joseph, *National Ingratitude Exemplified, in the Case of Gideon and his Family, and Applied to the Present Times. A Sermon Preached Nov 5, 1740*, 5th edn. (1754).

Some Thoughts on the Present State of our Trade to India (1754).

A True Blue Song, Upon True Blue Paper [ballad] (Oxford, 1754).

Welch, Saunders, *Observations on the Office of Constable with Cautions for the More Safe Execution of that Duty* (1754).

An Address to the Jurymen of London. By a Citizen (1755).

Advice to Posterity Concerning a Point of the Last Importance (1755).

An Answer to a Pamphlet called A Second Letter to the People (1755).

Fielding, John, *A Plan for Preventing Robberies within Twenty Miles of London* (1755).

Hayter, Thomas, *A Sermon Preached in the Parish Church of Christ Church, London, on Thursday May the 1st, 1755 Being the Time of the Yearly Meeting of the Children Educated in the Charity Schools in and about the Cities of London and Westminster* (1755).

The Important Question Concerning Invasions, A Sea War, Raising the Militia and Paying Subsidies for Foreign Troops (1755).

Mackay, James, *The Spirit of Loyalty, and of Rebellion, During some Late Troubles, Detected, in the Conduct of the Commissioners of Excise in Scotland: And of an officer, who distinguished himself in Behalf of the Government* (1755).

McCulloh, Henry, *A Miscellaneous Essay Concerning the Course Pursued by Great Britain in the Affairs of her Colonies* (1755).

—— *The Wisdom and Policy of the French in the Construction of the Great Offices* (1755).

Some Material and Very Important Remarks Concerning the Present Situation of Affairs between Great Britain, France and Spain (1755).

Merlin's Life and Prophecies . . . His Prediction Relating to the Late Contest about the Rights of Richmond Park (1755).

A Miscellaneous Essay Concerning the Courses Pursued by Great Britain in the Affairs of her Colonies (1755).

The Nature and Use of Subsidiary Forces fully Considered: In an Answer to a Pamphlet intitled A Second Letter to the People of England (1755).

The Present State of North America (1755).

Shebbeare, John, *A Letter to the People of England, on the present Situation and Conduct of National Affairs* (1755).

—— *Letters on the English Nation* (1755).

—— *A Second Letter to the People of England, on Foreign Subsidies, Subsidiary Armies, and their Consequences to this Nation* (1755).

Sybelline Leaves, or Anonymous Papers, containing A letter to the Lord Mayor of London (1755).

Talbot, George, *A Sermon Preached at the Cathedral of Glocester [sic] At the Opening of the Infirmary . . .* (1755).

Tucker, Josiah, *Element of Commerce* (1755).

—— *Reflections on the Expediency of Opening the Trade to Turkey* (1755).

Wade, Edward, *A Proposal For Improving and Adorning the Island of Great Britain* (1755).

An Address to the Electors of England (1756).

Admiral B—— Seiz'd with Pannick, at Captain A——s Ghost; or Who is Afraid to Come Home (1756).

Admiral Byng's Letter to Secretary Cleveland; or Who will Kick at the Coward [slip song] (1756).

Alcock, Thomas, *A Sermon on the Late Earthquakes, More Particularly that at Lisbon* (1756).

Allen, Dr John, *The Destruction of Sodom Improved, as a Warning to Great Britain. A Sermon Preached on the Fast-Day, Friday, February 6, 1756, At Hanover Street, Long Acre* (1756).

An Answer to a Pamphlet called A Third Letter to the People of England (1756).

An Appeal to the Sense of the People on the Present Posture of Affairs (1756).

Ashton, Thomas, *A Sermon Preached on Occasion of the General Fast Appointed by Royal Proclamation on Feb 6, 1756* (1756).

Bate, John, *The Practical Use of Public Judgements. A Sermon Preach'd at St Paul's, Deptford, Kent, on February 6, 1756* (1756).

The Block and Yard Arm. A New Ballad (1756).

Bulkley, Charles, *The Nature and Necessity of National Reformation. A Sermon Preached at the Barbican, Feb 6, 1756. Being the Day appointed for a General Fast* (1756).

Byass, William, *A Sermon Preach'd in the Parish Churches of Storrington and Parham in Sussex, on Friday, February 6, 17567. Being the Day Appointed for a Public Fast* (1756).

The Conduct of the Ministry Impartially Examined, In a Letter to the Merchants of London (1756).

Considerations on the Addresses Lately Present to His Majesty, on Occasion of the Loss of Minorca (1756).

Craddock, John, *A Sermon Preached in the Parish Church of St Paul, Covent Garden, on Friday, Feb 6, 1756. Being the Day Appointed by Authority for a General Fast* (1756).

Crudden, Alexander, *The Corrector's Earnest Address to the Inhabitants of Great Britain* (1756).

Dodd, William, *The Nature and Necessity of Fasting. being the Substance of Two Sermons Preach'd in the Parish Churches of West Ham, Essex, and St Olave's, Hart Street, London* (1756).

Downes, John, *The True National Evil: Or, Cowardice the Cry; but Corruption the Grievance. A Sermon Preach'd at the Temple Church, London* (1756).

A Fifth Letter to the People of England, on M[inisteria]l Influence and Management of National Treasure (1756).

Fontayne, John, *A Sermon Preached at the Cathedral Church of York, on Friday the 6th of February, 1756, Being the Day Appointed for a General Fast* (1756).

A Full and Particular Answer to all the Calumnies, Misrepresentations and Falsehoods contained in a Pamphlet, called A Fourth Letter to the People of England (1756).

German Cruelty. A Fair Warning to the People of Great Britain (1756).

Gilbert, Robert, *The Terms of National Happiness Stated and Recommended. A Sermon Delivered at Northampton, Feb the 6th, 1756* (1756).

Gittings, Daniel, *A Serious and Earnest Address to All Orders and Degrees of Men Amongst Us. Being a Sermon Preached on Occasion of the Late General Fast, February 6th* (1756).

A Grand Consultation of Physitians or, An Attempt to Assign the Cause of a Sickly & Languishing Constitution [ballad] (1756).

Hanway, Jonas, *Thoughts on The Duty of a Good Citizen with regard to War and Invasion* (1756).

How, James, *A Sermon on Occasioon of the Earthquake at Lisbon, in the Kingdom of Portugal, and the Present Situation of Affairs in Great Britain. Preach'd in the Parish Church of Milton, Near Gravesend, the Sixth of February, 1756* (1756).

An Impartial View of the Conduct of the M[inist]ry, in Regard to the War in America (1756).

Jones, T., *Repentance and Reconciliation with God Recommended and Enforced. In Two Sermons Preached at the Parish Church of St Saviours Southwark* (1756).

Maddox, Isaac, *The Duty and Wisdom of Remembering Past Dangers and Deliverances. A Thanksgiving Sermon for the Suppression of the Late Unnatural Rebellion . . . 9 October 1746*, 4th edn. (1756).

Memoirs of the Life and Actions of General W Blakeney: to serve as an introduction to a fuller history of certain transactions, wherein he had a share (London and Dublin, 1756).

Memoirs of the Life and Particular Actions, of that Brave Man, General Blakeney (1756).

A Modest Address to the Commons of Great Britain (1756).

Moss, Charles, *A Sermon Preached at the Parish Church of St James, Westminster, on Friday, Feb 6, 1756, Being the Day Appointed by His Majesty for a General Fast* (1756).

Nowell, William, *A Sermon Preached at the Parish Church of Wolsingham, in the Bishoprick of Durham, on the 6th Day of February, 1756* (Newcastle, 1756).

The Old British Foxhunter's Cry. Talio, Talio (1756).

Postlethwayt, Malachy, *A Short State of the Progress of the French Trade and Navigation* (1756).

The Progress of the French, in their Views of Universal Monarchy (1756).

Reflections Previous to the Establishment of a Militia (1756).

A Rueful Story, Admiral B——g's Glory, or Who Ran Away First. A New Ballad (1756).

Richards, T., *National Repentance Urged from the Prospect of National Judgements. A Sermon Preach'd at the Parish Church of All-Saints in Northampton, on February 6, 1756* (1756).

A Sequel to Hosier's Ghost: or, Old Blakeney's Reception into the Elysian Fields. A ballad; written by a Patriot of Ireland (London and Dublin, 1756).

A Serious Address to the Worthy Livery of London (1756).

A Serious Defence of Some Measures of the Administration: Particularly with Regard to the Introduction and Establishment of Foreign Troops (1756).

Shebbeare, John, *An Answer to a Pamphlet call'd, The Conduct of the Ministry Impartially Examined* (1756).

—— *An Appeal to the People, Containing the Genuine and Entire Letter of Admiral Byng to the Secr. of the A[dmiralt]y* (1756).

—— *A Third Letter to the People of England. On Liberty, Taxes and the Application of Public Money* (1756).

—— *A Fourth Letter to the People of England. On the Conduct of the M[iniste]rs in Alliances, Fleets and Armies, since the First Differences on the Ohio to the taking of Mihorea by the French* (1756).

—— *Lydia, or Filial Piety* (1756).

A Sixth and Last Letter or Address to the Parliament As well as to the People of Great Britain (1756?).

Squire, Samuel, *A Speedy Repentance the Most Effectual Means to Avert God's Judgements: A Sermon Preached at the Parish Church of St Anne Westminster, Feb 6, 1756*, 2nd edn. (1756).

Stebbing, Henry, *A Sermon Preached at Gray's Inn Chapel, on Friday, Feb 6, 1756, Being the Day Appointed by Authority for a Public Fast* (1756).

The True National Evil (1756).

Two Discourses Occasioned by the Cruel Oppression of the Protestants in France (1756).

Useful Remarks on Privateering. Addressed to the Laudable Association of Anti-Gallicans (1756).

The Voice of the People: A Collection of Addresses to His Majesty and Instructions to Members of Parliament by their Constituents (1756).

The Wonder of Surry! Or, Who Perswaded A—— l B——g to Run Away? [slip song] (1756).

The Wonder of Surry! the Wonder of Surry! Or the Genuine Speech of an Old British Oak [ballad] (1756).

Wonder upon Wonder: or, The Cocoa Tree's Answer to the Surrey Oak [ballad] (1756).

An Alarm to the People of England: Shewing Their Rights, Liberties and Properties to be in the utmost Danger from the present destructive, and unconstitutional Association for the Preservation of Game all over England, which is proved to be illegal (1757).

Ancell, James, *National Virtue, the Condition of National Happiness: A Sermon Preached in the Parish Churcho of Monks Kirkby, in the County of Warwick, the 1th of February* (1757).

Ball, Nathaniel, *True Religion, Loyalty, and Union Recommended to all Orders of Men; In a Sermon Preached at Pleshey, Feb 11 1757. Being the Day Appointed for a Public Fast on Account of the War Against France* (1757).

Brown, John, *An Estimate of the Manners and Principles of the Times* (1757).

Chafy, John, *A Sermon Preached at Broad Chalk, in Wiltshire, on Friday the 11th of February, 1757, Being the Day Appointed for a General Fast, On Occasion of the War* (1757).

The Contest in American Between Great Britain and France (1757).

Dupont, John, *National Corruption and Depravity the Cause of National Disappointments. In a Sermon Preach'd at Aysgarth, on Friday, the 11th of February, 1757, Being the Day Appointed by Proclamation for a General Fast* (1757).

The Father of the City of Eutopia, or the Surest Road to Riches (1757).

Fauquier, Francis, *Essay on the Ways and Means for Raising Money* (1756).

Fothergill, Thomas, *The Qualifications and Advantages of Religious Trust in Times of Danger. A Sermon Preached Before the Mayor and Corporation at St Martin's in Oxford, on Friday, February 11. Being the Day Appointed by Royal Proclamation to be Kept as a General Fast* (1757).

Frederick the Third [sic], King of Prussia (1757).

German Cruelty: A Fair Warning to the People of Great Britain (1757).

The Ghost of Ernest, Great Grandfather of Her Royal Highness, the Princess Dowager of Wales. With Some Account of his Life (1757).

Gilbert, Robert, *An Alarm to Great Britain; With an Invitation to Repentance From the Respite of Judgement. Represented in a Sermon Delivered at Northampton, February 11th, 1757* (1757).

Greenhill, Joseph, *A SERMON Preached on the SUNDAY Preceding the FAST DAY, February 11, 1757, in Preparation to the FAST* (1757)

A Guide to the Knowledge of the Rights and Privileges of Englishmen. With an Exhortation to the Christian and Independent Clergy, the Gentry, Freeholders and other Electors of Members to Serve in Parliament (1757).

Hervey, James, *The Time of Danger, and the Means of Safety: To Which is Added, the Way of Holiness. Being the Substance of Three Sermons, Preached on the Late Public Fast Days* (1757).

The Independent Freeholder's Letter to the People of England (1757).

A Letter to His Grace the D—— of N—— on the Duty he Owes Himself, his King, his Country and his God At this Important Moment (1757).

A Letter to a Member of Parliament on the Importance of the American Colonies (1757).

Milner, John, *Signs of the Times. In Two Discourses Delivered at Peckham in Surrey. On the General Fast, February 11, 1757* (1757).

The Morning's Thoughts on Reading The Test and Con-Test (1757).

Old English Valour: Being an Account of a Remarkable Sea Engagement, Anno 1591. Written by Sir Walter Raleigh (1757).

Postlethwayt, Malachy, *Britain's Commercial Interest Explained and Improved* (2 vols., 1757).

—— *Great Britain's True System* (1757).

Proposals for Carrying on the War with Vigour (1757).

The Prosperity of Britain Proved from the Degeneracy of its People (1757).

Some Particular Remarks upon the Affair of the Hanoverian Soldier (1757).

The Real Character of the Age, in a Letter to the Rev. Dr Brown, Occasioned by his Estimate of the Manners and Principles of the Times (1757).

A Refutation of the Sixth Letter to the People of England (1757).

Richards, T., *God's Goodness, and Man's Ingratitude, Consider'd, In a Sermon Preach'd at the Parish Church of All Saints, Northampton, On February 11, 1757. Being the Day Appointed by His Majesty's Proclamation for a Publick Fast* (1757)

A Sermon, preach'd at York, to a congregation of protestant dissenters, on the 27th of November 1757, just upon receiving the account of the King of Prussia's victory, on the fifth of that month. . . . By Newcome Cappe (1757).

Scott, Thomas, *Great Britain's Danger and Remedy. Represented in a Discourse Delivered at Ipswich, on the Day Appointed for a General Fast, February the 11th, 1757* (1757).

A Seventh Letter to the People of England. Upon Political Writing, True Patriotism, Jacobitism, and Evil and Corrupt Adm[inistratio]ns (1757).

Shebbeare, John, *A Fifth Letter to the People of England. On the Subversion of the Constitution, and the Necessity of its being Restored* (1757).

—— *A Sixth Letter to the People of England, on the Progress of National Ruin* (1757).

—— *The Occasional Critic* (1757).

A Tract on the National Interest, and Depravity of the Times (1757).

Trial of Lady Allured Luxury (1757).

A Word in Time to Both Houses of Parliament (1757).

Ashton, Thomas, *A Sermon Preached at the Parish Church of St Botolph without Bishopsgate on Friday, February 17, 1758. Being the Day Appointed by Proclamation for a General Fast* (1758).

An Authentic Account of our Late Enterprise on the Coast of France, 1758 (1758).

The Cries of the Public. In a Letter to His Grace the Duke of Newcastle (1758).

Dilworth, W. H., *The Life and Heroick Actions of Frederick III. King of Prussia. From his Birth to the Present Times* (1758).

Egmont, John, 2nd Earl of, *Things As They Are* (1758).

The Eulogy of Frederic, King of Prussia (1758).

An Explanatory Defence of the Estimate of the Manners and Principles of the Times (1758).

Fielding, John, *An Account of the Origins and Effects of a Police* (1758).

A Genuine Account of the Late Secret Expedition to Martinico and Guardeloupe under Commodore Moore and Hopson (1758).

A Genuine and Particular Account of the Late Enterprise on the Coast of France (1758).

A Letter of Consolation to Dr Shebbeare (1758?).

The Life of Admiral Vernon. By an Impartial Hand (1758).

Marteilhe, Jean, *The Memoirs of a Protestant Condemned to the Galleys of France for his Religion* (2 vols., 1758).

Massie, Joseph, *A Plan for the Establishment of Charity Houses for Exposed or Deserted Women and Girls and for Penitent Prostitutes . . .* (1758).

Occasional Reflections on the Importance of the War in America, and the Reasonableness and Justice of Supporting the King of Prussia & in Defence of the Common Cause (1758).

Plans and Proposals Transmitted to the Committee on the British Fishery. By Several Hands (1758).

Postlethwayt, Malachy, *The Importance of the African Expedition Considered* (1758).

A Proposal for the Encouragement of Seamen to Serve in the Navy, for Preventing Desertion, Supporting their Families, and the Easier Government of His Majesty's Ships (1758).

Rules and Orders of the Society, instituted at London for the Encouragement of arts, manufactures and commerce (1758).

Welch, Saunders, *A Proposal to Render Effectual a Plan, to Remove the Nuisance of Common Prostitutes From the Streets of the Metropolis* (1758).

Britain in Tears, for the Loss of the Brave General Wolfe [slip song](1759?).

Considerations on the Importance of Canada (1759).

A Dialogue betwixt General Wolfe, and the Marquis Montcalm, in the Elysian Fields (1759).

Douglas, John, *The Conduct of a Noble Lord Candidly Considered, A Seasonable Antidote against the Poison of Popular Censure* (1759).

The Encouraging General, A Song Sung by that Truly Galland Officer, General Wolfe, the Evening Before he Received the Mortal Wound which Occasioned his Death (1759?).

Hanway, Jonas, *An Account of the Marine Society* (1759).

The Honest Grief of a Tory Expressed in a Genuine Letter to the Monitor (1759).

The Life of Frederick III. King of Prussia (1759).

Memoirs of the Life of the Heroic Frederick III, King of Prussia (Nottingham, 1759).

Montagu, Edward Wortley, *Reflections on the Rise and Fall of the Antient Republicks. Adapted to the Present State of Great Britain* (1759).

The Newsman's Review of Transactions, for the Year, 1758 [ballad] (1759?).

Populousness with Oeconomy, the Wealth and Strength of a Kingdom (1759).

A Second Letter From Wiltshire to the Monitor on the Vindication of his Constitutional Principles (1759).

An Account of the Society For the Encouragement of British Troops, in Germany and North America (1760).

Admiral Hawke's Welcome to Old England, on Compleating the Ruin of the French Navy [ballad] (1760).

The Battle of Warburg. A New Song (1760).

Douglas, John, *A Letter Addressed to Two Great Men, on the Prospect of Peace; and on the Terms Necessary to be Insisted Upon in the Negotiation* (London and Edinburgh, 1760).

General Reflections Occasion'd by the Letter Addressed to Two Great Men and the Remarks on that Letter (1760).

The Interest of Great Britain Consider'd with Regard to her Colonies (1760).

A Letter from a Gentleman in the Country to his Friend in Town; on his Perusal of a Pamphlet addressed to Two Great Men (1760).

Pringle, Sir John, *The Life of General James Wolfe, the Conqueror of Canada: or, the Elogium of that Renowned Hero* (1760).

Reflections on the Present Posture of our Affairs in North America (1760).

Remarks on the Letter Addressed to Two Great Men (1760).

An Answer to a Letter to the Right Honourable the Earl of B—— (1761).

Cole, Thomas, *Discourse on Luxury, Infidelity, and Enthusiasm* (1761).

An Earnest Address to the People of Great Britain and Ireland Occasioned by the Dismission of William Pitt, Esq (1761).

Kippis, Andrew, *Observations Upon the Coronation. A Sermon Preached at the Chapel in Long Ditch, Westminster on Sept 20, 1761* (1761).

A Letter to His Grace the Duke of N——, On the Present Crisis of Affairs of Great Britain (1761).

A Letter to the Right Honourable the Earl of B——, On a Late Important Resignation, and its Probable Consequences (1761).

Lockman, John, *Charity and Pleasure* (1761).

The Reasons for Keeping Guadeloupe at a Peace, Preferable to Canada, Explained in Five Letters from a Gentleman in Guadeloupe to his Friend in London (1761).

The Right Honourable Annuitant Vindicated (1761).

Seasonable Hints From an Honest Man on the Present Important Crisis of a New Reign and a New Parliament (1761).

An Address to the Cocoa Tree, from a Whig (1762).

Considerations on the Approaching Peace, 3rd edn. (1762).

Dodd, William, *A Sermon on Job, xxix, ver 11–13. Preached at the Anniversary Meeting of the Governors of the Magdalen Charity, on Thursday, March 18, 1762* (1762).

Edwards, John, *The Safe Retreat from Impending Judgements. Being the Substance of a Sermon Preached at Leeds, March 12, 1762. Being the Day Appointed by His Majesty for a General Fast; Pursuant to the Declaration of War against Spain* (1762).

An Examination of the Commercial Principles of the Late Negotiations between Great Britain and France in 1761 (1762).

A Fair and Full Answer to the Author of Occasional Thoughts on the Present German War (1762).

Heathcote, George, *A Letter to the Right Honourable the Lord Mayor . . . of the City of London . . . From an Old Servant* (1762).

A Letter to a Member of the Honourable House of Commons, on the Present Important Crisis of National Affairs (1762).

Massie, Joseph, *An Historical Account of the Naval Power of France* (1762).

Pennick, Richard, *A Sermon Preached on the General Fast Day, March the 12th, 1762. At the Parish Church of St Catherine Cree* (1762).

A Political Analysis of the War, 2nd edn. (1762).

The Proper Object of the Present War with France and Spain Considered (1762).

Shebbeare, John, *The History of the Excellence and Decline of the Constitution, Religion, Laws, Manners and Genius of the Sumatrans* (2 vols., 1762).

—— *One More Letter to the People of England* (1762).

An Appeal to Knowledge: Or Candid Discussions of the Preliminaries of Peace, Signed at Fontainbleau, Nov 3, 1762, and Laid before Both Houses of Parliament. By a Member of Parliament (1763).

Campbell, John, *Candid and Impartial Consideration on the Nature of the Sugar Trade* (1763).

A Letter from a Member of Parliament in Town, to his Friend in the Country, upon the Three Great Objects of Present Attention, Peace, Parties, and Resignations (1763).

Propositions for Improving the Manufactures, Agriculture and Commerce of Great Britain (1763).

Reflections on the Terms of Peace (1763).

Tucker, Josiah, *The Case for Going to War, For the Sake of Procuring, Enlarging and Securing of Trade, Considered in a New Light* (1763).

Wesley, John, *A Sermon Preached before the Society Reformation of Manners* (1763).

Burgh, James, *An Account of the First Settlement, Laws, Form of Government, and Police, of the Cessares, A People of South America* (1764).

The History of the Robin Hood Society (1764).

Low Life, or One Half of the World Knows not How the other Half Live (1764).

A View of the Internal Policy of Great Britain (1764).

A Concise Account of the Rise, Progress, and the Present State of the Society For the Encouragement of Arts, Manufactures and Commerce (1765).

A Short Account of the Great Benefits which have Already Arisen to the Public, By Means of the Society Instituted in London, In the Year 1753, For the Encouragement of Arts, Manufacturers and Commerce (1765).

Smollet, Tobias, *History of England* (6 vols., 1758–65).

Fielding, Sir John, *Extracts from Such of the Penal Laws as Particularly Relate to the Peace and Good Order of this Metropolis* (1768).

Anderson, James, *The Interest of Great Britain with Regard to the American Colonies Considered* (1782).

Sinclair, John, *Thoughts on the Naval Strength of the British Empire* (1782).

Knox, John, *A View of the British Empire, More Especially Scotland; With Some Proposals For the Improvement of that Country, The Extension of the Fisheries, and the Relief of its People* (1784).

9th Earl of Dundonald, *The Present State of the Manufacture of Salt Explained* (1785).

Knox, John, *Observations on the Northern Fisheries with a Discourse on the Expediency of Establishing Fishing Stations, or Small Towns, in the Highlands of Scotland, and the Hebride Islands* (1786).

Scotland

Arranged chronologically. Published in Edinburgh unless otherwise indicated.

The British Fishery Recommended to Parliament (1734).

The Several Addresses of the Merchant Company and Corporations of Edinburgh to the Magistrates and Town Council thereof (1739).

A [Serious] Address to the Electors of Great Britain (1740).

Acts of the Town Council of Edinburgh for the Suppression of Vice and Immorality, made since the Happy Revolution, especially since 1700 (1742).

A Memoriall Concerning the Unnatural Rebellion Begun in the North West of Scotland. Read in the Church of Ormistoun, Nov 10, 1745 (1745?).

The Present State of Scotland Consider'd (1745).

Blair, Hugh, *The Wrath of Man Praising Man* (1746).

A Letter to the Author of the National Journal (1746).

A Letter to the Most Noble Thomas, Duke of Newcastle, on Certain Points of the Last Importance to these Nations (London, 1746).

An Appeal to the Common Sense of Scotsmen (1747).

A Letter to the Most Noble Thomas, Duke of Newcastle of the Dagners Arising from Popery and Disaffection (London, 1747).

Observations Upon a Bill, entitled, An Act for Taking Away, and Abolishing the Hereditable Jurisdications in that Part of Great Britain called Scotland (1747).

National Union Recommended (1747).

A Poem, Compos'd the Second of November, 1747, The Day the Honourable Archibald Stuart, Esq; was Assoilzied from his Second Trial (1747).

Remarks on the People and Government of Scotland (1747).

The Groans and Miseries of Great Britain Modestly Stated (1748).

A True Account of the Behaviour and Conduct of Archibald Stewart Esq, Late Lord Provost of Edinburgh (London, 1748).

The British Fishery Recommended to Parliament (1749).

Warden, John, *The Happiness of Britain Illustrated. In a Sermon* (1749).

Gillies, John, *An Exhortation to the Inhabitants of the South Parish of Glasgow, Wednesday, September 26th 1750* (Glasgow, 1750).

Dalrymple, Sir David, *Proposals for Carrying on a Certain Public Work in the City of Edinburgh* (1752).

Elliot, Sir Gilbert, *Proposals for Carrying on Certain Public Works in the City of Edinburgh* (1752).

Moncrieff, Alexander, *England's Alarm, which is Directed to Scotland and Ireland* (Edinburgh, 1756).

Witherspoon, John, *A Serious Enquiry into the Nature and Effects of the Stage. Being an Attempt to Show, That Contributing to the Support of a Public Theatre, is Inconsistent with the Character of a Christian* (Glasgow, 1757).

Carlyle, Alexander, *The Questions Relating to the Scots Militia Considered* (Edinburgh, 1760).

Girvin, John, *The Impolicy of Prohibiting the Exportation of Rock Salt from England to Scotland, to the Refined here, Illustrated* (1799).

Ireland

Arranged chronologically. All published in Dublin unless otherwise indicated.

A View of the Grievances of Ireland. By a True Patriot (1745).

The Necessity of a Well-Disciplined Militia in Ireland (1746).

Lucas, Charles, *The British Free-holder's Political Catechism: Addressed . . . to the Free Citizens, and Freeholders of the City of Dublin* (1748).

Brooke, Henry, *A First [to Tenth] Letter from the Farmer to the Free and Independent Electors of the City of Dublin* (1749).

—— *An Occasional Letter from the Farmer to the Free-Men of Dublin* (1749).

Cox, Richard, *A Letter from Sir Richard Cox to Thomas Prior, Esq* (1749).

A Freeholder's Fourth Address to the Merchants, Traders, and Others, the Freemen and Citizens of the City of Dublin (1749).

Lucas, Charles, *Addresses to the Free Citizens and Freeholders of the City of Dublin* (1748–9).

Some Considerations on the British Fisheries with a Proposal for Establishing a General Fishery on the Coasts of Ireland. Addressed to the Rt Honourable the Lord L[ieutenant] (1750).

A Critical Review of the Liberties of British Subjects. With a Comparative View of the Proceedings of the H[ous]e of C[ommon]s of I[relan]d, Against an Unfortunate Exile of that Country. By a Gentleman of the Middle Temple (London, 1750).

An Answer to the Late Proposal for Uniting the Kingdom of Great Britain and Ireland (1751).

Archdall, Nicholas, *An Alarum to the People of Great Britain and Ireland: In Answer to a Late Proposal for Uniting these Kingdoms* (1751).

Lord Hillsborough, *A Proposal for Uniting the Kingdoms of Great Britain and Ireland* (1751).

An Humble Address to the Nobility, Gentry and Freeholders, of the Kingdom of Ireland (1751).

Lucas, Charles, *The Political Constitutions of Great Britain and Ireland, Asserted and Vindicated; The Connection and Common Interest of Both Kingdoms, Demonstrated* (2 vols., 1751).

Honesty the Best Policy; Or the History of Roger (London, 1752).

A Vindication of the R——t H—— e and H—— L—ds and Gentlemen, Who have Lately been Basely Aspersed and Scandalously Misrepresented, in a Late Anonymous Work, Intitledd, The History of Roger (1752).

An Answer to a Late Pamphlet, intituled A Free and Candid Enquiry, Addressed to the Representatives &c of the Kingdom (1753).

Brett, John *Political Pastime; or, Faction Displayed. In a Letter to the Author of The Candid Enquiry* (1753).

Brooke, Henry, *The Spirit of Party* (1753) [4 parts].

Bruce, William, *Some Facts and Observations Relative to the Fate of the Late Linen Bill, last Session of Parliament in this Kingdom* (1753).

Dedication on Dedication: or the Second Dedication to his Grace the D[uke] of D[orset] (1753).

A Fourth Letter from a Free Citizen of Dublin, to a Freeholder of the County of Armagh (1753).

A Fifth Letter from a Free Citizen of Dublin, to a Freeholder of the County of Armagh (1753).

A Fragment of the History of Patrick (1753).

A Free and Candid Enquiry humbly addressed to the representatives of the several counties and boroughs of Ireland (1753).

Howard, George Edmund, *A Short Account of His Majesty's Hereditary Revenue and Private Estate in the Kingdom of Ireland* (1753).

A Letter of Advice to I[ri]sh Members (1753).

A Letter from a Free Citizen of Dublin to a Freeholder in the County of Armagh (1753).

A Letter to a Member of the H[ouse] of C[ommon]s of I[relan]d on the Present Crisis of Affairs in that Kingdom (London, 1753).

A Letter to a Person of Distinction in Town, From a Gentleman in the Country, Containing Some Remarks on a Late Pamphlet intitled A Free and Candid Inquiry &c (1753).

A Letter Upon Libels (1753).

The Life of Betty Ireland with her Birth, Education and Adventures, Together with Some Accounts of her Elder Sister Blanch of Britain (1753).

A List of Members of the H[ouse] of C[ommon]s of Ireland who voted on the Question Previous to the Expulsion of Arthur Jones Nevill, Esq, Late Engineer and Surveyor-General of that Kingdom (1753).

Lucas, Charles, *Free Will to Freeholders* (1753).

O'Connor, Charles, *Seasonable Thoughts Relating to our Civil and Ecclesiastical Constitution* (1753).

The Patriot (1753).

The R[o]y[a]l Mistake, or a Catechism for the I[ris]h Parliament (London, 1753).

Seasonable Advice to the Freeholders of the County of Armagh (1753).

A Second Letter from a Free Citizen to a Freeholder in the County of Armagh (1753).

A Second Letter to a Person of Distinction from a Gentleman in the Country (1753).

A Second Number of Queries Relative to the Present Crisis of Affairs, Humbly Addressed to all True Patriots (1753).

Short Observations upon a Letter Lately Publish'd, From Somebody to Somebody (1753).

A Third Letter from a Free Citizen to a Freeholder of the County of Armagh (1753).

An Address from Lilliput, to the P[a]rl[iamen]t of Ireland (1754).

An Address from the Free Electors of the Pro[vi]nce of Ul[st]eer to Anthony Malone, Esq; the Right Honourable Thomas Carter, & Bellingham Boyle, Esqs (London, 1754).

An Address From the Independent Electors of the County of Westmeath to Anthony Malone, Esq (London, 1754).

An Address from the Independent Freeholders of the P[ro]v[in]ce of M[u]ns[te]r, to Sir R[ichar]d C[o]x (1754).

An Address from the Influenc'd Electors of the County and City of Galway to the D[uke] of D[orse]t, L[ord] G[eorge], and the P[rimate] (1754).

An Address to Friends and Foes (1754) [2 parts].

Bindon, David, *An Answer to Part of a Pamphlet, intitled, the Proceedings of the Honourable House of Commons of Ireland, in rejecting the altered Money Bill* (1754).

—— *Some Observations Relative to the Late Bill for Paying Off the Residue of the National Debt of Ireland, Humbly Submitted to the Consideration of the True Friends of this Country* (1754).

Brett, John, *To all the Serious, Honest, and Well-Meaning People of Ireland, the Following Queries are Affectionately Addressed and Recommended to their Serious Perusal* (1754).

The Cabinet: Containing A Collection of Curious Papers Relative to the Present Political Contests in Ireland (1754).

A Clear and Reasonable Answer to that Disingenuous Pamphlet, call'd Considerations on the Late Bill for Payment of the Remainder of the National Debt (1754).

Common Sense: in a Letter to a Friend (1754).

The C[ourtie]r's Apology To the Freeholders of the Kingdom for their Conduct this S[e]ss[io]n of P[a]rl[iame]nt (1754).

Cox, Richard, *The Proceedings of the Honourable House of Commons of Ireland, in Rejecting the Altered Money Bill, on December 17, 1753, Vindicated* (1754).

A Defence of the Case Fairly Stated, Against a Late Pamphlet, intitled Truth against Craft, or Sophistry and Falsehood Detected (1754).

A Dialogue Between Dick —— and Tom ——, Esqs; Relating to the Present Divisions in I[relan]d (1754).

An Essay on Lying. Inscrib'd to all True Lovers of their Country (1754).

John Gast, *A Letter to the Tradesmen, Farmers, and Rest of the Good People of Ireland* (1754).

—— *A Second Letter to the Tradesmen, Farmers, and the Rest of the Good People of Ireland* (1754).

The History of the Ministerial Conduct of the Chief Governors of Ireland . . . from the Glorious Revolution of 1688, to the Never-to-be Forgotten 17th of December, 1753 (1754).

Howard, George Edmond, *A Letter to the Publick: With Some Queries, Humbly Offered to it's Consideration* (1754).

Leland, John, *The Case Fairly Stated: or, An Inquiry How far the Clause Lately Rejected by the Honourable House of Commons, would, if it had Passed, have Affected the Liberties of the People of Ireland* (1754).

A Letter from Dionysius to the Renowned Triumvirate (1754).

A Letter from a Gentleman at Cork, To his Friend in Dublin. Concerning the Loan Bill, Rejected on the 17th December 1753 (1754).

A Letter from a Prime Serjeant to a High Priest (1754).

A Letter to the Honourable the Lord ——, *Occasion'd by a Pamphlet just Published, Entitled Thoughts on the Affairs of Ireland* (London, 1754).

A Letter to the Right Honourable James, Earl of Kildare, on the Present Posture of Affairs (1754).

Moderation Recommended to the Friends of Ireland, Whether of Court or Country Party (1754).

The Modern Querists Examined, or a Word of Advice to the Scriblers of Both Sides of the Present Important, and Interesting Question (1754).

A New Litany For the People of I[relan]d, or a General Supplication to Caiphas, the High Priest, Pope ENOTS the First (1754).

Patriot Queries, Occasioned by a Late Libel entitled, Queries to the People of Ireland (1754).

The Patriots. A Poem (1754).

Queries to the Querist: or a Series of 141 Queries, in Vindication of the Conduct and Character of the Patriots of Ireland (1754).

A Question to be Considered Previous to the Rejection of the Bill for Paying off the National Debt, upon Account of Inserting to the Preamble His Majesty's Previous Consent (1754).

Remarks on a Pamphlet entitled, Considerations on the Late Bill for Paying the National Debt (1754).

The Review: Being a Short Account of the Doctrine, Arguments, and Tendency, of the Writings Offered to the Publick, by C[our]t Advocates, since Last September (1754).

To the Right Honourable Henry Boyle, Esq; Speaker of the House of Commons of Ireland, an Address from the Gentlemen and Traders of the City of Dublin (1754).

Robinson, Christopher, *An Answer to a Pamphlet, intitled, The Proceedings of the Hnourable House of Commons of Ireland, . . . So far, as the Same Relates to the Argument of a Pamphlet, intitled, Considerations on the Late Bill . . .* (1754).

—— *Considerations on a Late Bill for Paying the National Debt* (1754).

—— *Remarks on a Pamphlet, intitled, Considerations on the Late Bill for Paying the National Debt* (1754).

Stannard, Eaton, *The Honest Man's Apology to the Country for his Conduct* (1754).

Tyranny Display'd. In a Letter From a Looker-on Earnestly Recommended to the Serious Perusal of all True Lovers of their Country (1754).

The Universal Advertiser. Containing A Collection of Essays, Moral, Political and Entertaining: Together with Addresses from Several Corporate and other Bodies in Ireland, to their Representatives in Parliament, in relation to their conduct on the 23d of November and 17th of December 1753 (1754).

The Weaver's Letter to the Tradesmen and Manufacturers of Ireland (1754).

The Advertiser's Answer to the Quaker's Letter, Concerning a Coalition (1755).

A Few Thoughts on the Present Posture of Affairs in Ireland (1755).

Common Sense: in a Letter to a Friend, 4th edn. (1755).

The Conduct of a Certain Member of Parliament During the Last Session (1755).

Gast, John, *Faction's Overthrow: or More Fair Warning, and Good Advice, to the Nobility, Gentry and Commonalty of Ireland* (1755).

—— *The Haberdasher's Sermon* (1755).

Hezekiah Oldbottom to the Adviser of the People of Ireland (1755).

A Layman's Sermon, Preached at the Patriot Club of the County of Armagh, which Met at Armagh, the 3rd of September, 1755 (1755).

A Letter to the People of Ireland, Relative to our Present Feuds and Jealousies (1755).

The Moderator; Being a True Picture of Popular Discontents (1755).

O'Connor, Charles, *The Case of the Roman-Catholics of Ireland. Wherein the Principles and Conduct of that Party are Fully Explained and Vindicated* (1755).

Policy and Justice: An Essay being a Proposal for Augmenting the Power, and Wealth of Great-Britain, by Uniting Ireland (1755).

A Quaker's Letter, to the Universal Advertiser, Concerning the Coalition (1755).

Remarks on a Late Pamphlet, Entitled, The Case of the Roman Catholics of Ireland. By a Protestant (1755).

Advice to the Patriot Club, of the County of Antrim. On the Present State of Affairs in Ireland, and Some Late Changes in the Administration of that Kingdom (1756).

Advice to the Speaker Elect, or a Letter to John Ponsonby (1756).

A Few Thoughts on the Times. In a Letter From a Free-Citizen of Dublin to his Friend in the North (1756).

Lucas, Charles, *An Appeal to the Commons and Citizens of London. By Charles Lucas, the Last Free Citizen of Dublin* (London, 1756).

Memoirs of the Right Hon Lady Betty Ireland, with a Particular Account of her Eldest Son, Roger, Jemmy Gripe, and Fox, the Jugler (n.d., 1756?).

A Narrative of the Dispute in the Corporation of Kinsale. In a Letter from a Buff at Kinsale, to his Friend in Dublin (1756).

Remarks on a Late Pamphlet entitled, Advice to the Patriot Club of the County of Antrim, in a Letter from a Member of that Club to his Friend in Dublin (1756).

A Short but Full Defence of a Certain Great Man (1756).

The State of the Nation Considered, with Respect to a French Invasion (1756).

An Appeal to his Grace the Lord P—— te of all I—— d, Being a Short Vindication of the Political Principles of Roman Catholics (1757).

Pery, Edmund Sexton, *A Letter to his Grace the Duke of Bedford* (1757).

The Protestant Interest, Considered Relative to the Operation of the Popery Acts in Ireland (1757).

Serious Thoughts Concerning the Interests and Exigencies of the State of Ireland in a Letter to the Duke of Bedford (1757).

Sheridan, Thomas, *An Oration, Pronounced before a Numerous Body of the Nobility and Gentry, Assembled at the Musick Hall in Fishamble Street, Tuesday, 6th December 1757* (Dublin, 1757).

The King of Prussia's Confession of Faith, which he sent to all the Protestant Ministers of the Empiree, at Ratisbon. With a hymn, sung by His Prussian Majesty and his army . . . (1758).

The Proceedings of the Hiberian Society, Drawn up by their Order (1758).

Remarks upon Poyning's Law, and the Manner of Passing Bills in the P[arliamen]t of I[relan]d (1758).

Brooke, Henry, *An Essay on the Antient and Modern State of Ireland, with the Various Important Advantages Thereunto derived, under the Auspicious Reign of his Most Sacred Majesty, King George the Second* (1759).

Hints Relative to some Laws that May be for the Interest of Ireland to have Enacted. In a Letter to a Member of Parliament (1759).

The Drapier's Ghost's Advice to the Clothier's Letter (1760).

Lucas, Charles, *Seasonable Advice to the Electors of MPs in the Ensuing General Election* (1760).

Lucas, Charles, *An Address to the Free Electors of the City of Dublin* (1761).
The Question about Septennial Parliaments Impartially Examined in two letters to Charles Lucas (1761).
Skelton, Revd P., *The Necessity of Tillage and Granaries* (1761).
Some REASONS Against Raising an Army of Roman Catholicks in IRELAND in a Letter to a Member of Parliament (1762).

Secondary Sources

The following list comprises only the main works referred to above or which I have found very useful in thinking about the mid eighteenth century.

Andrew, Donna T., *Philanthropy and Police: London Charity in the Eighteenth Century* (Princeton, NJ, 1989).
Bartlett, Thomas, *The Fall and Rise of the Irish Nation: The Catholic Question 1690–1830* (Dublin, 1992).
Beattie, John, *Crime and the Courts in England, 1660–1800* (Oxford, 1986).
Black, Jeremy, *America or Europe? British Foreign Policy, 1739–63* (1998).
—— *Pitt the Elder*, 2nd edn. (1999).
Borsay, Peter, *The English Urban Renaissance: Culture and Society in the Provincial Town, 1660–1770* (1989).
Brewer, John, *The Sinews of Power: War, Money and the English State, 1688–1783* (1989).
Burns, Robert E., *Irish Parliamentary Politics in the Eighteenth Century*, ii, *1730–60* (Washington, DC, 1990).
Cannon, John, *Samuel Johnson and the Politics of Hanoverian England* (Oxford, 1994).
Clark, J. C. D., *The Dynamics of Change: The Crisis of the 1750s and English Party Systems* (Cambridge, 1982).
Clayton, T. R. 'The Duke of Newcastle, the Earl of Halifax, and the American Origins of the Seven Years' War', *Historical Journal*, 24 (1981), 571–603.
Colley, Linda, *Britons: Forging the Nation, 1707–1837* (New Haven, Conn. and London, 1992).
—— *In Defiance of Oligarchy: The Tory Party 1714–60* (Cambridge, 1982).
Connolly, S. J., *Religion, Law and Power: The Making of Protestant Ireland 1660–1760* (Oxford, 1995).
Connors, Richard, ' "The Grand Inquest of the Nation": Parliamentary Committees and Social Policy in Mid-Eighteenth-Century England', *Parliamentary History*, 14 (1995), 285–313.
Dickinson, H. T., *The Politics of the People in Eighteenth-Century Britain* (1994).
Gerrard, Christine, *The Patriot Opposition to Walpole: Politics, Poetry and National Myth 1725–1742* (Oxford, 1994).
Gould, Elijah H., *The Persistence of Empire: British Political Culture in the Age of the American Revolution* (Chapel Hill, NC and London, 2000).
Guest, Harriet, ' "Those Neuter Somethings": Gender Difference and Commercial Culture in Mid Eighteenth Century England', in Kevin Sharpe and Steven N. Zwicker (eds.), *Refiguring Revolution: Aesthetics and Politics from the English Revolution to the Romantic Revolution* (Berkeley, Calif. and London, 1998), 173–94.

Hancock, David, *Citizens of the World: London Merchants and the British Atlantic Community*, *1735–1785* (Cambridge, 1995).

Harris, Bob, 'Patriotic Commerce and National Revival: The Free British Fishery Society and British Politics (c.1749–58), *English Historical Review*, 114 (1999), 285–313.

—— *Politics and the Rise of the Press: Britain and France 1620–1800* (1996).

Harris, Michael, *London Newspapers in the Age of Walpole: A Study in the Origins of the Modern English Press* (London and Ontario, 1987).

Harris, Robert (Bob), *A Patriot Press: National Politics and the London Press in the 1740s* (Oxford, 1993).

Hill, Jacqueline, *From Patriots to Unionists: Dublin Civic Politics and Irish Protestant Patriotism, 1660–1840* (Oxford, 1997).

Hunt, Margaret R., *The Middling Sort: Commerce, Gender and the Family in England, 1680–1780* (Berkeley, Calif. and London, 1996).

Innes, Joanna, 'The "Mixed Economy" of Welfare in Early Modern England: Assessments of the Options from Hale to Malthus (c1683–1803)', in Martin Daunton (ed.), Charity, Self Interest and Welfare in the English Past (1996), 139–80.

—— 'Parliament and the Shaping of Eighteenth-Century English Social Policy', *Transactions of the Royal Historical Society*, 40 (1990), 63–92.

—— 'Politics and Morals: The Reformation of Manners Movement in Later Eighteenth Century England', in Eckhart Hellmuth (ed.), *The Transformation of Political Culture: England and Germany in the Late Eighteenth Century* (Oxford, 1990), 57–118.

Kelly, James, 'The Glorious and Immortal Memory: Commemoration and Protestant Identity 1660–1800', *Royal Irish Academy Proceedings*, 94 (1994), 25–52.

Kidd, Colin, 'North Britishness and the Nature of Eighteenth-Century British Patriotisms', *Historical Journal*, 39 (1996), 361–82.

—— *Subverting Scotland's Past: Scottish Whig Historians and the Creation of an Anglo-British Identity, c.1689-c.p349   3491830* (Cambridge, 1993).

Langford, Paul, *A Polite and Commercial People: England 1727–1783* (Oxford, 1989).

—— *Public Life and the Propertied Englishman, 1689–1798* (Oxford, 1991).

Lawson, Philip, *A Taste for Empire and Glory: Studies in British Overseas Expansion, 1660–1800* (Aldershot and Brookfield, Vt., 1997).

Lenman, Bruce, *The Jacobite Risings in Britain, 1689–1746*, 2nd edn. (Aberdeen, 1995).

Macinnes, Allan I., *Clanship, Commerce and the House of Stuart, 1603–1788* (East Linton, 1996).

—— 'Scottish Jacobitism: In Search of a Movement', in T. M. Devine and J. R. Young (eds.), *Eighteenth-Century Scotland: New Perspectives* (East Linton, 1998), 70–89.

McNally, Patrick, *Parties, Patriots and Undertakers: Parliamentary Politics in Early-Hanoverian Ireland* (Dublin, 1997).

Middleton, R., *The Bells of Victory: The Pitt-Newcastle Ministry and the Conduct of the Seven Years' War, 1757–1762* (Cambridge, 1985).

Munter, Robert, *The History of the Irish Newspaper 1685–1760* (Cambridge, 1967).

Murdoch, Alexander, *British History 1660–1832: National Identity and Local Culture* (1998).

—— *'The People Above': Politics and Administration in Mid-Eighteenth-Century Scotland* (Edinburgh, 1980).

Newman, Aubrey, 'Leicester House Politics, 1748–1751', *English Historical Review*, 76 (1961), 577–89.

Newman, Gerald, *The Rise of English Nationalism: A Cultural History 1740–1830* (New York, 1987).

O'Donovan, Declan, 'The Money Bill Dispute of 1753', in Thomas Bartlett and David Hayton (eds.), *Penal Era and Golden Age: Essays on Irish History 1690–1800* (Belfast, 1979), 55–87.

Owen, J. B., *The Rise of the Pelhams* (1957).

Pares, Richard, 'American versus Continental Warfare, 1739–63', *English Historical Review*, 51 (1936), 429–65.

Peters, Marie, *The Elder Pitt* (Harlow, 1998).

—— *Pitt and Popularity: The Patriot Minister and London Opinion during the Seven Years War* (Oxford, 1980).

Pocock, J. G. A., 'The Varieties of Whiggism from Exclusion to Reform. A History of Ideology and Discourse', in id., *Virtue, Commerce and History: Essays on Political Thought, Chiefly Eighteenth Century* (Cambridge, 1985), 215–310.

Rogers, Nicholas, *Crowds, Culture and Politics in Georgian Britain* (Oxford, 1998).

—— *Whigs and Cities: Popular Politics in the Age of Walpole and Pitt* (Oxford, 1989).

Shaw, J.S., *The Management of Scottish Society 1707–1764: Peers, Nobles, Lawyers, Edinburgh Agents and English Influences* (Edinburgh, 1983).

—— *The Political History of Eighteenth-Century Scotland* (1999).

Sekora, John, *Luxury: The Concept in Western Thought, from Eden to Smollett* (Baltimore, 1977).

Solkin, David H., *Painting For Money: The Visual Arts and the Public Sphere in Eighteenth-Century England* (New Haven, Conn. and London, 1993).

Speck, W. A., *The Butcher: The Duke of Cumberland and the Suppression of the '45*, 2nd edn. (Gwynedd, 1995).

—— *Literature and Society in Eighteenth-Century England: Ideology, Politics, and Culture, 1680–1820* (1998).

Stewart, A. T. Q., *A Deeper Silence: The Hidden Origins of the United Irishmen* 1993; (repr. Belfast, 1998).

Sutherland, Lucy, 'The City of London and the Devonshire-Pitt Administration', in Aubrey Newman (ed.), *Politics and Finance in the Eighteenth Century: Lucy Sutherland* (1984), 67–93.

—— 'The City of London in Eighteenth-Century Politics', in Aubrey Newman (ed.), *Politics and Finance in the Eighteenth Century: Lucy Sutherland* (1984), 41–66.

—— 'Sampson Gideon and the Reduction of Interest, 1749–50', in Aubrey Newman (ed.), *Politics and Finance in the Eighteenth Century: Lucy Sutherland* (1984), 399–413.

Szechi, Daniel, *The Jacobites* (1994).

Taylor, Stephen, 'Whigs, Bishops and America: The Politics of Church Reform in Mid-Eighteenth-Century England', *Historical Journal*, 36 (1993), 331–56.

Thomas, Peter D. G., *Politics in Eighteenth-Century Wales* (Cardiff, 1998).

Western, J. R., *The English Militia in the Eighteenth Century* (London and Toronto, 1965).

Wilson, Kathleen, 'Empire, Trade and Popular Politics in Mid-Hanoverian Britain: The Case of Admiral Vernon', *Past and Present*, 121 (1988), 74–109.

—— *The Sense of the People: Politics, Culture and Imperialism in England, 1715–1785* (Cambridge, 1995).

UNPUBLISHED THESES/PAPERS

Only works referred to more than once are listed.

Allan, D. G. C., 'The Society For the Encouragement of Arts, Manufactures and Commerce: Organization, Membership and Objectives in the First Three Decades, 1755–84', Ph.D. thesis (London University, 1979).

Connors, R. T., 'Pelham, Parliament and Public Policy, 1746–1754', Ph.D. thesis (Cambridge University, 1993).

D'Cruze, Shani, 'The Middling Sort in Provincial England: Politics and Social Relations in Colchester 1700–1800', Ph.D. thesis (Essex University, 1990).

Gee, Austin, 'English Provincial Newspapers and the Politics of the Seven Years War, 1756–1763', MA thesis (Canterbury University, New Zealand, 1983).

Innes, Joanna, 'William Payne of Bell Yar, Carpenter c1718–1782: The Life and Times of a London Informing Constable' (unpub.).

McCoy, J. G. 'Local Political Culture in the Hanoverian Empire: The Case of Ireland, 1714–1760', D.Phil. thesis (Oxford University, 1993).

Magennis, Eoin, 'Politics and Government in Ireland During the Seven Years War, 1756–1763', Ph.D. thesis (Belfast University, 1996).

Scott, Richard, 'The Politics and Administration of Scotland, 1725–1748', Ph.D. thesis (Edinburgh University, 1981).

Smyth, P. D. H., 'The Volunteer Movement in Ulster: Background and Development, 1745–85', Ph.D. thesis (Queen's University, Belfast, 1974)

Taylor, Stephen, 'Church and State in the Mid Eighteenth Century: The Newcastle Years 1742–1762', Ph.D. thesis (Cambridge University, 1987).

Index